W9-CDV-393

FOR REFERENCE ONLY
DO NOT REMOVE FROM THIS ROOM

The Encyclopedia of
AMERICAN RELIGIOUS HISTORY

Edward L. Queen II,
Stephen R. Prothero,
and
Gardiner H. Shattuck, Jr.

Foreword by
Martin E. Marty,
Editorial Advisor

0 66546

Ref
BL
2525
.Q44
1996
v 2

Book Producer: Marie A. Cantlon, Proseworks, Boston

WITHDRAWN

☑®

Facts On File, Inc.

AN INFOBASE HOLDINGS COMPANY

LEARNING RESOURCE CENTER
CHARLES COUNTY COMMUNITY COLLEGE
LA PLATA, MARYLAND

The Encyclopedia of American Religious History

Copyright © 1996 by Proseworks

All rights reserved. No part of this book may be reproduced or utilized in any form or by any means, electronic or mechanical, including photocopying, recording, or by any information storage or retrieval systems, without permission in writing from the publisher. For information contact:

Facts On File, Inc.
11 Penn Plaza
New York NY 10001

Library of Congress Cataloging-in-Publication Data

Queen, Edward L.
The encyclopedia of American religious history / by Edward L. Queen II, Stephen R. Prothero, and Gardiner H. Shattuck, Jr. ; foreword by Martin E. Marty.
p. cm.
Includes bibliographical references and index.
ISBN 0-8160-2406-5 (set) (alk. paper)
ISBN-0-8160-3545-8 (vol. 1)
ISBN-0-8160-3546-6 (vol. 2)
1. United States—Religion—Encyclopedias. 2. Religious biography—United States—Encyclopedias. I. Prothero, Stephen R. II. Shattuck, Gardiner H. III. Title.
BL2525.Q44 1996
200'.973—dc20   96-2487

Facts On File books are available at special discounts when purchased in bulk quantities for businesses, associations, institutions or sales promotions. Please call our Special Sales Department in New York at 212/967-8800 or 800/322-8755.

This book is printed on acid-free paper.

Printed in the United States of America

RRD VC 10 9 8 7 6 5 4 3 2 1

CONTENTS

Entries A to Z   1
Synoptic Index   757
General Index   765

M

Machen, John Gresham (1881–1937)

J. Gresham Machen was the leading intellectual voice of American FUNDAMENTALISM in the opening decades of the 20th century. A Presbyterian clergyman, educator, and New Testament scholar, Machen accused Protestant leaders of rejecting the traditional beliefs of Christianity and substituting a new religion, which he called "liberalism," in their place.

Machen was born in Baltimore, Maryland on July 28, 1881. He received a B.A. in classics from Johns Hopkins University in 1901 and a B.D. from Princeton Seminary in 1905. At Princeton, Machen was strongly influenced by Benjamin B. WARFIELD, the theologian who coined the term INERRANCY to describe the literal truth of the biblical text. Machen studied in Germany for a year at Marburg and Göttingen, but he was disturbed by the advanced notions of biblical interpretation he learned there. In 1906, he returned to Princeton to take a position in the New Testament Department, where he taught until 1929. He was ordained to the Presbyterian ministry in 1914 and, during the First World War, served for a year with the YMCA in France.

Machen was the author of several books on theology and New Testament interpretation, including *The Origin of Paul's Religion* (1921) and *The Virgin Birth of Christ* (1930). His most enduring work, however, was *Christianity and Liberalism* (1923), which placed him at the forefront of the controversy between fundamentalists and theological modernists. He feared that Presbyterians and other American Protestants were drifting away from their theological and spiritual moorings. He also believed that those who held beliefs contrary to his own definition of orthodoxy should not be allowed to remain members of his church.

As it turned out, Machen and his followers, not their liberal adversaries, left the mainline Presbyterian denomination. First, Machen withdrew from the Princeton faculty in 1929 and founded Westminster Theological Seminary in Philadelphia. Next, after becoming concerned that foreign missionaries were doctrinally lax, he formed the Independent Board of Foreign Missions in 1933. The Presbyterian General Assembly condemned that action a year later and called upon Machen to renounce his support of it. Since he refused to comply with the General Assembly's decision, he was judged guilty of violating his ordination vows, and his ministerial standing was revoked in 1935. In response, Machen helped organize a new denomination: the Presbyterian Church of America (later called the Orthodox Presbyterian Church).

Machen worked tirelessly in an effort to gain members for the church and explain its theological positions and rigorous conservatism. On a trip west to rally support, however, his health failed. He died of pneumonia at Bismarck, North Dakota on January 1, 1937.

GHS, Jr.

Bibliography: D. G. Hart, *Defending the Faith: J. Gresham Machen and the Crisis of Conservative Protestantism in Modern America* (Baltimore: Johns Hopkins University Press, 1994).

Madison, James (1751–1836)

In the years following the AMERICAN REVOLUTION, Americans grappled as seriously with the problem of religious freedom as earlier they had struggled over political freedom. James Madison, fourth president of the United States, sought to prevent the new government from providing any particular religion with formal recognition or support. Madison's efforts to undercut such attempts to establish religion, culminating in his work on the First Amendment, comprise a vitally important contribution to the growth of American religious liberty.

Madison came from the same upper ranks of colonial VIRGINIA as did his friend Thomas JEFFERSON. Born to James and Nelly Conway

James Madison, United States president and statesman who, with Jefferson, led the disestablishment forces in Virginia and in the Continental Congress. (Painting by Gilbert Stuart)

Madison on March 16, 1751, Madison gained his education from private tutors, and at the Presbyterian College of New Jersey (later Princeton) from 1769 to 1772, where he studied with John Witherspoon. In the years after graduation, having rejected both law and the ministry as career choices, Madison served the revolutionary cause working in the Virginia governor's office and as a Virginia delegate to the Continental Congress. He had also helped draft the Virginia constitution and the Virginia Declaration of Rights (1776), in which he proposed not merely that government encourage religious "toleration," but instead the far stronger claim: "all men are equally entitled to the full and free exercise of religion, according to the dictates of conscience."

In the aftermath of revolution, sharp disagreement arose over the most appropriate structure for the new country. Madison was concerned that the diversity of interests within the 13 original states would inevitably produce a weak, and not very long-lived, nation. As a Virginia delegate to the Constitutional Convention in Philadelphia in 1787, he was instrumental, along with Benjamin Franklin, James Wilson, and a few others, in designing the new federal government, which sought to balance powers and respect the plurality of interests among states, and groups that Madison referred to as "factions." Along with John Jay and Alexander Hamilton, Madison authored the widely read *Federalist Papers* (1788), which argued for the necessity of a strong national government and ratification of the new constitution.

While many of his fellow citizens saw religion as the key underpinning of such a government, Madison did not. Winning the Virginia seat in the first federal congress, in part by promising to introduce a bill of rights amending the Constitution, Madison went on to draft several versions of what became the First Amendment in June of 1789.

Madison's views on religious liberty are summed up best in a document that subsequent generations have nearly venerated, but which in his own day circulated anonymously, the Memorial and Remonstrance Against Religious Assessments (1785), written to combat Virginia governor Patrick Henry's continued influential advocacy of his General Assessment bill, a tax in support of "the Christian religion." Madison's argument against taxes levied in support of religion rested on the assumption not that religion was unimportant but that such policies would deprive people of the "unalienable" right to duty to worship as their own consciences required. Thus he made religion an area of human life beyond the reach of society or the state. Religion is "precedent, both in order of time and in degree of obligation, to the claims of Civil Society." As a republican, Madison believed that religion was the well-spring of morality and civic responsibility. The only way in which a liberty-loving society could endure, one in which citizens lived responsibly, was to insure that each individual's conscience was allowed the freedom of drawing on that religious well-spring as seemed best. In spite of the fact that Christian majorities, in Madison's day and later, have often chafed against the extension of this liberty to all, unbelievers and non-Christians, his thinking has shaped subsequent judicial approaches to religious liberty. As president and diplomat later in life, Madison's attention turned to other issues, though up to the time of his death, June 28, 1836, he was ready to respond in letters and statements to continuing challenges to religious freedom.

MG

Bibliography: Irving Brant, *James Madison,* 6 vols. (Indianapolis: Bobbs-Merrill Company, 1941–61); William Lee Miller, *The First Liberty: Religion and the American Republic* (New York: Paragon House, 1985); Robert Allen Rutland, *James Madison: The Founding Father* (New York: Macmillan, 1987).

Mahan, Asa (1799–1889)

Asa Mahan was a Congregational minister and the first president of Oberlin College in Ohio. An antislavery advocate, Mahan accepted the presidency of Oberlin in 1835 on the grounds that the school would be open to African-American students. After a profound religious experience, he began to emphasize the possibility of Christian perfection, a hallmark of the HOLINESS MOVEMENT then emerging within the American churches.

Mahan was born in Vernon, New York on November 9, 1799. He taught school to earn money for an education and eventually graduated from Hamilton College in 1824. Despite an orthodox Calvinist theological upbringing, a period of spiritual questioning led Mahan to reject the idea of predestination and affirm instead humanity's free will and moral autonomy.

He studied for the ministry at Andover Theological Seminary in Massachusetts and graduated in 1827. Mahan served as pastor of the Congregational church in Pittsford, New York from 1829 to 1831. During that time, he participated in Charles G. Finney's Rochester revival of 1830 and 1831, one of the most celebrated revivals of the Second Great Awakening.

In 1831 Mahan was called to the pastorate of the Sixth Presbyterian (later Vine Street Congregational) Church in Cincinnati, Ohio. While functioning on the board of trustees of Lane Theological Seminary in Cincinnati, he supported the group known as the "Lane Rebels." Led by Theodore Dwight WELD, those students withdrew from the seminary when they were prohibited from discussing slavery and the injustices of the slave system. Mahan's strong support of Weld and other antislavery advocates led to the invitation to become the president of Oberlin College, which had been founded on abolitionist principles in 1833. Eighty students from Lane followed Mahan to Oberlin. This led to the establishment of a theological department at the college and the appointment of Charles Finney as the professor of theology.

In 1836, Mahan and Finney together began to explore the doctrines of entire sanctification and perfection in the writings of Methodist founder John Wesley. Mahan published his *Scripture Doctrine of Christian Perfection* in 1839. In that book he described how believers might attain complete victory over sin through the spiritual presence of Jesus Christ within their hearts. The Oberlin community as a whole became excited by Mahan's views on holiness, and *The Oberlin Evangelist* was founded in 1838 to publicize those perfectionist ideas. Mahan's theological beliefs had social and political applications as well. He advocated the involvement of Christians in social reform, especially in activities promoting equality for African-Americans and women.

Mahan's personal tactlessness and poor relations with some faculty members at Oberlin forced his resignation from the presidency in 1850. He held several positions over the next few years. He served, first, as president of Cleveland University from 1850 to 1855; next, as pastor of the Congregational church in Jackson, Michigan from 1855 to 1857; then, as pastor of the church in Adrian, Michigan from 1857 to 1860; and finally, as president of Adrian College from 1860 to 1871. Adrian College was connected with the Wesleyan Methodist Church, and Mahan eventually joined that denomination. By 1870, when he published *The Baptism of the Holy Spirit,* Mahan's theology reflected the major themes of the HIGHER CHRISTIAN LIFE MOVEMENT and stressed the sanctified Christian's release from the power of sin.

In 1871 Mahan moved to England, where he spent the remainder of his life. In his later years, he edited a monthly magazine entitled *The Divine Life,* and he was a frequent speaker at Keswick meetings, the conferences that popularized holiness teachings in Great Britain. Mahan died at Eastbourne, England on April 4, 1889.

(See also HOLINESS MOVEMENT; KESWICK MOVEMENT; PERFECTIONISM.)

GHS, Jr.

Bibliography: Edward H. Madden and James E. Hamilton, *Freedom and Grace: The Life of Asa Mahan* (Metuchen, N.J.: Scarecrow Press, 1982).

Maharishi Mahesh Yogi   See
TRANSCENDENTAL MEDITATION.

mainline Protestantism   The term "mainline Protestantism" refers to the group of dominant Protestant denominations that long occupied the center of American religious life. Although not all commentators agree about the group's exact composition, the following church bodies are usually thought to compose it: Congregationalists, now the UNITED CHURCH OF CHRIST; the EPISCOPAL CHURCH; the PRESBYTERIAN CHURCH (U.S.A.); northern Baptists, now the AMERICAN BAPTIST CHURCHES IN THE U.S.A.; the UNITED METHODIST CHURCH; the Disciples of Christ (see CHRISTIAN CHURCH (DISCIPLES OF CHRIST)); and the EVANGELICAL LUTHERAN CHURCH IN AMERICA, the largest Lutheran body. Other terms employed to identify these seven churches include "religious mainstream" (denoting their position at the heart of American life); "liberal Protestantism" (describing their relatively liberal social and theological attitudes); and "Protestant establishment" (emphasizing not a formal state-supported establishment, but the central role the denominations have played in American history).

These churches, which have long controlled America's spiritual and cultural values, share a number of common characteristics. Shaped over the last century by progressive trends in theology, they exhibit an openness not only to other churches, but also to religions other than Christianity. They have traditionally been concerned with influencing American society as a whole and, as a consequence, have helped sponsor numerous moral and political reform movements. Although they all have adherents who are African-Americans and members of other races, the denominations have always been predominantly Caucasian. Finally, unlike theologically conservative evangelical, Pentecostal, and fundamentalist churches, which stress individual salvation and the need for evangelism, the mainline denominations have tended to de-emphasize soul-winning. Their current decline in membership, a combined loss of more than six million members over the past 25 years, may well reflect the unintended results of the liberals' inattention to a clearly defined religious mission.

Use of the term "mainline" is of fairly recent origin, a fact itself illustrative of one further attribute these churches share. Until the 1960s, historians usually discussed American religion with few references outside mainline Protestantism. It was commonly assumed that those churches simply *were* American religion and the standard against which all other groups should be measured. Nowadays, the fluid and multi-faceted character of American religion is often highlighted by scholars instead. As a result, the Protestant establishment is now believed to be faced with two major challenges. First, the rapid growth of evangelical churches and the emerging political strength of religious conservatives have both tended to reduce the prominence of the old mainline. Second, the celebration of pluralism and the recognition of the many diverse groups that compose America have challenged the idea that a "mainstream" has ever existed here. It is ironic, then, that these historic Protestant denominations have been labeled "mainline" only after the dominance they once enjoyed has been greatly diminished.

GHS, Jr.

Bibliography: William R. Hutchison, *Between the Times: The Travail of the Protestant Establishment, 1900–1960* (Cambridge: Cambridge University Press, 1989); Wade Clark Roof and William McKinney, *American Mainline Religion: Its Changing Shape and Future* (New Brunswick, N.J.: Rutgers University Press, 1987).

Malcolm X (Malcolm Little) (1925–1965)

Born Malcolm Little in Omaha, Nebraska on May 19, 1925, Malcolm X transformed the debate over the role of blacks in American society, and paved the way for a radical change in the CIVIL RIGHTS MOVEMENT, away from nonviolence to assertiveness and militant self-defense.

Malcolm's earliest memory was of the family's house being burned by night riders (1929). Two years later his father, Earl Little, a Baptist preacher and organizer for Marcus GARVEY's Universal Negro Improvement Association, was murdered by members of the Black Legion, a racist organization, in the family's home in Lansing, Michigan.

His mother became overwhelmed by ill health, poverty, and the care of 11 children. Several of her children, including Malcolm, were removed from her care by the state welfare agency. Malcolm was placed in a foster home, until he was sent to a detention home for putting a tack on a teacher's chair.

Although a good student and popular in school, he was dissuaded from his desire to become a lawyer by his English teacher, who, surprised to hear such a desire, told him, ". . . you've got to be realistic about being a nigger. A lawyer—that's no realistic goal for a nigger. . . . Why don't you plan on carpentry?" Such treatment began to affect Malcolm, and he became increasingly angry and hostile.

After finishing the eighth grade, he moved to Boston to live with his half-sister, Ella Little. Although she attempted to convince Malcolm to associate with the middle-class blacks of the Humboldt Avenue Hill section of Roxbury, he was more attracted to the poorer section. During this time he began his criminal activities by making extra money as a procurer while working as a shoe-shine boy at the Roseland State Ballroom.

In the late 1930s Malcolm began working as a railroad porter and immersed himself in the fast life in Harlem. Dealing drugs, running numbers, and pimping, he lived the life of a hustler. He managed to con a psychiatric deferment during World War II and avoided police pressure on his New York drug-dealing by using his railway identification card to travel along the Eastern Seaboard selling drugs to the jazz players he had met in New York. Returning to Boston, he organized a burglary ring that led to his arrest and conviction in 1946. The judge, infuriated by the fact that the ring included two upper-class white women, gave Malcolm the maximum sentence of 10 years, despite the fact that he had no previous convictions.

Malcolm entered prison as an incorrigible hustler and troublemaker. His foul mouth, blasphemous attitude toward religion, and active violation of prison rules soon earned him the nickname "Satan." The example of one black prisoner who, due to his knowledge, commanded respect from black and white prisoners as well as the white guards impressed Malcolm. At the suggestion of this prisoner he began correspondence courses and to read books from the library.

In 1948, letters from members of his family began to tell him of the teaching of one Elijah MUHAMMAD and the NATION OF ISLAM (NOI). Although originally hostile and unreceptive, he became increasingly convinced by Elijah Muhammad's teaching that the white man was the devil. He was soon converted, and began not only to conform to the strict, moral code the NOI demanded of its members, but also increased his efforts at self-education.

Paroled in 1952, he went to Detroit where he lived with his brother Wilfred and his family. An active Muslim, Wilfred introduced Malcolm to the daily routine of the Nation of Islam. Malcolm joined Temple Number 1 in Detroit, receiving his "X" to replace the slave name of Little that had been forced on his ancestors.

Malcolm soon attracted the attention of Elijah Muhammad, who led the Nation of Islam from the Chicago Temple. After expressing concern about the small size of the Detroit Temple, Malcolm received Elijah Muhammad's permission to begin active recruiting among the black youth of Detroit. The size of the Detroit Temple tripled, and in 1953 Malcolm X was appointed its assistant minister. He soon began working full-time for the Nation of Islam and attained notable success organizing temples in Boston and Philadelphia. The result was his appointment, in June 1954, as minister of Temple Number 7 in Harlem, which Malcolm soon turned into one of the most important mosques in the movement.

From the mid-1950s until 1964, the growth of the Nation of Islam was linked with the rise of Malcolm X, who became its National Representative and official spokesman. In 1961 he founded *Muhammad Speaks* as the official newspaper of the NOI. Still a relatively unknown organization outside the black community and the FBI, the Nation of Islam leaped into the public view with the 1959 TV documentary "The Hate that Hate Produced." This program, along with the publication of C. Eric Lincoln's *The Black Muslims in America,* brought the Nation of Islam to national consciousness.

As one of its most outspoken leaders and its New York minister, Malcolm X became the object of much media and public attention. His criticisms of white society and of the "integration mad negroes" in the civil rights movement earned him enemies in both the white and black communities who accused the Nation of Islam and Malcolm of being racists, "black fascists," and "hate mongers." Despite this opposition, his uncompromising delivery of the message of the Nation of Islam that whites were devils and would never accept blacks as equals also earned him a large following in the urban ghettoes.

However, conflicts were developing within the organization that would lead to Malcolm's break with it, and his eventual assassination. During the last four years of his life, Malcolm X underwent numerous personal transformations. Internal dissension within the NOI led to a decrease in Malcolm's responsibilities and access to Elijah Muhammad. Rumors of Elijah Muhammad's sexual indiscretions disturbed Malcolm. An off-the-cuff remark that President Kennedy's assassination resulted from the inherent violence in American society and that "the chickens had come home to roost," led to his official silencing by Elijah Muhammad. These events, combined with Malcolm's growing dissatisfaction with the official policy of "non-engagement" in responding to American racism, led to his official break with the NOI on March 12, 1964.

After announcing the formation of his own organization, the Muslim Mosque, Inc., Malcolm left the country to embark upon the *haj,* the pilgrimage to Mecca required of every orthodox Muslim. During this trip, which included visits throughout the Middle East and Africa, Malcolm was confronted with the differences between orthodox Islam and the teachings of the Nation of Islam as well as the lack of racial distinctions within Islam itself. This experience called forth a radical re-thinking on Malcolm's part regarding race, a re-thinking that was only beginning when he was shot and killed at a meeting of his newly organized Organization of African-American Unity on February 21, 1965.

EQ

Bibliography: George Breitman, *The Last Year of Malcolm X: The Evolution of a Revolutionary* (New York: Schocken, 1968); John H. Clarke, ed., *Malcolm X: The Man and His Times* (New York: Macmillan, 1969); Peter Goldman, *The Death and Life of Malcolm X* (New York: Harper & Row, 1973); Malcolm X, with Alex Haley, *The Autobiography of Malcolm X* (New York: Grove Press, 1965), ———, *Malcolm X Speaks* (New York: Grove Press, 1965), ———, *Two Speeches by Malcolm X*, 3rd ed. (New York: Pathfinder, 1990).

Manifest Destiny From the early 19th century to the present, the term "Manifest Destiny" has been used in a variety of ways to indicate the close association in American history between concepts of providential mission and geographical expansion. Used in its more circumscribed political sense, it refers to the vision of a free, confederated, self-governed republic spanning the North American continent, a goal that dictated federal policy in the mid-1840s, particularly under President James Polk. Although terms like it had been used previously, the precise phrase was coined and popularized in 1845 by John O'Sullivan, a journalist, lawyer, politician, and theoretician of westward expansion. As editor of the *Democratic Review,* O'Sullivan used the expression in a series of editorials in 1845 supporting the annexation of Texas, asserting that the United States had a divinely ordained right "to overspread and to possess the whole of the continent which Providence has given us." His reasoning provided a popular justification for the Mexican War that followed later in the decade, but the general concept has emerged in various guises from the early 19th century to the present.

Americans who supported the principles of this doctrine did not always agree on precisely what Manifest Destiny meant. In many respects, its genius lay in its ambiguity. For most people, the idea that Americans had the right to spread their political control to the "natural boundaries" of the nation meant that the United States should occupy the entire continent, extending to the Pacific Coast. Others argued for expansion throughout the hemisphere, including much of Latin America. And some even saw the doctrine as applicable to the claiming of American colonial possessions across the Pacific. Equally equivocal was the matter of how Euro-Americans, in spreading their culture that was presumed to be superior to any other, would relate to the native peoples whose lands they wanted to possess. While some assumed that Native American and others, as "naturally" inferior cultures, would eventually yield and be assimilated or exterminated in the onrushing tide of Euro-American migration, others, particularly Protestant mission leaders, advocated the education and regeneration of "backward" peoples so that they could become good American citizens. Finally, Americans also disagreed about how aggressively this expansion should take place. The most vocal supporters of the war with Mexico argued that only the initial use of force would allow the power of republican, democratic values to flourish in western territories. But many others saw military aggression as unnecessary. With their optimism about the self-evident superiority of American civilization, they firmly believed that the example of the republic would eventually win over its neighbors without bloodshed. Both sides, however, saw the eventual domination of American values on the continent as inevitable.

Religious values, and particularly those held by Protestant Americans, played an integral role in the formulation of notions of Manifest Destiny. Indeed, scholars have noted that the doctrine continued and built upon a longstanding tradition of seeing America as a missionary nation, playing a central part in sacred history. Like the Puritans before them, many Americans in the 19th century depicted America's religious and political forms as a beacon to the world, an example for others to follow. Because providence had smiled on the nation, some people argued that Americans were thereby obligated to a "higher calling," to spread the blessings of their political, social, and religious institutions to those less enlightened than themselves. In turn, the doctrine of Manifest Destiny shaped the views of religious organizations in 19th century America, particularly those of the Protestant evangelical denominations (see EVANGELICAL-ISM). Beginning in the early 19th century, evangelicals formed mission associations to spread the gospel of Christianity and American culture across the continent and throughout the world. In most cases, the goal of these organizations was not merely the reiteration of a narrowly defined Christian doctrine. It also encompassed the inculcating of the values of democracy, liberty of conscience, free trade, and other concepts that comprised American cultural life. At times, the tasks of missionaries even included statistical or geographical surveys of various territories for entrepreneurs or the federal government. Most mission organizations saw no inherent tension between their roles as disseminators of religious values and promoters of American economic and political expansion, because they believed that God had fortuitously and purposely connected the two in a divine plan for worldwide Christianization.

Reaching its peak of popularity during the Spanish-American War in the 1890s, in the 20th century the doctrine of Manifest Destiny as justification for aggressive expansion has become much less popular. But it is significant that certain aspects of the doctrine remain politically salient, particularly the idea of America as a superior civilization that can serve as an example to other nations in the world. From the Puritan era to the present, many Americans have continued to believe that the nation plays a unique and privileged role in history.

LMK

Bibliography: Conrad Cherry, ed., *God's New Israel: Religious Interpretations of American Destiny* (Englewood Cliffs, N.J.: Prentice-Hall, 1971); Frederick Merk, *Manifest Destiny and Mission in American History, A Reinterpretation* (New York: Vintage Books, 1963); Ernest Lee Tuveson, *Redeemer Nation: The Idea of America's Millennial Role* (Chicago: University of Chicago Press, 1968).

Mann, Horace (1796–1859)   Legislator and educator Horace Mann's vision of the task of education had a lasting effect on the growth of public schools in America well into the 20th century. Through his work on the Massachusetts Board of Education, Mann articulated a philosophy of public education that gained wide acceptance. Just as important, he provided public education with a democratic structure.

Mann was born into the modest home of Thomas and Rebecca Stanley Mann, in Franklin, Massachusetts on May 4, 1796. His own schooling came through self-study and tutoring at home and church, until his admission to Brown University in 1816. He took up law after graduating, being admitted to the bar in 1823, and served in the Massachusetts legislature for several years. As president of the Senate he helped push through a measure establishing a state board of education, and in the process began to make education his life work.

Although lacking any formal training in education himself, Mann was appointed secretary of the state board, and labored for 12 years to educate the Massachusetts citizenry on the need for public education, writing countless articles and speeches, editing a journal, and turning his influential *Annual Reports* into a major forum for the discussion of educational theory. While Massachusetts, through Mann's influence, came to provide an influential model for public education in America, Mann's own national prominence grew after he took up the stormy cause of abolition (see ABOLITIONISM) in Congress, having succeeded John Quincy Adams in the House of Representatives in 1848. In 1852 the founders of Antioch College in Yellow Springs, Ohio offered Mann the presidency of the new college. Lured west by the opportunity to work in the nonsectarian, coeducational, and racially integrated setting provided by the liberal Unitar-

ians and DISCIPLES OF CHRIST who governed
Antioch, Mann remained there until his death
on August 2, 1859.

Mann's ideas about education were shared by
many in his day. In common with the thinking
of American founders such as Thomas JEFFER-
SON, Mann saw education as the primary means
to create reasonable, responsible citizens, capable of living within the framework of liberty
without succumbing to the forces of economic,
religious, or sectional passion. While Mann
distanced himself from American Protestants'
frequent denominational quarrels (see EVANGEL-
ICALISM), he shared the millennial expectations
of the day, believing that education was the key
to an American future free of crime, immorality,
disease, and other social ills.

But whereas many in America saw the civic
function of education achieved through home,
church, or private institutions, Mann provided
the republic with a well-thought-out model of
public, or what he called "common," education.
Common education would enable Americans
of different class and religious backgrounds to
develop a set of common values and virtues.
Mann's vision of the common school's provisions was evangelical: piety rooted in scripture,
civility through awareness of shared history, in-
tellect grounded in reading, arithmetic, writing,
and hygiene. Given its functions, such an education could only be provided by the state's organizational powers. Mann understood that public
power over education depended not simply on
the agency of the state, but rather upon the
citizens themselves. He strove to create mecha-
nisms, such as local school boards, through
which parents themselves had a role in shaping
the schools' philosophy and task. Mann's contribution to the development of public education
was regarded highly by his contemporaries; and
his vision pervaded the public schools until well
into the 20th century, when a more secular
wave of thought took hold (see DEWEY, JOHN;
SECULARISM).

MG

Bibliography: Lawrence A. Cremin, *American Ed-
ucation: The National Experience, 1783–1876* (New
York: Harper and Row, 1980); Louis Filler, ed.,
Horace Mann on the Crisis of Education (Yellow
Springs, Ohio: Antioch Press, 1965).

Marechal, Ambrose (1764–1828)   The
third archbishop of Baltimore, Ambrose Marechal was born on August 28, 1764 in Ingres,
France. Although wishing to enter the priesthood, Marechal bowed to the wishes of his
parents and studied law until 1787 when he no
longer could resist the call and entered the
Sulpician Seminary in Orleans. Two years of
study there, followed by two years at the seminary in Bordeaux, led to the young man's ordination in 1792. By this time the French
Revolution had forced Marechal and other
priests to flee the country.

Marechal came to America to serve as a priest
in St. Mary's County, Maryland. He then went
on to become pastor and administrator of the
former Jesuit (see JESUITS) plantation at Bohemia Manor until 1799. In that year he was
appointed to the faculty of St. Mary's Seminary
in Baltimore, where he taught theology, until
he was transferred to Georgetown College in
1801. In 1803, with the religious situation in
France stabilized, he was recalled by his superior
general to aid in the reorganization of that
country's seminaries.

After returning to France he taught at various
seminaries until 1811, when Napoleon, in an
attempt to strengthen state control of education,
expelled the Sulpicians from France. Marechal
returned to the United States where he taught
at the Baltimore seminary and later served as
president of St. Mary's. Deeply committed to
his teaching, Marechal had refused offers to
become bishop of New York and Philadelphia,
but when he was named to become coadjutor
bishop of Baltimore, he relented. Official notifi-
cation of the appointment did not reach the
United States until after the death of the then
archbishop Leonard Neale. Upon receipt of his

appointment, therefore, Marechal was consecrated archbishop of Baltimore on December 14, 1817.

Responsible for the ecclesiastical oversight of the entire United States, Marechal faced numerous difficulties during his 11-year tenure. Chief among them was the ongoing issue of TRUSTEEISM, the complex problem of property ownership, and the question of who had the right to hire and fire the parish's priest. This was exacerbated by the constant influx into the United States of priests from Europe. Often Irish, these priests would accept a parish call without obtaining permission from the archbishop. Marechal viewed this breach of ecclesiastical authority as a danger to priestly discipline and to lay faith and took strong steps to end it.

His attempts to assert his episcopal prerogatives created much animosity. The Irish and Germans looked upon Marechal as a "foreign" bishop whose actions were designed to secure French control over the American Church. Marechal did little to allay their fears. He steadfastly refused to gather his bishops together for a provincial council, despite the obvious need for regularizing the rules and institutions of the rapidly growing American church.

Despite these troubles, and an ongoing conflict with the re-established Jesuits over the ownership of property, Marechal provided the American Church with strong management and administration. He traveled extensively through his vast archdiocese and managed to quell most threats to his authority. Marechal also obtained papal approval for the right of the American bishops to nominate candidates for open bishoprics. Although a far cry from John CARROLL's desire to have the priests elect bishops (with the right of papal veto), it did give the American Church greater say in its leadership. Taken ill in 1826 during one of his many trips, Marechal never recovered, dying on January 29, 1828 at home in Baltimore.

(See also ROMAN CATHOLICISM).

EQ

Bibliography: James Hennesey, *American Catholics: A History of the Roman Catholic Community in the United States* (New York: Oxford University Press, 1981); Ambrose Marechal, *Diary of Archbishop Marechal, 1818–1825* (n.p.: American Catholic Historical Society, 1960); Ronin John Murtha, *The Life of the Most Reverend Ambrose Marechal, Third Archbishop of Baltimore* (Washington, D.C.: Catholic University of America Press, 1965).

Marquette, Jacques (1637–1675)

A Jesuit missionary best remembered as the explorer who accompanied Louis Jolliet on the expedition that opened the Mississippi River to Europeans. Born on June 1, 1637 in Laon, France, he became a novice in the Society of Jesus (see JESUITS) in 1654. Trained in philosophy, he taught at several Jesuit seminaries in France until 1666 when he received his desired posting to Canada.

After three years at Trois-Rivières, Canada where he served as pastor and mastered six Algonkian dialects, Marquette was posted to the mission of La Pointe de St. Esprit on the southern shore of Lake Superior. There Marquette maintained a successful mission among the Ottawa and Huron, baptising many children and making contact with tribes further inland. He even attempted to establish contact with the eastern Lakota (Sioux) bands, but continuing Huron-Sioux conflicts led the former to abandon La Pointe. Marquette joined them and established a new mission at St. Ignace on the shores of the Straits of Mackinac (Michilimakinac) in modern-day Michigan.

While at St. Ignace, Marquette met Louis Jolliet (December 1672), who had been commissioned by the governor of NEW FRANCE to locate the great river described by the Illinois Indians. Marquette, whose earlier contact with the Illinois kindled his desire to establish a mission among them, was to accompany Jolliet as interpreter. Traveling from St. Ignace to Green Bay, they journeyed down the Fox River, making the portage to the Wisconsin, which they traversed to the Mississippi. They followed the great river south to the mouth of the Arkansas. At this time, informed that it flowed into the Gulf of Mexico and that the Spanish were present on the lower river, they headed back north. Returning via the Illinois River and the Chicago portage, they followed the shore of Lake Michigan up to the mission of St. Francis Xavier at De Pere, Wisconsin.

Seriously ill and terribly weak, Marquette remained there for a year. By October 1674 he felt well enough to return south to establish his long-desired mission among the Illinois. Although he managed to begin a small ministry among them, his illness returned and he felt compelled to return to St. Ignace. During this trip his strength failed and he died on May 18, 1675 near present day Luddington, Michigan. Two years later his remains were recovered and carried to St. Ignace, where they were re-interred at the chapel.

A gentle, even saintly man, Marquette was among those early missionaries who exhausted themselves in order to bring what they saw as the religious truth to the Native Americans. While many may consider his activities misguided, it is still possible to recognize the courage and faithfulness he manifested in his endeavors.

EQ

Bibliography: Joseph P. Donnelly, *Jacques Marquette, S.J. 1637–1675* (Chicago: Loyola University Press, 1968); Raphael N. Hamilton, *Marquette's Explorations: The Narratives, Re-examined* (Madison: University of Wisconsin Press, 1970); Jacques Marquette, *Father Marquette's Journal* (Lansing: Michigan Bureau of History, 1990); Francis B. Steck, *The Jolliet-Marquette Expedition, 1673* (Washington, D.C.: Catholic University of America Press, 1927).

Maryland (Colony)

Maryland (Colony) Planned by George Calvert, the first Lord Baltimore, as a refuge for English Catholics who suffered under legal and social liabilities at home, colonial Maryland had a turbulent history of civil war and rebellion interspersed with periods of legal and social tolerance (see ROMAN CATHOLICISM). Although this noble experiment was overwhelmed by external forces, Maryland became the center for Catholicism in British North America (see COLONIAL PERIOD).

George Calvert died before he could bring his plan to fruition; his son Cecilius (see CALVERT, CECILIUS) inherited the charter and in November 1633 sent two ships, the *Ark* and the *Dove*, to Maryland under the governorship of his brother, Leonard. Making land in March 1634, the two priests who accompanied the party of 20 mostly Roman Catholic gentlemen and 200 mostly Protestant laborers and artisans offered up in thanksgiving the first Mass in British North America.

In order to preserve the peace, Cecilius had directed his brother to allow complete religious freedom to all Christians. The Catholics also were warned to avoid antagonizing their fellow colonists and not to practice their religion too publicly. As added insurance against conflict, Calvert attempted to control the activities of the JESUITS, extracting from the Jesuit General the ruling that all priests must conform to the colony's laws and gaining veto power over appointments of priests to the colony.

Hostility from those in England who opposed a colony ruled by a Catholic, and from the colonists who chafed under the absolute rule of the proprietor, forced Cecilius to grant a measure of self-government to the colony, retaining only the right of veto over the colony's laws. This brought little respite, however, and until his death in 1675, Cecilius's energies were expended in attempting to control the colony. After a period of armed rebellion in the early 1640s, he re-established his control in 1647. In 1649 Leonard's successor, the Protestant William Stone, attempted to maintain peace by convincing the colonial assembly to pass an Act Concerning Religion (Act of Toleration of 1649) that allowed religious freedom for all those not denying the Trinity and made it illegal to disparage anyone's religion.

This act did not have the desired affect. In 1650, Protestants gained control over the colony's government and in 1654 forced the assembly to disenfranchise all Catholics and to outlaw "popery, prelacy, and licentiousness." The Calverts once again regained control of the colony in 1658. Maryland remained relatively peaceful and stable for the next 17 years, and when Cecilius died in 1675, the proprietorship passed to his son George.

The "Glorious Revolution" (1688) in England, which deposed the Roman Catholic King James II and replaced him with James's Protestant daughter Mary and her husband William of Orange, marked the end of Catholic proprietorship in Maryland. Galvanized by the revolution in England, a group of Maryland Protestants seized control of the government in 1689. In 1691 King William III relieved the Calverts of their grant and Maryland became a royal colony. In the following year, the Church of England was officially established and a series of laws limiting Roman Catholic political and religious rights soon followed. These anti-Catholic laws (see ANTI-CATHOLICISM) remained on the books until the AMERICAN REVOLUTION. With the achievement of independence and the adoption of the Constitution, Maryland's Catholics finally regained the legal rights they originally had allowed to others.

EQ

Bibliography: Jay P. Dolan, *The American Catholic Experience: A History from Colonial Times to the Present* (Notre Dame: University of Notre Dame Press, 1992); John Tracy Ellis, *Catholics in Colonial America* (Baltimore: Helicon Press, 1965); James Hennesey, *American Catholics: A History of the Roman Catholic Community in the United States* (New York: Oxford University Press, 1981); Aubrey C. Land, *Colonial Maryland: A History* (Millwood, N.Y.: KTO Press, 1981); Vera A. Foster Rollo, *The Proprietorship of Maryland: A Documented Account* (Lanham, Md.: Maryland Historical Press, 1989); John Gilmary Shea, *The Catholic Church in Colonial Days,* 2 vols. (New York: J.G. Shea, 1886).

Mason, Charles Harrison   See CHURCH OF GOD IN CHRIST.

Masonic Order   See FREEMASONRY.

Massachusetts Bay Colony   Now the state of Massachusetts, the Massachusetts Bay Colony was established by Puritans (see PURITANISM) fleeing religious persecution in England. Composed of numerous settlements established at various times, the colony had its true beginning on June 19, 1630 when John WINTHROP stood aboard the ship *Arbella* and delivered a sermon to a group of sick and weary passengers who were about to disembark and to begin a new life in the "howling wilderness" of New England. Winthrop reminded his listeners that their removal from England did not break their social and political ties, indeed those ties should become tighter and more closely follow the will of God. In speaking to his fellow Puritans this way, Winthrop desired to impress upon them the type of society that they were to struggle to build together in the colony of Massachusetts Bay. The colony was to be an ordered community, dedicated to realizing the will of God and to creating a model society for old England to emulate.

The rulers of old England were not desirous of following the Puritan lead. Both James I and Charles I were greatly suspicious of the Puritans, especially their rejection of bishops, which they saw as tantamount to rejecting royal authority. James I had his surfeit of rejection of episcopal authority while king of Scotland, having seen the Scottish Presbyterians remove his mother from the throne and place him upon it while still a youth, supervising his education and actions closely. When he succeeded to the throne of England, James knew that he wanted to retain the Church of England's bishops and promised to make his Puritan subjects conform or "harry them out of the kingdom or worse," as he put it. This anti-Puritanism was continued and expanded by his successor, Charles I. Charles and his archbishop of Canterbury engaged in a process of persecution that led to the "great migration" of thousands of English Puritans to British North America.

This migration, of which the *Arbella* and her sister ships were the first major group, led to the establishment of numerous Puritan colonies in New England, the most significant of which was Massachusetts Bay. Originally organized as a stock company with voting rights limited to stockholders who chose the colony's leaders, this changed soon after their arrival in America. Winthrop, who held the title of governor, gathered the colony's inhabitants on October 29, 1630 and by a show of hands gave all the freemen of the colony the right to elect the assistants, or legislators. This action, which soon encompassed nearly all adult males in the colony, gave Massachusetts Bay a much wider franchise than England and most of Europe, despite its limitation to male church members.

The Puritans desired to build an ordered community, under the watchful providence of God. This society was not, however, the theocracy that many have claimed. In fact, ministers in the Massachusetts Bay Colony had less formal power than anywhere in Europe, and did not constitute a recognized class with special privileges. This absence of inherited privileges was a significant factor in the life of the colony. Although the Puritans firmly believed that there were greater and lesser people, and titles such as Goodwife, Mistress, and Master constantly affirmed these divisions, the range was much less than in England. Sumptuary laws governed the nature of individual dress, limiting the colors, amount of gold, and jewelry a person could wear. These laws both affirmed social distinctions and limited ostentatious displays of wealth and power. When combined with the Puritan doctrine of human sin and of human equality before God, they resulted in much less overt social difference in Massachusetts Bay than the home country.

The desire to maintain harmony, stability, and social order was great. The magistrates enforced the laws against blasphemy and punished those who failed to attend church services. The nature of colonial settlement also served to strengthen social stability and cohesion. Land was allocated to each colonist for farming, but people lived in towns, traveling out to their farms each morning and returning in the evening. Towns centered on the meetinghouse, the church building, which functioned as the center of the community's social and political, as well as religious, life. The independent settler separated from the community that is the American stereotype was not acceptable in Massachusetts Bay. Such a settler, separated from the bonds of family, church, community, and government, was bound to lapse into barbaric and irreligious behavior. The godly life could be lived only with others.

Conflicts over the nature of that life, however, were such that the harmony desired by the colony's political elite was never realized. These conflicts emerged early in the colony's life. The first of these was the so-called ANTINOMIAN CONTROVERSY. Occasioned by the religious instruction that Anne HUTCHINSON provided in her home, and involving conflicts between the growing merchant class and the colony's political and religious elite, the antinomian controversy was typically Puritan in that it was fought over theology, and the role of social harmony in theology.

Similarly, the expulsion of Roger WILLIAMS from the colony was a response to theological differences the implications of which were seen as inherently destabilizing. Williams's belief that the government had no right to enforce the first half of the decalogue—the first four of the Ten Commandments dealing with worship—was seen as an assault upon the social stability of the colony. Indeed, many viewed any failure of the state to enforce these laws as an invitation to divine destruction. To outlaw blasphemy not only was an act of religious faith but also helped ensure social survival.

These conflicts, like those with other "socially disruptive" groups like BAPTISTS, Quakers (see FRIENDS, THE RELIGIOUS SOCIETY OF), and witches (see SALEM WITCHCRAFT TRIALS), were secondary struggles in the Puritans' attempt to build a viable society in a hostile land.

They struggled mightily to establish the social institutions that would provide for the colony's stability. Churches and towns were the first to appear. These were followed by a college (Harvard, 1638), printing presses, and schools. Soon Massachusetts Bay was an expanding and successful colony, kept alive by fishing, agriculture, timber, and even the slave trade.

Prosperity did not ease the difficulties of creating an ordered society pleasing to God, and tensions emerged within the New England way, not only among those outside but within it as well. The first concern was the perception that piety was declining within the colony. From the heroic period of settlement when the colony seemed to have been dominated by great men and high religious concern, there seemed to have been a decline by the mid-17th century. Many believed that religious interest had waned and that the number of visible saints had declined. This concern became so prevalent that the sermons preached about it have received their own name. These "jeremiads," as they are known, were directed against this perceived religious decline. Whether the decline was as great as the ministers claimed is debatable, but it is true that the colony experienced a shift from the time when people immigrated from religious conviction to a period when people simply were born into the society. A telling anecdote, probably apocryphal, describes this well. A Puritan minister once berated a man he caught unloading fish on Sunday, reminding him of the religious nature of the colony and its founders. The fisherman quickly responded, "My grandfather came here for God, I came here for cod."

There were other challenges to the colony as well. Chief among these were the local Indians and the French who, from their outposts in Canada, occasionally harried the colony's more distant settlements along with their Native American allies. These challenges ended with the eventual British conquest of France's North American colonies in 1759.

The removal of this external threat only exacerbated the internal one, the ongoing conflicts between the colonists in America and the mother country. This conflict was not to be taken lightly, and in Massachusetts it had its religious dimension. The late 17th century had seen an apparent victory of the "Puritan" party in its monarchical form in England. The glorious revolution of 1688 had removed the Catholic king James II and with it the threat to the colony's independent existence under James, who had revoked the colony's charter and had established an Anglican foothold at King's Chapel in Boston.

This, however, was not the only religious threat that England presented to the colony. If some contemporary writers are to be believed, the most significant conflicts and the true start of the American Revolution began with the rumor that England would send a bishop to the colonies. The imposition of a bishop was seen by many colonists as an inherent threat to their liberties. In Massachusetts Bay, where stories of episcopal persecution of Puritans were still remembered, this was the final assault on everything they had tried to create. Already forced to extend toleration to other Protestants, they now faced the final loss of their religious independence. The Puritan tradition of self-government, and the rule of law helped to set the stage for the American Revolution. The revolution in "the hearts and minds," as John Adams—a Puritan scion—wrote, already had occurred. It was no coincidence that a great deal of the revolutionary leadership came from Massachusetts. The colony and its Puritanism had helped to pave the way.

EQ

Bibliography: Timothy Breen, *Puritans and Adventurers: Change and Persistence in Early America* (New York: Oxford University Press, 1980); David Hall, *Worlds of Wonder, Days of Judgment* (New York: Knopf, 1989); Perry Miller, *Errand into the*

Wilderness (Cambridge: Belknap Press of Harvard University Press, 1956); Edmund Morgan, *The Puritan Dilemma: The Story of John Winthrop* (Boston: Little Brown, 1958); Samuel Eliot Morison, *Builders of the Bay Colony* (New York: Houghton Mifflin Co., 1930).

Mather, Cotton (1663–1728) Related to the Puritan minister and theologian John COTTON and son of Increase MATHER, minister at Boston's Second (Old North) Congregational Church, Cotton Mather attempted to live in both the older world of the MASSACHUSETTS BAY COLONY's Puritan founders (see PURITANISM) and the increasingly diverse and changing world of the 18th century.

Born in Boston on February 12, 1663, Cotton Mather was quick to learn the religious and cultural values of the Puritan way. After graduating from Harvard College at the age of 15, he joined his father as a minister at Second Church, a position he would hold until his death on February 13, 1728.

Mather was a complex and contradictory figure and has been viewed by many of his contemporaries and later historians as a self-righteous nag. He struggled to stop what he saw as the decline in religious fervor and activity through his preaching and writing. A prolific author of 469 published works, Mather wrote on subjects ranging from the reality of witchcraft and the history of New England to natural science and the usefulness of smallpox inoculation—which he defended against most medical men of the time.

Although an orthodox churchman and often viewed as backward-looking, Mather was a strong proponent of science. He was one of the first colonial members elected to the Royal Society of London (1713) and was honored by the University of Glasgow with an honorary D.D. in 1724. Such recognition provided Mather with little favor among his contemporaries, however, and his support of the SALEM WITCHCRAFT TRIALS and defense of the use of spectral (invisible) evidence in the trials, against the skepticism of his father, severely damaged his reputation.

Mather's greatest disappointment was his failure to receive appointment as president of Harvard College after his father stepped down in 1701. This turned him against the school, which he felt was drifting away from its religious roots. He became an active supporter of the Yale corporation, established in response to this perceived drift and designed to promote more orthodox Christian teaching.

The maintenance of this orthodoxy was the driving force in Mather's life. His sermons and writings were usually directed toward that end. Increasingly his pleas were ignored, and at the time of his death Mather appeared to be a man who had outlived his era.

EQ

Bibliography: Thomas Holmes James, *Cotton Mather: A Bibliography of His Works* (Cambridge: Harvard University Press, 1940); David Levin, *Cotton Mather: The Young Life of the Lord's Remembrancer, 1663–1703* (Cambridge: Harvard University Press, 1978); Richard Lovelace, *The American Pietism of Cotton Mather: The Origins of American Evangelicalism* (Grand Rapids: Christian University Press, 1979); Robert Middlekauf, *The Mathers: Three Generations of Puritan Intellectuals, 1596–1728* (New York: Oxford University Press, 1971).

Mather, Increase (1639–1723) As minister of Second Church in Boston for nearly 60 years and president of Harvard for 16, Increase Mather played a major role in trying to maintain religious orthodoxy in Massachusetts. In this role he deserves the description "the last American Puritan," given him by biographer Michael Hall.

Born in Dorchester, Massachusetts on June 21, 1639, Increase Mather left for Ireland after his graduation from Harvard. He received an M.A. from Trinity College, Dublin and served as a chaplain to the British army during the period of Puritan rule in England. The restoration of a Stuart king in 1661 ended his hopes

The "last American Puritan," Increase Mather was minister of Second Church in Boston for 60 years and president of Harvard from 1685 to 1701. (Painting by Jan Van Der Spriett)

for advancement in England, and Mather returned to America.

Upon his return he took up the cause of orthodoxy and tradition against his own father. Richard Mather and several other ministers had argued for a relaxation of the rules that limited baptism to those infants having at least one parent in full church membership (see HALF-WAY COVENANT). Increase, his brother Eleazar, and the president of Harvard, Charles Chauncy, led the opposition. All three maintained that such a relaxation would encourage the growth of irreligion. They were outvoted and the change was gradually adopted by all Congregational churches. Even Increase eventually was

reconciled and wrote two books defending the Half-way Covenant.

This would be the conundrum in which he would find himself throughout his life—how to maintain traditional forms of belief while responding to changes in society and the world. In his sermons, his writings (over 130 books and pamphlets), and as president of Harvard (1685–1701), Mather called the people to task for their sins with little long-term affect.

Mather also played a major role in ending the SALEM WITCHCRAFT TRIALS. While accepting the reality of witches, he was convinced that witchcraft was a rare phenomenon and rejected the use of spectral evidence (the claim by a witness that the defendant's specter had appeared to them and tormented them) as proof. His influence with the royal governor, Sir William Phipps, helped end the trials and executions.

Mather was also a public figure. When James II revoked the charter of Massachusetts in 1684 and appointed Edmund Andros as governor (1686), many rightly feared that self-government and religious purity were threatened. Andros immediately requisitioned a church for Anglican services, legalized Christmas celebrations, and installed a maypole on Boston Common. Such actions appalled the Puritans. With the Glorious Revolution in 1688 and the overthrow of James II, the Puritans (who learned of it in April 1689) imprisoned Andros. Mather, already in England pleading Massachusetts's case, negotiated a new charter with William III.

The new king, while more sympathetic to the Puritans than James, desired to retain as much royal control over the colony as possible. This made Mather's job all the more difficult. He managed to retain most elements of local government in the colony, but the new charter removed church membership as a requirement for voting, guaranteed religious toleration for all Protestants, and provided for a governor appointed by the king.

Mather received little applause for what he had gained. Returning to Boston in 1692, he faced growing criticism. Associated with an unpopular charter and religious traditionalism, his popularity waned. In 1701 he resigned as president of Harvard. Despite this loss of prestige, Mather continued his advocacy for traditional Puritan beliefs in the face of new religious forces and social changes until his death on August 23, 1723.

EQ

Bibliography: Michael Hall, *The Last American Puritan: The Life of Increase Mather, 1639–1723* (Middletown, Conn.: Wesleyan University Press, 1987); Robert Middlekauf, *The Mathers: Three Generations of Puritan Intellectuals, 1596–1728* (New York: Oxford University Press, 1971).

Mathews, Shailer (1863–1941)

The theologian and educator Shailer Mathews epitomized Protestant MODERNISM. A theological radical, he was also an active churchman. Rather than being hostile to tradition, he saw his work as firmly within the tradition of evangelical Christianity. For him modernism, as he wrote in *The Faith of Modernism* (1924), was nothing more than the use of "scientific, historical, social method in understanding and applying evangelical Christianity to the needs of living persons."

Mathews, born in Portland, Maine on May 26, 1863, stressed an historical approach to the doctrines of the Christian church. For him the doctrines reflected the historical period that gave birth to them. These traditional beliefs, therefore, needed to be reformed constantly by application to changing circumstances and adaption to new needs. Like his colleagues Edward Scribner AMES, Mathews believed that an individual's religious experience and the developmental process were more significant than metaphysical systems or revelation in determining authoritative religious standards. Jesus who lived completely for others provided the model for that life.

The churches, as the location of the Christian life, played a major role in Mathews's thought. Their purpose was to realize the religious goal of improving individual and social life, especially by transforming the values of industrial society in order to make them more Christian. These views led him to support the SOCIAL GOSPEL movement, which he understood as an important religious activity toward human progress.

Mathews was active as an educator, theologian, writer, and churchman. Between 1887 and 1894, with one year of study in Berlin (1890–1891), he was professor of rhetoric, history, and political economy at Colby College in Waterville, Maine. He left Colby to become a professor at the University of Chicago Divinity School, of which he was dean from 1908 to 1933, and where he remained until his death on October 23, 1941.

Mathews edited two major religious magazines, *The World Today* (1903–1911) and *Biblical World* (1913–1920). He also served on the boards of many organizations, and was especially concerned with the improvement of race relations, inner-city missions, and the Chautauqua Institute. Mathews's concern with the church is seen by his activity within his own denomination. He played a major role in the American Baptist Convention and was convention president in 1915. A vocal exponent of Christian unity (see ECUMENICAL MOVEMENT) he served as president of the Federal Council of Churches (1912–1916) and as a delegate to the 1925 Life and Work Conference in Stockholm and the 1927 Faith and Order Conference in Edinburgh (see NATIONAL COUNCIL OF CHURCHES; WORLD COUNCIL OF CHURCHES).

Mathews had his greatest impact as dean of Chicago's Divinity School. His teaching influenced numerous ministers and theologians, and his high profile, combined with his gentle personality, greatly furthered the spread and acceptability of modernist ideas.

EQ

Bibliography: Charles H. Arnold, *Near the Edge of the Battle: A Short History of the Divinity School and the Chicago School of Theology, 1866–1966* (Chicago: Divinity School Association, 1966); Joseph Jackson, *Many But One: The Ecumenics of Charity* (New York:

Sheed and Ward, 1964); Miles H. Krumbine, ed., *The Process of Religion: Essays in Honor of Dean Shailer Mathews* (New York: Macmillan, 1933); Shailer Mathews, *The Gospel and Modern Man* (New York: Macmillan, 1910); ———, *The Faith of Modernism* (New York: AMS Press, 1969); ———, *New Faith for Old: An Autobiography* (New York: Macmillan, 1936).

Mayflower Compact   Signed on November 11, 1620, the Mayflower Compact is generally understood as the starting point of the American ideal of self-government. Drawn up by the PIL-GRIMS prior to the establishment of their settlement at Plymouth Plantation, it became the basis for the colony's political and social organization and a means of asserting their continued loyalty to the British king despite their geographic separation. By signing it, the Pilgrims pledged "to covenant and combine our selves togeather into a civill body politick, for our better ordering & preservation. . . ." The colony would be held together by laws that its members would enact as required to accomplish the "general good of ye Colonie. . . ."

While the connection between the Mayflower Compact and the American ideal of representative democracy can be overdrawn—the Pilgrims limited political participation to the "saints" or members of the church, for example—it does suggest something significant. This is the idea that governments can be organized and created by the governed who gather together in a compact and agree to abide by the laws they will later adopt. As the first statement of that principle to be created in what later became the United States, the Mayflower Compact has a revered and well-deserved place in the national memory.

EQ

Bibliography: William Bradford, *Of Plymouth Plantation, 1620–1647: The Complete Text, with notes and an introduction by Samuel Eliot Morison* (New York: Knopf, 1952); George D. Langdon, Jr., *Pilgrim Colony: A History of New Plymouth, 1620–1691* (New Haven: Yale University Press, 1966).

Mayhew, Jonathan (1720–1766)   Described by John Adams as one of the first to promote the cause of American independence from England, Congregationalist minister Jonathan Mayhew was the descendant of Puritan ministers (see PURITANISM) who had given their lives to missionary work among the Indians on Martha's Vineyard. While born (October 8, 1720) and raised amid orthodox Puritan learning, Mayhew's life and thought signified a radical departure from Puritan orthodoxy.

His radical religious views were known early. When the young Harvard graduate was called to the ministry by West Church (Congregational) in Boston, there was difficulty in finding sufficient number of ministers to officiate at Mayhew's ordination for fear of providing the stamp of legitimacy to Mayhew's views.

There was good reason for that fear. Like his friend Charles CHAUNCY, Mayhew emphasized the reasonable nature of the Christian religion. He rejected the doctrine of eternal damnation, feeling that such punishment violated both the categories of reason and the existence of a just God. This was not all. Mayhew was also a nontrinitarian (see UNITARIAN CONTROVERSY). He rejected the belief that Christ was equal to God. Certainly Christ was a spiritual being superior to both humans and angels but not co-extensive and co-eternal with the Father.

Mayhew also emphasized human ability more than orthodox CONGREGATIONALISM. This emphasis brought Mayhew into conflict with the so-called New Divinity men, who emphasized the CALVINISM of their Puritan forebears and downplayed human ability. Mayhew was flatly Arminian (see ARMINIANISM), believing human action had a positive role to play in bringing about salvation and in doing good.

Mayhew's stress on human ability also led to a greater emphasis on human liberty and freedom. The implications were obvious in Mayhew's sermons. In 1750 he delivered a sermon entitled, "A Discourse Concerning Unlimited Submission and Non-Resistance to Rulers." The Scrip-

Jonathan Mayhew, Congregational minister at West Church in Boston whose opposition to English bishops and taxes greatly influenced New England's revolutionary leaders.

ture text was Romans 13, in which Paul admonishes the church at Rome against disobedience to the government, reminding it that all authority comes from God. This apparently clear-cut rejection of revolution was transformed by Mayhew, who argued that surely evil rulers were not of God. They must be of the devil. If so, resistance to them was virtue not sin.

Mayhew took his own advice and led the opposition to the appointment of a Church of England bishop in America. Here he combined the traditional Puritan hatred of bishops with the new emphasis on liberty. In sermons he denounced bishops as servants of tyranny, destroyers of liberty, and wondered where were the new worlds to escape to before being drowned in a deluge of bishops.

It was the Stamp Act of 1765 however, that provoked Mayhew's greatest political involvement. Opposition to the Stamp Tax imposed on the colonies by the British Parliament had been violent. In Boston, rioters destroyed the home and offices of the tax collector, prompting him to resign. In this atmosphere on August 25, 1765, Mayhew preached a sermon, "Ye Have Been Called unto Liberty." The "liberty" was renewed rioting that destroyed the home of Lieutenant Governor Thomas Hutchinson. Although Mayhew bemoaned the act of violence in an apology to Hutchinson, the colony's governor in his report to England labeled Mayhew as a leading agitator.

News of the repeal of the Stamp Act elicited a thanksgiving sermon from Mayhew. In "The Snare Broken," delivered on May 23, 1766, Mayhew emphasized the importance of freedom. He argued that God willed liberty for humanity, and that anything limiting that liberty displeased God. Mayhew did not live to see the fruits of the seeds he planted. Less than two months after delivering "The Snare Broken," he died on July 9, 1766. Although he missed the AMERICAN REVOLUTION by a decade, Mayhew deeply affected many of New England's revolutionary leaders. Josiah Quincy, John and Samuel Adams, James Otis, and James Bowdoin had been friends of the minister. In 1818 John Adams could still recommend Mayhew's 1750 sermon to Thomas JEFFERSON and reminisce about the impact it had on him as a 14-year-old boy.

EQ

Bibliography: Charles W. Akers, *Called Unto Liberty: A Life of Jonathan Mayhew, D.D.* (Cambridge: Harvard University Press, 1964); Alden Bradford, *Memoirs of the Life and Writings of Rev. Jonathan Mayhew* (Boston: C.C. Little, 1838); John Corrigan, *The Hidden Balance: Religion and the Social Theories of Charles Chauncy and Jonathan Mayhew* (Cambridge: Cambridge University Press, 1987); Clinton Rossiter, *Six Characters in Search of a Republic: Stud-*

ies in the Political Thought of the American Colonies (New York: Harcourt Brace & World, 1964).

McGready, James See CAMP MEETINGS.

McPherson, Aimee Semple (1890–1944)

Aimee Semple McPherson was a flamboyant Pentecostal (see PENTECOSTALISM) leader and the founder of the International Church of the Foursquare Gospel. She was the most famous female preacher of her day, and one of the greatest American evangelists of all time. McPherson emphasized faith healing and the importance of speaking in tongues as evidence of having been baptized by the Holy Spirit.

Aimee Kennedy was born on a farm near Ingersoll, Ontario in Canada on October 19, 1890. She was raised as a member of the Salvation Army but converted to Pentecostalism at a 1908 revival led by Robert James Semple. Soon thereafter she married Semple, was ordained, and traveled with him as a missionary to China. After her husband's death in Hong Kong, Aimee returned to the United States in 1911 with the intention of continuing her work as an evangelist. She then married Harold McPherson in 1912 but, finding her marriage confining, divorced him in 1921.

Between 1915 and 1923, Aimee McPherson conducted tent revivals throughout Canada and the United States. "Sister Aimee" knew how to use her good looks and theatrical oratory to draw thousands to her worship services. In 1917 she also began publishing *Bridal Call,* a monthly magazine that contained transcripts of her sermons and reports on the meetings she led. McPherson was one of the first evangelists to recognize the potential of radio, which, she said, carried "on the winged feet of the winds, the story of hope, the words of joy, of comfort, of salvation." By 1923 McPherson had made nine transcontinental tours and held preaching credentials from the ASSEMBLIES OF GOD, the METHODISTS, and the BAPTISTS.

On New Year's Day in 1923, McPherson opened the 5,000-seat Angelus Temple in Los

Aimee Semple McPherson. The flamboyant Pentecostal evangelist founded the International Church of the Foursquare Gospel in 1927. (Library of Congress)

Angeles, where she served as minister for 21 years. That site became the headquarters of the International Church of the Foursquare Gospel, a new denomination incorporated in 1927. The church's name refers to a vision McPherson experienced, when she saw the four-faced figures described in the Bible in Ezekiel 1:4–14. McPherson believed the faces in her vision symbolized the four roles that Christ's ministry fulfilled: Savior, Healer, Baptizer, and King. McPherson also founded a Bible institute known as L.I.F.E. (Lighthouse of International Foursquare Evangelism), which eventually trained over 3,000 pastors and evangelists. Her son Rolf McPherson assumed leadership of the denomination after her death, and it grew rapidly in the 1950s and 1960s.

After an alleged kidnapping in 1926, McPherson's mental health deteriorated precipitously. She suffered a nervous breakdown in 1930, was married for a third time in 1931, and was divorced four years later. While on a journey to help strengthen churches in her denomination, she succumbed to an accidental overdose of barbiturates, dying at an Oakland, California hotel on September 27, 1944.

GHS, Jr.

Bibliography: Edith L. Blumhofer, *Aimee Semple McPherson: Everybody's Sister* (Grand Rapids, Mich.: Eerdmans, 1993).

Mencken, Henry Louis (1880–1956)

Mencken's talent, the consummate production of vitriolic satire, let loose on all pieties and personalities of his day, found expression in a body of essays and newspaper columns. Acknowledging the wide resonance of Mencken's satire in the changing times of the 1920s, social critic Walter Lippman spoke of him as "the most powerful influence on this whole generation of educated people." As editor of the *Baltimore Herald* and other newspapers and magazines, Mencken produced a large number of essays, as well as several books, and an enduring scholarly contribution in three editions of *The American Language* (1919).

Mencken's grandfather emigrated from Germany in 1848, part of a large wave of Germans settling in Baltimore, Maryland. Born September 12, 1880, Mencken grew up in a successful middle-class family, with a strong belief in the superiority of German culture over that of non-German neighbors. Although thrust by his parents into the American Protestant world of Sunday school (see SUNDAY SCHOOL MOVEMENT) from an early age, in his youth Mencken also picked up a suspicion of all things religious from his father and grandfather, and a love of reading.

While apprenticed in his father's cigar factory, Mencken enrolled in a writing course, taking a job as a reporter for the Baltimore *Morning Herald* in 1899. Mencken's many years in journalism gave his prose its hard, direct edge. In *Newspaper Days* (1941), one of his three autobiographical works, Mencken referred to himself as "a critic of ideas," and in his striving to fill this role, he developed widely appreciated attacks on what he saw as the most pernicious influences on American culture, in particular PURITANISM and FUNDAMENTALISM. Writing for his magazine, the *American Mercury*, in the 1920s, Mencken reached an audience of approximately 65,000 people, being especially popular on the nation's college campuses.

Mencken, who valued the individualism and liberty at the heart of American life above all else, scorned those features of the culture that threatened to replace American's room for diversity and achievement with social conformity and mutual suspicion. A serious student of German philosopher Friedrich Nietzsche (1844–1901), he railed against what he saw as the mob's resentment of superior things and individuals, a tendency promoted by democracy's chief illusion—the idea that individuals are equal in fact. His *Diaries* also betray a lasting ANTI-SEMITISM. While a supporter of capitalism, he attacked the growing consumerism of his own day as an attempt to satiate the masses. He also lampooned the mindless turning to religious "quackery," whether forms of Christianity typified by popular evangelists (see SUNDAY, BILLY) or the eclectic blending of NEW THOUGHT in an age of science. As reporter for the *Baltimore Herald*, he covered the famous 1925 SCOPES TRIAL in Tennessee, where William Jennings BRYAN (see CREATIONISM) took on agnostic Clarence Darrow. Mencken's widely circulated sarcastic treatment of the trial provided many Americans with their primary exposure to the ideological conflict between modernists and fundamentalists.

By the Depression, Mencken's readership had declined; yet he remained an active writer, even though plagued by ill health from 1940 until his death on January 29, 1956. While his reputation has sometimes waned, members of later generations, dissatisfied with their culture, still find humor and insight in his biting critiques of American religious and political life.

MG

Bibliography: Carl Bode, *Mencken* (Carbondale: Southern Illinois University Press, 1969); George H. Douglas, *H. L. Mencken: Critic of American Life* (Hamden, Conn.: Archon Books, 1978); Marion E. Rogers, ed., *The Impossible H. L. Mencken: A Selection of His Best Newspaper Stories* (New York: Doubleday, 1991).

Mendes, Henry Pereira (1852–1937)

Although often overshadowed by men like Isaac Mayer WISE, Solomon SCHECTER, and Cyrus ADLER, Henry Pereira Mendes was a significant figure in 19th and 20th century American JUDAISM. Among the more traditional of the so-called Historical School, he served as a mediator between that school and the Orthodox (see CONSERVATIVE JUDAISM; ORTHODOX JUDAISM). He was instrumental in the founding of many of the institutions that strengthened traditional Judaism in the United States, and helped to bridge the difference between the older Sephardic and German Jewish communities and the newer Eastern European Jews who immigrated to the United States between 1880 and 1924.

Born in Birmingham, England on April 13, 1852 and descended from a long line of Sephardic rabbis, Henry Pereira Mendes came to the United States in 1877 as rabbi of Congregation Shearith Israel in New York City. During his 43-year tenure, Mendes labored to create a traditional yet decorous and Americanized Judaism. Working closely with Rabbi Sabato MORAIS, Mendes helped establish the Jewish Theological Seminary (1887), where he lectured on Jewish history and served as interim president (1897–1902) following Morais's death.

As rabbi of the oldest congregation in New York, Mendes took the lead in establishing the New York Board of [Jewish] Ministers, (now the New York Board of Rabbis) in 1882. He was also instrumental in the formation of the Union of Orthodox Jewish Congregations (1892) and served as its president until 1913. The U.O.J.C.'s statement of purpose to "advance the interests of positive Biblical, Rabbinical, Traditional, and Historical Judaism" can be read as Mendes's own vision for American Judaism.

Mendes was no parochial traditionalist. Reared in the cosmopolitan atmosphere of Sephardic Judaism, he had an abiding interest in promoting the cultural aspects of Judaism and serving the wider Jewish community. He contributed numerous poems, articles, and translations to the pages of the *American Hebrew*. Mendes also wrote pamphlets, children's books, and plays. He worked with a coalition of Reform, Orthodox, and Conservative Jews to produce the *Jewish Encyclopedia* and a new English translation of the *Tanakh*, the Hebrew Bible.

Mendes's concern for *klal Israel* (universal Israel) is seen in his early support of ZIONISM. Although more interested in its cultural and spiritual aspects as a means of revitalizing Jewish life, he lent his aid to political Zionism as a member of the Federation of American Zionists.

Poor health forced Mendes's retirement from public life in 1920. Although unable to continue most of his activities, he maintained an abiding interest in American Jewry. He continued his writing whenever his health allowed, publishing his last book, *Derech Hayim: The Way of Life*, three years before his death on October 20, 1937.

(See also REFORM JUDAISM.)

EQ

Bibliography: Moshe Davis, *The Emergence of Conservative Judaism: The Historical School in Nineteenth Century America* (Westport, Conn.: Greenwood Press, 1977); Nathan Glazer, *American Judaism*, 2nd ed., rev. (Chicago: University of Chicago Press, 1972); Eugen Markovitz, *Henry Pereira Mendes (1877–1920)* (Unpublished thesis, New York: Yeshiva University, 1961); David deSilva Pool, *H. Pereira Mendes: A Biography* (New York: s.n., 1938); Howard

Descendants of the radical, pacifist wing of the Reformation in Europe maintain a simple lifestyle in rural communities. The Mennonite church near Hinkletown, Pennsylvania in the 1930s. (Library of Congress)

M. Sachar, *A History of the Jews in America* (New York: Knopf, 1992).

Mennonites   One of the most successful movements to emerge out of the Radical Reformation in 16th-century Europe, the Mennonites now comprise the largest Anabaptist group in the United States. The Anabaptists were religious sectarians who exited what they saw as the corrupt state-churches of Switzerland, Germany, and Holland in order to form a group of true believers who would model themselves and their congregations after the patterns of the primitive church as described in the Bible. In addition to

attempting to maintain pure communities of visible saints apart from the impurities of society, Anabaptists typically practiced pacifism and attempted to live simply. Their practice of rebaptizing adults who could give accounts of their conversion experiences gave the Anabaptists (literally, rebaptizers) their name.

Mennonites derive their name from Menno Simons (1496–1561), a 16th-century Dutch convert from Roman Catholicism who established early Mennonite congregations in both the Netherlands and Germany. But their deepest roots are in Switzerland, where the Mennonites first emerged as dissenters from the religious establishment championed by the Swiss reformer and theologian Ulrich Zwingli and as pacifist opponents of the revolutionary Anabaptism of Melchior Hoffman, a radical reformer whose attempts to create out of Munster a "New Jerusalem" had ended in bloodshed.

Like other Anabaptist groups in 16th-century Europe, the Mennonites refused to participate in activities of the state, which they saw as "worldly." They objected to state-churches and vociferously championed the separation of church and state. Like the HUTTERITES and the AMISH, the Mennonites are included among the "peace churches" because of their refusal to participate in the military.

Mennonites first migrated to America in 1683. They were among a group of 13 families from Krefeld, Germany who responded to William PENN's promise of religious freedom in the Pennsylvania colony (see PENNSYLVANIA [COLONY]) by founding Germantown (now in Philadelphia), the first German-speaking settlement in America. Led by Francis Daniel Pastorius (1651–1720), these 13 families included both Mennonites and Quakers (see FRIENDS, THE RELIGIOUS SOCIETY OF), and by 1686 a meetinghouse to serve both these communities had been built in Germantown. Eventually these groups went their separate ways, and the first permanent Mennonite place of worship was established in Germantown in 1708.

The Mennonites' numbers in America were not increased through conversions, since for the most part they refused to proselytize. Their numbers were augmented instead by high birth rates and by three waves of immigration. In the colonial period, German-speaking Mennonites settled alongside their brethren in Pennsylvania. Eventually, these earliest Mennonites removed themselves to rural areas in present-day Lancaster County, Pennsylvania and from there moved south into Virginia and the Carolinas and west into Ohio, Indiana, and Ontario, Canada.

The religious freedom and economic prosperity enjoyed by America's first Mennonites prompted two additional waves of German-speaking Mennonite immigrants from Europe. The first group arrived after the Napoleonic wars and came from Alsace, Bavaria, and Hesse. The later group came from southern Russia in the 1870s. They were fleeing not the ravages of war but the indignities of a "Russification" campaign that threatened their folkways and sectarian religious practices. Both of these groups settled for the most part in the Midwest, and together they populated what is now the General Conference Mennonite Church of North America, a less stringent and smaller cousin to the so-called "Old Mennonites" of the Pennsylvania-based Mennonite Church.

Mennonites have split into numerous branches in America, typically over questions regarding the number and type of concessions that may be made to "worldly" contingencies. The Old Colony Mennonites, who quit Canada for Mexico in the 1920s in order to escape mandated governmental education, have clung tightly to their sectarian roots in Anabaptist dissent. They typically manifest their withdrawal from the corrupt "world" by dressing and speaking plainly and by shunning technological trappings such as radio and television. They also refuse to buy insurance, secure in the conviction that Mennonites can and must take care of one another in times of trouble. Other Mennonite groups have become both more "churchly" and more "Americanized." The Mennonite Church, for example, now conducts services in decorated churches rather than simple meetinghouses, and its liturgies proceed in English rather than German. Its members run colleges and seminaries, and sit on missionary boards. The largest Mennonite organization in the United States, the Mennonite Church reports over 100,000 members.

SRP

Bibliography: Harold S. Bender and Henry C. Smith, eds., *The Mennonite Encyclopedia,* 4 vols. (Scottsdale, Pa.: Herald Press, 1955–59); Cornelius J. Dyck and Dennis Martin, eds., *The Mennonite Encyclopedia,* 5 vols. (Scottsdale, Pa.: Herald Press, 1990).

Mercersburg Theology   See NEVIN, JOHN WILLIAMSON; SCHAFF, PHILIP.

Merton, Thomas (1915–1968)   Social commentator, poet, monk, and hermit are all words that describe Thomas Merton, one of the most enigmatic and intriguing figures in American religion. His audience, like that of Dorothy DAY, spread far beyond his ROMAN CATHOLICISM.

Merton's religious pilgrimage was a circuitous one. As described in his autobiography, *The Seven Storey Mountain,* it was a journey from worldliness and confusion to contemplation and clarity. Perhaps most significant was Merton's discovery that the deeper his withdrawal into contemplation, the more pronounced his engagement with the world.

Thomas Merton was born the son of artists in Prades, France on January 31, 1915. His father was a New Zealander and his mother an American. Shortly after his birth they moved to the United States to escape World War I. Merton's early life was marked by the death of his mother in 1921, extensive travel, temporary residences, and irregular education. His father's death in 1931 left Merton alone and depressed.

Entering Clare College at Cambridge University in 1932, Merton took too great advantage of the financial security provided by a trust set up by his grandfather. His dissolute and frivolous life led to his dismissal, and his guardian's demand that he return to America. On doing so, he entered Columbia University, where he majored in English. Active in literary affairs, journalism, and the avant-garde Communism of the day, Merton led a life typical of the rebellious intellectual of the 1930s. While at Columbia, however, he also encountered different views of the world, provided by two of his professors, Mark Van Doren and Daniel Walsh. Both of these men encouraged him to look at the medieval period and the Catholic intellectual world as an available option for interpreting the world and living one's life. This appreciation of the Catholic synthesis was strengthened by his reading of Etienne Gilson's *The Spirit of Medieval Philosophy.*

After entering Columbia's master's program in English, Merton began to focus his reading on Catholic authors, especially the English Jesuit Gerard Manley Hopkins. During this time he attended his first Catholic Mass and, after much internal struggle, decided to convert. Shortly after his conversion (November 16, 1938) he felt a call to the priesthood and was accepted by the Franciscans, who sent him to teach at St. Bonaventure College in upstate New York in order to experience the religious life. During that time he began to doubt his calling, and in a period of emotional turmoil (1941) made a Holy Week retreat to Our Lady of Gethsemani, a Trappist abbey in Kentucky. Impressed by the silent and contemplative life of the Trappists, Merton returned in December and after a two-month trial period became a novice monk in February 1942.

Brother Louis, as he was called, entered into the regimen of the Cistercian Order of the Strict Observance, as the Trappists are officially known. Silence, manual labor, regular devotions, and a simple life mark the daily existence of the members. Despite this or, as Merton himself claimed, because of this he began to write more. A book of poems and a guide to Cistercian life were followed by his spiritual autobiography. This work, *The Seven Storey Mountain,* brought fame to the young monk and renewed popular interest in monasticism, leading to an influx of young people into contemplative orders like the Trappists.

Despite the demands of the order and his positions as master of scholastics (1951–1955) and master of novices (1955–1965), Merton was a prolific author, producing 50 books and hundreds of articles. His interests were in two apparently divergent areas. The more widely known was his social concerns. Pacifism, racial equality, and economic justice all were topics of his writings. Deeply committed to nonviolence, he was a strong supporter of Martin Luther KING, JR. His pacifism was so absolute that he was silenced by his superiors in 1962 during the VIETNAM WAR. His deep spiritual commitment and the popularity of his autobiography allowed Merton's views on social issues to reach an audience that otherwise might have rejected them out of hand.

The spiritual depth of religious experience was the other aspect of Merton's writings. In the early 1960s Merton began serious study of monasticism and contemplation in the Asian religions, developing strong interests in ZEN, Sufism, and Taoism. In 1965 he received a dispensation from the corporate rule of the order and entered a hermitage located on the monastery's grounds. During this period he wrote several books on Zen and on the contemplative life. Invited to attend a conference on Asian Christian contemplation, he embarked on a whirlwind tour of the United States and Asia. While at the conference in Bangkok, Thailand he was electrocuted as he adjusted an electric fan in his room. He died on December 10, 1968, exactly 27 years after he had entered the monastery of Gethsemani. Although his death cut short his career, Merton's work continues to have a deep impact on people concerned about the spiritual life and the corrosive impact of materialism and violence on the human soul and human society.

EQ

Bibliography: Dennis Q. McInerny, *Thomas Merton: The Man and His Work* (Spencer, Mass.: Cistercian Publications, 1974); Thomas Merton, *The Seven Storey Mountain* (New York: Harcourt, Brace, 1948); Michael Mott, *The Seven Mountains of Thomas Merton* (Boston: Houghton Mifflin, 1984).

mesmerism   Mesmerism refers to a tradition of healing techniques and metaphysical speculation begun by the Austrian physician Franz Anton Mesmer (1733–1815) and popularized in the United States in the mid-19th century.

Mesmerism was first and foremost a technique for healing. According to Mesmer, diseases of both the body and the mind were caused by subtle imbalances in a fine fluid called "animal magnetism." The way to heal diseases and to foster life and health was, therefore, to redirect this fluid back to its natural and harmonious state. Mesmer's technique for accomplishing this realignment was to put the patient into a trancelike state and then to manipulate that patient's "animal magnetism" by passing his or her arms over the area of the disease.

Although Mesmer described his discoveries as scientific rather than religious truths, mesmerism possessed for its defenders a spiritual as well as a therapeutic allure. According to Mesmer, animal magnetism could promote not only healing but also seemingly supernatural insight into occult mysteries. It could also foster extraordinary mental abilities such as extrasensory perception.

Mesmer performed his first cures in 1773. His healing system became such a hit in Paris that the French Academy felt compelled to denounce him in 1784. This organized opposition caused Mesmer to have limited influence in Europe. But his ideas and practices were taken to America by the author Charles Poyen, whose books and lectures helped to popularize mesmerism in the United States in the 1840s. Poyen's advocacy attracted figures such as Andrew Jackson DAVIS, who began shortly after hearing the lecture of an itinerant mesmerist to cultivate the clairvoyant powers that would make him one of the most important figures in American SPIRITUALISM.

Like SWEDENBORGIANISM, mesmerism appealed primarily to educated, middle-class Americans who were able to follow its esoteric theories (and, in the case of mesmerism, afford its practitioners). Again like Swedenborgianism, it peaked in the middle of the 19th century before gaining a significant following. Through people like Davis, however, who integrated mesmerist ideas and practices into spiritualism, mesmerism made its way into other occult movements, including THEOSOPHY and phrenology. Mesmerism also played a role in the development of CHRISTIAN SCIENCE, hypnotism, and Freudian psychoanalysis. At least in this way, the work of Mesmer lived on well after his death in 1815.

SRP

Bibliography: Robert C. Fuller, *Mesmerism and the American Cure of Souls* (Philadelphia: University of Pennsylvania Press, 1982).

Methodist Episcopal Church, South
See UNITED METHODIST CHURCH.

Methodists   The Methodists are a group of churches that trace their origins back to 18th-century Church of England clergyman John Wesley (see WESLEYAN TRADITION, THE). Organized at first as societies under lay leadership within Anglicanism, Methodism eventually developed into a separate denomination after the American Revolution. The UNITED METHODIST CHURCH is the largest Methodist denomination in the United States at present. Several smaller churches, including the AFRICAN METHODIST EPISCOPAL CHURCH and the AFRICAN METHODIST EPISCOPAL ZION CHURCH, the major branches of black Methodism, also compose this denominational family.

In 1729 John Wesley joined a small association of Oxford University students (known derisively as "Methodists") who were seeking to deepen their religious faith. A number of years later, on the way to attend a church service in London in May 1738, Wesley felt his heart "strangely warmed" and sensed for the first time that God truly loved him. Soon afterward, he began traveling about the countryside with his brother Charles, a brilliant writer of hymns. He preached to large crowds of common people who gathered in open areas to hear his message about the saving grace of Jesus Christ. Wesley also developed an elaborate connectional system that spread Methodist ideas throughout England.

Inevitably, friction developed between Methodists and the Anglican establishment of which they were a part. American Methodist congregations had begun to meet regularly both in Virginia and in New York in the 1760s. Because

A worshiper at First Methodist Wesleyan Church, Washington, D.C. in the 1930s. (Library of Congress)

the War for Independence forced many Anglican priests to flee the colonies, Methodist societies were often left without access to baptism and holy communion, sacramental acts over which only clergy could preside. Although Anglican polity required a bishop to ordain a man to the ministry, Wesley and two other priests ordained clergy for the American church in September 1784. At the same time, Wesley appointed Thomas COKE and Francis ASBURY as superintendents over Methodists in the new United States. In December 1784 a gathering of preachers in Baltimore, Maryland, known afterward as the "Christmas Conference," established the Methodist Episcopal Church and confirmed Wesley's appointment of Asbury and Coke as superintendents.

Methodists soon were major participants in the SECOND GREAT AWAKENING, the remarkable series of revivals that sprang up in the early 19th century. Asbury, their most active leader, was an aggressive evangelist who traveled almost incessantly preaching the gospel and building up his denomination. He became a model for other circuit-riding preachers who spread Methodism across the Appalachian Mountains and into what was then the frontier. Asbury recognized the value of "circulation," prodding clergy to seek converts in even the most remote locations. He was also an advocate of CAMP MEETINGS, the extended outdoor revivals that helped establish Methodism as the most vigorous denomination of the period.

Despite the tremendous growth the Great Awakening inspired, conflicts began to emerge as Methodism expanded. One division was precipitated over the matter of race. Although African-Americans had been among the earliest participants in American Methodism, racial discrimination forced Richard ALLEN, a black preacher in Philadelphia, to leave his church. In 1816 he organized the African Methodist Episcopal Church and became its first bishop. In New York City in 1821, two other black Methodists, Peter Williams and James Varick, formed the African Methodist Episcopal Zion Church. Both these churches have had immense influence within the African-American community. The African Methodist Episcopal Church contains over 2.2 million members today, while the African Methodist Episcopal Zion Church now has a membership of 1.2 million.

The other major dispute within American Methodism concerned the authority of bishops. James O'Kelly, a Methodist minister, wished his church would adopt an egalitarian governing structure, one that did not contain bishops and was more in accord with the democratic ideology of the Revolution. When this protest failed, O'Kelly and his followers withdrew from the main denomination in 1794 and formed the Republican Methodist Church. This denomination later chose the name "Christian Church." It numbered about 20,000 people before part of it merged with the Disciples of Christ in the mid-19th century. In the 1820s, another Methodist party arose that sought both the elimination of the episcopate and greater authority for laity. This challenge also was unsuccessful, and as a result, about 5,000 Methodists formed the Methodist Protestant Church in November 1830.

John Wesley abhorred slavery, and the earliest rules of the Methodist Episcopal Church gave slaveholders one year to emancipate their slaves if they wished to be considered church members. Although Methodists moderated their views about slavery for a time, rising abolitionist sentiment in the North during the 1830s and 1840s again brought the issue to the center of denominational life. When the 1836 and 1840 General Conferences failed to adopt a strong antislavery position, Orange Scott, a prominent New England minister, convinced 15,000 Methodists in 1843 to organize a new denomination, the Wesleyan Methodist Church. In 1860, another group of antislavery Methodists left the main denomination and formed the Free Methodist Church. The group added "free" to its name to signify that it stood for freedom in worship as well as freedom for slaves. The Wesleyan Church (as the denomination is now called) and the Free Methodist Church, which were both strongly influenced by the HOLINESS MOVEMENT at the end of the century, contain about 110,000 and 75,000 members respectively today.

The greatest schism in the Methodist ranks occurred in 1845, when Methodists in the southern and border states created the Methodist Episcopal Church, South. At the 1844 General Conference, antislavery forces were able to require that James O. Andrew, bishop of Georgia, either discontinue functioning as a bishop or free the slaves he owned. Since Andrew had not bought his slaves but acquired them through marriage, he thought he should not have to comply. Gathering in protest at Louisville, Kentucky the following year, the Methodist annual conferences in the slaveholding states created a new church in which ownership of slaves was acceptable. The first General Conference of the Methodist Episcopal Church, South met in Petersburg, Virginia in May 1846. Although Union victory in the Civil War encouraged northern Methodists to attempt to win back the southern churches by force, white southerners resisted and maintained their ecclesiastical independence after 1865.

In 1870, African-Americans who formerly belonged to the Methodist Episcopal Church, South were encouraged by white southern Methodists to organize their own denomination. In cooperation with white Methodists, black Methodists formed the Colored Methodist Episcopal Church. They were given title to church property by white trustees, and African-American clergy were ordained by the southern Methodist bishops. This denomination altered its name in 1954 and, now known as the CHRISTIAN METHODIST EPISCOPAL CHURCH, contains over 700,000 members.

In the half-century after the end of the Civil War, the Methodist Episcopal Church and the Methodist Episcopal Church, South each grew four-fold—from one million to four million members in the North, and from 500,000 to two million members in the South. Despite such impressive figures of growth, defections from these churches also occurred, as discord over the Holiness movement challenged the comprehensiveness of the mainline denominations in the late 19th century. While most Methodists believed that the quest for personal holiness was a lifelong process, others insisted it could be an instantaneous experience. Since Wesley himself had admitted the possibility of a believer's attaining perfect sanctification in the present life, some Methodists believed they were justified in separating from their churches. These holiness advocates formed several new denominations, including the SALVATION ARMY, the CHURCH OF THE NAZARENE, and the Pilgrim Holiness Church.

During the last years of the 19th century, representatives of the northern and southern branches of mainline Methodism began to discuss reunion. As the animosities of the Civil War era started to fade, Methodists in both sections of the country realized that their shared theological ancestry and similar governing structures made unity once again feasible. Although preparations for the merger took several decades, a uniting conference in the spring of 1939 brought the Methodist Episcopal Church and the Methodist Episcopal Church, South (as well as the smaller Methodist Protestant Church) together.

The ecumenical trends of the 1950s and 1960s, moreover, culminated in another merger that further strengthened American Methodism. After a meeting in Chicago in November 1966, the union of the Methodist church with the Evangelical United Brethren Church, a denomination of German Pietist origin, was approved. This new denomination, called the United Methodist Church, came into being early in 1968. Despite a recent decline in membership, typical of all the denominations of mainline Protestantism over the past two decades, the United Methodist Church reported nearly nine million members in 1991.

GHS, Jr.

Bibliography: Harry V. Richardson, *Dark Salvation: The Story of Methodism as It Developed Among Blacks in America* (Garden City, N.Y.: Doubleday, 1976); Russell E. Richey, *Early American Methodism* (Bloomington: Indiana University Press, 1991); A. Gregory Schneider, *The Way of the Cross Leads Home: The Domestication of American Methodism* (Bloomington: Indiana University Press, 1993).

Metropolitan Community Church

The Universal Fellowship of Metropolitan Community Churches (M.C.C.) is a new Protestant denomination that ministers especially to lesbians and gays.

The M.C.C. was founded in 1968 by Troy D. Perry, a pastor at the Church of God of Prophecy in Santa Ana, California, who was ousted from his church after publicly acknowledging his homosexuality. Perry was born in Tallahassee, Florida. When he was 12 years old his father died, and he subsequently moved in with church-going relatives who introduced him to PENTECOSTALISM and the controversial practice of SNAKE HANDLING. Shortly thereafter, he experienced a call to the ministry. At the age of 13 he became an itinerant preacher in the Tennessee-based Church of God (see CHURCH

OF GOD [CLEVELAND, TENNESSEE]). He preached in Georgia, Alabama, Florida, and Illinois before being called at the age of 23 to the pastorate of the Church of God of Prophecy in Santa Ana.

Distraught over losing his church as well as his wife and two children following his avowal of his homosexuality, Perry attempted suicide. On October 6, 1968, he advertised a church meeting open to homosexuals at his home in Huntington Park, California. Twelve people attended, and the M.C.C. was born.

Now headquartered in Pasadena, California, the M.C.C. boasts approximately 27,000 members in 240 congregations in the United States and abroad. The AIDS crisis has swelled the denomination's ranks, as HIV-infected gays and lesbians have turned to a church that has embraced them unflinchingly. But that same crisis has also taken, through death, many of the denomination's parishioners and clergy.

Perhaps because of Perry's roots in Pentecostalism, M.C.C. churches tend to be rather conservative theologically. Most members view the Bible as the inspired word of God and affirm orthodox creedal positions such as the Trinity. On social issues, however, M.C.C. churches tend toward liberal stances. The denomination has supported, for example, a nuclear arms freeze. It has, moreover, spoken out against claims that the Bible condemns homosexuality. Paul, many M.C.C. members claim, was condemning not homosexuality in general but particular types of homosexuality in his letters to the Romans and the Corinthians. And the sin of Sodom and Gomorrah was not homosexuality but idolatry.

The M.C.C. has attempted unsuccessfully to join the NATIONAL COUNCIL OF CHURCHES. Nonetheless, the denomination has, by its very existence, forced more mainline Protestant denominations to address theological, ethical, and liturgical issues regarding homosexuality, including the "holy union" rites of same-sex couples in M.C.C. churches and the controversial assertion of M.C.C. members that "God made me gay."

SRP

Bibliography: Ronald M. Enroth and Gerald E. Jamison, *The Gay Church* (Grand Rapids: Eerdmans, 1974); Mel White, *Stranger at the Gate: To Be Gay and Christian in America* (New York: Simon & Schuster, 1994).

millennialism See ESCHATOLOGY; DISPENSATIONALISM; POSTMILLENNIALISM; PREMILLENNIALISM.

Miller, William (1782–1849) William Miller was a farmer and Baptist lay preacher in upstate New York whose prediction that the second coming of Jesus Christ would occur in 1843 created a flurry of religious excitement across the United States. The movement Miller created, which represented one of the most extreme instances of American millennial (see PREMILLENNIALISM) fervor, provided a nucleus for the formation of the SEVENTH-DAY ADVENTIST CHURCH.

Born on February 15, 1782 in Pittsfield, Massachusetts, Miller grew up in Low Hampton, New York. After his marriage in 1803, he worked as a farmer in Poultney, Vermont and served as an officer in the United States army during the War of 1812. In 1815 he returned to Low Hampton where he experienced a religious conversion and abandoned the skepticism of his youth. Following a lengthy period of biblical study, he announced in 1831 that the return of Jesus Christ would take place 12 years later. Miller was licensed as a lay preacher by the Baptist church in 1833 and published his computations about the second coming (*Evidence from Scripture and History of the Second Coming of Christ*) in 1836.

The revivals of the SECOND GREAT AWAKENING had already raised millennial expectations that the thousand-year reign of Christ might soon be realized. As a consequence, large crowds came flocking wherever Miller spoke. Joshua

William Miller, the founder of the Adventist Church who in the 1830s predicted the imminent second coming of Christ.

V. Himes, a Boston minister who publicized Miller's predictions, bought him the largest tent in the country and a chart on which to display his biblical calculations. Despite opposition from most clergy and the ridicule of many other Americans, people of all denominations joined Miller's intentionally nonsectarian movement. At the height of the Millerite excitement, over a million people are estimated to have viewed his teachings sympathetically.

As January 1843 began, Miller announced that Christ would return to earth sometime between March 21, 1843 and March 21, 1844. After the latter date passed, Miller confessed he had erred in his original computation and instead named October 22, 1844 as the correct date. When October 23rd dawned and the millennium failed to arrive, most of Miller's disciples abandoned their hopes, repudiated their leader, and simply went back to their ordinary lives. A few followers, however, remained faithful to his teachings. No longer desiring to predict a specific date for the second coming, they met in Albany, New York in April 1845 to continue the Millerite movement. Although this organization itself proved short-lived, one part of it under Ellen Gould White's leadership eventually helped establish the Seventh-day Adventist Church.

Miller himself played little part in the subsequent development of Adventism. Embittered by his experiences and virtually a forgotten man, he died at Low Hampton on December 20, 1849.

GHS, Jr.

Bibliography: Ronald L. Numbers and Jonathan M. Butler, eds., *The Disappointed: Millerism and Millenarianism in the Nineteenth Century* (Bloomington: Indiana University Press, 1987).

missions, foreign A phrase applied to a number of Christian missionary efforts during various periods of American history, foreign missions has most often denoted Protestant efforts to bring the message of salvation and/or the blessings of American civilization to those considered to be non-American. In general, Protestant foreign missions have focused on two sorts of cultural outsiders. During the colonial period and into the early 19th century, efforts centered around the conversion of "foreigners" on the North American continent, particularly Native Americans. In the decades following the American Revolution, Protestant missionary organizations began to extend their work to foreigners abroad, and outreach to Native Americans gradually was subsumed under the category of domestic or "home" missions. Indeed, the distinctions made between home and foreign mission fields have always been hazy at best, and most often have reflected current attitudes regarding racial difference and the potential for cultural assimilation.

During the colonial era, Protestant outreach to Native American peoples was largely limited to work among those in areas adjacent to European settlement, tribes that Anglo-American settlers hoped to civilize and enlighten with the blessings of Christianity. In general, these efforts encountered fierce native opposition and suffered the logistical problems created by cultural and linguistic differences. Moreover, missionaries also coped with land-hungry whites who exhibited little sympathy for Native American missions, and who favored cultural extermination over conversion.

Although the 17th-century Puritans were largely preoccupied with the welfare of their own religious community, within the first decades of settlement they initiated sporadic missions to Native Americans. Thomas Mayhew, Jr. established the first "foreign mission" on Martha's Vineyard in 1642. A more extensive effort was launched in 1646 when John ELIOT began to preach among the Massachusets tribe and to work on a translation of the Bible into the local tongue. He saw the conversion of the Native Americans as an integral aspect of sacred history that would help to usher in God's kingdom. Believing that civilizing and Christianizing went hand-in-hand, Eliot attempted to isolate Christian converts by organizing them into "praying towns" where they could be immersed in the values of a Christian culture. By 1671, over 3,500 Native Americans had congregated in 14 "praying towns," but these efforts were cut short by King Philip's War in 1675, in which an estimated 5,000 Native Americans were killed along with many Euro-Americans. Other colonial missions to Native Americans included John Sergeant's work among the Housatonics in Stockbridge, Massachusetts, beginning in 1734; Eleazer Wheelock's boarding school, established in 1743 in Lebanon, Connecticut; and David Brainerd's work in New Jersey in the mid-1740s.

Although colonial missionary efforts were neither sustained nor systematic, notable Protestant theologians followed Eliot's lead in seeing foreign missions as an important part of God's providential plan. Religious leaders such as Samuel Sewall and Cotton MATHER wrote about the importance of missions in the early 18th century. By mid-century Jonathan Edwards, perhaps the most famous colonial intellectual and theologian, and also a preacher to Native Americans in western Massachusetts, conceptually linked the missionary spread of the revivals of the GREAT AWAKENING with God's plan for the work of redemption. Gradually, Protestants came to see the evangelization of the rest of the world as an obligation placed upon America by virtue of its unique covenant with the creator.

Anglicans conducted more extensive, if not more successful, missionary efforts among Native Americans and African-Americans in the colonial period, as one aspect of their work in North America under the SOCIETY FOR THE PROPAGATION OF THE GOSPEL IN FOREIGN PARTS. Although the primary concern of the Church of England remained the organizing of unchurched Euro-Americans, in the first decades of the 18th century attempts were made to catechize and baptize Native Americans. When linguistic and cultural barriers rendered these efforts fruitless, missionaries focused on the slave population and experienced some modest successes. Most slaves defied Anglican instruction, but greater resistance came from slave owners, who worried that bringing Africans into the church would threaten their status as property and eventually necessitate manumission. In turn, clergy worked hard to convince both masters and slaves that Christianity and slavery were compatible institutions.

The 19th century is often called the "Great Century" of American missions, because within that period ideology and organization combined to form the first well-supported national foreign missions organizations dedicated to the task of evangelizing the rest of the world. The foreign mission movement was not entirely a creature of American soil; indeed, leaders depended on the British precedents of the Baptists, who formed a mission society in 1792, and especially the London Missionary Society (1795), for their inspiration. But local impetus sprang from the evangelical zeal ignited by the revivalism of the Second Great Awakening, a movement that promoted the connection between individual regeneration and Christian service to society as a whole. In 1806 a group of Williams College students, seeking shelter from a thunderstorm in a local haystack, prayed together (see HAYSTACK PRAYER MEETING) and promised to dedicate their lives to foreign missions. Out of this gathering arose the largely Congregational- and Presbyterian-sponsored American Board of Commissioners for Foreign Missions (1810), the first national society dedicated to the task of outreach overseas. In turn, after two of its first missionaries, Adoniram JUDSON and Luther Rice, were convinced of the theological importance of adult baptism en route to their field in India in 1812, American Baptists formed the Baptist Board of Foreign Missions (1814) to support foreign work. These societies were joined by the Methodists (1819), the Episcopalians (1821), and the Old School Presbyterians, who broke from the ABCFM to form their own denominational missionary society in 1837.

Inherent in all of these efforts were assumptions about America's providential role in the history of the world, many carried over directly from 18th-century Puritan theorists. To be sure, the missions movement as a whole, as William Hutchison has noted, was a New England-centered enterprise, despite the location of national offices in New York and Philadelphia. New Englanders had always been assured of the natural superiority of their own culture. After the founding of the nation, much of this assurance was transferred to the notion of the republic as the unique agent of God's will on earth. Thus it is not surprising that as the United States opened itself politically and economically to commerce with other countries, Protestants believed that the blessings of its superior culture, and especially its religion, should travel along as well. By mid-century Americans supported missions in China, Burma, India, Southeast Asia, the Sandwich Islands, Africa, South America, and Palestine.

Often overlooked in studies of the foreign mission enterprise is the crucial role that has been played by women. Prior to the Civil War, most societies did not commission single women for overseas posts. However, it was a common practice for women who wanted to carry the gospel abroad to marry men headed to foreign fields in order to work alongside them as "helpers." Schools such as Mount Holyoke trained women specifically for this occupation, and single men about to embark on their assignments were encouraged to choose spouses from these academies. Moreover, mission efforts were highly dependent upon financial assistance from home, and lay women frequently organized fund-raising efforts to support men and women in the field. In the postbellum era, when women were granted commissions as missionaries in their own right, they entered the field in large numbers and often brought a distinctive style to their Christian outreach by emphasizing education and the training of children. By 1900 women in some overseas missions far outnumbered their male colleagues. Moreover, beginning in the late 1860s Congregational, Methodist, Baptist, and Presbyterian women organized their own auxiliaries to the national denominational missions boards, enlisting millions of American women in the largest of the great 19th-century female voluntary movements.

If the early 19th century witnessed the birth of national missions organizations, the period from 1880 to 1920 marked the heyday of foreign missions interest and activity among American Protestants. At the center of this crusade was the STUDENT VOLUNTEER MOVEMENT (SVM), an instrument for recruiting college-age volunteers founded in 1888. By the mid-20th century, the SVM claimed to have sent 20,000 missionaries abroad to preach the gospel, and along with auxiliary fund-raising organizations, the work of able leaders such as John R. MOTT,

Arthur T. Pierson, and Robert E. Speer led to a sharp rise in voluntary giving to the cause of missions, which peaked at $45 million per year in 1924. Yet even at the pinnacle of its success, the evangelical missions movement was being eroded by internal ideological disputes. The relative harmony that had existed throughout the 19th century among people holding disparate theological opinions about missionary strategy began to unravel with the growing rift between conservative and liberal evangelicals.

For liberals, growing secularization and pluralism in American society meant that the notion of overseas outreach itself became increasingly problematic, and mainline denominations became less inclined to cooperate with the conservative emphasis on American preaching and baptizing as the principal means of foreign assistance. By the 1930s and 1940s, liberals increasingly favored handing over control of missions to native churches, and providing smaller-scale social services to supplement local expressions of Christian practice. Conservative evangelicals, on the other hand, have been joined by Holiness and Pentecostal Churches in recent years in a burgeoning program of outreach. In recent decades, these missions have achieved remarkable successes in Latin America, Africa, and Southeast Asia, and large numbers of natives have converted to evangelical Protestantism.

In the 20th century American Catholics also have organized to sponsor foreign missions. Although European-based missionary orders, such as the JESUITS, had been seeking American recruits prior to this time, in 1911 the Maryknoll Order established the first American-based association, the American Foreign Missionary Society. Prior to World War II, Maryknoll focused its efforts primarily on Asia, but in recent years the focus has shifted to Latin America and Africa. Beginning in the 1940s, lay missions within the church were instituted, and by the late 1950s Americans had organized a number of successful lay mission groups, including the Association for International Development in New Jersey, Lay Mission Helpers in Los Angeles, and the Papal Volunteers for Latin America. In 1970 the Church consolidated its missions outreach under the umbrella of the United States Catholic Missions Council.

LMK

Bibliography: Patricia R. Hill, *The World Their Household: The American Woman's Foreign Mission Movement and Cultural Transformation, 1870–1920* (Ann Arbor: University of Michigan, 1984); William R. Hutchison, *Errand to the World: American Protestant Thought and Foreign Missions* (Chicago: University of Chicago Press, 1987); Kenneth Scott Latourette, *A History of the Expansion of Christianity,* 7 vols. (New York: Harper & Brothers, 1937–1945).

missions, home The commitment to domestic or "home" missions has been an important aspect of Protestant church life throughout the history of Euro-American settlement in North America. The conversion of Native Americans was offered frequently as an ostensible reason for the exploration and colonization of the New World. Missionary efforts were sporadic during the colonial period, and in the eyes of religious leaders, they usually fell under the rubric of "foreign" missions because they were conducted among peoples of other cultures. The push for home missions, which initially connoted outreach to other Euro-Americans who remained outside the bounds of Protestant church life, was largely a product of 19th-century evangelical culture. The primary impetus for such outreach came from Christians in the Northeast, particularly New England, where the motivating vision of America as God's chosen nation remained clearest.

A number of social conditions in the post-Revolutionary nation contributed to the growth of interest in domestic missions. The notion of the United States as a unified republic with a shared destiny encouraged a conceptual separation between the conversion of those at home and those abroad. While both tasks were seen as important, the former took on added urgency after the disestablishment of churches in the early national period, an institutional rupture that left northern evangelicals fearful about the moral consequences of letting individuals find their own spiritual paths. Increasingly, the onus of communal religious guidance, and thus missionary outreach, fell upon the denominations, which were forced to compete for adherents in a newly opened marketplace of beliefs. Although they did vie for members, they also demonstrated a new willingness to cooperate interdenominationally. The resurgence of revivalism during the SECOND GREAT AWAKENING of the 1820s and 1830s, in which preachers emphasized the connection between individual salvation and social reform efforts, further reinforced the commitment to missions. And finally, the opening of western territories to settlement in the decades after the Revolution left large numbers of Euro-Americans in need of religious organization.

The establishment of missionary societies proceeded swiftly, beginning at the local and state levels. The New York Missionary Society (1796) was founded by Baptists, Presbyterians, and Dutch Reformed as the first interdenominational association dedicated to missions, and it was followed by societies in Connecticut (1798) and Massachusetts (1799). Initially devoting their attentions to both the evangelization of Native Americans and the establishment of churches in the new American settlements in western territories, these societies gradually turned over work among Native Americans to foreign missions organizations. The Connecticut Missionary Society, the largest and most expansive of the New England organizations in this period, concentrated the majority of its efforts on American settlers. Its first missionaries were sent on four- to eight-week tours, preaching the gospel and distributing Bibles and religious tracts. The itinerant work of Joseph Badger in Ohio, and Timothy Flint and Salmon Giddings in Missouri, reflected the circuit-style organization adopted by the societies to effectively cover large expanses of western land. In 1826 these state societies became auxiliaries of the newly established American Home Missionary Society, an association of churches from the reformed tradition that sponsored thousands of missionaries across the country. The Domestic and Foreign Missionary Society of the Protestant Episcopal Church (1821) and the American Baptist Home Missionary Society (1832) also reflected the increased tendency toward national consolidation of mission efforts, as well as a growing Protestant focus on church-building in western regions.

Out of the social ferment of the SECOND GREAT AWAKENING came many auxiliary interdenominational organizations that contributed to missionary efforts. The American Bible Society (1816) determined to supply Bibles to every family in the nation; the American Sunday School Union (1824) dedicated itself to establishing a Sunday school in every place in the United States with sufficient population; and the American Tract Society (1825) commissioned hundreds of colporteurs, or distributors of religious literature, to work throughout the Mississippi River Valley and in the territories beyond. In addition, the missionary impulse spurred the establishment of dozens of colleges and universities between 1815 and 1860, with the aim of inculcating morality and piety in young American citizens.

Increasingly, moral behavior and social reform also fell within the purview of missionary efforts, leading to the creation of temperance, antislavery, antigambling, and antidueling associations in the antebellum period. These crusades, meant to wipe out maladies that were defined as sinful, increasingly mobilized the support and voluntary efforts of lay Protestants, many stirred by the zealous calls for reform sounded in the revivals. The voluntary labor of women figured largely in these societies, inasmuch as these social ills were often depicted as direct threats to the welfare of the home and the family. Through "moral suasion" rather than coercion, American Protestants hoped to save the country from spiritual dangers that seemed to take an expanding variety of forms. Some scholars have attributed this increased apprehension of moral peril as a consequence of the lack of obvious external dangers to the nation, which led to a heightened tendency to fear internal subversion and to see it in many guises. To be sure, antebellum mission supporters did not lack for certitude about the righteousness of their work, and recent scholarship has indicated the extent to which "sinfulness" often was defined as anything falling outside the bounds of normative middle-class, Euro-American behavior. Whatever its causes and shortcomings, the antebellum mission effort remains unmatched in terms of the financial and human resources mobilized during this period. Some of these crusades endured into the 20th century, most notably the temperance cause, a movement that led directly to the work of the Women's Christian Temperance Union in the late 19th century. Other crusades reached their peak of support in this period and subsequently yielded to newer mission movements.

Both the focus of home missions and its organizational bases shifted dramatically in the years after the Civil War. The Protestant commitment to interdenominational cooperation gave way to an increasing denominational consciousness by mid-century. Thereafter, most missionary associations worked under denominational auspices. Several new social concerns also came to occupy religious attention. The most immediate was the education of newly freed slaves in the southern states, a cause that northern Protestants quickly placed at the center of their domestic agenda. The Congregational American Missionary Association led the way in offering education and "proper" Christianity to African-Americans, although its efforts frequently aroused the antagonism of southern blacks who viewed their help as patronizing. Northern black denominations, including the AFRICAN METHODIST EPISCOPAL (A.M.E.) and AFRICAN METHODIST EPISCOPAL ZION (A.M.E.Z.) Churches, also conducted extensive domestic missions in the southern states during Reconstruction. In general, educational efforts were quite successful, leading to the establishment of many schools and colleges, but southern blacks resisted attempts to promote northern, and particularly Euro-American, evangelical practices and beliefs, such as more formalized, less enthusiastic worship services. Similar efforts were also initiated among Native Americans in the postbellum period and have continued in some places into the 20th century.

A second, increasingly important field of home mission activity arose with increased immigration to the United States after 1880. Once again fearful about the effects of non-Protestants on American morality and piety, Protestant leaders initiated work among American immigrants. Yet the definition of this labor as a home mission field was dictated largely by prevalent racial theories of the period. Just as Native Americans in the early 19th century had been considered objects of foreign mission (see MISSIONS, FOREIGN) work, so now was outreach to Asian-Americans seen as a distinctly foreign field. Conversely, concern for European immigrants fell under the control of home missions agencies, and religious leaders initiated a broad array of social programs, Sunday schools, and language classes in an effort to "Americanize" new migrants. These exertions largely overlapped with increased Protestant interest in the welfare of Christians in the urban environment, where "institutional churches" were established to complete with employment offices, training programs, gymnasiums, and social centers to encourage Protestant morality. Bolstered by the rise of interdenominational Christian agencies such as the YMCA, YWCA, and the Salvation Army, urban missions became an integral component of Protestant outreach.

Although in the 20th century most Protestant denominations have boards or commissions assigned to deal with home missions, the intensive and broadly popular efforts that characterized 19th-century home missions have given way to specialized efforts that cover the social and theological spectrum. Mainline Protestants and more conservative evangelicals have come to view the missionary task in substantially different ways, with liberals emphasizing the social service component, and evangelicals concentrating on evangelization and the preaching of the gospel.

Indeed, among liberal Christians the notion of mission itself has become problematic, inasmuch as it implies a form of cultural imperialism that runs counter to liberal assumptions about the positive aspects of PLURALISM. Home missions in the older sense, as a crusade combining individual salvation with social transformation, have increasingly been left to conservative Protestants. Some scholars have suggested that aspects of the evangelical anti-abortion movement come close to replicating older models of American domestic missions, in which the vision of American destiny was intertwined with personal morality and spiritual striving.

LMK

Bibliography: Colin B. Goodykoontz, *Home Missions on the American Frontier, with particular reference to the American Home Missionary Society* (Caldwell, Idaho: The Caxton Printers, Ltd., 1939); Kenneth Scott Latourette, *The Great Century in Europe and the United States of America,* vol. IV of *A History of the Expansion of Christianity* (New York: Harper & Brothers, 1941); John P. McDowell, *The Social Gospel in the South: The Woman's Home Mission Movement in the Methodist Episcopal Church, South, 1886–1939* (Baton Rouge: Louisiana State University Press, 1982).

Missouri Synod Lutherans See
LUTHERAN CHURCH—MISSOURI SYNOD.

modernism (Protestant)
Modernism, an outgrowth of liberal theology (see LIBERALISM, THEOLOGICAL), was a theological movement of the late 19th and early 20th centuries, numbering Edward Scribner AMES, Shailer MATHEWS, Henry Nelson Wieman, and Douglas Clyde Macintosh among its leaders. It was a radical readjustment of Protestant theology in light of new intellectual and scientific developments. Darwinian EVOLUTION, historical research, biblical criticism, and the entire scientific world view threatened the belief in miracles, the literal truth of the Bible, and the Genesis view of creation (see BIBLICAL INTERPRETATION; SCIENCE AND RELIGION). Rather than rejecting or ignoring these new developments, modernists embraced them and reformulated Christian tradition in their light.

The modernists accepted the new ideas and formed an understanding of religion and of Christianity based upon them. Rather than destroying Christianity as their opponents claimed, modernists understood themselves to be "saving" it. They asserted that the truth of Christianity did not rest on the reality of miracles, the virgin birth, or the literal truth of the Bible. The conservatives and fundamentalists (see FUNDAMENTALISM), asserted the modernists, made a dangerous mistake by insisting on their centrality to the Christian message.

While the term "modernism" covers a wide range of individuals and perspectives, all shared certain views. The first was an emphasis on experience as the source of religious knowledge. Some located this in the realm of human feeling or psychology, others in the realm of empirical reality. Both emphasized that within certain human experiences—friendship, wisdom, kindness—an in-breaking of the divine occurs, pointing to God's actions in the world.

Modernists rejected attempts to ground religious understanding in traditional creedal formulations or appeals to authority. Since knowledge of religion is rooted in human experience, the traditional formulations of religious belief are expressions of the historical period that created them. While important, religious knowledge cannot be limited by them.

The emphasis on human experience sprang from their belief in the immanence of God: God's presence within the world, history, and human activity. This presence made it possible to experience religious feeling within human activities. The immanence of God and religious experience drove humanity in search of progress, of improvement—the search for something higher and better. This drive for progress was manifested both in the moral improvement of individuals and in social progress.

For Christianity, the possibility of what human beings could become was manifested in the person of the historical Jesus. Jesus, as a person who lived a life on earth subject to all the limitations of humanity, showed himself to be the moral example. He was the perfectly altruistic being whose life was lived completely for others, up to his death on the cross. The fact that one man could lead such a morally acceptable life demonstrated the possibility of its attainment by all.

Social morality also played a major role for modernists. Most were committed to the SOCIAL GOSPEL and felt that individual Christians and the churches had an obligation to work for the Christianizing of the social order. Prohibition, poverty, race relations, pacifism, and workers' rights all attracted the concern of modernists. This drive for moral reform was strengthened by their firm conviction of God's immanence. If God were working in human activity, in history, then the outcome eventually must be positive. This gave the modernists an optimism that was nearly unshakable.

Optimism was also visible in their understanding of sin. The modernists understood sin as error that could be overcome by education, training, or human activity. Sin was not an inevitable part of human existence. It was, in fact, alien to that existence as demonstrated by the life of the historical Jesus.

Given such an understanding of religion, sin, and Jesus, the modernists placed little emphasis on such traditional elements of Christianity as miracles, or the doctrine of the atonement. They did have a deep commitment to the church, however. The church was the location for the education of human beings to their moral obligations. Within the church people were brought face to face with the historical Jesus and the moral example that he set. The church had an especially important role in bringing people to awareness of the new moral obligations and duties incumbent upon them within industrial society.

The optimism that gave modernism its vitality and power proved to be its undoing. While modernism was able to defeat its theological foes, the fundamentalists, it could not defeat the problems caused by historical events, events that challenged its optimism and its understanding of God's immanence.

World War I, the Depression, and the rise of Nazism destroyed modernism. In the face of these events the belief in constant progress that was its hallmark was difficult to accept. If progress were constant, then how could one explain the reversion to barbarism in the war? If sin were mere error, how does one explain why so many educated persons welcomed the WORLD WAR I, and why Nazism in the land of Kant, Hegel, and Schiller? Modernism was challenged by a new theological movement, NEO-ORTHODOXY, that raised these questions and supplanted both modernism and the wider movement of liberal theology itself.

Not all the themes addressed by modernism collapsed. Its acceptance of historical research and science was adopted by Neo-orthodoxy. Also significant was its work on the psychology of religious experience. Drawing as it did on William JAMES, modernism has had a continuing influence on the study of religion. Finally, modernism's emphasis on social obligation exerted a major influence on Christian thought throughout the 20th century.

EQ

Bibliography: Sydney Ahlstrom, *Theology in America: The Major Protestant Voices from Puritanism to Neo-orthodoxy* (Indianapolis: Bobbs-Merrill, 1967); William R. Hutchison, *The Modernist Impulse in American Protestantism* (Cambridge: Harvard University Press, 1976); William R. Hutchison, ed., *American Protestant Thought in the Liberal Era* (Lanham, Md.: University Press of America, 1981); Shailer Mathews, *The Faith of Modernism* (New York: AMS Press, 1969); Bernard M. G. Reardon, *Liberal Protestantism* (Stanford: Stanford University Press, 1968).

Moody, Dwight Lyman (1837–1899)

Dwight L. Moody, a layman and evangelist, was the greatest revivalist (see REVIVALISM) of his day. He helped reconcile the "old-time religion" practiced in small towns before the Civil War to the flourishing urban and industrial environment of late 19th-century America.

Wright Lyman Moody, with singer Ira Sankey, rejuvenated revivalism, preaching to millions in 19th-century cities. (Library of Congress)

Moody was born in Northfield, Massachusetts on February 5, 1837. He had very little educational or religious training as a youth. In 1854 he left his home in western Massachusetts to work in his uncle's shoe store in Boston. While living in Boston, Moody experienced a religious conversion and began attending church. He moved to Chicago in 1856, where he not only continued his career as a shoe salesman but also began to throw himself into church work. Joining the Plymouth Congregational Church, he rented four pews every Sunday morning and filled them with anyone he could find on the street or in the city's boardinghouses. He took charge of a Sunday school in the Chicago slums in 1858, and two years later left his business in

order to devote himself fully to that missionary endeavor.

When the Civil War came in 1861, Moody served for four years as an agent of the United States Christian Commission, the evangelistic organization that ministered in both practical and spiritual ways to the Union troops. After the war, he became president of the Chicago YOUNG MEN'S CHRISTIAN ASSOCIATION, where he proved himself an able executive and fundraiser. He visited over 600 families in the city in one year to try to win their souls for Christ— an effort that earned him the nickname "Crazy Moody."

Following the 1871 Chicago fire that destroyed his YMCA building, Moody began his most important work as an itinerant revivalist. While in England on business for the YMCA in the spring of 1872, he was invited to preach in a London pulpit. When 400 people responded that day to his call to dedicate their lives to the Christian faith, Moody believed he had discovered his true calling. Having earlier persuaded Ira David SANKEY to join him as a chorister, Moody and his song-leader began a successful evangelistic tour of the British Isles between 1873 and 1875. Sankey, who popularized the gospel hymn, knew how to supplement the sermon with simple, moving lyrics and with melodies borrowed from dance and march rhythms. At least three million listeners are estimated to have heard the Moody-Sankey team in England, Scotland, and Ireland over that two-year period. And on returning to the United States, they began a series of revivals that filled auditoriums in every major northern and midwestern city.

Moody founded several educational institutions to help prepare others as evangelists. In his hometown he established the Northfield Seminary for girls in 1879 and the Mount Hermon School for boys two years later. He also created the Northfield Conferences in 1880. Those conferences provided lay men and women with opportunities for spiritual renewal and were instrumental in spreading religious teachings that were hallmarks of the early fundamentalist (see FUNDAMENTALISM) and Holiness (see HO-LINESS MOVEMENT) movements. Participants at the 1886 Northfield Conference also conceived the STUDENT VOLUNTEER MOVEMENT, an organization that promoted overseas missionary work. Finally, Moody started a Bible training school (see BIBLE SCHOOLS) (named Moody Bible Institute after his death) in Chicago in 1889.

Good businessman that he was, Moody preached a message that was simple, winsome, and relatively unemotional. He combined typical American optimism with a theology that stressed how individuals could, with God's help, effect their own salvation. He would hold up a Bible and assure his congregations that eternal life was available for the asking if they would merely "come forward and t-a-k-e, TAKE!" He eschewed discussion of all other topics, including doctrinal beliefs and political concerns. Moody was convinced that the salvation of individual souls was the only effective means of solving America's social problems. He described his ministry as essentially an other-worldly rescue operation: "I look upon this world as a wrecked vessel. God has given me a lifeboat and said to me, 'Moody, save all you can.' "

Although Moody's evangelism helped encourage the militantly conservative religious movement that would later be called fundamentalism, his own temper was irenic, and he maintained cordial relations with theological liberals throughout his lifetime. He literally rejuvenated the American revivalistic tradition. When a heart ailment forced him to curtail his activities in 1892, no figure of equal stature ever again appeared on the urban revival scene. Moody died in retirement at Northfield on December 22, 1899.

GHS, Jr.

Bibliography: James F. Findlay, Jr., *Dwight L. Moody: American Evangelist, 1837–1899* (Chicago: University of Chicago Press, 1969).

Moody Bible Institute   See BIBLE SCHOOLS.

Moon, Sun Myung (1920–)   The founder of the UNIFICATION CHURCH, the Reverend Sun Myung Moon is one of the most controversial leaders of a new religious movement in the United States today.

Born in 1920 in northwestern Korea, Moon was raised in a Presbyterian church (see PRESBYTERIANISM) influenced by PENTECOSTALISM. He graduated from high school and studied for a time at Waseda University in Tokyo. The defining event in his life occurred on Easter, 1936 when he was 16 years old. On that day, Moon reports, Jesus came to him in a vision, informing him that he had been selected to usher in the kingdom of God on earth. This incident set off a series of subsequent revelations in which Moon received instructions from angels, Moses, and even the Buddha.

Moon's career as an independent Christian minister and staunch anti-Communist began when he established the Kwang-ya Church in northern Korea in 1946. But Moon's ministry was interrupted shortly thereafter by his arrest and imprisonment. After two and a half years in prison at the hands of the Communist government of North Korea, Moon was freed in 1950 by United Nations forces fighting in the Korean War. Moon began once again to preach, first in Pusan and later in Seoul. In 1954 he founded the Holy Spirit Association for the Unification of World Christianity, popularly known as the Unification Church. Three years later he published his magnum opus, *The Divine Principle,* which now functions as sacred scripture for Unification Church members.

Although Moon sent missionaries to the United States as early as 1959, and toured the country twice beginning in the mid-1960s, his movement did not start to grow rapidly in the United States until his immigration in the early 1970s. Soon "Moonies," as members of his church are popularly called, seemed like permanent fixtures on urban street corners across America. These clean-cut devotees distinguished themselves from the hippies who had occupied those same street corners before them by shunning drugs, profanity and premarital sex. Viewing themselves as members of a divine family, they referred to Moon as "Father," his wife as "Mother," and God as the "True Parent." Despite the "All-American" image of his followers and his emphasis on family values, Moon's church was criticized by the media and by relatives of some of its members as a dangerous "cult."

Moon was convicted of tax evasion in 1982 and eventually served 13 months in prison. After his release, Moon deemphasized his American work and refocused his efforts on Asia. As a result, Moon's church in America has failed to maintain the membership that it enjoyed during its heyday in the 1970s. Moon still retains some influence over a number of church-affiliated institutions in the United States, including a conservative daily, the *Washington Times.*

SRP

Bibliography: Sun Myung Moon, *The Divine Principle* (Washington, D.C.: Holy Spirit Association for the Unification of World Christianity, 1973); Frederick Sontag, *Sun Myung Moon and the Unification Church* (Nashville, Tenn.: Abingdon, 1977).

Moorish Science Temple The Moorish Science Temple was one of several black religions founded in the United States preaching racial pride and calling American blacks to turn from Christianity to their true and original religion (see BLACK JEWS; NATION OF ISLAM). The first Moorish Science Temple was organized in Newark, New Jersey in 1913 by Noble Drew Ali (see DREW, TIMOTHY). Incorporated as the Moorish Temple of Science in 1925, and renamed the Moorish Science Temple the next year, it had branches in Detroit, Philadelphia, New York, and Pittsburgh, as well as several southern cities. At its height membership reached nearly 30,000.

The beliefs of the Moorish Science Temple were laid out in its *Holy Koran* written by Drew. The black people in America were not Africans but were correctly called Asiatics. Their true homeland was Morocco. Only after the so-called

Negroes were restored to their legitimate nationality could they know their true religion. Noble Drew Ali was in the line of all prophets including Jesus, Mohammed, Confucius, Buddha, and Zoroaster, and he came to restore his people to their rightful status on earth. The message of racial pride and identity was very strong, and in fact the Moorish Science Temple taught that Marcus GARVEY was to Noble Drew Ali as John the Baptist was to Jesus.

Conspicuous in their red fezzes and secure in their new-found identity, members of the Moorish Science Temple became an annoyance to the police departments in many midwestern cities, especially Chicago where the temple was headquartered. They would accost whites and declare that they were freed from white domination. While little violence ever transpired, the mere fact of proud black males sent many a police chief into hysteria. Drew finally was forced to inform his followers that they were merely sowing confusion and that he had come to "uplift the nation."

Drew's death in 1929—he was probably murdered by opponents within the temple—resulted in a split within the church. Some claimed to follow only the spirit of Noble Drew Ali. Others followed a new leader as Drew reincarnate. It also lost many members to the young Nation of Islam (NOI), especially since it was rumored that the founder of the NOI, W. D. FARD, was Drew reincarnated.

By 1990 the Moorish Science Temple had shrunk greatly. Although temples existed in over 14 cities during the 1940s, only two were known to remain in the 1980s, in Hartford, Connecticut and Chicago, Illinois. Small and insignificant in size, the Moorish Science Temple played a significant role in the creation of racially defiant black religion in America, a movement that reached its height in the early 1960s with the Nation of Islam.

EQ

Bibliography: Arthur H. Fauset, *Black Gods of the Metropolis: Negro Religious Cults of the Urban North* (New York: Octagon, Books, 1970); Wardell J.

Payne, *Directory of African American Religious Bodies: A Compendium by the Howard University School of Divinity* (Washington, D.C.: Howard University Press, 1991).

Morais, Sabato (1823–1897)

In his 46 years as rabbi at Mikveh Israel Synagogue in Philadelphia, Sabato Morais worked to establish the institutions necessary for the invigoration and maintenance of traditional Judaism in the United States. Associated with what is called the "Historical School" of Judaism, the precursor of CONSERVATIVE JUDAISM, Morais attempted to balance the demands of both tradition and modernity. Although orthodox (see ORTHODOX JUDAISM) in his opposition to family pews, organs, and his insistence on adherence to Jewish dietary laws and the Sabbath, he recognized the need for modifying other religious laws, calling for a clear, brief, and contemporary code "with due respect for our changed conditions."

Born in Leghorn, Italy on April 13, 1823, Sabato Morais trained privately as a rabbi until the age of 23, when he moved to London as a teacher of Hebrew. Five years later he was called to the pulpit of Mikveh Israel to replace Isaac LEESER. As rabbi of this distinguished Sephardic synagogue he devoted himself to the affairs of American Jewry and his new country.

Sabato Morais, a Sephardic rabbi, prolific writer, and one of the founders of Conservative Judaism in the United States.

Like many of his contemporaries, Morais viewed Jewish learning and education as instrumental in revitalizing American Judaism. He privately tutored many students and served as professor of biblical literature at the short-lived Maimonides College. Although suspicious of REFORM JUDAISM, he cooperated with Isaac Mayer WISE in the founding of Hebrew Union College in Cincinnati and served on its Board of Examiners. Shocked by the serving of unkosher food at the banquet honoring the college's first graduates, and even more by Wise's callousness to the injury, Morais decided that no cooperation with the Reformers was possible. Traditionalists would have to establish their own institutions. For Morais this meant preeminently a rabbinical school, an institution for the training of rabbis who would be both American and traditional. This need led to the creation in New York of the Jewish Theological Seminary in 1886, where Morais served as president and professor of Bible until his death on November 11, 1897.

Morais strongly desired the creation of a central organization for American Judaism. He felt that such an organization was necessary to sustain the community. He especially desired the creation of a distinctive ritual that would be both traditional and modern, to unify American Jewry. Although he did not live to see either unity or organizational coherence among supporters of traditional Judaism, the formation of the Union of Orthodox Jewish Congregations the year after his death owed much to Morais's activity.

An early Zionist, Morais raised funds for the establishment of Jewish agricultural colonies in Palestine. Suspicious of the secular, political Zionists, Morais was interested in the religio-cultural aspects of Zionism, belonged to Hovevei Zion (Lovers of Zion), and advocated ZIONISM from his pulpit.

Morais concerned himself with more than religious affairs. He was a vocal opponent of slavery and aided nearly every charity in Philadelphia. He vehemently opposed attempts to have Pennsylvania declared a "Christian State" and was among the most visible in providing assistance to the Eastern European Jews who streamed into the United States after 1880. His death left a void in American Judaism, and without his energetic and inspired leadership the Jewish Theological Seminary nearly closed. His work did not collapse, however, and he bequeathed to Conservative Judaism the identity and vision needed to transform itself into the largest branch of American Judaism.

EQ

Bibliography: Moshe Davis, *The Emergence of Conservative Judaism: The Historical School in Nineteenth Century America* (Westport, Conn.: Greenwood Press, 1977); Henry S. Morais, *Sabato Morais: A Memoir* (New York: Press of P. Cowen, 1898); Howard M. Sachar, *A History of the Jews in America* (New York: Knopf, 1992).

Moral Majority Established in 1979 by Virginia Baptist pastor Jerry Falwell, Moral Majority, was an educational and fund-raising organization dedicated to lobbying on behalf of right-wing political causes. The most visible embodiment of the ideals of the New Religious Right (see CHRISTIAN RIGHT), the organization advanced conservative theological and social views on a host of ethical issues troubling late 20th-century America.

Falwell, a Baptist minister, organized the Thomas Road Baptist Church in Lynchburg, Virginia in 1956. There he launched, first, a daily radio program and, later, a weekly television broadcast of his Sunday morning services (called the "Old-Time Gospel Hour"). In 1971 he also founded what is now Liberty University as a Christian undergraduate institution. Falwell's alarm at the changing mores of American society roused him into the forefront of political action in 1976. The "I Love America" rallies he staged during the Bicentennial celebration and the "Clean Up America" campaign he led the next two years were a prelude to the formation of the Moral Majority. His books, *How You Can Help Clean Up America* (1978) and *Listen, America!* (1980), summarized what he wished his organization to become: a coalition of God-fearing Americans dedicated to undertaking the moral reform of their society.

Despite its lobbying on behalf of candidates and its strong support from white fundamentalist Christians, the Moral Majority envisioned its agenda as neither political nor religious, but ethical. The organization was intentionally nonsectarian and claimed to represent a broad Judeo-Christian tradition. As a 1983 brochure stated, the Moral Majority was made up of Protestant ministers, Roman Catholic priests, Jewish rabbis, and ordinary citizens of all faiths who were united against a common enemy: "the moral decline of our nation." Committed to battling "amoral and secular humanists and other liberals . . . destroying the traditional family and moral values" on which the United States was built, Moral Majority members opposed the sexual revolution and the many "evils" it generated.

For a time, the objectives of the Moral Majority exactly mirrored those of the conservative wing of the Republican Party, and it was credited with aiding the victory of Ronald Reagan in 1980. Exultant, Falwell called the November 1980 election his "finest hour." After the 1984 elections, however, the influence of the Moral Majority began to decline as rapidly as it had grown. While legislators in Washington refused to act favorably on such key conservative issues as prayer in public schools and abortion, political liberals accused the Moral Majority of violating the time-honored separation of church and state. Despite strenuous efforts in the media, Falwell and his group were never able to transcend the relatively narrow religious base that nurtured them.

Pledging to devote more time to his pastoral and television ministries in Lynchburg, Falwell resigned from the presidency of the Moral Majority in 1987 and Jerry Nims succeeded him. In June 1989 Falwell, confidently claiming that his organization had accomplished all its original goals, officially dissolved the Moral Majority. The election of Bill Clinton in 1992, however, led him to reconsider that decision. In a 1993 sermon entitled "America Must Return to the Faith of Our Fathers," Falwell lambasted the Clinton administration and the United States Supreme Court. He declared that they had "raped the Constitution and raped the Christian faith and raped the churches." While the Moral Majority is formally defunct today, Falwell and other leaders of the religious right remain committed to keeping concern for what they call "traditional family and moral values" at the heart of American politics.

GHS, Jr.

Bibliography: Walter H. Capps, *The New Religious Right: Piety, Patriotism, and Politics* (Columbia: University of South Carolina Press, 1990); Frances Fitz-Gerald, *Cities on a Hill: A Journey Through Contemporary American Cultures* (New York: Simon & Schuster, 1986).

Moral Re-Armament   See BUCHMAN, FRANK NATHAN DANIEL.

Moravians   Probably the most influential pietistic denomination in the United States, the Moravians or Unitas Fratrum (Unity of Brethren) emerged out of the Hussite movement in Moravia in the 15th century. The Hussites borrowed their name from Jan Hus, a Catholic priest and university professor whose attempts to restore the Church to the primitive simplicity of apostolic times led to his excommunication in 1411 and his execution as a heretic in 1415.

The Moravians first organized themselves in 1457 at Kunvald, Bohemia as a reform movement within Roman Catholicism. In 1467, however, they broke irrevocably from Rome when they began to ordain their own ministers. Initially the Bohemian Brethren, as they were called, were rigidly sectarian. They refused to swear oaths or to bear arms, abjured higher education, and used legends of the martyred Hus to emphasize the state of war that existed between themselves and the "world." Later in the 15th century, however, the group decided to accommodate itself to "worldly" contingencies. As a result of this decision, the movement prospered, swelling to about 400 churches and over 100,000 adherents in the early 16th century.

The persecutions of the Counter-Reformation brought an abrupt end to the Moravians' period of early growth, but the tradition maintained an underground existence in Bohemia and Moravia until its reemergence in the 18th century. Under the direction of a Christian David (1690–1751), a lay person, a group of these secret Moravians escaped from religious persecution in 1722, gathering in Saxony on the lands of Count Nicolas Ludwig von ZINZENDORF (1700–60), which they called Herrnhut.

Soon Zinzendorf took charge of both this religious settlement and this second phase of Moravian history. Though a convert from Lutheranism, Zinzendorf attempted to instill in what came to be called the Renewed Moravian Church his own brand of christocentric Lutheran piety. Under Zinzendorf's direction, Moravians affirmed an evangelical theology and stressed hymn-singing, missionary work, and ecumenism (see ECUMENICAL MOVEMENT). Zinzendorf's attempts to find common ground between Lutherans and Moravians bore some fruit, but his decision to become a Moravian bishop in 1737 stretched the understanding of local Lutheran authorities to the breaking point.

Moravians first came to North America in 1735. Led by Augustus Gottlieb Spangenberg (1703–1792), who would eventually become Zinzendorf's successor, they arrived in Georgia hoping to cultivate both the lands provided by the colony and a mission to the Creeks and Cherokees. It was in Georgia that Spangenberg met John Wesley (see METHODISTS), introduced him to the Moravians' "heart-religion," and set him on the course to his famous conversion of 1738. Unfortunately for these first American Moravians, their Georgia experiment in communal living failed. So when in the midst of the first GREAT AWAKENING the grand itinerant George WHITEFIELD urged Spangenberg to take his followers north, the Moravians uprooted themselves to Philadelphia. Soon they had settled planned towns whose names—Bethlehem, Nazareth, and Emmaus in Pennsylvania, Hope in New Jersey, and Salem in North Carolina— demonstrated their commitment to both christocentric piety and biblical inspiration, and whose success demonstrated their commitment to communitarian living and hard work.

Following his banishment from Saxony, Zinzendorf joined his fellow Moravians in the New World. He was active in rooting Moravian settlements in the fertile soils of Pennsylvania, but he devoted most of his energies to attempting to unite all of the "Pennsylvania Dutch" into one nonsectarian Christian community, which he named the Congregation of God in the Spirit. Although he managed to gather at least a handful of German-speaking Protestant ministers into his ecumenical organization, his hopes for Christian union fared no better in the New World than they had in the Old.

From the time of the foundation of the Unitas Fratrum, Moravians have emphasized Christian unity. In the 16th century, Moravian churches allied, at least for a time, with Lutheran and Reform churches. And Zinzendorf himself was one of the earliest and the most committed of Protestant ecumenists. What fueled the Moravians' ecumenical vision was their pietistic emphasis on the experience of conversion and their relative lack of interest in creeds and doctrines. Like the Disciples of Christ (see CHRISTIAN CHURCH), however, whose attempt to incorporate all Christians into one great nonsectarian organization ended, ironically, in the formation of yet another denomination, the Unitas Fratrum fell short of its goal of uniting all Christian brethren.

In addition to being ecumenists, the Moravians have been avid missionaries. Beginning in 1732, Moravians from North America and Europe maintained missions to West Indians, Africans, and Native Americans. By some estimations, Moravians provided the majority of Protestant missionaries in the 18th century. They clearly did more missionary work in that century than any other Protestant denomination.

Despite their commitment to evangelization, Moravians have never reached large numbers in the United States. In 1978 the Moravian Church in America reported 145 congregations and 43,000 members. They are significant, therefore, not for their numerical strength but for their contributions to Protestant missions and ecumenism. They also influenced greatly American hymnody. Other Protestant denominations have adopted modified forms of their passionate hymns to a bodily Jesus who is simultaneously bloody and divine.

Moravians have also played an important part in the intellectual and spiritual development of theological luminaries such as the Methodist evangelist John Wesley and Friedrich Schleiermacher, the so-called "father" of liberal Protestant theology. Both of these men were greatly influenced by Moravian teachers who instilled in them the Moravians' characteristically pietistic emphases on the passion of Jesus Christ and the experience of conversion.

SRP

Bibliography: Gillian Lindt Gollin, *Moravians in Two Worlds* (New York: Columbia University Press, 1967); J. Taylor Hamilton and Kenneth G. Hamilton, *History of the Moravian Church: The Renewed Unitas Fratrum from 1722–1957* (Bethlehem,

Pa.: Interprovincial Board of Christian Education, 1967).

Mormons

Mormons   See CHURCH OF JESUS CHRIST OF LATTER-DAY SAINTS; REORGANIZED CHURCH OF JESUS CHRIST OF LATTER DAY SAINTS.

Mott, John Raleigh (1865–1955)

Mott, John Raleigh (1865–1955)   John R. Mott, often ignored today, was the most significant American voice in the movement for Christian unity, the ECUMENICAL MOVEMENT, and one of the most influential religious figures in America. Born May 25, 1865, Mott was involved in the creation of nearly every major interdenominational organization from the 1880s until his death on January 31, 1955.

Mott, with a group of mission-minded college students, spent a month at Dwight L. MOODY's school in Mt. Hermon, Massachusetts in 1886. While there, many, including Mott, were moved to commit themselves to serving in the foreign missions field. When asked what mission field interested him, Mott supposedly responded "the world." While never officially a missionary, Mott definitely had the world as his field.

In 1888, while serving as a secretary for the YOUNG MEN'S CHRISTIAN ASSOCIATION, Mott was involved in the formation of the STUDENT-VOLUNTEER MOVEMENT (S.V.M.), whose phenomenal growth was due to his leadership. The S.V.M. became an international movement in 1895 when the World's Student Christian Federation, of which Mott served as general secretary until 1920, was organized. This position, along with the many others he held, demanded constant international travel—by sea and rail in those days. It is estimated that Mott, despite being afflicted with seasickness, travelled 1.7 million miles just in his capacity as an officer of the W.S.C.F.

He helped organize the First World Mission Conference in Edinburgh (1910), and served as the chairman of its Continuation Committee. Mott and the committee's secretary, Joseph H. Oldham, maintained the committee during WORLD WAR I, keeping it sufficiently vibrant that it became the nucleus of the International Missionary Council in 1924, with Mott serving as chairman until 1946.

During the First World War Mott was equally busy in other fields. He served as chairman of the International Committee of the YMCA, and directed the United War Work Campaign that brought together American Jews, Catholics, and Protestants for religious work among American soldiers in Europe. During this time he was offered the post of ambassador to China, which he declined, but he did join former Secretary of State Elihu Root on a diplomatic mission to Russia in 1917 with the stipulation that he could limit himself to "religious, educational, and humanitarian contacts."

Following the war Mott worked to reinvigorate international religious cooperation. He presided over the second Life and Work Conference in Oxford in 1937, and served on the Consultative Committee that urged the merger of that conference with the Faith and Order Conference to create a WORLD COUNCIL OF CHURCHES. When the World Council was organized in 1948, Mott was chosen one of its first presidents. The title later was made honorary and given to him for life. The significance of Mott's devotion to international cooperation and ecumenical work is illustrated by his receipt of the Nobel Peace Prize in 1946.

EQ

Bibliography: Galen M. Fisher, *John R. Mott: Architect of Co-operation and Unity* (New York: Association Press, 1952); Charles Howard Hopkins, *John R. Mott, 1865–1955: A Biography* (Grand Rapids: Eerdmans, 1979); Basil J. Mathews, *John R. Mott: World Citizen* (New York: Harper & Bros., 1943); John R. Mott, *The Evangelization of the World in this Generation* (New York: Arno Press, 1972); ———, *Addresses and Papers of John R. Mott,* 6 vols. (New York: Association Press, 1946–1947).

Muhammad, Elijah (1897–1975)

Muhammad, Elijah (1897–1975)   The Honorable Elijah Muhammad, leader of the Lost-Found NATION OF ISLAM (NOI), the Black Muslims, for 41 years, was born near Sandersville, Georgia on October 7, 1897 as Elijah (Robert, according to some sources) Poole. One of 13 children born to ex-slaves, he dropped out of school in fourth grade to help support the family. He married Clara Evans (Sister Clara) in 1919, and in 1923 the young couple joined the black migration to the urban North, settling in Detroit. There, Poole worked in various factories until 1929 when the Depression put him out of work.

Around 1931 Poole met W. D. FARD, an itinerant peddler who wandered the black sections of Detroit preaching that Islam was the true religion of blacks, who shared a common bond with all Africans and Asiatics but had had their history and heritage stolen from them by the "white devils." Poole became a trusted follower of Fard, who made Poole his chief lieutenant, bestowing upon him his "true" Muslim name. Elijah Poole became Elijah Muhammad.

Although opposed by several of Fard's other assistants, Elijah Muhammad was chosen by Fard to oversee the nascent Nation of Islam. Shortly after this, Fard disappeared mysteriously in 1934. The result was schism and conflict within the small religious community. Fearing for his life, Elijah Muhammad led a large proportion of the membership to Chicago, where he transformed the two-year-old Temple Number 2 into the movement's headquarters.

From Chicago, Elijah Muhammad formalized and expanded the organizational and theological elements of the movement. He instituted a girl's training school, rebuilt the Fruit of Islam as its security branch, and re-organized the University of Islam. In this combination elementary and secondary school, boys were taught traditional subjects as well as black history. Here the lies of white "tricknology" were exposed.

Elijah Muhammad introduced the idea that Fard had been Allah come to earth to lead his black children to the truth, and that at his disappearance he had appointed Muhammad as his spokesman on earth. For this reason Elijah Muhammad often was referred to as the "Prophet" or the "Messenger [of Allah]." He

also oversaw the development of businesses owned and operated by the NOI as part of his message of black independence from the white man's world.

Rejecting the idea that white American society could possibly be a country for blacks, he advocated that blacks not fight in World War II against another colored people. The result was his conviction for violating the Selective Service Act and imprisonment from 1942 to 1946. After his release he was welcomed back as a martyr, and between 1946 and 1965 the movement underwent tremendous growth. By 1963 the NOI probably had a membership of half a million, as well as several million sympathizers. Much of this was due to the work of Muhammad's hand-picked lieutenant, MALCOLM X.

Declining health forced a move to Phoenix in the late 1950s, although Chicago remained the NOI's headquarters. A scandal over Elijah Muhammad's sexual relations with several of his secretaries rocked the puritanical movement, causing the loss of many members, especially from Temple Number 2. This, along with political differences, resulted in a schism between Malcolm and Muhammad, who is alleged to have ordered the former's assassination.

Less visible and aggressive after these problems, the Nation continued under Elijah Muhammad's leadership until his death on February 25, 1975 in Chicago. At that time the mantle of leadership fell upon his son Wallace Dean MUHAMMAD, who led the NOI toward orthodox Sunni Islam. The result was a schism within the movement, with a breakaway faction led by Louis FARRAKHAN returning to the beliefs and racial separatism that had distinguished the Nation of Islam during Elijah Muhammad's leadership.

EQ

Bibliography: C. Eric Lincoln, *The Black Muslims in America* (Boston: Beacon Press, 1961); Elijah Muhammad, *The Supreme Wisdom: Solution to the So-Called Negroe's Problem* (Newport News, Va.: National Newport News and Commentator, 1957); ———, *Message to the Blackman in Amer-*

ica (Chicago: Muhammad Mosque of Islam #2, 1965).

Muhammad, Warith Deen (1933–)

The fifth of Elijah MUHAMMAD's six sons, Wallace Deen Muhammad (born October 30, 1933 in Hamtramck, Michigan) succeeded his father as chief minister of the NATION OF ISLAM (NOI) on February 26, 1975. He wrought tremendous changes, transforming the former Nation of Islam into an orthodox Muslim organization. In doing so he became the most important Islamic leader in the United States (see ISLAM).

Raised in the center of the Nation of Islam, Warith Muhammad early assumed a major role in the movement. Named Wallace, after Wallace FARD, the founder, he gained a mystical aura within the Nation of Islam for his association with Fard, who was recognized as Allah incarnate. This significance was so great that when he moved the Nation of Islam toward orthodox Sunni Islam he dropped the name Wallace and adopted Warith as a way of signifying this break. In many ways his life was inseparable from that of the Nation of Islam. But his training in classical Arabic and his Islamic education led him, as it did his friend MALCOLM X, to develop doubts about its doctrines.

Troubled by the disclosure of his father's sexual relations with several of his secretaries, Wallace Muhammad joined with Malcolm in developing a response to those events. This resulted in the first of his three suspensions from the movement. Despite this he retained the trust of his father and most of the other leaders within the NOI, who recognized within Warith the same deep spirituality that Malcolm did. Not only was he put forward as his father's successor by the family, but the choice was unanimously ratified by 20,000 delegates at the NOI's 1975 meeting in Chicago.

Following this succession he began to take the Nation of Islam down a new path. In June 1975 he shocked delegates attending the annual convention by announcing that the NOI no longer viewed all whites as devils, and that it would be open to all people regardless of color. He disbanded the security force, the Fruit of Islam, and proceeded with a process of Islamicization throughout the organization. This included the adoption of traditional Islamic titles and names—temples became mosques (masjids), ministers became imams—and the Islamic calendar for the reckoning of feasts. The earlier rigid discipline also was relaxed. Women were allowed to travel after dark, and their status within the movement elevated. Military service was allowed and members were encouraged to participate in civic affairs. Warith reversed the view that the United States was an alien government for blacks, and members of the now named World Community of Al-Islam in the West (changed to the American Muslim Mission in 1980) were encouraged to view themselves as loyal Americans.

These changes met resistance. Some members drifted away. Others refused to give up the racial separatism of the NOI. Led by Louis FARRAKHAN, they re-appropriated the Nation of Islam name, along with the mythology of black superiority and white "deviltry."

Despite these losses, the American Muslim Mission under Warith Muhammad obtained a remarkable level of significance, if not within the consciousness of the United States at least within the wider Muslim community. Under his leadership the American Muslim Mission was accepted into the World Muslim Council (W.M.C.), and he received the title Mujaddid (renewer) to signify his role in vivifying Islam in the United States. The W.M.C. also gave him the position of certifying all Americans desiring to make the *hajj*, the pilgrimage to Mecca required of all Muslims. These titles were accompanied by economic muscle. Several of the Gulf states, including Saudi Arabia, appointed him the "sole conduit and trustee" for all funds to Muslim organizations engaged in propagating Islam in the United States.

Despite his importance in the Islamic world, most Americans are unfamiliar with his name. Mujaddid Muhammad remains undaunted by this fact, as well as by the incipient anti-Islamic attitude in the United States engendered by conflicts with the Islamic world over oil and the Palestinians. Committed to making Islam an American religion (he was a vocal supporter of America's involvement in the war against Iraq), he feels that it can surpass Judaism and become the second-largest religion in the United States.

EQ

Bibliography: C. Eric Lincoln, *The Black Muslims in America* (Boston: Beacon Press, 1961); Clifton E. Marsh, *From Black Muslims to Muslims: The Transition from Separatism to Islam, 1930–1980* (Metuchen, N.J.: Scarecrow Press, 1984); Warith Deen Muhammad, *As the Light Shineth From the East* (Chicago: WDM Publishers, 1980).

Muhlenberg, Henry Melchior (1711–1787)

Henry Melchior Muhlenberg was a German-born minister who came to the American colonies in the mid-18th century. Having worked diligently for the ideal of a united, self-sustaining Lutheran (see LUTHERANISM) Church, Muhlenberg is generally considered to be the patriarch of his denominational tradition in this country. A church historian once remarked that Muhlenberg's influence was so great that the history of the colonial Lutheran Church was "scarcely more than his biography."

Muhlenberg was born at Einbeck in the Duchy of Hanover in Germany on September 6, 1711. He graduated from the University of Göttingen in 1738 and, after training for the ministry at the University of Halle, was ordained in 1739. He served for two years as a minister at Grosshennersdorf. At Halle, Muhlenberg was influenced by Pietism, a Protestant religious movement that stressed individual spiritual renewal and attention to godly living. Pietist leaders convinced Muhlenberg of the need to undertake missionary work among Lutheran congregations in the New World. He arrived in South Carolina in September 1742, moved northward to Philadelphia that same year, and quickly began stabilizing the confused organization of his church in the colonies.

After Muhlenberg arrived in Philadelphia, he discovered that the three congregations to which he had been assigned were being pastored by other men, the most formidable of whom was the Moravian leader Count Nicolas von ZINZENDORF. The Moravians, representing one branch of the Pietist movement, were religious enthusiasts determined to create an interdenominational fellowship they called the "Congregation of God in the Spirit." Zinzendorf, moreover, while not ordained as a Lutheran minister, posed as one in America. Despite Muhlenberg's Pietist sympathies, he still wished to create an American church that was loyal to the traditional creeds and organizational structure of Lutheranism. Thus, he suppressed the Moravians and within a few years established control over Lutheran churches in Pennylvania, New Jersey, and New York.

Muhlenberg's greatest achievement was the creation of the Pennsylvania Ministerium in 1748, the first permanent governing body within American Lutheranism. Muhlenberg had always complained of a number of institutional deficiencies fostered by the American religious environment. The problems he cited included adults who were poorly educated in their faith and lay members who possessed too much power over church life. With the formation of the Ministerium, Muhlenberg addressed these concerns. A constitution was prepared that established procedures for calling ministers to vacant parishes and gave the laity a voice in church government that was subordinate to their clergy. A book of worship was also drafted that drew upon Lutheranism's rich liturgical heritage and deterred revivalism, which Muhlenberg despised, from gaining a foothold in the church.

As the War for Independence approached, Muhlenberg avoided making an overt political stand. He even resigned his pastorate in the revolutionary hotbed of Philadelphia and moved to rural Providence, Pennsylvania. Lutherans generally, however, supported the patriot cause. In 1775 Muhlenberg's clergyman son Peter dramatically left his parish in Virginia and joined the

Continental army, in which he was eventually commissioned a general. Throughout the wartime period, Henry Muhlenberg labored to maintain Lutheran congregations, encourage immigration from Germany, and recruit clergy for the American church. Although poor health forced his retirement in 1779, his authority in the church remained strong. He died at Providence on October 7, 1787.

GHS, Jr.

Bibliography: Leonard R. Riforgiato, *Missionary of Moderation: Henry Melchior Muhlenberg and the Lutheran Church in English America* (Lewisburg, Pa.: Bucknell University Press, 1980).

Muir, John (1838–1914)   John Muir, father of the American nature preservation movement, founded the Sierra Club and initiated the creation of the National Parks System, which became the most important model for the global National Parks movement.

Born April 21, 1838 in Scotland, Muir immigrated with his family to southeastern Wisconsin as a boy of 11. Early on he showed a genius for technological invention, leading to studies in the natural sciences at the University of Wisconsin in the early 1860s. But in 1867, after nearly losing his sight in an industrial accident, Muir turned from his technological path and focused all his attention on his foremost love since childhood, wild nature. By his late twenties, he began experiencing epiphanies in the wilderness, leading him inexorably toward a biocentric and pantheistic world view. In his 1868 *Thousand Mile Walk to the Gulf,* Muir noted that, contrary to Christian notions that the natural world was provided by a sovereign God for human use, nature was indifferent or fundamentally hostile to humans. Muir walked west, spending many years becoming intimate with the Sierra Nevada Mountains as a sheepherder, mountaineer, and naturalist. But by 1878, Muir had married and settled down on his wife's ranch in California's Central Valley, never again to spend extended time in his beloved mountains. Somehow his mountain experiences sustained his passions for

John Muir, a Scots immigrant whose love of the wilderness, pantheistic world view, and nature writings pioneered the environmental movement and led to the creation of the National Parks System. (Library of Congress)

the rest of his life. By 1901, although still cloaked in theistic language, Muir's pantheism was clearly established, woven through many of his writings. By the time of his death in 1914, shortly after the damming of the Sierra Nevada's Hetch Hetchy Valley (which he likened to the desecration of a holy temple), Muir had transformed public discourse over environmental issues.

Until recently, Muir was seen primarily as a popularizer of ideas from TRANSCENDENTALISM. Contemporary scholarship, however, asserts that although influenced by the transcendentalists (Henry David THOREAU more than Ralph Waldo EMERSON), Muir made several important if not original contributions to American reflection on wilderness. Most notably, Muir challenged the Christian anthropocentrism that confers value to nature only to the extent that it is useful to humans, asserting that ecosystems have intrinsic value apart from their usefulness to humans. Muir's wilderness experiences also led him to perceive that nature as a whole functions like a unified organism, and eventually to a pantheistic sense of the relatedness and sacrality of all being. This central ethics and perception were derived primarily from his own experiences in wilderness—most importantly from his empirical observations over the years but also from an affective, esthetic, and ultimately ecstatic religious experience of the sacred in nature.

Today Muir is recognized for being at the forefront of 19th-century evolutionary thought, especially regarding its moral implications—for him, biocentrism. But as provocative and innovative as his ideas were and are, his clearest long-term impact has resulted from his role in establishing the National Parks movement and its preservationist mission, founding the Sierra Club in 1892, and inspiring the formation of other groups since then. Muir served as the Sierra Club's president until his death, thereby contributing directly to the tradition of preservationist activism in the United States. He also inspired indirectly the formation of several other important environmental organizations that split off from the Sierra Club in the years since his death, usually when activists became convinced that the club had strayed too far from Muir's preservationist crusade. Moreover, Muir's naturalist and activist writings have been influential in and of themselves. Even when losing important battles, Muir's passionate writing contributed to shifts in public perceptions that help account for the continuing strength of preservationist sentiment in the United States. His thought has become nearly canonical within the contemporary environmental movement—and Deep Ecologists (see DEEP ECOLOGY) have posthumously adopted Muir as a central intellectual and spiritual elder—precisely for his "resacralization" of nature, a perceptive task they view as a prerequisite to the reestablishment of proper human behavior toward the natural world. Muir's influence on the Deep Ecology movement may turn out to be his most significant legacy.

BRT

Bibliography: Michael P. Cohen, *The Pathless Way: John Muir and American Wilderness* (Madison: University of Wisconsin Press, 1984); Stephen Fox, *The American Conservation Movement: John Muir and His Legacy* (Madison: University of Wisconsin Press, 1981); Frederick Turner, *Rediscovering America: John Muir in His Time and Our Own* (New York: Viking, 1985).

Murray, John Courtney (1904–1967)

Although recognized at his death as the most important American Catholic theologian of his time, John Courtney Murray long endured opposition and even silencing before attaining that status. Born in New York City on September 12, 1904, Murray studied at several minor Catholic seminaries and colleges before graduating from Weston College in 1926. After receiving his M.A. from Boston College the following year, he taught in the Philippines until 1930 when he returned to the United States.

Ordained in 1933, he began advanced theological studies at Woodstock College, completing them at the Gregorian Institute in Rome in 1937. He returned to Woodstock as a professor of dogmatic theology, a position he held until his death on August 16, 1967.

As a theologian, Murray was an expert on the Trinity, publishing numerous articles, but no books, on the subject. Despite the complexity of this specialty, Murray had an abiding interest in making theology accessible to the laity and helping them relate their faith to the secular world.

This concern about the role of faith in the world led Murray to reflect increasingly on the relationship between government and religion. Following a consistent, but generally unrecognized, strand of thought in Catholic social theory, Murray articulated a distinction between government and society. Given this distinction, it was the role of government to maintain the social peace, through the application of law. Incompetent in matters of religion, the state's role lay in ensuring that people could exercise their beliefs without fear or favor.

The state was thus a sub-section of society, which is composed of all the institutions—religious, trade, labor, families, etc.—in which human beings participate. Members of these institutions, through a process of dialogue and debate made possible by the laws of the state, are to struggle together to achieve the common good.

These views set Murray at odds with the predominant Catholic social theory—integralism. Integralism argued that religious truth, that is the Roman Catholic faith, is a primary social good and that the state, as the locus for creating and realizing the social or common good, had a moral obligation to promote that faith, even to the point of proscribing other religions. After his suggestion in the early 1950s that the Vatican recognize the legitimacy of the United States's separation of church and state, his superiors in the Jesuit order forbade him to lecture on church-state issues and required that all his writings be cleared with Rome. In 1963 he was barred from speaking at the Catholic University in Washington, D.C. He was sufficiently suspect that he was not invited to the early sessions of VATICAN COUNCIL II despite his stature as a theologian.

Rescued from this exile by Francis Cardinal SPELLMAN, who brought him to Rome as an advisor, Murray played the key role in drafting the council's Declaration on Religious Freedom (*Dignitatis Humanae,* 1965). In this document the Roman Catholic Church declared for the first time that "the human person has a right to religious freedom." Vigorously supported by the American bishops, its passage was the high-point of American participation in the council.

The council also represented the beginning of Murray's rehabilitation. He was chosen to be a concelebrant with Pope Paul VI of a Mass for the council participants and, upon returning home, received numerous honorary degrees and accolades from secular, Protestant, and Catholic quarters. He spent the last years of his life lecturing widely and serving as director of the LaFarge Institute, the purpose of which was to promote dialogue between blacks and whites, Protestants and Catholics, as well as Marxists and Christians.

(See also ROMAN CATHOLICISM.)

EQ

Bibliography: Robert P. Hunt and Kenneth L. Grasso, eds., *John Courtney Murray and the American Civil Conversation* (Grand Rapids: Eerdmans, 1992); Robert W. McElroy, *The Search for an American Public Theology: The Contribution of John Courtney Murray* (New York: Paulist Press, 1989); John Courtney Murray, *We Hold These Truths: Catholics' Reflections on the American Proposition* (New York: Sheed and Ward, 1960); David E. Pelotte, *John Courtney Murray: Theologian in Conflict* (New York: Paulist Press, 1975).

N

Nation of Islam (Black Muslims) Few religious movements have seared themselves as deeply into the American psyche as the Nation of Islam (NOI), or as they are more commonly called, the Black Muslims. Perhaps it is because no religious movement in American history has been so militantly hostile to the dominant social and political ethos.

The Nation of Islam had its genesis in Detroit in 1930 with the appearance of W. D. FARD. Blacks, he argued, were descendants of an honorable race that had been stolen from its homes and brought to America by the white devils. These devils also had stripped blacks of their own religion, Islam, and had forced Christianity upon them in order to have them accept their inferior status. Fard had been sent to America to awaken blacks to the real nature of the world and to free them from white domination.

Fard's talk of "white devils" and black superiority soon gained him a considerable following among poor southern blacks who had migrated to the North. During this time many followers of the late Noble Drew Ali (see DREW, TIMO-THY; MOORISH SCIENCE TEMPLE) also joined Fard's movement. Organizationally astute, Fard developed a strict procedure for admission into the temple as well as a hierarchy of command. By 1933 he had developed a ritual for the Nation of Islam, organized a school for boys and a training class for girls, and established a security organization, the Fruit of Islam, designed to protect the NOI from outsiders and enforce the strict code of behavior demanded of all Muslims.

Even in these early years the Nation of Islam was rent by external problems and internal conflicts. One group rebelled against Fard's teaching that blacks owed no allegiance to an America that denied them their rights. Led by a former lieutenant of Fard's, Abdul Muhammad, they formed a counter temple with loyalty to the American Constitution and the American flag as a guiding principle.

With the organization increasingly run by a group of his hand-picked ministers, Fard began to withdraw from public appearances. In June 1934 he disappeared completely, and was never seen again. According to the accepted history of the NOI, Fard had picked Elijah MUHAMMAD as Minister of Islam, second only to Fard himself. After Fard's disappearance Muhammad was the logical successor, but internal conflicts prevented a smooth transition of leadership. In fact, death threats forced Elijah Muhammad and his closest followers to flee Detroit in 1936. They went to Chicago, establishing Temple No. 2 as the NOI's headquarters.

In Chicago, Elijah Muhammad rebuilt the organizational infrastructure Fard had established. He also slowly gained control of the movement itself, including Temple No. 1 in Detroit. Muhammad stressed black economic independence. Under his direction the Nation of Islam purchased farms in several states from which they ran a food distribution company. The NOI also established stores, restaurants, and other businesses.

The Nation of Islam grew slowly during the 1930s and 1940s. Elijah Muhammad's imprisonment in 1942 for subversion (he had written that blacks had no obligation to fight for America against another colored man—the Japanese) weakened the movement for several years. After his release in 1946 he was welcomed as a martyr, and the fact of his imprisonment (as well as that of several of his sons during both World War II and the Korean conflict) aided the NOI's remarkably successful recruitment in prisons.

Representative of this success was the conversion of Malcolm Little from criminal to Muslim minister and international celebrity as MALCOLM X. With the encouragement of Elijah Muhammad, Malcolm X initiated an active recruitment campaign for the Nation of Islam. Intelligent, articulate, and committed, Malcolm helped to bring about a period of phenomenal growth. He

Founded in Detroit during the Depression, NOI preached separation from whites and economic independence for blacks. Malcolm Shabazz Temple, Harlem. (Pluralism Project of Harvard University)

organized temples in Philadelphia, New York, Boston, and Atlanta. Capable of speaking to any audience, he was in great demand on the college lecture circuit, and a successful recruiter among the poorest inner-city blacks. Much more militant and vocal about white abuses and black separatism than Elijah Muhammad, Malcolm also attracted many followers who never became members.

As minister of Boston's Temple Number 11 and later of Harlem's Temple Number 7, Malcolm became for many in America the face of the Nation of Islam. This role that was thrust upon Malcolm was acknowledged by Elijah Muhammad himself when he appointed Malcolm national messenger of the Nation of Islam. In 1959 the television documentary by Mike Wallace and Louis Lomax, "The Hate that Hate

Produced," brought the Nation of Islam to the attention of the wider American public. Americans both black and white were dumbfounded by the existence of such a movement. Most Americans simply could not believe that there existed a group of blacks who not only refused to be a part of white American society, but actively detested it.

By 1963 the Nation of Islam had reached the height of its expansion, with perhaps half a million members. There were, however, internal conflicts hidden from view. The first public sign of these tensions was Elijah Muhammad's silencing of Malcolm X in November 1963, ostensibly because of remarks Malcolm X made following President John F. Kennedy's assassination. Asked to comment on the killing, Malcolm responded that the chickens were coming home to roost—explaining that the violence in American society, directed primarily at blacks, had expanded until it consumed the country's own leader. Malcolm X was merely stating what many other commentators had said, but as a leader of what many viewed as a "hate" group he brought public condemnation down upon the NOI. The resulting negative publicity seemed to be the cause of his silencing by Elijah Muhammad.

More trouble was to come for the NOI. In 1963 Elijah Muhammad was named in paternity suits filed by two former secretaries. Although rumors of sexual indiscretions on the part of the leader had circulated since the mid-1950s they had been ignored. By the time the suits were filed, the Chicago temple had been experiencing a loss of members, although the rumors were barely noticed in Boston and New York. Malcolm confronted Elijah Muhammad and, according to Malcolm's *Autobiography,* obtained an admission of guilt. With the aid of Elijah Muhammad's son, Wallace D. Muhammad (see MUHAMMAD, WARITH DEEN), Malcolm worked out a strategy to respond to the potential problems. Unbeknownst to Malcolm, Elijah Muhammad was working to remove him from positions of power.

During his period of enforced silence Malcolm and his family joined the young boxer Cassius Clay at his training camp. Following his defeat of Sonny Liston, Clay announced his conversion and the adoption of a new name, Muhammad Ali. This conversion, along with that of several other leading sports celebrities, gave the Nation of Islam heightened visibility in the nation's press.

Malcolm, no longer welcome in the movement, announced his resignation in March 1964, as well as his formation of the Muslim Mosque, Inc. along the lines of Orthodox Sunni ISLAM. He was replaced as minister of Temple Number 7 and as national representative by Louis X (see FARRAKHAN, LOUIS). Distraught, Malcolm left the country, making the *hajj* (pilgrimage) to Mecca, and visiting several Middle Eastern and African countries before returning to the United States. Upon his return he announced that he had given up racial separatism and the belief that all whites were devils, although he remained a vocal critic of American racism and American foreign policy. Assassinated in February 1965, allegedly by three members of the Nation of Islam, he became more famous in death. The posthumous publication of his autobiography did much to enhance his fame, but within the Nation of Islam he was regarded as a traitor.

The late 1960s and early 1970s were periods of continued internal dissension and conflicts. Revelations of movement-directed assassinations also led to defections and public condemnation. Despite decreasing membership during this time, the Nation of Islam retained a certain aura, since it was associated vaguely in the public mind with the emergence of the "Black Power" movement and with Malcolm, who was understood as a harbinger of that movement.

Between 1965 and 1975 the Nation of Islam, despite declining membership, solidified its financial and economic holdings. The leadership transition following Elijah Muhammad's death seemed to be smooth when he was succeeded by his son, Wallace Dean Muhammad. In June of 1975, however, Wallace Muhammad shocked his followers by announcing that whites were no longer to be considered devils, and that they now could join the Nation of Islam. He then took a series of steps designed to move the Nation of Islam toward Orthodox Sunni Islam, culminating in 1980 with the movement's reorganization as the American Muslim Mission.

This resulted in a schism within the movement led by Louis Farrakhan, who reorganized the old Nation of Islam along separatist lines in 1978. Numbering about 20,000 members in 1994, the Nation of Islam is only a shell of its former self. The speaking ability and militancy of Minister Farrakhan have served to give it a level of visibility and apparent political strength that it had not seen since the early 1960s. He has been associated with many leading black politicians, including Jesse Jackson, and his outspokenness has created much public furor. While these involvements have not dramatically increased the membership, they have created a fairly sympathetic group of listeners among urban blacks who find themselves victimized by racism, poverty, and crime—the same ills that gave the Nation of Islam its initial strength in the 1930s.

The beliefs of the Nation of Islam were set out in two works of W.D. Fard, the *Secret Ritual of the Nation of Islam* and *Teaching for the Lost-Found Nation of Islam in a Mathematical Way.* The former work was generally transmitted orally and few manuscript copies exist. The latter was written in a symbolic language that needed to be interpreted by one of the organization's leaders. With only minor changes these works remain authoritative.

Central to the belief system of the Nation of Islam is the claim that blacks were the original human beings. Due to their divine origin, they are superior. These first black men were the tribe of Shabazz, and they built the earliest cities and began agriculture and all other forms of technology. Over 6,000 years ago, a leading "scientist" of this people, Mr. Yacub, rebelled against Allah, and his followers were exiled. To wreak his revenge, Yacub began an experiment in negative eugenics, producing a bleached-out, blue-eyed race of moral and physical degenerates, the ancestors of today's white people. When these people began to cause trouble, the original black people exiled them to Europe. God later sent Moses to civilize them, and it was written that this race of "blue-eyed devils" would be allowed to dominate the world for 6,000 years. Allah would then send a messenger to free his people, especially the Lost-Found Nation of Islam living in the wilderness of North America, who of all the black people in the world had suffered most from the evil of the white devils.

According to NOI doctrine, this 6,000-year period ended in 1914. The appearance of W.D. Fard in 1930 signified the beginning of the restoration of the original people to their right-ful status. He brought to blacks the knowledge that they were part of a great people whose history, heritage, and identity had been stolen from them. Fard had come to reveal their true identity.

Following Fard's disappearance and the stabilization of control in the hands of Elijah Muhammad, it was taught that Fard was Allah himself who had brought this message to the blacks of North America, who were divine in their origin. Elijah Muhammad had been left behind by Fard/Allah to be his messenger to his people.

The Nation of Islam has a rigid code of behavior and dress. Members are forbidden to eat certain foods—pork, cornbread, catfish, possum—that are symbols of their slavery and the sources of their enslavement. The ingesting of these foods causes moral degeneracy. Alcohol, tobacco, and drugs are forbidden, as are extra- and pre-marital sexual relations. Social intercourse between the genders is regulated strictly, and adult males are forbidden to be alone with nonrelated females. Women dress modestly and makeup is forbidden. The men usually wear dark suits, white shirts, and ties. Frugality, modesty, and self-discipline are central to the life-style of the Black Muslims.

Given the degeneracy of whites, it was necessary that blacks remove themselves as much as possible from contact with them. The ultimate goal was the establishment of an independent country for black Americans. The location of this country was vague and changing. Sometimes the Nation of Islam spoke of emigration, of a return to their true homeland. Most often Elijah Muhammad spoke of the establishment of a country carved from the United States in compensation for nearly 400 years of unrewarded toil. Perhaps no other element in the thought of the Nation of Islam enraged whites more than this demand for territory. Along with the existence of the Nation of Islam's security force—the Fruit of Islam—this demand conjured up images of secessionist warfare in the minds of many whites.

The result has been a failure to understand the Nation of Islam as a religious movement. When blacks ceased to be a major item on the national agenda in the 1980s, the Nation of Islam dropped from the public mind. The emergence of Louis Farrakhan as a public figure and companion to leading black politicians brought the movement back to public awareness. Additionally, his anti-Semitic (see ANTI-SEMITISM) and inflammatory remarks as well as those of several of his lieutenants have generated a great deal of public scrutiny and condemnation. This scrutiny is significant because, despite its relative smallness as a denomination, the Nation of Islam has served as a barometer of black frustration, signaling changes before they arrive.

(See also AFRICAN-AMERICAN RELIGION; CIVIL RIGHTS MOVEMENT.)

EQ

Bibliography: C. Eric Lincoln, *The Black Muslims in America* (Boston: Beacon Press, 1961); Malcolm X, with Alex Haley, *The Autobiography of Malcolm X* (New York: Grove Press, 1965); Clifton E. Marsh, *From Black Muslims to Muslims: The Transition from Separatism to Islam, 1930–1980.* (Metuchen, N.J.: Scarecrow Press, 1984); Muhammad, Elijah, *The Supreme Wisdom: Solution to the So-Called Negroe's Problem* (Newport News, Va: National Newport News and Commentator, 1957); ———, *Message to the Blackman in America* (Chicago: Muhammad Mosque of Islam #2, 1965).

National Association of Evangelicals

The National Association of Evangelicals is an organization of denominations, congregations, and individuals who affirm the divine inspiration of Scripture; the doctrine of the Trinity; the divinity, virgin birth, and resurrection of Christ; and Christ's atoning death for human salvation. The association was founded in 1942 at Moody Bible Institute (Chicago, Illinois) by several Neo-evangelicals (see EVANGELICALISM), including Harold J. Ockenga of Park Street Church in Boston and Carl F. H. HENRY of Fuller Theological Seminary, partly in response to Carl McIntire's fundamentalist (see FUNDAMENTALISM) American Council of Christian Churches. More importantly, however, the founders saw a need for an evangelical counter to the Federal Council of Churches (see NATIONAL COUNCIL OF CHURCHES) which, they believed, harbored theological liberalism and sacrificed doctrinal distinctiveness to further the cause of church unity.

The National Association of Evangelicals has served as a focal point for thoughtful and reflective conservative theological versions of Christianity. While maintaining strict doctrinal orthodoxy, the N.A.E. has avoided the separatism that marks most fundamentalist organizations. The N.A.E.'s willingness to extend membership to those Holiness and Pentecostal movements (see HOLINESS MOVEMENT; PENTECOSTALISM) traditionally spurned by fundamentalists is an example of this openness.

In 1988 the association, headquartered in Wheaton, Illinois, claimed a membership of four million individuals, 46,000 congregations, and 50 denominations. It serves as a major publisher of evangelical literature, and provides the primary institutional structure for American evangelicalism.

EQ

Bibliography: Robert P. Lightner, *Neoevangelicalism Today,* rev. ed. (Schaumburg, Ill.: Regular Baptist Press, 1978); George Marsden, ed., *Evangelicalism and Modern America* (Grand Rapids, Mich.: Eerdmans, 1984).

National Baptist Convention of America, Inc.

Known popularly as the "unincorporated body" or convention, and at one time as the "Boyd Convention," the National Baptist Convention of America, Inc. is the second-largest historically black denomination in the United States, with approximately 3.5 million members. The National Baptist Convention of America, Inc. (NBCA) was formed as a result of a split in the NATIONAL BAPTIST CONVENTION, U.S.A., INC. when it was discovered at the convention's 1915 meeting that the publishing house established under the auspices of the convention's Home Mission Board was not convention property, but was titled to the Reverend Richard Henry Boyd, the publishing house chairman.

Attempts by the convention to gain control over the publishing house were met with resistance by Boyd supporters, who began meeting in Salem Baptist Church in Chicago, eventually organizing the National Baptist Convention, Unincorporated on September 9, 1915. Reorganized in 1987 with its headquarters in Shreveport, Louisiana, it assumed its present name, the National Baptist Convention of America, Inc.

Although one of the first decisions of the newly renamed convention in 1987 had been to declare the publishing board independent of the convention, the following year saw a move to bring it and the National Baptist Sunday Church School and Training Union Congress under the control of the convention. The result was another schism, and the formation of the National Missionary Baptist Convention of America, comprising about 25 percent of the membership of the NBCA. The new convention supported the independent publishing house and Sunday School Congress, while the parent body organized two new institutions under its control.

A growing interest in social concerns has brought the denomination into a working arrangement with both the National Baptist Convention, U.S.A. and the PROGRESSIVE NATIONAL BAPTIST CONVENTION, INC. on issues relating to African-American survival. As a result it has begun to address more directly the problems of alcohol and drug abuse, family stability, violence, and racism.

The NBCA is strongest in Louisiana, Texas, South Carolina, Florida, Mississippi, and California and, like most of the historically black denominations, has a strong missionary presence in Africa and the Caribbean. It operates 15 colleges and seminaries, and in 1992 had 8,000 ordained ministers and 2,500 member churches.

(See also AFRICAN-AMERICAN RELIGION.)

EQ

Bibliography: C. Eric Lincoln and Lawrence Mamiya, *The Black Church in the African American Experience* (Durham N.C.: Duke University Press, 1990); Wardell J. Payne, *Directory of African American Religious Bodies: A Compendium by the Howard University School of Divinity* (Washington, D.C.: Howard University Press, 1991).

National Baptist Convention, U.S.A., Inc.

The largest historically black denomination, and reportedly the largest African-American organization in existence, the National Baptist Convention, U.S.A., Inc. is a dominant force in African-American religion. Claiming 8.2 million members (one-quarter of the black population and one-third of black church members in the United States), the National Baptist Convention, U.S.A. was organized in Atlanta, Georgia on September 28, 1895 through the merger of the Baptist Foreign Mission Convention of the U.S.A., the American National Baptist Convention, and the National Baptist Educational Convention of the U.S.A.

The convention was split early by schisms, a minor one in 1897, and a major division in 1915, when conflicts over the reelection of the convention's president, E. C. Morris (president from 1895 to 1922), and the ownership of the publishing house led a minority of the members to establish what is now the NATIONAL BAPTIST CONVENTION OF AMERICA, INC.

As the dominant black religious denomination, the NBC, U.S.A. has had a major influence on African-American life. In the early years of the 20th century, both Booker T. WASHINGTON and W. E. B. DU BOIS were frequent speakers at its annual conventions. The convention, however, was more drawn to Washington's accommodationism, reflecting perhaps the rural poverty of most of its members, and officially endorsed Washington's policy of black uplift through labor in 1909. Despite this, it remained a staunch supporter of the NAACP and outspoken in its support for black enfranchisement.

Throughout its existence the NBC, U.S.A. has been dominated by strong convention presidents. In its 95-year history it has had only six presidents. One of these, Joseph H. Jackson, served for 29 years. Elected in 1953, Jackson continued the convention's traditional gradualism and opposed Martin Luther KING, JR.'s campaigns of civil disobedience. Attempts by King and others to replace Jackson during the convention's annual meetings in 1960 and 1961 failed, and many of Jackson's opponents organized a separate convention, the PROGRESSIVE NATIONAL BAPTIST CONVENTION, INC. in 1961.

Under Jackson's successor, Dr. Theodore J. Jemison, the NBC, U.S.A. took on a greater role in the struggle for black equality, especially in voting rights and voter registration. It also began building its first permanent headquarters, the World Center Headquarters in Nashville, Tennessee, which was opened on May 1, 1989.

With 33,000 churches, 12 colleges, including Spellman and Morehouse in Atlanta, and an annual budget of nearly $5 million, the NBC, U.S.A. is a powerful force on the American religious landscape.

(See also AFRICAN-AMERICAN RELIGION; CIVIL RIGHTS MOVEMENT.)

EQ

Bibliography: C. Eric Lincoln and Lawrence Mamiya, *The Black Church in the African American Experience* (Durham, N.C.: Duke University Press, 1990); Wardell J. Payne, *Directory of African American Religious Bodies: A Compendium by the Howard University School of Divinity* (Washington, D.C.: Howard University Press, 1991).

National Catholic Welfare Conference

The National Catholic Welfare Conference (NCWC) began its life in August 1917 as the National Catholic War Council, whose purpose was to coordinate religious and social services for Roman Catholics (see ROMAN CATHOLICISM) serving with United States forces during World War I. At home the council worked with the Federal Council of Churches (see NATIONAL COUNCIL OF CHURCHES), the YMCA (see YOUNG MEN'S CHRISTIAN ASSOCIATION), and the Jewish Welfare Board to raise money and maintain home-front morale. Membership consisted of all the United States bishops, although ordinary activities were directed by a committee of four bishops. Father John J. Burke, a Paulist priest instrumental in its founding, was appointed as director.

Meeting after the war, the United States bishops were encouraged to continue the organization by a pastoral letter from Pope Benedict XV, who asked them to work for peace and justice in the world. Equally important was the work done by Father John RYAN in making the Church's statements on a just society an integral part of the American scene. Ryan in fact, wrote the "Bishops' Program on Social Reconstruction" that constituted the social agenda for the NCWC in its early days. This program called for the establishment of a guaranteed wage, unemployment, old age, and health insurance, as well as laws to protect labor unions and to limit child labor.

Although best known for its concern about social issues, especially during the time when John Ryan headed its social action department (1928–1945), the NCWC also served as a standing committee to deal with issues relating to the health and vitality of the Roman Catholic Church in America. This made it the first ongoing institution concerned with the affairs and policies of the Roman Catholic Church in the United States on a national level.

This raised several concerns, however, about the NCWC impinging upon the rights and autonomy of the bishops. Out of just such a concern, the pope threatened to suppress the NCWC in 1922. In response, the bishops issued a statement clarifying the NCWC's role. In a letter to the Vatican, the administrative committee of the NCWC pointed out that it was a voluntary organization, membership in which was the free choice of each bishop, and that the NCWC possessed no ecclesiastical jurisdiction or compulsory authority on either bishops, members of religious orders, priests, or laity. To dispel any further confusion about the organization's authority, the word "Council" was changed to "Conference."

Rome approved the changes in 1923, and the National Catholic Welfare Conference continued the activities of the earlier body. Until 1966 the NCWC had two main purposes. The first of these was to act as a source of information and locus of communication for the leaders of the American Catholic Church. In this role it functioned primarily as a bishops' organization, providing a continuity of policy and effort in the absence of annual episcopal meetings. Its second function was to act on behalf of the entire Church as a proponent of Catholic interests and concerns. In this role it took on the job of political lobbyist and watchdog to ensure that Catholic interests were protected.

By the mid-1960s these functions had become too diverse and numerous for one institution. In 1966 the NCWC was divided into two organizations. The first of these was the NATIONAL CONFERENCE OF CATHOLIC BISHOPS (NCCB), which took on the informational and policymaking role of the old NCWC. Composed of all the bishops and archbishops in the United States and its territories, the NCCB has much more authority and power than the old NCWC. Although most of that power is moral, it does have the authority to make statements juridically binding on all United States Catholics.

While much of its effort involves administrative matters of the Church, the NCCB has spoken out with vigor on controversial issues. The most significant were its pastoral letters on nuclear war (1983) and the economy (1986). Both of these struck many people as politically radical and as unnecessary religious meddling in politics. The latter charge also has been directed at the NCCB for its vocal and consistent opposition to abortion.

The lobbying work of the NCWC was vested in the United States Catholic Conference (USCC). Composed of laity, clergy, and members of religious orders, the USCC is concerned primarily with education, communication, and peace and social concerns. It is responsible for producing the Church's media programs, including television and radio, the training of Catholic religious educators, as well as human

rights, economic development, and political and legal affairs.

EQ

Bibliography: Jay P. Dolan, *The American Catholic Experience: A History from Colonial Times to the Present* (Notre Dame: Notre Dame University Press, 1992); James Hennesey, *American Catholics: A History of the Roman Catholic Community in the United States* (New York: Oxford University Press, 1981); E. K. McKeown, *War and Welfare: American Catholics and World War I* (New York: Garland Publishing, 1988).

National Conference of Catholic Bishops

Organized in 1966, the National Conference of Catholic Bishops (NCCB) is the successor organization to the NATIONAL CATHOLIC WELFARE CONFERENCE. When this reorganization took place, the NCCB took responsibility for all internal Church affairs, especially affairs related directly to the administration of the Roman Catholic Church (see ROMAN CATHOLICISM) in the United States, while the United States Catholic Conference (USCC) was given responsibility for political lobbying and policy implementation.

Composed of all local bishops and their associate bishops, the NCCB has several focal points. The first area involves liturgy and ritual. Here the decisions of the NCCB have the force of ecclesiastical law, and the bishops traditionally have spent much of their time on such internal church matters.

Similarly, the NCCB has responsibility for internal and public policy matters that affect the functioning of the Roman Catholic Church. Issues of primary concern to the bishops have included religious education, Catholic colleges and universities, and priestly formation. Although lobbying efforts on behalf of the Church are handled by the United States Catholic Conference, the NCCB gives the USCC direction on those matters. These include lobbying on behalf of aid to private education, opposition to abortion, and a concern for human rights.

The NCCB has been most visible as the source of moral teaching for the Roman Catholic Church in the United States. Here its work has been most controversial, especially its pronouncements on the economy (1983) and nuclear war (1983). In the pastoral letter on the economy, "Economic Justice for All: Catholic Social Teaching and the U.S. Economy," the bishops called for the establishment of an economic system that guaranteed all citizens a sufficiency of the goods necessary to live a human life. This was followed closely by the pastoral letter on nuclear war, "The Challenge of Peace: God's Promise and Our Response." This letter criticized nuclear deterrence as a strategy for achieving peace and argued that nuclear war could never be just since it violated the traditional Catholic teaching that a war to be just had to be conducted on the basis of proportionality. The bishops argued that the good achieved in winning a nuclear war could never be greater than the mass destruction it would cause and, therefore, never could be just.

Both of these letters drew vocal criticism from conservative Catholics and politicians, who argued that the bishops either had succumbed to a left-wing agenda or were too naive to know what they were saying. They were successful, however, in bringing these issues to the fore and engendering a tremendous amount of public discussion. In doing this they brought the questions of moral teaching and public policy into the foreground and worked to improve the quality of public debate in the United States.

EQ

Bibliography: Jay P. Dolan, *The American Catholic Experience: A History from Colonial Times to the Present* (Notre Dame: Notre Dame University Press, 1992); James Hennesey, *American Catholics: A History of the Roman Catholic Community in the United States* (New York: Oxford University Press, 1981); Thomas J. Reese, S.J., *A Flock of Shepherds: The National Conference of Catholic Bishops* (Washington, D.C.: FADICA, 1992).

National Council of Churches   The National Council of Churches of Christ in the U.S.A., organized in 1951, is the institutional setting of the ECUMENICAL MOVEMENT in America. In 1990 its membership consisted of 32 denominations, representing every branch of the Christian tradition except Roman Catholicism.

The forming of the National Council of Churches must be seen within the trajectory of both world and United States church history. On the world level it is the result of a disenchantment with the divisions within Christendom. The council is both an institutional response to this separation and an attempt to overcome it.

The formation of the NCC, and its precursor, the Federal Council of Churches, was the culmination of the growth of cooperative ventures during the 19th century. The impetus for this cooperation lay in the SECOND GREAT AWAKENING, the movement of religious revival that swept the United States in the early 1800s. The magnitude of Christianizing the frontier and converting (see CONVERSION) the world lay beyond the scope of any one denomination. To increase efficiency and reduce organizational duplication, denominations joined forces. American Protestants formed the American Board of Commissioners for Foreign Missions (1810), the American Bible Society (1816), the American Sunday School Union (1824), and the American Home Missionary Society (1826) to achieve that purpose.

Perhaps the most far-reaching of these joint ventures was the PLAN OF UNION worked out between the Presbyterians (see PRESBYTERIANISM) and Congregationalists (see CONGREGATIONALISM) in 1801. This plan, designed specifically to meet the needs of the unchurched frontier, allowed for unprecedented cooperation between the two denominations.

While many of these organizations, including the Plan of Union, foundered on the shoals of doctrinal conflicts or sectional tensions (see CIVIL WAR, THE), they set the tone for interdenominational cooperation. Cooperation was to be based primarily upon actions, upon what the churches could do together. Theological and doctrinal issues could be ignored while the denominations worked together on such general enterprises as missions, charity, combating infidelity, and moral reform.

Following the Civil War there was a resurgence of interdenominational organizations, especially those for people of college age. These included YMCAs and YWCAs (see YOUNG MEN'S CHRISTIAN ASSOCIATION; YOUNG WOMEN'S CHRISTIAN ASSOCIATION), the Interseminary Missionary Alliance, and the STUDENT VOLUNTEER MOVEMENT. Organized on an international level in 1895 as the World's Student Christian Federation, the last had a major impact on the ecumenical movement, for it created a core of educated, able, and adventurous young people committed to cooperation among churches.

In the United States these movements came together in December 1908 with the formation of the Federal Council of Churches of Christ in America. Originally composed of 33 denominations representing approximately 18 million people, the Federal Council was organized around issues of Christian activity, not questions of doctrine. In fact its constitution denied it "authority to draw up a common creed, form of government, or worship."

The early years of the council were periods of struggle; many wondered whether it would long survive. Oddly enough, WORLD WAR I proved the savior of the Federal Council. The mobilization of American soldiers demanded an organized response for their religious welfare. The institutional nature of the F.C.C. enabled it to provide the necessary religious and social services. Its high profile during the war gave the Federal Council greater credibility and importance.

The successful work of the Federal Council during the war did not exempt it from criticism afterward. Its commitment to action, designed to avoid doctrinal squabbles, instead immersed the council in controversy. The F.C.C.'s responses to child labor, poverty, unsafe working conditions, and racial prejudice all proved divisive.

Following the end of WORLD WAR II, the rapid growth of ecumenical and international concerns, illustrated by the formation of the United Nations and the World Council of Churches, brought home to ecumenically minded Americans the need for a more broadly based organization. To accomplish this a proposal was made in April 1944 that the eight major interdenominational agencies not affiliated with the F.C.C., including the Home Missions Council, the Foreign Missions Conference, and the International Council of Religious Education, merge with the council and form a new agency. By 1950 all these organizations had approved the plan. By that time four previously uninvolved agencies—Church World Service, the Protestant Radio Commission, the Protestant Film Commission, and the Inter-Seminary Movement—and three major Lutheran bodies had also decided to enter into the new union.

The new institution, the National Council of the Churches of Christ in the United States of America officially began its existence on January 1, 1951. Membership consisted of 29 denominations, 25 Protestant and four Eastern Orthodox.

Like its predecessor, the National Council of Churches has had numerous problems, including financial insecurity. The refusals of the Southern Baptist Convention and the Roman Catholic Church, the two largest denominations in the United States, to join the National Council have limited its representative nature. Like the Federal Council, the NCC has been criticized for its involvement in social issues. The NCC has been savaged as a Communist-infiltrated organization and denounced for its commitment to racial and social equality. During the 1980s the council's struggle with the issue of women's rights also brought it under fire. Despite these criticisms and attacks, the National Council has survived and grown, in both size and activity. It also has matured into a more representative organization. A sign of this maturity was the selection of the Very Reverend Leonid Kishkovsky of the Orthodox Church in

America as president of the National Council in 1990. This represented a significant move away from Protestant dominance within the National Council.

(See also NATIONAL ASSOCIATION OF EVAN-GELICALS; WORLD COUNCIL OF CHURCHES.)

EQ

Bibliography: Samuel McCrea Cavert, *The American Churches in the Ecumenical Movement, 1900–1968* (New York: Association Press, 1968); James F. Findlay, *Church People in the Struggle: the National Council of Churches and the Black Freedom Movement, 1950–1970* (New York: Oxford University Press, 1993); Henry J. Pratt, *The Liberalization of American Protestantism: A Case Study in Complex Organizations* (Detroit: Wayne State University Press, 1972); Wade Clark Roof and William C. Mckinney, *American Mainline Religion: Its Shape and Future* (New York: Oxford University Press, 1987); Ruth Rouse and Stephen C. Neill, *A History of the Ecumenical Movement,* 2nd ed. (Philadelphia: Westminster Press, 1967).

Native American assimilation and resistance   See ASSIMILATION AND RESISTANCE, NATIVE AMERICAN.

Native American Church   Although ritual use of peyote has a long history among Native Americans, it took on a new, institutionalized form in the early 20th century, particularly with the formation of the Native American Church in 1918. In spite of widespread efforts to prohibit the religious use of peyote, the Native American Church has grown throughout the century. In many places peyote religion has become the most predominant form of "Indian" religion, often replacing more traditional tribal religions and frequently synthesizing Christian symbolism with older native rituals.

Peyote, *Lophophora williamsii,* grows in the United States in a small region of southern Texas near the Rio Grande River, and in scattered locations southward into Mexico. The hallucinogenic properties of the cactus "buttons" commonly induce sensations of well-being or exhilaration and enhance the perception of color, although consumption of larger quantities may lead to extreme forms of behavior. Peyote's properties have been known among various native cultures since at least 1000 A.D., with some evidence suggesting a much earlier date. In historic times, its ceremonial use has been widespread among the Huichols and a number of other northern Mexican tribes. Huichol pilgrims continue to harvest it, bringing it back to the village for a tribal ceremony held in January in order to renew the corn and deer. Peyote-use also spread southward to the Aztecs well before the Spanish conquest of Mexico (see NEW SPAIN).

Unlike its long-standing diffusion throughout northern Mexico, peyote did not spread into the United States until the second half of the 19th century, although Lipan Apaches were acquiring it earlier. Mescalero Apaches in Texas apparently began bringing peyote back from Mexico around 1870. The buttons were kept for the use of shamans, individuals having the personal knowledge necessary to intercede with spiritual powers. Mescalero shamans used peyote primarily in their efforts to heal the sick, recover lost objects, or foretell an event's outcome, thus incorporating peyote in a completely different ritual complex than found in Mexico.

By 1880 or so, peyote had spread from the Lipans and Mescaleros to the Kiowas and Comanches, located on reservations in Oklahoma, who began using it in the context of tribal dances, but rapidly developed a set of rites devoted exclusively to peyote, which form the basis of native peyote rituals today. In accordance with a common tendency among Native Americans to make creative adaptations to imported cultural or religious elements, peyote use took on a number of different symbolic associations and ritual practices as it spread among Plains tribes (see NATIVE AMERICAN RELIGIONS: PLAINS).

Peyote religion traveled along a number of routes, but was effectively proselytized by "peyote men" such as John Wilson, a Delaware/

Caddo and Quanah Parker (1845?–1911). By 1875 Parker, a Comanche chief who had taken an active role in the southern Plains wars after the Treaty of Fallen Timbers (1867), became an active proponent of adaptation to reservation life. Successful as a farmer and rancher, Parker sought ways to combine Comanche and American values. Recovering from a serious illness in 1884, in spite of the failure of white medicine, he attributed his cure to peyote, and became a devoted follower of the new "Peyote Way." Parker and other proponents often viewed peyote in terms combining tribal with Christian symbolism.

Peyote rituals remain distinctive among various groups; however, the two main forms, the "Half Moon Way" and the "Cross Fire Way" (more explicit in its use of Christian symbolism) developed in the last century, have several common features. A "meeting" is essentially an all-night prayer session, led by a "road man" who erects a tipi and constructs an altar of sand in the shape of a crescent moon, on which the peyote is prepared for consumption.

Gathering at various times, and frequently in response to an individual's need for healing or other personal crisis, church members sit in a circle, while the road man recites various peyote myths, leads songs, and offers prayers. Small portions of peyote are circulated and consumed, enabling congregational members to "see God." Peyote itself is often identified as the divine being and is consumed with great humility, and often emotion. The meeting is broken into segments by breaks for water, since peyote induces great thirst, and concludes at dawn, followed by a ritual breakfast.

Peyotists have developed a religion that accomplishes a number of important symbolic tasks. Often characterized as a "Pan-Indian" movement, peyote religion focuses on the specific problems facing many American Indians in the last century. It promotes a life of self-discipline, attacking alcoholism and encouraging those who strive to participate in the white economy. At the same time, it emphasizes a number of continuities with tribal traditions. Its

syncretism, the combining of symbols and ritual elements from other cultural contexts, is itself a traditional native practice. But in the modern context, it enables members of many different tribes to see themselves sharing a common Indian identity. Its spread in the 20th century has made it the most common religion practiced today by native people.

Concern over the effects of peyote spread almost as early as the new religion itself, although the history of suppression dates back to 1620 when Catholic inquisitors prohibited its use in Mexico. In 1888 E. E. White, agent in charge of the Kiowa, Comanche, and Wichita Agency, issued the first United States order prohibiting peyote use, threatening to cut off annuities and rations, or even lease-money for those who violated the order. Urging federal legislation more comprehensive than available under the Court of Indian Offenses (see AMERICAN INDIAN RELIGIOUS FREEDOM ACT), White and others pushed for elimination of peyote as an impediment to "civilizing" the Indian. Federal legislation never came, despite numerous efforts by western legislators, but peyotists faced a continual series of punitive efforts from individual states and agency administrators seeking to prosecute peyote cases under existing liquor and drug laws.

The Native American Church itself emerged in response to this policing of Indian life on the reservations of Oklahoma. In 1907 Parker and other Indian peyotists persuaded Oklahoma and Bureau of Indian Affairs officials that peyote was not harmful. Seeking to extract their new religion from the wave of anti-peyote efforts, led by individual BIA agents, Christian missionaries, and Indian opponents, the peyote leaders incorporated the Native American Church in 1918, modeled to some extent on earlier efforts of groups like the Oto Church of the First Born to view peyote in Christian terms. Anthropologist James Mooney, who had studied both peyote and the GHOST DANCE, suggested the strategic need to make parallels between peyote and Christian traditions. Churches spread among various tribes across the Plains, further west and east, leading to reincorporation in 1944 as the Native American Church of the United States. Upon spreading to Canada in 1955, the church became the "Native American Church of North America."

In spite of peyote religion's growth, and the inability of the federal government to successfully outlaw its use, opposition has remained. California, for instance, passed anti-peyote legislation in 1959, New York in 1967. Opposition has also continued from various quarters. In addition to state officials and Christian missionaries, various native groups have sought to resist peyote by means of regulation or legislation. Some Christian Indians, such as the proponents of assimilation who formed the Indian Rights Association in the late 19th century, saw peyote as a step backward. Native traditionalists, concerned to preserve tribal distinctiveness, objected to the corruption of tribal traditions. On the Navajo reservation, where nearly half of the adult population came to practice peyote religion, peyote remained illegal until 1967. An Oregon prosecution of two Native American substance-abuse counselors from the Warm Springs reservation in 1986 led to a landmark 1990 U.S. Supreme Court ruling (*Employment Division vs. Smith*) that acknowledged states' right to prohibit religious use of peyote, although the Oregon statute itself was repealed the following year.

Although faced with continuing opposition from various quarters, the Native American Church and other groups of Indian peyotists continue to draw upon the power they find in this new religion to enable them to maintain contact with the past and face the future.

MG

Bibliography: James Slotkin, *The Peyote Religion: A Study in Indian-White Relations* (New York: Farrar, Straus and Giroux, 1975); Omer Stewart, *Peyote Religion: A History* (Norman: University of Oklahoma Press, 1987).

Native American religions

Native Americans developed rituals and sacred stories to order their personal and communal lives, to provide them with means of drawing on supernatural power, and to locate their lives within the specific landscapes of their history. Thus Native American religions are typically oriented around the specifics of environment and culture, economy, language, and kinship. Native American cultures embody a diversity of ideas and practices. Native American religions are intertwined with other elements of culture, making it difficult to generalize about characteristics of native religious experience. The history of interaction between indigenous peoples and the descendants of America's European colonizers often reflects the misunderstandings resulting from the tendency to obscure cultural differences. Consequently to understand Native American religions it is necessary to examine both the unity and diversity of native religions, as well as the image of the "Indian" held in the dominant American culture.

The best conservative estimates suggest the wellsprings of human culture in the Americas run back between 20,000 and 30,000 years. In that period of time, a large number of cultures have flourished and declined. Some, like the Adena and Hopewell in the Ohio Valley or the Anasazi in the Southwest left impressive architectural evidence. Others left traces more on patterns of vegetation, which the Europeans mistook for an environment untouched by human hand.

At the time of Christopher COLUMBUS's landfall in 1492, demographers estimate the Americas were home to some 75 million people, from six to 10 million in the area of the United States, who divided themselves into approximately 500 cultural groups, speaking at least 250 languages, nearly 100 of which are still in use today. While certain patterns were shared among those who dwelt in particular regions of the country, indigenous North Americans developed an enormous variety of religious ceremonies, technologies, agricultural and hunting practices, and forms of social organization. Anthropologists typically group tribes together in "culture areas," although these groupings are sometimes more convenient than accurate, since within any particular area a wide variety of beliefs, institutions, and practices is present. A simplified form of culture areas appears in this volume (see NATIVE AMERICAN RELIGIONS: EASTERN WOODLANDS, NATIVE AMERICAN RELIGIONS: INTERMONTANE/CALIFORNIA; NATIVE AMERICAN RELIGIONS: NORTHWEST; NATIVE AMERICAN RELIGIONS: PLAINS; NATIVE AMERICAN RELIGIONS: SOUTHWEST).

Constants among tribal religions are perhaps more evident in terms of functions and formal features than specific beliefs or practices regarding the supernatural. Rituals have provided effective means of healing individual illness and the removal of ills affecting communal life. The use of natural resources, whether through intricate agricultural practice, foraging, hunting, or fishing, gave rise to rituals of petition, purification, and thanksgiving, which made possible the annual renewal of life and the harvest of crops and game. Whether in elaborate annual communal rites like the Plains Sun Dance and the various forms of Green Corn Ceremony found in the Eastern Woodlands, or in the prayers and offerings of individual hunters, native peoples have acknowledged their dependence upon the beneficence of natural forces.

American Indian oral traditions passed on mythic stories to convey their understanding about the creation of the world, the dilemmas and pitfalls facing human beings, their own distinct group identities, and models for right living. Such stories emphasize the importance of upholding one's obligations to kin or social networks, and detail the countless ways in which supernatural beings intersect with the natural world. In some traditions transcendent beings may play a dominant role; in others the supernatural powers are embodied within the animate and inanimate things of this world. This ability to locate the sacred within things that Europeans thought simply profane has led to consistent misunderstandings of native beliefs and practices.

While Europeans and Americans have been most inclined to see religious knowledge and authority handed down through institutions such as churches, native traditions exhibit a variety of approaches. Some traditions are highly decentralized, encouraging individuals to gain their own insight and guidance through personal acts of prayer, rituals of fasting and purification, and vision quests. Some stress the role of specialists—shamans, who attain personal acquaintance with spirits through self-discipline, visions or other means, which enable them to serve as intermediaries for the group. Some have developed elaborate bodies of sacred teachings, controlled by groups of priestlike elders, who administer public ritual life, and assure the continuity of the oral tradition.

With the European arrival the long history of conflict, adaptation, and borrowing by which native cultures influenced each other took on new dimensions, stemming in part from misconceptions that both Europeans and indigenous peoples held of each other (see NEW FRANCE; NEW SPAIN). While significant linguistic and cultural differences marked off one tribal group from another, Europeans, especially those with little first-hand knowledge of the new land, accepted the term Columbus used: *los indios*—"Indians," as the name for the entire indigenous population, and often played down their cultural differences. Rather than seeing hundreds of different cultures, Europeans saw varieties of the same. Gradually realizing Columbus had not found his Asian goal, Europeans grappled with the problem of who these people were, drawing upon the authority of the Bible, scholastic philosophy and theology, science, and European folk traditions to account for their absence from the European stock of knowledge. Debates loomed large in European capitals as to whether the indigenous Americans were descendants of Noah's sons, or perhaps like the "Wild Man" or *l'homme sauvage* of folklore a kind of subhuman race, as many Spanish colonists suspected, a suspicion that made possible use of Indians as slaves in the gold mines of NEW SPAIN. Assuming all humans were descendants of Adam, and themselves possessors of a common Christian culture, Europeans were inclined to see a universal human nature, and to explain cultural differences in terms of derivation, or degeneracy, from a common Adamic source.

Due largely to this universalizing tendency in European thought of the day, the history of interaction between native cultures and Europeans is full of misunderstanding, frequent conflict, and tragedy (see ASSIMILATION AND RESISTANCE, NATIVE AMERICAN). The questions of who is Indian and what is Indian not only perplexed European minds, but played an active role in shaping the political, religious, and military strategies Europeans and their American descendants used in dealing with native groups. In the years following the AMERICAN REVOLUTION, Congress claimed the power to regulate "trade and intercourse," and establish treaties with Indian tribes. As a consequence the legislative and bureaucratic framework constructed to administer federal "Indian Affairs" depended for its success on viewing indigenous people as one distinct group, with common interests, problems, and lack of true religion.

This homogenizing of cultures has both created difficulties for tribes and, on occasion, served their needs to deflect the impact of government policy and cultural or religious pressure from the whites. Whereas Europeans and Americans used religion to link their personal identities and loyalty to large-scale nations and churches, native people most often saw their own personal identity tied to locales or small kinship groups. Thus in dealing with whites, many groups found they had little common interest, making alliance against colonial or later federal power difficult. For instance, most tribes, and sometimes even the various kinship groups within a tribe, such as the Hopis, had sacred accounts of their own origins as a people, and of the process by which they came to dwell in a given area of land. In this way indigenous cultures generally avoided conflicts for religious supremacy, since each tribe saw itself defined by its relationship to the spiritual powers of a particular place. But at the same time, because origin myths are local, members of one group might find little in common with another.

On many occasions, however, native people have creatively overcome the barriers of localism. New myths telling of a common origin among all "red" people enabled native groups in the East to unite in opposition to white encroachment on tribal territory during the early 19th century. HANDSOME LAKE and WOVOKA were only two of many prophetic leaders over the last four centuries who created new religious movements in which older tribal loyalties and animosities were recast in common resistance to white culture. Thus while the European idea of "Indian" made bureaucratic administration of lives and lands efficient, it also helped forge common identity among tribal people seeking ways to accommodate influences from the larger society, and even to spur on religious, cultural, or political resistance to the dominant order.

In addition to the problem of unity and diversity among native cultures, there is the boundary problem of how to distinguish between Indian and white. What is Indian? And often even more vexing in times of cultural change, what is "really Indian?" Such questions appear in the discourse of both the dominant culture and among Indian people themselves.

Historically tribal groups fixed the boundaries between themselves and others on the basis of sacred kinship obligations. Those who fulfilled obligations to each other were members of the group, regardless of their own original background. Thus the boundaries were somewhat fluid, as the many white captives adopted into families often found. Benjamin Franklin, for instance, noticed in 1753 the tendency of many white captives/adoptees to return to the tribes after their ransom, evidently most comfortable with the way of life learned during their captivity.

In the 1870s the government began to see Indian-ness as based on blood-quanta. Through intermarriage and religious conversion, government and church officials sought to "kill the Indian to save the man." Blood-quanta served to distinguish those with greater from lesser amounts of "Indian blood." Based on the assumption that as blood thinned, so would native culture and religion, government policies governing land-leasing or credit actually gave greater freedom and weight to those with less rather than more blood.

Increasingly in the later 20th century, Native Americans have replaced the government's emphasis on blood with a new focus on culture as the key determinant of being Indian. Rather than disappearing as often predicted and hoped for by expansionist Americans, the Indian population has climbed from a lowpoint of 250,000 in 1890 to nearly two million in 1990. In recent decades many have come to see a potential cultural revival, arising out of the tension between those who strive to retain or creatively renew traditional cultural practices, languages, or religious ceremonies, and those attracted or compelled to accept the values and practices of American culture. With growing political power and cultural prestige in the last few decades, Native Americans have gained the opportunity to reconfigure both their own identities and the constricting images often found in the dominant culture.

MG

Bibliography: Peggy V. Beck, Anna Lee Walters, and Nia Francisco, *The Sacred: Ways of Knowledge, Sources of Life* (Flagstaff: Navajo Community College Press/Northland, 1977); Brian Dippie, *The Vanishing American: White Attitudes and U.S. Policy* (Middletown, Conn.: Wesleyan University Press, 1982); Darcy McNickle, *Native American Tribalism: Indian Survivals and Renewals* (New York: Oxford University Press, 1973).

Native American religions: Eastern Woodlands
Eastern tribes bore the brunt of the original English and French advances into North America. Traditional Eastern Woodlands religions were often based on personal acquisition of sacred power. In some cultures, societies of shamans mediated access to the supernatural. In the southeast the religious life of several tribes centered around the yearly performance of the Green Corn Ceremony. However, more than three centuries of interaction with colonial powers and the expanding American society brought both the collapse and resurgence of tribal religions.

Anthropologists typically divide the Eastern Woodlands of the United States and Canada, running from the Atlantic Ocean to the Mississippi River, into two separate regions, the Northeast and the Southeast, divided roughly along the Ohio River, although in the area as a whole a number of common cultural patterns and linguistic similarities appear. Settlement in the Eastern Woodlands extends from approximately 16,000 B.C. Some features of these archaic cultures remain among contemporary Crees and other Algonquian-speakers north of the St. Lawrence River in Canada. Several early cultures developed elaborate urban centers after 1000 B.C. that stood at the center of great networks of trade, political, and religious influence, such as the Adena and Hopewell of the Ohio Valley. The Mexican-inspired Mississippians, builders of the great city of Cahokia (in Illinois), influenced the development of southeastern tribal ceremonial life into more recent centuries.

By the 16th century the Eastern Woodlands archaic cultures had been replaced by a large number of tribes. While many left little evidence of vanished ways of life, at least 68 languages were spoken by the groups encountering the Europeans. Eastern tribes exhibited a range of economies, a range that has its parallel in forms of religious practice as well. Mixed agricultural economies had developed by 1000 B.C., although corn only appeared among the Iroquois and Algonquians around 1300 A.D. Many Algonquian-speakers in northern New England were semi-nomadic hunters. The Iroquois, their southern Cherokee relatives, and the diverse group of southern Muskogean tribes dwelt in permanent towns. In either case, woodland tribes had successfully shaped many eastern micro-environments in order to increase their harvesting of game and crops, producing a landscape that early Europeans described as parklike. In all cases, religion enabled the people to interact with the surrounding environment.

While much of the available information on eastern tribes during the first centuries of contact with Europeans comes from the pens of colonizers themselves, a fairly detailed portrayal of religious life has been pieced together by historians and anthropologists. Common to Native Americans in general are the assumptions that the world is full of a wide variety of spiritual powers, and that human life is only possible when lived in recognition of these powers, called *manitou* by the semi-nomadic Algonquians of New England. The Massachussets and Wampanoags told large numbers of sacred stories detailing the ways in which power affected the world, but gave little effort to developing these stories into systematic form, and little attention to theological questions regarding a supreme being. Other tribes had cosmologies accounting for the world's creation, such as the Earth-Diver stories common around the Great Lakes and elsewhere.

The acquisition of *manitou* often required the work of a shaman, or *powwow* in Algonquian, an individual capable of addressing and influencing the *manitou* directly, either warding off malevolence, or insuring benevolence through the performance of many rituals. Individuals themselves also possessed the capability of ritual performance, such as those observances governing hunting, or the acquiring of insight through dreams, fasting, or isolation. Communal rituals necessary for the replenishment of game and the planting cycle, or those for passage through the stages of life or warding off evil, however, were left to the *powwow*. Some Algonquian tribes, like the Anishenabeg, or Chippewa of the Great Lakes area, developed medicine societies, the *Midewiwin*.

Among those tribes dwelling in more permanent towns, such as the Iroquois and Hurons of the north and the Cherokees, Muskogees, Seminoles, and others in the south, community life often revolved around a series of calendrical and periodic rituals. Some, such as the *Onanharoia*, of the Hurons and Iroquois, in which dreams were fulfilled, enabled a community to purge itself of antisocial tensions. Others, such as the diverse forms of the Green Corn Ceremony practiced throughout much of the southern region, combined many needs. The Muskogee *poskita* brought together an annual thanksgiving for the power of corn, the purifying of the community, and the reinforcement of gender boundaries. Some tribes relied upon various voluntary societies, like the Iroquois False Faces, to administer rituals and to cure disease or possession by witchcraft.

Native societies in the East existed in complex relations with each other, evident in extensive trade networks and the pull of political expansion, as among the Iroquois Confederacy. Competition, conflict, and cooperation were all crucial in creating a dynamic history prior to contact with Europeans. However, relations among the tribes, as well as social, economic, and religious life within tribal boundaries, altered under the impact of colonization in the 17th and 18th centuries. Confronted with missionaries, such as the French Jesuits in the north (see NEW FRANCE), tribal members found their unity destroyed as the new faith focused on personal salvation rather than upholding kinship networks. Many tribes took advantage of European desires for trade in furs, a crucial commodity in mercantile capitalism. Struggling for dominance in this network, many hunters found themselves overharvesting the game, eventually sinking into dependence upon the new European-controlled economic order.

While adopting elements of the new order's religion and economy aided some tribes, such as the Cherokees, in coping with the stresses of change, many tribes suffered dramatic declines in population and land-base. The Hurons, having accepted the Jesuits' ROMAN CATHOLICISM, collapsed under an Iroquois onslaught in 1648. Puritans (see PURITANISM) eliminated the Pequots and other New England tribes, or gave thanks when disease accomplished the same end.

Some tribes were able to forestall colonial expansion; the Iroquois were defeated only by the failure of their British ally during the AMERICAN REVOLUTION. Others, under leaders like the Shawnee Tecumseh (see ASSIMILATION AND RESISTANCE, NATIVE AMERICAN) forged great alliances among tribes. Others developed new religions (see HANDSOME LAKE) that provided enduring means of retaining distinctive cultural identity in the midst of the expansive American society.

However, during the first decades of the 19th century many remaining tribes were removed west of the Mississippi River, and as the American population continued to stretch its own desires for land, numerous eastern tribes were eventually confined within Oklahoma's "Indian Territory," where many Muskogees, Cherokees, Seminoles, Yuchis, and others continue to live. At the same time, while the national mythology of MANIFEST DESTINY often depicts an eastern region wiped clean of Indian people, reservations, often quite small except around the Great Lakes, remain in eastern states. Some peoples, notably the Iroquois, but also including smaller tribes like the Passamoquoddys and Penobscott, who first encountered Puritan colonization in the early 17th century, successfully sued for return of lands or compensation in recent years, in the process gaining renewed sovereignty and control over their lives.

MG

Bibliography: James Axtell, *The Invasion Within: The Contest of Cultures in Colonial North America* (New York: Oxford University Press, 1985); Charles Hudson, *The Southeastern Indians* (Knoxville: University of Tennessee Press, 1976); Elizabeth Tooker, *Native American Spirituality of the Eastern Woodlands* (Mahwah, N.J.: Paulist Press, 1979).

Native American religions: Inter-montane/California

Native Americans in the far western United States, an area of great diversity in terms of landform and climate, developed a correspondingly wide range of religious practices. Responding to the strains placed on traditional religions by encroaching Spanish, Mexican, and American colonists, Native Americans also created new, millennial religions to restore balance to the world, some of which remain in practice today.

Anthropologists typically discuss Native American cultures in the far west in terms of three cultural areas: the Great Basin of Nevada and western Utah, the Plateau area west of the Rocky Mountains (which extends north to the Canadian border), and California. The wide variety of cultural and linguistic groupings found in these regions reflects significant religious differences as well.

Great Basin tribes including the Monos, several groups of Paiutes, numerous Shoshones, Utes, and others, adapted to an arid climate, living in small family groups near water sources, and relying upon intricate, sophisticated methods (including irrigation) to promote and harvest a wide range of plants, animals, and other natural resources. Perhaps because of the rigors of life in the Basin, religion tended to focus on the personal acquisition of spiritual power, *puha* in Numic, which enabled one to lead hunts or cure illness or the evils associated with dreams or malevolent spirits. Basin people found *puha* present in many things—landforms, water sources, animals, plants, and people. The human task was to maintain connections with the sources of power found in the environment, and to use it in ways that benefited the group. While a tribe might hold occasional communal dances, which eventually provided the ritual basis for the GHOST DANCE, religious ceremonialism focused largely on either the curings of shamanic leaders (both male and female), personal or group acts of petition and thanksgiving used in harvesting pine nuts, game, or other resources, and rites associated with transitions in life.

Plateau religion provided villagers with means to draw upon spiritual beings for guidance. Fasting, purification, and all-night vision quests were encouraged among adults and children of both sexes, although after puberty a girl's source of power shifted from an external guardian spirit to one emanating from her own body. Shamans, most adept at maintaining personal contact with spiritual beings, were the primary religious authorities, able to cure disease and ward off the powers of witches, ghosts, or other evil beings. Both men and women could receive visions, as well as the personal instruction necessary from those more experienced, in order to specialize in specific shamanic cures.

Depending upon their particular economy, people living in the Plateau had reason to thank numerous spiritual powers for providing them with the resources necessary for life. Midwinter, when family groups returned to their permanent villages, provided the opportunity to perform a number of ceremonies inside large wooden lodges, led by various individuals possessing spiritual powers. Prayers, songs, and dances were offered up during ceremonies, often concluded with large feasts. While rituals helped to put the world right, myths often explained why human life was difficult. Coyote or mink stories tell of forces gone awry during ancient times. The Thompson River tribe for instance, in eastern Oregon, tell of Coyote's misguided efforts to insure human immortality. Crossing a series of mountains on his way back from the land of the dead, bringing back a bag full of departed souls, the trail becomes too steep, and he opens the bag to lighten the load, losing all the souls.

While shamanism provided all California tribes with religious specialists, the traditional religions of California took on a multitude of forms, far more than in other American regions. Tribes were very territorial and developed mythical stories of the world's creation with a pronounced local emphasis. Mythologies thus differed dramatically from tribe to tribe, along with any constants of belief. In the Northwest, cultures bore resemblance to those of tribes further north (see NATIVE AMERICAN RELIGIONS: NORTHWEST); an abundant salmon economy allowed for the growth of great mate-

rial wealth. Religious ceremonies often centered around a feast held by a wealthy tribal leader, emphasizing the wealthy person's generosity. Other ceremonies insured the renewal of game and crops, such as the Jumping Dance or the White Deerskin Dance. The Patwin of the Central Valley, much like the Hopis (see NATIVE AMERICAN RELIGIONS: SOUTHWEST), held a series of performances in which the village was visited by powerful spiritual beings who came to bless the community.

Like most others, southern Californians practiced initiation rites, focusing particularly on puberty and death. Boys among the Chumash, and "Mission Indians" such as the Gabrielinos, were given a hallucinogenic drug made from jimson weed (*Datura stramonium*—also used by numerous southwestern tribes for a variety of purposes) to assist them in obtaining visions during puberty rites. Among the Liuseno and Diegueno an elaborate ritual invoking the spirit Chinigchinich developed around the drug's use.

The diversity of far western tribes exceeds the capacity of generalization about common traditional characteristics. One commonality, however, were the crises, at once religious and social, stemming from the pressure of European and American colonialism (see NEW SPAIN; FRONTIER). Beginning with the Spanish advance into California in 1769, the Far West became the scene of intense missionary efforts by both Catholics and Protestants. The rapid influx of American settlers during the California Gold Rush of 1849 created enormous strain on tribal life. The Native population in California declined from 300,000 prior to Spanish settlement in the 18th century, to 150,000 by the American conquest of 1846, to 30,000 by 1870. Although reflecting increased Native American mobility, the 1990 census puts California's native population at more than 242,000.

Native people in California and throughout the West responded to the disruption of traditional lifeways in the second half of the 19th century by creating new prophetic movements, such as the GHOST DANCE, or that begun by the Wanapum chief Smohalla in 1855, who preached that Indians should avoid contact with white ways of life. Movements such as the northern California Bole Maru (Patwin for "dreamers") and Earth Lodge religions often combined native traditions and rituals with Christian symbolism. The frequent use of millennial ideas gave the followers of these religions a means to interpret the drastic social and environmental changes brought by the Americans, by portraying an afterlife restored to precontact circumstances.

In spite of the continuing impact from colonization and government intervention that resulted in a reduction of traditional landbases, extensive population loss, dissolution of tribal status, and prohibition of native religions, the Indian people endured throughout the 20th century in California and the intermontane region. The religions begun by dreamers and prophets in the 19th century continue in the present. Urban California gained a large Native American population during the 1950s and 1960s. With the state's numerous educational institutions, it became a focal point of the political and religious renewal sweeping the national Indian population during recent decades (see ASSIMILATION AND RESISTANCE, NATIVE AMERICAN).

MG

Bibliography: R. F. Heizer and M. A. Whipple, *The California Indians: A Sourcebook,* 2nd ed. (Berkeley: University of California Press, 1971); Jay Miller "Basin Religion and Theology: A Comparative Study of (Power) Puha," *Journal of Great Basin and California Anthropology* (5/1–2 (1983): 66, 86); Robert F. Ruby, *Dreamer-prophets of the Columbia Plateau: Smohalla and Skolaskin* (Norman: University of Oklahoma Press, 1989); William C. Sturtevant and Warren L. D'Azevedo, eds., *Handbook of the North American Indians: Great Basin,* Vol. 11 (Washington, D.C.: Smithsonian, 1986).

Native American religions: Northwest

The native people living on the Northwest coast of the United States share a number of common cultural and religious practices. Permanent settlements and a largely marine economy provided the opportunity to develop an elaborate social structure undergirded by a calendar of ceremonial festivals. Northwestern religion also depended heavily upon the powers of shamans to perform healings and ensure success. While ceremonial practices such as the potlatch were outlawed by the government in the late 19th century, many communities have held on to or revived traditional rituals.

In contrast to their linguistic diversity, northwestern peoples developed fairly similar economies, cultures, and religions. The outlines of historic cultures are evident by 1000 B.C.: the practices of intricate woodworking, construction of elaborate, permanent cedar housing, a marine economy based on salmon harvesting and hunting sea mammals (including whales in the north), and a widespread trade network. The abundance of natural resources allowed for the creation of stratified social structures in which the acquisition of wealth (and its reciprocal, its distribution) played a prominent role. People took their lineage from long lines of ancestors, traceable back to the mythical beings whose exploits are often depicted on the totem poles common across the region. Thus social rank reflected a degree of inherited spiritual power, and chiefs, called *gyigame* among the Kwakiutls—"being in front"—were ancestors incarnate. Residence and property were based on birth, and the great cedar houses, some recorded as being several hundred feet long, were filled with relatives sharing resources in common, dependent upon the wealthy leaders. Potlatches, elaborate ceremonial feasts, were held to commemorate changes of social status and death, in the process also honoring those whose generosity could make the feast possible.

Like many other Native Americans, people of the Northwest coast attached religious significance to activities seen by the European or American as secular. Success for whalers hunting on the violent northern ocean could only come to those who were protected by a spirit helper. The harvesting of food and resources was accompanied by personal rituals. Fundamentally, the world was a dangerous place, full of powers that could easily wreak havoc on human life. Accordingly, such powers had to be pacified, avoided, or overcome. The Kwakiutls, for instance, dwelt in a symbolic world full of faces. Totem poles and ceremonial masks depicting the open mouths of bears, ravens, eagles, killer whales, and other spiritually powerful animals created a world of symbols suggesting that everything eats. Humans are related to both animals and spirits in a mutual relation of eating. Thus humans are dependent upon those whom they eat, and recognize that their own position in the universe can become that of the prey.

Northwestern tribes relied upon shamans to cure illness and evil. While shamans, often under the patronage of village chiefs, acted on an individual level, they also formed societies responsible for the performance of the great winter ceremonies, which might take place over the course of the entire season. In the north, communities put great effort into various ritual efforts to push away the forces of darkness and death that seemed to descend during the long winters. Among some tribes, elaborate mythic accounts tell of the creation of the world; among others, humans confront a preexisting world populated by powerful spiritual beings. The Kwakiutl winter ceremonial, the *tsetega,* led by a secret society of shamans called the *hamatsa,* presented in dramatic form the effort to kill the Man-Eater spirit, who personified the insatiable hunger governing relationships among living beings. The elaborate ritual, spread over several days, enabled the community to overcome death and to maintain balance between humans/animals and summer/winter. The ceremonial also reinforced the relationship between nobles and commoners by underscoring the ritual role of community leaders in staving off hunger.

Northwestern coastal tribes retained autonomy in the years after they first encountered European explorers Juan Perez in 1774 and James Cook in 1778. Trading begun by the Hudson's Bay Company eventually created rivalries between villages that contributed to severe internal stress and increased competition between tribes. The influx of whites into the region in the 1850s, including Protestant and Catholic missionaries, resulted in a series of treaties between Vancouver Island tribes and the Canadian government, and between the Americans and the more southern tribes. Having ceded nearly all of their landbase, tribes were generally left with village sites and fishing rights, though these also came under pressure, and in late 1855 war broke out both on the coast and further inland, involving a number of tribes over the next three years.

In spite of the loss of landbase, many northwestern tribes have been able to hold on to their fishing economy, although dependency has also grown. In the second half of the 20th century, a number of factors have enabled Indians in the Northwest to endure, and in some cases prosper. Increased ability to tackle government policy has enabled tribes to fight successfully for the restoration of fishing rights, and for restitution for the taking of lands. Religious and cultural renewal, while tenuous in some communities, has grown. While both Canadian and United States tribes were forced to abandon many ceremonies, including the potlatch, performances have revived in many communities. Some have been able to provide needed means of economic development from the performance of public ceremonies and the growing interest in native art.

MG

Bibliography: Irving Goldman, *The Mouth of Heaven: an Introduction to Kwakiutl Religious Thought* (New York: Wiley and Sons, 1975); H.R. Hays, *Children of the Raven: The Seven Indian Nations of the Northwest Coast* (New York: McGraw-Hill, 1975); Stanley Walens, *Feasting with Cannibals:*

An Essay on Kwakiutl Cosmology (Princeton: Princeton University Press, 1981).

Native American religions: Plains The distinctive patterns of Plains culture and religion are relatively recent. Many elements of Plains religion, such as the pipe, vision quests, and more recently the Sun Dance, were shared by the various tribes that came to occupy the region. Following years of widespread warfare, Native Americans were confined to reservations, where federal officials enacted laws and policies prohibiting the practice of traditional religions. Many traditional religious practices became covert, resurfacing only in the later decades of the 20th century.

Although archeological evidence indicates that the grasslands in the center of North America were inhabited sporadically since at least 10,000 B.C., permanent settlement occurred only around 500 B.C. The presence of historic tribes associated with the region is quite recent compared with other patterns of settlement, beginning around A.D. 1400 when the Blackfeet began entering the grasslands for periodic hunts. The Missouri River country became the permanent home of Hidatsas, Arikaras, and Mandans, who built fortified towns and practiced a diversified agriculture in the north, Pawnees and Wichitas further south. Other groups, including Shoshones, Apaches, and Kiowas, also entered from surrounding areas.

It was not until the early to mid-1600s, however, that Plains culture took on some of the major characteristics for which it is often noted. With the displacement of large numbers of peoples as a result of conflicts with encroaching European colonizers to the east, the Plains became a vast haven. Numerous tribes migrated into the area, increasing competition for resources with tribes already present, but also promoting an interchange of religious ritual, technology, and the domestication of the horse, upon which Plains people came to depend.

Plains tribes came to embrace common subsistence patterns, either more nomadic bison-hunting or more permanent, generally riverine agriculture; however most tribes practiced forms of both. In social organization, Plains tribes relied upon a loose structuring. Tribes, based on shared dialects and culture, were often composed of fairly independent bands, based more on kinship. Bands themselves tended to be fairly small and mobile among the hunters. Within each social unit, voluntary societies were responsible for common enterprises. But, since Plains people prized individual autonomy as well as social solidarity, the authority of leaders was never absolute.

Religious life for Plains cultures centered around the acquisition of supernatural power, which was seen to fill the world, and upon which fragile humans had to depend in order to live well. Individuals, particularly males among the bison-hunters, sought power as a guide to life, relying upon vision quests to provide an independent spiritual source upon which to base life choices and engage in the activities of hunting and warfare. Power also came to individuals through various rituals marking passage from one phase of life to the next, as in the Lakota *tatanka lowanpi,* a girl's puberty rite that ensured young women the ability to be industrious, fertile, and hospitable.

While agricultural tribes such as the Mandans often held a series of calendar-based rituals in conjunction with the planting cycle, which also served to reinforce communal spirit, those whose subsistence economy depended on the vast migrating herds of bison had less opportunity for regular gatherings. The Sun Dance (a Lakota name), widely practiced, though not universal, among tribes by the late 18th to early 19th century, was often the only calendrical ceremony performed in many tribes. Held in midsummer in conjunction with the annual communal bison hunt, the Sun Dance, with its theme of sacrifice for the common good, enabled its Plains practitioners to purify themselves in order to beseech the sacred powers to renew the bison in the coming year, in essence renewing the world. The complexity of tribal symbolism, interweaving the people's history, the powers of the universe itself, and the natural processes of growth, provided many Plains rituals with a richness of function. Thus personal, social, and natural renewal could all be engendered through the performance of a vast, interlocking ritual framework, as in the Crow Tobacco ceremony.

Plains cultures developed elaborate mythological accounts of their origins as distinctive peoples, and the disposition of the sacred powers, some beneficent, some malevolent, affecting their lives. Many drew on tales of a "trickster" figure, a supernatural being both comic and malevolent, and often short-sighted. Through trickster stories the people learned appropriate conduct and the limitations of self-aggrandizement.

Plains tribes often embedded their search for supernatural power or their mythic self-understanding in particular places. Seeing human life in this world as transitory, or "as driftwood" in the words of a Crow saying, Plains people generally avoided construction of permanent sacred sites. Ritual structures such as those built for the Sun Dance or the Cheyenne Medicine Lodge fell apart, buffeted by wind, snow, and thunderstorm. But the land itself often revealed the sacred. Prominent features like buttes, mountains, lakes, or rivers were seen as sources of power. But there were also many sites unnoticeable to those not raised on the stories handed down from elders.

Given that Plains culture is itself a creative adaptation to the presence of European colonizers, it is interesting that the image of the Plains warrior is the most prominent example of "Indianness" in American culture. Plains tribes early on dealt with the presence of Europeans and Americans, from Coronado's trip through Kansas in the 1540s to French and American trappers, traders, and missionaries near the beginning of the 18th century. The federal government began making treaties with Plains tribes in 1825, and forcibly removing many eastern tribes out onto the Plains, encroaching upon territory and resources already claimed by western groups.

Although occasional hostilities broke out over the massive influx of westering Americans during the late 1840s Gold Rush, it was not until after the CIVIL WAR that the Euro-Americans turned their eyes to the Plains themselves as a region for settlement. A series of wars fought with both southern and northern tribes in the 1860s and 1870s ended with the creation of a vast reservation system overseen by the Office of Indian Affairs and an unofficial group of Christian missionaries. During this period of enormous stress, new religions, such as the GHOST DANCE and the "Peyote Way" spread widely among many members of Plains tribes.

During the years from 1883 to 1934, those confined to reservations were subject to government penalizing of traditional religious practice. Various important Plains rituals, such as the Sun Dance, were prohibited by the Court of Indian Offenses (see AMERICAN INDIAN RELIGIOUS FREEDOM ACT). Ritual performance became covert. Government intervention in the Lakota Ghost Dance culminated in the 1890 Wounded Knee massacre.

In subsequent years land bases continued to erode and economic conditions often grew precarious. Nevertheless, many Plains cultures have endured. Despite the difficulties of federal administration of Native life, members of many tribes experienced the cultural and political rebirth associated with the new emphasis on sovereignty and religious traditionalism during the 1960s (see ASSIMILATION AND RESISTANCE, NATIVE AMERICAN).

MG

Bibliography: Howard L. Harrod, *Renewing the World: Plains Indian Religion and Morality* (Tucson: University of Arizona Press, 1987); Peter J. Powell *Sweet Medicine: The Continuing Role of the Sacred Arrows, the Sun Dance and the Sacred Buffalo Hat* *in Northern Cheyenne Culture,* 2 vols. (Norman: University of Oklahoma Press, 1969); James R. Walker, *Lakota Belief and Ritual* (Lincoln: University of Nebraska Press, 1980).

Native American religions: Southwest

The American Southwest, an arid land of low and high deserts, rugged mountains, and high plateaus, has been home to a wide variety of indigenous cultures for thousands of years. Patterns of religious life range from the institutionalized performance of communal rituals among the Pueblos, to the more shamanic focus on personal healing or power among Apaches and other tribes, and the related "sing" among the Navajos. Influences from several ancient cultures have carried down through the centuries to many of the native tribes dwelling there today. While notable for the longevity of existing cultures, the area also has seen catastrophes of drought, population dislocation, war, and colonization, in the face of which native people have struggled to adapt creatively to changing circumstances.

The earliest inhabitants of the Southwest are known through stone tools, such as the Clovis and Folsom points discovered by archaeologists along the Rio Grande River in southern New Mexico, dating from approximately 15,000 B.C. Many historic southwestern tribes were agricultural, continuing practices of corn-planting that date back at least 3,000 years. In that time cultures like the Hohokam (ancestors of the Pimans in the south) and Anasazi (ancestors of the Pueblos in the north) developed agricultural technologies, distinctive esthetic styles, and religious understandings, particularly visible in the care with which they treated their dead. The Anasazi, the last of these older peoples, built adobe and stone towns, such as Chaco Canyon and Mesa Verde. Prominent between A.D. 300 and 1300, the Anasazi passed on many features of their way of life to the Pueblos—Spanish for "village dwellers."

Speaking six different languages—Tewa, Tiwa, Towa (all varieties of Tanoan), Hopi,

Young drummers being trained in the rituals of their ancestors at a Cheyenne and Arapaho Powwow, Conch, Oklahoma, August 1992. (Pluralism Project of Harvard University)

Zuni, and Keresan—the Pueblo peoples developed a complex, interwoven culture over many centuries. While diverse in terms of family and social organization, the Pueblo world view has a number of common features. Living in compact towns—each of which is an autonomous social as well as religious unit, relying upon an intricate form of agriculture—Pueblos attribute a high value to communal solidarity.

Pueblo religious life centers around maintaining a sense of place in the world. The specific contours vary from group to group, but in general Pueblos have drawn upon ceremony, art, mythology, and moral action to underscore the importance of retaining balance between the human and the life-bestowing powers of the natural world. The Pueblo world view divides everything into pairs such as male/female, summer/winter, wet/dry, day/night—dichotomies that also often form the symbolic basis of social division. Drought or misfortune was typically seen as the result of the people's failure to maintain balance or harmony within their groups or with the powers of the world. *Kivas,* circular underground rooms symbolic of the power-filled world beneath the earth's surface from which the people originally emerged, housed the voluntary societies active within each village. Within the *kivas* members prepared for the performance of public ceremonies above, often directed by priests who inherited their office. Ceremonies enabled Pueblo groups to thank the ancestral *katsina* or *kachina* spirits who brought rain and fertility, such as the Hopi *Powamu* ("bean-planting"), and to perform dramatic reenactments of mythical events that helped promote communal solidarity. During the half-year period in which people dressed as these *katsinas* came down from their mountain homes, they performed numerous dances in village squares, some humorous, some serious, all instructing the people in their duties to the group.

Other southwestern tribes developed lifestyles more nomadic than those of the Pueblos, although horticulture became central to nearly all southwestern tribes except such eastern Apaches as the Jicarilla, Mescallero, or Chiricahua. Pimans (Pimas and Papagos), Quechans, Mojaves, and others in southern Arizona, inheriting elements of the old Hohokam culture, dwelt in loosely scattered *rancherias,* often along the Gila and Salt rivers, developing extensive irrigation networks for corn and other crops, while Papagos and various groups of Pais adapted to the rigors of desert or mountain life. Utes, living primarily in the plateau country north of the Grand Canyon, drew on some aspects of the horse culture of the Plains (see NATIVE AMERICAN RELIGIONS: PLAINS), adopting the annual Sun Dance. The Apaches and Navajos, both speaking Athabascan dialects from the subarctic region, arrived late in the Southwest, conse-

quently existing in conflict with more settled groups, but often, particularly the Navajos, adopting features of Pueblo life, such as the story of origins from beneath the earth, and the acknowledgment of various desert peaks as the home of supernaturals, in the process creating a sacred place for themselves in the desert.

In contrast to the Pueblos, these other tribes developed religious practices often based on shamanism: individual acquisition of secret knowledge and spiritual power used for healing. Originally in both Apache and Navajo cultures a shaman, having gained power through dreams or an encounter with a powerful animal or mountain spirit, would be engaged by those sick, despondent, or suffering evil. Shamanic cures were discovered through individual inspiration. In the centuries since coming into the Southwest however, Navajos have developed a third religious form, based on the ritual chant or "sing." Like shamanism, Navajo curing is performed by trained individuals; however, their training comes from years of study with an accomplished singer, or *hataalii.* The symbolically rich Navajo chants are detailed, prescribed sets of ritual observances that incorporate ceremonial sand paintings and mythic recountings of the actions of supernatural beings, drawn from a vast body of sacred stories arising out of Navajo reflection on the landforms of the Southwest.

Under the impact of colonization, southwestern tribes experienced severe strain, leading at times to collapse, to revolt, to adaptation, and to creative rebirth. Since the 1530s southwestern tribes developed a variety of responses to Spanish ROMAN CATHOLICISM. The Franciscan Marcos de Ninza reached the Zunis in 1539. The Yaquis resisted Spanish forces from 1533 to 1609, when they concluded Jesuit missionary influence was desirable. However in 1740 another bloody revolt forced a temporary Spanish withdrawal from Yaqui territory. Taos Pueblos and others, whose villages were forcefully occupied by the Spanish, naming their colonial capital Santa Fe in 1610, revolted in 1680 and 1696.

The harsh conditions created by the colonizers turned the Tanoan Pueblos inward. Forcibly converted to Catholicism, they retained their traditions and languages in secret.

Between the conclusion of the Mexican War in 1848 and 1886, many native tribes resisted the movement of Americans into the Southwest. Apache spiritual leaders like Geronimo fought guerrilla wars with the army for a number of years. The Yaquis, south of the border, maintained a standing army until 1927. The Navajos, although resistant to United States designs to turn them into settled agriculturists, were relocated in 1864. Their forced march and four years of captivity at Fort Sumner in eastern New Mexico, during which they were expected, but refused, to adopt Anglo values and agricultural practices, resulted in the creation of a large, mineral-rich reservation. In the years since 1868, Navajos expanded both their population and land base, resulting in increased tensions with the Hopis and the federal government that remain unresolved.

The history of contact and conflict among tribal groups, and between those groups and encroaching Euro-Americans, has produced a complicated cultural landscape. Cultural, religious, and linguistic diversity remain strong among many tribes, and threatened among others. Within the region as a whole, while American institutions have come to play a dominant role in the lives of native people, they have failed to produce the intended outcome of complete assimilation.

MG

Bibliography: Bertha P. Dutton, *American Indians of the Southwest* (Albuquerque: University of New Mexico Press, 1983); Alphonso Ortiz, *The Tewa World* (Chicago: University of Chicago Press, 1969); Edward H. Spicer, *Cycles of Conquest: The Impact of Spain, Mexico and the United States on the Indians of the Southwest, 1533–1960* (Tucson: University of Arizona Press, 1962).

nativism   Nativism is a collective term applied to hostility manifested toward foreigners and immigrants. Nativism has ebbed and flowed during the course of American history, often linked to periods of economic dislocation and national insecurity. While nativism in the United States traditionally has been associated with Protestants of English descent, this has not always been the case. David Levin was one of the most outspoken anti-Catholic and anti-Irish nativists in the 19th century, and the Louisiana branch of the Know-Nothing Party, which reached the peak of its strength in 1855, split between those who were anti-immigrant but not anti-Catholic (led by Charles Gayarre) and those who combined the two (see ANTI-CATHOLICISM). Indeed Catholicism, the major foe of 19th-century nativists, was not the target of the first American nativists. They directed their attacks against "atheism" and "infidelity."

The French Revolution exacerbated the political divisions in the young United States. The Federalist Party saw in the Democratic-Republican Party an American version of the French Jacobins who had led the French Revolution into the period of terror. During the spring of 1798, when it seemed that France and the United States might go to war, the Federalists—who were in power—passed the Alien & Sedition Acts. These were directed against immigrants (primarily French) who were seen as hostile aliens and the Democratic-Republicans whose support for the French Revolution made them appear seditious during this time of American-French hostility.

In the same year, some claimed to have discovered a more sinister and insidious threat to the nation. On May 9, 1798, Jedidiah Morse announced to his congregation at New North Church, Boston that he had in his possession documents proving the existence of an international conspiracy to overthrow the United States. This conspiracy of the "Bavarian Illuminati," who wished to destroy Christianity, morality, and private property, already had brought about the French Revolution. Morse's allegations were picked up by the Congregationalist and Presbyterian clergy of New England.

Staunch Federalists, their worst fears were confirmed by this report. Among those who spoke out against the "malice of atheism and the sin of the enemies of Christ" was the future president of Yale, Timothy DWIGHT. With the Jeffersonian newspapers leading the attack, the conspiracy theory collapsed under scrutiny. Morse was forced into silence. The triumph of the Jeffersonians in the election of 1800 ended this period of nativism. This would not be the last time people would raise the specter of conspiratorial forces so immense that extreme measures would be necessary to meet them.

The next period of nativism was directly and virulently anti-Catholic. Many Americans doubted that European Catholics, who they believed had been raised in ignorance and servitude among princes and prelates, could adapt to a republican society. They feared that an increase of Catholic immigrants would damage American society and politics. Some even suggested that these immigrants were part of a papal plot to subvert the United States.

During the 19th century numerous nativist organizations were established including the Organization of United Americans (1844), Organization of United American Mechanics (1845), Order of the Star Spangled Banner—better known as the Know-Nothing Party (1850)—American Protective Association (1887), and the National League for the Protection of American Independence (1889). Despite some differences, all these organizations shared a hostility to foreigners whom they viewed as a threat to the nation. Despite virulent propaganda and occasional violence these organizations met with little long-term success. Even the Know-Nothing Party's political successes owed more to the political confusion of the 1850s than to any general acceptance of its nativist views.

None of these organizations were capable of changing American immigration laws. The late 19th and early 20th centuries, however, saw major changes in those laws, leading to the eventual closing of immigration in the 1920s. The first of these acts was directed against the allegedly most "unassimilable" groups—the Chinese and Japanese. Not only were these groups not Europeans, not "white," and not Protestant, they were not even Christians. In 1882 the "Exclusion Act" drastically cut the number of Chinese allowed into the United States. In the same year Congress placed the first limits on European immigration, forbidding the arrival of criminals, paupers, and the insane. In 1908 Theodore Roosevelt's "Gentleman's Agreement" with Japan limited the number of Japanese allowed into the country. Not until 1917 did any law pass that severely curtailed European immigration. In that year Congress overrode President Woodrow Wilson's veto and required that all immigrants be literate in some language. Within 10 years a series of laws would turn the flood of European immigration, over one million a year at its height between 1904 and 1907, into a trickle of 150,000 annually.

Two factors played a major role in accomplishing this. The first was the development of "scientific racism." Following the ideas of certain popularizers of Charles Darwin (see EVOLUTION), biologists and amateur scientists argued that the peoples of the world were inherently different. The races had different characteristics, and some races were superior to others. In the English-speaking world the Teutonic and Anglo-Saxon peoples—the Germans and the English—were discovered to be the superior species. These people, it was asserted, had given to the world democracy, science, and pure religion. Other peoples were lower, although in varying degrees. The consensus was that the Latins (Italians, Spaniards), the Greeks, the Slavs, and the Jews (see ANTI-SEMITISM) definitely were inferior to the descendants of the English who had founded the United States. Because they were inferior, they endangered the nation as a whole.

The second factor was the fear of radicalism. Many felt that every immigrant was either an anarchist or a Bolshevik (see COMMUNISM). From the round-up of political radicals during the Palmer raids in 1917, through the revival of the KU KLUX KLAN and the "return to normalcy" of the postwar period, the equation of radical and immigrant was a given. These immigrants were viewed as a threat to American society, and there was a strong movement to exclude them from the United States.

The door to massive immigration finally closed in 1927. In that year Congress passed, and Calvin Coolidge signed, the National Origins Act, cutting annual immigration to 150,000. By a carefully crafted percentage system, 60 percent of that was allotted to England and Germany, only 4 percent to Italy.

WORLD WAR II transformed American nativism. The most outspoken and virulent American nativists were viewed as treasonous and seditious because their anti-Semitism, hatred of Communism, and racial views drew them toward Hitler and the Nazis. During the war they were suspect and harassed. Nevertheless, the war did not end nativism. Hysteria allowed the Japanese to be rounded up and interned in 1942 out of an alleged fear that they were disloyal.

Despite this, the war did make hostility toward other peoples a questionable activity. The struggle against Nazi racism made it impolitic to express nativist views directly. Nativism did not die, however. It took on characteristics similar to the conspiracy of the "Bavarian Illuminati." In the postwar era the threat was from worldwide Communism; a sinister alien movement, foreign but aided by American citizens. Anti-Communism was a nativist position amenable to Catholics. The Roman Catholic hierarchy in the United States was vocal in its opposition to Communism, and Senator Joseph McCarthy from Wisconsin, while extreme, epitomized much lay Catholic anti-Communism (see ROMAN CATHOLICISM).

From the 1960s on, nativism diminished in intensity. Beginning in 1965 a series of immigration reform bills progressively removed discrimination against Asian immigrants and the legal preference for western Europeans. Sporadic outbreaks against immigrants continued. The economic problems of the late 1970s and early 1990s saw occasional outbursts of hostility against the Japanese. The growing numbers of immigrants, many illegal, from Mexico and Central America gave rise to fears that "American" culture would be drowned in the flood. Some Americans have argued for a crackdown on illegal immigrants. Others have responded to increasing immigration by pushing for the adoption of English as the nation's official language. The 1990s saw increasing opposition to immigration, and, although most politicians were careful to couch their desire to limit immigration in circumspect terms, it increasingly became a significant political issue. This was especially true in states like California, which in 1994 passed, by referendum, a strict law forbidding the expenditure of any governmental monies for services to illegal immigrants, including educational and most health services.

EQ

Bibliography: Ray A. Billington, *The Protestant Crusade, 1800–1860: A Study of the Origins of American Nativism* (Gloucester, Mass.: Peter Smith, 1963); Morton Borden, *Jews, Turks, and Infidels* (Chapel Hill: University of North Carolina Press, 1984); David A. Gerber, ed., *Anti-semitism in American History* (Urbana: University of Illinois Press, 1986); John Higham, *Strangers in the Land: Patterns of American Nativism, 1860–1925* (New York: Atheneum, 1963).

nature religion   Nature religion refers to diverse forms of religious expression in which nature constitutes the sacred symbolic center of reflection, experience, and ethical practice. Nature religion, or at least nature as a central religious symbol, has been decisive in the religious and moral sentiments of many Americans. Contending views of the religious and moral significance of the natural world, however, often become intertwined with disputes over land-use decisions and who should make them. Historically, the most important types of nature religion are those forms that (1) are ambivalent or fearful of nature, thus promoting human mastery of it, or conversely (2) view harmony with and preservation of nature as the central prerequisite to human happiness and spiritual contentment, or (3) become concerned with nature primarily as a means to discerning the other-worldly realities embedded (or concealed) in it, and thus remain aloof from disputes about land use and control.

Certainly nature functioned symbolically in very different ways among Native North Americans and Anglo-Puritans. In general, Native Americans tended to view nature as inhabited by a variety of kindred creatures and spirits and to see themselves as part of the natural world rather than as superior to and separate from it. Consequently, harmonizing their life with all the entities of nature seemed to be the obvious, appropriate path. Practically speaking, this usually contributed to environmentally sustainable lifeways. The Puritans (see PURITANISM; MATHER, COTTON), however, tended to be ambivalent toward the vast wilderness confronting them, viewing it as a place of spiritual danger (a haunt of Satan) and as a place of spiritual opportunity, the site for the construction of God's kingdom on earth.

Consequently, the wilderness had to be tamed and mastered. Practically speaking, this meant enclosing and privatizing the land, and exploiting its "natural resources"—often in environmentally unsustainable ways. Biblical passages suggesting that God gave humans "dominion" over the earth were used to justify such impulses.

During the revolutionary period and the early years of the United States republic, Americans combined a republican ideology of nature based partly on ENLIGHTENMENT notions of progress, "natural law," and "inalienable" natural rights with a millennial reading of the Bible that viewed America as the new promised land, given to European-Americans for a special, divine purpose. The combination provided the growing Anglo-American population with a powerful but pernicious ideology that justified the displacement of Native Americans and the institution of slavery. The power of the ideology of MANIFEST DESTINY was fueled by its connection with a sacred natural order, still unfolding. Many religious groups adopted and promoted such ideas including FREEMASONRY.

Another important form of nature religion is represented in HARMONIAL RELIGION, represented in United States religious history by 19th-century MESMERISM, THEOSOPHY, NEW THOUGHT, SPIRITUALISM, CHRISTIAN SCIENCE, and TRANSCENDENTALISM, and since the COUNTERCULTURE of the late 1960s, in the NEW AGE, DEEP ECOLOGY, and FEMINIST THEOLOGY movements, as well as in NEO-PAGANISM.

The tension between different types of nature religion—prioritizing mastery over or harmony with nature—is also reflected within the many nature religions that place a premium on harmony. For example, transcendentalism views nature as the "really real," and thus suggests that the ethical priority must be to preserve and live in harmony with it. But transcendentalism also includes a more metaphysical vision, suggesting that one can transcend nature by plumbing its spiritual secrets through the human mind—through mystical experience. And thus in transcendentalism and other nature religions the central priority for human life often remains confused as to whether to preserve and live in harmony with nature or seek the spiritual world through it, moving from nature to spirit by seeking correspondences between them.

Practically speaking, then, some organize their lives to promote this-worldly harmony, and especially nature preservation—while believing nature provides a pathway toward the even more real and valuable. Meanwhile, others commit themselves to the healing arts—some stressing the prevention and curing of disease through the physical manipulation of nature (e.g., the "sectarian" medical movements, including the thomosonians, homeopaths, hydropaths, osteopaths, and chiropractors); still others believe in the mental/spiritual mastery of nature and disease, sometimes by denying the very existence of disease and matter itself (see QUIMBY, PHINEAS; EDDY, MARY BAKER). This confusion over whether nature is "real" or "ideal" suggests that even among harmonial forms of nature religion, the desire for mastery of nature has been difficult to extinguish.

By the late 20th century, informed by the "new physics" that emphasizes the relatedness and interdependence of all matter, contemporary proponents of New Age religions and their metaphysical cousins seem to be moving toward a consensus that the confusion between matter and spirit can and must be resolved by rejecting any duality between them. Thus, today harmony remains the central axis for nature religion—but in a new way—matter and spirit themselves are being harmonized into a monistic divine universe as nature religions enter the 21st century.

BRT

Bibliography: Catherine Albanese, *Nature Religion in America* (Chicago: University of Chicago Press, 1989); Roderick Nash, *Wilderness and the American Mind* (New Haven: Yale University Press, 1967).

Neo-evangelicalism See EVANGELICALISM; HENRY, CARL FERDINAND HOWARD.

Neo-orthodoxy Neo-orthodoxy is a term used mainly in the United States and England to designate a theological movement that emerged in the post-WORLD WAR I era in reaction to the simplistic optimism of liberal theology (see LIBERALISM, THEOLOGICAL). Called "dialectical theology," or "crisis theology" on the European continent, Neo-orthodoxy is one of the few theological movements that has a definite beginning: the 1919 publication of Swiss theologian Karl Barth's *Commentary on Romans*. This book, as one commentator put it, "fell like a bomb in the playground of the theologians."

World War I and the uncritical support for it by German intellectuals and churches troubled Barth greatly. (There was a similar occurrence among American liberal theologians.) The devastation and horror of the war negated the easy optimism of liberal theology. The eruption of evil in the midst of civilization severely challenged liberalism's view of progress. The war seemed to undermine its emphasis on the immanence of God. As demonstrated by the unquestioning support that religious thinkers gave the war, liberalism tended to identify human activity with God's activity. This made it difficult to judge and to criticize the world.

Barth's "bomb" was the claim that God was the central point of the Christian message. Rather than center the study of religion on human religious experience, Barth returned to the Christian scriptures. There he found, in Paul's Epistle to the Romans for example, that the emphasis was on God's sovereignty, God's glory. God is not a God who validates and approves human activity but is a God who judges all human activity. God is a God who says "No!" to all human pretensions, a judge who rejects all claims of human society to absoluteness.

The Neo-orthodox theologians, by returning to the Bible and the Reformation, rediscovered evil and sin. Evil and sin were not, as the liberal theologians thought, mere mistakes, error, or ignorance. They were ingrained within the human condition and could not be overcome by education, reflection, or human action. Only God who is judge makes it possible to overcome sin. This, the Neo-orthodox theologians posited, is the message of the Gospel. God has come to human beings in the Christ, demonstrating that God is not only judge but also the source of mercy and forgiveness. This is the source of the dialectic. God not only says "No!"; God also says "Yes!" And not because of anything humans do, but because God is God.

In the United States Neo-orthodoxy emerged during the postwar era as well. The United States had been largely spared the horrors of World War I, but the magnitude of the 1930's Depression and the realization that the appeal to Christian love would not avoid war or end social injustice undermined liberal optimism. The appearance of Reinhold NIEBUHR's *Does Civilization Need Religion?* (1927) was the first step in a domestic critique of liberal theology. In this book Niebuhr criticized the liberal tendency to associate the existing world with God's will. Others echoed Niebuhr's criticisms, including Walter Marshall Horton at Oberlin Seminary, Edwin Lewis of Drew University, and Henry P. Van Dusen of Union Theological Seminary. The depth of the challenge to liberalism was demonstrated in 1935 when the country's most popular liberal preacher, Harry Emerson FOSDICK of Riverside Church in New York, published his sermon "Beyond Modernism." His plea that Christianity go beyond modernism, that Christians realize that Christ does not harmonize with modern culture but challenges it, signaled the death of liberalism's dominance. The most damning dismissal of liberal theology came two years later in H. Richard NIEBUHR's book *The Kingdom of God in America*. There he described liberalism as a theology in which, "A God without wrath brought men without sin into a kingdom without judgment through the ministrations of a Christ without a cross."

While United States Neo-orthodoxy began as a self-critical reflection on the failings of American liberal theology, it also adopted many themes from European theology. Barth certainly played a role, although the first English edition of his work did not appear until 1928 with Douglas Horton's translation of *The Word of God and the Word of Man*. An English edition of *The Epistle to the Romans* was not published until 1933. Other sources for American Neo-orthodoxy included the work of Soren Kierkegaard, which appeared in English translation in 1939. Kierkegaard's insistence on the distinction between the human and the divine, along with his view that faith was a leap across the abyss, greatly influenced American Neo-orthodoxy, as did his insistence upon the importance of paradox.

The work of both G.W.F. Hegel and Karl Marx influenced American Neo-orthodoxy as well. This was most obvious in the dialectical approach of Neo-orthodoxy. Dialectics, the understanding that contrary ideas can be true simultaneously, played a major role in the development of Neo-orthodox thought.

While Neo-orthodoxy influenced many American thinkers, it is most often associated with the names of Reinhold Niebuhr, H. Richard Niebuhr, and the German emigré theologian Paul TILLICH. None of these men were ever comfortable with the designation Neo-orthodox. All had serious theological disagreements with Barth and with each other. What held them together was their rejection of liberal theology. Despite this rejection, however, none of them, including Barth, rejected the liberal world view. Modern scientific methods and the historical-critical method of biblical interpretation were accepted by all the leading Neo-orthodox theologians.

What separated the Americans, especially Tillich and Reinhold Niebuhr, from Barth was their resistance to his claim that, apart from God's action, humanity has no knowledge of God. For Barth, God is known only in the revelatory event—for Christianity, in the coming of the Christ. This seemed to suggest the complete impotence of human activity. Humans must wait for God to act. But as Tillich is supposed to have posited, "What if God doesn't come?" Both Tillich and the Niebuhrs suggested that human beings could have some knowledge of God apart from the revelatory event. They maintained a place for human activity. For Tillich this comes about through his theory of correlation, for Reinhold Niebuhr from his position as a social ethicist and the realization (which he owed to his brother) that God is both in and out of history. Christians live in the world and must respond to it, with the constant awareness that their responses are conditional, imperfect, and tainted with sin.

Neo-orthodoxy dominated American religious thought through the 1950s and into the 1960s. To a great extent this was due to the public activity of Reinhold Niebuhr. There were deeper reasons. Most of the Neo-orthodox theologians had served as pastors and later taught in seminaries. Their ideas were diffused among younger ministers who combined a return to the language of sin and divine sovereignty with radical social criticism. Under the Neo-orthodox influence several denominations restructured their approach to religious education.

The Neo-orthodox emphasis on the church as the location for the proclamation of God's revelation provided a reason for church renewal and was especially significant for the ECUMENICAL MOVEMENT.

The significance of Neo-orthodoxy is even deeper. It dominated American religious thought into the 1980s. Just as liberal theology framed the debate for the Neo-orthodox theologians, Neo-orthodoxy framed it for its successors. Historical events seem to confirm Neo-orthodoxy's negative view of human nature, its bleak picture of human endeavor. Simultaneously, its radical critique of the existing human social order and its demand for human action helped to give birth to liberation theology. Its emphasis on divine transcendence and the God who says "No!" gave impetus to the radical theologies, including the DEATH OF GOD THEOLOGY. More than anything else Neo-orthodoxy ended the naive belief in human goodness that dominated liberal thought.

EQ

Bibliography: Sydney Ahlstrom, *Theology in America: The Major Protestant Voices from Puritanism to Neoorthodoxy* (Indianapolis: Bobbs-Merrill, 1967); Richard Fox, *Reinhold Niebuhr: A Biography* (New York: Pantheon Books, 1985); Donald B. Meyer, *The Protestant Search for Political Realism, 1919–1941.* (Berkeley: University of California Press, 1960).

Neo-paganism   Neo-paganism is a new religious movement in which devotees re-appropriate one or more pre-Christian nature religions, usually of European origin but also from ancient Greece, Egypt, and a variety of indigenous peoples. The primary goal of Neo-paganism is to re-harmonize and re-unite with the sacred—conceived of usually in pantheistic and/or polytheistic and/or animistic terms. It is generally believed that the western, Christian rejection and repression of pagan spiritualities has alienated humans from knowledge of their authentic selves as beings embedded in a sacred cosmos.

Persecution certainly played a major role in the decline of pagan spiritualities and witchcraft in Europe and America. The persecution of witches—beginning in the 11th century and escalating in brutality between the 15th and 18th centuries—was responsible for the murder of tens of thousands of suspected witches, who were mostly poor, single, older women. As the scientific world view gained ascendancy, belief in magical world views declined, and consequently fear and persecution of witches waned.

In the mid-19th century, however, interest in paganism was rekindled by writers who asserted that European witchcraft was a survival of pre-Christian religion. But the revival of modern witchcraft really began in earnest between 1920 and 1950 with Margaret Murray's *The Witch-Cult in Western Europe* (1921) and *The God of the Witches* (1934). Murray was describing what she claimed to be the surviving, old pagan religion of pre-Christian Europe. A small group in England felt great affinity with the spirituality she described, and drawing on these descriptions, they began to practice witchcraft as best they could. In the years after World War II Gerald Gardner emerged with Doreen Valiente as the major popularizers of this emerging tradition, and they were largely responsible for its export to America. Valiente's *Book of Shadows* became the central liturgical guide, and Gardner began publishing *Witchcraft Today* in 1954. Robert Graves's *White Goddess* contributed theories about matristic, goddess-worshiping societies, now central to the beliefs of many neopagans, buttressed recently by archeologist Marija Gimbutas's *The Goddesses and Gods of Old Europe* (1982), but much scholarly skepticism about the existence of such societies remains.

Contemporary witchcraft, or wicca, involves a great deal of creative invention in its various ritual forms; many if not most of the core practices involved in American witchcraft are derived from Gardner—although some claim to derive their craft from secret family traditions going back to colonial times and before then to Europe. Gardner's influence is waning, however, as witches borrow freely from practices derived from a variety of magical or nature-based religions, often known by means of the comparative study of religion.

Neo-paganism and witchcraft (its most prominent tradition) are anti-authoritarian and extremely pluralistic. Thus care must be taken in making generalizations. It is possible, however, to identify certain ideas and practices that are nearly universal within Neo-paganism.

Unifying the diverse types of Neo-paganism is a world view holding that the universe is sacred and interrelated; and since each part is related at a metaphysical level, each part affects every other part. (See also DEEP ECOLOGY and NEW AGE RELIGION for other contemporary spiritualities based on the metaphysics of sacred relatedness.) This provides the metaphysical basis for those Neo-pagans who believe in and practice magic—but magic is not usually thought to involve the "supernatural." Interrelation is natural, and explains how spells, psychic abilities, mental powers, and ritual manipulation of nature can affect seemingly distant realities. (Witches especially believe in the power of the mind, and sometimes of spells, principally for personal improvement and healing. A small minority may also employ spells against others—however this is rare since it apparently violates the neo-pagan ethic, "And ye harm none, do what ye will".)

Most Neo-pagans are polytheists, animists, or pantheists. They blame human maladies on their estrangement from nature, and see ritual as a means to restore human harmony with her. Many believe in reincarnation, and also that, since the earth and her natural processes are sacred, so is human sexuality. When performed sacramentally, the sexual "great rite" can help one to experience the divine, often referred to as "the goddess."

The major difference between witches and other neo-pagans seems to be that neo-pagans place greater emphasis on nature and environmental concerns, although this difference is narrowing in the wake of the more political versions of witchcraft promoted by two witches influenced by the COUNTERCULTURE and 1960s activism: Margo Adler and Starhawk. Indeed, the most fertile ground for Neo-paganism is found within the counterculture, and has been leading to increasing affinities and political alliances and activism between the Neo-pagan and Deep Ecology movements. Many Deep Ecologists also describe themselves as pagans or Neo-pagans or witches, and vice versa.

Fear of persecution, a consequent desire for anonymity, and the anti-authoritarian views within the Neo-pagan community make it seem unlikely that Neo-paganism will become a major religion in the United States. Conservative and fundamentalist Christians continue to fan the flames of fear, portraying Neo-pagans and witches as servants of Satan, ignoring the rejoinder that Satan is an entity that preoccupies Western religions but not those involved in Neo-paganism. Nevertheless, the secrecy cloaking Neo-paganism is gradually being drawn back, and the movement appears to be growing, particularly as a result of the invention of Neo-pagan festivals, the survival of Neo-pagan journals such as *Green Egg,* and the efforts of academic pagans within the feminist spirituality (see FEMINIST THEOLOGY) movement. By the early 1990s, estimates of those involved range from 83,000 to 333,000, suggesting that Neo-paganism is emerging as a small but important religious alternative.

BRT

Bibliography: Margot Adler, *Drawing Down the Moon: Witches, Druids, Goddess-Worshippers and Other Pagans in America Today* (Boston: Beacon Press, 1986); Ann L. Barstow, *Witchcraze: A New History of the European Witch Hunts* (San Francisco:

Harper, 1994); Jeffrey Burton Russell, *A History of Witchcraft: Sorcerers, Heretics, and Pagans* (London: Thames & Hudson, 1980); Starhawk, *The Spiral Dance: A Rebirth of the Ancient Religion of the Great Goddess* (San Francisco: Harper and Row, 1979).

Nevin, John Williamson (1803–1886)

John W. Nevin was a theologian at the German Reformed seminary at Mercersburg, Pennsylvania and, along with fellow professor Philip SCHAFF, the chief formulator of the movement known as the Mercersburg Theology. Nevin's focus on the institutional church and his critique of American REVIVALISM placed him in fundamental opposition to mainstream Protestant EVANGELICALISM in his day.

Nevin was born on February 20, 1803 near Shippensburg, Pennsylvania. He was raised in the Presbyterian Church. After graduation from Union College (1821) and Princeton Theological Seminary (1826), he taught the Bible and Oriental languages at Princeton for two years. He next served as a professor of biblical literature at Western Theological Seminary, a Presbyterian school in Allegheny, Pennsylvania, from 1828 to 1840. Nevin was strongly influenced by the writings of German church historian Johannes A. W. Neander, who taught that the church was an organic community, not a collection of individuals. Under Neander's influence, Nevin gradually became disgruntled with the ecclesiastical beliefs of Presbyterianism. Attracted to the German Reformed Church, he left Western Seminary, changed denominations, and in 1841 joined the faculty at Mercersburg.

Nevin taught that the church as an objective, historic institution was essential to the Christian life and provided men and women access to salvation. In *The Anxious Bench* (1843), he employed this idea to launch a full-scale assault on the popular revivalism of the day. He criticized the individualism, emotionalism, and devaluation of the church's sacramental life that the American revivals fostered. Nevin's most profound work, *The Mystical Presence: A Vindication of the Reformed or Calvinistic Doctrine of the Holy Eucharist* (1846), charged that the sacramental practices of nearly all the Protestant churches were faulty and had fallen away from the standards set by the great reformers of the 16th century.

Nevin edited the *Mercersburg Review* from 1849 to 1852. During that period, debates about his liturgical and theological views became so acrimonious that a schism within the German Reformed Church was threatened. Many of the journal's readers also believed that Nevin himself would convert to Roman Catholicism. Although Nevin remained loyal to the German Reformed Church, his positions were repudiated, and he withdrew from active teaching in 1853. However, after a lengthy period of recovery from the stress caused by the controversy, he returned to teaching. Nevin lectured at Franklin and Marshall College in Lancaster, Pennsylvania between 1861 and 1866. He also served as president of the college from 1866 until his permanent retirement in 1876.

Nevin died at Lancaster on June 6, 1886. Not until the 20th century, when his catholic ecclesiastical ideals were less threatening to American Protestants, did Nevin's thinking about the nature of the church gain the appreciation and respect it deserved.

GHS, Jr.

Bibliography: James Hastings Nichols, ed., *The Mercersburg Theology* (New York: Oxford University Press, 1966);—, *Romanticism in American Religion: Nevin and Schaff at Mercersburg* (Chicago: University of Chicago Press, 1961).

New Age religion

The New Age is a millennial religious movement whose origins can be traced to the spiritual ferment, quest for personal fulfillment, and interest in altered states of consciousness (related to the popularity of hallucinogens) during the 1960s. Although New Age spirituality can be understood as a new religious movement, it has also appropriated aspects of many earlier spiritual traditions, including Platonic metaphysics, diverse forms of occultism, 18th-century FREEMA-

SONRY, and 19th-century SPIRITUALISM and THEOSOPHY. During the 1970s the movement was especially interested in eastern spiritual teachers; during the 1980s the major attention was placed on "channeling" as numerous mediums reported that spiritual entities spoke through them. Shamanism as a means to altered states of consciousness and the appropriation of Native American religious traditions are also assuming increasing importance.

Central characteristics of the New Age include the millennial intention and hope for personal and planetary healing—both of which depend on the transformation of human consciousness. Like the devotees of NEO-PAGANISM and DEEP ECOLOGY, the hoped-for consciousness change would overturn dualistic, mechanistic (Newtonian and Cartesian) views of the cosmos, supplanting these with the perception of the universe as one, metaphysically interrelated, sacred, whole. What helps distinguish the New Age from Deep Ecology and Neo-paganism is its forward-looking, optimistic eschatology. New Age adherents tend to be much more optimistic, expecting a widespread change in human consciousness to precipitate human and planetary healing. Technology is also expected to play a positive future role.

The vehicles to the anticipated consciousness change are many. Transpersonal psychology (building upon humanistic psychology) and the related human potential movement have been especially important in connecting the spiritual development of individuals with the New Age's expectation for planetary healing and progressive social change. Humanistic psychology identified "peak experiences" as central to the healthy human personality—Gestalt psychology advocated living "in the moment" rather than fixating on the past—and both were seen as important to the full development of the human person. Transpersonal psychology focuses on how humans can transcend ego and thereby reveal their authentic natures as divine manifestations of the sacred universe. Such eco-transcendence has been promoted by consciousness-

altering techniques including biofeedback, meditation, hallucinogens, and, most recently, through meditative "breathwork" similar to ritual processes such as those developed by Stanislav Grof.

A variety of other practices common among New Agers are seen as means to the desired transformations—including yoga, massage, shiatsu, astrology, and crystal healing, and other alternative, "natural" healing arts. Although the vehicles to New Age consciousness for devotees may differ and change, and although great diversity of spiritual traditions are appropriated, the emphasis on personal and planetary transformation provides the core that makes it possible to identify the New Age as a new religious tradition.

Metaphysical, HARMONIAL RELIGION akin to the New Age movement seems to surge and wane in North America. Today's New Age may fade as did 19th-century spiritualism and theosophy. But whatever its long-term staying power, the New Age movement has already had a significant role in reshaping religious belief in North America, helping to popularize religious ideas such as reincarnation, astrology, and the belief in psychic powers. Still, it is difficult to foresee major political change resulting from New Age spirituality. Its magical world view and its tendency to deny the reality of sin and evil seem to undercut passion for political activism or resistance. Instead, the first priority of the New Age remains individual spiritual transformation—the expected social and planetary transformation will unfold naturally from the mass, spiritual evolution of individual human beings.

BRT

Bibliography: James R. Lewis and J. Gordon Melton, *Perspectives on the New Age* (New York: State University of New York Press, 1992); J. Gordon Melton, Jerome Clark, and Adian Kelly, eds., *New Age Encyclopedia* (Detroit: Gale Research, 1990).

New Divinity   The New Divinity (or Consistent CALVINISM as it was also known) was a theological system that developed within New

England Congregationalism in the mid-18th century. The New Divinity helped reconcile traditional Calvinist beliefs about human sinfulness and divine sovereignty to the egalitarianism of the evangelical (see EVANGELICALISM) movement. Originally used as a term of derision by its opponents, who believed an altogether novel system of theology had been devised by the disciples of Jonathan EDWARDS, the New Divinity hinged on a combination of views Edwards had expressed: orthodox teaching about God and humanity blended with an openness to the heartfelt piety of American revivalism.

After the waning of the GREAT AWAKENING, the series of revivals that swept through the churches of New England between 1735 and 1750, many theologians appropriated and reinterpreted Edwards's teachings. Closely tied by teacher-student relationships to Edwards, and often allied to one another by kinship and marriage, the New Divinity theologians tended to be graduates of Yale College serving as church pastors both in Connecticut and along the Connecticut River. Congregational clergymen such as Samuel HOPKINS, Joseph BELLAMY, Jonathan Edwards, Jr., and Nathanael Emmons sought to develop many of their mentor's ideas and pass them along to the next generation of New England Protestants.

Three concerns were critical for exponents of the New Divinity. First, these theologians emphasized the standard Calvinist doctrines of predestination, divine election, and human depravity in extreme and unbending forms. Second, they believed that God could turn the hearts of sinners to repentance through the means of revivals. And third, they accepted the moral rigor and reformism exemplified by Hopkins's concept of "disinterested benevolence," the belief that selflessness lay at the core of Christian virtue. As a result, the New Divinity represented a creative compromise between the doctrinal rigidity of conservative Congregational orthodoxy, the theological liberalism of the emerging Unitarian movement, and the unfettered emotionalism of the most extreme revivalists. However, because of the moderating position it occupied, the New Divinity also offended far more people than it pleased and was consistently ridiculed by critics.

Despite the negative reception of their views, Hopkins and his colleagues produced an important intellectual system for their time. They constructed what is now regarded as an essential bridge between the still recognizably Puritan teachings of Edwards in the early 1700s and the evangelical religious ethos that arose in the United States at the end of the 18th century.

GHS, Jr.

Bibliography: David Kling, *A Field of Wonders: The New Divinity and Village Revivals in Northwestern Connecticut, 1792–1822* (University Park: Pennsylvania State University Press, 1993); Mark Valeri, *Law and Providence in Joseph Bellamy's New England: The Origins of the New Divinity in Revolutionary America* (New York: Oxford University Press, 1994).

New France   As Spanish America (see NEW SPAIN) formed an arc across the southern United States stretching from Florida to California, it intersected another arc of European Roman Catholic settlement at the Mississippi River (see ROMAN CATHOLICISM). Stretching from Maine to Michigan's Upper Peninsula, through northern Wisconsin, then down the Mississippi River to Louisiana, the French colonial empire was immense. With the exception of Louisiana, French Catholicism in North America left little behind other than "a treasure of melodious but soon hopelessly mispronounced place-names," in the words of the historian Sidney Ahlstrom.

Lasting from 1604 to 1803, the history of French missionary and religious activity in France's North American empire is on one level a heroic one. The priests and friars who directed it led harsh and solitary lives. Explorers as much as missionaries, these priests, primarily JESUITS, opened up the interior of the continent. The Jesuits lived among the Indians, slowly learning their languages. Early active in southern Ontario among the Huron, they became, by association, enemies of the Iroquois, and many met harsh deaths at the latter's hands. French America produced numerous martyrs and saints, including the first Native American considered for sainthood, Kateri TEKAKWITHA, whose piety and austerities led her to an early death in 1680.

The Hurons and the French missionaries were, to some extent, victims of 17th- and 18th-century geopolitics. Catholic France and the Protestant Netherlands (see NEW NETHERLAND)—with the Hurons and Iroquois their respective allies—fought each other for God, country, and furs. This conflict continued with different players after the British replaced the Dutch in 1664, and the Iroquois adopted the British as their new allies. This alliance helped to destroy France's American empire, as France was forced to cede Canada to England and Louisiana to Spain in 1763 following the French and Indian War.

In the modern-day United States, French influence was strongest in Louisiana and especially in the city of New Orleans. There, social stability and the city's relatively large population buttressed French culture. Religiously, however, French Louisiana had little of the evangelistic fervor that marked religious activity in the North.

Although she regained most of this land in the 1783 Treaty of Paris that ended the American Revolution, France had little opportunity to develop the region before the French Revolution and the Napoleonic empire drew all of her energies. With the Louisiana Purchase in 1803, the history of French Catholicism in the United States ended, save for small cultural outposts in Louisiana, Alabama, and Mississippi.

EQ

Bibliography: James Axtell, *The Invasion Within: The Contest of Cultures in Colonial North America* (New York: Oxford University Press, 1985); Pierre François Xavier de Charlevoix, *History and General Description of New France* (Chicago: Loyola University Press, 1962); Cornelius J. Jaenen, *The Role of the Church in New France* (Ottawa: Canadian Historical Association, 1985); John Hopkins Kennedy, *Jesuit and Savage in New France* (New Haven: Yale University Press, 1950); Henry Schlarman, *From Quebec to New Orleans: The Story of the French in America* (Bellville, Ill.: Beuchlen Publishing, 1929); John Gilmary Shea, *History of the Catholic Missions among the Indian Tribes of the United States, 1529–1854* (New York: AMS Press, 1973).

New Harmony   See OWEN, ROBERT DALE; RAPP, GEORGE.

New Haven Theology   See DWIGHT, TIMOTHY; TAYLOR, NATHANIEL WILLIAM.

New Lights/Old Lights   The terms "New Light" and "Old Light" refer to factions that appeared within the Congregational churches of New England in the mid-18th century. The New Lights supported the GREAT AWAKENING and believed the revivals of the Awakening to be genuine works of God that strengthened American Christianity. The Old Lights, on the other hand, viewed revivalism as an unnecessary and disruptive element within church life.

The New Light/Old Light dispute symbolized the final dissolution of the Puritan social and theological system that had shaped New England religious culture for over a century. While each side claimed to be the genuine heir of PURITANISM, each in its own way was responsible for the reshaping of American Protestant thought. The Old Lights emphasized rationalism, which was born out of the ENLIGHTENMENT and signified orderliness, common sense, and self-control. The New Lights were representatives of the emerging evangelical (see EVANGELICALISM) movement, which stressed the emotions and was both pietistic and perfectionistic.

Jonathan EDWARDS, a pastor and theologian in Northampton, Massachusetts, was the great exemplar of the New Light party. His preaching in 1734 and 1735 sparked the beginning of the New England phase of the Great Awakening. In his writings Edwards not only defended the revivals themselves, but also emphasized how the heart, not the head, was the true basis of religious faith. In contrast to what he considered the overly intellectualized faith of the Old Lights, Edwards argued that true religious experience involved a new "sense of the heart," which transformed an individual's self-love into love of God.

CHARLES CHAUNCY, minister of the First Church in Boston, was Edwards's staunchest Old Light opponent. In his *Seasonable Thoughts on the State of Religion in New England* (1743), Chauncy denounced the revivals of the Awakening as a resurgence of the enthusiasm and antinomianism that once threatened to destroy law and order in the early Puritan settlements. Identifying the New Lights with the heretical teachings of Anne Hutchinson, who in the 1630s had claimed to receive direct revelations of the Holy Spirit, Chauncy insisted that Christianity was a religion of "the Understanding and Judgment, and Will," not of the emotions.

Following the early wave of revivals in New England, moderate voices for a time held Congregationalism together. The deep theological rift between the New and Old Light camps, however, could never permanently be healed. After the American Revolution, theological debates were renewed with fervor, and in the end this controversy helped divide the Congregational churches. Extreme evangelicals and rationalists eventually went their separate ways, forming, respectively, Baptist (see BAPTISTS) and Unitarian (see UNITARIAN CONTROVERSY) congregations out of many of the old Congregational parishes of New England.

(See also NEW SIDE/OLD SIDE.)

GHS, Jr.

Bibliography: Edwin Scott Gaustad, *The Great Awakening in New England* (New York: Harper and Row, 1957); C.C. Goen, *Revivalism and Separatism in New England, 1740–1800; Strict Congregationalists and Separate Baptists in the Great Awakening* (New Haven: Yale University Press, 1962).

New Netherland   Part of the Dutch colonial and commercial expansion of the early 17th century, New Netherland, present-day New York State, was claimed for the Dutch in Sep-

tember 1609, when Henry Hudson entered the river that now bears his name. By 1613 the Dutch had established several trading houses in Manhattan and a fort on Castle Island. Engaged primarily in the fur trade, they moved into what is now upstate New York, establishing a fort at what is now Albany.

In 1621 administration of the colony was given to the Dutch West India Company, and in 1623 the first permanent settlers arrived, settling primarily in the town of New Amsterdam, present-day New York City. The company attempted to encourage settlement by making large grants of land to the colonists. These landed gentry or *patroons,* as they were called, dominated the affairs of the colony and their large land grants ironically hindered settlement.

Religion played only a small role in the life of the colony, not surprising given its status as a commercial venture. The Dutch Reformed Church was established, but the Dutch West India Company sent no ministers until 1628. The first minister, Jonas Michaelius, served the fewer than 300 inhabitants of the colony for nearly five years until he returned home. His replacement, Everardus Bogardus, managed to stabilize the community's religious life and built a new stone church in New Amsterdam. Conflicts with the governor hampered his work, however. Both he and the governor sailed for home in 1647 to appeal their positions to the company's directors. Their ship was lost at sea.

The colony's next several years saw some growth in settlement. They also saw a new governor, Peter Stuyvesant, arrive in May 1647. Stuyvesant struggled to impose order and uniformity on the colony. A professional soldier, he was an honest and efficient governor who also was quite religious, and during his tenure the church grew to nearly 15 congregations served by 12 ministers.

His religious convictions led Stuyvesant to attempt to prevent the infiltration of Lutherans, Quakers, and Jews into the colony. He worked closely with pastor Jan van Mecklenburg to convince the directors of the West India Company of the need for religious uniformity for the colony. More interested in encouraging settlement than religious truth, the directors overruled the pastor and the governor.

By 1664 the expansion of English power in North America made the small colony increasingly isolated, and on July 27 of that year, four ships of the British navy sailed into the harbor of New York and demanded the colony's surrender. Vastly outnumbered and outgunned, the Dutch did so. Although they temporarily regained control of the colony in 1673, Dutch colonial settlement in North America had effectively ended. The 2,000 colonists now became British subjects. The victors, recognizing the previous history of the colony, allowed the inhabitants to continue their forms of worship, and although only five ministers remained, the Dutch Reformed Church (see CHRISTIAN REFORMED CHURCH; REFORMED CHURCH IN AMERICA) became a part of the American religious landscape.

EQ

Bibliography: Gerald Francis De Jong, *The Dutch in America, 1609–1974* (Boston: Twayne Publishers, 1975); A. Eekhof, *Jonas Michaelius: Founder of the Church in New Netherland, His Life and Work* (Leyden: A. W. Sijthoff, 1926); George L. Smith, *Religion and Trade in New Netherland; Dutch Origins and American Development* (Ithaca: Cornell University Press, 1973).

New Religious Right   See CHRISTIAN RIGHT.

New School/Old School

The New School and the Old School were two opposing factions in a bitter dispute that divided American Presbyterianism in the the mid-19th century. Following the SECOND GREAT AWAKENING of the 1820s and 1830s, the New School party was formed by Presbyterians open not only to revivalistic methods of worship, but also to the loose denominational structure and the social reform movements the revivals tended to spawn. The Old School party, on the other hand, was composed of Presbyterian traditionalists who were uncomfortable with liberalizing tendencies in theology and politics that the New School group advocated.

The origins of the New School/Old School controversy lay in the 1801 PLAN OF UNION, which created an alliance between Congregationalists and Presbyterians, allowing them to work closely together in evangelizing the American frontier. The Plan led many Presbyterians to see that their denomination's governing structure was simply too cumbersome to meet the religious and social challenges of the newly opened western territories. These men and women, who soon formed the core of the New School party, began to minister through interdenominational alliances and voluntary agencies, not through the Presbyterian hierarchy. The Old School faction, however, believed such institutional laxity posed a grave threat to the integrity of Presbyterian polity and doctrine.

The emergence of antislavery sentiment in the North in the 1830s also exacerbated internal differences within the Presbyterian denomination. While New School Presbyterians were attracted to abolitionism, the southern-oriented Old School was repelled by it. The Presbyterian controversy was brought to a head by the two heresy trials (1831 and 1835) of Albert Barnes, a New School Philadelphia pastor who supported the campaign against slavery. Although the Old School party accused Barnes of contradicting several traditional Calvinist doctrines, the New School party was able to obtain his acquittal at the General Assembly, the Presbyterians' highest decision-making body.

Barnes's vindication, as well as further New School aggressiveness at the 1836 General Assembly, only inflamed Old School sentiment. When the next General Assembly met in 1837, it was solidly in Old School hands. The Plan of Union was immediately rescinded and all joint ventures undertaken by the Congregational-Presbyterian consolidation were retroactively annulled. As a consequence, the four western synods formed under the provisions of the Plan of Union (553 churches, 509 ministers, and nearly 100,000 members) were removed from the Presbyterian rolls. Determined to prove its loyalty to Presbyterianism, the New School published a confessional document, the Auburn Declaration, and sought to rejoin the church. But when the 1838 General Assembly refused to recognize the New School representatives from the deposed synods, a separate New School jurisdiction was organized. Led by Nathan Beman, a minister in Troy, New York, it comprised slightly less than half of the total American Presbyterian membership.

The action of 1837 was a short-lived victory for Old School principles, for the coming of the Civil War brought further confusion to an already divided denomination. In 1857, the northern-dominated New School church watched its small southern contingent secede, while the Old School church itself split on sectional lines after the 1861 attack on Fort Sumter. Wartime pressures forced Old and New School Presbyterians in the South to reunite in 1864, while the northern Presbyterian parties came back together in 1869. Although the labels themselves no longer had meaning, the northern branch of Presbyterianism after the Civil War reflected a continuing New School influence, and the southern Presbyterian church remained the strongest bastion of the Old School ethos well into the 20th century.

GHS, Jr.

Bibliography: George M. Marsden, *The Evangelical Mind and the New School Presbyterian Experience: A Case Study of Thought and Theology in Nineteenth-Century America* (New Haven: Yale University Press, 1970).

New Side/Old Side   The New Side and the Old Side were opposing factions that appeared within American Presbyterianism in the mid-18th century. While the Old Side Presbyterians favored a confessional church, that is, a body based on strict adherence to doctrinal statements, the New Side Presbyterians held a more experiential view of the Christian faith and were,

as a consequence, comfortable with flexibility in matters of polity and theology. The revivals of the GREAT AWAKENING so severely aggravated this division that in 1741 the Old Side succeeded in ousting the New Side from fellowship with it.

Early in the 18th century, Presbyterians in America began to raise questions concerning the standards for ordination and discipline in their church. While Scottish and Scotch-Irish Presbyterians in the middle colonies tended to view adherence to the Westminster Confession of 1643, the classic summary of English-speaking Calvinist belief, as the essence of orthodoxy, those of English descent in New England and New York generally argued that the Bible by itself provided a sufficient rule for the church's faith and practice. The Adopting Act of 1729, the first creedal statement of American Presbyterianism, temporarily settled this dispute by making the Westminister Confession normative. Although those responsible for examining a candidate were allowed some discretion in distinguishing between essential and nonessential articles of faith, agreement with that doctrinal standard became a condition for ordination to the ministry.

The stability of the 1729 compromise was shaken, however, by the Great Awakening and the rising fame of three charismatic clergymen brothers, Gilbert, John, and William Tennent (see TENNENT, GILBERT) of New Jersey. The moderate revivalism, "experimental" piety, and nontraditional theological training (the so-called Log College) they favored heightened the fears of conservatives. Old Side Presbyterians in the Synod of Philadelphia, the official Presbyterian governing body in America, responded to the Tennents' challenge by requiring in 1738 that ministerial candidates without degrees from major universities submit their credentials to a reviewing committee before ordination. Next, they censured the presbytery of New Brunswick, New Jersey in 1739 for ordaining a Log College graduate without following those stated procedures.

When Gilbert Tennent attacked the opponents of the Awakening in an acerbic sermon, "The Danger of an Unconverted Ministry," in March 1740, he brought the controversy to a head. The Synod of Philadelphia officially rebuked Tennent at its 1741 meeting, concluding that both his followers and he had "no right to be acknowledged as members of this judicatory of Christ." Following that assertion, the Old Side party in the Synod declared that it alone spoke for Presbyterianism, thereby effectively ejecting Tennent and the New Brunswick presbytery from the church. In response, the New Side party organized a separate organization, which in 1745 was joined by the sympathetic New York presbytery to form the New Side Synod of New York.

The two parties engaged in a pamphlet war about the meaning of revivalism for several years, but the New Side's inherently greater zeal and the mobility of their itinerant preachers won the most popular support. While the New Side grew from 22 to 73 ministers between 1741 and 1758, the Old Side party shrank from 27 to 22 over the same period. The New Side not only carried the Great Awakening into Pennsylvania and Virginia, but the broad-based educational ministry the Log College symbolized also led to the 1746 founding of the College of New Jersey (now Princeton University).

Gilbert Tennent ultimately repented of his earlier militancy and helped open the way to ecclesiastical reunion. The schism was ended in 1758 when an entirely new Synod of New York and Philadelphia was formed along lines similar to the New Side's 1741 position. Although the reunion of 1758 in many ways marked a rebuff for the Old Side, that party's principles still remained vital over the decades ahead. The conservative faction eventually captured overall control of Presbyterian education, and Princeton in fact evolved into a bastion of strict doctrinal orthodoxy. The conflict between confessional and pietistic interpretations of Protestantism, moreover, became even more violent in the 19th century. This ongoing dispute was a significant factor in the NEW SCHOOL/OLD SCHOOL split of 1837, when revivalism, social reform, and antislavery agitation ruptured the Presbyterian ranks and kept Presbyterians separated along regional lines for nearly 150 years.

(See also NEW LIGHTS/OLD LIGHTS.)

GHS, Jr.

Bibliography: J. M. Bumsted and John E. Van de Wetering, eds., *What Must I Do To Be Saved? The Great Awakening in Colonial America* (Hinsdale, Ill.: Dryden Press, 1976); Richard L. Bushman, ed., *The Great Awakening: Documents on the Revival of Religion, 1740–1745* (New York: Athenaeum, 1970).

New South   See DABNEY, ROBERT LEWIS; HAYGOOD, ATTICUS GREENE; LOST CAUSE MYTH; SOUTH, THE.

New Spain   With the arrival of Christopher COLUMBUS in 1492, the North American continent was brought into the realm of ROMAN CATHOLICISM. The first explorers were Spanish, as were the first European churches in this hemisphere and on present-day United States territory—San Juan, Puerto Rico. Made a diocese in 1511, San Juan received North America's first bishop in 1513. The Spanish colonial church had a long history in the United States, spanning over three centuries. Although less successful than church work in Mexico and South America, it gave a distinctive cast to Catholicism in California, the Southwest, and Florida. Nearly moribund by 1800, it was reinvigorated in the 19th and 20th centuries by immigrants from Cuba, Mexico, and Central and South America.

Spanish settlement in the modern-day United States was meager, especially when viewed in light of Spanish efforts elsewhere. Early attempts to plant colonies along the Atlantic and Gulf coasts failed miserably. Bad weather, poor planning, and hostile inhabitants brought all attempts to naught. The settlement of a small group of French Protestants on the St. John's River near modern-day Jacksonville, Florida in 1564, however, gave the Spanish compelling reasons to colonize La Florida. The colony,

The Mission of San Juan Bautista, one of 21 missions organized by Junipero Serra and his Franciscan colleagues in California from San Diego to San Francisco. (Library of Congress)

named Fort Caroline, was designed as a refuge for French Protestants. It also served French national interest as a location from which to raid Spanish shipping (see NEW FRANCE). In response, the Spanish government sent Captain-General Pedro Menendez de Aviles to neutralize this threat. Sailing up the east coast of Florida, he planted a settlement he named St. Augustine on September 8, 1565. He then turned north and destroyed the French garrison at Fort Caroline and massacred the survivors. Menendez de Aviles returned to St. Augustine, which became the first permanent and most important settlement in the Spanish colony of La Florida.

Although the Spanish presence lasted until 1821 (with a 20-year interruption from 1763 to 1783 when it passed to British hands), Florida never became a major colony. Religious activity,

however, was significant if fairly unsuccessful. Spanish priests and friars attempted to bring religion to the colony, and religious orders were especially active among the native inhabitants. The first Jesuit superior in Florida was killed by Indians in 1566, and a Jesuit mission begun in 1570 at Ajacan in modern-day Virginia ended with the deaths of the seven Jesuit missionaries (see JESUITS). In 1572 the order terminated its work in Florida and the remaining members left for Mexico.

Franciscans replaced the Jesuits, but the problems remained. Spanish opposition to Indian traditions, notably polygamy, led to the Guale rebellion of 1597 that destroyed the Franciscan mission. Conflicts with the secular authorities also hindered the Franciscans' efforts. Obligated to protect the Indian converts, the Franciscans' opposition to enslavement and abuse resulted in decreased governmental support for their work. By 1708 the missions had declined dramatically. They, and Spanish Florida, never recovered. Caught up in the American versions of Europe's 18th-century wars, Florida became a political pawn more than a locus for religious activity. By the time Florida was ceded to the United States in 1821, religious life had ceased outside of Pensacola and St. Augustine.

Spanish colonial efforts in what is now the southwestern United States and California were slightly more successful. The missionary work in those areas produced great names, men whose efforts were heroic, although many now doubt the rightness of the goal and the morality of their means.

New Mexico well illustrates the problems. The Spanish movement into New Mexico, begun in 1598, met with armed resistance from the Native Americans that the Spanish bloodily suppressed. The Franciscans began successful work among the native inhabitants that continued until 1680, when a revolt by the Pueblo drove the Spanish from the region. Not until 1695 would the Spaniards regain control over Santa Fe. The brutality of the suppression alienated the people. The restored missions never regained their previous strength. Only 20 priests remained in 1776, too few to meet the population's needs. As a result many returned to their traditional beliefs or devised a syncretistic version of Spanish Catholicism and traditional religion that lasted into the 20th century.

Although never heavily populated during Spanish rule, Texas was the back door to Mexico and had major strategic significance for that colony. It also contained the most famous of all the Spanish missions, San Antonio de Valero. Better known as the Alamo, this was the largest mission in Texas and the center of Spanish activity in the region. Settlement in Texas primarily served a military function. In 1810, one-quarter of the 4,155 Europeans settled in the territory were soldiers. This tiny outpost of the Spanish empire would soon be overwhelmed by land-hungry Anglos who swarmed into the region following Mexican independence from Spain in 1821. As in Florida, those who founded and built the colony would find themselves aliens.

The Spanish missions in Arizona and California are inextricably linked with the names of two men—Eusebio KINO and Junipero SERRA. Kino began his work in Arizona in 1687, and his tireless efforts established numerous missions throughout the region, including San Xavier Del Bac near present-day Tucson. Kino claimed 30,000 converts, over 4,000 of whom he baptized personally. Although the missions declined following his death in 1711, they recovered in the next decade. Indian revolts in 1751 and the expulsion of the Jesuits from Spain in 1768 ended their work, however. The Franciscans attempted to continue, but Indian hostility and political conflicts hampered their activities. They withdrew in 1828, ending organized Catholicism for nearly four decades.

California proved no better. Here Father Junipero Serra and his Franciscan colleagues would organize 21 missions, extending from San Diego to San Francisco. Although successful at converting the relatively peaceful California Indians, the missions were less successful at keeping them alive. Forced to work on the mission farms, virtually enslaved and severely punished for the slightest infractions, California's Indians died in staggering numbers. By the time the missions were secularized in 1832 only 98,000 out of a pre-colonial population of nearly one million remained in all of California.

Within 40 years the Anglos who swarmed into northern California after the discovery of gold in 1849 had decreased this number to fewer than 21,000. These new settlers also changed California's religious and cultural life. As in the rest of Spanish America, California was transformed by the new immigrants, many of whom looked upon Roman Catholicism as a degenerate religion and the native Californios as degenerate beings.

The Mexican Revolution (1816–1821) ended Spanish control in Texas, Arizona, New Mexico, and California, severely weakening Spanish Catholicism in these areas. With the passing of these territories to United States control after the Texas Revolution (1835–1836) and the Mexican-American War (1846–1848), Spanish Catholicism became a mere vestige, lingering in the old missions and among the few remaining descendants of the Spanish settlers. This heritage, however, would be revived in the late 19th and 20th centuries as immigrants from Mexico and Central and South America brought back to the southwestern United States the Catholicism that had once dominated the region.

EQ

Bibliography: John F. Bannon, *The Spanish Borderlands Frontier, 1513–1821* (Albuquerque: University of New Mexico Press, 1974); Herbert E. Bolton, *The Mission as a Frontier Institution in the Spanish American Colonies* (El Paso: Texas Western College Press, 1960); ———, *The Spanish Borderlands: A Chronicle of Old Florida and the Southwest* (New Haven: Yale University Press, 1921); Maynard Geiger, *Franciscan Missionaries in Hispanic California, 1769–1848: A Biographical Dictionary* (San Marino, Calif.: Huntington Library, 1969); Mariano Picon-Salas, *A Cultural History of Spanish America from Conquest to Independence* (Berkeley: University of California Press, 1971).

New Thought   The quintessential American expression of what philosopher William JAMES called "the religion of healthy mindedness" and historian Sydney Ahlstrom analyzed as "harmonial religion," New Thought emerged out of CHRISTIAN SCIENCE in the 1880s.

New Thought received its first intellectual boost when Warren Felt Evans, a Swedenborgian (see SWEDENBORGIANISM) who had benefited from the mesmeric cures (see MESMERISM) of Phineas P. QUIMBY, began to champion as early as the 1860s an idealistic and optimistic metaphysics for spiritual and mental well-being. The movement was first institutionalized in 1882 when Julius and Annetta Dresser, also students of Quimby, founded their Church of the Higher Life. After the term "New Thought" gained currency in the 1890s, a number of New

Thought institutions and movements arose, including the Christian Science Theological Seminary of Emma Curtis HOPKINS, Malinda Cramer's Divine Science, the Unity School of Christianity of Charles and Myrtle Fillmore, and Ernest Holmes's Religious Science.

One thing that attracts Americans to New Thought is its insistence that individuals shun dogma and find their own paths to religious truths. For this reason, New Thought advocates are traditionally wary of institutionalizing their religious lives. In 1915, however, a number of local New Thought groups gathered into a loose federation called the International New Thought Alliance (I.N.T.A.). Two years later this organization's "Affirmations" promulgated something akin to a New Thought creed:

> We affirm the freedom of each soul as to choice and as to belief . . .
> The essence of the New Thought is Truth, and each individual must be loyal to the Truth as he sees it . . .
> We affirm the Good. . . . Man is made in the image of the Good, and evil and pain are but the tests and correctives that appear when his thought does not reflect the full glory of this image.
> We affirm health . . .
> We affirm the divine supply. . . . Within us are unused resources of energy and power. . . .
> We affirm the teaching of Christ and the Kingdom of Heaven is within us, that we are one with the Father, that we should judge not, that we should love one another. . . .
> We affirm the new thought of God as Universal Love, Life, Truth and Joy.

The New Thought movement recruited many of its early healers and teachers from Christian Science. But New Thought advocates differentiated themselves from Christian Scientists by refusing to cede the status of exclusive revelation to the writings of Christian Science founder Mary Baker EDDY. New Thought adherents typically respect and in many cases revere Eddy's work, but they do not accept her ideas as unerring doctrine. Moreover, they insist on the freedom to supplement her writings with other religious texts (including non-Christian scriptures) and with their own intuitions.

New Thought further differentiates itself from Christian Science by its unrelenting cosmic optimism. Although Eddy joined most New Thought teachers in affirming that evil and sins were illusions, in her view human beings still needed to be redeemed by Jesus Christ. At least in their unregenerate state, humans were, according to Eddy, estranged from God; "mortal mind" and "divine Mind" were not to be confused.

New Thought advocates generally view Eddy's positions on these matters as unduly pessimistic. They accept no essential division between God and humanity, since the human mind is for them "God within." They reject her argument that the mind can work for evil (through "malicious animal magnetism") as well as good. And to the extent that humans need saving, they can save themselves; humans have no need for any agent outside their own powers of positive thinking.

New Thought cannot claim many members in its loosely affiliated organizations, but millions of Americans have no doubt embraced the movement's optimistic gospel, which in secularized versions is virtually indistinguishable from the popular American myth of individual success. The enduring popularity of Ralph Waldo Trine's hugely successful *In Tune with the Infinite, or, Fullness of Peace, Power, and Plenty* (1897) and the appearance on best-seller lists of inspirational books like Dale Carnegie's *How to Win Friends and Influence People* (1936) and Norman Vincent Peale's *The Power of Positive Thinking* (1952) attest to the broader influence of New Thought on American popular culture.
SRP

Bibliography: Charles Braden, *Spirits in Rebellion: The Rise and Development of New Thought* (Dallas: Southern Methodist University Press, 1963); Donald Meyer, *The Positive Thinkers: Religion as Pop Psychology from Mary Baker Eddy to Oral Roberts* (New York: Pantheon Books, 1980).

Nichiren Shoshu Academy The largest Buddhist group (see BUDDHISM) in the United States, the Nichiren Shoshu Academy (N.S.A.) is an American branch of the Soka Gakkai ("Value Creation Society"), a lay organization established in Japan in 1930 in an effort to convert the world to Nichiren Shoshu ("True Nichiren") and usher in an era of world peace. Nichiren Shoshu is a sect within the Mahayana ("Great Vehicle") Buddhist school of North Asia that traces its origins back to the 13th-century Buddhist reformer and Japanese nationalist Nichiren Daishonin (1222–1282).

Nichiren Buddhists distinguish themselves from other Buddhists in at least four ways. They value the Lotus Sutra over all other Mahayana Buddhist texts. They tend to regard all other forms of Buddhism not merely as inferior faiths but as dangerous heresies. They are generally militantly nationalistic. Finally, they emphasize the instrumental benefits and absolute simplicity of Buddhist practice.

The Korean-born Masayasu Sadanaga, who would become the first general director of the N.S.A., established Soka Gakkai's first branch in the United States in 1960. At first, he attracted a predominantly Japanese-American clientele. But in 1967, he began an aggressive and successful missionary campaign to non-Asians, especially to blacks and Hispanics. Out of this campaign, Nichiren Shoshu of America emerged under Sadanaga's leadership as a vital new religious movement. In the 1960s and 1970s, N.S.A. grew rapidly, especially among the college-age population, by reaching out to occidental Americans through seminars and publications, including two periodicals, the *World Tribune* (established 1964) and the *NSA Quarterly* (established 1973). As the organization moved into Canada, Central and South America, and the Caribbean, it changed its name to Nichiren Shoshu Academy. The N.S.A. makes its headquarters in Santa Monica, California and maintains temples in Honolulu, Hawaii, Washington, D.C., New York City, Chicago, and Etiwanda, California. It claims 300,000 adherents.

Members, like Nichiren Shoshu adherents in Japan, believe that Buddhahood is achieved through faith in and reliance upon the Lotus Sutra. Their core ritual practices are reciting the Lotus Sutra and chanting the Daimoku: "Hail to the Mystical Teaching of the Lotus Sutra." Both of these practices are said to invoke the power of the Lotus Sutra to instill in the individual practitioner spiritual and material benefits. When members are initiated into the N.S.A., they receive a mandala called the Gohonzon, which is installed in their homes as a domestic shrine.

Although the N.S.A. maintains close organizational ties to its mother movement in Japan, it has supplanted the Soka Gakkai's militant Japanese nationalism with its own brand of American CIVIL RELIGION. Ironically, the N.S.A. is the most aggressively and self-consciously Americanized Buddhist movement in the United States. In 1972 Masayasu Sadanaga took the "American" name of George M. Williams. In his lectures, Williams stresses the common aspirations of American patriots and N.S.A. practitioners. Youth members march in a fife and drum corps and brass band, and the organization's "Junior Pioneers" participate in activities akin to those of the Boy Scouts. One N.S.A. convention around the time of the American Bicentennial was organized around the theme "The Spirit of 1776." And the American flag flies proudly atop all 40 N.S.A. centers in the United States.

Although the N.S.A. has been tarnished by critics who deride the organization as a dangerous "cult," it remains by most accounts the largest and most diverse Buddhist organization in America.

SRP

Bibliography: Emma McCloy Layman, *Buddhism in America* (Chicago: Nelson–Hall, 1976); Charles Prebisch, *American Buddhism* (North Scituate, Mass. Duxbury Press, 1979); George M. Williams, *The Gosho Reference* (Los Angeles: World Tribune Press, 1976).

Niebuhr, Helmut Richard (1894–1962)

Although overshadowed by his more outspoken and celebrated older brother (see NIEBUHR, REINHOLD), H. Richard Niebuhr had a profound impact on 20th-century American religious thought. Unlike Reinhold, whose life was a constant attempt to bring the Christian witness to bear on particular historical issues, H. Richard plumbed the depths of what was enduring.

Born September 3, 1894 in Wright City, Missouri, where his father was a minister in the German Evangelical Synod, H. Richard grew up in a German-speaking immigrant family. He studied at the synod's schools at Elmhurst College (1912) and Eden Seminary (1915). After leaving Eden he undertook graduate work at Washington University in St. Louis (M.A. 1918), during which time he also held a full-time pastorate, and Yale University (B.D. 1923, Ph.D. 1924). He later served on the faculties of both Eden as professor of theology 1919–1922, 1927–1931, and Elmhurst as president from 1924 to 1927. In 1931 Niebuhr was appointed to the faculty of Yale Divinity School, where he served as professor of Theology and Ethics until his death in 1962.

There are two significant strains in H. Richard Niebuhr's theology. The first is the awareness that religious thought and affirmation are historically conditioned. In this he remained within the tradition of liberal theology (see LIBERALISM, THEOLOGICAL) and was indebted to the thought of the German theologian Ernst Troeltsch (1865–1923). Niebuhr himself moved far beyond the historicism of liberal theology. As one considered to be within the camp of NEO-ORTHODOXY, Niebuhr rejected the liberal position that the truth of religion resided within human life and experience. Certainly individuals might have truth about God, but since God's position was absolute and the individual's position relative, no person, no creed, no faith could have complete knowledge of God.

This insight—that knowledge of God was always socially and historically conditioned—allowed Niebuhr to produce significant studies of Christian thought and belief in particular historical periods. In his books *The Social Sources of Denominationalism* (1929), *The Kingdom of God in America* (1937), and *Christ and Culture* (1951), Niebuhr developed typological analyses of Christian beliefs that illuminated the social and religious concerns of their times.

For Niebuhr, the contextual nature of humanity's understanding of God was not problematic. Problems and errors emerged, however, when human beings attempted to raise their limited perspective to the absolute. Here Niebuhr showed himself to be Neo-orthodox. God, in Niebuhr's radically monotheistic view, destroys all pretensions to absolutism. Only the principle of Being itself has any claim to be absolute. The claims of God are unchanging, but the claims of religion are not.

The significance of Niebuhr's life and work is great. Most obvious is the impact on his students, many of whom went on to be leading ethicists in their own right. The influence of his books analyzing the sociological-historical elements of Christianity has been immense. Their typologies have entered into the vocabulary of the study of religion, especially of religion in America.

The significance of Niebuhr's theological work, is perhaps even more important. His *Radical Monotheism and Western Culture* helped bring about a resurgence of interest in and concern about the doctrine and nature of God that American theological discourse had lacked for decades. Niebuhr was unable to finish his theological work. He died unexpectedly from a heart attack on July 5, 1962 with his final manuscript incomplete.

EQ

Bibliography: James W. Fowler, *To See the Kingdom: The Theological Vision of H. Richard Niebuhr* (Lanham, Md.: University Press of America, 1974); Libertus A. Hoedemaker, *The Theology of H. Richard Niebuhr* (Philadelphia: Pilgrim Press, 1970); H. Richard Niebuhr, *The Social Sources of Denominationalism* (New York: Meridian Books, 1957), ——, *The Kingdom of God In America*. 1937. Reprint. Middletown: Wesleyan University Press, 1988; ——, *Christ and Culture* (New York: Harper, 1951); ——, *Radical Monotheism and Western Culture* (New York: Harper, 1960); Paul Ramsey, ed., *Faith and Ethics: The Theology of H. Richard Niebuhr* (New York: Harper, 1957).

Niebuhr, Reinhold (1892–1971)

Reinhold Niebuhr, America's most famous 20th century theologian, was born on June 21, 1892 to Gustav and Lydia Niebuhr in Wright City, Missouri. His father, a German immigrant, was a pastor in the German Evangelical Synod. German was Reinhold's mother tongue, and his English remained accented throughout his life. His thinking on religion and society made him the most important religious thinker of his time with an influence that extended far beyond his denomination and even Christianity. For over three decades he advised the politically powerful and numbered among his friends some of the most important people of his time.

Niebuhr's early life was that of a small-town boy. In 1902 his family moved to Lincoln, Illinois where his father had accepted a pastorate. Here Niebuhr lived until 1907, when he was sent to Elmhurst College to prepare for entry into Eden Seminary, where ministers in the German Evangelical Church were trained.

Following his graduation from Eden (1913), Niebuhr moved on to Yale Divinity School, although the unexpected death of his father in that year had jeopardized these plans. Niebuhr's acceptance by Yale was the result of the school's attempt at rebuilding. No other major university accepted students from unaccredited colleges, and even Yale did not accept Eden's B.D. When Niebuhr entered Yale he did so as a third-year B.D. student. Despite the weakness of his education and English, Niebuhr did well at Yale and continued in the M.A. program from which he graduated in June 1915.

After leaving Yale, Niebuhr began a 13-year tenure as minister at Bethel Church in Detroit. During his pastorate Niebuhr, with the assistance of his mother and later his sister Hulda, turned the church from the smallest in the denomination into a thriving and dynamic congregation.

Among those Niebuhr impressed during his Detroit years was the president-general of the German Evangelical Church, who called upon Niebuhr to perform many denominational tasks including service on the synod's war board during WORLD WAR I, liaison to the new Federal Council of Churches (see NATIONAL COUNCIL OF CHURCHES), and speaking engagements for the synod. Niebuhr also was active in work for the YOUNG MEN'S CHRISTIAN ASSOCIATION, and contributed numerous articles to journals and magazines, especially the *Christian Century.*

While in Detroit, Niebuhr became increasingly radical in his economic and political views. He spoke out against the speed-up of the automotive assembly line, layoffs during periods of re-tooling, and the auto companies' refusal to allow unionization. Already influenced by the SOCIAL GOSPEL, Niebuhr began to see the need for a deeper critique of capitalist society, which he expounded in *Does Civilization Need Religion?* (1927).

In 1928 Niebuhr joined the faculty of Union Theological Seminary in New York City and began one of the most influential careers in American religious history. He was one of the most popular teachers at Union, and he and his wife, Ursula (nee Keppel-Compton), frequently entertained groups of students and friends at their home. A man of constant action, Niebuhr's activities were many and varied. He traveled constantly, preaching and speaking throughout the country. He founded the Fellowship of Christian Socialists (1930), edited its journal, and was a Socialist Party candidate for the New York Senate (1930) and the United States Congress (1932).

Niebuhr also served on the executive committee of the pacifist Fellowship of Reconciliation, but resigned in 1933 in response to the rise of Nazism and his increasing suspicion of the uncritical optimism of liberal theology. This change in Niebuhr's thought culminated in his resignation from the Socialist Party in 1940. The following year he founded the journal *Christianity and Crisis.* In 1941 he was the leader in organizing the Union for Democratic Action, which he served as national chairman.

An early and vocal opponent of the Nazis and an advocate of American aid to the allies, Niebuhr actively supported American policies in WORLD WAR II. He was a critic, however, of the massive bombings and wholesale destruction of German and Japanese cities. Niebuhr also signed the Federal Council of Churches statement criticizing the use of the atomic bomb. Privately, however, he suspected that its use was necessary to end the hostilities.

Following the war he served as an adviser to the State Department's Policy and Planning staff and its chairman, George Kennan. In doing so he helped to develop the United States's postwar understanding of the balance of power.

Although weakened by a stroke in 1952, he remained as active as his health allowed. Much was asked of him, for during the last two decades of his life Niebuhr was an internationally acclaimed religious and political figure, speaking throughout Europe and the United States. In 1964, in recognition of his work, he received the Presidential Medal of Freedom. During the 1960s he continued to write in support of the civil rights movement and in opposition to the Vietnam War. Increasing enfeeblement and pain marked Niebuhr's life until his death on June 1, 1971.

Reinhold Niebuhr constructed no complete theological system. His theology, like his life, was in constant motion, but there is one theme that connects all Niebuhr's thought. This is the question of how to apply Christianity to existing social and political conditions. In the search for an answer Niebuhr moved from the pietism of his youth, through liberal theology (see LIBERALISM, THEOLOGICAL), to a position of NEO-

ORTHODOXY (a term he hated) or Christian Realism.

As a Christian, Niebuhr understood history as linear. Events are distinctive and unique. For this reason Christians were constantly called upon to re-apply religious doctrines to new realities. Unlike the Renaissance and the ENLIGHTENMENT and their liberal theologian descendants, Niebuhr rejected the conviction that this linear movement included progress. Certainly there is improvement in technology and material conditions, but this is not to be confused with improvement in the human moral condition.

That type of progress is precluded by the reality of human sin. Sin, to Niebuhr, is not merely error or misunderstanding as some liberal theologians thought. Rather it is inherent within the human condition and illustrated by the will to power of individuals, social groups, and nations. Sin most often manifests itself as pride, the belief of individuals, classes, and nations that they have all possible knowledge, that they are completely right.

Human knowledge and ability, however, are always incomplete. Given this fact, any belief that one has all the truth and the right to implement that truth within the world is dangerous. This attitude, which Niebuhr referred to as utopianism, must be combated. Utopianism was the most visible manifestation of pride. Rejection of utopianism was not to be confused with political quiescence, or inaction. That would be the sin of sloth and allow for the possibility of the emergence of even greater evils that might need to be opposed. This was the reason for Niebuhr's rejection of pacifism in the face of the rise of Nazism.

According to Niebuhr, the obligation of the Christian is to determine the concrete application of love within particular historical situations. This love finds concrete application within justice, but justice needs love to prevent it from becoming rigid, legalistic, and eventually unjust. The involvement with political affairs inevitably involves Christians with the messy and imperfect world. Simultaneously Christians must remember that, given the imperfections of the world and the political realm, no political system ever deserves or should receive divine sanction. At best, all we can hope to accomplish is the most appropriate application of Christian love to existing conditions.

After he died on June 1, 1971 those attending his funeral included Arthur Schlesinger, Jr., William Shirer, and Lionel and Diana Trilling. Among the officiants at the memorial service was Rabbi Abraham HESCHEL. Such was the reach of the man that those of other religions and no religion came forward to honor him publicly. (See also NIEBUHR, HELMUT RICHARD.)

EQ

Bibliography: June Bingham, *Courage to Change: An Introduction to the Life and Thought of Reinhold Niebuhr* (New York: Scribner, 1961); Richard Wightman Fox, *Reinhold Niebuhr, A Biography* (New York: Pantheon Books, 1985); Hans Hoffman, *The Theology of Reinhold Niebuhr* (New York: Scribner, 1956); Dennis McCann, *Christian Realism and Liberation Theology: Political Theologies in Conflict.* (Maryknoll: Orbis Books, 1981); Reinhold Niebuhr, *Moral Man and Immoral Society* (New York: C. Scribner's, 1932); ———, *The Nature and Destiny of Man:* vol. 1, *Human Nature,* vol. 2, *Human Destiny* (New York: C. Scribner's, 1945); D. B. Robertson, *Reinhold Niebuhr's Works: A Bibliography* (Lanham Ma.: University Press of America, 1983); Nathan A. Scott, ed., *The Legacy of Reinhold Niebuhr* (Chicago: University of Chicago Press, 1975); Ronald Stone, *Reinhold Niebuhr: Prophet to Politicians* (Nashville: Abingdon Press, 1972).

North American Baptist Conference
See BAPTISTS.

Northern Baptist Convention See AMERICAN BAPTIST CHURCHES IN THE U.S.A.

Noyes, John Humphrey (1811–1886)
Best known for his founding of the Oneida community in western New York, John Hum-

John Humphrey Noyes, Christian radical and founder of the most widely publicized 19th-century utopian experiment, the Oneida Community in upstate New York.

phrey Noyes was also a writer, a preacher, and a social reformer. The son of wealthy, agnostic parents in Brattleboro, Vermont, Noyes attended Dartmouth College (1826–1830) and after graduating determined to study law. Within a year, however, he was converted during an evangelical revival, and decided to enter the ministry instead. After a brief stay at Andover Theological Seminary in Massachusetts, Noyes studied at Yale Divinity School and received his license to preach from the Congregational Church in 1833.

During his time in New Haven, Noyes gradually became dissatisfied with the evangelical faith that initially had ignited his piety. He struggled to find moral and spiritual perfection, and increasingly he looked to New Testament models,

and particularly the paradigm of earthly holiness exemplified by the apostle Paul, for his guidance. Eventually he concluded that Christ had returned in A.D. 70, thereby enabling human beings to achieve spiritual perfection during this life. The public espousal of this heretical conviction led to the revocation of his ministerial license in 1834, but it impelled Noyes to seek institutional means through which men and women could achieve a life of ordered holiness.

Noyes then moved on to Putney, Vermont, to develop his ideas, and gathered around him fellow spiritual seekers. Using the facilities of the Putney Bible School as well as finances from his father's estate, he gradually exerted control over a community that, by the early 1840s, counted some three dozen members. Noyes insisted on exercising complete authority over his flock, and he sought to provide followers with a combination of individual and environmental regeneration—including cultivation through work, leisure activities, and even diet—in order to facilitate their perfection. In 1846 he added the most controversial element of community life, a form of free cohabitation known as "complex marriage," in which monogamy was considered spiritual tyranny, emotional attachments between the sexes were frowned upon, and procreation was regulated by Noyes himself in a system called "stiripculture," which matched suitable partners for the conception of offspring.

The public uproar over Noyes's unorthodox sexual practices, including his indictment on charges of adultery, forced the community to relocate to Oneida, New York in 1848. There the community thrived for nearly three decades, gaining economic security through the manufacturing of steel traps and silverplate. Noyes published a series of tracts explaining his views of scientific propagation and its spiritual rationale, including *Essay on Scientific Propagation* (1872) and *Male Continence* (1872). By 1876 outside pressure forced Noyes to remove to Canada, where he remained for the rest of his life, and to transfer leadership of Oneida to a ruling committee. He also advised the colony to end the practice of complex marriage. Although Noyes's utopia dissolved in 1881, it reformed as a joint-stock company and became known for the manufacture of fine silver.

LMK

Bibliography: Maren Lockwood Carden, *Oneida: Utopian Community to Modern Corporation* (Baltimore: Johns Hopkins Press, 1971); Robert David Thomas, *The Man Who Would Be Perfect: John Humphrey Noyes and the Utopian Impulse* (Philadelphia: University of Pennsylvania Press, 1977).

O

occult movements See NEO-PAGANISM; NEW AGE RELIGION; ROSICRUCIANS; SANTERIA; SATANISM; SPIRITUALISM; VODOU.

O'Connor, Flannery See LITERATURE AND RELIGION.

O'Hair, Madalyn Murray (1919–) Madalyn Murray O'Hair became the most famous atheist in the United States in the years following WORLD WAR II (see ATHEISM and FREE THOUGHT). Her notoriety stemmed from her outspoken opposition to prayers in the public schools and from her general opposition to what she said was a concerted drive by government officials to make the country a Christian nation. Her successful challenge to the Baltimore school board in the 1963 case of *Murray vs. Curlett* outlawed prayers in the school system and lent credibility to her campaign against government support for religion.

Madalyn Mays was born in Pittsburgh, Pennsylvania on April 13, 1919, the daughter of a Presbyterian father and a Lutheran mother. Her reading of the Bible from cover to cover at the age of 13 convinced her of its "impossibility." After high school she attended several colleges, finally getting her baccalaureate degree in 1948 after serving as a cryptographer in the Women's Army Corps during World War II. Her marriage to William J. Murray during the mid-1940s ended in divorce. They had two sons, William J. Murray III and Jon Garth Murray. After obtaining a law degree from South Texas College of Law in 1953, she studied social work for two years at Howard University. Most of her career she spent as a psychiatric social worker and as an attorney for child welfare agencies, mental health clinics, and government agencies.

Madalyn Murray's coming to public attention resulted from her request that her older son, William, be exempted from daily prayers at Woodbourne Junior High School in Baltimore in 1960. An agreement to allow him to be excused during prayers fell through when students and adults taunted and harassed the family, and Murray brought suit to eliminate entirely "sectarian opening exercises" from the city's public schools. An 8–1 United States Supreme Court decision in 1963 upheld her position. Harassment of the family by irate neighbors and citizens continued in later months and years.

Following her victory, Murray expanded her campaign against organized religion, challenging the inclusion of the words "under God" in the Pledge of Allegiance, attacking the Federal Communications Commission for not forcing stations to sell time on the airwaves to atheists, and challenging the tax-exempt status of religious organizations. In 1965, after marrying Richard O'Hair, she founded the American Atheist Center, serving as its director from 1965 to 1973. In subsequent years Murray has continued to promote her point of view, hosting radio programs, giving public lectures, and writing tracts and numerous books.

MG

Bibliography: Madalyn Murray O'Hair, *Freedom Under Siege: the Impact of Organized Religion on Your Liberty and Your Pocketbook* (Los Angeles: J.P. Tarcher, 1974); Lawrence Wright, *Saints and Sinners: Walker Raley, Jimmy Swaggart, Madalyn Murray O'Hair, Anton LaVey, Will Campbell, Matthew Fox* (New York: Alfred A. Knopf, 1993).

Olcott, Henry Steel (1832–1907) Henry Steel Olcott, the president and cofounder of the Theosophical Society and a major contributor to the late-19th century Sinhalese Buddhist Revival in Ceylon (now Sri Lanka), is probably the only American who is remembered by his admirers as a bodhisattva ("enlightenment being") and a reincarnation of Gautama Buddha. He is undoubtedly the only such American who

Henry Steel Olcott, a cofounder, with Madame Blavatsky, of the Theosophical Society. (Theosophical Society)

has also been denounced in the *New York Times* as "a man bereft of reason."

A descendant of the Puritans, Olcott was born to Presbyterian parents in Orange, New Jersey in 1832. After dropping out of college, he moved to Ohio and became at the age of 20 a convert to SPIRITUALISM. In the two decades that followed his spiritualist turn he distinguished himself as an experimental agriculturalist, *New York Tribune* reporter, antislavery advocate, civil service reformer, government investigator of Lincoln's assassination, insurance lawyer, and chaste reviewer of raucous burlesque productions. Thus it was not without reason that one of his contemporaries dubbed him "that most progressive of all the Americans."

Olcott's theosophical career began when he met the Russian occultist Helena Petrovna BLAVATSKY (1831–1891). This fateful first meeting occurred in 1874 at a farmhouse in Chittenden, Vermont that many spiritualists believed housed loquacious spirits of the dead. After an early and failed attempt to reform spiritualism morally and philosophically from within, Olcott and Blavatsky founded their own organization, the Theosophical Society, in New York in 1875. While Blavatsky was clearly the charismatic genius behind the theosophical movement, Olcott was its organizational man. He oversaw the transplantation of the society from New York to Bombay to its present location in Adyar, a suburb of Madras, India. And he sustained it during its development from an organization devoted to investigating scientifically spiritual phenomena into the organization it is today: an eclectic body dedicated to preserving the ancient wisdom tradition and to promoting interreligious harmony.

In Ceylon in 1880, Olcott formally converted to BUDDHISM. Over the next few decades, he earned the respect of many Sinhalese Buddhists by founding Buddhist schools and by lobbying a series of British colonial administrators for Buddhist civil rights. Though Olcott claimed to be preserving "pure, primitive Buddhism," he contributed mightily to the creole religious tradition scholars now describe as "Protestant Buddhism." Like the gospel of the missionaries whose proselytizing he decried, Olcott's faith was activistic, optimistic, didactic, adaptationist, and progressivist. And like his hated missionaries, Olcott promoted his faith by founding voluntary associations, authoring and distributing catechisms, promoting the translation of Buddhist scriptures into the vernacular, establishing Sunday schools, preaching temperance, and conducting revivals.

Later in his career Olcott attempted to gather all the world's Buddhists into one grand "International Buddhist League." Olcott succeeded in garnering signatures of Mahayana ("Great Vehicle") and Theravada ("Way of the Elders")

Buddhists from across Asia onto an ecumenical Buddhist platform, in promoting a new Buddhist flag as a symbol for all Buddhists, and in founding the Mahabodhi Society with the Sinhalese Buddhist reformer Anagarika DHARMAPALA in 1891. But his broader, perhaps utopian hope for a "United Buddhist World" was never realized.

Olcott edited the magazine the *Theosophist* (established 1879) and wrote a six-volume history of the Theosophical Society entitled *Old Diary Leaves* (1895–1935), but he is best known for his *Buddhist Catechism* (1881), which has gone through over 40 editions and been translated into 20 languages.

Olcott died in his adopted homeland of India in 1907. He is remembered today not only by theosophists but by many Sinhalese who revere him as "the White Buddhist" who contributed in important ways to their nation's spiritual and political independence.

SRP

Bibliography: Henry Steel Olcott, *Old Diary Leaves: The History of the Theosophical Society,* 6 vols. (Adyar, India: Theosophical Publishing House, 1972–75); Stephen R. Prothero, *The White Buddhist: The Asian Odyssey of Henry Steel Olcott,* (Bloomington: Indiana University Press, 1996).

Old Catholic movement A disparate movement divided by numerous schisms and conflicting claims, the Old Catholic movement's official organization was formed in the 1870s in response to the doctrine of papal infallibility proclaimed at VATICAN COUNCIL I. Its doctrinal origins lay in the 1700s, however, when the bishop of Utrecht, Holland, Peter Codde, accepted into his diocese Jansenist refugees from the convent of Port Royal, France following their expulsion from that country.

Developing from the thought of the Dutch theologian Cornelius Jansen, Jansenism held to the doctrines of predestination and limited salvation, believing salvation was not available to all. Their views were condemned by several popes and they were hounded by their leading oppo-

nents, the JESUITS. The positive reception given to the Jansenists by the bishop of Utrecht, therefore, led to his deposition by the pope. Codde retained much of his following and with the arrival of Dominique Varlet, a French bishop with Jansenist leanings, there was a general confirmation of those who had followed Codde. Varlet returned to Utrecht in 1724 to consecrate a new bishop there and he later consecrated bishops in Haarlem and Deventer, guaranteeing apostolic succession for the movement that would become the Old Catholics.

Following the promulgation of papal infallibility in 1879, a group of theologians and churchmen who opposed the doctrine met in Munich, Germany. These delegates, including representatives of the Church of Utrecht and the Church of England, organized the Old Catholic Church along national lines. The ritual is that of the Roman Catholic rite, although clergy are allowed to marry. The national churches retain their autonomy with the bishop of Utrecht presiding over the episcopal conference. The Roman Catholic Church recognizes the validity of the ordination of Old Order Catholic (Utrecht) priests, but rejects the Church's right to consecrate bishops.

In the United States, the Old Catholic Church has become a jumble of schisms and irregular consecrations. To a great extent the movement in the United States has been a history of bishops without dioceses. These churches include the American Catholic Church, the American Catholic Church (Syro-Antiochean), the Christ Orthodox Catholic Exarchate of the Americas and the Eastern Hemisphere, two bodies under the name of North American Old Roman Catholic Church, and numerous others.

A major exception to the general rule is the Polish National Catholic Church of America. It is the only one of the American Old Catholic bodies in communion with the see of Utrecht and is by far the largest in the United States. It was organized in 1904 by the merger of several independent Polish Roman Catholic parishes that had been formed in response to a perceived hostility by American bishops to Polish Catholic sensibilities. The Polish National Catholic Church of America retains the ethos of pre-VATICAN COUNCIL II Roman Catholicism with a strong injection of Polish nationalism. Head-quartered in Scranton, Pennsylvania it numbers nearly 300,000 members in 162 parishes.

EQ

Bibliography: Peter F. Anson, *Bishops at Large* (New York: October House, 1964); J. Gordon Melton, *The Encyclopedia of American Religions* (Wilmington, N.C.: McGrath Publishing Co., 1978); Karl Pruter, *A History of the Old Catholic Church* (San Bernardino: Borgo Press, 1986); ———, *The Old Catholic Sourcebook* (New York: Garland, 1983); Jonathan Trela, *A History of the North American Old Roman Catholic Church* (Scranton: s.n., 1979).

Old Lights   See NEW LIGHTS/OLD LIGHTS.

Old School   See NEW SCHOOL/OLD SCHOOL.

Old Side   See NEW SIDE/OLD SIDE.

Old South   See PROSLAVERY THOUGHT; SLAVERY; SOUTH, THE.

Oneida Community   See NOYES, JOHN HUMPHREY.

Orthodox Christianity   Despite the activity of several million believers, Orthodox Christianity has attracted relatively little attention in North America. Obscured by what the historian Martin Marty has called the cocoon of ethnicity, the Orthodox in America have been perceived primarily as Slavs, Greeks, Aleuts, Romanians, and so on. Nevertheless, a family of Orthodox churches has taken root in North America during the 20th century. Large and stable communities have emerged from immigrant chaos and poverty, and an ancient Christian tradition has begun to grapple with American culture.

The first contact took place in the islands off Alaska during the 18th century. Organized Russian missions carried the faith across the Bering Sea beginning in 1794, and many indigenous peoples embraced Orthodoxy. However, most Orthodox living in North America today trace their roots to the vast diaspora of the late 19th and early 20th centuries, when waves of immigrants arrived from Eastern Europe and the Mediterranean. They carried with them a faith that, although the dominant form of Christianity in its homelands, was little known in the West.

The major historical legacy of the Byzantine Empire (324–1453), Orthodoxy prizes its unbroken continuity with the church established in Jerusalem on Pentecost. It claims to be the universal, unaltered, and normative expression of Christianity. And although composed of more than a dozen autonomous local or national churches, the Orthodox communion considers itself to be a single church bound together by a common doctrinal, ecclesiastical, and liturgical tradition.

Inextricably connected to the Byzantine state, Orthodoxy flourished throughout the medieval period. Its influence extended far beyond the empire's embattled borders as Byzantine missions converted the Serbs and the Bulgars, and, after the 10th century, spread the faith into the Ukraine and Russia.

Although contact with the church in Western Europe dwindled after the sixth century, much of the shared dogmatic heritage of Trinitarian Christianity was articulated by Eastern theologians. Thus, although the Roman Catholic and Orthodox churches still share a great deal, significant theological differences developed, notably disagreements about the nature of papal authority and the role of the Holy Spirit in the Trinity.

The rise of Islam and centuries of conflict with the Roman Catholic West eroded the position of the Byzantine Church, especially after the 12th century. The conflict with the West was particularly sharp. The bitter estrangement between Rome and Constantinople is symbolized by the Great Schism of 1054, the sack of Constantinople by Western Christians in 1204 during the Fourth Crusade, and long centuries of tension along the European borders between the Catholic West and the Orthodox East, which stretch from Serbia to Lithuania.

However, the massive dispersion of migrants at the end of the 19th century shattered the geographical isolation of the Orthodox. More than one million Orthodox from roughly two dozen ethnic groups established themselves in North America, including Albanians, Arabs, Bulgarians, Greeks, Romanians, Serbs, Russians, and Ukrainians.

In addition, hundreds of thousands of closely related Eastern Rite Catholics, also called Greek Catholics or Uniates, arrived during this period. While Orthodox in tradition and practice, they came from groups that had broken with Orthodoxy to join the Roman Catholic Church between the 16th and 18th centuries. Most Greek Catholics in America were Slav immigrants from the Austro-Hungarian Empire. Their relations with American Catholic bishops, who were unfamiliar with their traditions, were often strained.

As American Catholic bishops pressed them to conform with Western norms, many Greek Catholics considered rejoining the Orthodox Church. By 1890, the Russian Orthodox diocese in America was pursuing the Uniates eagerly (see BELAVIN, TIKHON). Eventually, several hundred Eastern Rite parishes rejoined Orthodox jurisdictions in several waves beginning in the 1890s.

The history of most Orthodox jurisdictions in America falls into three phases: a turbulent period of mass migration that ended soon after World War I, a period of intense struggle for survival during the 1920s and 1930s, and a period of consolidation following World War II.

Although diverse in language and ethnic identity, Orthodox immigrants shared two general challenges. The first was acculturation. Orthodox people typically held their religious and ethnic identities to be inseparable. As immigrants and their children lost touch with, for example, Greek or Syrian culture, they ran the risk of slipping away from Orthodoxy.

The second challenge was the continuing and often profoundly disruptive impact of events in the old homelands. Old World political struggles divided almost every Orthodox group in America at some point. The rise of Communist regimes in Eastern Europe proved to be devastatingly divisive.

During the period between 1880 and 1920, the Russian church took the lead. Supported from St. Petersburg, it oriented itself to serve immigrants pouring into the cities and industrial regions along the East Coast and around the Great Lakes. Russian bishops also attempted to build a single American Orthodox archdiocese with many ethnic subjurisdictions to serve the polyglot flock. And although most Greeks resisted this arrangement, the Russian plan achieved some success as many Syrians, Serbs, and other Slavs cooperated.

Local lay groups often took the initiative in forming Orthodox communities in the new land. Typically, religious or ethnic brotherhoods formed as a prelude to the organization of a parish that could provide the religious and cultural support the immigrants sought. The adjustment from homelands where a state-sponsored Orthodox church prevailed to the voluntaristic atmosphere of America proved often difficult.

The vigorous role of the laity in America gave parishes a loyal and active constituency, but clashes took place frequently among those from different regions of the homeland, and among laity, priests, and bishops. In the fluid circumstances of the diaspora, the canonical validity of parishes, clergy, and jurisdictions was often questioned. The search for stability and canonical good order remained a major challenge well into the 20th century.

Nevertheless, by 1910 a large Orthodox community was taking shape. Unfortunately, World War I brought disaster. The Russian revolutions of 1917 virtually destroyed the Russian church in America. Subsidies ended abruptly, and the Russian church at home and abroad was splintered by disagreements over how to respond to Communist domination. The three rival Russian-descended jurisdictions still persist. Greeks and Syrians also suffered schisms reflecting homeland politics during the 1920s. To compound matters, immigration restrictions enacted during the early 1920s cut off immigration from most Orthodox homelands.

As a result, the Orthodox in America fragmented into separate ethnic jurisdictions. A Romanian diocese formed in 1921, a Greek archdiocese in 1922, and others followed. These ethnic churches reflected the preferences of immigrants eager to maintain ties with their homelands, and the reality that the Orthodox community was divided by language and ethnicity.

The situation began to stabilize in the 1930s, as the Greek archdiocese and the largest Russian jurisdiction moved beyond internal quarrels and began to build an institutional base, including the opening of the first permanent Orthodox theological seminaries in the United States. Three jurisdictions emerged during the 1940s and 1950s as the leading Orthodox groups: the GREEK ORTHODOX ARCHDIOCESE OF NORTH AND SOUTH AMERICA, the Russian-descended group now called the ORTHODOX CHURCH IN AMERICA (OCA), and the Antiochian Orthodox Christian Archdiocese of North America (whose main constituency was of Arab origin). At least 11 additional Orthodox jurisdictions (including some groups divided by home-country politics or by theological debate) also function. Most now collaborate, but a single, unified American Orthodox church remains a distant goal.

For most Orthodox, the decades after World War II were marked by relative ecclesiastical peace. The American churches did not, however, live beyond the reach of events abroad. The rise of Communist regimes in Yugoslavia, Romania, and Bulgaria produced the same schisms over relations with Communist-controlled home churches that still crippled the Russians.

But despite these difficulties, Orthodox Americans began to move more comfortably in this culture. Their churches began to face important issues of acculturation, epitomized by the debate over how much English to use in worship. Across ethnic boundaries, several other "American" elements crept into Orthodox worship, including choral singing accompanied by organs, the use of fixed pews in churches, and the institutionalization of lay authority in parish councils.

The passage into American culture also sparked two distinct and occasionally conflicting movements within Orthodoxy. The first was the assertion of an Orthodox presence in American society, usually expressed though participation in the ECUMENICAL MOVEMENT. The second was the attempt to develop authentic Orthodox critiques of American and western society.

Driven by the desire to present Orthodoxy outside its accustomed cultural settings, these efforts stimulated a powerful theological revival in the diaspora. Scholars also struggled to translate the vast corpus of foundational Orthodox theological, liturgical, and spiritual texts needed by English-speaking believers and others interested in the faith.

The reassertion of traditional Orthodox themes has been the hallmark of this revival. The tendency is visible in theology, in worship, and even in church architecture. In theology, it took the shape of what the Russian-American theologian George Florovsky called the patristic revival. First articulated in the 1930s, it calls for the correction of "false developments" (mostly adaptations from the Protestant and Catholic West) that took place in the Greek church during the Ottoman period and in the Russian church after 1800.

Florovsky and other Orthodox thinkers in the West complained about the ecclesiastical ossification of the Orthodox world and of the tendency of Orthodox theologians to appropriate Catholic arguments to combat Protestants and Protestant arguments to oppose Catholics. Proponents of the movement argued that intensive study of theological and liturgical sources from the patristic and Byzantine periods would provide the most authentic guide for Orthodox renewal. An outpouring of groundbreaking historical studies, translations of source texts, and theological reflections followed.

Although most Orthodox leaders support cautious participation in the WORLD COUNCIL OF CHURCHES and other ecumenical activities, the Orthodox stance toward ecumenism is internally controversial. Conservatives, who harbor profound reservations about ecumenism, oppose concessions to modern scholarly methods, and bitterly condemn modifications in long-standing Orthodox norms (such as the decision taken by some national churches during the 1920s to adopt the Gregorian calendar).

The tendency to reemphasize tradition is also evident in a broad movement to renew sacramental practices. Many jurisdictions now encourage members to receive the eucharist frequently, rather than several times a year, as had gradually become customary. Liturgical reformers, most notably the Russian-American theologian Alexander SCHMEMANN, have not advocated the alteration of the liturgy, but rather criticized the accretion of pious customs that distract attention from the main themes of the liturgy.

The revival of traditional forms has also influenced church architecture, iconography, and even the design of vestments. Pioneering American communities often purchased and renovated structures built by others. While some obtained magnificent churches, most took over buildings poorly suited for Orthodox use. So, after World War II it became increasingly common for parishes to construct new structures, often in styles that blended architectural modernism with elements of traditional Orthodox design, such as "onion domes." This trend reached its pinnacle in Frank Lloyd Wright's Annunciation Greek Orthodox Church in Milwaukee, a circular structure built in the early 1960s.

However, a countertrend surfaced during the same period. Across jurisdictional lines, communities recreated, often scrupulously, traditional Orthodox architecture. Two churches built in the early 1960s proved to be powerful models: the OCA's St. Nicholas Cathedral in Washington, D.C., which replicates a church in the Russian city of Vladimir, and the chapel at the Greek Orthodox seminary outside Boston, which is modeled on surviving Byzantine churches in Greece.

Traditionalism is even more strongly marked in recent iconography, where there has been a decisive turn away from the Italianate style of the 19th and early 20th centuries. The neo-Byzantine style of the Greek iconographer Photios Kontoglou has been particularly influential. Among the Slavs, the style of Andrei Rublev and other pre-17th century Russian iconographers has been revived.

Current membership estimates are not highly reliable, but the major Orthodox jurisdictions claimed about four million members in 1990. The overwhelming majority are concentrated in three jurisdictions: the Greek archdiocese with about two million members; the OCA with about one million; and the Antiochian archdiocese with 250,000. About a dozen smaller jurisdictions claim about 700,000 members. There are more than 1,800 Orthodox parishes in North America.

AHW

Bibliography: John Meyendorff, *The Orthodox Church,* (Crestwood, N.Y.: St. Vladimir's Seminary Press, 1981); Alexander Schmemann, tr. Lydia W. Kesich, *The Historical Road of Eastern Orthodox* (Crestwood, N.Y.: St. Vladimir's Seminary Press, 1977); Timothy Ware, *The Orthodox Church* (New York: Penguin Books, 1984).

Orthodox Church in America The Orthodox Church in America (OCA) traces its origin to a mission established on Kodiak Island in Alaska in 1793 by eight Russian monks. The mission flourished during the early 19th century, especially under the charismatic priest John Veniaminov, who in 1840 became the first Orthodox bishop to serve in the Americas.

The Russian church neglected the mission after the sale of Alaska in 1866, but its interest was rekindled in the 1880s, when Orthodox and Eastern Rite Catholic immigrants began flooding into North America. To serve this booming population, the diocese shifted its seat from Sitka, Alaska to San Francisco in 1872, and then to New York in 1905.

Under a series of vigorous bishops, including Tikhon BELAVIN, the diocese sought to persuade Eastern Rite Catholics to return to Orthodoxy, and eventually more than 200 parishes did so.

Incorporated in 1897 as the Russian Orthodox Greek Catholic Church of America, the diocese remained a part of the Church of Russia. It aimed, however, to embrace members of all Orthodox churches. By 1910 it included groups of Arabs, Serbs, and Bulgarians, as well as its chief constituency of Slavs and Native Americans.

This pan-Orthodox structure disintegrated after the Russian revolutions of 1917, when subsidies were terminated and the chief source of clergy cut off. Extreme privation, compounded by intense political conflict, racked the Russian church during the 1920s and 1930s.

During this period, the Russian Orthodox split into three factions whose relations were extremely complex. A small group preserved ties with the church in the Soviet Union. Others leaned towards the Russian Orthodox Church Abroad, based in Yugoslavia. Most, however, steered a middle course, joining together in the so-called Russian Metropolia. For much of the period, the Metropolia was affiliated with the synod in exile, but tended to assert its ecclesiastical autonomy, despite questions about the canonical validity of that arrangement.

After World War II the Metropolia broke with both other groups and entered a long period of growth in which it moved away from its Slav and immigrant roots. The church spent much of the 1950s and 1960s evaluating its role in American society and in world Orthodoxy.

Spurred by the work of a talented generation of theologians, including George Florovsky, Alexander SCHMEMANN, and John Meyendorff, the Metropolia played an active role in the ECUMENICAL MOVEMENT and simultaneously campaigned for the creation of a single, independent Orthodox church in America. Turning initially to the Ecumenical Patriarchate in Constantinople and then to the Church of Russia, the Metropolia won its independence on April 10, 1970, when the Moscow patriarchate granted autocephally, or ecclesiastical independence, to the newly renamed Orthodox Church in America.

The OCA achieved a multi-ethnic character during the 1960s and 1970s, as smaller jurisdictions of Romanians, Albanians, and Bulgarians affiliated with its synod of bishops. It also collaborated closely with the Serb and Syrian Orthodox jurisdictions, particularly in the education of clergy at St. Vladimir's Seminary in New York.

The OCA sought to embody a new and indigenous American form of Orthodoxy, chiefly by promoting the use of English in worship and openly seeking converts. It established missions in areas of the United States with small populations of Orthodox ethnic groups, and by the 1980s, a large portion of its clergy and membership was composed of converts.

The OCA also renewed its Alaskan roots, where nearly half of the indigenous population still profess Orthodoxy. St. Herman's Pastoral School opened there in 1973 to train indigenous clergy and lay leaders and to coordinate translations.

The church claims one million members in about 520 parishes in the United States and Canada. It also supervises parishes in Mexico, South America, and Australia.

AHW

Bibliography: Constance J. Tarasar, ed., *Orthodox America, 1794–1976: Development of the Orthodox Church in America* (Syosset, N.Y.: Orthodox Church in America, 1975).

Orthodox Judaism   It is symptomatic of the state of American religion that what is simply Judaism in the rest of the world is Orthodox Judaism in the United States, one of the three denominations or branches of Judaism. Orthodoxy, the oldest form of Judaism in the country by 200 years, has been the least studied. Scholars often have pronounced its death, but it has sprung back to life with renewed vigor and strength.

Simply put, Orthodox Judaism is the branch of Judaism that maintains the Jewish laws, Halachah, and the traditional forms of religious ex-

The interior of a synagogue in Colchester, Connecticut in 1940 after a small weekly service. (Library of Congress)

pression. These laws are drawn from the Torah; the commentaries on the Torah, the Mishna; and commentaries on the commentaries, the Gemara. Together these comprise the Talmud, the authoritative text for Judaism. The very complexity and length of the Talmud led to attempts during the Middle Ages to codify these laws. One of the most important of these was Rabbi Moses ben Maimon's (Maimonides, 1135–1204) Code formally known as the Mishneh Torah and popularly as the Yad Ha-Hazaka ("The Mighty Hand"). Designed as a definitive statement of the Jewish religion, it also includes a list of the 613 *mitzvot* (commandments or directives) imposed upon the observant Jew.

This book, steeped in the philosophical concerns of 12th century Sephardic (Spanish) Jewry, was inaccessible to the majority of the Jewish people. In order to make the law more easily understood, Rabbi Joseph Caro (1488–1575) undertook a more direct outline of the laws in the 16th century. This codification, the Shulhan Aruch (1564–1565), became the basis for determining the life of an observant Jew. Its importance cannot be overestimated. Orthodoxy is inherently a religion of practice, of behaviors. The religious laws guide every element of a

Jew's life from awaking in the morning to going to bed at night. Even sexuality is regulated. For example, it is forbidden for a male to sleep with his wife during menstruation.

The arrival of several families of Dutch Jews in New Amsterdam in 1654 marks the beginning of Orthodoxy in North America. The religion of these settlers, descendants of Jews expelled from Spain (1492) and Portugal (1496), was different from that of the Central and Eastern European Jews who arrived two centuries later. These Sephardic Jews followed a different ritual from that of Eastern European Jews, maintained a decorousness in worship, and came from a region where, until the 1490s, they had known (relative) comfort and security under both Muslim and Christian rulers. They were more outward-looking and more willing to integrate into the wider society and did so with evident ease. During the time of the American Revolution, a Hessian soldier serving in Newport, Rhode Island (the second Jewish community in the United States) could write, the Jews "are not distinguishable by their beards and attire . . . while their women wear the same French finery as the other faiths. . . ."

While these first settlers and their descendants would dominate America's Jewish community until the 1820s, there were early conflicts between them and Ashkenazic (Central and Eastern European) Jews. As early as 1738 a minister in Savannah, Georgia remarked on the conflict between the Spanish and German Jews there. "They want to build a synagogue, but cannot come to terms. The Spanish and Portuguese Jews are not so strict as far as eating is concerned. They eat, for instance, the beef that comes from the warehouse. The German Jews, on the other hand, would rather starve than eat any meat they do not slaughter themselves."

The arrival of increasing numbers of these Ashkenazic Jews altered the character of American Judaism. Although many were drawn into the orbit of Reform Judaism, itself a German product, large numbers were strictly Orthodox in behavior. This was especially true of those

Jews from Poland, Romania, Lithuania, and Russia who arrived by the hundred thousands between 1880 and 1924. These new arrivals, whose entire existence had been structured by the tight-knit Jewish communities of the region, the *shtetls*, overwhelmed the older communities. While certain congregations retained their ancient Sephardic rites, for example Shearith Israel in New York, Orthodoxy in the United States became synonymous with Eastern European Jewry.

Organization is both unnecessary and imperative within Orthodox Judaism. Although contradictory, this statement is nonetheless true. For worship to occur, all that is required is the presence of 10 adult Jewish males, a *minyan*—no minister, no building, no externals are needed. But the requirement of 10 members means that a community must exist, a community that can create all the necessary elements of Orthodox life. These elements include: a *shehitah*, a ritual slaughterer (before the days of refrigeration); a *mikveh*, a pool for ritual purification; and a cemetery. Some form of religious education is also required, so that the children can be raised in the knowledge of the faith. Theoretically it is possible for such a community to be self-contained with no organizational connections with other communities. In reality this is quite difficult. The complexities that emerge in ritual and dietary laws often require outside sources of adjudication and some manner of determining authority. Patterns of religious training link individuals and communities with particular schools of thought and practice. Additionally, in the Old World, Jews, despite their persecuted and minority position, were a distinctive community, and most countries recognized an individual or group of individuals as authoritative for the community. Faith, practice, and authority served to link Jewish communities together.

Such a situation did not obtain in the United States. The government was forbidden to dictate to any religious community, and the social makeup of the country imposed weak penalties on deviance. To maintain the structures of Orthodoxy meant that the Orthodox had to choose to do so; the community ceased to be a given and became a creation.

The organizations necessary for an Orthodox religious life were formed early. Several congregations following the Sephardic rite emerged in the colonial towns. The first Ashkenazic rite synagogue was formed in Easton, Pennsylvania in 1761, followed in 1802 by Rodeph Shalom in Philadelphia, and in 1825 by B'nai Jeshurun in New York. As early as 1731 Shearith Israel formed the first religious school. All this activity took place without benefit of officially sanctioned rabbis. Not until 1840 did the first Orthodox rabbi come to serve a congregation in the United States when Abraham Rice arrived from Germany to take the a pulpit in Baltimore. There he locked horns with the radical reformer David EINHORN, and his own less-than-observant flock. Their violations of the religious laws grieved Rice greatly, and he despaired of "whether a Jew may live in a land such as this."

There was much reason for that despair. The period between 1840 and 1880 was a time of change. Jews who rejected the *Halachic* prescriptions as outdated, unnecessary, and superstitious had the upper hand. These years saw the rise and dominance of REFORM JUDAISM in America, and the more traditionally oriented found themselves in retreat.

The wave of Jewish immigration that swept the United States from 1880 to 1924 changed this. During that time 2.5 million Jews came to America, nearly all of them from Eastern Europe. Although the majority did not continue the religious traditions of Europe upon arriving, large numbers did, breathing new life into a weakened Orthodoxy. Most of these immigrants organized their religious life around small *shuls*, as the Yiddish-speaking Jews called their synagogues. These *shuls* generally were organized on patterns of similarity, a shared region of birth—the *Rumanische* (Romanian) *shul*—or occupation—the India rubber *shul*, so-called because most of its members peddled suspenders.

This rapid growth caused tremendous chaos and attempts were made to impose some order. As early as 1845, Isaac LEESER, cantor of Mikveh Israel in Philadelphia, had urged the appointment of a chief rabbi but with no success. By the mid-1880s a central authority seemed so necessary in New York, with nearly 120,000 Orthodox families, 130 synagogues, and only three or four rabbis, that 15 congregations banded together into the Association of American Orthodox Hebrew Congregations. Their goal was to bring the distinguished Vilna rabbi, Jacob Joseph, to the United States as chief rabbi, by offering a salary of $2,500 a year to be raised from certificates on kosher food, licensing of slaughterers, and *gittim* (the certificates of divorce). The result was a fiasco. Other congregations appointed their own chief rabbi; housewives and butchers complained about rises in prices; the secular and Reform Jews mocked the undertaking. Rabbi Joseph attempted to ignore the controversy and proceed with his work, with little success. Ruined in spirit and health, he died in 1902, penniless. Similar attempts were made in other communities, including Baltimore (1908–1910), Los Angeles (1919–1920), and Albany, New York (1918–1921), but with little positive result. There was no way to impose order on such a diverse community.

There were some achievements, however, notably the creation of a school to train rabbis for Orthodox congregations—Rabbi Isaac Elchanan Theological Seminary. Founded in 1897 the school struggled along for two decades. Even its recognition by the Union of Orthodox Rabbis (Augudat ha-Rabbanim) as the only acceptable school of higher learning in America helped little. A merger with Etz Chaim Academy in 1915 and the appointment of a new president who saw the school as both Orthodox and American led to a period of phenomenal growth. Problems remained, however. The addition of secular education in 1928 alienated the ultra-Orthodox. Their antagonism to the secular world led to the creation of another rabbinical union, the Rabbinical Council of America, in 1935, an outgrowth of the seminary's alumni association. Joined in 1942 by graduates of Hebrew Theological College founded in 1921, the Rabbinical Council of America became the dominant rabbinical organization in America, representing what is known as "modern Orthodoxy."

The Orthodox synagogues themselves found their voice in the Union of Orthodox Jewish Congregations. Founded in 1898, the Union originally included men like Henry Pereira MENDES and Cyrus ADLER. Too much separated these men and their congregations from the Eastern Europeans, and following the death of Mendes, many left to found what is known as CONSERVATIVE JUDAISM.

The Union affirmed its belief in the divine revelation of the Bible and the Jewish law and its commitment to them. It took a swipe at Reform by declaring that the Jews were a people as well as a religion and that they looked forward to the restoration of their homeland. Although the Union grew slowly, and suffered a major setback with the founding of the United Synagogue of America (see UNITED SYNAGOGUE OF CONSERVATIVE JUDAISM) by 1980 the Union included 1,000 congregations and represented most of America's one million Orthodox Jews.

While commitment to the totality of Jewish law would seem to insure unity among the Orthodox, such has not been the case. Divisions that existed in Europe persisted in the United States. New divisions emerged as well. Despite the numerous divisions, Orthodox in the United States can be grouped into three broad categories, "modern Orthodox," "traditionalists," and "sectarians" or "ultratraditionalists."

The modern Orthodox are by far the largest group, and are predominant within the Union of Orthodox Jewish Congregations and the Rabbinic Council of America. These Orthodox Jews follow Jewish law but are neither hostile to secular education nor indifferent to the wider social world. Traditions not specifically Halachic have been jettisoned, and certain Halachic demands have been modified. Their rabbis use

English in their sermons, women probably do not wear head-coverings outside the synagogue, and some even dispense with sex-segregated seating in the synagogue. These modern Orthodox Jews are acculturated, predominantly middle-class Americans who have made peace both with their tradition and with their society.

The traditionalists, on the other hand, maintain a rigid commitment to religious ritual and law. They also embrace secular education, and are significantly represented in the natural and physical sciences. In fact the most truly traditionalist organization is the Association of Orthodox Jewish Scientists. This group is interesting in that embrace of secular education has made their traditionalism possible. While the socioeconomic cost of a rigid Orthodoxy was too high for earlier generations, the economic stability of this group makes their uncompromising attendance to religious law feasible.

The ultra-traditionalists or sectarians show a different face of Orthodoxy. Many did not arrive in the United States until the Nazi era, and they are closest to the European scene, both in terms of heritage and lineage. Comprised of the various Hasidic (see HASIDISM) groups as well as non-Hasids affiliated with traditional-style yeshivas (religious schools), these Orthodox Jews try to retain traditional Eastern European folkways, both religious and otherwise. They cluster together, look with suspicion on other Orthodox groups, and especially the non-Orthodox and non-Jewish world. They eschew much of contemporary society, including television. The Hasids owe their allegiance to their various *rebbes,* the religio-social leaders of the Hasidic movements. Similarly, the lives of the non-Hasidic sectarians center on traditional right-wing yeshivas and the *Gidolim,* the "Torah leaders," who head those institutions. Most characteristic of these ultratraditionalists is their refusal to exercise independent thought on religious, social, or political issues. On questions of importance the final decision rests with the religious leaders. While it might be expected that these groups would follow the traditional pattern and

make greater concessions to the wider world as they become more Americanized, developments in the United States since the 1960s suggest that this pattern may not hold. The ultratraditionalists show a vitality that suggests not only a maintenance of their position but also the possibility of expansion.

Orthodox Judaism in the United States, since the 1960s, has shown a remarkable vibrancy and growth, especially among the more ultratraditionalist elements. This growth has come both from the relatively high birth-rate and their appeal to many alienated secular Jewish youth. This vibrancy has brought about a level of self-confidence and aggressiveness traditionally lacking among Orthodox Jews in the United States. The result has been a greater willingness to criticize and attack the less observant members of the Reform and Conservative movements, and to lay claim to being the only true form of Jewish religious expression. Whether this movement can sustain itself is unclear. Certain elements suggest it can. Pushed from the right, organizations such as the Rabbinic Council of America and the Union of Orthodox Congregations have become increasingly conservative in their views.

The institutional framework of Orthodoxy, especially the elementary schools, seems to be acculturating the younger generation into the movement, and, as the traditionalists illustrate, there seem to be fewer economic reasons for deserting Orthodox practice. Finally, there are growing connections with Orthodoxy around the world, especially in Israel. This universal connection, particularly the position of the chief rabbi of Israel, may serve to close the biggest gap in the Orthodox system—the absence of a final arbiter of Orthodoxy.

There are countervailing forces as well. The appeals of American society make it difficult to retain the loyalty of the second and third generations. As the ultratraditionalists move further from their European heritage and the leaders born in Europe are replaced by the American born, adaptations to the American situation could take place. Finally, Orthodoxy, especially the ultratraditional, finds itself at a point of decision. It must decide whether to continue its more outward-looking, aggressive, proselytizing stance, or its exclusive insularity designed to protect it from contamination.

Whichever direction it takes, Orthodox Judaism has developed impressive strength, with about one million adherents in 1990. This fact alone means that Orthodox Judaism will play a greater role in American Judaism and American religion than it has in the past.

EQ

Bibliography: Murray Herbert Danzger, *Returning to Tradition: The Contemporary Revival of Orthodox Judaism* (New Haven: Yale University Press, 1989); Nathan Glazer, *American Judaism*, 2nd ed. rev. (Chicago: University of Chicago Press, 1972); William B. Helmreich, *The World of the Yeshiva: An Intimate Portrait of Orthodox Jewry* (New York: Free Press, 1982); Arthur Hertzberg, *The Jews in America, Four Centuries of an Uneasy Encounter: A History* (New York: Simon & Schuster, 1989); Jacob Neusner, ed., *Sectors of American Judaism: Reform, Orthodoxy, Conservatism, and Reconstructionism* (New York: KTAV, 1975); Howard M. Sachar, *A History of the Jews in America* (New York: Knopf, 1992).

Orthodox Presbyterian Church   See
PRESBYTERIANISM.

Owen, Robert Dale (1801–1877)

Often overshadowed in life by the larger reputation of his father, Robert Dale Owen was an enthusiastic antebellum reformer dedicated to a variety of causes including free thought, state-sponsored education, women's rights, and SPIRITUALISM. His father, Robert Owen (1771–1858), was a pioneer socialist and inspirer of communitarian experiments in both Britain and the United States. The elder Owen, born in Wales, became a cotton textile manufacturer in Manchester, England. As a young man Robert Dale enjoyed the benefits of his father's financial prosperity. He was educated by private tutors and later completed his education at the elite and socially conscious Fellenberg School in Switzerland.

In 1825 Owen accompanied his father to New Harmony, Indiana, a property recently purchased from the Rappites, where they put into practice his father's perfectionist (see PERFECTIONISM) and socialist theories. Robert Dale edited the community's newspaper, the *New Harmony Gazette*. Increasingly, he saw inequality of education as the real cause of poverty, and his later work as a journalist, politician, and advocate of workers' rights reflected his sense that the poor needed a good state-supported school system. In 1827 he met Frances Wright, a female British socialist reformer, and the two embarked on a radical critique of traditional Christianity, the sectarian school system, and the oppression of women.

Greatly influenced by perfectionist ideas of the antebellum era, but equally formed by his own upper-class background, Owen looked to proper education as the solution to the problems of the working classes. He called for state intervention in public schooling, and recommended that all children, but particularly those in the poor areas of cities, be moved from their homes at age two into government-run boarding schools, where they could learn and develop unhindered by the debilitating effects of the urban environment. He also promoted the traditionally Protestant virtues of hard work, thrift, and temperance, although he deplored the religious self-righteousness of evangelical reformers who espoused the same causes. In 1830 he authored *Moral Physiology*, a text that at once advocated birth control and attacked the sexual license of the lower classes.

Although he condemned most of the religious institutions and authorities of his day, Owen also had an intense interest in spirituality. In 1856, while traveling in Italy, he witnessed his first demonstration of "animal magnetism," a popular form of hypnosis. In 1860 he published *Footfalls on the Boundary*, a defense of the spiritualist movement then sweeping the country, and he followed with *The Debatable Land Be-*

tween This World and the Next, a further analysis of the spiritualist inquiry into the afterlife. Like many antebellum "seekers," Owen yearned for religious certainty yet rejected the traditional forms that such certainty had taken. More moderate in his socialism than his father, Owen freely quoted from the Bible and showed a measured respect for religion. But he is perhaps best remembered as a tireless promoter of social reform who kept his distance from the most popular religious reform movements of his day, instead seeking his own path.

LMK

Bibliography: Richard William Leopold, *Robert Dale Owen: A Biography* (Cambridge: Harvard University Press, 1940); Anne Taylor, *Visions of Harmony* (New York: Oxford University Press, 1987).

Oxford Movement   See ANGLO-CATHOLICISM.

P

Pacifism See PEACE REFORM.

Paganism See NEO-PAGANISM.

Paine, Thomas (1737–1809)

Of modest English origins, Thomas Paine gained an international audience as one of the strongest champions of revolution and the power of reason in the 18th century. He played a prominent role in the AMERICAN REVOLUTION, and wrote several widely read rationalist attacks on Christianity.

Paine was born at Thetford in Suffolk on January 29, 1737; his father, Joseph, was a farmer and corset-maker and came from a Quaker family. His mother, Frances Cocke, was a member of the Church of England. The Quaker tradition had a lasting impact on Paine's life, making him a lifelong opponent of slavery and supporter of humane treatment of animals (See FRIENDS, THE RELIGIOUS SOCIETY OF). While he lacked formal education, he later said the Quaker influence provided him "an exceeding good moral education and a tolerable stock of useful learning."

For many years Paine struggled to make ends meet. Upon the recommendation of Benjamin Franklin, he immigrated, reaching Philadelphia in December 1774. Franklin found him employment as the editor of a small paper. He completed his first American work, *Common Sense,* in the fall of 1775. Influenced by English dissenters, he came to play a prominent role during the revolution, serving in the army, as a secretary to Congress, and on a diplomatic mission to France in 1781. In addition, his reputation grew with the spread of his pamphlets, collectively entitled *The American Crisis,* sixteen of which were written during the course of the war.

With the war's end Paine again traveled to Europe, arriving in France at the outbreak of the revolution in 1789. Greeted as a hero, he was presented by Lafayette with the keys to the Bastille as a present for George Washington. For the next few years he moved between France and England, at which time he wrote the first half of *The Rights of Man,* his famous defense of the French Revolution. With English publication of the second half of that work in 1792, the government sought his arrest for sedition and he fled to Paris, where he held French citizenship and a position in the National Convention. However Paine also made many enemies in France by denouncing plans to execute Louis XVI. He spent a year in French prison, which interrupted his writing of *The Age of Reason,* his great plea for religious rationalism. Returning to America in 1802, Paine spent his last years still plagued with controversy and financial difficulties. He was denied the vote in 1806 by enemies in the New York legislature. He died in New Rochelle, New York on June 8, 1809.

Paine sought an end to the rule of oligarchs both domestic and foreign, and his writings appealed to a broad spectrum of Americans. He urged extending the franchise to all "freemen," far beyond the bounds set by colonial elites. Paine's witness of the Terror during the French Revolution had convinced him that modern democratic government depended upon a rational religious basis, which he found in Deism (see ENLIGHTENMENT, THE). In *The Age of Reason* he attacked a number of Christian doctrines and the revelatory stature of the Bible, pointing out inconsistencies that indicated human authorship. Paine argued for global human benevolence, stemming from the conviction that nature itself was a sure guide to the divine intention. He looked forward to an age in which humanity would abandon superstition and conflict, forming a kind of international republic. Hostility greeted the book in England, where it was portrayed as destroying the foundations of government. In America, however, thousands of copies sold, contributing to the expansion of

Deism well beyond the confines of elite society. Even though the supernatural theology guiding the revivals that spread across America in the early 19th century eclipsed Paine's appeal to rational religion, his commitment to equality continued to influence popular revivalists. In subsequent years Paine has become a hero of American free thinkers (see ATHEISM AND FREE THOUGHT).

MG

Bibliography: Gregory Claeys, *Thomas Paine: Social and Political Thought* (Boston: Unwin/Hyman, 1989); Thomas Paine, *The Thomas Paine Reader* (New York: Penguin, 1987).

Palmer, Phoebe Worrall (1807–1874)

Phoebe Palmer was a mid-19th century lay Methodist evangelist and one of the early leaders of the HOLINESS MOVEMENT in America. She preached a religious doctrine known as "entire SANCTIFICATION" that was based upon the teachings of Methodist founder John Wesley. Palmer believed that a Christian could attain spiritual perfection if she simply followed biblical commandments and consecrated herself wholly to God.

Phoebe Worrall was born in New York City on December 18, 1807. At age 19 she married Walter C. Palmer, a New York physician. In 1835, her sister Sarah Worrall Lankford began a series of weekly prayer meetings for Methodist women in her home. These meetings, called the "Tuesday Meeting for the Promotion of Holiness," soon became a center for the emerging Holiness movement. The gatherings featured Bible reading, prayer, and personal testimonies by the participants. Palmer took over the direction of this group after she experienced sanctification on July 26, 1837, a moment she later called "the day of days." Eventually, the Tuesday Meetings were opened to men as well as to women, and they attracted leaders from every Protestant denomination.

Palmer wrote 10 books in all. Between 1862 and 1874 she edited the *Guide to Holiness,* a magazine that had 30,000 subscribers at the

height of its popularity. Palmer's first and undoubtedly most important book was *The Way of Holiness,* published in 1843. In her view, holiness was immediately available to the believer through faith in Jesus Christ. Conversion was the first blessing of God's grace. Complete consecration occurred next, when a believer surrendered everything to God and laid her soul upon the "altar" of Christ. Although some criticized the terminology Palmer employed, the simplicity of the process she described won many disciples. She stressed the importance of trusting in God's pledge to honor promises made in the Bible and awaken faith.

Palmer's commitment to spiritual perfection impelled her as well into social reform programs. While she always sought the promotion of holiness as her principal aim, Palmer also advanced the public role of women in American religious life. Her most impressive work was in the Five Points district of New York, the city's worst slum. She served on the board of the Ladies' Home Missionary Society of the Methodist Episcopal Church. Through that agency, she helped establish a mission house, which contained a chapel, school, baths, and rent-free apartments, in 1850. However, despite defending the right of women to participate fully in church work and despite demonstrating great individual compassion for the poor, Palmer remained neutral on the two most controversial social issues of her day: feminism and slavery.

After 1850 both Palmers became increasing involved in camp meetings and religious revivals. They were active participants in the so-called Prayer Meeting Revival, the great spiritual awakening that swept through northern cities in 1857 and 1858. Palmer's Tuesday Meetings also proved increasingly popular after the Civil War. Following Phoebe's death, her sister Sarah (who later married Walter Palmer) again assumed leadership of the gatherings, and by 1886, 200 were in operation across the United States.

In poor health when she composed *The Way of Holiness,* Palmer believed that her life had been spared to be of greater service to God. She died in New York City on November 2, 1874.

GHS, Jr.

Bibliography: Charles Edward White, *The Beauty of Holiness: Phoebe Palmer as Theologian, Revivalist, Feminist, and Humanitarian* (Grand Rapids, Mich.: F. Asbury Press, 1986).

Parham, Charles Fox (1873–1929)

Charles F. Parham was the founder of modern American PENTECOSTALISM, the spiritual phenomenon that one historian has called "*the* popular religious movement" of the 20th century. Following the outbreak of speaking in tongues at his Bible institute in Topeka, Kansas on New Year's Day in 1901, Parham pronounced that charismatic gift to be the definitive evidence of a person's having been baptized in the Holy Spirit.

Parham was born at Muscatine, Iowa, a frontier farming community, on June 4, 1873. He experienced a religious conversion when he was 13 years old and soon afterwards became active in the Methodist church. He entered Southwest Kansas College in 1890 to study for the Methodist ministry. Although poor health and financial difficulties forced Parham's withdrawal from the college before graduation, he was licensed as a Methodist preacher in 1893. Two years later, he resigned and became an independent Holiness (see HOLINESS MOVEMENT) preacher instead. In poor health throughout much of his life, Parham believed he had been miraculously cured of illness, and his early teaching as a consequence emphasized the possibility of divine healing.

In 1900 Parham founded the Bethel Bible School in Topeka in order to pursue his interest in Spirit baptism. Parham concluded that, according to the New Testament Book of Acts, baptism in the Holy Spirit, the work of divine grace that follows a person's conversion, was distinguished by the ability to speak in tongues. He also insisted that tongues were actual foreign languages bestowed on believers to evangelize

people in foreign lands. This, however, became only a minority opinion among American Pentecostals. Most Pentecostals believed that speaking in tongues (or glossolalia) was an unintelligible form of speech, a divine language known only to God.

On January 1, 1901 Parham believed that the miracle for which he and his followers had prayed took place. "Fire fell" from heaven, he claimed, and a student, Agnes N. Ozman, began to speak in tongues. In the following months, his Bible school gained attention as others including Parham himself experienced that gift. The "Apostolic Faith Missions" he organized soon spread, and about 25,000 adherents espoused Pentecostalism. Parham opened a Bible institute in Houston, Texas, where itinerant preacher William J. Seymour attended for a few weeks in the fall of 1905. Seymour was to gain Pentecostalism further distinction by carrying the movement to an African-American Holiness mission in Los Angeles, site of the famed AZUSA STREET REVIVAL of 1906.

Parham soon lost control over the movement he launched. Charges of sexual misconduct led in 1907 to the repudiation of his ministry. Accused of homosexuality, he was able to retain leadership over just a handful of Apostolic Faith churches. He served in relative obscurity for the next 20 years as a pastor in Baxter Springs, Kansas. After he toured the Holy Land in late 1927, Parham's health rapidly declined. He died at Baxter Springs on January 29, 1929.

GHS, Jr.

Bibliography: James R. Goff, Jr., *Fields White unto Harvest: Charles F. Parham and the Missionary Origins of Pentecostalism* (Fayetteville: University of Arkansas Press, 1988).

Parker, Theodore (1810–1860)

Unitarian minister, social reformer, and one of the most important figures in the transcendentalist (see TRANSCENDENTALISM) movement of the mid-19th century. Parker's humanistic faith, while controversial among American Unitarians in his day, eventually won recognition as an

Theodore Parker, an innovative antebellum theologian who spoke for the humanist wing of the Unitarian movements.

essential characteristic of his denomination by the end of the century.

Parker was born in Lexington, Massachusetts on August 24, 1810. Admitted to Harvard College, he was too poor to attend classes. He engaged in private study instead and passed the examinations for his degree in 1831. After teaching school for two years, he enrolled at Harvard Divinity School. Following his graduation in 1836, he accepted a pastorate at the Unitarian church in nearby West Roxbury.

Parker almost immediately became engaged in an acrimonious public debate with other Unitarian ministers over the nature of the Christian faith. He had been heavily influenced both by the German idealistic philosophy exemplified by Georg W. F. Hegel and by the emerging "higher criticism" of the Bible (see BIBLICAL INTERPRETATION). As he argued in May 1841, when he preached at the ordination of Charles Shackford at the South Boston Church, everything that is historically rooted within Christianity is imperfect. Parker's sermon, later published as *The Transient and Permanent in Christianity,* attempted to distill the great ethical truths of the Christian religion from its mere dross. Christianity, he said, was not grounded on miracles, on any special revelation, on the deity of Christ, or even on the actual existence of the historical Jesus. Rather, true and enduring faith came only from a person's innate intuition and perceptions of the divine.

The commotion that followed Parker's sermon led to ostracism by his fellow ministers and their refusal to exchange pulpits with him. Undeterred, he continued to argue his views, and in 1845 he accepted the invitation of a group of progressive Unitarians to preach in Boston's Melodeon Theatre. This position was soon regularized through the formation of the Twenty-Eighth Congregational Society, and in 1852 Parker's congregation moved into the large Music Hall in Boston. Over the next decade, he produced a vast corpus of essays, lectures, and sermons articulating his beliefs. It became increasingly clear, however, that Parker and the "Christian" Unitarians were irrevocably at odds over the issue of biblical authority. In 1853 the executive committee of the American Unitarian Association officially condemned Parker's opinions and declared its own belief in "the Divine origin . . . of the religion of Jesus Christ."

Not only was Parker a fervent theological innovator, he was also passionately committed to social reform, especially the emerging antislavery movement. He thought slavery was a crime against nature, and calling resistance a religious duty sanctioned by a higher, divine law, he excoriated the Fugitive Slave Law of 1850 and later backed John Brown's insurrectionary activities in the South. Parker may well have worn himself out by his ceaseless reformist activities. He suffered a hemorrhage of the lungs in 1859 and was forced to seek recovery in Italy.

Despite a period of recuperation, Parker died in Florence, Italy on May 10, 1860. He was still so unpopular at the time of his death that the alumni of Harvard Divinity School, when learning of his impending demise, refused to pass a motion conveying their sympathy.

GHS, Jr.

Bibliography: Henry Steele Commager, *Theodore Parker, Yankee Crusader* (Boston: Little, Brown, 1936).

peace reform   From the time of the Puritan migrations to the present, Americans have seen themselves as a people of peace, committed to establishing a world in which nations need not resort to armed conflict in order to solve their differences. However, since government most directly shapes the policies by which peace has been pursued, political leaders often tend to view peace as merely one available option by which to advance the national interest. In contrast to government's strategic interest in peace, and often in tension or conflict with it, a small but influential number of American citizens have pursued peace on their own, creating voluntary societies and professional organizations, forming informal networks, marshalling the resources of media, scholarship, and religious institutions, and organizing protest and resistance movements when their concerns seemed unheeded by those in official circles.

American peace activists have drawn on basically two general sources for their intellectual foundations: religious traditions and international law, sources which remain distinct in theory if not always in fact. While many religious groups in America have viewed peace as an important element of their religious vision, most Christian denominations have also found religious rationales for supporting war, and thus been able to accommodate their views to the state's use of violence. By contrast, some groups as a matter of principle have adopted pacifism, renouncing the use of violence in any form. Beginning in the COLONIAL PERIOD, several groups brought a pacifist ethic of nonresistance to violence into Pennsylvania (see RELIGIOUS SOCIETY OF FRIENDS, THE; WOOLMAN, JOHN; PENN, WILLIAM; MENNONITES; MORAVIANS; CHURCH OF THE BRETHREN). While Friends, or Quakers, sought to create a social order based on pacifist principles, other sectarian groups, basing their nonviolence on a reading of the biblical ethic of Jesus, saw their own nonviolent commitment upheld best by voluntary isolation from the state, consequently giving Penn little support in his efforts to create a peaceful social order. Sectarian pacifists have remained small in number, but their communities have continued to provide a "witness" to nonviolence throughout American history, even though often faced with legal consequences and social derision of their refusal to bear arms.

In addition to the religious commitment, and sometimes strategically in complement to it, other Americans have based their commitment to peace on ideas of international law developed during the ENLIGHTENMENT. Internationalists, reflecting the millennial faith in progress common in American culture, have expected a change in moral outlook to make war obsolete. While religious pacifists tend to make pacifism a consequence of faith, internationalists have seen pacifism following simply from the dictates of reason itself. This secular commitment to peace grew away from specifically "Christian" influences in the years since the CIVIL WAR.

Americans influenced by both intellectual traditions found it necessary to establish organizations in order to promote their peace concerns. Beginning with the American Peace Society (1828), American peace activists have struggled not simply with what they saw as a culture geared towards war, but amongst themselves—debating both the meaning of peace and the most appropriate strategies for obtaining it. Consequently peace activists have forged alliances with reformers of various stripes: abolitionists and feminists in the years prior to the Civil War, leftists and environmentalists in the 20th century. Organizations have flourished and dissipated over lack of funds as well as ideological conflict. But in spite of the difficulties of agreeing on strategies for achieving their concerns, some American organizations, such as the Fellowship of Reconciliation (established 1915), and the American Friends Service Committee (established 1917) have put in decades of work for the cause of peace.

The task of peace activism in America has developed in response to changing needs and social conditions. William Lloyd Garrison and others made common cause between peace and abolition as the question of SLAVERY came to dominate American political life between 1830 and 1860. But the linking of causes had the drawback of turning the concern for peace into support for the Union war effort, in effect destroying the movement. The war also destroyed optimistic views of the American future.

In the following decades of industrial and territorial expansion, a new generation of peace workers came to identify the cause of peace with the expansion of American civilization, promoting cooperation among European powers achieved through diplomacy, the codification of international law, and establishment of procedures for arbitration of disputes. In 1889 American activists such as Frances WILLARD, president of the Women's Christian Temperance Union, attended the first Universal Peace Congress in Paris. Activists had regained their optimistic faith in America as the world's best hope for moral insight. Both supporters and opponents of America's military interventions in the Spanish-American War (1898) often spoke of the superiority of Anglo-Saxon values, as in the case of the Anti-Imperialist League, begun in Boston in 1898, which forged alliances among feminists, conservative populists such as William Jennings BRYAN, labor activists, and industrialists such as Andrew Carnegie (see GOSPEL OF WEALTH).

In history's most violent century, the 20th, peace workers have increasingly come to rely upon both international organizations and the development of a cosmopolitan moral vision, underscoring the oneness of humanity, in order to halt the spread of war. But American national-ism (see CIVIL RELIGION) fueled by the global context of war (see WORLD WAR I; WORLD WAR II) has been quite resistant to the concerns of peace activists. During both global wars, in spite of the general climate of isolationism which preceded American involvement, opposition to the war effort remained unpopular. In recent decades, peace concerns, whether focused on actual shooting wars or the COLD WAR climate, have met with frequent resistance. Charges of Communist conspiracy were levelled against antinuclear activists during the 1950s, and federal officials such as FBI chief J. Edgar Hoover and presidents Lyndon Johnson and Richard Nixon continually sought to show that the large-scale opposition to the VIETNAM WAR was inspired by Communists.

Despite periods of popularity in response to particular wars, the movement for peace reform in American culture has never been capable of establishing a lasting base for itself. Even though relying upon many of the same symbols and values which figure so prominently in the nation's civil religion, such as individual liberty and dignity, justice and divine law, peace activists have been less successful at tapping America's conscience than those who have argued for war. In spite of this, they have made lasting contributions to the nation's efforts to embody its ideals.

MG

Bibliography: Merle Curti, *Peace or War: The American Struggle, 1636–1936* (New York: Garland Publishers, 1972); Charles DeBenedetti, *The Peace Reform in American History* (Bloomington: Indiana University Press, 1980); Lawrence S. Wittner, *Rebels Against War: The American Peace Movement, 1933–83* (Philadelphia: Temple University Press, 1984); Valarie H. Ziegler, *The Advocate of Peace in Antebellum America* (Bloomington, Ind.: Indiana University Press, 1992).

Peale, Norman Vincent   See POSITIVE THINKING.

Penn, William (1644–1718)   Quaker activist and founder of the colony of Pennsylvania,

One of England's leading Quakers, William Penn founded the colony of Pennsylvania to be a model of religious toleration, pacifism, and fair treatment of Native Americans. (Library of Congress)

William Penn is one of the mythical figures of American history. Born in London, England on October 14, 1644, Penn had all the advantages available to the son of a wealthy war hero. His father, Admiral Sir William Penn, had served with distinction under William Cromwell, Charles II, and James II.

After attending private school, he entered Oxford in 1660. While there, he was drawn toward PURITANISM and was expelled two years later for his unconventional religious views. He was then sent to school in France in order to become "more worldly." While there he continued to develop his interest in religion. Sent to Ireland to oversee his father's estates, he encountered a group of Irish Quakers (see FRIENDS, THE RELIGIOUS SOCIETY OF) whose faithfulness under persecution moved him greatly. He soon became one of the leading English Quakers and

a major controversialist for the cause, writing numerous books and tracts defending Quaker beliefs as well as a minor devotional classic, *No Cross, No Crown* (1669). Jailed four times for his religious views, his 1670 trial became the occasion for a leading civil rights case. In that year a jury repeatedly returned a verdict of "not guilty" despite the fact that the judge had directed them to return a guilty verdict and repeatedly threatened them with punishment for failing to do so. The case enshrined in British common law the right of a jury to determine its verdict free from judicial interference.

Despite his unconventional religious beliefs, Penn was a favorite of both Charles II and James II, as well as the radicals John Locke and Algernon Sydney. It was Charles II who repaid a debt to the Penn family by deeding a parcel of land in North America to Penn (1681). Here Penn founded the colony of Pennsylvania in the light of Quaker theology. It soon became one of the most successful colonies in British North America.

Pennsylvania offered religious toleration to all its colonists, had no militia, and attempted to deal fairly and equitably with the local Delaware Indians. Penn hoped to make this colony into the ideal form of a Christian society, which he set out in his *Frame of Government* (1682).

Conflicts with the settlers forced Penn to make the colony's government (originally set up as an oligarchy, with most of the authority vested in the proprietor) more democratic, and he established an elected assembly in 1701. Although Penn had arrived with a group of colonists in 1682, disagreements over the boundaries of the colony caused him to return to England two years later. While he was away, the taxes owed him by the colonists nearly ceased, and he was thrown into debtors prison. He returned to Pennsylvania for another two years in 1699, during which time he viewed a thriving colony, albeit one that was still lax in paying its taxes.

Back in England he continued to agitate in support of both the Quakers and his colony until 1712 when a massive stroke left him nearly incapacitated. He lived for another six years, dying in London on July 30, 1718.

EQ

Bibliography: Mary M. Dunn, *William Penn: Politics and Conscience* (Princeton: Princeton University Press, 1967); Melvin B. Endy Jr., *William Penn and Early Quakerism* (Princeton: Princeton University Press, 1973); William T. Hull, *William Penn: A Topical Biography* (London: Oxford University Press, 1937); William Penn, *No Cross, No Crown* (Boston: Rogers and Fowle, 1747).

Pennington, James William Charles (1807–1870)

Born a slave on the eastern shore of Maryland in 1807, Pennington's life as a slave was notably brutal. He was given to his master's son at the age of four and experienced the rage that a young master could vent. Trained as a stonemason and a blacksmith, he avoided some of this torment by being hired out. He escaped from slavery in either 1827 or 1828 and settled in Pennsylvania where he was aided, as were so many other fugitive slaves, by a Quaker family (see FRIENDS, THE RELIGIOUS SOCIETY OF).

Another Quaker taught him the rudiments of reading and writing, and Pennington continued this education by attending night schools and through reading. During the early 1830s, he taught school in New York and Connecticut, while studying theology. Ordained as a Congregational minister, he served as pastor in Newtown, New York (1838–1840) and Hartford (1840–1847), where he also was president of the ministerial association and of the Union Missionary Society.

Taking part in antislavery activities, Pennington was a delegate to the World's Anti-Slavery Convention (1843) and the World's Peace Society (1843). While in London attending the latter, he was feted widely; one tea given in his honor attracted over 500 guests. Leaving England for the continent, he lectured and preached in Paris and Brussels. He returned to the United States and became pastor of the First (Shiloh) Presbyterian Church in New York City (1847–1855). He continued his antislavery work, organizing a conference of black leaders to condemn the American Colonization Society's plans to return freed slaves to Africa and to lobby the New York legislature against state support for black colonization.

In 1849 he published his memoirs, *The Fugitive Blacksmith, or, Events in the History of James W. C. Pennington, Pastor of a Presbyterian Church, New York, Formerly a Slave in the State of Maryland, United States.* The passage of the Fugitive Slave Law the following year endangered Pennington, who traveled to Europe to avoid capture as a fugitive slave. During this sojourn he gave antislavery lectures in Scotland, England, and Germany. There he attended the World Peace Conference at Frankfurt-am-Main. While in Germany he may have been awarded a Doctor of Divinity degree from Heidelberg.

Following the payment of $150 to the estate of his former master, Pennington returned home. From this time on Pennington became increasingly militant in his demands for equal rights. In 1855 he helped organize the New York Legal Rights Association that helped blacks obtain more equitable treatment on public transportation. He applauded John Brown's attack at Harper's Ferry (1859) and in an editorial in the *Anglo-African Magazine* urged blacks to pray for Brown.

After 1856 Pennington was increasingly debilitated by alcoholism and slipped from public view. The minutes of the Presbyterian General Assembly list his address during this period variously as Hartford, New York, and Maine. In an attempt to regain his health, Pennington traveled to Jacksonville, Florida in 1869 or 1870. There he organized a Presbyterian congregation that he served as pastor until his death in October 1870.

EQ

Bibliography: Jane H. Pease and William H. Pease, *They Who Would Be Free: Blacks' Search for Freedom* (New York: Atheneum, 1974); J. W. C. Pennington, *The Fugitive Blacksmith, or, Events in the History of*

James W. C. Pennington (London: Gilpin, 1850); ———, *A Text Book of the Origin and History, &c. &c. of Colored People*. (Hartford: L. Skinner, 1841); Benjamin Quarles, *The Black Abolitionists* (New York: Oxford University Press, 1969)

Pennsylvania (Colony)   Founded in 1681 by William PENN as a haven for Quakers (see FRIENDS, RELIGIOUS SOCIETY OF), Pennsylvania quickly became a model for both religious tolerance and commercial success. The colony had its start early in 1681 when Penn convinced the English King Charles II to discharge a debt owed to the Penn family by providing a grant of land in British North America. Penn hoped to make this land, located west of Delaware between 40°N and 43°N, into a holy commonwealth built on Quaker principles. These principles included religious tolerance, nonviolence, and democratic government, all under the watchful care of Penn as proprietary governor.

Following the grant of land, Penn quickly began establishing his colony. The deputy governor arrived with a load of settlers in July 1681. Penn arrived in the autumn of 1682, and by the close of that year he had begun to lay out the city of Philadelphia, a colonial assembly had been brought into session, and the colony had adopted a formal plan of government.

Although Quakers were the majority in the colony and predominated in its political and economic systems, Pennsylvania soon contained within its borders the most diverse array of religions in the colonies. Penn desired that the colony's dealings with the Native Americans be equitable and tolerant, and the colony's early life was not threatened by hostile natives. Neither did the Quakers attempt to force them to convert and punish them for failing to uphold "Christian" standards, as was the case in the MASSACHUSETTS BAY COLONY. In Pennsylvania, European Christianity and the faiths of the Native Americans lived together in relative harmony.

Not only was this an unusual occurrence, but different types of Christians, who were slaughtering each other in Europe, lived peacefully alongside each other in the Quaker commonwealth. In fact, Pennsylvania was where many of the most exciting and significant events in American religious history took place. Early settlers to the colony included Scotch-Irish immigrants who brought with them their staunch Presbyterianism, and in Philadelphia they would organize the first presbytery in what would become the United States. Baptists also were strong in Pennsylvania. The Philadelphia Association, organized in 1707, was a dominant force in American Baptist life until the SECOND GREAT AWAKENING weakened the Calvinist (see CALVINISM) hold on American Baptists. Equally significant was the presence of Roman Catholics in the colony. Although small and operating under some political liabilities, Catholics in Philadelphia were well organized and, by 1734, had one of the few resident priests in British America outside Maryland (see ROMAN CATHOLICISM).

As victims of religious persecution, the Quakers had a particular sensitivity to other persecuted groups, and Pennsylvania soon became haven for many of the smaller religious groups of Europe. These included the MENNONITES and AMISH, the Schwenkfelders, and the Moravian Brethren (see MORAVIANS). All of these groups found a safe haven in Pennsylvania, and while some of them would move into other areas of the country, Pennsylvania remained the locus of their population.

Along with these primarily German-speaking sects, Pennsylvania also became an early center for both German LUTHERANISM and the German Reformed Church (see REFORMED TRADITION). By 1730, nearly 15,000 Germans of Reform background lived in Pennsylvania. For years dedicated laymen and a few minsters had attempted to organize and maintain congregations, but this work was hampered by the lack of a central organization, the appeal of the pietist sects, and by the work of Count Nicolas von ZINZENDORF, who attempted to merge all of the German-speaking Protestants into a single "Congregation of God in the Spirit."

The collapse of that plan and the arrival of Michael Schlatter led to the creation of the first organization of the German Reformed Church in America. In September 1747 in Philadelphia, representatives of 12 German Reformed churches came together in an association, placing themselves under the control of the synod of Amsterdam.

They were followed shortly in this organizational development by the German Lutherans. Lutheranism had a long history in what became British North America, existing as the state church of New Sweden and as a barely tolerated church in New Netherland. German Lutheranism had its early strength in New York, which had swallowed up both New Sweden and New Netherland. It was soon surpassed, however, by the German migration to the Quaker colony, beginning in the second decade of the 18th century.

Like most new settlers in British North America, German Lutherans suffered from a dearth of pastors and institutions. A call from one of these overworked pastors led to the arrival in America of Henry MUHLENBERG in 1742. Muhlenberg, a man of numerous abilities and indefatigable strength, was the individual most responsible for the creation of American Lutheranism in the 18th century. Traveling across the vast wilderness of Pennsylvania and preaching before numerous small Lutheran congregations, he was insistent upon appropriate church discipline, doctrine, and organization. It was under his auspices that the Pennsylvania Ministerium was created in 1748, an event that some view as the most important single event in American Lutheran history. With this creation, the colony with the largest Lutheran population now had the organization to help meet its religious needs.

As an experiment in religious tolerance, Pennsylvania was an overwhelming success. For Penn personally, and for the Quakers as well, Pennsylvania was a mixed blessing. The rents that all settlers were required to pay to Penn were exceedingly difficult for him to collect, and he often found himself at odds with the colonists. Disgusted with governing the colony, he traveled to it in 1699, provided it with a constitution that made it self-governing, and returned to England.

As a whole, however, the colony was a commercial success. Business boomed and the strict discipline of its Quaker commercial class produced great wealth. Simultaneously, it led them to a decreasing interest in the strict spiritual discipline of their early days. The reality of being the colony's commercial and political elite raised other problems for the Quakers. Committed as they were to nonviolence, they had eschewed force as a basis of maintaining social order. Yet with the growing numbers of colonists the need for force appeared to increase. As the French and their Indian allies menaced the colony in the early 1750s, the issue of colonial defense also became a troublesome one. Although the Quaker majority managed to prevent the formation of a colonial militia until 1755, the establishment of the militia in that year and the refusal of several prominent Quakers to pay taxes for its support led to a spiritual crisis among the Friends. In response they decided to give up the political and social power that they had, and return to the inward life in a way far more total than previously. Pennsylvania, which under the Quakers modeled what the United States would become religiously, would now be required to carry on under different leadership.

EQ

Bibliography: Edwin B. Bronner, *William Penn's Holy Experiment* (New York: Temple University Press, 1962); James H. Hutson, *Pennsylvania Politics, 1746–1770: The Movement for Royal Government and its Consequences* (Princeton: Princeton University Press, 1972).

Pentecostal Holiness Church, International   See PENTECOSTALISM.

Pentecostalism   Pentecostalism is a 20th-century Protestant religious movement distinguished by its emphasis on the experience of

Spirit baptism. Baptism in the Holy Spirit is usually characterized by ecstatic speech in unknown languages, a phenomenon called speaking in tongues, or glossolalia. The AZUSA STREET REVIVAL, which occurred in Los Angeles between 1906 and 1909, is now recognized as the starting point of modern Pentecostalism. Today there are more than 300 Pentecostal denominations in the United States. Although most are small sects, the two largest denominations, the African-American CHURCH OF GOD IN CHRIST and the ASSEMBLIES OF GOD, together claim nearly nine million members.

In its early history, Pentecostalism fused together a number of diverse strands in American religion: the desire for spiritual transformation, the plausibility of faith healing, and the expectation that the second coming of Jesus Christ was near. Pentecostals commonly cited certain key biblical passages to support these beliefs. They accepted, for example, that anyone who undergoes Spirit baptism will manifest the supernatural gifts to which St. Paul refers in 1 Corinthians, e.g., healing, prophecy, and speaking in tongues. Pentecostals also quoted the Old Testament prophet Joel, who prophesied that a "former rain" and a "latter rain" (2:23) would fall upon God's people. They interpreted the "former rain" as the events described in Acts 2, when the Holy Spirit enabled Jesus' disciples to speak in tongues on the day of Pentecost. Meanwhile, the "latter rain" was thought to be the glossolalia that had appeared in modern times.

The immediate antecedents of Pentecostalism are found in the HOLINESS MOVEMENT of the mid-19th century and in the efforts of American Protestants to attain Christian perfection. These ideals, which were expressed in the writings of Methodist founder John Wesley, spoke of the possibility of a person's achieving perfection in the present life and becoming (as Wesley said) "perfect as our Father in heaven is perfect." Phoebe Worrall PALMER, a lay Methodist evangelist, most effectively adapted Wesley's ideas to religious life in the United States.

In Palmer's view, holiness was available to the believer through faith in Jesus Christ. She spoke of "entire sanctification," a moment when one surrendered everything and received God's blessing. By the time of the Civil War, the phrase "baptism in the Holy Spirit" also became popular, used as a term synonymous with the blessing to which Palmer referred. In the optimistic moral climate of that day, the expectation that a Christian *could* overcome sin seemed completely reasonable, and the simplicity of the message Palmer preached won many disciples to the Holiness cause.

As the 19th century drew to a close, Americans associated with the Holiness movement were committed to experiencing baptism in the Spirit. The critical moment in the emergence of Pentecostalism occurred in 1900, when Charles Fox PARHAM began to identify speaking tongues as the definitive sign of Spirit baptism. On January 1, 1901, according to Parham, the miracle for which many had prayed took place: "fire fell" from heaven, and a student at Parham's Bible school in Topeka, Kansas spoke in tongues. In the following months, Parham's school gained attention as others experienced the gift of tongues there. Parham founded a fellowship of churches called the "Apostolic Faith Movement," and several thousand adherents soon espoused Pentecostal doctrines.

Parham opened a Bible institute in Houston, Texas that itinerant preacher William Joseph SEYMOUR attended for a few weeks in 1905. In January 1906 Seymour accepted an invitation to lead a black Holiness mission in Los Angeles, where the Pentecostal movement burst out in full force. In April 1906 and for another three years thereafter, crowds flocked every day to a rundown building on Azusa Street and were gripped by the religious enthusiasm at its services. At the height of the revival excitement, worship was held from mid-morning until past midnight. According to Parham, miraculous healings and a spiritual delirium (which Parham described as "Holy Ghost Bedlam") marked the event. Jennie Moore, the first woman to speak in tongues and later Seymour's wife, gave this report: "The power of God fell and I was baptized in the Holy Ghost and fire. It seemed as if a vessel broke within me and water surged through my being, which when it reached my mouth came out in a torrent of speech."

The revival on Azusa Street finally began to wane in 1909. By then many had visited the site, participated in worship, and brought the Pentecostal message back home with them. Among the visitors to Los Angeles was C. H. Mason, pastor of an African-American Holiness congregation in Memphis, Tennessee. Mason had been instrumental in forming a loose confederation of Holiness congregations named the Church of God in Christ. Mason traveled to Los Angeles in 1907, and there he experienced baptism in the Spirit and spoke in tongues. When he returned to Memphis, he began to hold all-night religious meetings. Soon even the city's white newspapers took notice of this activity, as people came to Mason's church to witness to their faith, to be healed of their illnesses, and to speak in tongues.

Despite a dispute over the use of the name "Church of God in Christ," the group Mason led was incorporated in the fall of 1907. Mason was elected general overseer of the church, a post he held until his death in 1961. Composed primarily of African-Americans, this church is the oldest Pentecostal denomination in the United States, as well as the largest black Pentecostal body in the world. Although it has never conducted a systematic census and its statistics may not be wholly accurate, the Church of God in Christ claims to have over six million American members today.

The CHURCH OF GOD (CLEVELAND, TENNESSEE) is the second oldest Pentecostal denomination. It originated in the mountainous region that covers eastern Tennessee and western North Carolina, when a group of Baptists joined together in 1886 and dedicated themselves to the ideal of restoring primitive Christianity. The Baptists later united with a similar group of believers who had spoken in tongues at a revival held near Camp Creek, North Carolina in 1896. This organization might well have remained in obscurity if it had not been for the leadership of A. J. TOMLINSON, an itinerant preacher who assumed control over it in 1907. He renamed the organization the Church of God to emphasize that it was the only true church, a community in continuity with New Testament Christianity.

The acceptance of faith healing and glossolalia quickly set the Church of God apart from other churches in the area. Tomlinson was convinced that God would not only help believers overcome sin in the present life, but would also bring healing to their bodies. After Tomlinson experienced baptism in the Spirit and spoke in tongues in 1908, glossolalia became a regular feature of worship in the Church of God. Although Tomlinson was deposed by the church in 1923 and organized his own Church of God of Prophecy, the main denomination remained strong. Headquartered in Cleveland, Tennessee and still heavily concentrated in Tennessee and North Carolina, the church now contains approximately 620,000 members.

The Pentecostal Holiness Church, International is the third oldest American Pentecostal denomination. It was formed in 1911 by a merger of two southern Holiness sects: the Fire-Baptized Holiness Church, founded in South Carolina in 1898 by B. H. Irwin, and the Pentecostal Holiness Church, organized in North Carolina in 1900. The leading figure in the early history of this group was former Methodist minister Gaston B. Cashwell, who attended the Azusa Street revival. When Cashwell returned home to North Carolina, he conducted a fiery preaching tour of the South and numbered A. J. Tomlinson among his converts. Although Cashwell left the Pentecostal Holiness Church in 1909, the composition of the denomination was completed in 1915 when several Presbyterian congregations in South Carolina also joined it. The church moved its headquarters to Oklahoma City in 1973, and it presently reports a membership of nearly 120,000 people.

The ASSEMBLIES OF GOD, which is now the largest Pentecostal denomination in the world, was organized in April 1914 out of several Pentecostal groups in the Midwest and Southwest, including Charles Parham's Apostolic Faith movement in Texas. William Durham, who—like so many other early Pentecostal leaders—experienced Spirit baptism at the Azusa revival, was undoubtedly the most significant figure in the shaping of the Assemblies of God. He rejected the then-common idea that human sin was eradicated when a believer experienced sanctification. Hoping to keep Pentecostalism from falling prey to charlatans and fanatics, the founders of the Assemblies of God realized that an organization was needed to provide discipline and guard against heterodox opinions. As a consequence, they adopted a Statement of Fundamental Truths in 1916 and ratified a formal constitution in 1927. The church expanded rapidly, reaching a membership of 300,000 by 1950 and now reporting approximately 2.2 million people.

An early schism in the Assemblies of God over the church's baptismal rite suggests the broad range of beliefs that developed within American Pentecostalism. Denominational leaders debated whether believers should be baptized in the name of the Trinity (Father, Son, and Holy Spirit), as the Gospel of Matthew prescribed, or only in the name of Jesus, as the Book of Acts suggested. The "Jesus only" faction (also known as the "Oneness Pentecostals") argued for their position by insisting that there is but one person in the Godhead—Jesus Christ. Since those who chose that formula explicitly denied the traditional Christian doctrine of the threefold nature of God, they were expelled from the Assemblies of God in 1916. They later organized themselves as the United Pentecostal Church, International, a denomination of about a half million members today.

Another important Pentecostal denomination is the International Church of the Foursquare Gospel, which developed out of the ministry of flamboyant evangelist Aimee Semple MCPHERSON. The most famous female preacher of her day, "Sister Aimee" knew how to make the most of her good looks, exciting oratory, and theatrical worship services. In 1923, she opened the 5,000-seat Angelus Temple in Los Angeles, which served as the headquarters of the denomination she organized. The "Foursquare Gospel" refers to a vision McPherson experienced, when she saw the four-faced figures described by the Old Testament prophet Ezekiel (1:4–14). She believed the faces symbolized the four facets of Christ's ministry: Savior, Healer, Baptizer, and King. McPherson died in 1944, but her son assumed leadership after her death. The International Church of the Foursquare Gospel grew rapidly in the 1950s and 1960s, and it now contains approximately 200,000 members.

Pentecostalism has always represented a broad, popular impulse within American Christianity, and it has enabled many to obtain a sense of spontaneity and spiritual excitement rarely found within the formal structures and worship of the mainstream churches. While several religious currents coalesced in the formation of the Pentecostal denominations between, roughly, 1900 and 1925, Pentecostalism has also proved capable of adjusting to changing social and cultural circumstances in the second half of the twentieth century.

After World War II evangelist Oral ROBERTS, for example, expanded the appeal of faith healing beyond traditional Pentecostal religious communities. The founding of the Full Gospel Business Men's Fellowship International in 1953, moreover, helped Pentecostal beliefs gain acceptance among middle-class Americans in non-Pentecostal denominations. Indeed, beginning with Episcopal clergyman Dennis Bennett's experience of baptism in the Spirit with speaking in tongues in 1959, charismatic (see CHARISMATIC MOVEMENT) renewal has even appeared within Episcopal and Roman Catholic parishes. And in recent years, membership in Pentecostal churches has increased most rapidly among the

American Hispanic population, an ethnic group once identified almost exclusively with Roman Catholicism.

An important recent development within the Pentecostal movement was the decision of the largest denominations to form an organization called the Pentecostal-Charismatic Churches of North America. This action was intended to heal the racial divisions that split Pentecostalism in the mid-1920s. Although the Pentecostal Fellowship, which was formed in 1948, excluded the predominantly black churches from its membership, leaders of the major Pentecostal churches voted in October 1994 to disband that association and organize a racially inclusive one instead. The new alliance includes members of the Assemblies of God, the Pentecostal Holiness Church, the International Church of the Foursquare Gospel, and the Church of God in Christ.

GHS, Jr.

Bibliography: Robert Mapes Anderson, *Vision of the Disinherited: The Making of American Pentecostalism* (New York: Oxford University Press, 1989); Donald W. Dayton, *The Theological Roots of Pentecostalism* (Metuchen, N.J.: Scarecrow Press, 1987); Vinson Synan, *The Holiness-Pentecostal Movement in the United States* (Grand Rapids, Mich.: Eerdmans, 1971).

perfectionism   The term "perfectionism" describes the Christian teaching that complete holiness is attainable by divine grace to every believer. This doctrine, which grew out of the writings of Methodist founder John Wesley, took on its principal expression in the 19th-century HOLINESS MOVEMENT. Wesley had emphasized how Christians might reach a point in their lives when God sanctified (see SANCTIFICATION) them and released them from all *intentional* sin. At that moment, their motives would be perfected, and they would be filled with love so complete that they became (as Wesley said in a 1733 sermon) "perfect as our Father in heaven is perfect."

Methodist lay evangelist Phoebe Worrall PALMER was one of the first Americans to lay stress on Christian perfectionism. She proclaimed that believers could attain perfect love if they would simply follow biblical commandments and consecrate themselves wholly to God. Palmer had undergone an experience of sanctification in 1837, following which she assumed leadership of prayer meetings for the "promotion of holiness" in New York City. These weekly meetings drew together many who were attracted by the optimistic doctrine of "entire sanctification" she preached. Participants in Palmer's group, moreover, included not only Methodists, but also Baptists, Presbyterians, and Quakers.

As Palmer's success suggests, perfectionism, while certainly a distinguishing characteristic of Methodist belief in the early 19th century, was never limited exclusively to Methodists. The growth of REVIVALISM during the SECOND GREAT AWAKENING inspired American Christians of all denominations to consider the possibility of being sanctified by the Holy Spirit. Congregationalist Asa MAHAN, who had participated in revivals led by Presbyterian minister Charles G. FINNEY, wrote a book on the *Scripture Doctrine of Christian Perfection* (1839). In that book Mahan described how believers might attain complete victory over sin through the presence of Jesus Christ within their hearts. Later in his life, Mahan published *The Baptism of the Holy Spirit,* which emphasized the sanctified Christian's release from the power of sin.

Belief in the spiritual perfectibility of humankind roused Protestants to consider how their society might also be improved by applying divine laws to political conduct. Wesley had consistently condemned the institution of slavery, calling it "the sum of all villainies." The antislavery campaign, therefore, became the most notable of the several reform movements into which American Christians threw their energies. Perfectionism also influenced other reform causes such as temperance, peace, and women's rights.

Perfectionism was such a powerful influence on 19th-century American religious life that the major Protestant denominations were eventually unable to contain every expression of it. Perfectionists often moved outside Christian orthodoxy altogether. John Humphrey NOYES provides a prime example of the antinomian potential of perfectionism. Converted by a revival in 1831, Noyes insisted that sinless perfection freed the individual from all conventional social mores. His view that perfection once attained could never be lost led him to found the communitarian society at Oneida, New York. There, Noyes instituted the practice of "complex marriage," freeing men and women from the sexual exclusivism of ordinary matrimony. More orthodox perfectionists like Mahan and Finney took pains to distinguish their beliefs from Noyes's practices, especially following the indictment of Noyes on adultery charges.

Debates over perfection fostered a number of schisms within 19th-century Methodism. Both the formation of the Wesleyan Methodist Church in 1843 and the organization of the Free Methodist Church in 1860 ostensibly concerned the refusal of the Methodist Episcopal Church to take a strong antislavery position prior to the Civil War. Declining interest in holiness and the alleged worldliness of the main denomination, however, were other factors in the departure of several thousand Methodists from their church. After the Civil War, further withdrawals occurred. Perfectionist Methodists insisted that sanctification was not a gradual and lifelong process, but an instantaneous gift of holiness experienced at the time of conversion. Several new denominations, such as the SALVATION ARMY, which began in England in 1865, and the Church of the Nazarene, which was founded in 1908, adopted this doctrine as central to the Christian life.

A final stage in the development of American religious perfectionism took place early in the 20th century. Just as the Holiness movement had underscored the possibility of eradicating sin in the present life, so emerging PENTECOSTALISM equated speaking in tongues as concrete evidence that a believer had received the desired baptism of the Holy Spirit. The first Pentecostals were drawn from the ranks of the Holiness churches, and the message they preached expressed perfectionist longings nurtured within the Holiness revival. The origins of Pentecostalism are generally linked to the ministry of Charles F. PARHAM in Topeka, Kansas, where on New Year's Day in 1901 one of his disciples spoke in tongues. The most publicized event of the early Pentecostal movement was the AZUSA STREET REVIVAL in Los Angeles in 1906.

GHS, Jr.

Bibliography: Charles Edwin Jones, *Perfectionist Persuasion: The Holiness Movement and American Methodism, 1867–1936* (Metuchen, N.J.: Scarecrow Press, 1974).

Phelps, Elizabeth Stuart (Ward) (1844–1911)

Elizabeth Stuart Phelps was a best-selling novelist and writer of fiction with religious themes in the post-Civil War era. Obsessed with questions relating to the afterlife, Phelps's most famous work, *The Gates Ajar*, challenged traditional Calvinist teachings about sin, divine election, and heaven and hell. Her writings represented a very popular expression of late 19th-century Protestant liberal theology (see CALVINISM).

Phelps was born in Boston on August 31, 1844. Daughter of Congregational minister Austin Phelps and his wife, Elizabeth Stuart (herself the daughter of Andover Seminary professor Moses Stuart), Phelps was originally named Mary Gray, but took her mother's name after her premature death in 1852. She married Herbert Dickinson Ward in 1888, but their relationship quickly soured and Ward moved to South Carolina. Phelps remained in Massachusetts, where she lived for the rest of her life.

As early as age 10, Phelps had written stories for religious weeklies. She published numerous novels over her lifetime, but her fame today rests principally on her first novel, *The Gates Ajar* (1868). Prompted by the death of her sweetheart in the Civil War, Phelp's novel told the story of Mary Cabot, whose brother Royal was killed in battle before he could experience a religious conversion. According to orthodox theological views, Royal ought to have been doomed to hellfire. The heroine Mary, however, refused to accept that God was such a cruel tyrant. As the book's narrative reveals, Mary's intuition is correct and Royal's soul is safe in heaven.

Although Phelps's father and other clergy denounced her for publishing heresy, thousands of Americans whose loved ones had died in the Civil War found *The Gates Ajar* provided immeasurable comfort. The book was reprinted over 50 times between 1869 and 1884. Phelps also penned a sequel, *Beyond the Gates* (dedicated to her recently deceased brother Stuart), which discussed death and a busy, productive heaven that resembled the most pleasant aspects of life on earth. The response to all Phelps's writings reveals how much she captured the religious mood of Gilded Age America, a generation that wished faith to provide not ethical or theological rigor, but security in the midst of an insecure world.

Most of Phelps's books showed her discontent with traditional Protestant faith and practice. She demonstrated, furthermore, an early sensitivity to changing social conditions and compassion for people unable to prosper in an industrializing nation. Her 1871 novel, *The Silent Partner,* which exposed the poverty of workers in a Massachusetts factory town, proved to be a pioneering effort in the movement later known as the Social Gospel. Although few women held leadership positions in churches in her day, Phelps's success discloses how women did affect 19th-century American theology and religious thought, albeit through subtle means such as religious literature.

Living in virtual seclusion for long periods of time, Phelps wrote and published prolifically. In 1910, she composed her last collection of stories, *The Empty House*. She died in Newton Center, Massachusetts on January 28th of that year.

GHS, Jr.

Bibliography: Carol Farley Kessler, *Elizabeth Stuart Phelps* (Boston: Twayne, 1982).

Pietism   Pietism was a renewal movement that took shape primarily within German LUTHERANISM in the late 17th and early 18th century. At the outset it involved a protest against the cold intellectualism and formalism of the officially established churches. It stressed personal religious experience, including the admission of one's unworthiness before God and the desire to grow in holiness. Emphasizing a religion of the heart, Pietism's influence soon transcended Lutheranism. It has also had an important impact on denominations of the free church tradition such as the MORAVIANS, on Methodism, and on American evangelical (see EVANGELICALISM) Protestantism generally.

Philipp Jakob Spener usually is considered the founder of Pietism. Born in 1635, he had studied at Geneva and Strasbourg before coming as a Lutheran pastor to Frankfurt-am-Main in 1666. He drew inspiration from Johann Arndt's 1606 devotional classic *Wahre Christentum* (*True Christianity*), which insisted that Christians should be instructed in a practical, living faith rather than in sterile doctrinal controversies, typical of Lutheranism at the time. Spener instituted religious meetings in his house, with devotional circles of prayer and Bible reading. In 1675 he published the first edition of his own famous work, *Pia Desideria* (*Pious Longings*), an event that effectively marks the beginning of the Pietist movement.

In 1691 Spener was called to a church in Berlin, a post he held until his death in 1705. At Berlin, he helped found the University of Halle, which became not only the intellectual center of the Prussian state, but also the international mecca of Pietism. In 1692, August Hermann Franke, who was to become the great organizer of Pietism, came to Halle to serve as both pastor and professor. Franke had experienced a religious conversion in 1687. One Sunday evening, he fell on his knees and, as he later wrote, felt himself "overwhelmed . . . with a stream of joy." Franke influenced Pietism as a preacher and writer, stressing the so-called repentance-struggle (*Busskampf*) leading up to the experience of new birth.

At the heart of the Pietist movement was the question, "How do I know I am saved?" Since Protestant orthodoxy tended to be extremely rationalistic, emphasizing God's remoteness and inscrutability, questions of religious assurance, naturally, were raised. Pietists proposed a form of religious life in which a direct, heartfelt encounter with God was central. They encouraged Bible study and formed small groups within parishes as a means to deepen devotion. Pietists sought to transform the pastor from being merely the administrator of sacraments and the protector of pure doctrine into a shepherd of souls and a preacher of salvation.

The Moravian Church, led by Nicolas Ludwig, Graf von ZINZENDORF, was the most important denomination to emerge out of the Pietist movement. Zinzendorf was born into a Prussian noble family in 1700, baptized by Spener, and educated at Halle. Acquiring an estate he called Herrnhut (the Lord's Protection) in 1722, he provided a refuge for members of the Moravian *Unitas Fratrum* (Unity of the Bethren), a religious party that extended back to the late Middle Ages. The Herrnhut community revived ancient Christian patterns of worship and placed stress on daily scripture readings and hourly prayers. Eventually Zinzendorf traveled to Pennsylvania in 1741, where a community had been founded through the work of Augustus Gottlieb Spangenberg. Zinzendorf served as the pastor of a Lutheran church in Philadelphia. He also organized several meetings of German Protestants in Pennsylvania in 1742 and 1743 in an attempt to effect Christian unity in the New World.

Pietism ultimately helped revivify Protestantism both on the Continent and in England and America in the 18th century. It inspired Methodist founder John Wesley, who held religious conversations with Spangenberg and the Moravians. Wesley also traveled to the Salzburger settlement in Georgia, where he engaged in dialogue with Austrian refugees whose pastor had been trained at Halle. When he returned to England he made contact there with Moravians, who sought to know whether he had received the assurance of pardon they believed was at the heart of true Christianity. On his way to a Moravian service on Aldersgate Street in London on May 24, 1738, Wesley felt his "heart strangely warmed," the experience that transformed his life.

Pietism influenced American religion not only through the Moravians and other sectarian groups, but also through contact with several mainstream Protestant denominations. Theodorus FRELINGHUYSEN of New Jersey, one of the early heralds of the Great Awakening of the mid-18th century, had been profoundly influenced by Dutch Reformed Pietism. Frelinghuysen in his turn attracted Presbyerian ministers William and Gilbert TENNENT, who became revival leaders in their denomination. Links to the Methodists included both Wesley himself and Jacob Albright, an 18th-century German Lutheran whose Evangelical Association eventually merged with the United Methodist Church in the 20th century.

Although Pietism disappeared as a distinct movement by the 19th century, its particular emphases continue to have an impact on evangelicalism in the United States today. American Protestants who believe in the importance of spiritual rebirth and a "born again" experience certainly understand the religious concerns that motivated the early Pietists. Like John Wesley, they are moved by the thought that Jesus Christ died to take away "*my* sins, even *mine,* and saved *me* from the law of sin and death."

GHS, Jr.

Bibliography: Ted A. Campbell, *The Religion of the Heart: A Study of European Religious Life in the Seventeenth and Eighteenth Centuries* (Columbia:

University of South Carolina Press, 1991); F. Ernest Stoeffler, *Continental Pietism and Early American Christianity,* ed., (Grand Rapids, Mich.: Eerdmans, 1976).

Pilgrim Holiness Church   See HOLINESS MOVEMENT.

Pilgrims   The Pilgrims were English separatists (see PURITANISM) who came to British North America in 1620 to escape religious persecution and who founded the settlement of Plymouth Plantation. English separatists, like the Pilgrims, despaired of the possibility of reforming the Church of England (see ANGLICANISM) and broke with the state church to form their own congregations based on their own readings of the Bible. The congregation from which the Pilgrims came was formed in Scrooby, England sometime in 1606. Richard Clifton was head minister; John Robinson and William Brewster were his assistants. Among the early members of this church was William Bradford, who later served as the long-term governor of Plymouth Colony.

From the beginning, the Scrooby congregation suffered persecution from civil and religious authorities. In response they decided, in the fall of 1607, to emigrate to Holland. Unfortunately, the captain and crew of the ship they hired for the journey proved untrustworthy, robbing them and turning them over to the local authorities. Most of the congregation were released after a month's imprisonment, but seven, including Robinson and Bradford, were held until spring.

The second attempt, in the spring of 1608, was only slightly more successful. For security reasons, the men and women separated while awaiting the ship hired to smuggle them out of England. The women, who were to join the group by water off the coast at Hull, were trapped by a storm and failed to arrive at the meeting place. The men, boarding from land, were surprised by a posse while boarding. The ship sailed away with those already aboard. During the voyage a storm drove them all the way to the coast of Norway. Thus it took them 14 days to reach Holland, during which time many feared they were lost.

The women, children, and remaining men were imprisoned by the English authorities. Upon their release they were driven from town to town as paupers since they had no possessions (having sold all their belongings). They soon become so tiresome to the authorities that they were allowed to leave and eventually between 60 and 125 arrived in Amsterdam.

In 1609 the Pilgrims moved to Leiden (their petition for residency was approved February 12) where they worked in the cloth industry. By 1617, fear of renewed warfare between Spain and Holland, economic depression, and disgust with the "licentiousness" of the Dutch made them look with favor on moving to America. The plans for such a removal were finalized, and in July 1620 those going to America returned to England. The Pilgrims and several other colonists left England in two ships, the *Speedwell* and the *Mayflower,* on August 5, 1620 but were forced to return to port when the *Speedwell* began to leak. They finally decided to continue the voyage with just one vessel, and on September 6 the *Mayflower* left England.

After a harrowing voyage she arrived off Cape Cod on November 21. The Pilgrims spent the next three weeks searching for a suitable place for settlement, which they found near modern day Plymouth, Massachussetts. They joined themselves together in a social contract (see MAYFLOWER COMPACT) and demonstrated their complete independence from all "popish" festivals by beginning construction of a common house on Christmas Day.

The winter of 1620–1621 was particularly cruel to the new settlers. Fifty of the 102 colonists died during that time. Fortunately they happened upon a native American who knew English, having been kidnapped by English fishermen and taken to England earlier in his life. Squanto acted as an emissary between the Pilgrims and the surrounding Native Americans, taught them about local agriculture, and helped to ease their difficulties.

For a people who believed themselves blessed by God, the Pilgrims had infinite problems. Food shortages were chronic. They were constantly cheated by their financial backers in England. New colonists were sent out with insufficient provisions, and many of the non-Pilgrims sent to increase the colony's number proved no end of trouble. These included Thomas Morton who sold guns to the native population, held orgies at his settlement of Merrymount several miles from Plymouth, and encouraged servants to leave their masters. Even the minister, John Lyford, sent by the company played them false. When it was discovered that he was not ordained, that he was an adulterer and fornicator, and that he had sent false letters about the colony to the stockholders in England, the Pilgrims ran him out of the colony.

Given these difficulties, the slow growth of the colony is not surprising. Not until 1622 were the losses of the first winter regained. By 1643 the colony still comprised only 2,500 people scattered through 10 towns. By this time Plymouth was increasingly overshadowed by the MASSACHUSETTS BAY COLONY, of which it became a part in 1691.

Despite this, no group is more wrapped in American mythology than the Pilgrims. That such a small group of people should loom so large in the consciousness of a nation is surprising. Perhaps their appeal lies in the fact that they were simple people fleeing persecution and overcoming numerous difficulties. Their weakness gives them an air of innocence allowing people to cherish them unreservedly. Finally, the observance Thanksgiving associated with them is an all-encompassing holiday. Not bound to a particular religion, not attached to war or nationalism, Thanksgiving well mirrors the innocence and simplicity associated with the Pilgrims themselves.

EQ

Bibliography: William Bradford, *Of Plymouth Plantation, 1620–1647: The Complete Text, with notes and an introduction by Samuel Eliot Morison* (New York: Knopf, 1952); George D. Langdon, Jr., *Pilgrim Colony: A History of New Plymouth, 1620–1691* (New Haven: Yale University Press, 1966).

Pittsburgh Platform Adopted by a conference of Reform rabbis meeting in Pittsburgh on November 1885, the "Pittsburgh Platform" became the theological basis of REFORM JUDAISM for half a century. This was a surprising achievement since only 15 rabbis attended the conference and none of the major Reform institutions—Hebrew Union College (HUC), the Central Conference of American Rabbis (CCAR), or the Union of American Hebrew Congregations (UAHC)—ever officially adopted the statement.

The Pittsburgh meeting, ostensibly designed to unify America's rabbis, served the opposite purpose. Dominated by radical Reformers, it irrevocably divided Reform Judaism from the more traditionally minded. Although Isaac Mayer WISE served as chairman of the meeting, the framing of the statement was the work of others more radical than he, most notably Kaufmann KOHLER. Kohler, rabbi at Temple Beth-El in New York, was the meeting's guiding spirit, and in his opening paper he submitted a 10-point program for Reform Judaism. Some points were purely organizational, calling for improved religious education, greater religious observance at home, and wider dissemination of Jewish literature. Others, such as the one calling for a revision of the scripture readings for Sabbath and holy day services "omitting all passages that might when translated, give offense . . ." were more extreme. Most importantly, Kohler called for the adoption of a platform that would "declare to the world what Judaism is and what Reform means and aims at." Crafted under his leadership, the statement of principles expressed the rationalism and progressivism that distinguished "classical" Reform Judaism.

While recognizing attempts to grasp the "infinite One" in every religious system, the statement declared that "Judaism presents the highest conception of the God-idea." The mission of the Jewish people is to serve as priests of the one God. The doctrines of Judaism are not incompatible with the discoveries of modern science. Judaism is declared a "progressive religion, ever striving to be in accord with the postulates of reason." The Bible, while a "most potent instrument of religious and moral instruction," is not considered authoritative for science or history, since it reflects "the primitive ideas of its own age . . . in miraculous narrative."

The Mosaic laws regulating dress, diet, and purity are deemed outmoded, as are all religious laws not "adapted to the views and habits of modern civilization." The resurrection of the body, and the existence of Gehenna and Eden (hell and paradise), also are rejected although the immortality of the soul is affirmed.

Most significantly, the statement rejected the idea of the Jewish nation. The Jews are declared to be a "religious community, and therefore expect neither a return to Palestine, nor a sacrificial worship under the administration of the sons of Aaron, nor the restoration of any of the laws concerning the Jewish state."

The adoption of such a statement of principles had a significant impact on American Judaism. It signaled a complete break between the Reformers and the more traditional members of American Judaism, leading to the latter's creation of the Jewish Theological Seminary the following year.

It even unsettled many of the Reformers. Isaac Wise, who called it the "Declaration of Independence for American Jews," used his position as president of both Hebrew Union College and (later) the Central Conference of American Rabbis to prevent either institution from adopting it as their statement of principles.

The Pittsburgh Platform eventually became integrated into Reform Judaism, becoming part of its ritual and prayer book, and remained the basis of Reform Judaism until the 1930s when parts of it, including its anti-Zionism (see ZION-ISM), were repudiated in the "Columbus Plat-

form" adopted by the CCAR in 1937. The principles, however, continued to exert an influence on much of Reform thought throughout the 20th century.

EQ

Bibliography: Nathan Glazer, *American Judaism*, 2nd ed., rev. (Chicago: University of Chicago Press, 1972); Beryl Harold Levy, *Reform Judaism in America: A Study in Religious Adaptation* (Ph.D. dissertation, Columbia University Press, 1933); Julian Morgenstern, *As a Mighty Stream: The Progress of Judaism Through History* (Philadelphia: Jewish Publication Society, 1949); Kerry M. Olitzky, Lance J. Sussman, and Malcolm A. Stern, eds., *Reform Judaism in America: A Biographical Dictionary and Sourcebook* (Westport, Conn.: Greenwood Press, 1993); W. Gunther Plaut, *The Rise of Reform Judaism*, 2 vols. (New York: World Union for Progressive Judaism, 1963–65); Howard M. Sachar, *A History of the Jews in America* (New York: Knopf, 1992).

Plan of Union   The Plan of Union was an alliance instituted in 1801 between the Presbyterian (see PRESBYTERIANISM) and Congregational (see CONGREGATIONALISM) churches of the United States. It effectively united the two denominations in a joint effort to evangelize the territories of what is now the Midwest. Although theological tensions within the Presbyterian Church curtailed the union in 1837, the plan helped transplant religious and political influences from New England to portions of upstate New York, Ohio, and Indiana in the early 19th century.

By the late 1700s, most American Presbyterians and Congregationalists considered themselves to be members of virtually the same denomination. They possessed a common Calvinist theological heritage and divided simply over matters of church organization. Fraternal ties, the formation of joint committees, and the exchange of delegates between the churches' respective decision-making bodies indicated a strong, albeit informal, connection. As a result of the Plan of Union, Congregational and Presbyterian settlers in frontier communities were officially allowed to join together in a single congregation. The majority of church members could decide to organize themselves as either a Congregational or a Presbyterian parish. No matter what structure was chosen, the church was also free to call a minister from either denomination as its pastor.

The plan functioned well for three decades, and there was but one "presbygational" denomination in New York, Ohio, Indiana, Michigan, Illinois, and Wisconsin. The plan tended to favor the establishment of Presbyterian parishes in the Midwest, since the greater organizational consciousness of that denomination usually won the upper hand among church members. Yet most clergy serving in the fluid social environment of the frontier preferred the theological openness and moral reform emphases of Congregationalism to the doctrinal conservativism Presbyterians tended to value. The Accommodation Plan of 1808 further strengthened this arrangement. Congregationalists were given a free rein in proselytizing the New England states, while Presbyterianism established itself as the dominant religious force in the West. The decline of interdenominational rivalry also benefited higher education. Colleges such as Western Reserve, Knox, Grinnell, and Ripon were all founded in the Midwest during that period.

Theological disputes among the Presbyterians eventually led to the abolition of the plan. The southern-oriented Old School Presbyterians (see NEW SCHOOL/OLD SCHOOL) began to fear that the alliance not only prevented them from having control over western missionary ventures, but also strengthened the New School party, whose liberal social and theological views were encouraged by close contact with New England Congregationalists. When the Old School faction gained control of the General Assembly in 1837, they severed all connections to the Congregationalists and expelled synods in New York and Ohio that had been formed under the plan. Although Congregationalists maintained an accord with the New School Presbyterian denomination that was formed in 1838, they too voided the Plan of Union in 1852, because

they feared it had benefited Presbyterianism far more than their own church.

Despite its relatively short existence, one of the plan's most lasting contributions to American life was the settlement of numerous "little New Englands" in midwestern towns throughout the early 19th century. Working under the the "presbygational" system, Congregational ministers helped carry the cultural values of the New England states to parts of the Midwest in the decades preceding the Civil War.

GHS, Jr.

Bibliography: George M. Marsden, *The Evangelical Mind and the New School Presbyterian Experience: A Case Study of Thought and Theology in Nineteenth-Century America* (New Haven: Yale University Press, 1970).

pluralism   Pluralism is an idea with a variety of meanings, all of which point to the complex texture of contemporary American society. In its most basic form, pluralism is used to point to the fact that there are a wide variety of ways in which Americans orient themselves to the world. More specifically, religious pluralism refers to the fact that Americans adhere to a great many different religious traditions, faiths, and belief systems. Pluralism, however, also conveys an ideal about how America might be as a nation, one in which the distinctive religious differences that exist between people are understood and respected. American society is now more radically pluralistic than at any time in its history, but pluralism as an American ideal has a much longer history.

There has always been a degree of religious pluralism in America. In old New England, Puritans (see PURITANISM) struggled among themselves over the question of orthodoxy. In the 19th century, Reform and Orthodox Jews differed as to how to interpret their traditions, and Catholic immigrants brought with them to America a wide array of distinct devotional traditions (see ROMAN CATHOLICISM and JUDAISM). Around the 1920s, the split between fundamentalists (see FUNDAMENTALISM) and liberals (see MAINLINE PROTESTANTISM) resulted in there being very different ways to be both Protestant and religious. However, this older kind of religious pluralism was muted around the middle of the 20th century, when a Cold War consensus was built on a common set of Judeo-Christian values thought to be shared by those in the American mainstream.

Developments in the last four decades seriously called that consensus into question. Despite moves toward cooperation and formal unity, American Protestants remain deeply divided along a variety of theological, doctrinal, and political lines. The decentralized Jewish community, which includes REFORM JUDAISM, CONSERVATIVE JUDAISM, ORTHODOX JUDAISM, HASIDISM, and a variety of secularist orientations, is well known for its diversity. Despite a centralized church, Catholics differ considerably, whether those differences point to tensions between progressives and traditionalists or to distinctive religious emphases related to ethnicity. Three additional developments helped to push the idea of religious pluralism into the foreground. Pluralism became a byword during the 1960s when African-Americans and white ethnics alike shared in a revival of ETHNICITY. The current interest in pluralism is also related to mass IMMIGRATION and the recent upsurge in Asian traditions on the American scene. A third development is related to a rise in the number of Christian sects and movements and New Age groups (see NEW AGE RELIGION) and to the ubiquity of free-wheeling religious sensibilities that have been on the rise in recent decades.

The idea of a religiously plural America burst into mainstream consciousness only recently, but pluralism as cultural and political ideal has a much longer pedigree. Cultural pluralism is an idea associated with Horace KALLEN, who in 1915 argued that the promise of American democracy was to preserve the cultural integrity of its diverse peoples. Kallen's idea of cultural pluralism resonated with the values of some liberal Protestant reformers, cultural anthropol-

ogists, and social commentators in the early decades of the 20th century, but only resurfaced as a powerful ideal in the 1960s. The idea of political pluralism is most closely associated with the name of Robert A. Dahl. In *Who Governs?* (1961), Dahl described how Americans can both subscribe to a universal creed of democracy and tolerate great inequities in wealth, power, and the capacity to influence political decision-making. He concluded that American democracy has become politically pluralistic, that is, it has been restructured to address the needs of different constituencies through interest groups, some based on class and others on ethnicity. This idea gained a wider audience through such noted books as *Beyond the Melting Pot* (1963) by Daniel Moynihan and Nathan Glazer, in which interest groups are portrayed as mediating the democratic process in New York City for many different constituencies.

These traditions of pluralistic thought paved the way for a consideration of America as a religiously pluralistic nation. But, religious pluralism has been most rigorously explored by scholars involved in the interfaith movement such as Paul Knitter and Alan Race, whose insights have only recently begun to be applied to understanding American religious history. For instance, it may be meaningful to talk about a common Judeo-Christian tradition in the American mainstream, but this does not negate the facts that Judaism and Christianity are different religions with deeply contested understandings of scripture and theology and that these differences have in the past led to conflict and hostilities. Catholics and Protestants, however much they share a common Christian heritage, appeal to different theological traditions, scriptural interpretations, and models of religious authority. Religious differences become pronounced when Asian religions are introduced into the equation. Muslims (see ISLAM) share many sensibilities with Jews and Christians. However, they understand their religion to be a revelation that began in the ancient Hebrew Bible and continued in the Christian New Testament, but finds its highest expression in the Koran. Hindu theology (see HINDUISM) derives from its own unique scriptural sources and gains expression in ways that are largely incommensurate with Christian theism. The Buddhist (see BUDDHISM) traditions are not, in any conventional, Judeo-Christian sense of the term, theistic at all, even though their religious values rest upon profoundly spiritual foundations. These more nuanced insights into religious pluralism are likely to become important in the United States as Asian-Americans begin to play a more prominent role in the nation's religious history.

Pluralism, therefore, is an idea with cultural, political, and religious implications which has only recently come of age in America, although it has been a long time in the making. Religious pluralism is a heightened awareness to the fact that different ideas, practices, and sacred traditions motivate different peoples. Pluralism is also an American ideal, whose goal is to encourage understanding and respect for the religious traditions and values of different peoples. Much of the recent controversy about religious and cultural pluralism is a direct result of the collapse of an older sense of Judeo-Christian consensus that only thinly masked perennial tensions. New and different elements are, moreover, constantly being added to the American scene, which insures that the debate over pluralism in America is likely to continue well into the next century.

RHS

Bibliography: Robert A. Dahl, *Who Governs?: Democracy and Power in an American City* (New Haven: Yale University Press, 1961); Paul Knitter, *No Other Name?: A Critical Study of Christian Attitudes Toward the World Religions* (New York: Orbis Books, 1985); Daniel Patrick Moynihan and Nathan Glazer, *Beyond the Melting Pot; the Negroes, Puerto Ricans, Jews, Italians, and Irish of New York City* (Cambridge: MIT Press and Harvard University Press, 1963); Alan Race, *Christians and Religious Pluralism: Patterns in the Christian Theology of Religions* (Maryknoll, N.Y.: Orbis Books, 1983).

politics, religion and   See CHRISTIAN RIGHT; CHURCH AND STATE, RELATIONS BETWEEN; CIVIL RELIGION; CONSTITUTION, THE UNITED STATES.

positive thinking   The positive thinking movement preaches the power of mind over matter. Philosophically idealistic, theologically monistic, and temperamentally optimistic, positive thinking lacks many of the institutional trappings of other religious movements, but its inspirational gospel of health, wealth, and individual success has spread widely across the United States through the mass media.

Although many associate positive thinking with post-World War II best-sellers by Dale Carnegie and Norman Vincent Peale, the movement has its roots in 19th-century American movements such as TRANSCENDENTALISM, CHRISTIAN SCIENCE, and NEW THOUGHT.

Though Ralph Waldo EMERSON would no doubt shrink from the slogans popularized in the sentimental novels and popular tracts of positive thinkers, many transcendentalist notions—self-reliance, the unity of the individual with the divine, the common foundation of all religions, and the fundamental goodness of both human beings and the cosmos—made their way into positive thinking.

The most influential early figure in the positive thinking tradition was Ralph Waldo Trine (1866–1958), a New Thought advocate who borrowed more than his first two names from Emerson. His *In Tune with the Infinite, or, Fullness of Peace, Power, and Plenty* (1897), which argued for both the commonality of religious traditions and the unity of God and humans, established the precedent of placing the message of positive thinking on best-seller lists.

Of the 20th-century authors who have spread the optimistic gospel of positive thinking, Dale Carnegie (1888–1955) and Norman Vincent Peale (1898–1993) were undoubtedly the most influential. Carnegie applied the principles of positive thinking to the business world in newspaper columns, radio programs, and his now-famous Dale Carnegie Course, but he is best known for popular instructional manuals, such as *How to Win Friends and Influence People* (1936) and *How to Stop Worrying and Start Living* (1948).

Peale, a minister of the Reformed Church in America, was equally eclectic in his reliance on mass media. He used television and radio, the pulpit and the phonograph to turn positive thinking into something of a postwar vogue. His *A Guide to Confident Living* (1948) and *The Power of Positive Thinking* (1952) both became best-sellers, and his *Guideposts* magazine still enjoys a circulation in excess of one million. The simplicity of Peale's "you can win!" message was both its greatest strength and its greatest weakness. While many everyday folk in America found Peale's commands to "have faith in yourself!" and "believe in your abilities!" inspirational, critics called his gospel vapid. To those who found troubling Eisenhower's probably apocryphal insistence that "Our government makes no sense, unless it is founded in a deeply felt religious faith—and I don't care what it is," Peale's slogans were, because of their runaway popularity, perhaps the most problematic example of the generic "faith-in-faith" of the placid decade.

Though the positive-thinking tradition has thrived for the most part inside the Protestant mainstream, it found an eager audience among other religious groups in the postwar period. Both Rabbi Joshua Liebman and Fulton J. Sheen, a Roman Catholic priest, championed their own versions of the cult of reassurance in best-sellers. The spirit of positive thinking has also migrated into EVANGELICALISM, FUNDAMENTALISM, and PENTECOSTALISM. The "possibility thinking" preached by Robert Schuller at his Crystal Cathedral in California is clearly based on Peale's "positive thinking," and the gospels of health and wealth preached by Oral Roberts and Pat Robertson all are outgrowths of this diffuse movement, whose popularity testifies not only to the power of positive thinking but also to the power of therapeutic culture in 20th-century American life.

SRP

Bibliography: Carol V. George, *God's Salesman: Norman Vincent Peale and the Power of Positive Thinking* (New York: Oxford University Press, 1993); Donald Meyer, *The Positive Thinkers: A Study of the Quest for Health, Wealth, and Personal Power from Mary Baker Eddy to Norman Vincent Peale* (Garden City, N.Y.: Doubleday & Company, 1965).

postmillennialism   Postmillennialism is the belief that the second coming of Jesus Christ will occur after the millennium, or thousand-year period of peace, described in the 20th chapter of the New Testament Book of Revelation. It was the most common eschatological (see ESCHATOLOGY) teaching in American Protestant thought between, roughly, the Great Awakening of the 1730s and the Civil War. Christians holding postmillennial beliefs tended to be optimistic about human progress and committed themselves to moral and social reforms they hoped would begin the era of peace on earth. Postmillennialism is commonly contrasted with PREMILLENNIALISM, whose adherents generally have been dubious about human efforts to improve society prior to Christ's second coming.

The basic outlines of postmillennial thought were first formulated by Puritan theologians in the 17th century. Jonathan Edwards, who argued that he saw signs of the coming millennium in the revivals of the Great Awakening, gave important intellectual shape to this tradition in the mid-18th century. The revivalist, missionary, and reform movements that followed the Second Great Awakening of the early 19th century carried postmillennial ideas to further prominence. The postponement of God's eventual judgment gave American Protestants the time they thought was needed to evangelize the world and fulfill America's providential mission. Postmillennialism assured believers that the golden age for which they longed would be a logical continuation of the best features of the present era. It gave these Christians energy to create their own future and became a critical force in the formation of the values of the American nation.

Until the last third of the 19th-century, post-millennialism functioned as an effective compromise between opposing theological emphases, a view that harnessed ancient symbolism to a modern vision of secular progress. However, despite its onetime popularity, the postmillennial synthesis began to break apart during the period of widespread disillusionment that is now styled "the spiritual crisis of the Gilded Age." The emergence of the theological controversy between Protestant modernists and fundamentalists, moreover, effectively sounded the death knell of postmillennialism. Liberals, on the one hand, questioned the value of interpreting the Bible literally and thus took an increasingly "amillennial" (no millennial beliefs) approach to eschatology. Conservatives, on the other hand, found the old postmillennial trust in progress an empty hope and considered premillennialism to be a more satisfying alternative in the modern era. As a result, postmillennialism proved neither theologically advanced enough to please 20th-century modernists nor sufficiently biblical to capture the allegiance of fundamentalists in the 20th century.

GHS, Jr.

Bibliography: James H. Moorhead, "Between Progress and Apocalypse: A Reassessment of Millennialism in American Religious Thought, 1800–1880," *Journal of American History* 71 (1984), 524–542.

Powell, Adam Clayton, Jr. (1908–1972)

One of the more controversial figures in recent American political life, Adam Clayton Powell, Jr. was an important African-American religious and political leader from the 1930s to the 1960s. The son of Mattie (Fletcher) and Adam Clayton POWELL, SR., Powell was born in 1908 and grew up in New York City, where his father was minister of the Abyssinian Baptist Church. Like Martin Luther KING, JR., Andrew Young, and numerous other black leaders, Powell emerged from the black church to become a major national figure.

Powell attended Colgate University, where he experienced a major turning-point in his life. While at Colgate, Powell attempted to pass as white, until a check into his background by the fraternity he pledged uncovered the truth and kicked him out. This experience turned him into an activist for African-American rights.

After graduating from Colgate (1930), he returned to New York City where he served as assistant pastor at Abyssinian Baptist Church and manager of its numerous projects, including a free kitchen and a relief agency that provided clothing, food, and fuel to people during the Depression. Powell early demonstrated his opposition to racial discrimination and was instrumental in convincing several companies in New York to hire blacks. He also helped persuade Harlem Hospital to hire black doctors and nurses for the first time.

Powell succeeded his father as minister of the Abyssinian Baptist Church upon the latter's retirement in 1937. This position only heightened his visibility as a civil rights activist. In 1939 he led the picketing against the executive office of the World's Fair in New York, forcing them to open employment to blacks. Convinced that he could accomplish more in politics, and using his position as minister of one of the country's largest and most prestigious black churches as a power base, Powell ran for the New York City Council in 1940 and he was elected easily. He followed this with a successful campaign for the United States House of Representatives in 1944.

When he arrived in Washington, D.C. in 1945, Powell encountered numerous discriminatory practices, including those of Congress itself. Technically barred from the congressional dining room, the barbershop, and the showers, he insisted on using these facilities and encouraged his staff to do likewise. Powell understood himself to be a voice for civil rights, and he fought for an end to racial discrimination. He sponsored the Powell Amendment to deny federal funds to any project where racial discrimination existed. Its successful adoption as part of the Flanagan School Lunch Bill made it the first piece of legislation proposed by a black to be adopted since Reconstruction.

In 1960, Powell became chairman of the House Committee on Education and Labor. In this position he was instrumental in assisting Presidents Kennedy and Johnson in passing some of their most significant social legislation.

Powell's outspokenness on racial issues, his increasingly flamboyant lifestyle, and legal difficulties led to his censure by the House and a refusal by the 90th Congress to seat him. He was, however, seated in 1968, and in 1969 the United States Supreme Court ruled that the House's action had been unconstitutional.

Powell increasingly neglected his congressional duties to relax on Bimini. Photographs of him on his boat there during important legislative debates in Congress eroded his electoral support. In 1970 he was defeated by Charles Rangel in a close race. Powell retired to Bimini and died two years later in Miami.

EQ

Bibliography: Charles V. Hamilton, *Adam Clayton Powell, Jr.: The Political Biography of an American Dilemma* (New York: Macmillan, 1991); Wil Haygood, *King of the Cats: The Life and Times of Adam Clayton Powell, Jr.* (Boston: Houghton Mifflin, 1992); Andy Jacobs, *The Powell Affair, Freedom Minus One* (Indianapolis: Bobbs-Merrill, 1973); Peter J. Paris, *Black Religious Leaders: Conflict in Unity: Insights from Martin Luther King, Jr., Malcolm X, Joseph H. Jackson, and Adam Clayton Powell, Jr.* (Louisville: Westminster/John Knox Press, 1991); Adam Clayton Powell, Jr., *Adam by Adam: The Autobiography of Adam Clayton Powell, Jr.* (New York: Dial Press, 1971); Andree E. Reeves, *Congressional Committee Chairmen: Three Who Made an Evolution* (Lexington: University Press of Kentucky, 1993).

Powell, Adam Clayton, Sr. (1865–1953)

Remembered today chiefly as the father of the United States Representative from Harlem (see POWELL, ADAM CLAYTON, JR.), during his life Adam Clayton Powell, Sr. was not only the leading black clergyman in America, but one of the most important clergymen in the United States. Born in Soak Creek, Franklin County, Virginia on May 5, 1865, this son of former slaves led a life similar to that of most blacks in the postbellum South, one of hard work and exertion.

Much of that exertion he directed toward education. Rejected by Howard University Law School, he continued his education while working at a Washington, D.C. hotel as a janitor and waiter. He entered Wayland College and Seminary (Washington, D.C.) in 1888. Graduating in 1892, Powell entered the ministry and, following a short pastorate at Ebenezer Baptist Church in Philadelphia (1893), he accepted the call to Immanuel Baptist Church in New Haven, Connecticut.

Powell had a very productive tenure at Immanuel and while there spent two years as a special student at Yale Divinity School. His success as a pastor was so great that Virginia Union University, which had merged with his alma mater, awarded him an honorary D.D. in 1904. It also led to his next pastorate.

At that pulpit, Powell would reach his true heights. The Abyssinian Baptist Church in New York City was the most venerable black Baptist pulpit in America. When Powell assumed its pastorate on December 31, 1908, the church was a shell of its former self. Membership had dwindled to 1,600 and it was $100,000 in debt. Powell's preaching and organizational activity reinvigorated the congregation. Realizing that the black population of New York was becoming centered in Harlem, he convinced the congregation in 1920 to purchase several lots at 138th Street for a new church building. The church, dedicated in the summer of 1923, cost over $300,000, but it was the project of a now-solvent congregation.

Powell firmly committed the church to social action, and Abyssinian became a social and political center for Harlem. During the Depression, the church operated soup kitchens and agitated for better jobs and services for the Harlem area. The church continued to grow throughout the Depression. By the mid-1930s it had over 14,000 members, making it the largest Protestant congregation in the United States.

During his pastorate at Abyssinian, Powell taught at several colleges and universities, including Colgate University and Union Theological Seminary, where he lectured on race relations. As vice-president of the NAACP, he was a major figure in the fight for black equality. An international figure, he traveled and wrote on social conditions in England, France, Germany, Switzerland, and Central America. Powell retired in 1937, and was succeeded by his son, Adam Clayton Powell, Jr. He remained pastor emeritus at Abyssinian Baptist and a respected figure in American religion until his death on June 12, 1953.

(See also AFRICAN-AMERICAN RELIGION.)

EQ

Bibliography: Charles V. Hamilton, *Adam Clayton Powell, Jr. The Political Biography of an American Dilemma* (New York: Macmillan, 1991); Adam Clayton Powell, Sr., *Palestine and Saints in Caesar's Household* (New York: R. R. Smith, 1939).

Prabhupada, Abhay Charanaravinda Bhaktivedanta Swami (1896–1977)

Born Abhay Charan De to a Bengali family in Calcutta, India in 1896, A.C. Bhaktivedanta Swami Prabhupada is revered in America by "Hare Krishna" devotees as the founder of the INTERNATIONAL SOCIETY FOR KRISHNA CONSCIOUSNESS (ISKCON).

As a young man in India, Prabhupada took a guru and began a life of devotion to Krishna, the Hindu God who is typically represented as one of many avatars, or human incarnations, of the deity Vishnu (see HINDUISM). In 1932, during a pilgrimage to Vrindavan, a city of Vaishnavites or worshippers of Vishnu, Prabhupada took the name of Abhay Charanaravinda ("one who fearlessly takes shelter at the feet of the Lord"). In 1956 he left behind his work as an Indian businessman, took the vows of a *sannyasin* or world renunciant and received the name of A. C. Bhaktivedanta Swami Prabhupada.

Urged by his guru to take his inexhaustible love of Krishna to the West, Prabhupada arrived in New York City in 1965 at the age of 69. One year later he began ISKCON out of a New York City storefront and began to publish *Back to Godhead* magazine. Prabhupada has published numerous books and translations through the agency of the Bhaktivedanta Book Trust (established 1972). His best-known work is *Bhagavad-Gita As It Is* (1972), a commentary on the most revered Hindu scripture of Krishna devotees.

Prabhupada's devotional Hinduism has proven to be more easily assimilated in America than the philosophical Hinduism preached by the VEDANTA SOCIETY of Swami Vivekananda (see VIVEKANANDA, SWAMI). While Vivekananda urged his students to realize their fundamental unity with an impersonal and ultimately nontheistic Brahman, Prabhupada instructs his readers and listeners to devote their lives to worshipping Krishna as "the Supreme Lord."

Following Prabhupada's death in 1977, the leadership of the movement passed to a Governing Body Commission, which now oversees an international organization that boasts an American following of approximately 3,000 core members living on its various properties and a quarter-million nonresidential lay devotees.

SRP

Bibliography: A.C. Bhaktivedanta Swami Prabhupada, *Bhagavad-Gita As It Is* (New York: Bhaktivedanta Book Trust, 1972); Larry D. Shinn, *The Dark Lord: Cult Images and the Hare Krishnas in America* (Philadelphia: Westminster Press, 1987).

preachers, Protestant

Viewed from a theological perspective, preaching is the action by which the word of God and the teachings of the Bible are communicated to men and women in the present day. While not every American preacher has been ordained, preaching has generally been considered the principal public function of clergy in the Protestant tradition. Clergy have tended to be some of the best-educated and most thoughtful members of their community. As a result, many of them (e.g., Jonathan EDWARDS, Charles G. FINNEY, and Martin Luther KING, Jr.) have assumed critically important roles in the development of American culture.

John WINTHROP, governor of the Puritan settlement of Massachusetts Bay, delivered the first important sermon in American history. Preaching aboard the ship *Arbella* on the way to New England in 1630, Winthrop's "A Model of Christian Charity" introduced the idea of America's unique national calling. Winthrop declared that God's providence had led the Puritans to the New World. He envisioned that the settlers of New England had made a covenant, or agreement, with God. If they maintained their side of the bargain, God would reward them with prosperity. Citing the New Testament, Winthrop proclaimed that the Puritan colony would be "a city upon a hill" with the eyes of the whole world fixed upon it.

Two generations later, at the end of the 17th century, Cotton MATHER, pastor of the Second Church of Boston, preached to as many as 1,500 people each Sunday morning. A prolific writer, Mather wrote enormous amounts of material, including the monumental *Magnalia Christi Americana* (1702), in which he reviewed the early history of Puritan New England. Mather feared that New Englanders had abandoned the piety of the founders of their colony and were straying from the covenant the original settlers had made with the God. In numerous sermons of lamentation called "jeremiads" (named for the biblical prophet Jeremiah), Mather called upon his people to seek spiritual renewal. He urged them to abandon their growing worldliness and dedicate themselves to honoring God's laws.

The outbreak of the Great Awakening, the revivals that stirred the churches of America in the middle decades of the 18th century, helped fulfill Mather's hopes for New England. Congregationalist Jonathan Edwards of Northamp-

ton, Massachusetts, the most learned preacher of his day, reasserted Puritan values and spoke to his congregation about the need for their religious conversion. The sermon he delivered at Enfield, Connecticut in 1740, "Sinners in the Hands of an Angry God," contains one of the most memorable images ever employed by an American preacher. He described the soul of a sinner, held by God over the pit of hell as a person holds a spider over a roaring fire. Only divine grace ("a slender thread") prevented the sinner from falling headlong into hell and being consumed by its flames. As Edwards intended, his sermon's graphic illustration evoked powerful emotions that impelled many in his congregation to confess their sins and seek God's forgiveness.

Another prominent preacher of the Great Awakening, Anglican priest George WHITEFIELD, had gained renown by speaking in fields and other open spaces in England. In America during his seven evangelistic tours of the colonies, Whitefield's extemporaneous preaching style excited thousands of hearers wherever he went. He estimated that 20,000 people came to hear him on Boston Common in October 1740. At Philadelphia in November of the same year, he spoke to thousands in an auditorium specially built for his visit. Whitefield's eloquence even made Jonathan Edwards weep when he preached at his church in Northampton.

Whitefield's Anglican colleague John Wesley, the founder of Methodism, developed an organization of lay preachers to aid him in the evangelization of England and America. Having created what he called "circuits," geographic districts that contained a number of Methodist societies, Wesley commissioned itinerant preachers, or circuit riders, to visit every local society on a monthly basis. Francis ASBURY, the first bishop of the Methodist Episcopal Church, was the prototype of many later American circuit riders. Asbury was an aggressive evangelist and itinerant minister who traveled almost incessantly, preaching the gospel and building up his denomination. It is estimated that he covered more than 300,000 miles and delivered over 16,500 sermons in his career.

Asbury was also an early advocate of CAMP MEETINGS, which became the most important institution of Protestant outreach on the frontier in the early 19th century. Camp meetings were open-air revivals where participants settled for several days at a site and heard almost continuous preaching. A large gathering congregated at Cane Ridge, Kentucky in August 1801, for example, and took part in an event some observers likened to the biblical day of Pentecost. Wooden preaching platforms were constructed and a clearing made near a small Presbyterian church. There, Methodist, Baptist, and Presbyterian ministers all preached together for a week and converted hundreds of souls among the assembled throng.

Presbyterian Charles G. Finney was the most celebrated preacher of the Second Great Awakening, the extended period of revivals spanning the first three decades of the 19th century. After undergoing a religious conversion in 1821, Finney abandoned a law career and set to work instead as an itinerant missionary in upstate New York. He had remarkable physical characteristics that he put to good use as a preacher. A commanding figure in the pulpit, he spoke in plain language to everyone, pleading with them to change their hearts and surrender to God. He called people forward to the "anxious bench," a front-row pew where they struggled publicly to acknowledge their sins. Finney made enemies who opposed his revivals on a number of counts, especially his abandonment of traditional Calvinist teachings about predestination and his willingness to allow women to preach and pray.

Preaching has always been tremendously important in the African-American religious tradition. Francis Asbury, for instance, traveled with a black preacher named Harry Hosier, who would preach to blacks at settlements where both slaveholders and their slaves were gathered. In 1785, Asbury also asked the young Richard ALLEN to accompany him. Since Allen would have been assigned to slave quarters when he accompanied Asbury on preaching tours of the South, he refused the request. Allen instead settled in Philadelphia, and in 1787 organized an independent black church, the beginning of the African Methodist Episcopal denomination.

Among African-Americans in the South, slave preachers helped keep hope alive for many who were held in bondage. The slaveholders' fear that Christianity might encourage rebellion was confirmed when two charismatic preachers, Denmark VESEY in 1822 and Nat TURNER in 1831, organized slave revolts. Some of Turner's religious ideas are recorded in the "confession" he made to the court that tried him for insurrection and murder. Despite his claim that God had inspired the revolt, Turner's white interrogators asked what seemed to them an obvious question: didn't capture and impending execution confirm that he was wrong? Turner knew the Bible well and understood how God's prophets had suffered at the hands of the wicked. He did not reply directly but asked his captors his own question: "Was not Christ crucified?"

Among white clergy in the same period, no preacher was better known for applying biblical teachings to the abolition of slavery than Congregationalist Henry Ward BEECHER. Beecher believed above all else that religious thought should be adapted to the culture and times in which Christians lived. Beecher preached openly on issues relating to social reform, including rights for women and an end to slavery. During the controversy in the 1850s over the admission of the Kansas territory to the Union, he also raised money from his pulpit to provide rifles (called "Beecher's Bibles") for the protection of antislavery settlers in Kansas. Throughout the Civil War he was an outspoken supporter of the northern war effort. In February 1865, Beecher was asked to deliver an address at the flag-raising in Fort Sumter in Charleston, South Carolina, the event that symbolized the end of the southern slaveholders' rebellion.

Along with Beecher, the most notable preacher in the middle years of the 19th century was Episcopalian Phillips BROOKS, rector of Trinity Church in Boston from 1869 to 1891. Brooks's thinking suited his parish well, for it blended optimism about the human condition with conservative social views. He believed in the goodness and nobility of humankind, and faith in progress kept him untroubled by the obvious social inequalities in America during the Gilded Age. Brooks published *Lectures on Preaching*, which had been delivered at Yale University in 1877, and a number of volumes of his popular sermons. He was also author of the beloved Christmas carol "O Little Town of Bethlehem."

Other preachers analyzed American society at the turn of the century in ways far different from Brooks's benign trust in human progress. Evangelist Dwight L. MOODY, whose preaching served as a harbinger of the fundamentalist movement emerging in American Protestantism, was convinced that the salvation of individual souls was the only effective means of reforming America. Eschewing the discussion of all other topics, he described his ministry as essentially an otherworldly rescue mission: "I look upon this world as a wrecked vessel. God has given me a lifeboat and said to me, 'Moody, save all you can.' " The message Moody preached was relatively unemotional, for he believed that people could, with God's help, attain salvation. He would hold up a Bible and assure people that eternal life was available for the asking, if they would merely "come forward and t-a-k-e, TAKE!"

Preachers of the Social Gospel movement, on the other hand, attributed poverty to the sinfulness of the wealthy and called on them to repent. Solomon Washington GLADDEN, minister of a Congregational church in Columbus, Ohio between 1882 and 1914, was one of the first to bring Christianity actively to bear on all areas of life, political and economic as well as spiritual. Walter RAUSCHENBUSCH served for 11 years as pastor of a German Baptist church in the Hell's Kitchen neighborhood of New York City. He preached about the need for Christians to take seriously their responsibilities in establishing God's kingdom on earth. Although he left the parish ministry to become a professor at Rochester Seminary, Rauschenbusch provided a systematic defense of the Christian social position he espoused in *A Theology of the Social Gospel*, published in 1917.

Harry Emerson FOSDICK was another early 20th-century preacher whose sermons contained liberal social and theological emphases. Beginning his career as pastor of a Baptist church in Montclair, New Jersey, Fosdick was involved in a labor union dispute shortly before World War I. While serving at the First Presbyterian Church in New York City, moreover, he became embroiled in the controversy over fundamentalism that divided the Presbyterian denomination in the 1920s. His sermon on May 21, 1922, "Shall the Fundamentalists Win?", won national attention. Although Fosdick intended his sermon to be a plea for tolerance, his challenge to the fundamentalists' belief in an infallible Bible only exacerbated the dispute and forced his resignation from the Presbyterian pulpit. He eventually won even greater fame as minister at New York's interdenominational Riverside Church, a magnificent gothic structure built with the financial assistance of John D. Rockefeller, Jr.

After World War II, Billy GRAHAM gained recognition as America's most influential preacher. He first gained national attention in 1949, when he undertook an evangelistic campaign in Los Angeles. In the early 1950s, he became an increasingly popular figure in Protestant circles. "The Hour of Decision," his radio program, went on the air in 1950, and he emerged as the unofficial spiritual advisor to President Dwight D. Eisenhower. In the summer of 1957, Graham led a series of religious gatherings in New York City, one of the earliest evangelistic crusades to be broadcast on television. Graham's theologically conservative approach fit the mood of the time. He believed that the first step in improving the world was for individuals to accept Jesus Christ as their savior. When enough individuals had repented, he thought, social betterment would inevitably follow.

Although Graham remains a respected preacher, he has been outshone in recent years by the flashier televangelists of the so-called ELECTRONIC CHURCH. Using the media, these preachers have achieved audiences far larger and exposure far broader than has ever been possible before. Robert Schuller, a minister of the Reformed Church in America, for example, broadcasts his weekly "Hour of Power" from the spectacular Crystal Cathedral in Garden Grove, California. Fashioning an optimistic theology he calls "possibility thinking," Schuller has recast the Christian gospel into a relatively inoffensive form that appeals to the age-old quest for self-esteem and success. By contrast, Jerry Falwell, pastor of a Baptist church in Lynchburg, Virginia, used his television preaching ministry, the "Old-Time Gospel Hour," as a springboard for the creation of the MORAL MAJORITY. An educational and fund-raising organization dedicated to political lobbying, Falwell's Moral Majority blended fundamentalist religious beliefs with rigidly conservative views on a host of ethical issues troubling late 20th-century Americans.

Martin Luther KING, Jr. undoubtedly the most influential preacher of the 20th century, as well as one of the most important ministers in all American history, emerged in the late 1950s as the acknowledged leader of the civil rights movement. King's sermons inspired millions of Americans, including many of his fellow clergy, to march and sit-in on behalf of black freedom. He was the embodiment of the black preaching tradition, combining appeals to social responsibility with classic theological themes.

No speech in recent memory has been as important as King's 1963 "I Have a Dream" address, virtually a sermon, delivered in front of the Lincoln Memorial in Washington, D.C. King the preacher combined biblical imagery with an evocation of American democratic ideals reminiscent of John Winthrop's sermon on the *Arbella* in 1630. Concluding with a thrilling call to "let freedom ring" across the United States,

King moved not only the hundreds of thousands who heard him in person that day, but also millions of others who have listened to recordings of his address since that time. Referring to the religious overtones of her late husband's speech, Coretta Scott King once commented: "At that moment it seemed as if the Kingdom of God appeared."

GHS, Jr.

Bibliography: DeWitte T. Holland, ed., *Preaching in American History: Selected Issues in the American Pulpit, 1630–1967* (Nashville: Abingdon Press, 1969); DeWitte T. Holland, *The Preaching Tradition: A Brief History* (Nashville: Abingdon Press, 1980); Harry S. Stout, *The New England Soul: Preaching and Religious Culture in Colonial New England* (New York: Oxford University Press, 1986).

predestination   See CALVINISM; ELECTION.

premillennialism   Premillennialism is the belief that the second coming of Jesus Christ will occur before the beginning of the millennium, the thousand-year period of peace and righteousness depicted in the New Testament Book of Revelation. It is the most popular form of ESCHATOLOGY taught among conservative Protestant groups in the United States today. Contrary to the socially progressive views encouraged by POSTMILLENNIALISM, once the dominant outlook in American Protestant thought, premillennialism tends to foster pessimism about human society by stressing the church's urgent need to save souls.

Premillennialists interpret biblical texts quite literally and expect the fulfilment of apocalyptic prophecies that foretell the destruction of the present age, the overthrow of Satan, and the establishment of God's kingdom on the earth. They are subdivided into two major groups. Some think that many biblical prophecies about the end-times have already been fulfilled in the history of the Christian church. Others believe that none of these prophecies has yet come to pass, for the eschatological events predicted in the Old and New Testaments lie entirely outside history. This latter group teaches that the Antichrist will gain control of the world and begin a reign of terror, called the tribulation, that will be ended by the triumph of the forces of God. They also think that at some point before Christ's second coming the RAPTURE of the true church will occur, and the saints will ascend to heaven, a prophecy found in the New Testament (1 Thessalonians 4:15–17).

A theory known as DISPENSATIONALISM is the most common form of premillennial teaching in 20th-century America. Developed by Anglican clergyman John Nelson Darby in the mid-19th century, this belief separates history into eras, or dispensations. The American biblical scholar Cyrus I. SCOFIELD, whose *Reference Bible* provides premillennialists with a useful tool for studying the Scriptures, defined a dispensation as a period marked off by some change in God's dealing with humanity. In recent years, Hal Lindsey's best-selling *The Late Great Planet Earth* (1970) has helped popularize dispensationalism among a new generation of Americans concerned about prophecies in the Bible.

Premillennialists were once caricatured as representing the most disadvantaged segments of society and being less socially concerned than other Christians. While this characterization still fits a denomination like the JEHOVAH'S WITNESSES, other groups who have espoused forms of premillennialism, the Mormons (see CHURCH OF JESUS CHRIST OF LATTER-DAY SAINTS), for example, or the Seventh-day Adventists (see SEVENTH-DAY ADVENTIST CHURCH), no longer are considered to be outside the mainstream of American life. And several spokesmen of the New Religious Right who adhere to premillennial beliefs (notably, Jerry Falwell and Pat Robertson) have changed markedly over the past decade and emphasize, rather than disparage, the importance of Christians' engaging in political activity.

GHS, Jr.

Bibliography: Paul Boyer, *When Time Shall Be No More: Prophecy Belief in Modern American Culture* (Cambridge: Belknap Press, 1992); Timothy P. Weber, *Living in the Shadow of the Second Coming: American Premillennialism, 1875–1982,* enl. ed. (1979; Chicago: University of Chicago Press, 1987).

Presbyterian Church (U.S.A.)   The Presbyterian Church (U.S.A.) is the largest and most theologically liberal of the diverse group of American denominations that adhere to the traditions of PRESBYTERIANISM. The church was formed in 1983 by the merger of the United Presbyterian Church in the United States of America (the main Presbyterian body in the North after the Civil War) and the Presbyterian Church in the United States (often popularly called the Southern Presbyterian Church).

Presbyterianism first took shape in the British Isles after 1558, when John Knox of Scotland adapted that system to the Scottish Church. An interest in presbyterian church government came to the forefront in England during the Puritan ascendancy in the mid-17th century. At the same time, Presbyterian sentiment also gained favor in America. Several Presbyterian churches were established when Puritan leaders migrated from Congregationalist-dominated New England to other colonies.

Under the leadership of Scotch-Irish missionary Francis Makemie, some of these early Presbyterian churches in America were brought together in 1706 to create the Presbytery of Philadelphia. Two additional presbyteries were organized over the next decade, and they formed the Synod of Philadelphia in 1717. Presbyterians then numbered approximately 3,000 members and 40 churches. A large-scale influx of Presbyterian immigrants from northern Ireland began in 1720. Their movement into the middle colonies, then southward through the Shenandoah Valley to the Piedmont region of the South, not only increased the vitality of Presbyterianism generally, but also assured the denomination's main strength would lie outside New England. American Presbyterianism had no generally accepted doctrinal standard until 1729. In that year, the Adopting Act of the Synod of Philadelphia established the Westminster Confession of 1643, the classic expression of English Calvinist (see CALVINISM) belief, as the official creedal position of the church.

From its beginning, the Presbyterian Church in America embraced two conflicting traditions. The Scots and Scotch-Irish emphasized precise theology and church governance, while religious piety characterized the English and Welsh experience. The outbreak of revivals during the Great Awakening of the 1730s and 1740s immediately split the new denomination along this inherent fault line. Presbyterian minister Gilbert TENNENT became one of the chief spokesmen for the revivals, and his 1740 sermon on "The Dangers of an Unconverted Ministry" is remembered for the vehemence with which he assailed his clerical opponents. Tennent's animosity greatly contributed to the NEW SIDE/OLD SIDE division of 1741, when Tennent and his presbytery were ejected from the church. Although the two Presbyterian factions reunited in 1758 and eventually established a General Assembly in 1788 (comprising over 200 congregations and 16 presbyteries), institutional problems still plagued the denomination as the 18th century drew to a close.

Following the American Revolution, some Presbyterians established ties with the Congregationalist churches on the basis of a common Calvinist theological tradition. Although separated by matters of organization (Congregationalists believed in the absolute independence of the local congregation), many Presbyterians and Congregationalists still considered themselves part of the same denomination. As settlers moved westward in the early 19th century and the evangelization of the new territories began, all technical distinctions about church government seemed pointless. A PLAN OF UNION, implemented in 1801 and reinforced in 1808, effectively united the two denominations in New York and the midwestern states. Never popular with doctrinal conservatives, however, the Plan of Union, coupled with divisiveness already aroused by the Second Great Awakening, soon

became a focus for renewed strife within Presbyterianism.

The Second Great Awakening, a diverse series of revivals that swept the United States from the 1790s through the 1830s, was especially costly for the Presbyterian church as an institution. Despite the fact that Presbyterian minister Charles Grandison FINNEY was the leading revivalist of the day, the church's leadership generally opposed the emotionalism and inattention to theology the Awakening fostered. Alienated by their denomination's formality and intellectualism, some Presbyterians even chose to leave their church and join the revival-oriented Baptists and Methodists instead. An independent Cumberland Presbytery was also formed in 1810 to nurture Presbyterians engaged in revivals in Tennessee and Kentucky.

Finally, in 1837, conflicts regarding revivalism, relationships with other denominations, social reform, and antislavery activity led to the abrogation of the Plan of Union and the expulsion from the General Assembly of four synods formed under the agreement with the Congregationalists. This NEW SCHOOL/OLD SCHOOL split embodied deep divisions not simply over polity and theology, but over political and sectional tensions as well—a prelude to the Civil War. The Old School party demanded strict conformity to the theological and organizational standards of Presbyterianism. In expelling the New School faction from the church, the southern-dominated Old School thought a double victory had been won: It both removed an internal opponent from the denomination and silenced northerners who were demanding the abolition of slavery.

Immediately before and during the Civil War, the New School and Old School churches each experienced further change. Political issues that rent the United States as a whole led in 1857 to the New School denomination's dividing South and North. The Old School denomination was split, too, following the beginning of the war in 1861. The Old School church in the South adopted the name Presbyterian Church in the Confederate States of America in 1861. It merged with congregations of the small southern New School Assembly in 1864 and, after the defeat of the Confederacy in 1865, renamed itself the Presbyterian Church in the United States. The Old School/New School schism was effectively healed in the North when Presbyterians there reunited in 1870 under the name Presbyterian Church in the United States of America.

More than any other Protestant body at the end of the 19th century, Presbyterians in the North were shaken by passionate disputes over the interpretation of the Bible. In 1870, Presbyterian pastor David Swing of Chicago challenged his denomination to rethink its doctrinal positions. He argued that religious creeds, like all human expressions, were imperfect and might contain errors. Tried for HERESY, Swing was acquitted but, nevertheless, chose to withdraw from his church. Swing's heresy trial was merely a prelude to the greater controversy that engulfed Charles Augustus BRIGGS, a professor at the Presbyterians' Union Seminary in New York City. Although he never questioned the overall inspiration of the Scriptures, Briggs specifically denied the authenticity of a number of biblical passages. For this assertion, he was charged with heresy. His trial extended over three years, and in 1893 he was suspended from the ministry. Briggs soon entered the priesthood of the Episcopal Church, and he retained his position at Union when the seminary simply severed its relationship with the Presbyterians.

The fundamentalist controversy in the first quarter of the 20th century also profoundly divided the denomination. The Presbyterian seminary at Princeton (see PRINCETON THEOLOGY) had long expounded conservative interpretations of the Bible and Christian doctrine, but when J. Gresham MACHEN, a professor of New Testament studies, militantly objected to growing liberal tendencies in his denomination, a schism occurred. Machen left Princeton in 1929 and founded Westminister Theological Seminary in Philadelphia. There, theological students were instructed in his ultraconservative interpretation of the Presbyterian faith. Machen's followers also created a new denomination, the Presbyterian Church of America (later known as the Orthodox Presbyterian Church), in 1936.

Meanwhile, the Presbyterian church in the southern states grew from approximately 80,000 to over one million members between 1869 and 1962. This denomination's most distinctive theological statement, the doctrine of "the spirituality of the church," had received its classic formulation shortly before the Civil War by theologian James Henley THORNWELL of South Carolina. In order to protect their church against the zeal of northern antislavery advocates, Thornwell and most southern Presbyterians argued that the Christian church should hold no corporate position on social or political matters. Thus, long after the Civil War had ended, the Presbyterian Church in the United States said little even about Sabbath observance or temperance, the great Protestant crusades of the 19th and early 20th centuries. Only in the 1930s, when the sectional hostility that had sparked Thornwell's teaching was virtually forgotten, was the church in the South able to direct attention away from its internal life toward wider social concerns.

Despite the defection of fundamentalists like Machen, northern Presbyterianism grew during the 20th century as it joined with other smaller Presbyterian bodies. In 1910, it reunited with the Cumberland Presbyterians following a long separation. Next, the church merged in 1958 with the United Presbyterian Church of North America, a denomination of Scottish heritage founded in the mid-19th century. And although discussions between northern and southern Presbyterians in the 1970s led to the defection of a number of conservative congregations from the southern church (forming in turn the Presbyterian Church in America), the thinning of the conservatives' ranks actually helped speed the process of denominational reunification. The two major branches of Presbyterianism, North and South, were at last joined with the birth of the present united church in June 1983. According to its 1990 annual report, the Presbyterian Church (U.S.A.) contains a total membership of nearly 3.8 million people and 11,500 congregations, making it one of the largest Protestant denominations in the United States today.

GHS, Jr.

Bibliography: Randall Balmer and John R. Fitzmier, *The Presbyterians* (Westport, Conn.: Greenwood Press, 1993); Bradley J. Longfield, *The Presbyterian Controversy: Fundamentalists, Modernists, and Moderates* (New York: Oxford University Press, 1991); Ernest T. Thompson, *Presbyterians in the South,* 3 vols. (Richmond, Va.: John Knox Press, 1963–1972).

Presbyterian Church in America See PRESBYTERIANISM.

Presbyterian Church in the United States See PRESBYTERIAN CHURCH (U.S.A.); PRESBYTERIANISM.

presbyterianism Presbyterianism is a type of church government that arose out of the Protestant Reformation of the 16th century. The word itself derives from the Greek term for "elder" (*presbuteros*). It is based on the Protestant doctrine of the priesthood of all believers, that is, the belief that every Christian shares in the leadership of the church. Presbyterianism was the prevailing form of organization among churches of the Reformed Tradition (see REFORMED TRADITION, THE) in the Netherlands, Switzerland, France, and Scotland in the 16th century. The immigration of Presbyterians from the British Isles to the New World helped establish this tradition in America by the mid-17th century.

In contrast to both the localism of the congregational (see CONGREGATIONALISM) system and the authoritarian tendencies implicit in the episcopal (see EPISCOPACY) system, presbyterianism stresses uniformity, universality, and democracy. Thus, ministers and elected laity (elders and deacons) together govern at all levels, maintaining theological orthodoxy and discipline within the church. Presbyterian church government begins with the local congregation, then extends upward to the presbytery (a geographical district composed of many local congregations), the synod (composed of clergy and laity elected by the presbytery), and the general assembly, where all synods unite on the national level.

Presbyterianism first took shape in the British Isles after 1558, when John Knox of Scotland adapted the system he had observed in Calvin's (see CALVINISM) Geneva to the Scottish Church. Presbyterianism, which had always been present among segments of the Church of England, came to the forefront during the Puritan ascendancy after the Long Parliament in 1640. Unlike the Congregational establishment in New England and the Anglican establishment in the southern colonies, the Presbyterian presence in 17th-century America was a relatively weak one. However, the influx of Scotch-Irish Presbyterian immigrants after 1714 began swinging the ethnic and ecclesiastical balance in the English-speaking colonies. A group of Presbyterian ministers under the leadership of Francis Makemie, who had been ordained in northern Ireland as a missionary to America, organized the first American presbytery in Philadelphia in 1706. By 1716, two other presbyteries were established (at New Castle and Long Island) and a synod was formed.

The formulation of the SAYBROOK PLATFORM in New England in 1708 was a further symbol of Presbyterianism's expansion in America. Although this agreement was the handiwork of a convention of Connecticut Congregationalists, it eliminated the longstanding practice of absolute independence for the churches adopting it and opened the way for connections between local congregations—a system akin, therefore, to Presbyterian government. As a result of the

Saybrook Platform, many Congregationalists linked themselves with other churches and ministers. This action helped them recognize how the Calvinist theological heritage they shared with Presbyterians outweighed technical differences between their respective church governments. Presbyterians and Congregationalists later institutionalized this relationship in the 1801 PLAN OF UNION, a missionary alliance that helped establish a Presbyterian presence in upstate New York and the Midwest.

Beginning with the GREAT AWAKENING of the 18th century, the history and development of Presbyterianism in America has been marked by a series of divisions along both theological and ethnic lines. The outbreak of revivals in the 1730s split American Presbyterianism between those who desired theological precision and those who valued simple piety. Presbyterian minister Gilbert TENNENT, for example, became one of the most prominent leaders of the Awakening. His animosity toward his allegedly "unconverted" fellow church members contributed to the NEW SIDE/OLD SIDE split of 1741. Although the two factions reunited in 1758, ecclesiastical tensions were never fully resolved.

The SECOND GREAT AWAKENING of the early 19th century proved even more challenging for Presbyterians. The Cumberland Presbyterian Church emerged out of disputes over the importance of REVIVALISM, when Presbyterians converted in the revivals in Tennessee and Kentucky chose to form a new denomination. Organized in February 1810 in Dickson County, Tennessee, the Cumberland Presbyterian Church established its first synod in 1813. The church grew rapidly between 1835 and 1860. While two-thirds of the church's members eventually rejoined the main body of American Presbyterians early in the 20th century, a sizable minority continued a separate denominational identity. The Cumberland Presbyterian Church still teaches a liberalized version of Calvinism. Its membership, which traditionally has been strongest in the upper South, numbers roughly 100,000 people today.

In 1837, further conflicts led to another split in the Presbyterian ranks, when the conservative, antirevivalist Old School (see NEW SCHOOL/ OLD SCHOOL) faction expelled the theologically and politically progressive New School faction from the church. When the Civil War came in 1861, the Old School Presbyterian Church also broke apart, and a new church, the Presbyterian Church in the Confederate States of America, was formed in the South. After the war, this denomination renamed itself the Presbyterian Church in the United States.

Although the major portion of that church reunited with Presbyterians in the North in 1983, a minority adamantly opposed the social and doctrinal liberalism they perceived in the northern church. As a result, they withdrew from their denomination while the discussions of reunion were still in progress and formed a new church, the Presbyterian Church in America. Extremely conservative in its theological beliefs, the Presbyterian Church in America is now the second-largest Presbyterian denomination in the United States. It numbers approximately 224,000 members in over 1,160 congregations, still mostly in the South.

More than any other Protestant body at the end of the 19th century, northern Presbyterians (then known as the Presbyterian Church in the United States of America) were shaken by theological disputes between modernists and fundamentalists over the meaning of religious doctrines and the interpretation of the Bible. As a result of this multifaceted controversy, the denomination divided once again in the 20th century.

In 1936 J. Gresham MACHEN, a professor at Princeton Seminary, formed a new, doctrinally rigorist denomination called the Presbyterian Church of America. Despite an almost immediate schism, when archconservative Carl McIntire and his followers withdrew to form the Bible Presbyterian Church, Machen's denomination was able to maintain its institutional integrity. A court action forced the Presbyterian Church of America to change its name in 1939. Now known as the Orthodox Presbyterian Church, this denomination has approximately 19,000 members, concentrated mainly in eastern Pennsylvania and New Jersey. McIntire's church, on the other hand, underwent several metamorphoses and eventually joined the Presbyterian Church in America in 1982.

Another small but vital Presbyterian denomination is the General Synod of the Associate Reformed Presbyterian Church. This body derives its identity from protests and political divisions within Scottish Presbyterianism in the 17th and 18th centuries. When separatist Scots settled in America, they continued to hold themselves aloof from other Presbyterians. Although some parts of this church eventually merged into the United Presbyterian Church of North America in 1858, the synod of the Carolinas retained the denomination's original name and heritage. The church's strength is still highly localized. Most of the reported 38,000 members of the Associate Reformed Presbyterian Church live in the western, mountainous regions of North and South Carolina.

Finally, the most theologically liberal of the Presbyterian denominations is the PRESBYTERIAN CHURCH (U.S.A.). Despite the defection of fundamentalists like Machen, Presbyterianism in the North grew in the 20th century by absorbing several smaller Presbyterian bodies. First, it reunited in 1910 with the majority of the Cumberland Presbyterians. Next, it merged in 1958 with the Presbyterians of Scottish lineage who composed the United Presbyterian Church of North America. Then, despite the defection of a number of conservative southern congregations, the two major branches of Presbyterianism, North and South, joined in June 1983 and healed the breach caused by the Civil War. According to its 1990 annual report, the Presbyterian Church (U.S.A.) contained nearly 3.8 million members. It is by far the largest Presbyterian denomination and one of the leading churches in American Protestantism today.

GHS, Jr.

Bibliography: Maurice W. Armstrong, Lefferts A. Loetscher, and Charles A. Anderson, *The Presbyterian Enterprise: Sources of American Presbyterian History* (Philadelphia: Westminster Press, 1956); Randall Balmer and John R. Fitzmier, *The Presbyterians* (Westport, CT: Greenwood Press, 1993); Lefferts A. Loetscher, *The Broadening Church: A Study of Theological Issues in the Presbyterian Church Since 1869* (Philadelphia: University of Pennsylvania Press, 1954).

Primitive Baptists See BAPTISTS.

primitivism Primitivism is the impulse within American Protestantism that seeks the restoration (see RESTORATION MOVEMENT) of the original Christian church described in the New Testament. Primitivists believe it is possible to remove the accretions of history and return Christianity to the pristine state of ancient times. Although the terms "primitivism" and "restorationism" have sometimes been used interchangeably, restorationism usually refers only to the 19th-century movement of which the present-day Christian Church (Disciples of Christ) and Churches of Christ are a continuation. Primitivism, on the other hand, is a broad tradition linked to a number of denominational families.

Religious primitivist themes appear throughout American history. From the days of its earliest settlement, America promised a land of new opportunities reminiscent of the biblical garden of Eden. As British philosopher John Locke said, "In the beginning, all the world was America." New England PURITANISM, which sought to reestablish ancient ideals of political life and Christian order and worship, epitomizes this phenomenon. In the 18th century, primitivism also appeared within elements of both the Methodist and the Baptist churches, notably in their emphasis on lay leadership and the democratization of church life.

The most significant example of the American primitivist impulse emerged in the restorationism promoted by Alexander CAMPBELL and Barton STONE early in the 19th century. Campbell had great confidence in the human ability to understand the Scriptures and restore the purity of the apostolic age. Stone's stress was somewhat different, for he was more interested in God's rule over human affairs than in actual church order. Still, these men shared many common concerns, notably the desire for church unity based not on doctrinal grounds, but on the essential truths expressed in the New Testament. Campbell's and Stone's movements joined forces in 1832 upon the basis of their mutual pursuit of a primitive Christian harmony.

The reappearance of primitivism in the 20th century can be linked to disillusionment both with contemporary religious life and with American culture generally. As a consequence of these modern trends, some Christians have become increasingly interested in discovering the lost purity of the early church. The Jesus movement of the 1960s, for instance, desired to return to the simple lifestyles of the first-century Christian community. PENTECOSTALISM, moreover, has proclaimed primitivist ideals in its claim to have restored the original gospel of healing, speaking in tongues, and baptism in the Holy Spirit. Pentecostals affirm that the manifestations of divine power they experience are irrefutable demonstrations of the restored faith of apostolic times.

Primitivism is a tradition that finds expression within a wide spectrum of denominations and theological positions. This impulse is so strong that some American religious historians believe it is the single most important intellectual presupposition underlying the development of Protestantism in the United States.

GHS, Jr.

Bibliography: Richard T. Hughes and C. Leonard Allen, *Illusions of Innocence: Protestant Primitivism in America, 1630–1875* (Chicago: University of Chicago Press, 1988).

Princeton Theology

In 1812 the Presbyterian Church established a denominational seminary at its college in Princeton, New Jersey. A unique theological tradition was cultivated at Princeton Seminary over the course of the 19th and early 20th centuries. Archibald Alexander, Charles HODGE, his son A. A. Hodge, Benjamin WARFIELD, and J. Gresham MACHEN were key figures in the formation of the so-called Princeton Theology. Their theological system was based upon SCOTTISH COMMON SENSE REALISM. This philosophy proved crucial to the development of conservative attitudes toward the Bible, especially in arguments for the INERRANCY of Scripture, an essential belief of 20th-century fundamentalism.

The Princeton Theology emerged out of the debate between Old and New School Presbyterians in the first half of the 19th century. While New School advocates sought a flexible version of Calvinism more in accord with their emphasis on revivalism and religious emotions, the Old School party stressed stable, objective theological standards. Old School Presbyterians tended to view truth as precisely stated propositions, expressed in written language, that conveyed the same message at all times and in all places. As Old School leader Charles Hodge proudly remarked about Princeton, "a new idea never originated in this Seminary."

Common Sense Realism, a philosophy that developed in the Presbyterian stronghold of Scotland, supported this concept of unchanging intellectual objectivity. Following the inductive methods of 17th-century scientist Francis Bacon, Common Sense philosophers asserted that the external world was just as it appeared to be. This theory was also applied to the Bible. Princeton theologians accepted the statement of Reformed theologian Francois Turretin, who wrote: "The Scriptures are so perspicuous in things pertaining to salvation that they can be understood by believers without the external help of . . . ecclesiastical authority." Turretin's works, which were used extensively at Princeton, reinforced the idea that everyday perceptions were reliable in reading and interpreting the Bible. This view of the infallible correctness of the biblical text was given its classic expression in 1881 when A. A. Hodge and Benjamin Warfield

A 19th-century predecessor to fundamentalism, Princeton Theology vigorously defended the Reformed Tradition and scriptural innerancy. (Billy Graham Center Museum)

published their defense of the "inerrancy" of Scripture.

The theological militancy of the Princetonians, coupled with a general conservative reaction in the late 19th-century churches to new forms of thought, led to heated debates in Presbyterian denominational circles. The Princeton theologians vehemently defended the errorless nature of the Bible against attacks by liberal biblical critics who pointed out obvious errors and historical discrepancies within it. Although the Protestant liberals wanted to bolster, not undermine, the Christian faith by appealing to lofty religious ideas not necessarily found in the Bible, conservatives insisted simply upon the objective truth of both the Bible and the traditional creeds. In 1910 the General Assembly, the Presbyterians' highest ranking judicial and legislative body, affirmed the Princeton position on inerrancy and declared it to be the church's official teaching on the Bible.

Over the next 10 years, however, significant changes occurred within the Presbyterian church and American Protestantism generally, and liberalism was able to gain ground. In this period Princeton professor J. Gresham Machen, who had assumed Warfield's mantle of leadership in 1906, responded to new threats to orthodoxy by suggesting that theological liberals had ceased to be true Christians and should leave their churches. But conservatives like Machen no longer had the voting power they once possessed in the denomination. Alienated from his church, Machen withdrew from the Princeton faculty in 1929 and founded an alternative school, Westminister Theological Seminary, in Philadelphia. There, he intended to maintain the intellectual emphases of the "Princeton" Theology.

Machen's departure represented a watershed at Princeton. Princeton Seminary in the 20th century, while still relatively conservative among mainline Protestant theological schools, no longer endorses the theological methodologies it militantly espoused in the 19th century. However, the positions for which the school once stood, particularly the stress on scriptural inerrancy, have hardly died out in American religious thought. Inerrancy remains strong in many evangelical denominations and has been adopted as the official teaching of both the Southern Baptist Convention and the Lutheran Church—Missouri Synod.

GHS, Jr.

Bibliography: Mark A. Noll, ed., *The Princeton Theology, 1812–1921: Scripture, Science, Theological Method from Archibald Alexander to Benjamin Breckinridge Warfield* (Grand Rapids, Mich.: Baker Book House, 1983).

Progressive National Baptist Convention, Inc. Organized in Cincinnati, Ohio on November 15, 1961, the Progressive National Baptist Convention, Inc. (PNBC) was created due to a schism within the NATIONAL BAPTIST CONVENTION, U.S.A., INC. The rupture was caused when a group of younger ministers, notably Martin Luther KING, JR., Benjamin Mays, and Ralph ABERNATHY, attempted to replace the NBC, Inc.'s longtime president, Joseph H. Jackson, with a candidate more receptive to the goals of the CIVIL RIGHTS MOVEMENT. Stopped by a series of parliamentary and legal maneuvers and removed from positions of leadership in the convention by Jackson, they formed a new denomination.

This new denomination, the Progressive National Baptist Convention, Inc., dedicated itself to support of the civil rights movement and, in order to prevent the conflicts over the presidency that had dominated the life of the NBC, Inc., limited convention presidents to two one-year terms. More politically active than the other two main black Baptist conventions, it was a vigorous opponent of apartheid in South Africa, and vocal in its support for civil rights legislation and organizations, including the Martin Luther King, Jr. Center for Nonviolent Social Change.

More urban-centered than the other two historically black Baptist conventions, the Progressive Convention has 1.8 million members and 1,800 congregations, making it the third-largest black Baptist denomination. Although without affiliated seminaries, the convention provides financial support to several of the most prestigious black seminaries, including Howard Divinity School and the Morehouse School of Religion.

(See also NATIONAL BAPTIST CONVENTION OF AMERICA, INC.; AFRICAN-AMERICAN RELIGION.)

EQ

Bibliography: Taylor Branch, *Parting the Waters: America in the King Years, 1954–1963* (New York: Simon & Schuster, 1988); C. Eric Lincoln and Lawrence Mamiya, *The Black Church in the African American Experience* (Durham, N.C.: Duke University Press, 1990); Wardell J. Payne, *Directory of African American Religious Bodies: A Compendium by the Howard University School of Divinity* (Washington, D.C.: Howard University Press, 1991).

prohibition See TEMPERANCE.

proslavery thought "We who own slaves honor God's law in the exercise of our authority," wrote James Furman, a Baptist in South Carolina, to a fellow slaveholder in 1848. Proslavery religious thought in the antebellum South (see SOUTH, THE) rested on a three-fold base of biblical teaching, moral philosophy, and natural law. These ideas were expressed not only through arguments that God had blessed slaveholding, but also in missionary efforts to convert slaves to the Christian faith of their masters.

Although many in the generation of Protestants who had been converted during the revivals of the Great Awakening of the 1760s had routinely attacked SLAVERY as contrary to the principles of both Christian morality and the American Revolution, by the 1830s numerous factors led white southerners to reconsider that earlier stance. The increasing economic dependence of the South on the slave system, the rising volume of abolitionist (see ABOLITIONISM) rhetoric in the North, and slave insurrections led by Denmark VESEY (1822) and Nat TURNER (1831), both forceful and charismatic religious teachers, all forced ideological changes. As a consequence, a new argument for the sanctity of slavery emerged.

Southern Christians declared that God had sanctioned slavery in biblical times, first, among the Old Testament patriarchs and, later, in the society in which Jesus and the apostles lived. Even the apostle Paul himself had returned a runaway slave to his master Philemon and implicitly blessed slavery as an institution. Nineteenth-century moral teaching, furthermore, emphasized duties and rights, a useful philosophy for men and women concerned about the relationship between masters and their slaves. Finally, natural law demonstrated that slavery had been in existence throughout human history and that forms of submission were to be found in all societies.

In order to erect an even higher barrier against northern antislavery attacks, white southerners also formulated a doctrine advocating the strict noninterference of churches in political affairs. Referring to Jesus' words in the Gospels, southern Christians argued that the church should not involve itself in the "things which are Caesar's." The state alone had a God-given sanction to govern society, while the church possessed a similar calling to superintend the spiritual sphere. Presbyterian minister James Henley THORNWELL of South Carolina gave this concept its classic formulation in his so-called "doctrine of the spirituality of the church." The church was a spiritual body concerned exclusively with eternal salvation, Thornwell reasoned, and as a consequence possessed no social or secular relevance at all. Churches had no authority to discuss the legitimacy of institutions such as slavery but must simply accept society as they found it.

Although proslavery religious thought was intended primarily to keep abolitionists in the North at bay and to relieve the troubled consciences of Christian slaveholders in the South, that was not its only focus. The evangelization of slaves, an outgrowth of the American Protestant home missionary enterprise, was another important facet of proslavery ideology. In bringing the Christian gospel to African-Americans, preachers sought both to save individual souls and to bring the religious beliefs of slaves into line with what their masters believed. Although some whites in the early 19th century feared that conversion to Christianity would cause slaves to become unruly, southerners generally assumed that evangelization improved the master-slave relationship. Methodist minister William Capers was one of the first to make successful missionary advances to slaves. Presbyterian clergyman Charles Colcock JONES, perhaps the best known of the evangelists to blacks, wrote a popular catechism for use in the slave quarters.

At its best, the slaveholding ethic helped ameliorate in small degrees an indefensible and otherwise degrading institution. Although racist ethnologists in the 19th century argued that African-Americans were mere savages, most religious proslavery advocates at least conceded that blacks were human beings who possessed souls. Southern white Protestants often asserted that their region was more Christian than the North, for southern leaders, unlike the ruling class in the North, were genuinely concerned with the moral and religious state of their laborers. Southerners believed that, if they continued to comply with their divinely sanctioned slaveholding duties, God would bless their region with prosperity—a hope eventually shattered, of course, by the outcome of the Civil War.

GHS, Jr.

Bibliography: Anne C. Loveland, *Southern Evangelicals and the Social Order, 1800–1860* (Baton Rouge: Louisiana State University Press, 1980); Donald G. Mathews, *Religion in the Old South* (Chicago: University of Chicago Press, 1977); Larry E. Tise, *Proslavery: A History of the Defense of Slavery in America, 1701–1840* (Athens: University of Georgia Press, 1987).

Protestantism   See MAINLINE PROTESTANTISM; REFORMATION, THE.

Puritanism   Puritanism, a complex religious movement of the 16th through 18th centuries,

Early New England Puritans going to worship armed. 1867 painting by George Henry Boughton. (Library of Congress)

played a major role in the development of American culture. Despite its influence, Puritanism is difficult to define. Indeed the Puritans have been appraised differently by each American generation in light of its own views of society and religion. They have been seen as priggish, cold, and dry, as the harbingers of political democracy, and as the source of all the defects and virtues in the American character. There is, perhaps, no greater proof of their importance than the fact that they have been impossible to ignore.

At the simplest level the Puritans were English Protestants, loyal in their own eyes to God, king, country, and the Church of England, who desired to continue the religious reforms begun during the reign of Henry VIII. The direction of this continuation was a point of disagreement among the Puritans themselves. Some, probably the majority, desired to retain the church as Elizabeth I had organized it, minus bishops. This was the view of the Presbyterians who, basically satisfied with the Elizabethan church, desired only to replace the bishops with a Presbyterian structure such as existed in Scotland (see PRESBYTERIANISM).

The other two major forms of Puritanism—Separatism and Congregationalism—sought greater changes. They not only opposed the EPISCOPACY, but also rejected any form of church organization superior to the individual congregation. They also opposed "human" accretions, primarily the vestiges of Catholic ritual and inclusive church membership, that had been introduced into the Church. They saw no biblical basis for these and wanted them removed from the established church.

For Separatists the church was not to include everyone within the parish or community, but was to be composed of regenerate, saved, members only. Congregationalists were unwilling to go that far, at least originally. Unable to judge who was saved, they were stricter than the established church in requiring members to assent to the rules of the congregation and to avoid scandalous living. After arriving in America, however, the Congregationalists would require evidence of a conversion experience as a criterion for church membership.

Separatists, of whom the PILGRIMS are the best known, were the most radical of the Puritans. Convinced that the existing English church was irredeemable, they separated from it completely and formed their own local congregations. Greatly persecuted during the reign of James I (1603–1625), many Separatists emigrated to the Netherlands, including the congregation that later became the basis for the Pilgrim settlement at Plymouth Plantation.

To remove bishops from the established Church of England and to base church practice on the Bible was not easily accomplished. The English monarchs understood the threats such a change posed for the hierarchical society of England. James I, who had experienced these challenges while king of Scotland, described their results succinctly, "No bishops, no King."

The destruction of an ordered and hierarchical society was far from the mind of the Puritans during the early 1600s. Although increasingly persecuted, they accepted that the civil authorities were ordained by God. This they explained in numerous pamphlets and petitions. The monarchs saw otherwise, realizing that once church polity and belief were removed from their hands the church became the superior power. God and the Bible would be above the monarch, and the Bible's interpreters—the ministers—became the true masters.

Persecution of the Puritans increased under Elizabeth's successors, reaching its height during the reign of Charles I. Combined with economic decline, this led to the "Great Migration" of Puritans to the New World—the colonies of British North America (see MASSACHUSETTS BAY COLONY). In America, Puritanism—primarily in its Congregational form—reached its highest level of theological, political, and social expression.

In coming to America the Puritans hoped to create the model of the godly society. Although Massachusetts Bay (established in 1630) was preeminent, the other Puritan colonies—New Haven, Connecticut, and Plymouth Plantation—also attempted this, often with different results. What all the Puritan colonies managed to create were ordered communities whose traditions of self-governance and an educated laity

would be long felt in the life and history of the United States.

While the Puritans considered themselves to be nothing less than orthodox in Christian doctrine, there were three distinctive elements of Puritan life that not only set them apart but would become central to American religious history. The first of these, the emphasis on the individual congregation composed of saved members as the model of the New Testament Church, already has been mentioned. The remaining elements were the centrality of the vernacular Bible and the sermon.

The Puritans were committed to the ancient doctrines of Christianity, the Westminster Confession—the primary faith statement of Presbyterianism—and especially the Bible, which had a central place in their religious understanding. The English Bible—originally in its Geneva version (1560) and then much later the King James Version (1611 first printing)—became the hallmark of Puritan spirituality. Read and studied by individuals and by groups (family Bible reading was central to Puritan culture), it also was the basis for determining religious and social truths.

This emphasis on the Bible inevitably led to inappropriate interpretions (see ANTINOMIAN CONTROVERSY; BIBLICAL INTERPRETATION). Here the role of the minister as the expounder of the Bible in the sermon became critical. Despite the popular understanding of New England as dominated by ministers, the clergy actually had less political power there than anywhere in Europe. They did have moral power through the sermon, delivered in a style comprehensible to the congregation. Drawing from scripture, the minister expounded principles or doctrines directly applicable to the life of the congregation or the community as a whole. In this manner the minister became a moral voice to the community, speaking on topics ranging from the punishment that awaited the unconverted, to the sinfulness of frivolity, to the need for careful reflection in choosing political leaders (see PREACHERS, PROTESTANT). Religion for the

Puritans was inherently a religion of the word, both written in the Bible and spoken in the sermon. This word was instrumental in the forming of human life in all its aspects and was fought and argued over by ministers and laity alike.

The result was the creation of numerous colonies where reading, thought, and social involvement were encouraged. The engagement of their citizens in the functioning of both religion and government would have a major impact on the future of British North America.

(See also CAMBRIDGE PLATFORM; COTTON, JOHN; COVENANT THEOLOGY; HALF-WAY COVE-NANT; HOOKER, THOMAS; MATHER, COTTON; MATHER, INCREASE; SAYBROOK PLATFORM; WINTHROP, JOHN.)

EQ

Bibliography: Carl Bridenbaugh, *Vexed & Troubled Englishman, 1590–1642* (New York: Oxford University Press, 1968); David Hall, *Worlds of Wonder, Days of Judgment* (New York: Knopf, 1989); Perry Miller, *Errand into the Wilderness* (Cambridge: Belknap Press of Harvard University Press, 1956); ———, *The New England Mind: the Seventeenth Century* (New York: Macmillan, 1939); Edmund Morgan, *The Puritan Dilemma: The Story of John Winthrop* (Glenview, Ill.: Scott, Foresman, 1958).

Q

Quakers See FRIENDS, THE RELIGIOUS SOCIETY OF (QUAKERS).

Quimby, Phineas Parkhurst (1802–1866)

A self-taught mesmerist and hypnotist, Phineas Parkhurst Quimby inspired through his mind-cure techniques a host of new religious movements, including CHRISTIAN SCIENCE and NEW THOUGHT.

Born in Lebanon, New Hampshire in 1802, Quimby was raised in Belfast, Maine. He received little formal education and earned his living as a clockmaker until falling ill with con-

Phineas Parkhurst Quimby, an early explorer of the science of mental healing who influenced Mary Baker Eddy.

sumption in the early 1830s. After turning to a medical doctor whose prescription of a medicinal powder called calomel did him more harm than good, Quimby healed himself. He was unable to explain his nascent powers, however, until attending a lecture on MESMERISM. Based on the theory that humans could be healed through the manipulation of a subtle fluid called "animal magnetism," mesmerism originated with the Austrian physician Franz Anton Mesmer (1733–1815) and had been brought from France to New England by the author Charles Poyen.

In 1859 Quimby opened an office in Portland and became an accomplished non-medical healer. At his lecture-demonstrations, Quimby would hypnotize an assistant named Lucius Burkmer, who would go into a trance and then diagnose diseases and suggest prescriptions.

As Quimby effected what to many were "miraculous" cures, he came to the conclusion that disease was psychological rather than physiological. His patients, he now believed, were actually healing themselves through the substantial powers of their own minds. His only contribution was to use his considerable powers of suggestion to prompt in his patients a belief in their fundamental well-being. After this breakthrough, Quimby continued to use magnetic passes and other mesmeric techniques in his healing practice, but he now utilized them to enhance his patients' faith in his talents and, consequently, their suggestibility to healing.

Quimby confined himself to therapy rather than theology, so he is best remembered among historians of American religion as the healer and teacher of three thinkers who creatively adapted his theories and practices: Horatio and Anetta Dresser, the founders of the first New Thought organization, The Church of the Higher Life, and Mary Baker EDDY, the founder of Christian Science.

During the 1880s, Dresser accused Eddy of pilfering Quimby's theories and marketing them as Christian Science. Though the Dressers were undoubtedly correct in finding important intellectual links between Eddy and her mentor (it was Quimby who coined the term "Christian Science"), Christian Science cannot be so easily reduced to Quimbyism. Eddy was first and foremost a theologian who devoted much of her time to Biblical interpretation, while Quimby taught a largely secular healing technique and demonstrated an almost complete indifference to the Bible.

One reason why Christian Scientists and their critics continue to fight about Eddy's intellectual debts is that Quimby never systematized or published his theories. Some of the notes that he shared with his students have survived in *The Quimby Manuscripts,* which were published posthumously in 1921.

SRP

Bibliography: Annetta Gertrude Dresser, *The Philosophy of P. P. Quimby, with Selections from His Manuscripts and a Sketch of His Life* (Boston: George H. Ellis, 1895); Phineas P. Quimby, *The Quimby Manuscripts* (New York: Thomas Y. Crowell Co., 1921).

R

Rapp, George (1757–1847) A pietist religious leader with mystical leanings, George Rapp founded the communitarian Harmony Society, a group that established three settlements in America during the antebellum period. Rapp, along with most of his followers, was a German immigrant. He was born Johann Georg Rapp in Württemberg, one of five children of a farmer. As a young man he apprenticed as a weaver, married in 1783, had two children, and settled down to a quiet life.

But Rapp's deeply held religious convictions and his strong opinions quickly brought him into conflict with the local Lutheran authorities. Yearning for a "closer communion with Christ," and finding the established church cold and informal, Rapp withdrew from communion and began holding his own services. The group he gathered around himself beginning in 1785 practiced a mystical, devotional Protestant faith that centered on union with God. Religious authorities warned him to cease holding separate meetings, and his refusal led to years of increasing persecution and harassment: several members were fined and even jailed for their expressed hostility to the church. But suppression only increased Rapp's following; by 1802, it was said to number 10,000 to 12,000, and Rapp termed himself the chief and bishop of the Separatists of Lower Württemberg.

In 1803 Rapp led a scouting party to America, to find a place where he and his flock could live and worship freely. They settled on a 5,000-acre site near Pittsburgh, Pennsylvania and named their colony Harmony, establishing the Harmony Society in 1805. Some 750 original members turned over all their possessions and pledged obedience and cooperation to the community. After 1807, celibacy was also required of all members. In 1814–1815 the colony moved to southern Indiana in search of better land, and there built New Harmony. Although this second community also prospered, the set-tlers sought out a better location, and moved back to western Pennsylvania in 1825 to found their third village, Economy.

Rapp lived to the age of 90, and his benevolent leadership style gained him the affection and confidence of his flock. Although a schism in 1832 reduced the population of Economy by one-third to around 500 members, the colony thrived during his life, and fell into a gradual decline after his death. In 1905 George Rapp's community dissolved its formal ties.

LMK

Bibliography: Karl J. R. Arnst, *George Rapp's Harmony Society, 1785–1847* (Philadelphia: University of Pennsylvania Press, 1965).

rapture, the The rapture of the church is a belief held by millions of American Christians who trace this idea to a passage in the New Testament (1 Thessalonians 4:15–17): "The Lord himself . . . will descend from heaven, and the dead in Christ will rise first. Then we who are alive . . . will be caught up in the clouds together with them to meet the Lord in the air." Members of the true church will be carried up to meet Christ at the time of his second coming.

American dispensationalists (see DISPENSATIONALISM), that is, theologically conservative Christians who believe all history is divided into seven eras or "dispensations," predict that events prophesied in the Bible concerning the end of the world are about to take place. Human society has been declining gradually over the centuries, and a time is approaching when the personification of absolute evil (the Antichrist) will gain control of human society. He will throw the world into a reign of terror known as "the tribulation," but just before the tribulation begins, the rapture will occur. The saints will then be translated into heaven, where they will be safe from the catastrophes happening on earth. At the end of the tribulation, the power of evil will at last be destroyed by the triumphant coming of Christ who, accompanied by the church descending again to earth, will establish his millennial (thousand-year) reign.

Belief in the rapture came to prominence at the end of the 19th century when many of the traditional teachings of American Protestantism seemed under attack by an increasingly secular nation. The doctrine of the imminent return of Jesus gave preachers a powerful evangelistic tool, for the rapture of the church impelled the wavering to make a quick decision for the Christian faith. The impending arrival of Christ also filled those already converted with renewed hope to live holy lives and save themselves from the evils that might soon arrive. Dispensationalists, unlike Protestant liberals, refused to see themselves caught up in some long evolutionary stream leading inexorably (but distantly) to perfection. Rather, they believed themselves to be living on the edge of eternity, perhaps merely a second away from Christ's appearance in the clouds above their heads.

This tradition remains strong in fundamentalist circles in America today. It owes its present acceptance mainly to two 20th-century sources: C. I. SCOFIELD's 1909 *Reference Bible* and Hal Lindsey's 1970 best-seller, *The Late Great Planet Earth*. Dispensationalism has a popular appeal as well. A bumper sticker that warns, "In the event of rapture, this car will empty," appears on automobiles driven by many conservative Protestants in the late 20th-century.

(See also PREMILLENNIALISM).

GHS, Jr.

Bibliography: Paul Boyer, *When Time Shall Be No More: Prophecy Belief in Modern American Culture* (Cambridge, Mass.: Harvard University Press, 1992).

Rauschenbusch, Walter (1861–1918)

A Baptist preacher turned seminary professor, Rauschenbusch became one of the most prominent Protestant voices of his own day. His writing on the SOCIAL GOSPEL provided that movement with its most articulate expression.

His ministry in Hell's Kitchen in New York City (1886–1897) inspired Walter Rauschenbusch's passionate preaching of the Social Gospel. (American Baptist Historical Society)

Born to a family of German immigrants on October 4, 1861, Rauschenbusch descended from several generations of Lutheran pastors, although his father became a Baptist early in life, and eventually a professor at New York's Rochester Theological Seminary. Significantly for his own theological development, Walter Rauschenbusch grew up in a home that maintained ties to German culture. His education included adolescent years in Germany, and an intense religious experience at this time inclined him toward the ministry and evangelism.

Completing both his undergraduate and seminary education at Rochester in 1886, he was sent to New York as pastor of the Second Baptist Church in Hell's Kitchen, a deeply impoverished neighborhood. Almost immediately he began to question the assumptions that had guided his own seminary education, which had focused on providing rural parishioners with personal salvation. Confronted with stark urban poverty, he became involved in economic reformer Henry George's campaign for mayor in 1886. Becoming a committed socialist, he turned to authors such as Tolstoy and Edward Bellamy for insight. A sabbatical at the German universities of Marburg, Berlin, and Kiel enabled him to delve into such German intellectual resources as the historical-critical approach to the Bible, the theology of Albrecht Ritschl, and the work of various socialist thinkers. Leaving his congregation in 1897, he accepted a position in New Testament at Rochester Theological Seminary. In 1902 he became professor of Church History, a position he retained until his death from cancer on July 25, 1918.

Confronted with the destructive side of the enormous social changes brought by the rise of industrial capitalism, Rauschenbusch found most Christians strangely silent at a time when he thought religion needed to offer the nation humane guidance on social policy. In *Christianity and the Social Crisis* (1907), he sought to provide his contemporaries with an understanding of why Christianity was silent on issues of wealth and poverty. He contrasted the original impetus of the biblical prophets and Jesus to establish a just "Kingdom of God" with a church that had become influenced by alien (bourgeois) social forces, "clogging" its "revolutionary moral power." For Rauschenbusch the history of the church reflected an unwise separation of religious and moral fervor.

Rauschenbusch saw the present historical moment as offering Christians an opportunity to reconnect with their biblical heritage, and at the same time encourage those modern developments in science, politics, and economics that could lead to the "social redemption of humanity." His arguments reflected a form of millennial thinking in America that saw the kingdom of God as something human beings could help bring about. But his optimism was strained by

the outbreak of World War I. In his final book, *A Theology for the Social Gospel* (1917), he sought to understand the continued presence of evil in modern life. In that book, the most systematic expression of the social gospel, he portrayed sin as a historical force corrupting institutions as well as individuals, consequently requiring social as well as personal salvation. He contrasted "prophetic" and "priestly" forms of religion, the first challenging unjust social orders and the other perpetuating them. Claiming the church too often had been the purveyor of the priestly form, he concluded by arguing that the prophetic form could unite with modern democracy to overturn the spread of economic and political injustice. For his detractors, Rauschenbusch came to symbolize a kind of naive belief in human perfectibility. He saw himself as a translator of the core of Protestant faith into 20th-century terms.

MG

Bibliography: Walter Rauschenbusch, *Christianity and the Social Crisis* (1907; reprint New York: Harper and Row, 1964); ———, *A Theology for the Social Gospel* (1917; reprint Nashville: Abingdon, 1987).

Reconstructionism, Christian   See CHRISTIAN RIGHT.

Reconstructionist Judaism

One of the four major branches of American JUDAISM, Reconstructionist Judaism is the extension of the work and ideas of one man, Mordecai M. KAPLAN. Its goal is to make Judaism more meaningful to Jews in the modern world by dispensing with all that is supernatural, retaining the traditions of Judaism, and furthering the continuation of the Jewish people. Although not a distinctive movement separate from CONSERVATIVE JUDAISM until the late 1960s, by 1995 Reconstructionist Judaism had a membership of 60 congregations, 50,000 individuals, and 150 rabbis in the Reconstructionist Rabbinical Association.

Kaplan never intended to form a separate movement within Judaism. For nearly 40 years,

Kaplan did everything in his power to prevent the split from Conservative Judaism. From his position at Jewish Theological Seminary where he was dean of the Teachers Training Institute and professor of homiletics, Kaplan attempted to reinvigorate Judaism, to make it more meaningful to Jews in the modern world.

The first institutional development in what became Reconstructionist Judaism were the Jewish Centers. The first of these was built in 1917 on West 86th Street in New York City. Kaplan, its first rabbi, viewed the Jewish Center as more than a synagogue. The place was to serve the recreational, educational, and social needs of its members. Conflict over Kaplan's increasingly unorthodox views of religion and his criticism of the labor practices of some his congregants led to conflicts within the center. Although supported by a majority of the congregation, Kaplan resigned. Over 20 families resigned with him, and formed the Society for the Advancement of Judaism (SAJ) which became the nucleus of the Reconstructionist movement.

The SAJ was no typical synagogue, and Kaplan insisted on the title "leader" rather than rabbi. To disseminate Kaplan's views, it published a magazine, the *SAJ Review,* that soon had an influence well beyond the congregation. Forced to fold during the Depression, the *SAJ Review* was replaced in 1935 by a new magazine, *Reconstructionist.* The name came from a article Kaplan had written in 1928 wherein he called for American Jewry to "reconstruct the Jewish civilization." For that reason, wrote Kaplan, "the SAJ prefers to be considered a branch of the Reconstructionist movement in Jewish life."

To maintain and support the magazine, the Jewish Reconstructionist Foundation was organized in 1940. The next year Kaplan published a New Haggadah (Passover service). In it Kaplan transformed the story of the exodus of the Jews from Egypt from one of miracles and plagues, to that of freedom and liberation. This was followed by a Sabbath prayer book in 1945. Orthodox (see ORTHODOX JUDAISM) rabbis viewed the new prayer book as blasphemous,

primarily because it changed certain prayers dealing with miraculous and supernatural events. A meeting of Orthodox rabbis pronounced a ban of *herem* (excommunication) on Kaplan and burned a copy of the book.

The 1940s and 1950s were difficult times for the movement. The horror of WORLD WAR II and the Holocaust made many of Kaplan's ideas about progress and human development look naive. Also, the growing traditionalism of REFORM JUDAISM made it look capable of fulfilling the goal of reconstruction. There were, however, Reconstructionists in both the Reform and Conservative movements. In 1950 a Reconstructionist Rabbinical Fellowship was organized, followed at the end of the decade by the Fellowship of Reconstructionist Congregations. Despite these developments, Reconstructionism lost ground. The percentage of students at the Jewish Theological Seminary who had Reconstructionist sympathies decreased between 1920 and 1967, and in 1961 a rabbi had to be brought from London to take over the SAJ.

This decline began to change after Kaplan's retirement from teaching in 1963. His followers convinced him that the Reconstructionists needed their own rabbinical school. Reconstructionist Rabbinical College opened in Philadelphia in 1968. Although its early years were tentative, the college has become a solid institution, producing a new generation of Reconstructionist rabbis and thinkers.

The reconstruction of Jewish civilization was the goal Kaplan outlined in his *Judaism as a Civilization* (1934). This book, considered by many to be the most significant on Judaism and the Jewish people written in America, articulated Kaplan's view of Judaism as "an evolving religious civilization." It is a civilization because it contains within itself a culture. It is religious because it has a transcendent element that enables Jews to actualize what is best within themselves. In order to accomplish this, however, Judaism must speak to the existing situation of the Jewish people. Judaism has always evolved, Kaplan argued. It must continue this evolution in order revitalize Judaism and provide meaning and value to modern Jews.

Kaplan called for the replacement of outmoded concepts, especially supernatural understandings of God and the Torah, with new ideas, albeit in a "deliberate and planned fashion" in order to use them to breath new life into the old forms. The old forms should be retained because they helped "to maintain the historic continuity of the Jewish people and to express, or symbolize, spiritual values or ideals which can enhance the inner life of Jews."

Kaplan's most controversial ideas were his naturalist understanding of God as the name for man's collective ethical ideal and his rejection of the chosenness of the Jewish people. To many, the abandonment of supernaturalism seemed to be a rejection of the very basis of Judaism, if not religion itself. While the debate over supernaturalism was primarily an intellectual, elite phenomenon, the rejection, or transvaluation, of the idea of the chosenness struck deeper.

Kaplan felt that the traditional understanding of chosenness was pernicious and undemocratic, implying genetic superiority. Judaism's chosenness, he believed, involved not the peoplehood of Jews through birth, but their striving to be a people in the image of God, desirous of awakening in themselves and others a "sense of moral responsibility in action."

Reconstructionist ideas have had a major influence on American Judaism. Their views on God, Judaism as a civilization, and the unity of the Jewish people are those of most American Jews. Kaplan's views on incorporating women into the religious services have been adopted by both the Conservative and Reform movements. The fact that Reconstructionist views predominate among many Jews accounts for its weakness as an institutional movement. There is no need to join, when one can achieve the same results where one is.

As Reconstructionist Judaism becomes more distinct from Kaplan's personality and attempts to respond to new historical realities, it faces an uncertain future. Debates over naturalism-supernaturalism, the idea of "chosen people," and of altering Kaplan's version of the prayer book already have pushed the movement in new directions. Much depends on the newer generation of rabbis and leaders, trained after Kaplan's death.

EQ

Bibliography: Ira Eisenstein and Eugene Kohn *Mordecai Kaplan: An Evaluation* (New York: Jewish Reconstructionist Foundation, 1952); Emanuel S. Goldsmith, Mel Scult, and Robert M. Seltzer, eds., *The American Judaism of Mordecai M. Kaplan* (New York: New York University Press, 1990); Mordecai Kaplan, *Judaism as a Civilization* (New York: Schocken, 1967); Richard Libowitz, *Mordecai M. Kaplan and the Development of Reconstructionism* (Lewiston, N.Y.: Edwin Mellen Press, 1983); Jacob Neusner, ed., *Sectors of American Judaism: Reform, Orthodoxy, Conservatism, and Reconstructionism* (New York: KTAV, 1975); Mel Scult, *Judaism Faces the Twentieth Century: A Biography of Mordecai M. Kaplan* (Detroit: Wayne State University Press, 1993).

Reform Judaism   Reform Judaism is one of the three main branches or denominations within American Judaism. Its roots lie in the attempt to accommodate Judaism with the modern world. From the 1840s until the turn of the century, it was the predominant branch of American Judaism. Overwhelmed by the massive immigration of Eastern European Jews between 1880 and 1920, it lost its dominance, giving way to the Conservative movement (see CONSERVATIVE JUDAISM). In 1995 the Reform movement counted nearly 2 million members in 853 synagogues.

Reform Judaism emerged from the intellectual, social, and political changes that marked Europe in the late 18th and early 19th centuries. Intellectually, Reform Judaism originated in the ENLIGHTENMENT emphasis on the moral aspects of religion and deemphasis of the supernatural as well as ritual and religious distinctiveness. The general European Enlightenment had its specifically Jewish counterpart in the Haskalah, the so-called Jewish Enlightenment. In this movement Jews who had received university educations, primarily in Germany, began to apply their secular learning to their own tradition. Most significant in this regard was the Wissenschaft des Judentums (Science of Judaism) movement, an attempt to apply the new forms of scholarship, especially historical scholarship, to the Jewish tradition. This movement served as an intellectual support for reforming tendencies by demonstrating that certain "traditional" elements in Judaism were of recent origin, or that apparently "radical" reforms had earlier roots within the tradition.

These intellectual elements converged with social and political concerns. Socially, some Jews, primarily upper-class German Jews, wanted to establish a Jewish service similar to that of their Protestant neighbors—more decorous, shorter, and less alien to the wider culture.

Politically, the issue was whether Jews, considering themselves a people apart and viewing themselves in exile from their true homeland, could be citizens of the country in which they resided. While France answered this question positively following the French Revolution (1789–1794), emancipating the Jews from the legal limits imposed on them, and Napoleon reaffirmed this for the regions under his control, other countries were more hesitant. As part of the struggle for legal equality, the reformers minimized the idea of Jewish peoplehood, emphasizing Judaism as a religion. They were Germans (or French, or Italians) of the Jewish faith, just as their fellow citizens were Germans of the Catholic, Lutheran, or Reformed faith.

The Reform movement, however was not predominant among the German-Jewish community. The nature of the Jewish community and the conservatism of the German states limited its ability to gain strength in the synagogues there. In America, to which many German Jews immigrated between 1820 and 1860, Reform found fertile soil.

Reform Judaism in the United States had its own indigenous roots. In 1824 several members of Charleston's Congregation Beth Elohim, seeking shorter services, increased use of English, and mixed seating of men and women, withdrew from the congregation and formed the Reformed Society of Israelites—the first Reform organization in the United States. This organization was the exception. The main catalyst for the growth of Reform in the United States was the immigration of German Jews.

As these reform-minded Germans arrived, they organized Reform Vereine (Reform Societies) that eventually became temples, as they called synagogues. In 1846 Temple Har Sinai in Baltimore became the first synagogue in the United States to be organized as Reform. It was followed by Emanu-El of New York (1845) and Sinai in Chicago (1858).

Other Reform temples were formed through internal conflict and secession. At Congregation Beth-El in Albany, New York, an attempt by a young rabbi from Bohemia, Isaac Mayer WISE, to lead his congregation down the path of Reform led to dissension and conflict. Wise, along with several members of his congregation, withdrew to found Congregation Anshe Emeth along reform lines. In 1854, Wise accepted the position of rabbi at B'nai Jeshurun in Cincinnati, Ohio. From this pulpit, he gave institutional form to American Reform Judaism. Wise was widely read and reflective, and his strengths lay in organization and publicity. David EINHORN and Kaufmann KOHLER would be more successful in articulating the meaning of Reform; Wise gave it institutional existence.

The activities of Wise produced the three major institutional centers of Reform Judaism in the United States: the Union of American Hebrew Congregations (1875), Hebrew Union College (1877), and the Central Conference of American Rabbis (1889). While the first two originally were created to serve the entire Jewish-American community, the tensions between the more traditionally minded and the reformers proved too great for cooperation. The more conservative elements withdrew, leaving the UAHC and HUC to the reformers.

Reform Judaism in the United States transformed Judaism, radically changing Jewish practice, belief, and ritual. Wise contributed to this transformation with the publication of a revision of the Jewish prayer book, *Minhag America* (American Ritual), in 1857. Although the most widely used Reform prayer book until the adoption of the *Uniform Prayer Book* by the UAHC in 1894, it had a competitor in the more radical *Olat Tamid* (1858) of David Einhorn. Einhorn, rabbi of Har Sinai in Baltimore, was Wise's opponent on the left. Where Wise was a practical organizer, Einhorn was an intellectual radical who believed that Reform needed a rigid intellectual base and a clear annunciation of its principles. These Einhorn and others attempted to provide. Meeting in Philadelphia in 1869, they adopted a statement rejecting the hope for the restoration of Israel and the temple cult, declared that the "messianic aim" was the union of all the children of God. They downplayed the dietary laws and rejected the requirement of circumcision for males.

Although viewed as unnecessarily antagonistic by Wise, and with horror by the more traditionally minded, this statement became the basis for the development of American Reform until superseded by the so-called PITTSBURGH PLATFORM in 1885. That document, which Wise called the "Jewish Declaration of Independence," was drafted primarily by Einhorn's son-in-law, Kaufmann Kohler, rabbi of Temple Beth-El in New York City. The platform rejected all parts of Jewish law not in keeping with "the views and habits of modern civilization." It declared that the Jews were not a nation, but a religious community that expected "neither a return to Palestine, nor a sacrificial worship under the administration of the sons of Aaron, nor the restoration of any of the laws concerning the Jewish state." Judaism was deemed "a progressive religion, ever striving to be in accord with the postulates of reason."

The rationalism that underlay Reform is quite obvious in the Pittsburgh Platform. For many

of the reformers, Judaism had become nothing more (or less) than an ethical monotheism. But if Judaism were not a distinctive religious form, why continue it as such? Some followed this thought to its logical conclusion. Among the most important was Felix ADLER who, finding no reason to continue Judaism as a distinctive religion, founded the Ethical Culture Society in 1876.

This rationalism was a major problem for the Reform movement. At the height of its organizational development, it was losing the people in the pews. Distilled down to an essence of ethical monotheism, Reform Judaism seemed to offer little comfort, support, or group identification. At just this time, however, Reform Judaism was saved from itself by a massive influx of Jewish immigrants from Eastern Europe. Although this wave of immigration ended the dominance of the Reform movement in American Judaism, it eventually provided it with a new sources of growth and passion.

The relationship between the Americanized German Reformers and the Eastern European Orthodox immigrants (see ORTHODOX JUDAISM) could not have been more inauspicious. The two groups eyed each other with suspicion. The former viewed the latter as superstitious, vulgar rabble; while the immigrants looked upon Reform Jews as pagans. As the newer immigrants underwent the process of Americanization, however, many would drop their Orthodoxy and some of them, or their children, would enter the Reform movement.

The results were a growing acceptance of ZIONISM within the Reform movement, and an increasing return to traditional religious elements. Zionism, the movement for the creation of a Jewish homeland in Palestine, was antithetical to the Reform movement's claim that the Jews were no longer a people in exile. In 1897 the Reform movement had explicitly rejected Zionism. By the mid-1930s this had changed to a position of neutrality, and in 1937 the Central Conference of American Rabbis adopted a new statement of Reform principles that included a call for the creation of a Jewish homeland in Palestine.

This statement also reversed the Pittsburgh Platform's rejection of the idea of Jewish peoplehood. "Judaism is the soul of which Israel [the Jewish people] is the body. Living in all parts of the world, Israel has been held together by the ties of a common history, and above all by the heritage of the faith. . . ." In that same year the UAHC passed a resolution calling for the restoration of traditional Jewish symbols and customs into the synagogue service.

This latter event also demonstrated the impact that the immigrants and their children were having on Reform Judaism. Although accepting Reform's rejection of many religious laws governing diet and activities, these Eastern European Jews were less willing to renounce their Jewish cultural and ethnic identity. The result was the return of many of the symbols of traditional Judaism and an increasing emphasis on Jewish culture and learning.

After World War II, Jews joined the American exodus to the suburbs. Synagogue membership increased and synagogues became centers for both the religious expressions and cultural affirmations of their members. They also became a locus for the political and social concerns of the Reform community. Having expressly committed itself to social justice since the adoption of the Pittsburgh Platform, the Reform movement became involved in causes like the civil rights movement and opposition to the Vietnam War. From the 1940s on, polls showed a steady decrease in ANTI-SEMITISM and life in the suburbs seemed calm and peaceful as most Reform Jews integrated into American middle-class life.

This was altered by the 1967 war between Israel and its Arab neighbors. The threat to Israel's existence brought both Israel and the Holocaust to the forefront for Reform Judaism and the Jewish-American community as a whole. From the late 1960s on, these two realities

became major themes within Reform Judaism, and accelerated its concern with maintaining Jewish traditions and the Jewish people. The result has been increased emphasis within the Reform movement on Jewish identity and Jewish survival—a survival that appears linked to the survival of Israel as a Jewish state.

The relationship between Israel and the American Reform movement has not always been peaceful, however. Despite the fact that Israel is a secular state, issues of marriage and divorce are in the hands of religious institutions. Since Judaism in Israel is Orthodox Judaism in the United States, Reform and Conservative rabbis are unable to perform marriages in Israel. Even more nettlesome is the debate over conversions performed by Reform and Conservative rabbis, the so-called Who Is a Jew? debate. The Orthodox in Israel have demanded that the state refuse to recognize such conversions, and given the fragmented nature of Israeli politics, the small religious parties have nearly succeeded in bringing this about. Despite these conflicts Reform Judaism has been increasingly supportive of the Jewish state, both financially and politically, although following the Israeli invasion of Lebanon in 1982 it also became increasingly willing to voice its criticism of Israeli government policies.

While this marked concern for the survival of the Jewish people and Jewish traditions has resulted in greater individual cooperation among Jewish-Americans, there have been growing religious conflicts. These have been caused by the increased self-confidence and aggressiveness of the Orthodox, as well as disagreements over issues of Jewish law. Disagreements concern the role of women within the tradition, the response to gays and lesbians, and the criteria for determining Jewishness. Decisions within the Reform movement to ordain women as rabbis (1972), to consider children with a Jewish father and a Gentile mother as Jewish (1983), to recognize congregations ministering to homosexuals (1977), and to consider ordaining homosexuals as rabbis (1990) increased tensions with the Orthodox and to some degree with the Conservative movement as well, although the latter also ordains women. These actions by the Reform movement serve well to illustrate that, despite a return to more traditional religious forms, the movement continues its heritage of adapting Judaism to meet the changing demands of society.

EQ

Bibliography: Nathan Glazer, *American Judaism*, 2nd ed., rev. (Chicago: University of Chicago Press, 1972); Beryl Harold Levy, *Reform Judaism in America: A Study in Religious Adaptation* (New York: Ph.D. Dissertation, Columbia University, 1933); Julian Morgenstern, *As a Mighty Stream: The Progress of Judaism Through History* (Philadelphia: Jewish Publication Society, 1949); Kerry M. Olitzky, Lance J. Sussman, and Malcolm A. Stern, eds., *Reform Judaism in America: A Biographical Dictionary and Sourcebook* (Westport, Conn. Greenwood Press, 1993); W. Gunther Plaut, *The Rise of Reform Judaism*, 2 vols. (New York: World Union for Progressive Judaism, 1963–65); Howard M. Sachar, *A History of the Jews in America* (New York: Knopf, 1992).

Reform, Social   See SOCIAL GOSPEL.

Reformation, the   The Reformation refers to a series of extraordinary religious and social changes that occurred in western Europe in the 16th century. During that period, a number of Christian leaders who were attempting to reform the church led successful revolts against the authority of the pope. The term "Protestant" was first used in 1529, when a group of German princes protested against the activities of Roman Catholic rulers who opposed them. Today, approximately half of the American religious population identifies itself as Protestant, that is, as heirs of the Reformation.

The Reformation is generally considered to have begun in October 1517 when the German monk Martin Luther nailed a placard inscribed with 95 theological theses on a church door in Wittenberg. Four years later, when summoned before the Holy Roman Emperor at Worms,

Luther refused to rescind his attacks on the papacy. Luther was forced to flee Worms under the threat of death but was given asylum in Saxony. There, under the protection of Frederick, his prince, he was able to continue the church reforms he had earlier proposed. Although Luther always denied that he intended to found a "Lutheran" (see LUTHERANISM) church, he inspired the religious tradition that later bore his name. News of Luther's accomplishments quickly spread beyond the borders of Saxony and aroused intellectual and spiritual ferment throughout northern and western Europe.

Luther's most important contribution to the Reformation was his teaching on justification by grace through faith. He was obsessed with the question of how a person could ever earn God's love or find eternal salvation. Like all the original Protestant reformers, he believed that the Bible contained all Christians needed to know about their religion. After meditating on the New Testament Epistle to the Romans, Luther decided that human beings could actually do nothing to save their souls. He concluded that God alone "justifies," that is, redeems human beings from sin. Faith, he said, was the divine gift by which God reveals his gracious character and leads a person to depend upon him for salvation. As a consequence, he rejected many of the religious customs and traditions of medieval Catholicism because he thought they obscured, rather than illuminated, God's true nature.

At the same time Lutheranism started to gather force in Germany, Swiss reformer Ulrich Zwingli took control of church affairs in Zurich. Lutheran influences clearly encouraged Zwingli's efforts at reform. As Luther did, Zwingli appealed to the Bible to support his work and envisioned a return to the primitive purity of early Christianity. His denunciations of the religious practices of the Middle Ages and of the hierarchy of the church, however, far surpassed anything that Luther had intended. Zwingli felt little respect for the immediate past or for traditional ways of worship and set out to transform completely the church in Zurich. He had statues and images of the saints smashed, altars stripped bare, and worship conducted in German, not Latin. Only Zwingli's death in battle in 1531 brought a premature end to the radical reforms he envisioned.

After Zwingli's death, leadership of the Swiss Reformation fell upon exiled French Protestant John Calvin (see CALVINISM). Around the year 1534, Calvin underwent a conversion experience and renounced his institutional connections with Roman Catholicism. At the same time, he began the composition of his *Institutes of the Christian Religion,* an imposing work that soon became recognized as the most systematic statement of Protestant theology. Calvin completed the first edition of the *Institutes* in 1536, the same year he arrived in Geneva and began the reformation of the church in that city. Over the next three decades, until his death in 1564, he devoted himself to transforming Geneva into what Scottish reformer John Knox called "the most perfect school of Christ that ever was on earth since the days of the Apostles."

Calvin borrowed heavily from the theological ideas of Augustine of Hippo, the fourth-century Christian theologian. He adopted Augustine's stress on the omnipotence of God and the passivity of humankind in the process of eternal salvation. The credit for salvation, Calvin said, belonged solely to God who, from eternity, had predestined the fate of every soul. Only God knew who would be saved and who would be damned. Without divine grace, no person could repent and become a Christian, yet grace was a gift that only the predestined elect received. Although Calvin's teaching on predestination appeared to undercut participation in the church, he contended that the elect would inevitably lead pious, Christian lives. He counseled people not to dwell on their failings, but simply to trust in the all-sufficient grace of God.

Calvin's theological emphases had an important influence on the next generation of Swiss reformers Theodore Beza, who succeeded him in Geneva, and Heinrich Bullinger,

Zwingli's successor at Zurich. The so-called Reformed (see REFORMED TRADITION, THE) branch of Protestantism, dependent heavily on Calvin's theology, spread into France, Germany, Holland, Scotland, and England over the course of the 16th century. Calvinism shaped the formation of a number of Protestant traditions in those countries: Dutch Reformed, German Reformed, French Reformed (or Huguenot), and Presbyterian (see PRESBYTERIANISM).

A third manifestation of the Reformation appeared in England in the 1530s. The English, or Anglican (see ANGLICANISM), Reformation was originally more a political than a religious revolution. Following his dispute with the pope over the legitimacy of divorcing Catherine of Aragon, Henry VIII repudiated the authority of the papacy over the Church of England. Although parliamentary action in 1534 declared Henry to be supreme head of the English church, little change in either theological doctrine or liturgical practice occurred at first, since Henry was intensely conservative in those matters.

After Henry's death, during the brief reign of his son, Edward VI, the process of church reform accelerated in England. Upon Edward's death in 1553, however, Henry's daughter "Bloody Mary" Tudor assumed the throne and set grimly to work to restore Roman Catholicism. Between 1553 and 1558, hundreds of refugees fled for their lives to Protestant areas on the continent. Attracted especially to Calvin's Geneva, they imbibed there Calvin's ideas on theology and church government, which they brought back to England after Mary's death. Thanks both to the horrors of Mary's persecution and to the instruction many exiles had received under Calvin, most English Christians were thoroughly committed to Protestantism by the mid-16th century.

With the accession of Elizabeth I in 1558, Anglicanism began to develop into its present form. Much of the organization of medieval Christianity was retained, and uniformity was enforced through the use of a common English-language prayer book. Considerable theological flexibility was also allowed. In opposition to the emerging Puritan (see PURITANISM) movement, on the one hand, which desired the Church of England to be more fully reformed, and to the continuing Catholic loyalist presence, on the other hand, Anglicans sought what they called a *via media,* a middle way, between the extremes of the papacy and the rigorous Protestants. Anglicans chose to find authority in the interaction between three religious sources: the Bible, ancient Christian traditions, and contemporary human reason.

The fourth branch of the Reformation had, by its very nature, less internal organization than Lutheran, Reformed, or Anglican Protestants possessed. Even the name of this branch has been under debate for many years. Opponents in the 16th and 17th centuries called that group of reformers "enthusiasts," "spiritualists," or simply "fanatics." Today, scholars refer to them as the "Radical Reformation" or the "left wing" of the Reformation, because they tended to reject all established religious and political authority in their day. Many of the radicals also bear the label "Anabaptist," since they repudiated the practice of infant baptism and rebaptized adults who joined their movement. Finally, some who rejected traditional Christian belief in the Trinity are known as "Unitarians" or "Socinians" (named for reformer Faustus Socinus).

The radical reformers were almost universally persecuted, threatened with death by Catholics and Protestants alike, who feared the threat they posed to the social order. The most notorious of all the radicals were those who briefly ruled the German city of Münster in 1534 and 1535. The city's inhabitants at first attempted to reinstitute church life according to descriptions contained in the New Testament Book of Acts and other early Christian writings. All food and property were held in common, and the use of money was outlawed. Later, on reading the Old Testament, the people of Münster claimed to have found a mandate for practicing polygamy.

Eventually the city was attacked and nearly all of its inhabitants slaughtered. Although Münster was hardly typical of the Radical Reformation as a whole, it became a symbol for the movement and was used as justification for its suppression throughout Europe.

The four major branches of the Reformation were all transmitted to America in the 17th century. The English settlers who established colonies in Virginia in 1607 and Massachusetts in 1630 were Anglicans. Although the Puritan settlements in New England rapidly adopted a congregational form of church government, those in Virginia continued loyal to Anglican polity and liturgical forms. The earliest Lutherans in America came from Sweden and the Netherlands in the 1620s. By 1669 the two oldest Lutheran congregations in America, at present-day Albany, New York and New York City, had been founded. The Dutch, then the principal trading power of Europe, established a post on Manhattan Island in 1626. Three years later, the Dutch Reformed Church was recognized as the official church of the New Netherlands. Pennsylvania was the great center of German immigration to America. Although Lutheran and Reformed emigrants did not come there until the early 18th century, a settlement of Mennonites, followers of Anabaptist leader Menno Simons, were the first Germans to establish a presence in that colony, arriving in 1683.

The denominations of 20th-century American Protestantism are heirs of the Reformation that began nearly 500 years ago. Although the Roman Catholic Church is now the largest Christian denomination in the United States, all the other major religious bodies in this country (among them, the Southern Baptist Convention, the Baptist churches with an African-American heritage, the United Methodist Church, and the Evangelical Lutheran Church in America) trace their historical roots back to the Reformation.

GHS, Jr.

Bibliography: Martin E. Marty, *Protestantism* (New York: Holt, Rinehart and Winston, 1972);

Lewis W. Spitz, *The Protestant Reformation, 1517–1559* (San Francisco: Harper & Row, 1985).

Reformed Church in America The denomination now known as the Reformed Church in America was formally organized in 1792 as the "Reformed Protestant Dutch Church." This church had its beginnings in the migration of settlers from the Netherlands to New York in the early 17th century. The denomination nominally parted from its ethnic heritage in 1867 by choosing to drop "Dutch" from its name and no longer uses the Dutch language in its worship. It has resisted merger with other Reformed (see REFORMED TRADITION, THE) groups, however, and continues to be the largest body of American Christians adhering to the Dutch Calvinist tradition.

After winning independence from Spain in 1609, the Dutch people became the principal trading power of Europe, establishing a post at the site of present-day Albany, New York in 1624, and two years later founding New Amsterdam on the tip of Manhattan Island. The first minister at these settlements, Jonas Michaelius, arrived in New Amsterdam in 1628 and there organized the "church in the fort" (the Collegiate Church today). Michaelius was followed by other pastors, who accompanied the movement of Dutch settlers north to Albany, east into Long Island, and west into New Jersey. In 1629, the Dutch Reformed Church was recognized as the officially established church of New Netherland.

When their colony surrendered to the English in 1664, Dutch Reformed congregations in New York lost their privileged status and strenuously resisted efforts by the Church of England to strengthen itself. Eventually, the Dutch Reformed influenced legislation tolerating non-Anglican churches in the colony and successfully earned legal recognition. Although few settlers came to America from the Netherlands after 1664, the Dutch population continued to grow by natural increase. Eleven in number in 1664, the Dutch Reformed churches in the New York area grew to 29 in 1700, the largest denominational body in that colony. By the mid-18th century there were over a hundred Dutch Reformed churches along the Eastern Seaboard.

The relation of the denomination to its Dutch roots caused much discussion and internal conflict, first, with the coming of the English and, later, during the period of the American Revolution. At issue was the authority of Americans to ordain their own ministers and conduct business independent of control by the church's headquarters across the Atlantic in Amsterdam. In 1747, the colonists formed their own coetus (association of churches). Under the leadership of Theodorus J. FRELINGHUYSEN, a minister who had come to America in 1720 and been a herald of the Great Awakening, the Americans declared themselves wholly free from Dutch control in 1755. In response, however, a small group of ministers formed the "Conferentie," a party of loyalists who remained allied to the Netherlands.

During the War for Independence, the Dutch Reformed congregations by and large supported the American cause. Both their innate patriotism and a century-old distrust of the English and their church affected the position Dutch-Americans assumed in the Revolution. Victory over England also helped assure their final release from ecclesiastical control in Amsterdam. A denominational college (Queen's College, now Rutgers University) had already been founded at New Brunswick, New Jersey in 1766, and in 1784 New Brunswick Theological Seminary, the oldest Protestant seminary in the United States, was organized. John Henry Livingston, often called the "father of the Reformed church," was the last American to travel to Holland for ordination. He helped reunite the two warring factions in his denomination in 1772, shaped a new constitution and hymnal, and in 1810 served as president of Rutgers.

The Dutch Reformed churches remained concentrated within their original strongholds in New York and New Jersey during the early 19th century. The similarity of their theology to that of the Congregationalists and Presbyterians, the resemblance of their governing structure to presbyterianism, and the inevitable ties to Dutch culture all made the task of winning new church members difficult. Only the entrance at mid-century of two groups of Dutch immigrants into Michigan and Iowa, some of whom merged in 1850 with the Reformed Dutch in the East, helped the church grow again. Led by ministers of a separatist movement that had earlier seceded from the state church of the Netherlands, many of these settlers soon formed the staunchly conservative True Holland Reformed Church (now the CHRISTIAN REFORMED CHURCH) at Zeeland, Michigan in April 1857.

Without this migration from the Netherlands to the American Midwest, the Dutch Reformed denomination might well have merged with some other church and (like the German Reformed) entirely lost its ethnic distinctiveness in the United States. As it was, a proposed federation with the German Reformed Church failed in 1892, and three similar approaches to Presbyterian denominational bodies similarly collapsed in the 20th century. Still, the church's strong ethnic identity limited its appeal. The strength of the Reformed Church in America today, therefore, is mainly restricted to descendants of the first Dutch settlers in three geographic areas: New York and New Jersey; Michigan, Wisconsin, Illinois, and Iowa; and California.

In many ways, the Reformed Church in America is a study in contrasts. It has participated, for example, in such liberal ecumenical ventures as the Federal Council of Churches (1908) and the NATIONAL COUNCIL OF CHURCHES (1950). Two of its most prominent ministers in the present century, Norman Vincent Peale and Robert Schuller, furthermore, while otherwise conservative in political and social outlook, have popularized the "POSITIVE THINKING" movement that has smoothed away much of the harshness of traditional Calvinist orthodoxy. Yet the denomination has also adhered strictly to the 16th- and 17th-century

Calvinist confessions that shaped its life in colonial and early national America. A relatively small denomination that maintains an identity replete with intellectual rigor, the Reformed Church in America reported approximately 325,000 members in 924 congregations in 1990.

GHS, Jr.

Bibliography: James D. Bratt, *Dutch Calvinism in Modern America: A History of a Conservative Subculture* (Grand Rapids: Eerdmans, 1984).

Reformed Church in the United States
See GERMAN REFORMED CHURCH.

Reformed Episcopal Church See
EPISCOPAL CHURCH.

Reformed tradition, the
The Reformed tradition is one of the principal theological and denominational streams to emerge out of the Protestant REFORMATION of the 16th century. The Reformed ethos has undoubtedly shaped American intellectual and social attitudes more than any other European religious tradition in the United States. For nearly four centuries, denominations, churches, and leaders committed to Reformed theology have played prominent roles in the development of American religion and culture.

The beginnings of the Reformed tradition are found in Switzerland in the reforms initiated by Ulrich Zwingli of Zurich in 1523 and by John Calvin of Geneva in 1536. These reformers believed they were restoring Christianity to the pure beliefs and practices found in New Testament times. Calvin's *Institutes of the Christian Religion* (1536) articulated Reformed theology in its classic form, and over the next century CALVINISM spread into France, Germany, the Netherlands, and the British Isles. The Scottish reformer John Knox, who had lived in exile in Geneva, brought Calvin's ideas back to Scotland when he returned home in 1558. The Puritan (see PURITANISM) movement in England also relied upon Reformed thought. Its beliefs were most fully expressed in the creed composed by the Westminister Assembly of Puritan leaders that met in London in 1643. This document, known as the Westminster Confession, soon became the normative theological statement of English-speaking Calvinism.

In matters of worship, Reformed Christians insisted that all statues, crosses, candles, and church decorations, which were reminders of the medieval Catholic past, had to be removed from church buildings. Of the seven sacraments of medieval Catholicism, only baptism and holy communion were still accepted as truly authorized by Jesus Christ. Contrary to Roman Catholic, Lutheran, and Anglican teaching, the bread and wine of communion were not considered the actual body and blood of Christ but simply symbols of Jesus' presence in the hearts of believers. While the physical elements of worship were being displaced, the verbal (the word of God expressed both in the Bible and in the sermon) became recognized as the appropriate focus instead.

A number of prominent intellectual themes have run through Reformed teaching and given it a unique character both in Europe and in America.

First, Reformed theologians have emphasized the absolute sovereignty, utter transcendence, and inscrutable power of God. God has determined from eternity the fate of every creature, choosing some for salvation and others for damnation. Salvation comes by God's gracious decision alone, not through any effort or cooperation on the part of human beings.

Second, Reformed Christians believe in total human depravity, a doctrine that further illuminates the awesome chasm and radical discontinuity between God and humankind. Human beings by their sins willfully rebel against God's sovereignty and their own status as creatures, thus further cutting themselves off from divine love.

Third, Christians in their personal behavior must be obedient to the laws of God that are revealed in the Bible. The church, too, should conform itself to the mandates of Scripture and eradicate all ceremonies that lack a clear biblical precedent.

Fourth, the Reformed tradition has consistently emphasized that religion is not merely a private affair, but demands an engagement with society as well. Church and culture function together in creative tension. Despite its fallen state, the world belongs to God, and Christians must help to transform it into the image of God's kingdom.

Fifth, Reformed theology has always affirmed the importance of precise doctrinal formulations and creeds. Because of this concern for theological orthodoxy, denominations within the Reformed tradition have often been disrupted by schisms and disagreements over the content and meaning of their beliefs.

The Reformed tradition became well established in America in the century and a half between the arrival of the PILGRIMS in Plymouth, Massachusetts in 1620 and the outbreak of the War for Independence in 1775. During this period, thousands of Dutch Reformed (see REFORMED CHURCH IN AMERICA), German Reformed (see GERMAN REFORMED CHURCH), and French Reformed (Huguenot) (see HUGUENOTS) settlers streamed into the American colonies.

In America, the Reformed tradition adapted to new conditions and evolved. Since the Huguenots' identity, for example, was far more religious than ethnic or national, most quickly abandoned their French roots and joined other denominations such as the Dutch Reformed Church. The church in the Netherlands also provided important assistance to German Reformed emigrants who came to the New World in the colonial period. Puritans in America were eventually divided between those who chose a congregational (see CONGREGATIONALISM) form of church government and those who were presbyterians (see PRESBYTERIANISM). The latter group was eventually strengthened by the arrival of Scottish and Scotch-Irish Presbyterian immigrants in the late 17th century. Finally, although the GREAT AWAKENING of the mid-18th century aroused violent controversies within several denominations, it also helped extend and intensify the hold of the Reformed faith over the American religious population as a whole.

The Reformed tradition today manifests its presence through four main denominational families. Certainly most prominent of these has been the Presbyterian household. The Presbyterian Church (U.S.A.) is now the largest Presbyterian body in the United States, while a number of smaller denominations maintain their own distinctive interpretations of the essentials of this faith. Next in size and historical importance is the United Church of Christ, which is the historic continuation of the Congregational churches founded under the influence of New England Puritanism. The United Church of Christ also subsumed the third major Reformed group, the German Reformed, which (then known as the Evangelical and Reformed Church) merged with the Congregationalists in 1957. Fourth and finally, the Dutch Reformed school finds its major institutional expression in the Reformed Church in America, as well as in the smaller and more conservative Christian Reformed Church.

American denominations upholding the Reformed Tradition report a combined membership of approximately six million people at the present time. Since large numbers of Baptists, Episcopalians, and members of other, independent churches also believe many of the principles of Reformed theology, this tradition's influence actually extends far beyond mere denominational affiliation. And while many liberal Protestants have jettisoned what they view as the most objectionable doctrines of Calvinism, its emphasis on Christian engagement in political and social affairs is more strongly stressed among theological liberals today than among conservatives in American Protestantism.

GHS, Jr.

Bibliography: Donald K. McKim, ed., *Major Themes in the Reformed Tradition* (Grand Rapids, Mich.: Eerdmans, 1992); David F. Wells, ed., *Reformed Theology in America: A History of Its Modern Development* (Grand Rapids: Eerdmans, 1985).

Regular Baptists   See BAPTISTS.

Religious Zionists of America   Religious Zionists of America (RZA) is a national organization devoted to support of the state of Israel within the context of Jewish law. Formed in 1957, the RZA has its roots in older Zionist organizations composed of Orthodox Jews (see ORTHODOX JUDAISM; ZIONISM).

The first of these was organized in 1901, when a group of Orthodox religious leaders seceded from the Federation of American Zionists to found the United Zionists of America. When representatives of the United Zionists traveled to the 1903 World Zionist Congress, they made contact with members of Mizrahi, the Orthodox faction within the World Zionist Organization. Formed the previous year by Rabbi Isaac Reines, Mizrahi—an acronym from *merkaz ruhani* ("spiritual center")—was designed to infuse political Zionism with a religious influence.

These delegates constituted themselves the first American members of Mizrahi, and upon their return to the United States organized chapters in New York, St. Louis, and Pittsburgh. By the second decade of the 20th century there were over 100 chapters in the United States, and the movement established affiliates for youth (B'nei Akivah, Mizrahi Hatzhair), women (Mizrahi Women's Organization), and labor (Hapoel Hamizrahi).

These affiliates merged with Mizrahi in 1957 to form the Religious Zionists of America. Numbering about 20,000 members in 1980, the RZA has moved to enlarge its activities on behalf of Israel and to strengthen its ties to Israel's National Religious Party (NRP), formed by Mizrahi in 1956. An important swing vote in Israeli politics, the NRP has been able to wring major religious concessions from the technically secular state.

Until his death in 1993, the spiritual leader of the RZA in the United States was Rav Joseph SOLOVEITCHIK, who had been its honorary president since its creation. On matters of religious law and the relationship between religion and politics, Soloveitchik's pronouncements were considered binding. His death left an intellectual and administrative void in the organization.

The RZA works to provide Orthodox schools with Zionist material, and to have religious Zionism incorporated into the curriculum. To further this goal it publishes *Jewish Horizon*, and maintains educational and social facilities in Israel for American Orthodox Jews.

EQ

Bibliography: Arthur Hertzberg, *The Jews in America, Four Centuries of an Uneasy Encounter* (New York: Simon & Schuster, 1989); *Religious Zionism: Challenges & Choices* (Jerusalem: Oz Veshalom, 1983); Mosheh Weiss, *Rabbi Zvi Hirsch Kalisher: Founder of Modern Religious Zionism* (New York: Religious Zionist Organization of America, 1969).

Reorganized Church of Jesus Christ of Latter Day Saints

The Reorganized Church of Jesus Christ of Latter Day Saints (the RLDS Church) is the largest and most moderate of the many Mormon groups that split off from the CHURCH OF JESUS CHRIST OF LATTER-DAY SAINTS (the LDS Church), founded in 1830 by Joseph SMITH, JR. The approximately 250,000 members of the RLDS Church, which is based in Independence, Missouri, are often referred to as "Missouri Mormons" to distinguish them from the "Utah Mormons" of the Salt Lake City-based LDS Church.

The roots of the RLDS go back to the intra-Mormon controversy precipitated by Joseph Smith's murder in a jail in Carthage, Illinois in 1844. At issue in this controversy were two key questions: Who would succeed Smith as the Mormons' temporal and spiritual leader? And in what direction would the Mormon church move?

On one side of the controversy stood Brigham YOUNG, who argued that Smith's successor should come from the Mormon's chief governing body, the Council of the Twelve Apostles. Young also contended that the Mormon movement should continue to distinguish itself from more mainstream Protestant denominations by persisting with controversial practices instituted by Smith while the Mormons were centered in Nauvoo, Illinois. Because many of these practices—polygamy or "plural marriages," temple ordinances such as marriage for eternity, theocratic rule, and the ordination of a patriarch—were derived by Smith from Old Testament examples, it is fair to say that Young envisioned a Mormonism that freely mixed Christian and Jewish themes.

The other side in the controversy insisted that only a descendant of Smith should follow the founder as the movement's prophet. Lineage rather than office should determine Smith's successor, who should come not from the Young-led Council of the Twelve Apostles but from Smith's family. This contingent contended, moreover, that Smith had never instituted some of the notorious post-1830 innovations, most notably polygamy and associated practices such as marriage for eternity. Their Mormonism was, therefore, less Jewish and more distinctively Christian than the Mormonism of the Young contingent. It was, as one scholar has noted, a "reformation" rather than a "radical restoration." While RLDS members joined LDS members in their hope of restoring the primitive Christian church, they distinguished themselves by harboring no hope of restoring ancient Israel as well.

Although many of Smith's family members, including his first wife, Emma Smith, aligned themselves against "the Brighamites," in the end it was Young who emerged from this battle victorious. He was ordained the president of the LDS church in 1847, and led the "Utah Mormons" westward to their current headquarters in Salt Lake City one year later. Those who refused to recognize Young as Smith's successor organized a conference at Zarahemla, Wisconsin in 1853 and established what they called the "New Organization." They eventually tapped as their leader Joseph Smith III (1860–1914), who became president and prophet of the Reorganized Church of the Latter Day Saints (also known as the "Reorganization") upon its inception on April 6, 1860.

From the beginning, LDS and RLDS members agreed on many things. Both groups accepted the *Book of Mormon* and the Bible ("in so far as it is translated correctly") as divinely inspired scripture; and both saw revelation as an ongoing process in which God revealed his will to his people through prophets like Joseph Smith. Over time, moreover, the two main divisions in the Mormon church came together on key issues. In 1890, for example, the LDS Church, under pressure from the federal government, joined the Reorganized Church in repudiating the institution of plural marriage.

Utah Mormons and Missouri Mormons continue to quarrel, however, about many matters. LDS members still call their president from the Council of the Twelve Apostles, and RLDS members still insist that their president be a direct descendant of Joseph Smith. The Reorganized Church also rejects some of Mormonism's later doctrinal developments—the plurality of gods and the eternal progression of humans toward divinity, e.g.—as unbiblical. Finally, the Reorganized Church has also tended to be more liberal on social questions. Unlike the LDS Church, which excluded African-Americans from ordination to the priesthood from 1847 until 1978, the Reorganized Church has never set up racial barriers to ordination. And while the LDS Church continues to bar women from ordination, the RLDS Church now welcomes female priests.

SRP

Bibliography: Alma R. Blair, "Reorganized Church of Jesus Christ of Latter Day Saints: Moderate Mormonism," in F. Mark McKiernan, et al., eds., *The Restoration Movement: Essays in Mormon History* (Lawrence, Kans. Coronado Press, 1972); Inez Smith Davis, *The Story of the Church* (Independence, Mo.: Herald House, 1964).

Republican Methodist Church. See METHODISTS.

restoration movement The restoration movement was the expression of diverse religious impulses arising in the early 19th century that sought the reestablishment of the primitive (see PRIMITIVISM) Christian church of New Testament times. Restorationists relied on the absolute authority of the Bible as their handbook of faith and practice. Thomas Campbell, one of the first leaders of this movement, coined the phrase that best describes its intent: "Where the Scriptures speak, we speak; where the Scriptures are silent, we are silent." In 1831 the major restorationist strands in the United States coalesced into the denominational body commonly called the Disciples of Christ (see CHRISTIAN CHURCH [DISCIPLES OF CHRIST]).

The idea of restoring the original purity of the New Testament paralleled secular understandings about the meaning of the new American nation. From the days of its earliest settlement, America had promised a land of new opportunities reminiscent of the biblical garden of Eden. Restorationism also fit well with the optimistic mood in the United States immediately after the Revolution. Political ideals of justice and equality encouraged the POSTMILLENNIALISM emerging within Protestant communities—the sense that American Christians might shortly establish God's kingdom on earth.

The beginnings of restorationism are found among those who withdrew from the Methodist Episcopal Church in 1792 and, under the leadership of James O'Kelly, briefly formed the Republican Methodist Church. In a conference in

1794, the new denomination chose the name "Christian Church" instead and announced that the Bible would be its only guiding principle. About 20,000 people had joined that group by 1810. At the same time, a number of Baptists in New England became dissatisfied with the theological emphases of their church. Led by Elias Smith and Abner Jones, they desired to follow only the Bible and work for Christian reunification. These Baptists joined with O'Kelly's Christians in 1811.

The most significant contributions to the early restoration movement were made by two refugees from Presbyterianism: Barton STONE and Alexander CAMPBELL. Stone was a Presbyterian clergyman whose ministry was shaped by the frontier revivals of Kentucky and Tennessee. Despite the fame he won for organizing the great revival at Cane Ridge, Kentucky in 1801, many of his fellow Presbyterians questioned both the theology that underlay the revivals and the emotional excesses the revivals encouraged. Stone and others chose to abandon the Presbyterian denominational label altogether, and in 1804 they began calling themselves simply "Christians." They eschewed all creeds except the Bible and practiced adult baptism by full immersion in water, as in New Testament times. Stone's group later united with elements of the Smith-Jones fellowship in 1826, and by 1830 Stone's Christians numbered about 10,000 members.

The final element in the formation of the American restorationism was provided by Presbyterian ministers Thomas and Alexander Campbell. Thomas Campbell had come to western Pennsylvania from Ireland in 1807. Disturbed by petty theological quarrels within Presbyterianism, however, he soon withdrew from his denomination and formed the Christian Association of Washington in 1809. The purpose of the association was to promote Christian union on biblical principles, and the name of its township (Washington County, Pennsylvania) was intended to be the group's sole distinguishing feature. After the arrival of his son Alexander

in America, Thomas eventually handed leadership of the movement to him.

Alexander Campbell always emphasized a Christianity based upon the New Testament, a faith free from doctrinal hairsplitting and ecumenical in focus. He was noted as well for his detailed expositions of the structures and practices of primitive Christianity. He was convinced that human beings, when they read the Bible, could put its precepts into action and reconstruct the first-century church. Appealing especially to Baptists, he formed groups of believers called "Disciples of Christ." The Disciples became one of the fastest growing American religious organizations during the expansive SECOND GREAT AWAKENING period.

Walter Scott, a Scottish Presbyterian minister who migrated to the United States in 1818, was another Presbyterian minister active in the Disciples of Christ movement in this period. He became Alexander Campbell's most distinguished assistant in 1821. Scott developed a "five-finger" summary of the Gospel that defined the Disciples' plan of salvation: (1) believing, (2) repenting, and being (3) baptized in order to receive the (4) forgiveness of sins and (5) eternal life. Scott was the movement's greatest early evangelist, attracting hundreds of new converts in Ohio in the late 1820s. By 1830, the Disciples numbered approximately 12,000 people in all.

Campbell encountered Barton Stone in 1830 and realized that common ground existed between his Disciples and Stone's Christians. As a result, the two groups were united in fellowship at a meeting held in Lexington, Kentucky on January 1, 1832. While its internal organization was not completed until 1849, a new denomination emerged out of the self-consciously nondenominational movements Campbell and Stone launched. Expanding rapidly, the Disciples of Christ (also known as the Christian Church) numbered 118,000 members in 1850.

Problems immediately presented themselves, however, concerning the merger of the two restorationist groups. While baptism by immersion was practiced by the Christians, it was not universally accepted among the Disciples. The Disciples, moreover, took a more rationalistic approach to Christianity than did the revival-oriented followers of Stone. They rejected the idea that the regenerating work of the Holy Spirit necessarily preceded baptism. Finally, the Campbellites celebrated communion on a weekly basis, but the Stonites allowed each local church the freedom to decide its own policies regarding the Lord's Supper. Because of these obstacles, about half of the original Stonite congregations refused to follow their leader into the union. Calling themselves the Christian Connection, this group remained an independent body for the rest of the century. The Christian Connection eventually merged in 1931 with the Congregational Church, a denomination that in turn helped form the United Church of Christ in 1957.

Alexander Campbell's theological beliefs were to dominate the Disciples of Christ for several decades to come. By 1860, the Disciples had become the sixth largest religious body in the United States with nearly 200,000 members. Although they had little strength in the East, they were highly successful recruiting members on the western frontier, being numerically strongest in what is now the Midwest and upper South. However, by the end of the 19th century, a number of other factors, including continued growth, sociological diversity, and doctrinal disputes, threatened the unity of the denomination.

The most outstanding figure of the late 19th and early 20th century was the Tennessee preacher David LIPSCOMB. Lipscomb, like Alexander Campbell earlier in the century, advocated absolute trust in the teachings of the Bible. He thought loyalty to the plain teachings of Scripture required that believers take no active role in earthly affairs, and he prophesied a time when God would overthrow all human governments. Lipscomb also attacked the use of instrumental music in worship and the formation of

church missionary societies. He considered church organs as worldly contrivances with no warrant in the Bible, and he believed that ecclesiastical agencies only routinized the sacred.

Although Lipscomb's positions revealed a clear division in the ranks of his denomination, the true issue was not so much the use of musical instruments or the importance of missionary work, but how biblical teachings were to be applied to present-day church life. Many conservative congregations in league with Lipscomb refused to follow what they believed were modern innovations. By the end of the 19th century, most of those churches had separated into a small, extremely puritanical sect. In 1906 after prodding from Lipscomb, the United States Census Bureau officially recognized the existence of two separate denominations within the restorationist tradition: Lipscomb's militantly anti-modern CHURCHES OF CHRIST and the more theologically liberal Disciples of Christ.

As the 20th century progressed, the movement again divided and a third restorationist path became clearly established. For a second time, the question pertained to the role of the Bible. In the first decades of the 20th century, during the heyday of the fundamentalist (see FUNDAMENTALISM) controversy, conservatives accused the leadership of the Disciples of undercutting the traditional authority of the Scriptures. Since the traditionalists did not think their concerns were given a fair hearing, they formed their own alternative denominational body, the North American Christian Convention, in 1927. This third wing of American restorationism is generally known as the independent Christian Churches and Churches of Christ today.

The noninstrumental (so called, because they oppose the use of musical instruments in worship) Churches of Christ grew rapidly after 1906 and now compose the largest segment of the restoration movement. Over 13,000 autonomous congregations with a membership of nearly 1,700,000 people, most in the upper South, presently belong to this denomination. The independent Christian Churches are a heterogeneous collection of congregations, most of which resemble the mainstream of 20th-century American EVANGELICALISM. This denominational body today comprises about 5500 congregations with more than a million members. Finally, the Disciples of Christ occupy a position among the denominations of mainline Protestantism. Like other theologically liberal churches, the Disciples have experienced a numerical decline over the past three decades. At the present time, they number about 4,100 congregation and a million members.

GHS, Jr.

Bibliography: Alfred T. De Groot, *The Restoration Principle* (St. Louis: Bethany Press, 1960); Richard M. Tristano, *The Origins of the Restoration Movement* (Atlanta: Glenmary Research Center, 1988).

revivalism   Revivalism, a major American religious phenomenon, is a method, predominantly Christian and Protestant, whereby a speaker attempts to bring people to a CONVERSION experience—an acceptance of God's saving grace. While periods of religious awakening—revival— have occurred throughout the history of Christianity and are common to all religions, the development of a method designed to cause such an awakening is distinctive to the United States.

A revival is a religious event that occurs separately from regular Sunday services and follows a set pattern. Generally held in the evening, it continues for several days and is led by a professional evangelist who travels from place to place leading revivals. During the course of the event, daily prayer meetings, workshops on evangelization, and visits throughout the community are organized to support the revival and distinguish it from regular religious services.

The revival must first of all be promoted and advertised in order to insure a good crowd. Through prayer, music and preaching, those attending a revival are led to a state of emotional and spiritual agitation over their lives and things religious, especially the status of their souls, that results finally in conversion.

Revivalism as a method dates only from the 1830s when Charles Grandison FINNEY introduced what Lyman BEECHER, a defender of Protestant orthodoxy, referred to as "dangerous new measures." In fact, of the four major periods of American revivalism, the first GREAT

A banner announcing a revival meeting in front of a church in Lawrenceburg, Kentucky, July–August 1940. (Library of Congress)

AWAKENING (1730–1760) was based on the completely opposite assumption, that a revival was an act of God. One could pray for a religious refreshening, but its appearance rested in God's hands. The first Great Awakening was a period of renewed emphasis on human inability to bring about spiritual renovation.

All the four major figures of the Great Awakening—Theodore J. FRELINGHUYSEN, Gilbert TENNENT, Jonathan EDWARDS, and George WHITEFIELD—preached a stricter CALVINISM than their peers. They rejected what Edwards would call "spiritual self-reliance," emphasizing instead human depravity and God's sovereignty. Their views are perhaps best expressed in the title of Edwards's 1737 book on the phenomenon, *A Faithful Narrative of the Surprising Work of God in the Conversion of Many Hundred Souls in Northampton*. Not only was the event surprising, it was the work of God, not of the man. None of these men believed that conversion involved human activity. They could only preach the word and the hearts of the hearers would be opened or hardened as God chose.

This view changed during the next period of American revivalism, the SECOND GREAT AWAKENING. Spanning a period from the 1801 revival at Cane Ridge, Kentucky (see CANE RIDGE REVIVAL) through the 1840s, the Second Great Awakening transformed American Protestantism, and American society itself. During this time revivalism became a method, something human activity could bring about. God offered salvation to all, people either accepted or rejected it. The purpose of a revival was to bring people to the point of acceptance. As Charles Finney, the man most responsible for this new attitude toward revivals wrote, "[A] revival is not a miracle; it consists entirely in the right exercise of the powers of nature. . . . The connection between the right use of means for a revival and a revival is as philosophically sure as between the right use of means to raise grain and a crop of wheat." This emphasis on human ability repudiated the Calvinism that had dominated American Protestantism until this time.

ARMINIANISM, in various forms, became the dominant thrust of American Protestantism. Its emphasis on human ability fit well the expanding and optimistic new nation.

During this period of revivalism some, including Finney, took the emphasis on human ability to the point of perfectionism. They argued that just as human beings could choose to be saved, they equally could choose not to sin. Such a strong view of human activity gave rise to numerous reform movements. If human beings could choose to be saved, if they could choose to turn away from sin, then they could choose to create a good society. Abolitionism, women's rights, as well as prison and education reform were all linked to the perfectionist impulse in the Second Great Awakening.

The third period of American revivalism, from roughly 1870 through 1920, was dominated by two men—Dwight L. MOODY and Billy SUNDAY. Sunday achieved a high level of popularity due to his homespun delivery and fusion of religious and nationalistic sentiments, but he left no long-term organizational legacy. Moody, on the other hand, initiated the first great period of urban revivalism in the United States and left behind a significant institutional structure. To his revivals Moody brought the organizational savvy and convincing eloquence that had made him a successful shoe salesman. Focusing on the industrial cities of the United States and Great Britain, Moody had one of the most successful evangelistic careers in American history. Moody and his peers, however, had a vision different from the revivalists of the 1830s. Gone was the optimism that had resulted in the profusion of reform movements. For Moody the world was not getting better, and probably could not. As he once put it, "I look upon this world as a wrecked vessel. God has given me a lifeboat and said to me, 'Moody, save all you can.'"

This stress on decline, on things falling apart, signaled a change in American revivalism. Although the emphasis on human ability had not changed, the expectation that society could experience a regeneration declined among the theologically conservative Protestants most involved in revivalism. Individuals could be saved and reformed, and perhaps if enough were saved (converted) the world might improve, but that was unlikely.

This pessimism was the result of the increasing acceptance of PREMILLENNIALISM among conservative Protestants. The feeling that the world was nearing the end created by premillennialism gave a powerful sense of urgency to the evangelists. There was no time to save the ship, the passengers must be loaded on to the lifeboats. Moral decay, political corruption, atheism, communism, and foreign ideas were clear evidence that the world was sliding away from God and would soon face God's wrath.

By the time of Billy GRAHAM's rise to prominence during the 1950s, the fourth major period of American revivalism, evangelism, had become a formulaic and ritualistic phenomenon. Graham better than anyone combined the ritual elements of revivalism with a message that made few enemies. In his "Crusades," Graham talked about moral decay, the failings of individuals, and the imminent end of the world (although that lessened during the 1980s), pointing out that the only way to change the world was through the conversion of individuals, for everyone has fallen away from God, away from the path of righteousness. Graham told his audiences that life could be better, more satisfying, more fulfilling. Not with more money, flashier clothes, sex, or drugs, but by saying yes to God. The message of the revivalist is "Say yes to Jesus who died for you on the Cross, to remove your sins and save you from eternal damnation."

Today, revivals occur regularly throughout the United States. From Alaska to Florida evangelists say nearly the same thing and get the same responses from nearly the same types of people. Revivals have become so ingrained within the American religious mind that everyone involved knows the parts. The evangelists, the pianists, the choir, and the audiences all know how the system works. In fact it works because all know their roles. This more than

anything demonstrates the success of Finney's "new measures."

EQ

Bibliography: Whitney R. Cross, *The Burned Over District: The Social and Intellectual History of Enthusiastic Religion in Western New York* (New York: Harper & Row, 1965); James F. Findlay, *Dwight L. Moody: American Evangelist, 1837–1899* (Chicago: University of Chicago Press, 1969); Charles Grandison Finney, *The Memoirs of Charles G. Finney: The Complete Restored Text* (Grand Rapids: Academic Books, 1989); Edwin Gaustaud, *The Great Awakening in New England* (New York: Harper, 1957); David Edwin Harrell, Jr., *All Things Are Possible: The Healing and Charismatic Revivals in Modern America* (Bloomington: Indiana University Press, 1975); David S. Lovejoy, *Religious Enthusiasm and the Great Awakenings* (Englewood Cliffs: Prentice Hall, 1969); William Martin, *A Prophet With Honor: The Billy Graham Story* (New York: W. Morrow & Co., 1991); William G. McLoughlin, *Billy Sunday Was his Real Name* (Chicago: University of Chicago Press, 1955); ———, *Modern Revivalism: Charles Grandison Finney to Billy Graham* (New York: Ronald Press Co. 1959); ———, *Revivals, Awakenings, and Reform: An Essay on Religion and Social Change in America, 1607–1977* (Chicago: University of Chicago Press, 1978); Timothy L. Smith, *Revivalism and Social Reform in Mid-Nineteenth Century America* (New York: Abingdon Press, 1957).

Revolutionary War   See AMERICAN REVOLUTION/REVOLUTIONARY WAR.

Rhode Island (Colony)   See WILLIAMS, ROGER.

Right, Christian   See CHRISTIAN RIGHT.

Right to Life movement   See SEXUALITY.

Ripley, George (1802–1880)   A Unitarian minister, transcendentalist, utopian visionary, and journalist, George Ripley was one of the best-known and foremost advocates of liberal Protestant reform in the 19th century. His life and work can be divided up into four distinct phases, and the trajectory of his religious thought and action stands as representative of the transformation of American Protestantism as a whole during this period.

Ripley was born in Greenfield, Massachusetts, the child of a prosperous merchant. On his mother's side, the family had many ties to distinguished Anglo-Americans, including Benjamin Franklin and Ralph Waldo EMERSON, who was George's first cousin. Although the Ripleys were devout Congregationalists, they were sympathetic to the Unitarian theology then gaining ground in the eastern part of the state. At once very serious and inclined toward religious reflection, George studied at Harvard College (1819–1823) and then entered the Divinity School to train for the Unitarian ministry (see UNITARIAN UNIVERSALIST ASSOCIATION). He was ordained in 1826 and assumed the pulpit of the Purchase Street Church in Boston.

By the early 1830s, Ripley grew dissatisfied with the "impractical" nature of Unitarian theology, which he felt did not engage the emotions and could not address the many social ills of the urban environment. From 1833 to 1836 Ripley published *Discourses on the Philosophy of Religion,* a series of reflections that took issue with some of the central teachings of Unitarian thought. In 1836, along with his close friends Ralph Waldo Emerson, Bronson ALCOTT, and Theodore PARKER, Ripley helped organize the Transcendentalist Club, a gathering of disaffected intellectuals who yearned to move beyond the narrow confines of Boston Unitarianism. As one of the group's main organizers, Ripley helped establish *The Dial* (1840–1844), a short-lived journal dedicated to disseminating transcendentalist principles.

But Ripley soon grew dissatisfied with the intense individualism of Emerson and his other colleagues. Seeking a community setting in which to actualize his religious theories, Ripley withdrew from the ministry in 1841 and established Brook Farm, a farming cooperative in West Roxbury, Massachusetts, near Boston. Basing the colony on a joint-stock model of ownership, Ripley's purpose was to unite the best qualities of the laborer and the intellectual, to educate both the human mind and the body. But Brook Farm sank heavily into debt within a few short years, and in 1844 its members voted to convert it to a Fourierist phalanx. By 1847 the community was dissolved.

After the demise of his utopian colony, Ripley returned to journalism as a vocation. He spent the remainder of his life writing articles and reviews for some of the most influential journals in the nation, including the *New York Tribune, Harper's New Monthly Magazine,* and *Putnam's Magazine.* He also coauthored the *New American Cyclopedia* with Charles Dana, a 16-volume work published between 1858 and 1863.

LMK

Bibliography: Charles Crowe, *George Ripley: Transcendentalist and Utopian Socialist* (Athens: University of Georgia Press, 1967).

Roberts, Granville Oral (1918–) Oral Roberts is a Protestant clergyman, faith healer, college president, and the one of most widely known religious figures of the late 20th century. A pioneer in religious broadcasting, Roberts's use of sophisticated production methods helped popularize television evangelism and enabled his ministry to attain national exposure by the mid-1950s.

Roberts, the son of a Pentecostal minister, was born in Pontotoc County, Oklahoma on January 24, 1918. Although he rebelled against his religious upbringing as a teenager, Roberts chose to become a minister like his father following what he regarded as a divine cure from tuberculosis in 1935. Roberts served faithfully as a pastor and itinerant evangelist in the Pentecostal Holiness Church for the next 12 years. Bothered, however, by the restraints placed upon him by his denomination, he chose in 1947 to start an independent healing ministry. His ability to help the sick and his reputation for honesty quickly brought him to the forefront of the faith-healing movement. Roberts offered a simple message, typical of American Pentecostalism as a whole: God possesses power to work miracles in anyone who is willing to trust and believe in him.

Roberts has demonstrated a canny ability to update his ministry to meet shifting American social and religious trends. Certainly his decision in 1954 to broadcast his healing services on television placed him in the forefront of popular evangelism in the United States. Sensing in the late 1950s that interest in his faith-healing was waning, Roberts turned his attention to education and founded Oral Roberts University, which opened in Tulsa, Oklahoma in 1965. In 1968, he left the Pentecostal Holiness Church and was ordained a minister of the decidedly less flamboyant, but more respectable, United Methodist Church. Finally, Roberts acknowledged that modern medicine could assist Christian prayer in bringing healing to the sick. The addition of a medical school to Oral Roberts University, and the construction of a hospital and medical center (known as the City of Faith) in 1978, declare his present commitment to the interrelationship of religion and healing.

While continuing to maintain his status as a celebrity, Roberts and his almost billion-dollar financial empire have come increasingly under criticism both in the secular press and among conventional religious leaders. Roberts's high-pressure fund-raising techniques and claims to direct divine guidance have undermined the esteem in which he was once held. The comment of an Oral Roberts University official epitomizes the image that Roberts has projected, and that some have questioned, in recent years: "You can't be much of a witness [for Christ] if you are a loser." Although Roberts's reputation is now diminished, his financial success and many contributions to American popular Christianity are undeniably impressive.

GHS, Jr.

Bibliography: David Edwin Harrell, Jr., *Oral Roberts: An American Life* (Bloomington: Indiana University Press, 1985).

Robertson, Marion Gordon (Pat)   See CHRISTIAN RIGHT; ELECTRONIC CHURCH.

Roman Catholicism   The story of Roman Catholicism in the United States has a complex and twisting plot. It arrived in North America as the only form of Western Christianity but was soon displaced by those it viewed as schismatics and heretics, and barely hung on in the fringes of the modern United States, in the French and Spanish colonies. Proscribed in most English colonies, it entered the new nation freed from legal liabilities, yet suspect. For the first 150 years of United States history, Roman Catholicism was viewed by many as an alien religion dominated by foreign rulers and opposed to American values. By the 1950s it had become one of "America's three faiths" in the words of Will Herberg, an accepted way of being American religiously. With the election of the first Roman Catholic president, John F. Kennedy, in 1960, the faith's integration into American culture was irreversible.

With the arrival of Europeans, the North American continent was brought into the realm of Western Catholicism. The European explorers were Catholic and the first European church in this hemisphere was Catholic. This work was that of Spain, and the Spanish colonial church had a long history in the United States, spanning over three centuries. Although less successful than church work in Mexico and South America, it gave a distinctive cast to Catholicism in present-day California, the Southwest, and Florida. Nearly moribund by 1800, it was reinvigorated in the 19th and 20th centuries by immigrants from Cuba, Mexico, and Central and South America (see NEW SPAIN).

As Spanish America formed an arc across the southern United States stretching from Florida to California, it intersected another arc of European Roman Catholic settlement at the Mississippi River. Stretching from Maine to Michigan's Upper Peninsula, then down the Mississippi River to New Orleans, the French colonial empire was immense. Like its Spanish counterpart, however, French Catholicism in North America left little behind other than an impressive history.

The Spanish explorer Pedro de Aviles Menendez established the first colony in what was to become the United States at St. Augustine, Florida in 1565. As in Spain, church and state were closely identified.

The history of French missionary and religious activity in its North American empire is a heroic one, however. The priests and friars who directed it led harsh and solitary lives. Explorers as much as missionaries, these priests, primarily JESUITS, opened up the interior of the continent during the 17th century. The Jesuits lived among the Indians, slowly learning their languages. Early active among the Huron they became, by association, enemies of the Iroquois, and many met harsh deaths at the latter's hands. French America produced numerous martyrs and saints, who braved hardship and death to bring Christianity to France's American empire (see NEW FRANCE).

If Roman Catholicism found itself linked with the state in both French and Spanish America, just the opposite was the case in the British colonies. While the first British explorations in the Western hemisphere occurred prior to the Reformation, not until after England joined the Protestant fold in the 1530s was the first permanent English colony (Jamestown, Virginia, 1607) established in the present-day United States. For many Englishmen there was divine providence in this. God had reserved the discovery of the "New World" until the dawn of the Protestant Reformation so that it might be freed from popish superstitions. To a great extent the settling of British North America was an act of religious and nationalistic fervor designed to prevent England's Catholic enemies from controlling the region.

As a result, the British colonies originally held little or no promise for Roman Catholics. The law of MASSACHUSETTS BAY COLONY was the most direct, decreeing "perpetual imprisonment" for any priest entering the colony. But in 1625 George Calvert, friend of King James I and a member of his privy council, converted to Catholicism. This act, inexplicable given the social and political liabilities under which English Catholics labored, was followed by one even more inexplicable—Calvert retained the favor of James I and his successor, Charles I, both Protestants.

George Calvert planned to found a colony in America, but died before obtaining permission to do so. His son Cecil, also a Catholic, did gain a charter for a colony that he named Maryland (see MARYLAND [COLONY]), after Charles I's Catholic wife, Henrietta Maria. Although there were more Protestants in Maryland than Catholics, the colony became the center of Roman Catholic life in British North America.

Small Roman Catholic communities existed in colonies other than Maryland. Virginia's Catholics contained both Irish-Catholic indentured servants and the influential and wealthy Brent family, whose Catholicism did not limit their political significance in the colony. Unlike

Virginia, whose Catholics were scattered and unorganized, Pennsylvania had a well-organized, albeit small, community. This was especially true in Philadelphia, which had its own resident priest and by 1734 its own permanent chapel, St. Joseph's, and a Catholic population of over 1,300 by 1757.

Smaller pockets of Catholics resided in New York and modern-day New Jersey, but political difficulties culminating with the 1689 rebellion led by Jacob Leisler, following upon William and Mary's accession to the throne of England, ended organized Catholic activity in New York until the AMERICAN REVOLUTION, with the exception of a colony of Scots Highlanders in the Mohawk Valley who arrived in 1773.

At the outbreak of the American Revolution, the Catholic population in the 13 British colonies numbered less than 25,000 (roughly one percent of the population) and was served by 24 priests. It was a community struggling for its survival.

The suppression of the Jesuits (1773) ended the corporate existence of the most influential missionary body in the Roman Church. The blow fell particularly hard on the American clergy, all but one of whom were Jesuits. One young American Jesuit, Father John CARROLL, returned to America following the suppression and soon wrote a new chapter in American Catholicism.

While Roman Catholicism in British America was weakened by internal conflicts, its external enemies were even greater. Few in the colonies had a kind word for the faith. Roman Catholicism was viewed with suspicion, if not hostility, by Puritans, Baptists, Deists, and Quakers alike. Considered inimicable to liberty and a breeding ground of tyranny, it had few supporters in the 13 colonies.

The colonists' rebellion did have supporters among Roman Catholics. Chief among these were the Marylanders, Charles Carroll of Carrolton, the wealthiest man in America and the only Catholic to sign the Declaration of Independence, and his cousin, Father John Carroll, who joined Benjamin Franklin on a diplomatic mission to Canada designed to convince the Canadians to join the rebel cause.

Numerous other Catholics rallied to the Continental Congress. Their actions, French aid, and the efforts of Catholic emigre volunteers, including Lafayette, Casimir Pulaski, and Tadeus Kosciusko, changed many people's views of Catholicism. The Congress itself attended four masses, giving many their first view of the rituals of the "arrant whore of Rome and all her blasphemies," as the *New England Primer* had it. Roman Catholics looked less like servants of a foreign and tyrannical system and more like fellow citizens who helped to secure liberty for the new nation.

While the American Revolution changed the attitudes of many toward Catholics, it left the organizational life of American Catholics in disarray. The dissolution of the Jesuits, the ending of ties with England, and American hostility to foreign control all argued for the establishment of a native hierarchy, an American bishop. Rome was amenable to this, already having sent out feelers through the French government and Benjamin Franklin as to the opinion of the young government. Congress responded by stating that the appointment was a spiritual affair with which it had no concern. In response the Vatican issued a decree in July 1788 authorizing the American clergy to nominate a candidate for bishop. Meeting at Whitemarch Plantation, a former Jesuit estate in Maryland, the American clergy chose John Carroll—who had been serving as vicar-apostolic, or overseer, in the United States—by a vote of 24–2. The nomination was accepted by Pope Pius VI who issued the bull *Ex Hoc Apostolicae* on November 6, 1789 naming Carroll as bishop of the See of Baltimore. Consecrated in England the following year, he was installed in Baltimore on December 12, 1790. The United States had its first Roman Catholic bishop.

The choice of Carroll was fortuitous. Descended from a distinguished family, related to signers of both the Declaration of Independence and the Constitution, orthodox in doctrine, and committed to the American system of government, Carroll envisioned a distinctly American Roman Catholicism. While the realities of curial politics prevented its realization until the late 20th century, his work as bishop provided for the Church's future growth and stability.

At the time of Carroll's installation, the Roman Church in the United States faced difficulties, many of which would persist for the next 150 years. Carroll's greatest need as an administrator was to impose discipline and order, but many factors mitigated against this. First was the radically different social and political system in the United States. Bishop Carroll could not rely upon the civil authorities to aid him. Neither did he control the finances of the various parishes. Churches were built and run by the members, many of whom felt that they, thereby, should have the right to choose their priest. Conflicts over TRUSTEEISM, the control of Church property by lay trustees, intermittently troubled the Church's hierarchy for decades.

This problem was exacerbated by the overwhelmingly Protestant culture. Protestant suspicions of Roman Catholicism as a despotic religion hostile to republican government lurked below the surface.

The mix of different ethnic groups in America also raised problems unknown in Europe. Although incipient during Carroll's tenure as bishop, tensions already existed between Irish and German Catholics, both of whom had their own particular religious culture with special saints and feast days. As Poles, Italians, and others arrived later in the century, these tensions increased.

Finally, the inability of the Church's Roman hierarchy to understand the United States's political and cultural realities hindered the work of Carroll and his successors. Although more fortunate than later bishops in this regard, Carroll spent much time and effort explaining America to the Curia, the papal bureaucracy.

By Carroll's death in 1815, the American Church was on a much stronger footing. The United States, excluding the Louisiana territory, had roughly 70,000 Roman Catholics served by 70 priests in 80 churches. Within three decades, however, it would be transformed by immigration from Europe and become the largest denomination in the country.

Carroll's successor as archbishop of Baltimore, Leonard Neale, survived him only by two years. He was succeeded by Ambrose MARECHAL, one of the many French Sulpicians who had come to aid the American Church. Pious, learned, and an able administrator, Marechal provided the American Church with a period of stability but failed to respond to the needs of numerous Irish immigrants whom he referred to as "*la canaille irlandaise*" ("the Irish rabble").

If their co-religionists manifested a distaste for the Irish, most other Americans loathed them. Fears that these immigrants were part of a plot to conquer America and turn it into a Catholic empire merged with stereotypes of Irish drunkenness, laziness, and depravity. Irish and Catholic became linked with all that threatened American liberty and purity, leading to an outbreak of ANTI-CATHOLICISM from the 1830s through the 1850s (see NATIVISM).

Although anti-Catholicism destroyed itself on the rocks of American politics, it reminded Catholics that to many they were aliens. Catholicism needed both to make itself more American and to protect itself from the sea of Protestantism that constantly threatened to wash it away.

The most significant development in American Roman Catholicism during this period, however, was its growth. By 1865 there were 15 dioceses in the east, and as the population moved westward, dioceses were organized in Cincinnati (1821), St. Louis (1826), Detroit (1833), Vincennes (1834), Nashville (1837), Chicago and Milwaukee (1843), Oregon City (1846), and San Francisco (1853). Others followed as the population filled out the vast region between the seas.

In Louisiana, California, and New Mexico the expanding nation (and Church) encountered

Roman Catholic institutions in the United States were built by working-class immigrants from many nations. A nun solicits donations at a shipyard gate in Baltimore, Maryland. (Library of Congress)

Roman Catholic cultures of long duration very different from the Anglo-Irish culture predominant in the American Church. The Anglo-Irish who dominated the Church were no more sympathetic to different traditions than the French had been. The result was conflict. The first American archbishop of New Orleans met with such resistance that he centered his rule in St. Louis. In New Mexico, a long-standing Catholic Native American culture that retained much of 16th-century Spanish Catholicism, including self-flagellation, was forced underground by ecclesiastical opposition. Similar conflicts emerged in California and left long-simmering tensions to re-emerge in the late 20th century.

While the Roman Catholic Church added some adherents through the westward course of the American empire—15,000 in the Louisiana Purchase, 26,000 in the Mexican secession—its greatest growth was from immigration. Although the poverty of many of these immigrants helped to fuel anti-Catholic and nativist move-

ments, their needs forced the Roman Church in the United States to greater organization.

Some organizations were created outside the United States—the Society for the Propagation of the Faith (France, 1822), the Leopoldine Foundation (Austria, 1829), and King Ludwig's Mission Society (Bavaria, 1838)—others were American in their roots. Many of these societies were women's religious orders, beginning with Mother Elizabeth Ann SETON's Sisters of Charity, and including the Sisters of Loretto, as well as Third Order Dominicans and Sisters of the Sacred Heart who, along with the Ursulines, provided most female education. In many areas these orders were the locus of institutional Catholicism and their labors maintained Catholic life and practice in an age of insufficient priests.

Catholic colleges also grew during this time, including Georgetown Academy (1789, now Georgetown University), Mount Saint James (1836, now Holy Cross), and in 1842 Notre Dame du Lac in Indiana. Numerous other small colleges dotted the landscape from Alabama to Detroit and Massachusetts to Missouri. All served as part of the infrastructure necessary to maintain Roman Catholic life and practice.

The clergy were themselves subject to institutional organization. Beginning in 1829 the United States Catholic hierarchy held the first of eight triennial provincial councils, supplemented by plenary councils in 1852 and 1866. While much of the work of these councils was mundane and repetitive, they provided coherence and uniformity to a widely dispersed and disparate Church. While attentive to the distinctiveness of the American political scene, the American hierarchy was attracted to the centralizing work of Pius IX and his successors. They viewed it as the only way to control their rapidly growing and diverse flock.

One issue about which the Church did not speak with uniformity was that which most agitated America in the 1840s and 1850s, SLAVERY. In Maryland and Louisiana where Catholicism was most strongly rooted, slavery was a part of life among laity and clergy. In both states there existed a significant number of black Catholics, and two orders of black women religious. The Oblate Sisters of Providence and the Sisters of the Holy Family (New Orleans, 1842) directed their missions to black education and care for black orphans and the elderly.

Nationally, however, geography helped to determine Catholic attitudes, and Bishop John England of Charleston published a spirited defense of slavery, while Bishop John Purcell opposed it. Officially, the hierarchy maintained silence, and when the CIVIL WAR broke out, Catholics volunteered to serve on both sides of the conflict. At the battle of First Manassas (Bull Run), the predominantly Catholic "Montgomery Guards" of the First Virginia Infantry battled the Irish Catholic 69th New York Regiment.

Their commitment to a worldwide communion prevented a split in the American Catholic Church of the kind that affected so many other denominations. Catholic commitment on both sides of the conflict also helped lessen latent hostilities. Catholics had proved their loyalties, at least among their co-regionists, and emerged from the war unified and secure.

In 1866 the Second Plenary Council of the Roman Catholic Church in the United States convened in Baltimore on October 4. When it ended two weeks later at a solemn assembly attended by President Andrew Johnson, the council had defined the agenda for American Catholicism. Concerned preeminently with pastoral issues, it called for positive action to aid immigrants, to improve the moral training of children, and to elevate the religious education of church members.

Interestingly the council's documents made no mention of the Pius IX's *Syllabus of Errors* that, by condemning certain errors of the modern world including freedom of religion and speech, was apparently at odds with the American political system. The document represented the European-centered views of the Roman Catholic Church's hierarchy. Buffeted by events in Europe, from the French Revolution to the unification of Italy and the loss of the papal states, European Catholicism began a withdrawal from and an attack upon the so-called modern world—an attack that was religious, political, and intellectual. Organizationally the Church turned inward. Authority was increasingly centralized in Rome, as the European governments that had once supported the Church now were hostile.

Most of the American bishops supported the centralizing tendency in the Church. The relationship of Catholics and the Church to the non-Catholic world, however, was another matter. Here disagreements divided the American hierarchy and exacerbated other conflicts within the church. A key conflict, often referred to as the "Americanist Crisis" (see AMERICANISM), resulted from numerous threads woven into the tapestry of United States Catholic history. Personal, theological, and practical differences within the American Church hierarchy became heresy when viewed from the perspective of Rome, although never was heresy so ambiguously defined or heretics so difficult to locate.

One segment of the hierarchy, led by Archbishop John IRELAND and supported by James Cardinal GIBBONS, felt that all Catholics in the United States should conform to a single Catholic culture, a culture open to the possibilities and promises of the United States. This group, known as Americanists, believed that the failure to create such a culture threatened episcopal authority, endangered morals, and embarrassed the Church within the wider society. This singular culture would be both American and Catholic. It would create a unified church, no longer foreign and alien.

The opponents, primarily Bishops Michael Corrigan (1885–1902) of New York City and Bernard McQuaid (1868–1909) of Rochester, New York, while equally committed to episcopal authority, believed that any concession to the wider culture threatened Catholics and Catholicism. The world was hostile to everything Roman Catholics believed and the greater the contact with it, the greater the threat of apostasy.

Although ascendant in the early years of Leo XIII's pontificate, the Americanists soon found themselves under suspicion, signaled unmistakably by the papal encyclical LONGINQUA OCEANI (January 6, 1895). Although formally a letter praising the strength and growth of the American Church, it pointedly stated that the Church would be even stronger if it "enjoyed the favor of the laws and the patronage of public authority." For Rome, obviously, the United States was not the model for nations or the Church.

In January 1899 the encyclical *Testem Benevolentiae,* which specifically condemned the existence of a religious heresy known as "Americanism" that suggested the Church should change in essentials to accommodate the modern world and should make itself more democratic. Although no one was named as holding these views and Cardinal Gibbons, writing for the American church, explained to the pope that none of its bishops held such views, the result of the condemnation was a half-century of cul-

tural and intellectual hibernation for American Catholicism.

If the condemnation of attempts to reconcile Roman Catholicism with the modern world served to isolate American Catholics from American culture, it could not prevent them from participating in that society. Catholics participated as equal citizens in American politics, and in some cases came to dominate the political life of northeastern and midwestern cities.

Catholics saw themselves as loyal Americans who answered their nation's call to arms when necessary. Although both the Civil War and the Spanish-American War had proved this, WORLD WAR I was a watershed for Roman Catholicism, and indeed the United States, in this regard.

The effects of World War I on the religious communities in the United States were immense. The war called for an unprecedented degree of interreligious cooperation, as well as occasioning much intrareligious organization. Roman Catholics participated equally in both.

Catholic individuals and organizations quickly took up their share of Red Cross work, Liberty Bond sales, and Belgian relief. The need to organize work among Catholic soldiers following United States entry into the war led to the formation of the National Catholic War Council in August 1917. Destined to outlive the war as the National Catholic Welfare Council (see NATIONAL CATHOLIC WELFARE CONFERENCE), it was the first national Catholic organization dedicated to social and political work.

Responsible for organizing war work among Catholics, the council provided chaplains, recruited volunteers, and raised money. Its head, John J. Burke, also served as permanent chairman of the Committee of Six, a religious advisory board to the secretary of war. Its members included officials of the Federal Council of Churches (see NATIONAL COUNCIL OF CHURCHES), the YOUNG MEN'S CHRISTIAN ASSOCIATION, the Jewish Welfare Board, and an Episcopal bishop.

Many Catholics emerged from their wartime experiences strengthened in the view that their unified and ordered religion was destined to overtake divided Protestantism. The insularity of American Catholic culture, resulting from the condemnation of "Americanism," went far toward explaining this smugness, but it also served to protect the community from the attitude of defeat and despair permeating the United States after the failure of Wilson's (and America's) attempt to make the world safe for democracy. It also helped to protect the community during the 1920s, when the "return to normalcy" ushered in a new period of nativism and anti-Catholicism.

Three events marked American Roman Catholicism in the 1920s. The resurgence of nativism, the end of immigration, and the presidential candidacy of Alfred E. Smith. The meaning of all three of these was mixed, and indeed one could argue that the outcomes were, in the long run, positive.

The end of World War I saw the a resurgence of anti-immigrant and anti-Catholic agitation, centered on a rejuvenated KU KLUX KLAN. This new Klan made anti-Catholicism one of its main precepts and clamored for immigration restrictions. By 1923 the Ku Klux Klan had three million members. Despite its size, the Klan had little success in turning its anti-Catholicism into political successes. While Alabama passed a convent inspection law that was probably Klan inspired, the only state law passed directly under Klan auspices (although its main sponsors were the state's Masons) was an Oregon law requiring all children between the ages of eight and 16 to attend public schools. Passed by referendum in 1922, it was struck down by the United States Supreme Court (*Pierce v. Society of Sisters*) in June 1925, before it even took effect.

By that time the Klan had begun to disintegrate. Shaken by internal divisions and crippled by criminal indictments against its national leaders, by 1928 it was a shell of its former self. But during its resurgence it had demonstrated to many American Catholics that, despite everything, many of their neighbors considered them suspect at best, and dangerous to the American way of life at worst.

Such suspicion was not limited to the Klan, however. Many allegedly enlightened and liberal persons and institutions tended to look upon the Roman Church as "alien to American ideals." But it was not Catholics alone that were seen as alien. The continued influx of immigrants, especially from Eastern and Southern Europe, seemed poised to overwhelm the country. These immigrants, it was assumed, brought with them dangerous ideas—anarchism and Communism—and unenlightened superstitions, including Roman Catholicism. They were considered to be the failures of already degenerate peoples.

The call went out for a massive reduction in the number of people entering the United States lest it be overrun. The result was a series of laws that restricted immigration, culminating with the National Origins Act of 1927, which effectively ended immigration from Southern and Eastern Europe.

The end of immigration profoundly affected the American Catholic Church. Although for many, the intent of the law was to weaken Catholicism, the long-term effect was just the opposite. The end of immigration transformed American Catholicism from a church in flux, constantly forced to respond to the immediate needs of an immigrant population, into a stable institution, secure within itself, and increasingly rooted to the American context. This stability enabled the Roman Catholic Church to gain acceptance after WORLD WAR II.

Nothing better illustrates the ambiguous status of American Catholicism in the 1920s than the 1928 presidential candidacy of Alfred E. Smith. A New York Catholic associated with Tammany Hall and an outspoken opponent of prohibition, Smith had been denied the 1924 Democratic Party nomination for just those reasons. In 1928 the nomination was his. As a Catholic who possibly would become the leader of the United States, Smith was forced to respond to Protestant fears of a Catholic takeover. These fears, while practically unfounded, had serious intellectual roots. Had not papal documents decried the separation of church and state as well as freedom of the press, speech, and religion? In fact did not the leading Roman Catholic liberal, Father John RYAN, in his book *The State and the Church* reiterate Leo's teaching in *Immortale Dei* that "error had no rights" and that where feasible and expedient, non-Catholics could be limited in their religious if not civil rights?

These questions were addressed to Smith in an open letter appearing in the *Atlantic Monthly* of April 1927. Responding in the next month's issue of the same magazine, Smith stated that as a devout Catholic all his life he had never heard of those documents until mentioned in the letter to him. He claimed that despite his Catholicism and his belief in the rightness of the Catholic faith, he was completely committed to the American ideal of the separation of church and state and rejected any claims by the Church to "interfere with the operations of the Constitution." In his response, Smith spoke for most American Catholics, who saw no conflict between their commitment to American political structures and their Catholic faith. The Church's official pronouncements remained, however, and many Americans simply would not vote for a Catholic.

Smith went down in defeat in 1928, as had every Democrat since 1860, except Grover Cleveland and Woodrow Wilson. While his religion definitely played a role in people's voting, whether it was decisive is doubtful. There were many other things working against him, including America's seeming prosperity under Republican governance. Smith's opposition to prohibition, and his affiliation with a political machine widely viewed as corrupt, played a greater role in his defeat than religion.

While the anger remained, more threatening events distracted the attention of Catholics and the entire country. In October 1929 the stock market crashed and the United States sank deeper into economic depression. By 1932 one-third of the work force was unemployed, thousands lost their savings as banks collapsed. Foreclosures dispossessed thousands more. President Herbert Hoover, who had worked miracles with European relief following World War I, seemed incapable of grasping the enormity of the crisis.

Alone among American denominations, the Roman Catholic Church had a well-articulated view of the right functioning society and economy, as well as a national organization dedicated to social and political concerns. Enunciated in the social encyclicals of Pope Leo XIII, most notably *Rerum Novarum* (1891), and reiterated by Pius XI in *Quadregesimo Anno* (1931), the Roman Catholic Church understood society as a system of parts united for the social good. While condemning socialism and Communism and affirming the right to private property, the Church also affirmed that property was a limited right that society could control. Workers were owed a living wage and the weaker segments of society deserved to have their needs met through forms of social welfare.

In the United States the implications of these documents had been worked out in the positions of the National Catholic Welfare Conference, and especially in the work of Father John Ryan. Ryan had been instrumental in formulating the social policies of the American Church since World War I. He had drafted the bishops' statement on social reconstruction for the postwar period, to which President Roosevelt often referred in defense of New Deal policies.

Even more radical than the corporativist policies of the encyclicals were the economic and social views of the CATHOLIC WORKER MOVEMENT. Guided and inspired by Peter Maurin and Dorothy DAY, the Catholic Worker movement articulated a radical vision of Christianity rooted in the preaching of Jesus, personalism, and voluntary poverty. Living in a series of settlement houses, the Catholic Worker groups lived lives of what would later be called "solidarity with the poor." Although numerically small, the movement exerted an influence far beyond Catholicism.

At the other end of the spectrum were those Catholics whose social views were grounded in the encyclicals but who took the corporate model of society much more seriously. For these Catholics, Mussolini's Italy and even Hitler's Germany provided attractive models for overcoming the economic chaos of the Great Depression.

The most visible of these was Father Charles COUGHLIN of the Shrine of the Little Flower outside Detroit. A dynamic speaker, Father Coughlin attracted a following in the hundreds of thousands for his radio sermons. Originally a supporter of Franklin Roosevelt, Coughlin called for massive government involvement to pull the nation out of its economic collapse. By 1936, however, Coughlin, turned against Roosevelt and began to denounce him as a tool of the international banking conspiracy. Coughlin also became increasingly anti-Semitic in his radio programs, blaming the nation's problems on Jewish bankers and a worldwide Jewish conspiracy. Silenced by the archbishop of Detroit for his ANTI-SEMITISM and stridency, Coughlin receded into relative obscurity.

Father Coughlin was only the most extreme example of the complexity within Roman Catholic economic and social thinking. While in the hands of a John Ryan, these views could be construed as progressive, they were much more compatible with a medieval world view that understood society as hierarchical, ordered, and uniformly Catholic. The messiness of democracy and pluralism presented problems for Roman Catholic thinking, problems that were most visible during the interwar years in the radical divergence of Roman Catholics from their fellow citizens on the issue of the Spanish Civil War.

What most Americans viewed as a war for democracy against tyranny, was interpreted by most Roman Catholics as a struggle of religious and social truth against the forces of infidelity and anarchy. The suspicion many Americans had of Hitler and Mussolini was not quite as widespread among Catholics, who still felt that the international enemy was atheistic Communism, against which Hitler and Mussolini acted as bulwarks. These differences led to some political tensions. Roman Catholics generally opposed easing the arms embargo to Europe, lend-lease, and any policy that seemed to aid the Soviet Union. While these views antagonized many Americans who viewed fascism as the problem of the moment, and caused some to view Catholics as suspect on Nazism (especially given the papacy's rather tepid condemnation of Hitler and its *modus vivendi* with Mussolini), it would serve the American Church well in the post–World War II era when it parlayed its unremitting anti-Communism into an asset.

The Church was capable of doing this since after hostilities began, its support for American entry into World War II was wholehearted. By then illusions had receded, and Roman Catholics rallied to the flag just as they had done in the earlier world conflict.

If World War I had gained for the Roman Catholic community entry into the American mainstream, World War II cemented this position. The Roman Catholic response to the American call-up was near-universal. Among the Roman Catholic media the sole dissenting voice was from the *Catholic Worker*, which continued its pacifist stance and set up work camps where Catholic conscientious objectors could perform their alternative service. Not that there were a great number of them—in fact the percentage of Catholic conscientious objectors was far below their percentage of the general population.

Despite this, the hierarchy did not lose sight of its teachings on war, nor did it ignore the Church's universal mission. The bishops condemned the massive bombing of German cities, of which the Dresden firebombing (February 1945) was the most severe example, and opposed the unconditional surrender policy promulgated by the allies. Such war practices and aims violated the just war doctrine of proportionality that had guided the Church's thinking since the time of Thomas Aquinas. Protests fell on deaf ears and as the Allied advance increasingly uncovered the magnitude of the Nazi evil fewer and fewer were willing to oppose the destruction of the Axis powers (and even the German nation) by any and all means. As a result, the atomic bombing of Nagasaki and Hiroshima met with little condemnation, although many have argued that such bombings blatantly violated the rule of proportionality.

The bombings, however, led to peace with Japan and the end of the war. As American troops demobilized, they returned to a nation and indeed a world radically different from the one existing before the war. This was especially true of Roman Catholics who found themselves viewed with much less suspicion 'than earlier. Although significant conflicts would emerge in the future, Roman Catholicism was well on its way toward full acceptance.

From the war's end until the early 1960s, two policy issues most concerned the American Church. On the domestic front, federal funding for education reopened a long-festering wound. Originally designed to enable returning servicemen to attend college or vocational school, these funds were made available to those attending both public and private colleges and universities. This was a boon to Catholic colleges, as it was to all colleges. It increased the number of students and led to expansion of facilities and programs. The increasing number of Catholics who attended college helped to transform the community itself. The higher levels of education moved many Catholics out of their traditional blue-collar jobs and into white-collar positions, helping to end much of their cultural isolation.

If aid to higher education was a boon, attempts to provide federal aid to elementary and secondary education resulted in conflict. Roman Catholics clamored for a share to aid their schoolchildren. Failure to provide money

equally to private and public schools, they argued, would be unfair. Those who chose to send their children to private schools were taxed twice for doing so.

Although legislative and judicial action prevented the allocation of governmental funds to parochial schools, the issue was never settled definitively and the fight continued into the 1990s. The issues of church-state (see CHURCH AND STATE RELATIONSHIP; FIRST AMENDMENT) relations that the debate highlighted led to the emergence of what many have been seen as a new form of anti-Catholicism. Represented by Protestants and Other Americans United for Separation of Church and State, these organizations and individuals opposed not Catholics, but Catholicism—the institution whose policies and views were at odds with church-state separation and religious liberty. Catholic demands for federal aid to parochial schools and attempts to appoint an ambassador to the Vatican were obvious proof of Catholic mingling of church and government.

While some might warn against Catholic power, many felt that the real threat to the American way of life in the decades following World War II was Communism and the Soviet Union, which following Hitler's defeat had overrun Eastern Europe. The suppression of religion in that predominantly Catholic area, and the maltreatment of religious leaders such as Josef Cardinal Mindszenty of Hungary only flamed Catholicism's anti-Communist passions.

Catholicism had earned its anti-Communist badge early, and while the junior senator from Wisconsin, Joseph McCarthy (a Catholic himself), and his ilk were warning of Communist infiltration in the State Department and the National Council of Churches, both bastions of the Protestant establishment, the American Catholic Church could proclaim that not one of its priests was a Communist. This staunch anti-Communism was reinforced by the public pronouncements of Francis Cardinal SPELLMAN of New York and most of the Catholic press which, with the exceptions of the liberal *Commonweal, The Catholic Worker,* and the often virulently anti-Communist Jesuit weekly *America,* were supportive of McCarthy.

Ironically, McCarthy was brought down in part by that instrument which helped bring about greater integration of Roman Catholics into American society—television. While television exerted a uniforming influence on Americans of all stripes, it brought certain clerical figures into great public prominence. Cardinal Spellman, an eloquent spokesman for the Church, often appeared on television. Monsignor (later archbishop) Fulton J. SHEEN's "Catholic Hour" attracted large audiences, including numerous Protestants. The appearance of Roman Catholic spokesmen in their living rooms helped to dissipate perceptions of Catholic strangeness and foreignness.

While suspicions of Catholics did not end, as evidenced by the uproar that greeted attempts to appoint a United States ambassador to the Vatican and the long-simmering conflict over federal aid to education, the 1950s saw a gradual dissipation of anti-Catholicism. In fact the 1960s would end with the event that signified the death-knell of anti-Catholicism as a social-political force in the United States: the election of John F. Kennedy as president.

It must be said first of all that Kennedy's election did not prove that anti-Catholicism was dead. In fact, some scholars argue that Kennedy's Catholicism nearly cost him the election. The issue was muted, however, by Kennedy's straightforward responses to those suspicions and his opposition to aid to religious schools. The charm and vibrancy of the young president, along with his tragic assassination, served to stigmatize anti-Catholicism for what it was, bigotry. The 1950s and 1960s also saw a series of events that transformed the Church. This transformation was so great that its implications are still being worked out.

These changes began with the election of Angelo Giuseppi Roncelli, as Pope John XXIII

in 1958. Originally viewed as a caretaker pope, the 77-year-old pontiff called for *aggiornamento* (awakening) within the Roman Church. The Church was to open its windows to the cleansing breezes of the modern world. In order to bring this about, he called a Church council that convened in the Vatican in 1962 (see VATICAN COUNCIL II).

While theologically unsophisticated when compared to many of their European counterparts, the American bishops played a major role in the formulation and adoption of several major statements at the council. These were the Declaration on Religious Liberty and the Declaration on the Relation of the Church to Non-Christian Religions, statements that were rooted in the historical and political realities of the American experience.

While such statements affected American Catholics by bringing Church statements into line with American practice, the radical liturgical and doctrinal formulations of the council more dramatically affected their religious lives. The use of English instead of Latin in the Mass, the ending of meatless Fridays, greater openness in religious forms and practice, as well as a decrease in the authoritarianism within the Church (especially that between priest and laity) confused many Catholics. Occurring at the beginning of the social and political upheavals of the 1960s and 1970s, the loss of old verities threw much of the Church into turmoil. Many priests and nuns left their offices; others picked up new vocations.

The opening to the world encouraged by Vatican II led many to recognize the existence of troubling social and economic problems. These women and men, many influenced by Dorothy Day and the Catholic Worker movement, threw themselves into the struggles for racial equality, civil rights, and economic justice, and against the war in Vietnam. Such activities served to create greater turmoil in the Church. Many saw their faith deepened by such social Catholicism; others saw it as anarchy engendered by changes in religious practice.

Into this maelstrom of change the successor to John XXIII, Paul VI, dropped yet another bombshell, a rejection by the Roman Church of all forms of artificial birth-control. In the encyclical *Humanae Vitae* (July 25, 1968), Paul VI rejected the suggestions of his appointed commission that questions of contraception be left to the consciences of Christian parents, and reiterated the Church's teaching that any artificial barrier to the generative act is a violation of natural and divine law. Coming amidst the Church's radical transformation, this decision caused tremendous dismay. Many American Catholic academics openly condemned it. Large numbers of priests, although bound to the Church's position, continued to counsel couples to follow their consciences in this area. Most significantly, it was simply ignored by large numbers of the Church membership. The opening of the Church and its greater collegiality, proclaimed by John XXIII and even Paul VI, found its greatest statement in the refusal of Church members to follow a teaching they viewed as inappropriate and wrong-headed.

Contraception was not the only issue of sexual morality that affected the Church. In fact, questions of sexual morality were a major element of debate throughout the last half of the 20th century. The so-called sexual revolution of the 1960s and 1970s saw many attacks on the Church's traditional opposition to sexual intercourse outside marriage. The Church refused to budge on this teaching, although it became obvious that large numbers of its members ignored it just as they did its teachings on contraception. While troubling, it did not appear to have major consequences until the outbreak of the AIDS epidemic in the 1980s. This illness combined numerous elements of human sexuality—non-marital intercourse, contraception (prophylaxis), and homosexuality—within the context of a fatal disease. The hierarchy of the American Church refused to reconsider its opposition on the use of condoms, in this case as a prophylactic measure, arguing that to do so would be tantamount to condoning non-marital

sex and homosexuality. This position brought the hierarchy into conflict with homosexuals and AIDS activists, as well as many health officials. This was especially true of the archbishop of New York City, John Cardinal O'Connor, who, because of his outspokenness on this issue, became a target for condemnation and abuse.

Cardinal O'Connor was a major player in another issue of sexual morality that dominated the political arena: abortion. Following the United States Supreme Court's ruling in *Roe v. Wade* (1972) restricting legal limits on abortion, the fight over abortion became an increasingly volatile issue in American political and religious life. Roman Catholic clergy and laity were early opponents of the decision, although as time passed they became joined increasingly by fundamentalist and evangelical Protestants. While some, like Joseph Cardinal Bernadin, the archbishop of Chicago, attempted to place opposition to abortion within the context of opposition to war and capital punishment, others emphasized abortion alone.

Abortion became a complex issue for Roman Catholics, especially Catholic politicians. Many, while convinced personally of the immorality of abortion, affirmed the right of women to make the choice individually, arguing that the state had no compelling interest (and perhaps no right) to adopt laws limiting this choice. This view brought several politicians into public conflict with Cardinal O'Connor, most notably Geraldine Ferraro, the Democratic vice-presidential candidate in 1984, and Mario Cuomo, the governor of New York, whom O'Connor threatened to excommunicate in 1991.

The Church's positions on contraception and abortion also were part of the debate over the role of women in the Church, an issue of such volatility that the bishops were unable to complete their pastoral letter on women, despite the fact that they had been able to issue very controversial letters on nuclear weapons (1983) and economics (1986).

Many viewed the teachings on contraception as symptomatic of the Church's denigration of women, and a result of its domination by un-married men. Beyond this was the failure of the Church to accept women as equal participants in the community of the people of God. The continuing refusal of the Church to ordain women as priests was the most emotional issue in this regard, but subtler conflicts emerged as well. Could women and girls participate in conducting the Mass? Could girls be altar-girls, could women be lectors? Could they serve at the Mass? These arguments were of deep theological import and how they were answered said much about the Church. They also had immediate practical implications for parish life. The priest shortage required many parishes to rely increasingly on lay members to assist in the running of congregational affairs, including services. How could a priest refuse the assistance of half of his congregation, especially when to do so was to risk losing them?

This highlights a major difficulty the Church had to face as it approached the 21st century, the shortage of priests. Since the Council of Trent, called to formulate the Roman Catholic response to the Reformation, the Roman Church had been clerically centered. The functioning of the Church depended upon priests, and to a lesser extent brothers and nuns. Lay involvement was to be subordinated to the priests, who supervised all parish activities. The priest also controlled the preeminent functions of the Church—the sacraments, especially the performance of the Mass and the distribution of the eucharist. The loss of many priests during the 1960's and 1970s, and the drastic decline in the numbers of men studying for the priesthood, presented a major challenge to the Church. To continue to meet the needs of its members in the face of this shortage, the Church needed to rethink its views on the centrality of priests, yet to do this was to challenge the very understanding of the nature of the Church itself.

Another major challenge to the Roman Catholic Church in the United States at the close of the 20th century was the change in the Church's composition. Although throughout the 19th and early 20th centuries the Roman Church's makeup changed constantly due to immigration, it found no way to accommodate to the different expectations and demands of the various ethnic groups. This failure led to new problems as the Church faced a growing Hispanic population that was destined to became a majority of its members. The inability of the Church to adjust to this new population threatened its hold on these members and the future of the Church.

The last decades of the 20th century also saw a return to those political questions that seemed to have been exorcised a quarter-century earlier. This debate centered upon the perceived inability of the Roman Church to accommodate to the values of the American political system. This resurgence was due to two main issues, abortion (again) and academic freedom. The church's vocal opposition to abortion and the intrusion of that opposition into the political realm caused many to raise issues long thought moribund. Preeminent among these was, "Does the very nature of Roman Catholicism mean that the Church is capable of exerting undue influence on its members who take political positions at odds with the teachings of the Church?" Cardinal O'Connor's highly publicized conflicts with leading Democratic politicians were only the most visible hints that such might be the case.

Along similar lines, a subtle anti-Catholicism ran through the debate over Clarence Thomas's nomination by President George Bush to the Supreme Court. A subtext of much pro-choice opposition to Thomas was due to his Catholic upbringing, which many feared would lead him to be an unfairly biased justice when it came to court cases dealing with the question of abortion.

Less politically volatile but no less significant was the debate over intellectual and academic freedom within the Roman Catholic Church. The most celebrated of these cases involved Father Charles Curran, professor of Roman Catholic Moral Theology at the Catholic University of America. Father Curran, who earlier had been in conflict with the hierarchy over his opposition to Humane Vitae, was removed from his position as one entitled to teach Roman Catholic seminarians due to his disagreement with the Church's teaching office, the Magisterium, over what he considered its (potentially) fallible teachings. This raised issues of academic freedom which later spilled over into the secular academic world when the president of Auburn University, where Curran had been given an endowed position, refused to grant him the tenure that usually accompanied that appointment. Rumors that the Church had "gotten to" the president abounded, and hints of insidious Catholic influence in political affairs were heard.

Although Father Andrew Greeley's claim that "anti-Catholicism is the anti-Semitism of the intellectuals" is a gross exaggeration, it appeared during the late 20th century that while negative attitudes toward Catholics themselves bordered on nonexistent, suspicion of Catholicism and its institutional forms was increasing, not only outside the Church but within it as well. This is perhaps a significant illustration of how much the Roman Catholic Church had become an accepted part of the American scene. It had reached a point where internal debates could comfortably be made public, and that external critics did not risk charges of bigotry by raising their criticisms. How the Church would meet these new pressures remained unclear as it entered its third millennium.

EQ

Bibliography: Jay P. Dolan, *The American Catholic Experience: A History from Colonial Times to the Present* (Garden City, N.Y.: Doubleday, 1992); John Tracy Ellis, *Documents of American Catholic History* (Milwaukee: Bruce Publishing Co., 1956); ———, *Catholics in Colonial America* (Baltimore: Helicon, 1965); James Hennesey, *American Catholics: A History of the Roman Catholic Community in the United States* (New York: Oxford University Press, 1981).

Rosicrucians Because Rosicrucians compose a secret fraternity, their history is difficult to untangle. Some historians, in fact, contend that no Brotherhood of the Rosy Cross ever actually existed. Rosicrucianism typically refers, therefore, not to a set of institutions but to a cluster of ideas regarding magic, science, and religion that creatively combines elements from Romanticism and the ENLIGHTENMENT, Christian PIETISM, and Renaissance occultism. At the core of this Rosicrucian synthesis is the individual's heroic quest for secret yet ostensibly scientific wisdom.

Legend traces the genesis of Rosicrucianism (from the Latin *rosa* [rose] and *crux* [cross]) to one Christian Rosenkreuz, who was supposedly born in Germany in 1378 and initiated into occult mysteries during travels in the Middle East. He then founded the Order of the Rose and the Cross in 1408. Although Rosenkreuz supposedly recruited monks into his order and constructed a sanctum called the House of the Holy Spirit, both his secret wisdom and his movement died with him in 1484.

Rosicrucianism was "revived," however, in the early 17th century. The faithful attribute this "revival" to the discovery of the lost tomb of Rosenkreuz in 1604; historians generally trace the 17th-century Rosicrucian vogue to the writings of Johann Valentin Andreae (1586–1654), a Lutheran pastor and theologian from Württenberg, Germany. These works, which began with *The Fama Fraternitas of the Meritorious Order of the Rosy Cross* (1614), comprised a manifesto of sorts for the burgeoning Rosicrucian movement. In them, Andreae told the story of the legendary Rosenkreuz, articulated the rules of his secret order, promoted social and political reforms, and hinted at an occult synthesis of Christian pietism, Renaissance hermeticism, magic, and alchemy.

Rosicrucianism made its way to the New World when German settlers founded The Chapter of Perfection, a Rosicrucian association, in 17th-century Pennsylvania. But the movement floundered in the United States until its conflation with FREEMASONRY in the 19th century. Eliphas Levi (1810–1875) was one key figure in this modern rediscovery of Rosicrucianism. His books, beginning with *The Doctrine of*

Transcendental Magic (1855), emphasized the links between Rosicrucianism and magic. Rosicrucian novelists such as the British-born Sir Edward Bulwer-Lytton also contributed to the 19th-century Rosicrucian vogue. Bulwer-Lytton's *Zanoni* (1842) did much to popularize among the uninitiated such Rosicrucian ideals as the elixir of immortality and the philosopher's stone that turns iron into gold.

The writings of Levi and Bulwer-Lytton prompted R. Swinburne Clymer of Quakertown, Pennsylvania to establish, in the first decade of the 20th century, the Fraternitas Rosae Crucis, the oldest Rosicrucian association in America. The largest Rosicrucian group, which was founded in 1915 in San Jose, California, is The Ancient and Mystical Order Rosae Crucis (A.M.O.R.C.). Both these groups are far less secretive than the legendary order of the mythical Rosenkreuz.

Rosicrucianism has never attracted large numbers of American adherents. But along with allied occult movements such as THEOSOPHY, it provides evidence of the strength and endurance of an alternative tradition of spirituality in the United States.

SRP

Bibliography: Frances A. Yates, *The Rosicrucian Enlightenment* (St. Albans, Vt.: Paladin, 1975).

Royce, Josiah (1855–1916)

Josiah Royce became the leading proponent of idealist philosophy in America in the course of a prolific career as a teacher and writer. Royce summed up his life in a 1915 speech in Philadelphia by saying he was a "born non-conformist." While Royce has sometimes been seen by subsequent generations as an outdated popularizer, his own remark best describes his course of life, his intellectual commitments, and his influence on American culture.

Born November 20, 1855 in the mining camp of Grass Valley, California, Royce was the inheritor of his father's restlessness and his mother's desire for education and culture. Josiah Royce Sr. and Sarah Bayliss Royce, both originally from England, settled in upstate New York, and were deeply affected by the moral and religious fervor coursing through that region in the first part of the 19th century (see SECOND GREAT AWAKENING). Emigrating to Grass Valley during the 1849 Gold Rush, Josiah Sr. tried his hand first as a miner and then as a traveling salesman, while Sarah opened her own private school and headed up the Royce household. From his mother, whom biographers and relatives count as the dominant influence in his life, Josiah Jr. gained a love of learning and a mystical conviction born from intense evangelical piety. For Royce himself, however, conviction of the divine presence was to lead away from organized Christianity and toward the writings of German idealist philosophers such as Immanuel Kant and G. W. F. Hegel.

When he was 11 years old, Royce's family moved to San Francisco. Graduating from the University of California in 1875, he studied abroad at the German universities of Leipzig, Heidelberg, and Göttingen. Returning to the United States in 1876, he enrolled in the new Ph.D. program at Johns Hopkins University, and after two years study received at the age of 22 one of the first degrees conferred there. He then accepted a position at the University of California, teaching literature and composition, and offering an occasional lecture in philosophy. Correspondence with William JAMES, with whom he had formed a friendship prior to leaving for Germany, eventually resulted in a temporary, and then a permanent, offer from Harvard in 1882, where he taught for the rest of his life.

Royce wrote prodigiously, ranging over logic, epistemology, metaphysics, and philosophy of religion. He is best known for his defense of metaphysical idealism—the view that the mind can grasp the nature of reality—and his philosophy of loyalty. Royce argued that beneath the variety of experiences, yearnings, and impressions that characterize our perception of the world there was an absolute that bound all life together. A systematic thinker, his own efforts to provide the foundations of certainty and hope to modern people disenchanted with orthodox Christianity were rapidly superseded by the popularity of the philosophies of pragmatism and positivism. However, the change in American philosophy since the time of his death has obscured both the extent of his importance as an original thinker and the similarities to his pragmatist contemporaries. William James once said to Royce "the only thing we see differently is the absolute, and surely such a trifle as that is not a thing for two gentlemen to be parted by."

Late in life he realized that his thinking had been primarily concerned with what he called "the Idea of the Community," that is, how individual fulfillment is only possible through commitment to something greater than the self. His crowning works, *The Philosophy of Loyalty* (1908) and *The Problem of Christianity* (1913), were sustained efforts to turn from metaphysics to the problems of community in the modern world. With the outbreak of WORLD WAR I, Royce's concerns became increasingly practical, especially following the German sinking of the British ocean liner *Lusitania* in May 1915. He made frequent addresses on behalf of what he called "the party of humanity," condemning an act that struck him quite personally since several of his students had been aboard. He died September 14, 1916 in Cambridge.

MG

Bibliography: John Clendenning, *The Life and Thought of Josiah Royce* (Madison: University of Wisconsin Press, 1985); Frank C. Oppenheim, *Royce's Mature Philosophy of Religion* (North Bend, Ind.: University of Notre Dame Press, 1987); Josiah Royce, *Basic Writings,* 2 vols. (Chicago: University of Chicago Press, 1969).

Russell, Charles Taze (1852–1916)

Charles Taze Russell was an evangelist and founder of the Zion's Watch Tower Bible and Tract Society, the millennialist (see PREMILLENNIALISM) religious movement from which the Jehovah's Witnesses later emerged. Russell preached that Jesus Christ had returned in an invisible, spiritual manner in 1874 and that God's faithful followers should prepare for the world to end in 1914.

Russell was born on February 16, 1852 in Allegheny, Pennsylvania, now a suburb of Pittsburgh. Raised as a Presbyterian, he experienced a loss of faith during his teenage years and rebelled against many of the religious teachings of his youth, especially the Calvinist doctrine of eternal punishment. Influenced by Adventist beliefs, which predicted the imminent return of Jesus Christ, Russell began a lengthy period of independent Bible study. He began disseminating his own unique interpretations of the Scriptures in 1872 and, rejecting some classic Christian doctrines such as the Trinity (Jesus was not God incarnate, he argued), quickly attracted many like-minded followers.

In his 1886 book, *Millennial Dawn,* Russell described the ages over which the divine plan for humankind had evolved. He insisted not only that Christ's second coming had already occurred, but also that true Christians were to preach judgment and await the final defeat of the forces of evil at an approaching cosmic battle. Russell was highly successful in spreading these views through publications and frequent travels across the United States, Canada, and Europe. He edited a periodical, *The Watch Tower and Herald of Christ's Presence* (sometimes called *Zion's Watch Tower*), between 1878 and 1916. Over 15 million copies of his writings, including the seven-volume *Studies in the Scriptures,* have been printed and distributed throughout the world, while over 1,200 churches were founded under the influence of "Pastor" Russell's teachings.

Although the outbreak of World War I in 1914 heralded a cataclysm of tremendous violence and destructiveness, the apocalyptic day of retribution Russell foretold never materialized. His unexpected death on October 31, 1916 during an evangelistic campaign in Pampa, Texas, moreover, prevented him from revising his predictions. However, Joseph Franklin ("Judge") Rutherford, Russell's legal advisor and successor as leader of the Jehovah's Witnesses (the name the movement assumed in 1931), stepped forward to vindicate his position. Rutherford argued that Satan had been defeated in a war that began in *heaven* in 1914 and afterward had been banished by God to reign on earth.

GHS, Jr.

Bibliography: M. James Penton, *Apocalypse Delayed: The Story of Jehovah's Witnesses* (Toronto: University of Toronto Press, 1985).

Russian Orthodox Church   See
ORTHODOX CHURCH IN AMERICA.

Rutherford, Joseph Franklin   See
JEHOVAH'S WITNESSES.

Ryan, John Augustine (1869–1945)
Raised on a Minnesota farm, John Augustine Ryan early developed the deep Catholic faith and the concern for economic justice that were to be the hallmarks of his life. Between 1898 and his death in 1945, Ryan did more than anyone to create an interest in social issues among American Roman Catholics. His involvement with organizations such as the American Civil Liberties Union, American Indian Defense Association, and the Labor Defense Council helped to break down the stereotype of the conservative ghettoized Catholic priest and to integrate Catholic social teaching into American political debate.

Born on May 25, 1869 in Vermillion, Minnesota to Irish immigrants, John Ryan grew up on a farm in one of the rural colonies that were the pet projects of Bishop John IRELAND. During the 1880s and 1890s, Ryan was influenced deeply by the principles of the Populist movement and its concern for farmers, small shopkeepers, and laborers. He also was imbued with his family's deep religious faith. Of his parents' six children, three became priests and two nuns.

Ryan began his seminary training at St. Thomas Seminary in 1887, continuing his studies at St. Paul Seminary until 1898. During this time he encountered the social encyclicals

John Augustine Ryan, the foremost promoter of concern about social and economic issues among Roman Catholics in the first half of the 20th century. (Library of Congress)

(pronouncements) of Leo XIII. Of these, Rerum Novarum, with its insistence on the dignity of human labor and the right to a living wage, would be the center of Ryan's life work.

Graduating from seminary and ordained in 1898, Ryan continued his studies at the Catholic University of America. In 1906 he received his doctoral degree. His dissertation, published as *A Living Wage: Its Ethical and Economic Aspects,* not only made a name for the young priest, but would become the basis for later American Catholic views of the economy.

From 1902 until 1939, Ryan served as a professor of moral theology, first at St. Paul Seminary (1902–1915) and then at Catholic University (1915–1939). Although deeply committed to teaching, Ryan supported numerous other causes. Most significantly, he served as director of the Social Action Department of the NATIONAL CATHOLIC WELFARE CONFERENCE from 1920 until his death in 1945. The department was a direct outgrowth of an official policy statement adopted by American Catholic bishops in 1919. Drafted by Ryan, it detailed specific policies to be enacted in order to create a more just society. Although often ignored by clerics and laity, it did provide the ground for greater Roman Catholic involvement in political affairs. Franklin Roosevelt often used this statement, along with the social encyclicals, to rally support for his policies, and in fact 11 of the 12 major recommendations of the bishops' program were enacted into law during Roosevelt's presidency.

Although often accused of socialism or worse by his enemies, Ryan was an orthodox Catholic, believing that his social views correctly expressed papal teaching on the economy. In his book *The State and the Church,* he argued the orthodox position on the state. As stated by Pope Leo XIII in the encyclical Immortale Dei, the state had an obligation to recognize the Catholic religion as the religion of society. Equally, in a Catholic society there could be times when it would be "feasible and expedient" to proscribe "non-Catholic sects." Published in 1922, this book became part of the anti-Catholic furor that surrounded Al Smith's 1928 presidential nomination, despite the fact that Ryan did not believe the teaching applied to the situation in the United States, which was not a Catholic state and would never be one.

Disgusted with Herbert Hoover's failure to respond to the Depression and bitter about the 1928 campaign, Ryan was highly visible in his support of Roosevelt and the New Deal. He delivered the benediction at Roosevelt's second and fourth inaugurations, becoming the first Catholic priest to do so. A member of the National Recovery Administration's appeals board and an advisor to Roosevelt, Ryan, who had become a monsignor in 1933, was so close to the administration that he often was referred to as "the Right Reverend New Dealer."

Although very active in projects to establish international peace, the victories of the Axis powers in 1939 and 1940 convinced him of the need for a military response. He joined the Committee to Defend America by Aiding the Allies and publicly supported the Lend-Lease Bill. In the time before Pearl Harbor, Ryan often was critical of his fellow Catholics for their hesitancy in supporting the Allies.

After it became obvious that the Allies would be victorious, Ryan looked forward to a major transformation of the American economy in order to create a more just society. Illness prevented him from taking an active part in the discussions about the postwar world. He died on September 16, 1945.

EQ

Bibliography: Francis L. Broderick, *Right Reverend New Dealer: John A. Ryan* (New York: Macmillan, 1963); John A. Ryan, *A Living Wage: Its Ethical and Economic Aspects* (New York: Arno, 1971), ———, *Social Doctrine in Action: A Personal History* (New York: Harper & Brothers, 1941).

S

Sabbatarianism Sabbatarianism refers to the scrupulous observance of the Sabbath as a divinely ordained day of rest. It is a view that insists people should abstain from all activity, except for what is absolutely necessary for the benefit of society, on the Sabbath. Sabbatarianism in its most rigid form is a development of the Reformation in England and Scotland and was brought to America by the Puritans in the 17th century.

The Sabbath is the seventh day of creation described in the Old Testament Book of Genesis. According to the Bible, the Sabbath has a double purpose: It is a day set apart both for the worship of God and for human rest and recreation. Sabbath observance was codified among the ancient Hebrews in the fourth of the Ten Commandments (Exodus 31:12–17). Among the Jewish people Saturday, the seventh day of the week, is observed as the Sabbath. Although the earliest Christians continued to keep Saturday as their Sabbath, the emperor Constantine decreed in 321 that the first day of the week, the day when Jesus Christ rose from the dead, would become Christianity's day of rest and prayer. Since Constantine's time, most Christians have considered Sunday as their Sabbath day.

The excessive strictness that eventually came to be associated with Sabbath observance was a product of 16th-century English Puritanism. The beginning of modern Sabbatarianism is connected with the publication of Nicholas Bound's *True Doctrine of the Sabbath* in 1595, a work that advocated the rigorous enforcement of Sunday worship and prayer. Although the theologically moderate party within the 17th-century Church of England approved of recreation on Sundays, their position was vehemently opposed by the Puritans. During the Puritan ascendancy in England, Parliament passed successive acts in 1644, 1645, and 1655 prohibiting all recreation on Sunday. Only after the restora-tion of the Stuart monarchy in 1660 were those restrictions again relaxed.

The Puritans who migrated to America in the early 17th century brought their concern for Sabbath observance with them to the New World. Arriving in New England, they enacted laws forbidding the desecration of the day. In 1656 the colony in New Haven, Connecticut passed statutes pertaining to Sundays. Printed on blue paper, those regulations became the basis of the so-called blue laws that continued to restrict activity on Sundays for several centuries to come. Although strict observance of Sundays remained a feature of American life until the mid-19th century, the limited attention to Sabbath-keeping after the Civil War was symbolic of the general decline of the Protestant hegemony in American religion.

In recent years, opponents of the blue laws have argued that regulations restricting business on Sundays violate the FIRST AMENDMENT guarantees on religious freedom and the separation of church and state. A 1961 Supreme Court decision, however, allowed states to restrict business activities on the basis of secular considerations. The Court argued that closing businesses once a week was socially desirable and would improve family and community life. Despite this ruling, many state laws that closed stores on Sundays have been repealed in recent years, and Sunday as a consequence has become heavily commercialized. Even in districts where blue laws remain technically in force, local authorities have tended to ignore them and have allowed business to be conducted freely on Sundays.

The observance of Sunday as the Christian Sabbath, moreover, has never been a universal custom in America. As early as 1671, a Seventh-day Baptist Church was founded in Newport, Rhode Island. Seventh-day Baptists differed from mainstream Baptists because they chose to make the "seventh day" (i.e., Saturday) as their day of rest. The Ephrata Community, which was

The witchcraft hysteria that seized Salem in 1692 resulted in the death of 20 men and women. (Library of Congress)

founded by Johann Conrad Beissel in 1732, also observed Saturday as their Sabbath. This practice was typical of several radical religious groups in the 17th and 18th centuries. Finally, in the 19th century, the Seventh-day Adventist Church was founded upon the principle of observing Saturday, rather than Sunday, as the Christian day of worship. Ellen Gould White, the founder of the Seventh-day Adventists, received a vision in which an angel informed her that Christianity's failure to observe Saturday as the Sabbath had delayed the return of Jesus Christ to earth.

GHS, Jr.

Bibliography: Winton U. Solberg, *Redeem the Time: The Puritan Sabbath in Early America* (Cambridge: Harvard University Press, 1977).

Salem witchcraft trials
Few events in colonial American history have riveted the imagination as much as the Salem witchcraft trials. From

a play by one of America's foremost playwrights—*The Crucible* by Arthur Miller—to several episodes of the 1960s situation comedy "Bewitched," the events at Salem, Massachusetts in 1692 have provided material for both popular culture and serious reflection. Scholars of American religion also have struggled with these events and their meaning, finding in them the ways in which both group hysteria and individual animosity can use religious values and understandings for evil ends.

The Salem witch hunt began when several young girls were discovered playing at fortune-telling with a crystal ball. To avoid punishment the girls claimed that they had been tormented by witches. The attempt by authorities to locate the witch, or witches, responsible for the girls' suffering quickly accelerated. The community's elite did little to restrain the frenzy. Indeed, the town's new minister, Samuel Parris—whose

West Indian slave Tituba was one of the first accused—did much to fuel the hysteria, warning his parishioners during one sermon that witches were everywhere, even in "this very church."

By the time the search for witches had run its course, over 150 people had been imprisoned— 50 of whom confessed to "having signed the Devil's book"—and 19 convicted witches hanged and one pressed to death. Most of the victims were people with little standing in the community or members of families who had opposed Parris's ministry. A large number were middle-aged women with no male relatives to defend them or to take revenge on their accusers. Another favorite target were the cranky and irritable. In the midst of the hysteria, people accused their neighbors on the slightest pretext. Even more troublesome was the introduction of spectral or invisible evidence—where witnesses were allowed to claim that a spirit or specter had appeared before them accusing someone of witchcraft.

The trials reached their apex in late summer of 1692 when several of the colony's leading citizens were accused of witchcraft. After an inquiry into the proceedings, the governor of the MASSACHUSETTS BAY COLONY, Sir William Phipps, forbade the use of spectral evidence and dissolved the special court hearing the witchcraft cases. Following this action the numbers of accusations soon dwindled to none.

The end of the trials and an increasing realization of the enormity of the undertaking's horror soon led to a major reappraisal of the trials. Many of the clergy and the general population came to recognize that the trials were a farce and that people guilty of nothing more than an occasional disagreement with their neighbors had been killed. Even Cotton MATHER, who had supported the trials and continued to defend the use of spectral evidence, admitted things had gone too far. Although witchcraft remained a capital offense in the colony, the Salem witches were the last to be executed in New England. Twenty years later the colony annulled all the convictions of the Salem "witches" and paid out reparations to the survivors.

EQ

Bibliography: Paul Boyer and Steven Nissenbaum, *Salem Possessed: The Social Origins of Witchcraft* (Cambridge: Harvard University Press, 1974); ———, eds., *The Salem Witchcraft Papers: Verbatim Transcripts of the Legal Documents of the Salem Witchcraft Outbreak of 1692,* 3 vols. (New York: Da Capo Press, 1977); ———, eds., *Salem-village Witchcraft; A Documentary Record of Local Conflict in Colonial New England* (Belmont, Calif.: Wadsworth, 1972).

Salvation Army   The Salvation Army is a Protestant denomination widely known for its social and evangelistic work in American cities. It was founded in London in 1865 by British Methodists William and Catherine Mumford Booth. Brought to the United States in 1880, the Salvation Army emphasized theological ideas typical of the 19th-century HOLINESS MOVEMENT.

William Booth (1829–1912) was licensed as a Methodist minister in 1852 but withdrew in 1861 to devote himself to the work of an

Evangelistic urban rescue missions are dedicated to those left behind by industrialization. A Salvation Army member with guitar on the streets of San Francisco. (Library of Congress)

independent evangelist. He and his wife Catherine organized the Christian Mission in London's rundown East End in 1865. They soon began bombarding the neighborhood with brass bands, preachers, and Hallelujah Lasses (as the Mission's controversial female evangelists were known). After the Booths changed the name of their organization, calling it "a Salvation Army" in 1878, the military trappings and a heirarchical organization were added that make the denomination distinctive today. William and Catherine Booth and their eight children all eventually held high rank in the Army.

The Booths intended the elaborate charitable system they developed to supplement evangelism and speed the work of saving the souls of the downtrodden. Their primary focus was on converting individuals to belief in Jesus Christ and guiding them to experience SANCTIFICATION, the second work of divine grace emphasized by Methodist founder John Wesley. Acts of social relief were thought both to symbolize God's love for sinful, fallen humanity and to respond to the New Testament commandment to care for the poor in Jesus' name. Practical relief efforts demonstrated to the poor that the Salvationists took both the spiritual and the social aspects of Christianity seriously. William Booth's famous *In Darkest England and the Way Out* (1890) boldly proclaimed his goal: to save souls among a class of people often ignored by the more traditional Christian churches.

Evangeline Booth (1865–1950), seventh child of William and Catherine, is the person most responsible for establishing the Salvation Army in America. After directing operations in Canada from 1896 to 1904, she was placed in charge of the Army in the United States. She served as American field commissioner between 1904 and 1934. In that period, she first brought the Army to prominence by caring for American soldiers in France during World War I. After the war, she helped homeless alcoholics, unwed mothers, and neglected children, and in the 1930s the Army provided widespread assistance to the destitute during the Great Depression.

Evangeline Booth was elected in 1934 as the fourth general of the International Salvation Army, the last of the Booths to lead the denomination.

Despite an internal dispute that led Ballington and Maud Booth (son and daughter-in-law of William and Catherine) to withdraw in 1896 and form a new agency, the Volunteers of America, the Salvation Army in the United States is by far the largest and most active branch in the organization. The Army's social welfare services are especially well developed and offer an effective collection agency of used clothing and furniture for poor Americans. During the Christmas season, moreover, the Army's musicians and bell ringers are seen in many city squares, reminders of the movement's original, flamboyant street-corner ministry. So successful, in fact, is the practical ministry of the Salvation Army that most Americans view the church as a charitable, rather than as a religious, organization.

Salvationists today accept the Army's statement of faith ("Articles of War") and pledge themselves to evangelistic efforts and a simple, disciplined style of life. Although the denomination does not observe the customary Christian sacraments of communion and baptism, its worship services are analogous to those held in other evangelical Protestant churches. In recent years, moreover, leaders have considered modifying the militaristic imagery they use in order to make it clear that the Salvation Army is a church. The Salvation Army reported nearly 450,000 members and over 1,100 congregations in the United States in 1990.

GHS, Jr.

Bibliography: Edward H. McKinley, *Marching to Glory: The History of the Salvation Army in the United States, 1880–1980* (San Francisco: Harper & Row, 1980); Norman H. Murdoch, *Origins of the Salvation Army* (Knoxville: University of Tennessee Press, 1995).

sanctification   The term "sanctification" is related to the Latin word *sanctus,* which means "holy." Sanctification is the process by which someone or something is made holy. There are numerous references to sanctification in the Christian Scriptures, and it is presented as a quality that true believers possess. Christian theologians have usually employed the word to refer to God's action in transforming a person's heart and soul. The ideal of the holy life, of course, is not solely the preserve of Protestants, since both Roman Catholic and Eastern Orthodox spiritualities place stress upon attaining sanctity. However, among Christians in the United States, the doctrine of sanctification has had its greatest impact upon members of the denominations most affected by 19th-century EVANGELICALISM, especially American Methodists.

Protestants have customarily taught that there are two major stages through which Christians pass on the way to salvation: JUSTIFICATION and sanctification. At the first stage, God justifies the sinner, that is, sin is forgiven and the guilt that sin has caused is removed. A person is made righteous in God's eyes and thus is "saved." Lutherans and heirs of the Calvinist theological heritage in America have tended to lay stress on this first stage of salvation. The second stage, known as sanctification, is the moment when God releases believers from the power of sin and enables them to live godly lives. According to Puritans in the early 17th century, sanctification was a lifelong process and involved a slowly developing awareness that divine grace was at work within an individual's soul.

Emphasis on sanctification has been the consistent hallmark of Methodism. As John Wesley, the founder of the denomination, said, justification is what "God does for us," while sanctification is what "God does in us." Wesley believed that sanctification would culminate in a dramatic experience, a "second blessing" after conversion in which the Christian would be filled with perfect love. Although Wesley did not think Christian perfection meant complete sinlessness in the present life, he did consider that freedom from all conscious or intentional sin was a pos-

sibility for the person who had been sanctified.

The SECOND GREAT AWAKENING in the early 19th century inspired Americans in every major Protestant denomination to give attention to the idea of sanctification. Methodist Phoebe PALMER of New York City, for example, underwent an experience of sanctification in 1837. Her weekly prayer meetings for the "promotion of holiness" drew together many who were attracted by the optimistic doctrine of "entire sanctification" that she preached. Presbyterian revivalist Charles G. FINNEY thought human beings both could and should strive to seek divine blessing. Asa MAHAN, a Congregational minister and Finney's colleague at Oberlin College, wrote in his book *Scripture Doctrine of Christian Perfection* that believers might attain complete sanctification when Christ was present within their hearts.

Debates about sanctification eventually fostered a number of divisions in American Protestantism in the late 19th and early 20th centuries. Many Methodists committed to perfectionist beliefs began to insist that sanctification did not have to be a gradual process, but could often be received as an instantaneous gift from God. Several new Holiness (see HOLINESS MOVEMENT) denominations, such as the Church of the Nazarene, which was founded in 1908, adopted this doctrine as central to their understanding of the Christian life. In the same period, beginning with the AZUSA STREET REVIVAL in Los Angeles in 1906, men and women involved in the Pentecostal (see PENTECOSTALISM) movement offered an even more radical interpretation of the experience of sanctification. Pentecostals described "baptism in the Holy Spirit," an event usually manifested by the phenomenon of speaking in tongues, as definitive evidence of the believer's sanctification.

Sanctification continues to be an important theme among American evangelicals. The idea certainly motivates much popular Christian spirituality and piety, inspiring people to strive for personal holiness. Disagreement over the meaning of sanctification, however, still remains.

Must sanctification be a sudden event, or can it be a gradual process? And can a person achieve perfection in his or her lifetime, or does that occur only after death?

GHS, Jr.

Bibliography: Melvin E. Dieter, *Five Views on Sanctification* (Grand Rapids: Zondervan, 1987).

Sanitary Commission   See CIVIL WAR, THE.

Sankey, Ira David (1840–1908)   Ira San-
key, an associate of late 19th-century revivalist Dwight L. MOODY, was the song-leader of the most celebrated American evangelistic team of his day. Using his clear baritone voice to sing moving lyrics with infectious melodies, Sankey added immensely to the sentimental appeal of Moody's famous preaching. Compiler of so-called gospel hymns, Sankey helped popularize this musical genre, making it an essential element in the revivalist tradition of the United States.

Sankey was born on August 28, 1840 in Edinburgh, Pennsylvania. After joining the Methodist church in Newcastle, Pennsylvania in 1855, he became the leader of the church choir, superintendent of the Sunday school, and director of the YMCA. He served in the Union army during the Civil War and, after returning home, worked as an assistant in the bank where his father was president. Sankey and Moody met in 1870, when Moody heard him sing at a YMCA convention in Indianapolis. He soon made Sankey his full-time music director and organist, and the two worked together for the next 25 years. Between 1873 and 1875, Moody and Sankey conducted a highly successful tour of Great Britain, during which three million people are estimated to have attended the revivals they led.

Although he only occasionally wrote lyrics, Sankey composed the music for some of the best-known hymns of his day. His first publication was *Sacred Songs and Solos,* released in 1873. Beginning in 1875, in collaboration with Phillip P. Bliss and other composers, he edited

Ira David Sankey, the musical half of the Moody-Sankey revival team, whose hymn writing contributed greatly to their success.

a work that proved to be the musical backbone of late 19th-century REVIVALISM. Completed in 1895, Sankey's series of six song-books entitled *Gospel Hymns* contained over 700 entries. A best-seller, Sankey's collection of musical favorites was noted for its many simple, but memorable, lyrics and rousing refrains.

After Moody's death in 1899 and the onset of his own blindness in 1903, Sankey's active career came to an end. The influence of his music, however, remained strong in conservative Protestant circles for many years. Sankey died in Brooklyn, New York on August 14, 1908.

GHS, Jr.

Bibliography: Ira David Sankey, *My Life and the Story of the Gospel Hymns* (Philadelphia: P. W. Ziegler, 1907); Sandra S. Sizer, *Gospel Hymns and Social Religion: The Rhetoric of Nineteenth Century Revivalism* (Philadelphia: Temple University Press, 1978).

Santería   Santeria ("the way of the saints") is a New World religion forged in Cuba but with roots in Roman Catholicism and the Yoruba religious traditions of West Africa. Following the revolution of 1959, many Cubans came to the United States and brought Santería with them. The tradition is now widely practiced among Cuban immigrants in cities such as New York and Miami.

Santería grew out of Cuban socio-religious clubs called *cabildos*. In these *cabildos*, Yoruba and Cuban beliefs and practices met and mingled and the syncretic tradition of Santería emerged. The most distinctive element of this new tradition, which in Cuba is called *Lucumi* (from the greeting, *oluku mi* or "my friend"), consisted of devotion to Yoruba spiritual beings called *orishas*. These *orishas* were worshiped, however, in the forms of Catholic saints. Thus, for example, Ogun (the Yoruba deity of iron and war) was revered as St. Peter; and Shango (the fierce god of thunder and lightning), as Saint Barbara. The theory that supported this syncretic practice, which also occurs in Haitian VODOU, was that the *orisha* and the saint were actually two manifestations of one spiritual entity.

The priests and priestesses of Santería practice ancestor veneration, initiation, spirit possession, animal sacrifice, and divination. Each of these ritual practices is rooted in traditional religions of West Africa and each has survived the passage to American cities. In rituals of initiation, the initiate's deity of choice is said to "take its seat" in that person's body. During this *asiento,* the initiate is possessed by the spirit of the deity. He or she then dances in a trancelike state to the music of the deity. Spiritual beings (ancestors and deities alike) are venerated and sustained in Santería through the ritual sacrifice of animals, a practice that has earned American Santeros the wrath of members of the American Society for the Prevention of Cruelty to Animals. In Ifa or divination, the *babalawo* ("father of the mystery") casts nuts or cowrie shells and offers readings of a client's future based on an elaborate numerology centering around the auspicious number of 16. One's destiny is thought by practitioners of Santería to be controlled by Olodumare ("owner of all destinies"), the Yoruba high god who is conflated with the Almighty God of Roman Catholics.

Santería shares much with Vodou, another New World religious creation that combines West African and Roman Catholic beliefs and practices. Like practitioners of vodou, Santeros maintain retail shops that support even as they promote their religious traditions. These *botanicas,* where consumers can purchase healing herbs and icons of orishas/saints, serve as the public face of Santería in the United States. The vast majority of the rituals of Santería, however, take place behind closed doors, typically in the homes of priests and priestesses, who sustain their religious tradition in the Americas by preserving dances and prayers, leading worship services, and practicing the healing and divining arts.

SRP

Bibliography: Joseph M. Murphy, *Santería: An African Religion in America* (Boston: Beacon Press, 1988).

satanism   Perhaps more than most other religious impulses, satanism means many things to many people. To its opponents, satanism has been associated with the abuse and even the murder of children. To satanists themselves, however, satanism refers to a tradition that affirms as good the natural desires and impulses that Christians have for centuries denounced as evil. Given the disparity in these definitions, it makes sense to refer to two satanisms: the satanism affirmed by practitioners; and the satanism denounced by detractors.

The former type of satanism is most visible in The Church of Satan, founded in 1966 by Anton S. LaVey (1930–   ). Before his incarnation as the self-appointed high priest of satanism, LaVey spent some time in the circus. He apparently extracted from his employment there both a flair for the dramatic and a keen sense of self-promotion. LaVey achieved national renown in 1967 when he conducted the first openly satanic rituals—a wedding and a funeral—in the United States. Two years later he published *The Satanic Bible* (1969), which contains a simple satanic creed that defines satanism as the perfect antidote to Christianity. According to LaVey, satanism affirms indulgence over abstinence, vengeance over turning the other cheek, and this life over the next. Its key rituals include the black mass (a parody of Roman Catholic holy communion) and celebrations of individual satanist's birthdays. LaVey has responded to criticisms of the satanic tradition by explicitly instructing members of the Church of Satan scrupulously to obey the law. LaVey's efforts have earned him a role as Hollywood's adviser of choice for horror movies; and he has appeared as Satan himself in silver-screen cameos.

The second type of satanism is both much more controversial and much more difficult to locate. In part a response to LaVey's popularization of satanism, conservative Christian groups began in the 1970s and 1980s to accuse satanists of operating clandestine rings devoted to kidnapping, abusing, and even murdering children. According to these detractors, the key religious ritual of satanism is child molestation; and each disappearance of a child from home is interpreted as evidence of this claim.

The most generous response that scholars can make to such allegations is that they have not yet been proven. In fact, the only truly observable phenomenon associated with this second type of satanism is not satanism itself but the denunciation of satanism by conservative Protestants and Roman Catholics. In keeping with the recent tendency to refer to the period of the witch trials in Salem, Massachusetts as an era of "witch-hunting" rather than "witchcraft," it might make sense to refer to the supposed "revival" of satanism as a time of satanist-hunting rather than a time of satanism per se. The fact that the satanic "revival" and the MORAL MAJORITY seem to have peaked roughly simultaneously would lend credence to the thesis that the more nefarious form of satanism may exist primarily in the minds of its opponents.

SRP

Bibliograpy: James T. Richardson, Joel Best, David G. Bromley, eds, *The Satanism Scare* (New York: A. de Gruyter, 1991).

Saybrook Platform   The Saybrook Platform was a response by the Congregational (see CONGREGATIONALISM) churches of Connecticut to a perceived decrease in religious piety and church discipline. Written by a synod authorized and summoned by the colony's legislature in 1708, the Saybrook Platform fundamentally altered the nature and structure of church organization. The 12 ministers and four laymen involved rejected the extreme congregationalism that had been the ideal of church polity and replaced it with a more presbyterian system (see PRESBYTERIANISM). This new organization was composed of local ministerial associations and consociations comprised of ministers and lay members from local churches within a particular region. The ministerial associations were given the authority to examine candidates for the ministry and to oversee ministerial behavior, while the consociations were to impose discipline on local churches and to judge disputes arising within congregations.

This assault on traditional congregational independence led many to resist implementation of these policies. Despite the colonial government's support for the platform and the penalties it provided, including disfellowship of churches refusing to accept consociational rulings, many congregations ignored its provisions.

However, resistance by individual congregations eventually succumbed to organizational strength, and the consociation became the method of Congregational governance well into the 19th century, surviving even after Congregationalism was disestablished as Connecticut's official church.

EQ

Bibliography: Williston Walker, *The Creeds and Platforms of Congregationalism* (Philadelphia: Pilgrim Press, 1960).

Schaff, Philip (1819–1893)   Philip Schaff was the founder of the American Society of

Church History and one of the most influential scholars and church leaders in 19th-century America. Along with his colleague John Williamson NEVIN at Mercersburg Seminary in Pennsylvania, Schaff was instrumental in developing a form of religious thought known as the Mercersburg Theology.

Schaff was born at Chur, Switzerland on January 1, 1819. Educated at the universities at Tübingen, Halle, and Berlin, he began a promising teaching career at Berlin in 1842. In 1843, Schaff accepted an invitation to come to Mercersburg, the newly formed seminary of the German Reformed Church in America, where he served until 1865. Schaff later taught and lectured at Andover, Drew, Union, and Hartford seminaries. In 1870 he accepted a professorship at Union Theological Seminary in New York City and remained there until his death.

Schaff's first major publication was *The Principle of Protestantism* (1845), an expansion of his inaugural address at Mercersburg. Translated into English and introduced by Nevin, *The Principle of Protestantism* became a virtual manifesto for the Mercersburg Theology. Schaff had been influenced at Tübingen by Georg W. F. Hegel's teachings on historical development. His book discussed the Reformation as a flowering of elements within medieval Catholicism. Contrary to the standard Protestant view that the Reformation had thoroughly repudiated the corruptions of Roman Catholicism, Schaff emphasized that there were valuable lessons to be learned in every age of church history.

Schaff's next significant publication appeared in 1846. In *What Is Church History?* he summarized interpretations of ecclesiastical history since the 16th century, placing his own work in the new "historical school." This book represented a milestone in American historical writing, for in it Schaff stressed how historians must not impose the values of their day on events of the past. However, the most conservative wing of the German Reformed Church viewed Schaff's ideas as reprehensible and raised the cry of "heresy" against him. Conflict over these

views eventually forced Schaff's departure from Mercersburg.

Schaff's publishing record was truly extraordinary. While at Mercersburg, he participated in the writing and editing of a number of publications, including the *Mercersburg Review* (1857–1861) and the first of eight volumes of his *History of the Christian Church* (1858). Later in his career, he published a number of significant works: *Church and State in the United States* (1876), an interpretation of the American commitment to religious liberty; the first edition of his three-volume *Creeds of Christendom* (1877); the 14-volume series *A Select Library of the Nicene and Post-Nicene Fathers* (1880–1886); and the original edition of the *Schaff-Herzog Encyclopedia of Religious Knowledge* (three volumes, 1882–1884). Schaff also helped organize what would eventually be the 13-volume *American Church History* series, which was released between 1893 and 1897.

Schaff remained in the forefront of American Protestantism throughout his long and productive life. In addition to his contributions to American religious thought through his writings and teaching career at Mercersburg and at Union, he founded the American Society of Church History and served as its first president from 1888 to 1893. He was also involved in numerous social reform and ecumenical activities. He worked, for example, with the New York Sabbath Committee, the Evangelical Alliance, and the American Revised Bible translation committee.

Active in church affairs until the end, Schaff died at New York City on October 20, 1893.

GHS, Jr.

Bibliography: George H. Shriver, *Philip Schaff: Christian Scholar and Ecumenical Prophet* (Macon, Ga.: Mercer University Press, 1987).

Schechter, Solomon (1847–1915)

By the time of his arrival in the United States to assume the presidency of the Jewish Theological Seminary (JTS) in 1902, Solomon Schechter was recognized as the preeminent Hebrew

Solomon Schecter. A preeminent Hebrew scholar, his presidency of the Jewish Theological Seminary (1902–1915) reinvigorated Conservative Judaism in the United States. (Jewish Theological Seminary of America)

scholar of his time. In his 13 years at the seminary, Schechter invigorated the academic study of Judaism and exerted a formative influence on the institutions and ideas of what became CONSERVATIVE JUDAISM

Born December 7, 1847 in Focsani, Romania, Solomon Schechter was raised in a traditional Hasidic family (see HASIDISM). He began his rabbinical training at an early age and in 1875 moved to Vienna for further religious study. There he received an introduction to secular learning, which he continued during advanced studies in Berlin.

Invited to England in 1882 by Claude Montefiore, the English Jewish philanthropist and industrialist, as his private tutor, Schechter began a scholarly career that led to an appointment in rabbinics at Cambridge University (1890). In 1897, Schechter made history with his excavation of a long-abandoned Cairo *genizah*. (A *genizah* is a place where unusable Jewish holy books are entombed in order to prevent their profanation.) This brought to light thousands of ancient and medieval manuscripts relating to Jewish culture and religion, many previously unknown or lost.

Academic respectability did not mean financial security, however. Financial woes, combined with a desire for a more Jewish environment in which to raise his children and a distaste for British classism, led Schechter to accept the presidency of the Jewish Theological Seminary in 1902.

Upon arriving in the United States, Schechter found "a demoralized institution with virtually no full time faculty, [and] little broad support among the laity." Undaunted, Schechter expressed his vision of the school in his inaugural address. The seminary was to combine rigorous scholarly method with a concern for Judaism and the Jewish people, open to all segments of the community and to all views. "I would consider my work . . . a complete failure if this institution would not in the future produce . . . a raving mystic who would denounce me as a sober philistine, . . . an advanced critic who would rail at me as a narrow-minded fanatic, while a third devotee of strict orthodoxy would raise protest against any critical view I may entertain." With this vision, Schechter and the men he hired turned the school into one of the premier centers of Jewish learning, and graduates of JTS soon exerted tremendous influence within the Jewish-American community.

Beyond his scholarly achievements as a philologist and interpreter of the Jewish tradition, Schechter was a creative thinker who believed that Judaism could withstand the secularizing and assimilationist tendencies of modernity only by addressing them directly. This view led him to demand that the work done at the seminary should meet the highest canons of scholarship. It should have "that scientific thoroughness and finish which alone deserves the name research." Only by responding to modernity, rather than withdrawing from or avoiding it, could Judaism meet those social and intellectual forces Schechter viewed as "often more dangerous to [Jews] than pogroms and direct persecutions."

Judaism, however, did not have to fear all change, Schechter asserted, because Judaism always had been a religion in process. This did not mean that everything could be altered. The traditions of Judaism were important because they expressed the values of the community, *klal* Israel (universal or "catholic" Israel). More precisely, the traditions of Judaism were created by the people Israel in order to realize the eternal values within the Torah. Since these traditions inhered within a living people, rather than in dead books, the community itself had the right to alter or change the tradition in order to bring it into line "with the ideal aspirations and religious needs of the age."

The Orthodox (see ORTHODOX JUDAISM) erred and dishonored the community by refusing to respond to the religious needs and demands of the time. The Reformers (see REFORM JUDAISM), on the other hand, failed to realize that some changes were incompatible with Judaism and never could be legitimate because they violated the community itself. To make those changes would be to commit cultural-religious suicide.

By the time of his death on November 19, 1915, Schechter had helped to reinvigorate Conservative Judaism in the United States. By transforming the JTS into a vibrant center of Jewish learning dedicated to intellectual rigor and a commitment to Judaism, Schechter helped to provide Conservative Judaism with a creative power that led it to become the largest branch of American Judaism.

EQ

Bibliography: Norman Bentwich, *Solomon Schechter: A Biography* (Cambridge: Cambridge University Press, 1938); Herbert Parzen, *Architects of Conservative Judaism* (New York: J. David, 1964); Solomon Schechter, *Studies in Judaism* (Freeport, N.Y.: Books for Libraries Press, 1972); ———, *Aspects of Rabbinic Theology Papers* (New York: Schocken Books, 1961); Marshall Sklare, *Conservative Judaism: An American Religious Movement* (Lanham, Md.: University Press of America, 1985).

Schmemann, Alexander (1921–1983)

Born and educated in Europe, Father Alexander Schmemann made an influential career in America as an Orthodox liturgical theologian, professor, and church leader. A crucial figure in the establishment of the independent ORTHODOX CHURCH IN AMERICA in 1970, he inspired a liturgical revitalization movement whose impact was felt beyond the boundaries of Orthodoxy.

Born in Estonia in 1921, Schmemann grew up in the Russian emigré community in Paris and was educated at the Orthodox Theological Institute ("St. Sergius") and at the University of Paris. Influenced by his teachers, including A. V. Kartashev, Nicholas Afanasiev, and George Florovksy, Schmemann committed himself to the reexploration of the Byzantine and patristic roots of Orthodoxy. He was also influenced by the lively French Catholic liturgical movement of the period.

Ordained to the priesthood in 1946, he joined the faculty of St. Sergius as a church historian before emigrating to the United States in 1951 to take a position at St. Vladimir's Orthodox Theological Seminary in New York. Along with several others trained at St. Sergius, Schmemann made St. Vladimir's a world center of Orthodox education and served as its dean from 1962 to 1983. He became the most important intellectual figure in the Russian Orthodox Greek Catholic Church of America (also known as the Russian Metropolia).

Often called "the father of Orthodox liturgical theology," Schmemann's scholarly and popular works fueled a liturgical and eucharistic revival among the Orthodox. Major works emphasizing his central theme, the power of the Orthodox liturgy, include: *For the Life of the World* (1964), *Introduction to Liturgical Theology* (1967), and *The Eucharist* (1984). Scores of those trained at St. Vladimir's carried his views into the churches.

He based his work on *resourcement,* the attempt to recapture the theological spirit of the pre-medieval church. In particular, he aimed to purge Orthodox theology of fragments of Protestant and Catholic argumentation that he considered inauthentic and inorganic. He was particularly passionate in his criticism of "Western" secularism, which he described as "a lie about the world."

Schmemann argued that the Orthodox liturgy, which he described as an eschatological action, is the lifespring of the faith, the central vehicle through which Christian identity is formed and expressed. Its purpose "is to manifest the Kingdom of God, to make people taste its celestial beauty, truth, and goodness."

His ideas were influential outside Orthodoxy, especially among Catholics, and Schmemann was also an important, if often critical, figure in the ECUMENICAL MOVEMENT.

Despite his aversion to secularity, Schmemann was an advocate of the selective accommodation of Orthodoxy to American culture. He was especially troubled by the fragmentation of the church and argued vehemently that Orthodox ecclesiology required the formation of a single American church.

Although few outside the Metropolia shared his sense of urgency, Schmemann and other leaders of the Metropolia worked to secure such a church. During the late 1960s, he played a crucial role in the negotiations between the Metropolia and the Patriarchate of Moscow that paved the way for the independence of the newly named Orthodox Church in America.

AHW

Bibliography: Alexander Schmemann, *The Historical Road of Eastern Orthodoxy* (New York: Holt, Rinehart and Winston, 1963); ———, *For the Life of the World: Sacraments and Orthodoxy,* 2nd ed. (Crestwood, N.Y.: St. Vladimir's Seminary Press, 1973); ———, *The Eucharist,* (Crestwood, N.Y.: St. Vladimir's Seminary Press, 1984).

Schmucker, Samuel Simon (1799–1873)

Samuel Schmucker was a minister and theologian who played a critical role in the development of American Lutheranism in the first half of the 19th century. He was instrumental in helping establish both the General Synod, the church's first national governmental body, and Gettysburg Seminary in Pennsylvania, now the oldest Lutheran theological school in America. Schmucker was also a controversial figure who wished to shape his denomination in the popu-

Samuel Simon Schumucker, a brilliant theologian and president of Gettysburg College who helped define American Lutheranism.

lar, democratic mold of mainstream American Protestant EVANGELICALISM.

Schmucker was born on February 28, 1799 in Hagerstown, Maryland. His father, John George Schmucker, was a Lutheran minister who was active in reform and benevolent activities in the early 19th century. Samuel graduated from the University of Pennsylvania in 1819 and from Princeton Seminary a year later. He was ordained to the ministry in 1821 and served a group of congregations near New Market, Virginia from 1820 to 1826. Possessing more formal schooling than any other Lutheran minister of his time, Schmucker was called in 1826 to be founding president and professor at Gettysburg Seminary. He later took a leading role in organizing Pennsylvania (now Gettysburg) College, serving as its president between 1832 and 1834. He remained at the seminary for nearly 40 years and helped prepare several hundred students for the Lutheran ministry.

Schucker sought to relate Lutheranism to the evangelical movement that dominated the religious landscape of the United States. He had been influenced by PIETISM, the 17th-century Protestant religious movement that stressed individual spiritual renewal and attention to godly living. He believed that Lutherans, who had initiated the REFORMATION in the 16th century, should continue their evangelistic efforts and spread the Christian gospel in America. As Lutheran congregations were created as settlers moved westward, Schmucker desired to bring them into communion with the central governing body of the denomination, the General Synod that had been organized in 1820.

Swayed by the heady religious environment of the young American republic, Schmucker opposed the narrow doctrinal conservatism of the "Old" or "Historic Lutherans" who insisted upon staunch adherence to the 1580 Book of Concord, the classic Lutheran creedal statement. Schmucker argued that the genius of the new "American Lutheranism" would lie in its ability to adapt to changing cultural and religious circumstances. While still allowing that the Bible contained the essential doctrines of Lutheranism, Schmucker believed that Lutheran ministers should not have to be bound simply to "the minutiae of any human creed." Such evangelical impulses also impelled Schmucker into the advocacy of Christian union. He published his *Fraternal Appeal to the American Churches* in 1838, a pioneering work calling for cooperation among the major Protestant denominations in the United States. And he attended the meeting of the Evangelical Alliance in 1846 in order to strengthen the cause of church unity.

As theologically conservative Lutherans flooded into the United States from Europe, however, Schmucker the evangelical liberal soon found himself isolated from most members of his church. Although Schmucker was once regarded as the savior of American Lutheranism, his fellow church members had virtually repudiated his leadership by mid-century. Nevertheless, he remained resolutely committed to the ideals he championed. Schmucker retired from his seminary professorship in 1864, and he died at Gettysburg on July 26, 1873.

GHS, Jr.

Bibliography: Paul P. Kuenning, *The Rise and Fall of American Lutheran Pietism: The Rejection of an Activist Heritage* (Macon, Ga.: Mercer University Press, 1988).

Schneerson, Menachem Mendel (1902–1994)

As the head, or *rebbe*, of Lubavitcher or Habad HASIDISM, Menachem Mendel Schneerson exerted tremendous influence on American JUDAISM after his arrival in the United States in 1941. He oversaw the massive outreach campaigns run by the Lubavitchers, their adoption of modern technology—including cable television—and their singular openness toward nonobservant Jews. All these activities have been designed to bring about greater religious observance among Jews, and to create a more holy world in preparation for the coming of the Messiah, the desire for which constitutes a major element of Lubavitch thought. The significance of the Lubavitcher rebbe ran far deeper than that of spiritual-communal head of the 30,000 to 50,000 members of the movement. The rebbe was a distinguished and respected figure among the Orthodox community (see ORTHODOX JUDAISM) at large, and had a rather large cadre of supporters among nonobservant and secular Jews, who looked upon him and Lubavitch as dynamic forces in maintaining Judaic life and culture in the United States.

Menachem Mendel Schneerson was born in Nikolaev, Russia on April 18, 1902. He was a descendant of the founder of Habad, Schneur Zalman of Lyady and great-grandson of the third rebbe. At an early age he showed great scholarly abilities, and by the time of his bar-mitzvah, was considered an *ilui,* or Torah genius. Persecution of the sect in Russia led to his removal to Warsaw, Poland where in 1929 he married the daughter of the then rebbe Joseph Itzhak Schneerson. (The rebbe's last name is the same as his father-in-law since both are related to Schneur Zalman. Schneerson is derived from the surname Schneuri, or Schneur's son.) Although a distinguished religious scholar and aide to his father-in-law, Schneerson took the most unusual step of attending a secular university, studying at both the University of Berlin and the Sorbonne, from which he received a degree in engineering.

Following the outbreak of WORLD WAR II, he came to the United States (1941) where he joined his father-in-law, who recently had been released from a Soviet prison. They settled in the Crown Heights section of Brooklyn, and Schneerson was placed in charge of the Lubavitch education programs. Following the death of Joseph Itzhak in 1950, Schneerson became the seventh Lubavitch rebbe.

Schneerson took the most organizationally sophisticated of all the Hasidic movements and made it into a powerful force in American Judaism. The rebbe himself was a powerful presence. For years he granted audiences to all comers on Tuesday and Thursday nights from nine until past midnight, but declining health and advancing years forced him to curtail this activity. Until

his stroke in 1992, he continued to dispense advice, comfort, and support to his supporters through the mail, a task made easier by his fluency in 10 languages.

While the more separatist Hasidic groups click their tongues at Habad's openness toward nonobservant Jews (as well as Schneerson's secular education), the rebbe is reported to have remarked that he recognizes only two types of Jews, those who are observant Habadniks, and those who are not yet observant Habadniks. This attitude, made possible by the theological bases of Habad, has led to active proselytization among nonobservant Jews.

Habad Houses exist on numerous college campuses, and Mitzvah Mobiles cruise the streets of New York City with Habad members who encourage Jews to follow the religious commandments. The rebbe has sent prayer books to Jews in Panama, a *mohel* (one who performs the ritual circumcision) to a tiny Caribbean island, and members of Lubavitch to small Jewish communities around the world. These activities are driven by Habad's kabbalistic theology, which emphasizes the divine spark in everyone. This spark is increased by the performance of any religious act.

Habad's messianic expectations fuel this desire to bring all Jews into conformity with the divine law. Every religious act not only brings the individual Jew closer to God, but also moves the world closer to the messianic age. As greater numbers of people follow the divine laws the world becomes "a more hospitable place for the Messiah."

This messianic desire, manifest on billboards and bumper stickers announcing, "We want *Moshiach* [Messiah] now!" led to some speculation that Schneerson himself was a messianic candidate. There were several reasons for this speculation. The first was sociological. Given the dynastic nature of Hasidism, the childlessness of the rebbe and his wife, Hannah (Chana), could prove fatal to the movement, especially since Schneerson appointed no successor. If, however, he were to usher in the messianic age, then continuation of the dynasty would be irrelevant.

There were theological issues as well. Since there is the tradition within Judaism that each generation has its potential Messiah, the possibility that it is Schneerson is not too far-fetched. He matches all the criteria for the Messiah set out by Maimonides in his *Book of Judges*. Schneerson is a descendant of the House of David, he mediated upon and scrupulously observed all the commandments, and he attempted to bring all of Israel into unity with the way of the Torah.

During the late 1980s and early 1990s, the messianic fervor reached a crescendo. Schneerson's messianic status seemed to be borne out by his predictions that the 1991 Gulf War would be short and that Israel would be spared, that the Soviet Union would collapse, and that Ethiopian and Russian Jews would launch an exodus to Israel. The expectations received a setback in the winter of 1992 when Schneerson suffered a stroke, but as he slowly recovered the expectations rose yet again. Schneerson's death in June 1994 caused tremendous grief and distress among his followers and created numerous tensions between those who continued to believe he would yet reveal himself as the Messiah and those who believe that the world had proved itself unworthy.

During his life, Schneerson's influence extended well beyond the United States. He had a substantial following in Israel and an impact on Israeli politics. Although he never visited the country, and viewed its secular government with suspicion, he believed strongly that the land of Israel belonged to the Jews. After he announced that it would violate religious law to relinquish any land (meaning the occupied territories of the West Bank and Gaza), a small religious party composed of Lubavitchers provided the votes to bring the hard-line government to power in 1990.

Within the United States, Schneerson's prestige extended beyond the Lubavitchers and orthodoxy to many secular and nonobservant Jews, whose financial support made much of the movement's activities possible. These Jews, concerned about the continuation of Jewish life and Jewish culture, viewed Schneerson and the Lubavitchers as bulwarks against assimilation. As a result Schneerson's significance within American Judaism was much greater than mere numbers could tell.

EQ

Bibliography: Edward Hoffman, *Despite All Odds: The Story of Lubavitch* (New York: Simon & Schuster, 1991).

science and religion   The relationship between religion and science in the United States has been complex and multi-faceted. They have been partners and opponents. Practitioners of each have alternately viewed the other as threat and partner, as critical and irrelevant.

The first European settlers in the present-day United States inhabited a radically different mental and scientific world from that of the late 20th century. Intellectually rooted in the cosmological works of Aristotle and Ptolemy as well as the Bible, they believed that the sun and planets revolved around the earth. For them the universe was naturally static and was actively governed by a God who used the natural world to manifest his power and majesty.

By the time of the American Revolution, this world had been turned upside down, and religious leaders had been active participants in that transformation. Copernicus and Galileo had demonstrated that the earth was not the center of the universe. Isaac Newton had explained the natural movement of objects. To a great extent, in Puritan New England at least, religion paved the way for the acceptance of these major intellectual breakthroughs. By the 1650s Harvard College, founded to train future ministers, taught the Copernican theory of the universe, and ministers such as Cotton MATHER and Jonathan EDWARDS took an active interest in scientific and medical developments. Mather was elected to the Royal Society of London, and Edwards wrote several botanical essays notable for their attention to scientific detail. Both also promoted the cause of smallpox inoculation—such an inoculation, in fact, caused Edwards's death.

This relationship remained fairly close through the antebellum era. Science and religion shared several basic assumptions. Each believed the world was orderly and understandable. They also shared a commitment to a Baconian view of knowledge. Science worked on the basis of gathering facts that produced a solution or answer. This non-theoretical view of the world meshed well with the SCOTTISH COMMON SENSE REALISM that predominated among the country's leading religious thinkers.

In the United States, Protestant religious thinkers saw science as a means of demonstrating the glory and power of God, while most scientists saw little or no conflict between their (usually Protestant) religious beliefs and their scientific work. When conflicts did emerge, they usually were over who was more qualified to interpret scripture rather than who was more qualified to interpret scientific evidence.

This harmony was broken by the publication of Charles Darwin's *On the Origin of Species* (1859), and especially his *The Descent of Man* (1871). While the books originally provoked much scientific debate about organic evolution, they met little widespread religious condemnation. By the turn of the century nearly all American scientists had become convinced of the doctrine of organic evolution, as had most religious liberals (see LIBERALISM, THEOLOGICAL) and many evangelicals (see EVANGELICALISM) although not necessarily in its Darwinian version. Even among those who rejected organic evolution, believing it incompatible with the Christian understanding of human nature, no major thinker accepted the literal biblical story of a recent six-day creation.

Early in the 20th century, this began to change. The increasing naturalism in science and the growing gulf between scientific knowledge and religious thought brought the issue of evolution to the forefront. Evolution in its Darwin-

ian form increasingly seemed to strike at the very heart of biblical religion. By seeing the evolution of the species as simply a random series of adaptations to external stimuli, Darwinian evolution appeared to deny a purposive creation that was the result of divine action and that the universe was part of a divine plan. This was particularly problematic when applied to human beings. If human development were the result of random evolutionary forces, the belief that human beings were created in the image of God was denied, as was the unity of humanity.

Many religious people were particularly disturbed by the last two implications of Darwin's theory. If development were solely the result of conflict, then war and violence were not only the norm for human behavior but positive goods, necessities for the improvement of the race. Human evolution, in the view of this social Darwinism, depended on conflict and on weaker peoples being destroyed by the stronger. The poor and the weak were detriments to human progress.

Many Christians recoiled at this doctrine, including William Jennings BRYAN, who saw both the social ills he had spent his political career fighting and German belligerence in WORLD WAR I as caused by this doctrine. Following the war, Bryan spent much of his energy campaigning against evolution.

Opposition to evolution was linked with the growing conflict between FUNDAMENTALISM and MODERNISM in Protestant Christianity. The decision already had been decided for the Catholic Church with the pope's condemnations of AMERICANISM in 1899 and of Catholic modernism in 1907. Both these condemnations and the campaign against evolution were part of a defense of traditional Christian doctrines against a science that seemed increasingly hostile to any supernatural claims. For many, the first line of this defense was the truth of scripture, including the doctrine of the special creation of human beings.

This conflict came to a head at the SCOPES TRIAL held in Dayton, Tennessee in 1925. The trial of John Scopes for violating the state's law against teaching evolution in schools became a platform for the wider conflict, with Bryan and Clarence Darrow the opposing heroes. Darrow's humiliation of Bryan and the concomitant pillorying of the anti-evolutionists in the public press drove the movement underground.

This underground movement reemerged in the late 20th century. Spurred originally by the 1960 publication of *The Genesis Flood: The Biblical Record and Its Scientific Implications* by Henry Morris and John C. Whitcomb, Jr. and strengthened by the formation of the Creation Research Society (1963) and Creation Science Research Center (1970), the fundamentalist fight against evolution, now proceeding under the name of CREATIONISM or creation science, attempted to have the biblical story of creation taught alongside evolution in public schools. They attained some success when this was mandated by the state of Arkansas. This law, however, was declared unconstitutional in 1982 by a federal appeals court that was convinced by the testimony of several leading Christian theologians that the very doctrine of creation implies a creator and was therefore a religious doctrine not a scientific theory.

Despite the predominance of scientific naturalism in education, the response of most people to the changes in science has been one of indifference. For many people, whether the sun moves around the earth or the opposite is basically irrelevant. Polls suggest that many Americans are scientifically illiterate, with large numbers agreeing with statements such as "God created man pretty much in his present form at one time in the last 10,000 years." The dominant role of physics in the 20th century and the resulting introduction of Einsteinian relativism, the uncertainty principle, and confusing concepts such as "black holes" and "quarks" broke the common bond that science and religion seemed to share in an earlier age. Religion remained committed to truths while science increasingly spoke of probabilities. Given these shifts, contact between them became increas-

ingly tenuous. Although there have been some attempts to reconnect religious and scientific issues, the major movement between science and religion during this century has been away from each other. Science and religion increasingly have come to inhabit radically different spheres and have lost the connections that had marked earlier periods.

EQ

Bibliography: Ian G. Barbour, *Issues in Science and Religion* (Englewood Cliffs: Prentice Hall, 1966); David C. Lindberg and Ronald L. Numbers, eds., *God and Nature: Historical Essays on the Encounter Between Christianity and Science* (Berkeley: University of California Press, 1986); Ronald L. Numbers, *The Creationists: The Evolution of Scientific Creationism* (New York: Alfred A. Knopf, 1992); Jon R. Roberts, *Darwinism and the Divine in America: Protestant Intellectuals and Organic Evolution, 1859–1900* (Madison: University of Wisconsin Press, 1988).

Scientology   Founded in 1953 by the Nebraska-born science fiction writer L. Ron Hubbard (1911–1986), the Church of Scientology aims to spread the self-help philosophy/religion first outlined in his best seller, *Dianetics, The Modern Science of Mental Health* (1950).

The goal of Scientology as described in *Dianetics* is to uproot unhappiness, which results, according to Hubbard, when an individual is induced by the "engrams" (brain records of prior experiences, including events in past lives) that operate on his or her "reactive mind" habitually to repeat destructive behaviors. This goal is accomplished by a number of techniques aimed at eradicating one's engrams and uprooting the effects of the reactive mind. These techniques include a thorough "auditing" or accounting of engrams and a systematic "clearing," through education and counseling, of all traces of those engrams from the individual. Scientologists who reach this end are called "Clears."

In the 1960s Hubbard added to this basic therapy a more elaborate metaphysics that described the spiritual essence of the human being as a "thetan." In keeping with this understanding, Scientologists strive to become not only "Clears" but also "Operating Thetans" (O.T.s). Freed from the ill effects of the "reactive mind," O.T.s are thought by Hubbard to possess extraordinary powers, including the ability to bring into existence MEST: Matter, Energy, Space, and Time.

Scientology has been criticized both by Christian groups and by the media as a dangerous "cult of greed." In 1967 the Internal Revenue Service ruled that the Church of Scientology was not a tax-exempt religious organization, and the United States Supreme Court upheld that ruling in 1988. In the early 1980s Hubbard's wife and 10 other leading Scientologists were put in prison. The charge was illegally interfering in investigations of their organization by government agencies.

Although these scandals have hurt, they have not killed the organization. Both the National Council of Churches and the American Civil Liberties Union have come to Scientology's defense, and a number of prominent Hollywood celebrities, including actors Tom Cruise and John Travolta, have endorsed Hubbard's teachings. In 1993 the IRS granted the church and its related corporations tax-exempt status.

The death of Hubbard in 1986 seems only to have strengthened the movement. Now lead by David Miscavige and headquartered in Los Angeles, the Church of Scientology maintains approximately 700 centers in 65 countries. The organization claims about eight million members, but critics fix the membership figure at approximately 50,000.

SRP

Bibliography: L. Ron Hubbard, *Dianetics, The Modern Science of Mental Health* (New York: Hermitage House, 1950); June D. Littler, *The Church of Scientology and L. Ron Hubbard* (New York: Garland Publications, 1992).

Scofield, Cyrus Ingerson (1843–1921)

C. I. Scofield was a minister and author of *The Scofield Reference Bible,* unquestionably the most important work to arise out of the American premillennialist (see PREMILLENNIALISM) move-

ment. Scofield insisted that every word of the Bible contained divine truth, and his *Reference Bible* outlined the various "dispensations" (see DISPENSATIONALSIM) of God's self-revelation to humankind. His views on the infallibility of the Scriptures also contributed significantly to the growth of fundamentalism in the United States in the early 20th century.

Scofield was born near Clinton, Michigan on August 19, 1843, but his parents later moved the family to middle Tennessee. Scofield served in the Confederate army during the Civil War. After the war, he settled first in St. Louis, where he studied law and was married, and then in Atchison, Kansas. He was admitted to the Kansas bar in 1869, elected to the Kansas state legislature in 1870, and appointed United States attorney for his district in 1873. However, in 1879 Scofield left his wife (whom he divorced in 1883) and two children behind in Kansas and returned to St. Louis.

The details of Scofield's life in this period are unclear, and alcoholism may well have contributed to the sudden end of his marriage and law career. In any case, he experienced a religious conversion in 1879, rejected his previous lukewarm affiliation with the Episcopal Church, and became a Congregationalist. After joining the evangelistic campaign of revivalist Dwight L. Moody, Scofield served as acting superintendent of the St. Louis YMCA and worked at the Hyde Park Congregational Church in the city from 1880 to 1882. In 1882 he moved to Dallas, where he was ordained a minister and had a successful tenure as pastor of the city's First Congregational Church.

During his years in Dallas, Scofield established his reputation as an outstanding conservative interpreter of the Bible. He conceived of the Bible as an encyclopedic puzzle, a dictionary of facts that could be sorted out in a scientific fashion and made to disclose the progressive revelation of divine secrets. In 1888 Scofield published *Rightly Dividing the Word of Truth,* a book that systematized those teachings he believed the Scriptures contained. He also composed a three-volume correspondence course on the Bible. Between 1895 and 1915, several thousand subscribers enrolled in this program, which was eventually sold to the Moody Bible Institute.

Moody convinced Scofield to leave Dallas in 1895 and come to Northfield, Massachusetts to lead the Congregational church Moody attended. While in that town, Scofield became involved both with the Northfield Conferences, the summer missionary conferences Moody had founded, and with the Niagara Conferences, the Bible and prophecy meetings held each summer in Niagara-on-the-Lake, Ontario. As early as 1901, Scofield indicated his interest in editing a Bible that would explain the millenarian ideas taught at the Northfield and Niagara conferences. Although he returned to his former church in Dallas in 1902 and served there five more years, he left the church again in 1907 to devote his full energies to the composition of his most important work.

The Scofield Reference Bible was published by Oxford University Press in 1909. Central to its approach was Scofield's belief that God had divided history into seven dispensations, lengthy periods in which men and women were tested in respect to their obedience to God's will. At the end of each of the first five dispensations, all described in the Hebrew Scriptures, the enormity of human sinfulness had led to divine condemnation and catastrophe. Scofield said that the world is presently in the midst of the sixth dispensation, the dispensation of grace that began with the death and resurrection of Jesus Christ. At the end of this dispensation, the rapture of the church will occur and, following a period of great tribulation, Christ will return and his millennial (thousand-year) reign will begin.

Scofield's thought had, and continues to have, a tremendous influence on American fundamentalism. After the publication of the *Reference Bible,* he moved from Dallas to New York City, where he founded the New York Night School of the Bible. In 1914 he also cofounded the

Philadelphia School of the Bible, and in that period he was highly popular as a lecturer and conference speaker. Although declining health forced him to curtail his activities, Scofield also edited the tercentenary edition of the King James Version of the English Bible in 1911 and revised his *Reference Bible* in 1917. He died at his home in Douglaston, New York on July 24, 1921.

GHS, Jr.

Bibliography: Ernest R. Sandeen, *The Roots of Fundamentalism: British and American Millenarianism, 1800–1930* (1970; Grand Rapids: Baker Book House, 1978); Charles Gallaudet Trumbull, *The Life Story of C. I. Scofield* (New York: Oxford University Press, 1920).

Scopes trial   The trial of John T. Scopes, a science instructor accused of illegally teaching the theory of biological evolution to students in Dayton, Tennessee, was a pivotal moment in the history of 20th-century American FUNDAMENTALISM. Often called "the Monkey Trial," this event was also one of the first media extravaganzas in history. Hundreds of reporters flocked to a little southern town to observe the great Christian statesman William Jennings BRYAN spar with defense attorney Clarence Darrow over the truth of the biblical account of creation and the descent of humankind from apes.

Following the appearance of *On the Origin of Species* in 1859, Christians had long been arguing whether Charles Darwin's theories of evolutionary development necessarily contradicted teachings in the Book of Genesis and other parts of the Bible. While some theologians asserted that God might well have used certain forms of evolution to create the human race, other, more conservative interpreters insisted that Darwin's ideas and Christianity were absolutely incompatible. The controversy over Darwinism raged in the United States for many decades after the Civil War.

Matters came to a head in the 1920s, when several southern states introduced legislation that banned the teaching of evolution in public

The campaign by fundamentalist churchgoers to halt the teaching of evolution in the public schools became a media circus when the trial was held in July 1925 in Dayton, Tennessee. Worshipers leave church in Dayton. (Library of Congress)

schools. The Tennessee law that Scopes violated had been passed early in 1925. It forbade teachers from mentioning "any theory that denies the Story of Divine Creation of man as taught in the Bible." Scopes, a new biology teacher in a small mountain town, chose to challenge the law. He was supported by the American Civil Liberties Union, which supplied three of the most eminent lawyers of the day, including noted trial lawyer and religious skeptic Clarence Darrow. William Jennings Bryan, a three-time loser as Democratic candidate for president and one-time secretary of state, on the other hand, was a pious Christian believer who had earlier taken up the antievolution cause. Bryan jumped at the opportunity to challenge the forces of unbelief.

The Scopes trial was a study of contrasts between two opposite world views. On one side was small-town America, southern, rural, poorly educated, and militantly conservative in its religious faith; on the other side was the urban North, intellectual, sophisticated, and religiously forward-looking. When Bryan was called as a witness to testify on the veracity of the biblical text, Darrow's cross-examination tore his testimony to shreds. Darrow believed he was helping modern liberal culture fight back against the intellectual oppression of "bigots and ignoramuses." In the eyes of the press covering the trial, Bryan appeared to be simply a benighted yokel with little understanding of either modern biblical interpretation or science.

Although Scopes was convicted of the charges against him, the verdict was later overturned by a higher court in the state. Bryan won his case but died a few days after the verdict was reached. For the rest of the century, the fundamentalism Bryan championed at Dayton would be branded as hopelessly obscurantist. However, neither the fundamentalist movement nor the antievolution forces believed themselves defeated by the Scopes trial. A handful of states in the South continued to pass legislation against evolution. Despite the overturning of many of those laws in the 1960s, the rise of "creation science" (see CREATIONISM) in the 1980s reveals the continuing strength of the opposition to Darwinist biological views.

GHS, Jr.

Bibliography: Lawrence W. Levine, *Defender of the Faith: William Jennings Bryan,* 1915–1925 (New York: Oxford University Press, 1965).

Scottish Common Sense Realism

Scottish Common Sense Realism (also known as Common Sense philosophy or Baconianism) was an 18th-century philosophical school. It was crucial not only in shaping popular Protestant thought in America between the end of the War for Independence and the Civil War, but also in laying an intellectual base for the rise of FUNDAMENTALISM at the end of the 19th century. In opposition to both philosophical skepticism and philosophical idealism, Scottish

Common Sense Realism argued that ordinary human beings were capable of gaining knowledge of the real world through the use of their senses.

The Common Sense philosophy emerged out of controversies in Enlightenment (see EN-LIGHTENMENT, THE) thought in the mid-1700s. Philosophers had long debated about the basis of human knowledge. John Locke (1632–1704), for example, had argued that "ideas" existed in an intermediate position between human beings and the real world. Since these "ideas" were the true objects of human thought, external things, he said, could only be known in one's mind. Locke's philosophical system was modified by George Berkeley (1685–1753), who insisted that ideas were the only things in existence and the only things that people could ever know. David Hume (1711–1776), however, swiftly demolished Locke's rationalism and Berkeley's idealism. He asked, first, how people could know that a real world existed and, second, if a real world did exist, how they could know anything about it. It was at this point that Thomas Reid (1710–1796), a Scottish Presbyterian clergyman, entered the philosophical fray.

Reid and the philosophers who followed him tried to give solid metaphysical content to common-sense observations people always made. The ability to know the world, Reid said, was as natural as the ability to breathe air. His philosophy was both utilitarian and democratic, for it postulated that ordinary men and women were capable of comprehending a rational and predictable universe. Following the inductive methods of 17th-century scientist Francis Bacon, moreover, the Common Sense philosophers asserted that the external world was just as it appeared to be.

The fundamentally optimistic temper of Scottish Common Sense Realism perfectly fit the American intellectual and religious mood at the end of the 18th century. The philosophy, of course, had developed within the context of Calvinist (see CALVINISM) theology. While it

appeared, on the one hand, to contradict the strict Calvinist view that sin limits the human ability to know what is right, its belief in an innate moral sense was, on the other hand, a helpful building block for a system of ethics. Calvinists in America thus gladly reconciled their views about determinism and depravity to match the new philosophy. Common Sense also provided the foundation for a rational, scientific confirmation of the truths of the Bible. A person could simply believe whatever he or she read in the Bible; no further knowledge or expertise was needed.

Many Americans employed the Common Sense method in the early days of the American republic. However, John Witherspoon, a Scottish-born clergyman who served as president of what is now Princeton University, brought the philosophy to prominence. After 1812, moreover, when the Presbyterian Church established a seminary at Princeton, Common Sense became the intellectual underpinning for theological instruction at that school. Princeton theologians saw themselves as champions of scientific impartiality against the challenge to biblical authority raised by liberals in their church. Teachers such as Charles HODGE, his son A. A. Hodge, and his protege Benjamin B. WARFIELD argued that the inspiration of Scripture depended upon the written words the Bible contained. Their doctrine of the INERRANCY of the biblical text, consistent with Common Sense belief, taught that the Bible was (as Charles Hodge put it) a "store-house of facts."

American fundamentalist thought in the late 19th and early 20th century was closely linked to Common Sense assumptions about the world. Combined with the biblicism of the Princeton theologians, Scottish Common Sense Realism led to supreme confidence about religious questions. Although fundamentalists might have appeared anti-intellectual in their refusal to accept Darwinist theories of evolution, their adherence to the "objective" standards of the biblical account of creation was—in their own estimation—highly rationalistic. Common Sense philosophy gave American fundamentalists what they believed was a secure bastion from which to defend the "old-time religion" and its conception of truth.

GHS, Jr.

Bibliography: Theodore Dwight Bozeman, *Protestants in an Age of Science: The Baconian Ideal and Antebellum American Religious Thought* (Chapel Hill: University of North Carolina Press, 1977); Henry F. May, *The Enlightenment in America* (New York: Oxford University Press, 1976).

Scripture See BIBLICAL INTERPRETATION.

Seabury, Samuel (1729–1796) Samuel Seabury was the first Anglican (see ANGLICANISM) clergyman in the United States to be consecrated bishop after the American Revolution. He made significant contributions both to the organization of the Episcopal Church and to the composition of that denomination's Book of Common Prayer.

Seabury was born on November 30, 1729 in Groton, Connecticut. Son of a Congregationalist minister who had converted to the Church of England, Seabury was himself ordained in 1753. He served as a missionary of the SOCIETY FOR THE PROPAGATION OF THE GOSPEL in parishes in Long Island and Westchester County, New York. He was also involved in the unsuccessful effort to obtain an Anglican bishop for the colonies in the 1760s. During the Revolution, he volunteered as a chaplain to American Loyalists serving in the British army.

After the war ended, Seabury took an active role in reconstructing Anglicanism in the new nation. Chosen by the clergy of Connecticut in 1783 to seek consecration as their bishop, he sailed to England. Because English church law at that time required all clergy to swear an oath of allegiance to the British king, Seabury was unable to obtain the office he sought. Undaunted, he went north to Scotland, where on November 14, 1784 he was consecrated to the

Consecrated in Scotland in 1784, Samuel Seabury became the first bishop of the Protestant Episcopal Church of America.

episcopate (see EPISCOPACY) by three bishops of the Scottish Episcopal Church. Seabury signed a concordat with the Scottish church pledging to incorporate its "high church" theological principles, notably, a strong episcopate, clerical control over the church, and emphasis on the sacrament of holy communion, into the structure of the new American Episcopal Church. Although the Episcopal General Convention at first refused to recognize that Seabury had been validly consecrated, since the Scottish Episcopal Church was not in communion with the Church of England, he was eventually accepted as a bishop in 1789.

Besides overseeing the church in Connecticut, Seabury extended assistance to Episcopalians throughout New England and assumed charge of parishes in Rhode Island in 1789. Ill health eventually overtook him. Seabury collapsed during a pastoral visit to New London, Connecticut and died there on February 25, 1796.

GHS, Jr.

Bibliography: Bruce E. Steiner, *Samuel Seabury, 1729–1796: A Study in the High Church Tradition* (Athens, Ohio: Ohio University Press, 1971).

Second Coming   See ESCHATOLOGY.

Second Great Awakening

The "Second Great Awakening" refers to the series of revivals (see REVIVALISM) that occurred in various localities throughout the United States between roughly 1790 and 1830. Like the GREAT AWAKENING of the mid-18th century, the Second Awakening had a corporate as well as an individual dimension. Revivalists emphasized not only that God wished to save the souls of those who repented of their sins, but also that a special divine blessing had been placed upon America. Consistent with the self-reliant spirit of the early republic, moreover, leaders of the 19th-century revivals stressed the innate ability of individuals to reform both themselves and their society.

The Second Great Awakening had three distinct phases and locales: the relatively sedate revivals among New England Congregationalists in the first two decades of the 19th century; the raucous CAMP MEETINGS on the southern and western frontier during roughly that same period; and the "new measure" revivals inspired by Charles G. FINNEY in the so-called BURNED-OVER DISTRICT of upstate New York in the 1820s and 1830s.

Historians usually date the beginnings of the Second Awakening among the scattered revivals that appeared in remote sections of Connecticut and New Hampshire in the late 1790s. Although the New England phase of the Awakening seemed to wane at the turn of the century, it gained force again in 1801 under the direction of Timothy DWIGHT, the president of Yale Col-

Dartmouth College's beginnings sprang from the missionary zeal that swept New England during the 1790s. (Billy Graham Center Museum)

lege. Dwight believed that many Yale students had fallen into "freethinking," and he determined to launch a counterattack against that tendency. Yet even Dwight was surprised at the reaction his preaching provoked, for a third of the student body soon professed that they had experienced a religious conversion. As one student wrote in a letter to his family, "Yale College is a little temple."

Although the excitement at Yale quickly flagged, Dwight helped motivate other Connecticut clergy to join the revival campaign. Dwight's protege Moses Stuart, for example, led a revival at the First Church in New Haven in 1807 and 1908. Later, Lyman BEECHER and Nathaniel William TAYLOR became leaders of the movement—Beecher being the great organizer and promoter of revivalism in New England, and Taylor providing the most coherent intellectual defense of that phenomenon.

The leaders of the New England revivals sought to maintain the theological emphases of their great exemplar, Jonathan EDWARDS, who was the first to kindle religious enthusiasm during the Great Awakening. The followers of Edwards believed that the preaching of "plain gospel truths" would convince sinners to seek God's grace and lead to an eventual outpouring of the Holy Spirit. They emphasized that the revivals were the work, not of human beings, but of God. They underscored this belief by insisting that worshipers maintain their decorum and eschew hysterical demonstrations of religious fervor. A renewed spiritual seriousness and the reformation of morals were viewed as the only genuine fruits of a revival.

As the Second Great Awakening spread west and south of New England, however, the eastern clergy's innate conservatism began to seem irrelevant to the social environment of the frontier. As a result, changes appeared in the method by which revivals were raised. Preachers viewed the successful revival more as a matter of technique than as a purely divine gift, and they introduced procedures whereby people might be induced to come to a decision for Christ. The western revivals were also marked by outbursts of undisciplined emotionalism. Held, for example, in unsettled areas among a generally unruly population, these revivals were said to attract those who preferred their "whiskey straight and . . . politics and religion red hot." Typical of this stage of the Second Great Awakening was the gathering in August 1801 at Cane Ridge (see CANE RIDGE REVIVAL), Kentucky. Over 10,000 people took part in a mass religious event that some participants later called the greatest outpouring of the Holy Spirit since the biblical day of Pentecost.

Cane Ridge became the symbol of tremendous religious changes occurring in the United States. Revivals broke out throughout Kentucky, Tennessee, and southern Ohio, and thousands of previously unchurched settlers were incorporated into the Protestant denominations. Methodist revivalist Peter CARTWRIGHT, for instance, took part in countless camp meetings in this period. In his autobiography, Cartwright described groups of clergy of many different denominations uniting to preach at one time. On those occasions, he saw "more than a hundred sinners fall like dead men," while hundreds of other believers stood around "all shouting aloud the high praises of God at once."

Despite the success of the western revivalists, the emotional excesses the camp meetings encouraged eventually convinced leaders of the Presbyterian Church to condemn the phenomenon. In 1805 the Presbyterian General Assembly, declaring that "God is a God of order and not of confusion," censured not only the looseness of revivalistic worship, but also the general disregard for educational standards for ordination that revivalism encouraged. The General Assembly decried as well the tendency of Presbyterian revivalists to accept Arminian (see ARMINIANISM) theological notions, that is, the idea that sinners had free will either to accept or reject faith in Jesus Christ. This controversy over revivals was a central factor in schisms that split Presbyterianism in Kentucky and Tennessee. Barton STONE and others, calling themselves "Christians only," withdrew from the Presbyterian Church in 1804, and revivalist members of the Cumberland Prebytery formed their own Cumberland Presbyterian Church in 1805.

Over the next 20 years, the revivals of the Awakening continued both in their conservative, New England form under the leadership of Congregationalists Lyman BEECHER and his colleague Asahel Nettleton, and in their more exuberant western pattern, then almost exclusively under Methodist direction. The Awakening entered its third major—and in some ways most significant—phase in 1821, when Charles G. FINNEY, a lawyer in Adams, New York, experienced a conversion to Christ and felt a call to preach the gospel.

Finney was ordained by the Presbyterians and began a series of evangelistic tours throughout western New York State. He was a physically imposing figure who drew large crowds wherever he traveled. He told his congregations that God had given men and women the opportunity to effect their own salvation, if they would merely decide to surrender themselves to the Lord. He believed that common sense revealed how the human will was free to make up its own mind about spiritual matters. Finney's theological views also led him to rethink the revivalistic process itself. He did not emphasize the miraculous nature of a revival, but the natural means needed to achieve the desired results. He introduced several controversial features that became known as his "new measures," and he scandalized many by encouraging women to testify and pray in public.

Finney was a highly skilled practitioner of the revivalistic art. In 1825 he moved into the Mohawk Valley, and cities such as Rome, Utica, and Troy successively "caught fire." Wave after wave of religious excitement swept over the area, earning it the sobriquet "Burned-Over District." Finney soon became a national figure and later traveled to Philadelphia, New York City, and Boston to lead revivals. Only an illness stopped Finney, but when he curtailed his activities in 1832, the Second Great Awakening as a distinct phenomenon effectively came to an end.

The revivals Finney led had a far-reaching impact not simply on American religion, but on American society as well. The remarkable wave of social reform activity that followed the Awakening was in part inspired by Finney's teachings, for he had always suggested the possibility of a person's attaining perfection (see PERFECTIONISM) in the present life. Although Finney himself was hesitant about applying his beliefs

directly to the political sphere (no law could ever produce a perfect society, he thought), his emphasis on the human will and on dedicating oneself to the advancement of God's kingdom on earth certainly was open to concrete social interpretations. Optimistic about the progress of revivalism and the increase of church membership across the United States, moreover, Finney even predicted in 1835 that the start of the millennium (see POSTMILLENNIALISM), the thousand-year reign of Christ, was only three years away—a further stimulus to the reforming impulse.

Thousands of American Protestants, animated by the revivals of the Second Great Awakening, quickly set to work to fulfill Finney's prophecy. The whole cluster of national societies that arose between 1816 and 1833, in fact—education, missions, peace, temperance, antislavery, and others (usually termed the "benevolent empire")—were responding to social challenges the Awakening had raised. As French commentator Alexis de Tocqueville remarked in 1835 after visiting America, religion was certainly "the foremost of the political institutions" of the United States. The Awakening had roused many Americans to spread the gospel and so transform their nation into a truly Christian republic, on which God would bestow favor.

(See also EVANGELICAL UNITED FRONT; EVANGELICALISM; NEW SCHOOL/OLD SCHOOL; RESTORATION MOVEMENT.)

GHS, Jr.

Bibliography: John B. Boles, *The Great Revival, 1787–1805: The Origins of the Southern Evangelical Mind* (Lexington: University Press of Kentucky, 1972); Whitney R. Cross, *The Burned-Over District: The Social and Intellectual History of Enthusiastic Religion in Western New York* (Ithaca, N.Y.: Cornell University Press, 1950); Nathan O. Hatch, *The Democratization of American Christianity* (New Haven: Yale University Press, 1989); Paul E. Johnson, *A Shopkeeper's Millennium: Society and Revivals in Rochester New York, 1815–1837* (New York: Hill and Wang, 1978).

Second World War   See WORLD WAR II.

secular humanism   The term "secular humanism," coined by conservative Protestants, refers to a world view that in their eyes eclipses the Christian God and elevates the worship of humanity itself. According to those who use the term, it is a pernicious ideological viewpoint undercutting modern American society. Secular humanism is seen to be particularly entrenched in the media, the educational establishment, government, and even many liberal religious groups. Throughout the 1980s conservative religious-political coalitions (see CHRISTIAN RIGHT) sought to mobilize opinion in a campaign to undercut the influence of secular humanism on public life.

In response to the social turmoil created by the 1960s COUNTERCULTURE, during the late 1970s and 1980s conservative Protestants affiliated with the New Religious Right became politically active. Southern Baptist minister Jerry Falwell, founder of the MORAL MAJORITY, began speaking out against the growing influence of "secular humanism": a godless, human-centered world view. Many activists drew on a diagnosis of Western culture made by conservative Presbyterian theologian Francis Schaeffer—whose most notable predecessor was J. Gresham MACHEN.

In Schaeffer's writings, such as *A Christian Manifesto* (1981) or *How Should We Then Live?* (1976), Western culture has been in a state of decline from its high point during the Protestant REFORMATION. According to Schaeffer, westerners, including Americans, lost their grounding in the absolute truth and moral standards provided by the biblically based REFORMED TRADITION. While many Americans have regarded the ENLIGHTENMENT with some ambivalence, Schaeffer found in its SECULARISM the definitive source of most modern social and spiritual ills.

In particular, the Enlightenment world view of humanism, which really only became firmly entrenched in America in the last few decades, inverted what earlier Protestants knew to be most important. For Schaeffer, humanists literally elevated the status of the human and dis-

placed the transcendent God. Consequently in recent decades moral standards collapsed and truth dissolved. Schaeffer's followers see a variety of social problems—sexual license, abortion (see SEXUALITY), drug use, and rising crime, all of which exemplify the permissiveness resulting from a lack of strong individual and family values—spreading across the land. This decline in values is especially disturbing because it has sapped America's spiritual strength, evident in the lack of will in the VIETNAM WAR, growing toleration for COMMUNISM, and a failure of patriotism (see CIVIL RELIGION).

In terms similar to those used by earlier generations to counter the spread of Catholicism (see ANTI-CATHOLICISM; NATIVISM) conservative Protestants, such as Tim LaHaye in *Battle for the Mind* (1980), claim secular humanism is a wide-ranging conspiracy entrenched within American institutions, threatening to dilute the country's Christian heritage. Increasingly throughout the 1980s conservative activists mobilized to ferret out secular humanism from public life. Contending that secular humanism is in fact a religion (and a dangerous one), activists argued that its pervasive influence in the public schools, government agencies, and publicly funded media violates the First Amendment. In 1987 Judge W. Brevard Hand of Alabama agreed, banning 31 textbooks from Alabama schools because they promoted "the religion of secular humanism." Though the decision was overturned, those opposed to secular humanism were encouraged to continue their efforts to remove dangerous titles from school libraries. According to a *New York Times* study, by 1986 "watchdog" groups had successfully removed 239 titles from public schools across the country.

The term "secular humanism" is occasionally used by members of the AMERICAN HUMANIST ASSOCIATION as a valid way of distinguishing their own beliefs from those of religious liberals, such as the Unitarians (see UNITARIAN UNIVERSALIST ASSOCIATION) who signed the HUMANIST MANIFESTO in 1933. In 1980 humanist Paul

Kurtz launched the journal *Free Inquiry,* including a "Secular Humanist Declaration" in order to meet Falwell's charges head on, and to try to reclaim the symbolic importance of humanism to American values. Nevertheless, the term remains more of a pejorative label than an accurate description of a distinct set of ideas. Most Americans who hold some form of the secular ideal also retain elements of a religious outlook. At bottom the struggle against secular humanism represents the continuing conflict to define America's fundamental religious legacy as either Christian or pluralist (see PLURALISM). Americans of many tendencies, whether liberal or conservative, religious or secular, continue to identify their own religious outlook with the nation's fundamental values.

MG

Bibliography: Robert Basil, Mary Beth Gehrman, Tim Madigan, *On the Barricades: Religion and Free Inquiry in Conflict* (Buffalo, N.Y.: Prometheus Books, 1989); Walter H. Capps, *The New Religious Right: Piety, Patriotism and Politics* (Columbia: University of South Carolina Press, 1990); Francis Schaeffer, *A Christian Manifesto* (Westchester, Ill.: Crossway Books, 1981).

secularism "Secular," from the Latin *saeculum,* literally means this present age or generation and, by implication, things of this age or world, as opposed to one still to come. Hence the term, like the word "profane," is often used in polar opposition to the word "religious" or "sacred." This opposition is commonly taken to be part of a long-term historical process that social scientists have labeled "secularization," by which societies supposedly lose their "traditional" moorings in religion on their way to becoming "modern." Secularism consequently means the belief that the outcome of secularization is beneficial, an ideal for human beings to achieve. Many social scientists and historians have seriously called into question the idea of secularization, arguing that it is not in fact a long-term irreversible process, or that the rigid conceptual distinction between religion and the secular are in fact not visible within actual societies. Nevertheless, if secularization remains elusive, the belief in its benefits borrowed originally from the European ENLIGHTENMENT has exerted a profound impact on American culture over time.

Secularism as an ideal emerges first in the Enlightenment world view incorporated by American Deists into the revolutionary struggle. While Deist revolutionaries largely avoided the strident anticlericalism and atheism that grew in Europe during the 18th century, many of them agreed with the typical Enlightenment effort to contrast reason with tradition, faith, superstition, or dogma. Accordingly, leaders such as Benjamin Franklin, Thomas JEFFERSON, and Tom PAINE were quite critical of Christianity's claims to be a revealed religion. As the radical Deist Elihu Palmer (1764–1806) put it, traditional religion was "an empire of superstition."

At the same time, almost all revolutionary leaders saw religion as necessary to promote civic virtue. For Jefferson or James MADISON, this task was best undertaken indirectly. The conflicts between religious groups suggested that it had to be kept out of any direct role in a stable government (see ESTABLISHMENT, RELIGIOUS). The ideal of a secular society, based on reason, was thus partly at work in shaping the Constitution, which avoided mentioning religion or a divine being from whom the fledgling government derived its legitimacy. At the same time however many Christians themselves, particularly BAPTISTS such as Isaac BACKUS, also championed the cause of religious liberty.

Between the Revolution and the CIVIL WAR the secular ideal diminished, its power usurped by the creative energy unleashed by disestablished denominations. In the wake of the SECOND GREAT AWAKENING's revivals and reforms, Christians, primarily Protestants, eagerly accepted the role of providing for the public good bequeathed to them by the more secular-minded Jefferson. Thus religion proved capable of flourishing under the secular conditions of disestablishment.

A second period marked by the secular ideal emerged in the years following the Civil War. The rise of industrial capitalism, the growth of science, urban centers, and an enormous influx of non-Protestant immigrants all contributed to profound transformations in American life. In the midst of the changes the secular ideal re-emerged, centered in the new views of knowledge contained within the emerging public universities. Many disciplines adopted the evolutionary theory developed by Charles Darwin (see Darwinism), which challenged much traditional religious belief, occasioning bitter conflicts over SCIENCE AND RELIGION. Religious modernists during the Progressive era prior to WORLD WAR I, largely Protestants, but also Catholics and Jews such as Horace KALLEN or Felix ADLER sought to claim the new social conditions for their own, much as had their antebellum evangelical predecessors, confident that true religion could not only coexist with but even lead a secular, science-driven society.

While religious modernists found their influence rapidly eclipsed outside the small circle of church bureaucracies or the budding ECUMENICAL MOVEMENT, during the same period a number of far more influential intellectuals abandoned their own religious backgrounds and embraced the secular ideal (see DEWEY, JOHN; JAMES, WILLIAM; HUMANIST MANIFESTO). But even here secularism was rarely appealed to in bald form, as the appreciation for nondogmatic religious experience in Dewey's *A Common Faith* (1934) and James's *Varieties of Religious Experience* (1901) testify.

Admittedly the confluence of institutionalized modern science, the state, the economy, and the mass culture produced by the media have created a form of society no longer conceptually dependent upon religion. But apart from largely university-based intellectuals, the secular ideal is not widely shared by the majority of the American population, who manage to live both religiously and secularly by trying to keep each in its place, a frequently difficult task since there remains profound disagreement about the public role of religion. Surveys indicate that the percentage of people actually holding atheistic or agnostic views (see ATHEISM AND FREE THOUGHT) is quite small. But if secularism rarely exists in a pure form, it has recently loomed large in the world view of resurgent conservative Protestants who see it as a powerful force destroying an essentially Christian society (see FUNDAMENTALISM; SECULAR HUMANISM).

Secularism has certainly contributed to the shape of American institutions, and to such important values as religious liberty and free speech. But whether seen in the struggles of the revolutionary era or in more modern times, in pure form it is rarely a powerful ideological force in American life. Ironically, the impact of secularism is most noticeable when combined with some form of the religious.

MG

Bibliography: Mary Douglas and Steven M. Tipton, eds., *Religion and America: Spirituality in a Secular Age* (Boston: Beacon Press, 1982); Martin E. Marty, *Modern American Religion: The Irony of It All, 1893–1919* (Chicago: University of Chicago Press, 1986); Rodney Stark and William Sims Bainbridge, *The Future of Religion: Secularization, Revival and Cult Formation* (Berkeley: University of California Press, 1985).

segregation   Segregation in the context of American history generally has meant the requiring of separate public facilities for whites and blacks, with a resulting relegation of blacks to inferior services and facilities. By the 1940s this separation had become so complete in parts of the United States that whites and blacks lived in nearly separate societies, and in certain areas whites never saw blacks except as domestics or in other servile positions. Until dismantled by law during the 1950s and 1960s, segregation was a dominant fact of American life, the effects of which still linger.

Despite segregation's deep hold in the United States, especially in the South, religious defenses of it were not generally popular, although there were those who attempted them and those who believed them. The religious justifications that were offered were rooted in arguments of biblical curse and racial inferiority.

The first of these religious justifications involved the curse of Cain, Genesis 4:15. Here it was argued that the "mark of Cain" was the making of his skin black. The second was the curse upon Ham, the son of Noah who "looked upon his father's nakedness," (Genesis 9:22). Noah's curse upon Ham, that he be a slave to his brothers and that his descendants would also be slaves, was applied to Africans, since Ham's grandson Cush was understood to be the father of the African people (Cushites) and since Africa was referred to as the land of Cush. Used originally by apologists for black SLAVERY, these texts also were marshalled to argue for the inherent inferiority of blacks, as was Jeremiah 13:23, "Can the Ethiopian change his skin, or the leopard his spots?" Some interpreted this verse as suggesting there was nothing Africans could do to overcome their inherent inferiority.

All these biblical arguments explicitly relied upon an assumption of black inferiority and white superiority. The one argument that did not immediately imply a natural inferiority of blacks was one based upon the fact that people of different races lived in different regions. Drawing from the biblical story of the tower of Babel, this argument claimed that God's confounding of the people's language implied a divine commandment of separation for different peoples. This was buttressed by references to biblical citations, like Leviticus 19:19, that seemed to require that unlike things be separated. By analogy, the conclusion was that God wanted the races separated in all things. The main point that this argument ignored was that Europeans were not particularly inclined to stay where they were put and that whites essentially were doing the assigning of places.

All these arguments had biblical mandates against them as well. Preeminent among these was the fundamental theological claim of the divine creation of humanity—the fact that the biblical story of creation affirmed a common lineage. Additionally, the Pauline argument that in Christ there is neither Jew nor Greek, slave nor free, male nor female (Galatians 3:28–29), seemed to belie any scriptural support for segregation. For these reasons most denominations in the United States never publicly supported segregation as biblically based. Even those denominations dominated by white southerners rarely argued that segregation was religiously mandated, although it might be allowed. There were, however, individual members of established denominations who did view segregation as religiously sanctioned, if not commanded. During the 20th century they tended to break away from existing denominations in order to organize new ones, such as the Association of Independent Methodists (1965), in order to avoid racial integration.

A major exception to the reluctance to argue that segregation was biblically mandated has been those religious bodies affiliated with white supremacists, preeminently the Identity movement (see KU KLUX KLAN). Rooted in 19th-century Anglo-Israelitism, which argued that Anglo-Saxons were the true Jews, the Identity movement affirms the superiority of the white race and their identity as the chosen people of God. The "mixing of the races" is understood to be a violation of divine law and a threat to racial purity. With no more than 15,000 to 20,000 members in several loosely affiliated organizations including the Covenant, the Sword, and the Arm of the Lord (C.S.A.); the Church of Jesus Christ, Christian, Aryan Nations; and the Order, the Identity movement has had a limited influence, but is the most developed attempt to maintain a religiously sanctioned defense of segregation.

(See also AFRICAN-AMERICAN RELIGION; CIVIL RIGHTS MOVEMENT.)

EQ

Bibliography: Branch, Taylor, *Parting the Waters: America in the King Years, 1954–1963* (New York: Simon & Schuster, 1988); Charles Carroll, *"The Negro a Beast" or "In the Image of God"* (Salem, NH: Ayer, 1991); James Coates, *Armed and Dangerous: The Rise of the Survivalist Right* (New York: Hill & Wang, 1987); Winthrop D. Jordan, *White Over Black: American Attitudes toward the Negro, 1550–1812* (Chapel Hill: University of North Carolina Press, 1968); Gunnar Myrdal, *The American Dilemma* (New York: Harper, 1944); C. Vann Woodward, *The Strange History of Jim Crow,* 2nd. ed., rev. (New York: Oxford University Press, 1966).

Self-Realization Fellowship Founded in 1920 by Swami Paramahansa Yogananda (1893–1952), the Hindu-based Self-Realization Fellowship aims to spread the teachings of the Yoga Sutras and the practices of *kriya yoga* to the West.

Born Mukunda Lal Ghosh to a wealthy Bengali family in Gorakhpur, India, Swami Paramahansa Yogananda made a pilgrimage as a young man to Benares where he took a guru and began to study and practice *kriya yoga*, a tantric spiritual discipline in which a student, under the direction of a qualified guru, seeks to "awaken" his or her *kundalini* or spiritual power by arousing it from its "sleep" between the anus and the genitals and then pulling it up from the base of the spine into the spiritual center at the top of the head. Such an awakening is said by practitioners of *kriya yoga* to culminate in *moksha* or the spiritual liberation that comes from union with the divine.

Around the time of his graduation from college in 1914, Yogananda took the ascetic vows of a *sannyasin* or world renunciant and became a member of the Swami Order of Swami Sri Yukteswar (1855–1936). His guru then gave him the name of Swami Yogananda (literally "bliss of spiritual discipline").

Like Swami VIVEKANANDA who first came to the United States to attend the WORLD'S PARLIAMENT OF RELIGIONS in Chicago in 1893, Swami Yogananda traveled to the United States to address an ecumenical religious conference.

In his lectures at the International Congress of Religious Liberals in Boston in 1920, Yogananda echoed Vivekananda in championing the real unity underlying the apparent particularities of the world's religions. Unlike Vivekananda, who eventually returned to India, Yogananda took up residence in America, thus becoming a full-time Hindu missionary to the United States. In personal encounters and public lectures, Yogananda taught *kriya yoga* as a practice compatible with Christian doctrine.

Yogananda established the Self-Realization Fellowship (S.R.F.) in Los Angeles in 1925 as an American outgrowth of his Yogoda Satsanga Society of India (established 1917). Incorporated in 1935, the fellowship now has over 100 centers in the United States. Members aim to achieve the bliss of self-realization, which they equate with God-realization. Their Church of All Religions meets on Sundays and mixes Christian and Hindu practices. Its liturgies focus on meditation and incorporate readings from the New Testament, the *Bhagavad Gita*, and Yogananda's most widely read book, *Autobiography of a Yogi* (1946). A countercultural hit in the 1960s (see COUNTERCULTURE), Yogananda's autobiography continues to be read by Americans inspired by its message of the unity of all religions and the effectiveness of the techniques of *kriya yoga*.

After Yogananda's death in 1952, his physical body was said by his followers to have resisted decay for 20 days. He was succeeded, first, by James J. Lynn (Swami Rajasi Janakananda) and then, after Lynn's death in 1955, by a nun named Faye Wright (Sri Daya Mata or the "Mother of Compassion").

SRP

Bibliography: Swami Paramhansa Yogananda, *Autobiography of a Yogi* (Los Angeles: Self-Realization Fellowship, 1946).

Separates See BAPTISTS; GREAT AWAKENING.

Separatists See CONGREGATIONALISM; PILGRIMS.

Serra, Junipero (1713–1784)

Junipero Serra was one of the countless priests and monks who attempted to bring the Catholic faith to the colonial and indigenous inhabitants of Spain's New World possessions. Driven by a missionary zeal and faithfulness alien to contemporary sensibilities, Serra struggled to bring the Native Americans into conformity with Spanish religion and civilization.

Born on the Spanish island of Majorca in 1713, he was christened Miguel Jose, but adopted the name Junipero, after a companion of St. Francis of Assisi, upon becoming a Franciscan in 1731. After several years of study at the Pontifical University and the Lullian University in Palma, Spain, Serra was appointed to the Duns Scotus chair of philosophy at the Lullian.

Junipero Serra, a Spanish Franciscan who organized mission stations among Native Americans, opening up vast areas of California to Roman Catholicism and colonization.

A promising academic career lay before the young priest, but the call to a mission field proved too great, and in 1649, after six years as a professor, Serra left for Mexico, arriving there on January 1, 1750.

For 17 years he labored in existing missions, until the papal suppression of the JESUITS opened up vast areas in California and the present-day southwestern United States to the Franciscans. Russian and English incursions along the California coast convinced Spanish officials of the need to solidify their control in that region, and Serra, who had been appointed to supervise the mission work, joined an expedition designed to pacify and colonize the region. In 1769 he established Mission San Diego, the first of nine such missions he organized in the region. Many of these missions eventually became major cities in California—San Diego, San Francisco, Santa Clara, and San Luis Obispo.

Around these missions Serra gathered the resident Native Americans, introducing them to agriculture and European customs. While a critic of governmental and military abuse of the inhabitants, Serra failed to recognize the toll that his relocation had on them. The missions, while outwardly prosperous, were a source of disease and death for California's native population.

An active pastor and able minister, Serra worked tirelessly. He claimed to have baptized over 6,000 Indians and confirmed 5,000. He visited his missions often and during one such trip died at Mission San Carlos de Monterey on August 28, 1784.

(See also NEW SPAIN; ROMAN CATHOLICISM.)

EQ

Bibliography: Omer Englebert, *The Last of the Conquistadors: Junipero Serra, 1713–1784* (New York: Harcourt, Brace, 1956); Maynard J. Geiger, *The Life and Time of Fray Junipero Serra, O.F.M., or The Man Who Never Turned Back, 1713–1784,* 2 vols. (Washington, D.C.: Academy of American Franciscan History, 1959); Theodore Maynard, *The Long Road of Father Serra* (London: Staples Press, 1956); Junipero Serra, *The Writings of Junipero Serra,* Antoine Tibesar, ed. (Washington, D.C.: Academy of American Franciscan History, 1955–66); Winifred E. Wise,

Fray Junipero Serra and the California Conquest (New York: Scribner, 1967).

Seton, Elizabeth Ann Bayley (1774–1821)

The first Roman Catholic (see ROMAN CATHOLICISM) saint born in the United States, Elizabeth Seton began her life as Elizabeth Ann Bayley in New York City on January 25, 1774. Her mother, Catherine Bayley, died when Elizabeth was three and she was raised by her father, Richard Bayley, a leading American physician.

She early showed a concern for the poor and weak, a trait that was encouraged by her father's educational methods, which were designed to encourage unselfishness and a sense of responsibility. In 1794 she married a New York businessman, William Magee Seton, and within nine years had borne three daughters and two sons. Despite the demands of domestic life, Seton engaged in charitable activities among the poor and sick of New York, helping to found the city's first charitable organization, the Society for the Relief of Poor Widows with Small Children (1797).

By 1800 her husband's business was bankrupt, and he was ill with tuberculosis. A family trip to Italy failed to restore his health, and he died in Pisa in December 1803. Comforted by Roman Catholic friends, she developed an affection for the Church, and upon returning to the United States the following year, she continued her education in the faith, becoming a Catholic on March 15, 1805.

Family and friends, shocked by her conversion, abandoned the young widow and her children. Forced to open a school to feed her family, Seton struggled along until 1808, when she was invited to open a girl's boarding school in Baltimore. Under the patronage of Bishop John CARROLL, Seton's school was successful, and she began to consider seriously the creation of a religious order. With four companions she established the Sisters of St. Joseph on March 25, 1809.

Relocating to Emmitsburg, Maryland that summer, the women adopted a modified version

The first Roman Catholic saint to be born in the United States, Elizabeth Ann Seton founded the Sisters of Charity to educate, nurse, and minister to the poor.

of the rule of the Sisters of Charity and dedicated themselves to education and aid to the sick and destitute. At Emmitsburg, Seton reconstituted her boarding school and introduced a free school for poor children, an activity that earned her the title "foundress of the parochial school system in the United States."

As superior of this first United States order, the Sisters of Charity of St. Joseph, Seton oversaw its growth through much of the northeastern United States, where the sisters organized schools, nursed the sick, and cared for orphans and the poor. By the time of her death on January 4, 1821 she was recognized as one of the pillars of the American Catholic community and a woman of deep spiritual power.

In 1940 she was formally introduced as a candidate for canonization. Beatified by John XXIII in 1963, she was proclaimed St. Elizabeth Seton by Paul VI on September 14, 1975, becoming the first saint born in the United States.

EQ

Bibliography: Joseph I. Dirvin, *Mrs. Seton: Foundress of the American Sisters of Charity* (New York: Farrar, Straus and Cudahy, 1962); Louise Malloy, *The Life Story of Mother Seton* (Baltimore: Carroll, 1924); Annabelle M. Melville, *Elizabeth Bayley Seton, 1774–1821* (New York: Jove Publications, 1951); Elizabeth M. Seton, *Elizabeth Seton: Selected Writings,* Ellin M. Kelly and Annabelle M. Melville, eds. (New York: Paulist Press, 1987); Elaine Murray Stone, *Elizabeth Bayley Seton: An American Saint* (New York: Paulist Press, 1993).

Seventh-day Adventist Church

The Seventh-day Adventist Church is a Protestant denomination that grew out of religious revivals in the mid-19th century and the predictions of self-taught Bible scholar William MILLER about the second coming of Jesus Christ. The denomination teaches the necessity both of preparing for the coming of Christ and of observing Saturday, rather than Sunday, as the Christian day of worship. The church derives its name from its emphasis on those beliefs: the Sabbath being the seventh day of creation described in the Old Testament Book of Genesis, and "advent" meaning arrival or coming.

The Seventh-day Adventists trace their roots back to the preaching of William Miller, who prophesied that the millennium (see PREMILLENNIALISM), the thousand-year reign of Christ, would begin in either 1843 or 1844. At the height of the excitement that arose prior to October 22, 1844, the day Miller eventually predicted Christ would appear, over a million Americans counted themselves among the "Millerites." Although the cataclysmic event Miller foretold never occurred and most of his followers subsequently resumed their normal lives, a few remained faithful to his millennial vision. Miller himself, however, died in 1849 and had no part in the later development of the denomination his prophecy spawned.

Ellen Gould WHITE, who was converted to Miller's doctrines in 1842, was the true founder of the Seventh-day Adventists. Along with her husband, James, she helped form the inchoate movement into a denomination. After a vision in which an angel informed her that Christianity's failure to observe Saturday as the Sabbath had delayed the return of Christ, Ellen White convinced other disappointed Millerites to adopt that practice. In 1855, the Whites moved from Rochester, New York to Battle Creek, Michigan, where the new church's headquarters were established. The term "Seventh-day Adventist" was officially accepted in 1860, and by 1863 there were over 100 churches and more than 3,000 members pledged to the denomination's distinctive teachings.

Ellen White's own struggle with illness assured that health reform would become one of the Seventh-day Adventists' central concerns. Advocating vegetarianism as well as the avoidance of alcohol, coffee, and tobacco, White was convinced that rigid dietary and hygienic precepts were central to maintaining a holy life. The elect, she argued, should pay heed not only to their theological doctrines, but also to their diet. The denomination spread throughout the United States in the second half of the 19th century, most quickly in the West, establishing hospitals and schools in many locations. Towns like Loma Linda, California and Battle Creek became settlements where Adventists maintained good health in anticipation of the imminent return of Christ. One of Whites' disciples, John Harvey Kellogg, achieved fame, moreover, by transforming Battle Creek into the breakfast-cereal capital of the United States.

By 1900 the denomination's missionaries had spread across the globe and garnered many converts. So successful were the evangelistic efforts of the Seventh-day Adventists overseas, in fact, that the church founded churches in over 200 other countries. Despite believing that Christ's return is very near, the church has also invested heavily in medical, educational, and publishing ventures both at home and abroad. The expansion of the denomination in the early 20th century brought administrative changes and reorganization that signaled respectability for the church. A new structure was established in which local churches were grouped together into conferences, conferences combined into unions, and unions into a general conference at the national level.

In 1903 the Seventh-day Adventist headquarters moved from Battle Creek to Takoma Park, Maryland, just north of the nation's capital. Although the denomination's fastest expansion at present is overseas, where there are more than seven million members, the church has also continued to grow in size in the United States. Now centered in Silver Spring, Maryland, the Seventh-day Adventist Church reports over 780,000 American members and about 4,200 churches.

GHS, Jr.

Bibliography: Edwin S. Gaustad, ed., *The Rise of Adventism: Religion and Society in Mid-Nineteenth-Century America* (New York: Harper and Row, 1975).

Seventh-day Baptists   See BAPTISTS.

sexuality   The significance attached to human sexuality in American culture has shifted over time. Sex became a problem requiring the sustained attention of religious and medical authority, and the intervention of the state, only in the 19th century. This intervention gave rise to a variety of counter currents, such as the "free love" movements of the late 1800s and the "sexual revolution" of the 1960s. Whether Americans have seen sexuality in a negative or positive light, as sinful or liberating, they have drawn on religious discourse, symbolism, and rituals in order to make it a significant part of their lives.

The Europeans who settled in America during the COLONIAL PERIOD brought with them an understanding of human sexuality shaped by Christianity, classical culture, and European folk beliefs. In the orthodox formulation given by Saint Augustine in Book XIV of *The City of God* (413), sex was a necessary part of human life, and hence intended by God as a part of the natural order of creation. But sex, intended for reproduction, was marred by the presence of lustful passion, concupiscence. Thus Christian tradition, both Catholic and Protestant, came to regard sexual acts ambivalently, as part of the divine order of creation, and as the cause or expression of sin.

During the Colonial period, Protestant Americans viewed sex as a fundamental feature of married life, enabling reproduction as well as providing an outlet for feelings. Colonists assumed marriage itself was the normal state of mature individuals. In situating sex within divinely ordained marriage, early Americans gave it a crucial role in the development of the colonial enterprise: expanding the population base. As a consequence, women bore children throughout much of their lives, contraception rarely being practiced except among the upper classes. In addition colonists emphasized the limits of appropriate sexuality by contrasting their own Christian perspective with what they imagined to be the barbaric sexual practices of Native Americans. Additional limits were emphasized by condemnation of "solitary living" and fornication, unless the couple was engaged to be married. A variety of sexual acts were punishable by death, including adultery, bestiality, and sodomy or "buggery." Records indicate several youths in Massachusetts suffered execution for having sex with animals. Other colonies were less severe.

In the early 19th century Americans began refiguring their sexuality, drawing upon the expansion of medical knowledge during the ENLIGHTENMENT to undergird a wave of social reform. Medical language came to complement or even replace the previously dominant religious language used to speak of sex. However the previous dichotomy between sex as divinely ordained and sex as sin continued in medical form, as Americans associated sex with health and disease. As the society grew more urban, sex became a potential social problem, and medical experts actively prescribed means to curb sexual desire among the unmarried and to counteract the spread of prostitution. For the most part, doctors, particularly those active in the new field of gynecology, continued to view reproductive sexuality as normal, in the process acquiring their own professional status by viewing women as reproductive beings and performing surgeries, such as female castration, in order to reduce the unhealthy, and socially destabilizing, expression of female sexual passion.

Doctors took on important public roles, advocating social policies based on their reproductive view of women, such as the limitation of new means of birth control, and lobbied successfully for antiabortion legislation in 40 states. Another focus of the growing medical interest in sex was deviance. Increasingly doctors came to see acts of sodomy, which earlier Americans had regarded as sinful (and hence which any person might be capable of performing and repenting), as symptomatic of underlying disorders. Thus "homosexuality" and "pervert" became words defining classes of persons.

Religious reformers also adopted the new medical approach to sex. Sylvester Graham (1794–1851) developed theories relating diet to sexuality, which were widely spread by SEVENTH-DAY ADVENTISTS such as Ellen White and dry cereal producer John Kellogg (see WHITE, ELLEN GOULD HARMON). Food products such as the "Graham cracker" or dry cereal were thought to reduce the otherwise uncontrollable sexual drive in children. Advocates of women's rights such as Susan B. Anthony, and even moderate Julia Ward HOWE, fighting in the years after the CIVIL WAR for the abolition of prostitution and an increase in the legal age of consent, had an ambiguous relationship with the medical establishment. Supporting the growing emphasis on education in relation to hygiene, sexuality, motherhood, and prostitution, they resisted physicians' efforts to confine women to the home.

Other groups developed communal visions as alternatives to modernizing American life (see COMMUNITARIANISM). SHAKERS, Oneida Community members, Mormons (see CHURCH OF JESUS CHRIST OF LATTER-DAY SAINTS), and others advocated either celibacy, communal marriage, or what John Humphrey NOYES called "scientific propagation." Marriage itself came under attack by advocates of "free love," led by Frances Wright, an ardent abolitionist and free thinker (see ATHEISM) who argued that love alone ought to be the basis for sexual relations.

In the early 20th century a number of social and technological developments affected the framing of American sexuality. Increasing numbers of single male and female adults, given opportunity for mobility by the expanding industrial economy, found themselves in cities, and possessing leisure time. The automobile provided adolescents with privacy, and Margaret Sanger's widespread advocacy of "birth control" enabled sexual activity outside the family, as well as population control for racial minorities and the lower classes.

By the 1920s Americans had begun to concur with H. L. MENCKEN's evaluation of Puritan (see PURITANISM) ancestors as "prudes," consequently glorying in public expressions of sexuality, as newly developed popular media made a constant theme of sex in song and film. Hollywood continually felt the pressure from religious groups opposed to public sexuality, such as the Catholic-based National League for Decency, founded in 1934 to monitor the moral content of motion pictures, which one leader claimed were "perhaps the greatest menace to faith and morals in America today." Catholics were urged to promise to abide by the league's film ratings.

Increasingly over the decades Americans came to view pleasure as a distinct and more fundamental component of sexuality than reproduction. The "sexual revolution" inspired by the COUNTERCULTURE in the 1960s simply extended the range of circumstances under which pleasure could be sought. The explosion of how-to-do-it books, such as Alex Comfort's *The Joy of Sex* (1972), continued the longstanding American pattern of regarding sex as a problem for which one sought expertise, though now the source might be a popularized tantric mysticism or the Kama Sutra as Americans turned East for inspiration. The focus on sexual pleasure spread to the churches as well. Protestant fundamentalists, as in the popular book *The Total Woman* (1975) by Marabel Morgan, spoke of sexual ecstasy as the hallmark of Christian marriage.

At the same time, sexuality became hotly contested in American life. In the climate of the sexual revolution, both women and homosexuals began to press for greater social rights and the freedom to live fulfilled lives apart from the old norm of marriage. While earlier women's rights advocates had achieved important reforms in terms of political rights or the improvement of child labor conditions, groups such as the Woman's Christian Temperance League (see WILLARD, FRANCES) had not been able to overturn what they often recognized as fundamental sexual inequalities in American life. Feminists in the 1970s took on the task of abolishing "patriarchy," an ideology of male privilege shaping American religious, political, and economic institutions, replacing it with what Mary DALY called "gyn/ecology," a spiritual world view more healthful for women as well as the earth itself (see FEMINIST THEOLOGY).

Homosexuals, compelled to hide their sexual identity in earlier years, adopted the strategies of the CIVIL RIGHTS MOVEMENT after the New York City Stonewall Riot in 1969, acknowledging their sexuality publicly and organizing demonstrations for "gay liberation" and the reform of discriminatory social policies and cultural practices. In addition to pressing for greater acceptance among various denominations, many of which continue to define homosexuality as a sin and prohibit homosexuals from careers in the ministry, homosexuals organized numerous gay churches and synagogues, the largest denomination by the late 1980s being the METROPOLITAN COMMUNITY CHURCH, founded in 1968 by Los Angeles Pentecostals (see PENTECOSTALISM).

In recent years public conflict over sexuality has intensified, most notably in the debate over abortion. As part of a growing reaction to the turmoil of the 1960s (see VIETNAM WAR), a broad-ranging alliance of conservative Protestants, Catholics, and Jews began exerting public pressure on both social policies and cultural currents that they saw destroying the nation's values. Organizations such as the MORAL MAJORITY mobilized previously unpolitical fundamentalist Protestants (see FUNDAMENTALISM). Media "watch-dog" groups began campaigning, as in the 1930s, against Hollywood's exploitation of sexuality in the mass media. But the fight over abortion in the years since the Supreme Court, in *Roe v. Wade* (1973), ruled that women had a constitutional right to abortion has become the most protracted public debate since prohibition (see TEMPERANCE). Originally opponents were primarily Catholics, who traditionally had regarded abortion as murder, but by 1976 a variety of Protestant groups became involved, mobilizing thousands to engage in political action and protest to repeal legalized abortion. The largest organization, the National Right to Life Committee, claims over 3,000 member groups across the country. While abortion often appears to be an issue posed between liberals ("pro-choice") and conservatives ("pro-life"), it has split many political and religious groups down the middle. The conflict has continued to grow in intensity since 1983 when protests at abortion clinics turned violent.

The conflicts over sexuality found throughout American history have left an unsettled legacy. Sexuality remains an important terrain for the exercise of social control, both by religious groups and the state, as can be seen in the nation's response to the AIDS crisis in the 1980s. The changing religious, economic, medical, and personal significance given to sex have significantly altered American family relations. Sexuality will likely remain a source of political, cultural, and religious conflict for some time.

MG

Bibliography: John D'Emilio and Estelle B. Freedman, *Intimate Matters: A History of Sexuality in America* (New York: Harper and Row, 1988); Peter Gardella, *Innocent Ecstasy: How Christianity Gave America an Ethic of Sexual Pleasure* (New York: Oxford University Press, 1985).

Seymour, William Joseph (1870–1922)

One of the first leaders of the Pentecostal movement (see PENTECOSTALISM) in the United States. His storefront church in Los Angeles became the site of the famed AZUSA STREET REVIVAL, the 1906 event that symbolized the emergence of Pentecostalism as a major force in American religion.

Exact biographical information about Seymour is spotty. The son of freed slaves, he was born in Centerville, Louisiana in 1870. He received no formal education and worked for a time as a waiter in Indianapolis, Indiana. In 1900 he moved to Cincinnati, Ohio, where he came under the influence of the HOLINESS MOVEMENT and underwent an experience of sanctification. Serving as an itinerant Holiness evangelist, Seymour settled next in Houston, Texas. There, he attended Charles F. PARHAM's Bible Institute in the fall of 1905 and adopted Parham's beliefs. Seymour became an advocate of Parham's Pentecostal teaching that speaking in tongues was definitive evidence that a believer had received baptism in the Holy Spirit.

In January 1906 Seymour accepted an invitation to an African-American Holiness mission in Los Angeles. In April 1906 and for another three years thereafter, thousands flocked to a rundown building on Azusa Street and were gripped by religious enthusiasm. At a time when few white Americans worshiped at churches led by black ministers, Seymour's revival was remarkable for its interracial makeup. Services were characterized by prayer and singing, speaking in tongues, and healing of the sick. As one participant wrote about her remarkable experiences during the revival, "the power of God fell and I was baptized in the Holy Ghost and fire. . . . I sang under the power of the Spirit in many languages." Seymour's early ministry at the Azusa Street mission is now generally believed to have sparked the growth of the Pentecostal movement in the early 20th century.

The revival began to wane after 1909, and Seymour's influence over Pentecostalism likewise declined. White worshipers gradually ceased coming to Azusa Street, and the church soon became exclusively black. Seymour, however, continued to conduct regular services at the mission until his death in 1922.

GHS, Jr.

Bibliography: Randall K. Burkett and Richard Newman, eds., *Black Apostles: Afro-American Clergy Confront the Twentieth Century* (Boston: G. K. Hall, 1978).

Shakers

One of the most enduring organizations to arise out of the apocalyptic fervor that accompanied the American Revolution, the United Society of Believers in Christ's Second Appearing, or Shakers, are a celibate religious order best known today for their manufacture of furniture and the austere architectural style of their villages. Although by the early 1990s they numbered only a handful of followers in a colony in Sabbathday Lake, Maine, at their peak in the early 19th century the movement consisted of some 19 communities spread over 1,500 miles from Maine to West Union, Indiana, and later as far south as Narcousee, Florida.

The movement had its roots during the 1760s in a small evangelical British sect popularly called the "shaking Quakers," because they were known for expressing their religious enthusiasms through ecstatic visionary experiences and abrupt bodily movements. Beginning in 1770, one member, a young woman named Ann LEE, received a series of revelations that disclosed the source of human sinfulness to be the act of sexual intercourse. She also came to believe that

The Shaker communities founded by Mother Ann Lee have left a strong mark on American art and music. (Library of Congress)

the revelation of this truth ushered in the millennial kingdom on earth, and that human beings could live in God's spiritual realm now if they would abstain from the sin of carnal love. Fleeing persecution and poverty, in 1774 Lee and a small group of her followers migrated from Manchester to Niskeyuna, New York (near Albany), where they practiced celibacy and pacifism within their small colony.

Only after Lee's death in 1784 did the United Society of Believers organize as a community with its base in New Lebanon, New York, and begin to seek converts through missionary efforts. Under the leadership of Joseph Meacham and Lucy Wright, the Shakers prospered, gaining followers from among the many displaced New England migrants moving into western rural settlements after 1790. Like other evangelical groups (see EVANGELICALISM) of the era, including the Methodists, Baptists, and Presbyterians, the Shakers increased their numbers through the many revivals (see REVIVALISM) that "burned over" newly established western territories. By the 1840s, at the height of the movement, between 5,000 and 6,000 adherents lived in Shaker communities. From 1837 to 1847,

Shakers experienced a spiritual revival known as "Mother's Ann's Work," in which believers affirmed that "Mother" Ann Lee had been the second coming of Christ. But after the 1850s community membership began to decline slowly.

While Shakers shared with many other Americans in the early national and antebellum periods the concern to unite religious ideals with perfected social environments, their beliefs and practices were also quite distinctive. Because they believed that the teaching of celibacy and strict separation from the sinful world would allow members to live within God's kingdom in the present, they promoted complete economic independence and lifetime support of all believers. All goods were held in common, and work itself was seen as a form of sacrament. Farming provided the economic base for most of the early communities, but villages later diversified by selling quilts, furniture, and other handicrafts. Because financial security was assured, the movement prospered by taking in orphans and sometimes single mothers who could not sustain themselves independently. These converts, as well as the poor, found the security of life in the villages particularly appealing. But Shaker communities also attracted those who had become disillusioned with the economic and social competitiveness of an increasingly market-oriented culture, and who sought spiritual simplicity in its myriad forms.

The Shakers were also distinctive for their belief in the bipartite nature of God and the strict separation of the sexes that followed from it. God was depicted as both Father and Mother, and Christ had also been revealed as both male and female in the persons of Jesus and Mother Ann. Shakers published numerous tracts, pamphlets, and other literature that explained their theology to the outside world. In turn, communities were organized along gendered lines, with a male and female leader in each community to oversee the welfare of his or her own sex. Men and women slept, ate, and worked apart, and even entered common buildings through separate doorways and staircases, and they united only for the highly ordered worship services characterized by ritualized singing and dancing. Although members remained celibate, they were organized into separate-sex family groupings within the communities.

Given their rejection of procreation as a means of increasing the size of the Society, the Shaker movement has lasted for an extraordinarily long period of time, making it the longest-lived communitarian experiment in American history. Although their numbers steadily decreased after 1850, those remaining held to the original teachings and maintained self-supporting communities as long as possible in a rapidly urbanizing and industrializing society. Many of their villages have since been converted into museums or sold. Along with the Mormon (see CHURCH OF JESUS CHRIST OF LATTER-DAY SAINTS) and CHRISTIAN SCIENCE churches, the Shakers are one of the few indigenous American religious organizations.

LMK

Bibliography: Edward Deming Andrews, *The People Called Shakers* (New York: Oxford University Press, 1953); Stephen J. Stein, *The Shaker Experience in America* (New Haven: Yale University Press, 1992).

Shaku, Soyen   See BUDDHISM; ZEN.

Sheen, Fulton J. (1895–1979)   One of the early masters of religious radio and television, Fulton J. Sheen was born in El Paso, Illinois on May 8, 1895. Although baptized as Peter, he later adopted his mother's maiden name, Fulton, which he used throughout his life. His parents were hard-working Irish-American farmers and merchants who inculcated Sheen with a deep Roman Catholic piety (see ROMAN CATHOLICISM). After graduating from St. Viator College in Bourbonnais, Illinois (B.A. 1917, M.A. 1919), he completed his studies at St. Paul's Seminary in Minnesota and was ordained on September 20, 1919 in the diocese of Peoria. From there he was sent to the Catholic University of America, where he received degrees in both theology and canon law. Further study followed in Europe, first at Louvain (Ph.D. 1923) and then at the Collegio Angelico in Rome (S.T.D. 1924).

Appointed to the faculty of St. Edmund's College in England, the young theologian published his first book (he eventually would publish 60), *God and Intelligence in Modern Philosophy*. This work earned him the Cardinal Mercier Prize in International Philosophy and an appointment as *agrégé* (lecturer) *en philosophie* at Louvain, the first American to receive such an honor. Recalled to a Peoria parish in a test of obedience, Sheen served as a pastor until the end of 1926, when he was allowed to take the chair of apologetics at the Catholic University of America. For nearly a quarter-century he would teach philosophy and theology there. Although widely respected for his intellectual abilities, Sheen would make his most important contributions elsewhere.

In 1930 he began to appear on the "Catholic Hour," a radio program on the NBC network. A commanding presence and a folksy approach to the issues soon made him a media celebrity and his broadcasts reached an estimated audience of over four million. In 1952 he expanded his audience to the new medium of television, with a weekly program called "Life Is Worth Living." This Emmy Award-winning program, which ran for 13 years and had an average audience of 30 million, made Sheen a popular religious figure whose reputation spread beyond Catholic circles. Sheen also wrote two syndicated newspaper columns, "Bishop Sheen Writes" and "God Loves You," both of which had a wide and varied readership.

Sheen's success among the American public was matched by his advancement within the Church. By 1934 he had been made a papal chamberlain and a monsignor. In June 1951 he was consecrated as an auxiliary bishop of New York, a position he held along with that of United States Director of the Society for the Propagation of the Faith until 1966. Responsible for missions in this position, he edited two magazines, *Missions* and *Mission World,* and raised vast amounts of money for mission work. Sheen was helped in this fund-raising not only by his celebrity status, but by his friendship with numerous wealthy and famous people, as well as his role of confidante to celebrated converts, including Clare Boothe Luce and Heywood Hale Broun.

Appointed bishop of Rochester in 1966, Sheen attempted to introduce changes into the diocese. The climate of resistance and hostility was so bad that after three years he resigned, at which time he was honored as titular archbishop of Newport, Wales. The remaining 10 years of his life were spent writing, teaching, and lecturing. He died of heart disease in Manhattan on December 9, 1979 and was buried in the crypt of St. Patrick's Cathedral in New York City.

It is not difficult to identify the reason for Sheen's popularity. He was a dynamic and eloquent speaker who was able to put difficult ideas into a language understandable to all. His anti-Communist and anti-materialist message played well in the 1950s. Equally important was the fact that American culture was becoming increasingly less hostile to religious differences. Sheen's ability to speak as a Catholic to themes important to most Americans—patriotism, faith, and morality—emphasized common values and made it possible for non-Catholics to listen to his programs without necessarily turning to Catholicism. In this regard he resembles no one as much as Billy GRAHAM. While each was a vigorous proponent of his particular brand of Christianity, both projected a message that moved beyond particularity. In Sheen's case, the universal appeal of his message can be seen as a major element in decreasing ANTI-CATHOLICISM and in making Roman Catholicism part of the religious and cultural mainstream in the United States.

EQ

Bibliography: Fulton J. Sheen, *Treasure in Clay: The Autobiography of Fulton J. Sheen* (Garden City: Image Books, 1980).

Sheldon, Charles Monroe (1857–1946)

Author of the novel *In His Steps,* which sold several million copies, Sheldon attempted to articulate the relevance of New Testament ethics to the industrial social order. He used fiction, the most accessible literary vehicle, to popularize the themes of the SOCIAL GOSPEL movement.

Sheldon was born in Wellsville, New York on February 26, 1857. His father, a Congregational minister (see CONGREGATIONALISM), moved the family to South Dakota while Sheldon was quite young. Schooled at home early on, Sheldon went east to college, graduating from Brown University in 1883, and having decided on the ministry, from Andover Newton Seminary in 1886. After serving a small congregation in Waterbury, Vermont for two years, Sheldon returned to the Great Plains, taking a position at the Central Congregational Church in Topeka, Kansas, where he remained from 1889 to 1916.

Sheldon began writing stories to replace Sunday evening sermons early in his ministry, and some were printed in *Advance,* a religious magazine based in Chicago. In one such series of

An influential advocate of the Social Gospel, Charles Monroe Sheldon wrote the 19th-century best-seller *In His Steps.*

stories Sheldon, seeking to attract young people to his church, focused his concern on the many social problems of industrial America's urban centers. Collected together they became *In His Steps* (1897). Sheldon lost control of the copyright and the book was pirated into numerous editions and some 20 foreign translations, selling at least six million copies over the years. By his own overly generous estimate in 1933, sales reached 23 million. But even by the more conservative estimate the book's popularity has been extraordinary. By 1965 its sales among fiction were surpassed only by *Peyton Place,* and in nonfiction by the Bible.

Literary fiction has served the cause of social reform in other eras. The spread of ABOLITION-ISM was due in great part to the influence of *Uncle Tom's Cabin* (see STOWE, HARRIET BEE-CHER). *In His Steps* continued the literary attack on American injustices, as did a number of literary efforts to make popular the reformist zeal of the Social Gospel movement. Books such as *Christ Came to Chicago* by William Stead (1894), *The Silent Partner* by Elizabeth S. Phelps (1871), as well as numerous periodicals and popular hymns such as Washington Gladden's "O Master Let Me Walk with Thee" suggested that New Testament principles, if adopted by well-meaning individuals, would result in profound social transformations. Sheldon's characters, members of a fashionable, middle-class church, are confronted one Sunday by a "shabby-looking young man," who soon dies in the home of the pastor, Henry Maxwell. Stirred by his encounter with poverty, Maxwell resolves to take his religion more seriously, and he challenges his parishioners to do the same. Several characters accept the pastor's challenge to ask themselves "What would Jesus do?" before making any decisions. The novel ends with Maxwell seeing in a vision "the regeneration of Christendom," made possible by the faithful choosing to follow Jesus "all the way, walking obediently in his steps."

Sheldon wrote 30 novels addressing Social Gospel themes, though none of them were nearly as successful as *In His Steps.* After concluding his ministry in Topeka, he served as an editor for the *Christian Herald* until his death in Topeka, February 24, 1946. In later decades his reputation remained strong as he championed causes such as prohibition (see TEMPER-ANCE), pacifism (see PEACE REFORM), and ecumenical cooperation (see ECUMENICAL MOVEMENT). Never adopting the critiques of social structures made by Walter RAUSCHEN-BUSCH's version of the Social Gospel, or in the NEO-ORTHODOXY of Reinhold NIEBUHR, Sheldon continued to advocate the personal appropriation of New Testament values as the surest cure for modern social ailments, in the process giving middle-class Americans assurance that older religious patterns could still make sense of the complexities of their new urban lives.

MG

Bibliography: Wayne Elzey, "What Would Jesus Do?: *In His Steps* and the Moral Codes of the Middle Class," *Soundings* 58 (Winter 1975): 463–89; Charles M. Sheldon, *In His Steps* (Nashville, Tenn.: Broadman Press, 1966).

Sikhism The approximately 250,000 Sikhs in America trace their religious roots back to the 16th-century Hindu reformer and founder of Sikhism, Guru Nanak (1469–?). Guru Nanak was the first in a series of Ten Gurus that culminated with Gobind Singh (?–1708). Sikhs, literally "disciples" of these Ten Gurus, practice a syncretic tradition that borrows from Hindu devotionalism and the Sufi mysticism of Islam.

The *Granth Sahib,* the scripture of the Sikhs compiled by the fifth guru in 1604, enjoins all believers to shun idol worship and to pray to one God, whom Sikhs invoke with the phrase *Wahi Guru* ("Hail Guru"). Known for their military prowess, Sikhs have been particularly ardent advocates, first, of Indian independence and, more recently, for a Sikh state independent from Hindu India. Although Sikh males in India typically distinguish themselves from Hindu men by refusing to shave or to cut their hair, most Sikhs in America do not have beards or long hair.

Drawing on both Hindu and Islamic traditions, Sikhism was brought to the New World in the 20th century by Indian devotees. A *gundwara* (temple) in Atlanta, Georgia. (Pluralism Project of Harvard University)

Though HINDUISM has had a greater impact than Sikhism among American intellectuals, Sikhs preceded Hindus to the United States. Asian Indian immigrants came to the United States as early as 1820, but they did not arrive in significant numbers until western railroad projects of the late 1890s provided them prospects for employment. Most of this first wave of immigrants came from northern India and most of them were Sikhs. By 1909 they had established the first Sikh *gurdwara* or temple in America in Stockton, California. A second temple followed in El Centro, California in 1948. In addition to these temples, American Sikhs established cultural organizations such as the Pacific Coast Khalsa Diwan Society and the India American Cultural Center.

Between the passage by the United States Congress of the Asian Exclusion Act of 1917 and its repeal in 1965, few Asian Indians came to the United States. In the late 1960s, however, a second and much larger immigration wave commenced, carrying hundreds of thousands of Indian immigrants, many of them Sikhs, to cities across the United States.

Unlike Hinduism, which has made some inroads among Caucasian Americans, Sikhism in the United States is almost entirely a religion of Indian-Americans. Sikhs now maintain temples in New York, Washington, D.C., Chicago, Houston, and a number of California locations. The largest of these institutions, located in Yuba City, California, is also the biggest Sikh temple in the world. Many United States Sikh temples are organized under an umbrella organization, the Sikh Council of North America.

Like other religious traditions from India, Sikhism has spawned gurus and movements in the West that combine its beliefs and practices with elements of other faiths. One of the most influential Sikh-influenced gurus is Yogi Bhajan, who came to the United States in 1968 and established the Los Angeles-based Healthy, Happy, Holy Organization (3HO). Yogi Bhajan mixes traditional Sikh practices such as ritual bathing with kundalini yoga.

The most numerous Sikh-influenced movement in the United States is the Radhasoami Satsang. This movement was established in 1861 in Agra, India by an Indian banker, Seth Shiv Dayal Singh (1818–1878). Like members of 3HO, Radhasoamis preach a mixture of Hindu and Sikh practices. Their movement has attracted Christians and Muslims as well as Sikhs and Hindus. Radhasoamis represent God as a mystical union of Radha (the consort of the Hindu God Krishna and a symbol of the perfect devotee's soul) and Soami (the "master" and creator). They distinguish themselves from more orthodox Sikhs by revering living masters as well as the Sikh's founding Ten Gurus. Radhasoamis practice two spiritual disciplines: devotion to the guru and meditation on divine sounds audible only to the concentrated mind.

After the death of its founder in 1878, the Radhasoami movement split into numerous branches. One branch originated in 1891 when Jaimal Singh (1839–1903) founded a Radhasoami Satsang at Beas in Amritsar, India. This group made its way to America in 1910.

Like most Indian gurus, Jaimal Singh was largely uninterested in recruiting and instructing non-Indian students, so the Radhasoami Satsang, Beas failed to gather any significant American following. After Jaimal Singh's death, however, Kirpal Singh (1894–1974) took the movement to the West under the banner of his own organization, the Delhi-based Ruhani Satsang (established 1951).

Kirpal Singh wrote books in English and recruited western disciples while in India. In 1955 and 1963, he toured America, lecturing and gathering disciples. The Ruhani Satsang responded to Kirpal Singh's death in 1974 by splintering into three groups: the Sawan Kirpal Mission, the Kirpal Light Satsang, and the Sant Bani Ashram. These organizations are based in Virginia, New York, and New Hampshire, respectively.

Together with more orthodox practitioners in America's Sikh temples and more syncretistic devotees of Sikh-influenced gurus, these Radhasoami members keep alive the Sikh tradition in the United States.

SRP

Bibliography: Yogi Bhajan, *The Teaching of Yogi Bhajan: The Power of the Spoken Word* (New York: Hawthorn Books, 1977); W. H. McLeod, *The Sikhs: History, Religion and Society* (New York: Columbia University Press, 1989); Kirpal Singh, *The Godman* (Delhi, India: Ruhani Satsang Sawan Ashram, 1967).

Simpson, Albert Benjamin   See HOLINESS MOVEMENT.

slavery   The nature of New World slavery was such that it caused immense problems for religion. Perpetual servitude for oneself and one's descendants without the hope that religious conversion would end enslavement was forbidden in Judaism and generally considered to be so in Islam. Many also believed that it was equally incompatible with Christianity. Slavery challenged religion in other ways as well. Not only did the process of capture, transportation, and enslavement in a faraway land wreak havoc with the Africans' traditional religious beliefs and practices, the religion of slaveowners was challenged also. Did the slavemaster have a duty to provide religious instruction to his slaves? Although most religious leaders answered yes, many slaveowners were hesitant, fearing that English law forbade enslaving Christians and that Christianity somehow ruined slaves.

Most religious leaders countered the opposition to Christianizing enslaved persons by pointing out that the Bible itself sanctioned slavery and that the Apostle Paul explicitly tells servants to obey their masters. Christianity, they argued, would improve slaves, causing them to do willingly what they previously had done only under coercion.

This was the message of the SOCIETY FOR THE PROPAGATION OF THE GOSPEL IN FOREIGN PARTS (SPG). Founded in England in 1701 to spread the gospel among the heathen, the SPG was the first organization to attempt systematic proselytization among the slaves in British North America. The SPG met with little success. The long process of Anglican catechizing, too few priests, and the indifference, if not suspicion, of both planters and slaves hindered the mission. Hostility from African-born slaves was so great that the SPG increasingly ignored them and expended its efforts on their American-born children. Finally, the opposition of the Anglican elite to the AMERICAN REVOLUTION ended any possibility that it could maintain a favored status. The Anglican Church would be replaced by denominations more in keeping with the democratic ethos of the new nation.

Methodists and Baptists achieved the earliest successes in evangelizing the slaves. Both opposed slavery in their early years, and preached a gospel of equality before God that seemed to challenge the accepted social order in the southern colonies. Like the Quakers (see FRIENDS, THE RELIGIOUS SOCIETY OF), the most outspoken of predominantly white religious groups in opposing slavery, Methodists and Baptists did not see religious power and authority as linked to political and social prestige. They early recognized the conflict between their message of religious equality and slavery. Their opposition to slavery, however, led most slaveowners to forbid them access to their slaves, thereby placing the denominations in a quandry. Should they maintain their opposition to slavery and thus endanger the souls of slaves who would never hear the gospel, or weaken their opposition to slavery to achieve that greater purpose? The majority of Baptists and Methodists, in the South at least, chose the latter. They, along with most southern religious groups, removed slavery from the moral to the political realm and continued their evangelism. Slavery ceased to be understood as a moral evil and came to be seen as a positive good, the means by which Africans were brought from heathenism and barbarity to Christianity and civilization.

Such accommodationism was not part of the African-American religious experience under slavery. Because of slavery, blacks read the biblical story differently from whites. While most

The Bible was appealed to by both plantation owners and slaves to justify and condemn the practice of slavery. A plantation preacher. (Billy Graham Center Museum)

whites searched the scriptures for passages that sanctioned slavery, the attention of blacks was drawn to the story of the Exodus of the Israelites from Egypt—from slavery to freedom—and the story of the resurrection. Their God was a God who freed the captives and brought women and men from death to life.

Christianity provided a message of ultimate redemption, both after death and in this life. While some blacks spiritualized this redemption—heaven would provide compensation for unjust suffering in this world—most viewed redemption as occurring both here and in the hereafter. This gave the slaves a distinct understanding of the biblical message embedded in the religious music of African-Americans, "If the Lord delivered Daniel from the lion's den, why not every man?"

For some slaves the Christian message of redemption became a message of apocalyptic deliverance. The blacks themselves were to act as the instruments of God's wrath against the evil of slavery and slaveholders. This explains the critical role religion played in the numerous slave revolts America experienced (see TURNER, NAT; VESEY, DENMARK).

Redemption and judgment also played a role in the religious impetus behind ABOLITIONISM. Rooted in the PERFECTIONISM of the SECOND GREAT AWAKENING, most abolitionists viewed slavery as a moral evil, and preached a radical version of nonaccommodation to it. Civil disobedience and moral suasion were their weapons. Other abolitionists saw slavery as an insult to God that needed to be stamped out by other means. As Frederick Douglass phrased it, "By ballots if possible, by bullets if necessary."

By the time of the Civil War (1861–1865), these visions had merged into one. Originally a war, as President Abraham LINCOLN argued, to "maintain the Union," it soon became a religious crusade against slavery. This was epitomized by Julia Ward HOWE's "Battle Hymn of the Republic," with its line, "As he died to make men holy, let us die to make men free."

The victory of the Union in the Civil War and the ratification of the Thirteenth Amendment to the CONSTITUTION (December 1865) ended slavery in the United States. Solving the problems bequeathed to the nation by slavery was another matter. A century would pass before most of these would be addressed, and even today the legacy of slavery troubles the land.

(See also CIVIL RIGHTS MOVEMENT.)

EQ

Bibliography: Gilbert H. Barnes, *The Antislavery Impulse, 1830–1844* (Gloucester, Mass.: 1933); David B. Davis, *The Problem of Slavery in Western Culture* (Ithaca: Cornell University Press, 1966); Eugene D. Genovese, *Roll Jordan Roll: The World the Slaves Made* (New York: Pantheon, 1974); Donald G. Mathews, *Slavery and Methodism: A Chapter in American Morality, 1780–1845* (Princeton: Princeton University Press, 1965); Benjamin Quarles, *The Black Abolitionists* (New York: Oxford University Press, 1969); Kenneth M. Stampp, *The Peculiar Institution: Slavery in the Antebellum South* (New York: Knopf, 1972); Allen Weinstein and Frank O. Gatell, *American Negro Slavery: A Modern Reader* (New York: Oxford University Press, 1968).

Small, Albion Woodbury (1854–1926)

Selected by William Raney Harper to chair the fledgling University of Chicago's Department of Sociology in 1892, Small was highly regarded in his own day as a leading light in the development of progressive social thought, as well as for his important contribution to the SOCIAL GOSPEL movement's attraction to the methods and claims of social science.

Born to Albion Keith Parris Small, a Baptist minister, and Thankful Lincoln Small in Buckfield, Maine on May 11, 1854, Small came from old Yankee stock. His life reflected the influences of both pre-Darwinian piety and the newer faith in science that spread rapidly in America in the late 19th century (see EVOLUTION; SCIENCE AND RELIGION; SECULARISM). Small graduated from Colby College in Maine and, intending to follow his father into the ministry, entered the Baptist Theological Seminary in Newton, Massachusetts in 1876. Upon graduation, however, Small's love of the new social sciences proved more powerful, and he moved to Germany to study sociology. At the time, German sociology

was dominated by an ethical, social reformist approach, which Small found congenial to his own liberal Protestant (see LIBERALISM, THEOLOGICAL) views. Upon his return he taught at Colby College, and eventually completed his Ph.D. at Johns Hopkins in 1889. After returning to Colby as its new president, Small came to the attention of William Raney Harper, who was using money from John D. Rockefeller to provide the new University of Chicago with an already distinguished faculty. Small remained at Chicago from 1892 until his death on March 24, 1926.

Small, like many academics of his day, saw the university as an institution with almost unlimited potential to bring about social reform. He took an active role in many civic organizations, and participated in numerous conferences held by Social Gospel leaders. While convinced that social science was at bottom an ethical endeavor, he distanced himself from contemporaries who spoke of sociology as specifically Christian work, as well as from what he saw as the utopianism of socialist radicals. Small looked to sociology to provide society with a rational basis for change, replacing competition with cooperation, individualism with community. Small sought to develop a systematic account of a rational society in his major works, *An Introduction to the Science of Society* (1894), *The Meaning of Social Science* (1910), and *The Origins of Sociology* (1924), as well as in a poorly selling novel, *Between the Eras* (1913), which attacked the moral premises of capitalism.

While he supported the reform efforts of the clergy, he saw his own role as providing an objective, empirical analysis for use in the formation of social policy, rather than making sociology itself a partisan enterprise. In spite of the ethical commitment that shaped the desire to study society, he thought the social scientist had the duty, and the capability, of remaining out of the political fray. Though never abandoning his own Protestant liberalism, over time he did move beyond his early argument that "the tendency in sociology must be toward an approxi-

626   Smith, Hannah Whitall

mation of the ideal of social life contained in the Gospels." He replaced the belief that Christianity provided a blueprint for a modern industrial society's social values with the assumption that a university-based social science would discover and articulate the values most capable of overcoming the conflicts of economic and political interest rocking American life.

He saw both religion and science contributing to the task of reform, but at different levels, since they were fundamentally different activities. The wellsprings of religion lay in the "affections" of the heart, while science was more public and self-critical. The university's task was to discover ultimate standards of value, religion's was to "impress the importance and authority of that ultimate standard," as he put it in an address to Phi Beta Kappa members in 1906. Thus, his commitment to the Protestant Social Gospel may have been overshadowed by his influence as a teacher supporting the growing secularism of American public culture in the 20th century.

MG

Bibliography: George Christakes, *Albion W. Small* (Boston: Twayne, 1978); Vernon K. Dibble, *The Legacy of Albion Small* (Chicago: University of Chicago, 1975).

Smith, Hannah Whitall   See HIGHER CHRISTIAN LIFE MOVEMENT.

Smith, Joseph, Jr. (1805–1844)   The translator of the BOOK OF MORMON and the founder of the CHURCH OF JESUS CHRIST OF LATTER-DAY SAINTS, Joseph Smith, Jr. was the inspiration behind America's most controversial and influential new religion. Mormons, as members of the LDS Church are popularly known, remember Smith, in light of a mixture of Hebrew Bible and New Testament models, as both seer and prophet, president and military commander, church elder and high priest, founder and apostle.

Smith was born the fourth of nine children to a farming family of modest means in Sharon, Vermont on December 23, 1805. His mother,

Joseph Smith, Jr., founder of the Church of Jesus Christ of Latter-day Saints, the most successful religion originating in America.

Lucy Mack Smith, and his father, Joseph Smith, Sr., moved their family many times before settling near Palmyra in western New York in 1816. Smith reached maturity, therefore, in an area of religious ferment frequently referred to as the BURNED-OVER DISTRICT. In Palmyra, Smith's mother joined the Presbyterian Church. But his father remained an unaffiliated "seeker," searching for religious truth in a variety of Protestant denominations even as he refused to pledge his fidelity to any of them. The problem of religious PLURALISM was, therefore, a live issue in the Smith household. This problem was only compounded, moreover, by the broader religious climate in which spiritual options as diverse as SPIRITUALISM, SWEDENBORGIANISM, Shakerism (see SHAKERS), UNIVERSALISM, FREEMASONRY,

REVIVALISM, and Christian PRIMITIVISM and Restorationism (see RESTORATION MOVEMENT) flourished. Also prospering among the area's adventurers were practices associated with magic and the occult. Smith took in many of these influences. He was troubled as a youth about which of the religious options that whirled around him was true, which could provide him eternal salvation.

Smith began to turn in the direction of the religious tradition that would become Mormonism while he was still a teenager. Starting in 1820, when he was only 14 years old, he had a series of visions that resolved his uncertainties into faith. In his famous "First Vision" of 1820, Smith reportedly encountered a "Father" and a "Son." He asked them whether he was saved and which of the Christian denominations he should join. Smith was offered assurance of his own salvation, but on the denominational question he was informed, as Smith later wrote, that "I must join none of them, for they were all wrong." In subsequent visions, Smith reportedly conversed with John the Baptist, who initiated him into the "lesser" priesthood of the Hebrew patriarch Aaron. Peter, James, and John appeared subsequently to confer on Smith the "higher" Old Testament priesthood of Melchizedek. In this way he received the authority to restore not only the primitive church but also ancient Israel.

In addition to Christian apostles and Hebraic patriarchs, a series of angels also reportedly appeared to Smith. In 1823, an angel named Moroni came to Smith, informing him of gold plates buried in Manchester, New York in the Hill Cumorah. These plates were inscribed in hieroglyphics, but were accompanied by two stones ("Urim" and "Thummim") that would enable their interpretation. Smith took possession of the plates and began translating them in 1827. The *Book of Mormon,* as Smith's translation was titled, narrated the adventures of ancient Israelites in the New World in the context of a post-Calvinist theology that rejected Reformed verities such as irresistible grace and original sin in favor of more liberal views of God and human nature. This new revelation first appeared when Smith was only 24 years old, in March of 1830. That same year in Fayette, New York, Smith founded "The Church of Jesus Christ," which, following Smith's insistence that true Christian saints were living in the last days before the return of Jesus Christ, would later be renamed the Church of Jesus Christ of Latter-day Saints.

Unlike many other founders of new religious traditions, Smith was not required to leave his family behind in order to pursue his spiritual calling. In fact, Smith's parents and siblings were among his earliest and his most important converts. Smith's father was ordained the first "patriarch" of the LDS church in 1833; his mother eventually produced a controversial but nonetheless influential study of her beloved son entitled *Biographical Sketches of Joseph Smith, the Prophet, and His Progenitors for Many Generations* (1853); and Emma Hale Smith, who became, in January of 1827, the first of his many wives, also was an influential Mormon.

Immediately after the publication of the *Book of Mormon* and the founding of his church, Smith received a number of revelations that together transformed Mormonism from a reform movement within Christianity to an entirely new religious movement. These revelations were collected and published, first, as *The Book of Commandments* (1833) and, later in an expanded form, as *Doctrine and Covenants* (1835). These books, along with a later compilation of Smith's revelations and translations entitled *The Pearl of Great Price* (1851), are now regarded by Mormons as divinely inspired scripture. In these texts, Smith preached distinctive doctrines (the corporeality of god, the "eternal progression" of humans toward divinity, the ongoing nature of revelation, etc.) and practices (baptism of the dead by proxy, polygamy, marriage for eternity, etc.) that distinguished Mormonism from other religious movements.

Under Smith's direction, the Mormon movement soon began to look not only like an attempt to restore the apostolic church but also like an effort to restore ancient Israel. In 1830 and 1831 Smith introduced the idea of "gathering" the Mormon community into one place and put that idea into practice by moving with his followers to Kirtland, Ohio. Later Smith would join his fellow Mormons in migrating from Kirtland to locations in Missouri and then, in 1839, to Nauvoo, Illinois. Smith's successor, Brigham YOUNG, would follow his mentor's example by transplanting the LDS church to the basin of the Great Salt Lake in 1848. At Kirtland, however, Smith persisted in injecting Hebraic models into Mormon life by orchestrating the building not of a church but of a temple. Smith's intermingling of Jewish and Christian themes into Mormonism was especially evident during the ceremonies marking the opening of the Kirtland Temple in 1836. In an event that paralleled the transfiguration described in the Gospel of Matthew, Smith and his important early associate Oliver Cowdery saw not only Jesus but also Moses and other Jewish patriarchs. And though they described the Kirtland temple as a reconstruction of the temple of Solomon built by the Jews, they incorporated into their dedication the early Christian ritual of foot-washing.

Although Smith's combination of Christian and Jewish beliefs and practices with Burned-Over District concerns attracted Mormon converts, it also precipitated anti-Mormon hostility. Smith was tarred and feathered in Hiram, Ohio in 1832 and arrested and jailed on subsequent occasions. But he seemed to devote as much energy to flaming anti-Mormon sentiments as he did to escaping from religious persecution. Perhaps because of his awareness that the hostility of the "Gentile" world to Mormon beliefs and practices functioned to knit the Mormons into a cohesive community, Smith often went out of his way to supply his opponents with reasons to hate him. Among the actions that brought wrath upon the Mormon church were Smith's institution of the practice of "plural marriage" or polygamy in Nauvoo, Illinois and

his proclamation in 1844 of his candidacy for the presidency of the United States. Smith's most provocative act, however, was probably his order, carried out on June 11, 1844, to destroy the printing press of the *Nauvoo Expositor,* which had published in its first and only issue articles hostile to the LDS church.

Local authorities responded to this provocation by arresting Smith and his brother Hyrum. On June 27, 1844, a mob broke into the jail in Carthage, Illinois where they were being held and lynched both Smith and his brother. Thus Smith was transformed at the age of 38 from prophet to martyr.

After Smith's death a struggle ensued over both the leadership and the direction of the Mormon movement. This battle resulted in the division of Mormonism into its two main divisions: the Church of Jesus Christ of Latter-day Saints (the "Utah Mormons"), which followed Brigham Young and affirmed controversial practices such as polygamy, and the much smaller REORGANIZED CHURCH OF JESUS CHRIST OF LATTER DAY SAINTS (the "Missouri Mormons"), which followed Smith's son, Joseph Smith III, and denounced polygamy.

Smith is remembered today by critics as a charlatan and by followers as a latter-day prophet sent by God. Defenders and debunkers agree, however, that Smith was one of America's premier religious innovators.

SRP

Bibliography: Fawn M. Brodie, *No Man Knows My History: The Life of Joseph Smith, the Mormon Prophet* (1948; New York: Knopf, 1971); Richard L. Bushman, *Joseph Smith and the Beginnings of Mormonism* (Urbana: Illinois University Press, 1984).

Smith, Robert Pearsall   See HIGHER CHRISTIAN LIFE MOVEMENT.

Smyth, Newman (1843–1925)   Newman Smyth was a Congregational minister and one of the most respected modernist (see MODERNISM) theologians of the late 19th century. Known for his insistence that religious teachings could be harmonized with science, Smyth argued that the Bible was thoroughly scientific in its approach to truth. He believed that Christianity could accept the discoveries of science without any fear of undermining its own supernatural authority.

Smyth was born in Brunswick, Maine on June 25, 1843. Following his graduation from Bowdoin College in 1863, he served as an officer in the Union army during the Civil War and saw active service at the close of the conflict. He graduated from Andover Theological Seminary in 1867 and worked for a year as minister of a Congregational church in Providence, Rhode Island. In 1869 Smyth traveled overseas to study theology at the University of Berlin and the University of Halle. After his return to the United States, he worked as pastor, first, at the Congregational church in Bangor, Maine and, later, at the First Presbyterian Church in Quincy, Illinois. Although Smyth was asked to come to Andover Seminary as a professor of theology in 1881, he declined that offer. He always considered himself to be as much a pastor as a theologian and chose instead to become minister of the First Church in New Haven, Connecticut in 1882.

Smyth consistently preached that adaptation to science found warrant both within the nature of religion in general and within the particular history of the Judeo-Christian tradition. As he wrote in his first book, *The Religious Feeling* (1877), "ideas gained primarily through the feeling of absolute dependence are the conditions of all . . . scientific knowledge." Smyth's argument for the scientific foundation of Christianity reached a climax in his next book, *Old Faiths in New Light* (1879), in which he asserted that the biblical authors had taught a form of EVOLUTION.

During his period of study in Germany, Smyth had been profoundly influenced by Isaac August Dorner, whose ideas about the development of Christian doctrines made historical criticism one of the foundations for theological discussion. Dorner believed that religious truth evolved over the centuries and that knowledge

of God was possible through the scientific study of historical records. Later in his career, Smyth's interest in Dorner's teaching about the dynamic processes of history led him to become a spokesman for the emerging ECUMENICAL MOVEMENT. Ecumenism was the subject of his 1908 book *Passing Protestantism and Coming Catholicism*. He believed that cooperation among the existing churches was essential, for Christian orthodoxy could not be circumscribed by any single denomination. Only an ecumenical consensus could reflect the truths about God that every church's creed imperfectly sketched.

Smyth retired in 1908, but he remained active in the affairs of both the First Church and nearby Yale University for the remainder of his life. He died at New Haven on January 6, 1925.

GHS, Jr.

Bibliography: William R. Hutchison, *The Modernist Impulse in American Protestantism* (1976; Durham, N.C.: Duke University Press, 1992); Newman Smyth, *Recollections and Reflections* (New York: Charles Scribner's Sons, 1926).

snake-handling Snake-handling is a religious practice that involves holding and lifting up copperheads, rattlesnakes, and other poisonous serpents as a demonstration that one has received a special blessing by God. It is a form of Christian worship, usually accompanied by loud rhythmic music and dancing, found mainly among members of independent Pentecostal (see PENTECOSTALISM) churches in the Appalachian region of the United States. This practice developed out of a literal reading of a New Testament passage (Mark 16:17–18) in which Jesus commands his disciples to use snakes as a symbol of their faithfulness: "And these signs will accompany those who believe: . . . they will pick up snakes in their hands, and if they drink any deadly thing, it will not hurt them."

The snake-handling movement first appeared in 1913 under the leadership of George W. Hensley, a self-trained preacher in eastern Tennessee who believed he had been baptized in the Holy Spirit and been given special powers by God. When Hensley joined Ambrose Jessup TOMLINSON's Church of God, he introduced snake-handling into that denomination. The practice received Tomlinson's tentative approval in 1917. Although Hensley left the Church of God a few years later, snake-handling quickly became popular in many Pentecostal churches in poor rural areas throughout the South. It was often combined with fire-handling and the drinking of strychnine as a vivid manifestation of God's control over the lives of believers.

Snake-handlers place serpents on top of their heads, wrap them around their necks, and even throw them to other worshipers. Bites, considered to be the result of a person's lack of faith, are surprisingly infrequent, and when they do occur, medical treatment seldom is sought. At least 63 people are known to have died from snakebites suffered during religious services since the beginning of Hensley's movement. Snake-handling today is legally prohibited throughout the South, but the practice continues to draw new members in the most economically depressed parts of the country. Those who participate in these activities trust that, since they are acting in obedience to biblical commandments, God has power to heal them and they will suffer no lasting harm.

GHS, Jr.

Bibliography: Thomas J. Burton, *Serpent-Handling Believers* (Knoxville: University of Tennessee Press, 1993).

Social Gospel

Social Gospel The Social Gospel movement refocused Protestant concerns for social reform away from the arena of the individual soul and toward the structures shaping American society. Reflecting and responding to rapid social and economic changes that were transforming the nation from a rural, agrarian society at the end of the CIVIL WAR to an urban, industrial order by the start of WORLD WAR I, social Christianity arose in the United States during the last several decades of the 19th century and achieved its high point between the turn of the century and 1920.

Though participating in currents of thought common to Europeans at the same time, the Social Gospel (the term that gradually displaced "social Christianity") was a typically American movement—idealistic, practical-minded, action-oriented, and melioristic in approach. Much influenced by the pragmatic spirit, which interpreted and judged ideas by their measurable results, the Social Gospel shifted the emphasis of traditional Protestantism from the imperative to love God to one of loving one's neighbor. In the words of Shailer MATHEWS, it involved "the application of the teaching of Jesus and the total message of the Christian salvation to society, the economic life, and social institutions . . . as well as to individuals."

The effort to apply Christian principles in everyday life was not new, going back at least as far as the apostle Paul. What was innovative during these decades was the emphasis given to social reform and the theological support given to social activism. Intense scrutiny was not directed at social evils of every type; the Social Gospel sought improvement through individual and cooperative action, like ABOLITIONISM earlier, while the more secular progressive movement sought change through political reform.

Faith in the power of information and education to transform people and force them to action was integral to the mindset of social Christianity. Even before 1902 its advocates had been studying social problems, but in that year the muckraking movement was launched with articles on political corruption and business malfeasance beginning to appear in popular periodicals in increased numbers. A decade of muckraking newspaper and magazine articles and books exposing social evils of every type fed into the growing momentum of the Social Gospel movement. Muckrakers touched the social conscience of people with a vocabulary paralleling that of clergy, with a heavy emphasis on terms such as "righteousness," "sin," "greed," "guilt," "corruption," and "conversion."

The Social Gospel's origins date from the 1870s, with the teachings of Solomon Washington GLADDEN, the minister of a large Congregational church in Columbus, Ohio. Urging his parishioners to confront directly the conditions of the urban slum, he preached a social Christianity that applied Christ's teachings to social problems wherever they existed. During the wave of violent strikes that occurred during 1877, he sought to bring resolution to the conflict between business and labor.

Our Country, a best-selling book published in 1885 by Josiah STRONG, another Congregational minister, served as a primary document for Protestant reform in succeeding years. Other pioneering leaders of the movement included George D. Herron, a popular preacher as well as a professor of applied Christianity at Iowa College (later Grinnell); William Dwight Porter Bliss, Congregational minister and sociologist who took the lead in founding the American Fabian Society and who edited the *Encyclopedia of Social Reform* (1897); and Richard T. Ely, a professor of political economy at Johns Hopkins, Wisconsin, and Northwestern and one of the most influential academics of his time. Gladden, Bliss, Ely, and other leading clergy and political economists organized the Society of Christian Socialists in Boston in 1889, but most people who participated in the Social Gospel movement refused to go so far as to identify themselves as socialists.

For the most part, this was a minority movement within Protestantism, although some Catholics and Jews were also involved. Denominations especially involved in its activities included the Congregationalists, Episcopalians, Methodists, and the northern branches of the Baptists. In addition, nondenominational groups such as the YOUNG MEN'S CHRISTIAN ASSOCIATION, the YOUNG WOMEN'S CHRISTIAN ASSOCIATION, and the SALVATION ARMY fed into the energy of the movement.

One of the most popular and influential works produced by the social gospelers was Charles M. SHELDON's *In His Steps* (1897), a book describing the radical transformation that would come to American society if only people would

ask, and base their actions on, the single question: "What would Jesus do?" The Social Gospel's leading theologian and theoretician, however, was Walter RAUSCHENBUSCH, whose social consciousness was raised by his observations of the neighborhood surrounding his Baptist parish in the notorious Hell's Kitchen area of New York City. Later, as professor at Rochester Theological Seminary, he penned the most significant single document of the movement, *Christianity and the Social Crisis* (1907), which became a sort of "Bible" for its members.

In 1908, the Social Gospel took institutional form with the establishment of the Federal Council of Churches (see NATIONAL COUNCIL OF CHURCHES, WORLD COUNCIL OF CHURCHES). During the period before World War I, this organization emerged as a voice for mainstream American Protestantism and began to serve as a liaison between progressive government officials and socially conscious churchpeople. By the 1920s it had lobbyists in Washington exercising influence on public policy. With American entry into World War I, the primary phase of the Social Gospel came to an end. The foundation that it had laid by that time, however, meant that its organizing principles and underlying commitment to social justice would play an increasingly influential role within American Protestantism during succeeding decades, particularly through the National Council of Churches that suceeded the Federal Council of Churches in 1951.

MG

Bibliography: Donald G. Gorrell, *The Age of Social Responsibility: The Social Gospel in the Progressive Era, 1900–1920* (Macon, Ga.: Mercer University Press, 1988); Charles Howard Hopkins, *The Rise of the Social Gospel in American Protestantism, 1865–1915* (New Haven: Yale University Press, 1940); Ronald G. White, Jr. and C. Howard Hopkins, *The Social Gospel: Religion and Reform in Changing America* (Philadelphia: Temple University Press, 1976).

Society for the Propagation of the Gospel in Foreign Parts
Founded in 1701 by

Thomas Bray (1656–1730), the Society for the Propagation of the Gospel in Foreign Parts (SPG) was a missionary organization established to promote and sustain Anglican piety and institutional life (see ANGLICANISM) in the North American colonies, including Canada and the West Indies, in the decades prior to the Revolutionary War. Although the society endured through the end of the 19th century, after the American Revolution its missionary interests moved away from the United States to other areas of British colonial rule.

The SPG originated as part of an aggressive and broad-based effort to expand British colonial control and consolidate power in North America in the late 17th century. One aspect of this push was the effort to bolster the strength of the Church of England as the religious arm of the government. Anglican officials had become increasingly alarmed at the spiritual indifference, tolerance of religious dissent, and institutional disarray evidenced in its American possessions. The church first asserted its authority by designating "commissaries" to several colonies, church officials who could assess and organize the religious needs of the population in lieu of a local bishop. Thomas Bray, appointed commissary of Maryland in 1696, realized that more resources would be necessary in order to establish the Church of England in the colonies. In 1699 he and a gathering of Anglican priests founded the Society for Promoting Christian Knowledge, an organization that founded schools and printed and distributed religious literature. In 1701 the same group established the SPG in order to train and support Anglican missionaries for work overseas.

Several aims guided the work of the SPG in its North American phase. A primary goal was to supply ministers to unchurched Anglicans, those New World subjects who were already loyal to the church. But of equal importance was outreach to Euro-American dissenters, particularly PURITANS, Quakers (see FRIENDS, THE RELIGIOUS SOCIETY OF), and Roman Catholics (see ROMAN CATHOLICISM), whose presence

threatened the authority of the crown. In 1702 George Keith, an ex-Quaker, was sent out to survey the status of colonial churches. Keith conducted a preaching tour from Maine to North Carolina, "preaching and disputing publicly," and devoting particular attention to Quakers. Subsequently, ministers were sent out with a modest sum of money and a parcel of books to locations where the need seemed most pressing. The SPG committed itself to supporting missionaries financially as long as was necessary.

Outreach to Euro-Americans met with mixed success. Because VIRGINIA and MARYLAND were relatively well covered with clergy, work in the South focused intensively on North and South Carolina, and the newly established colony of Georgia, where the young John Wesley served in the 1730s under the SPG. Anglicanism also spread effectively into the mid-Atlantic colonies. By 1750, New York boasted 20 churches, New Jersey 18, Delaware 14, and PENNSYLVANIA 19. In 1754 King George II chartered King's College, an Anglican school in New York that later became Columbia University. New England, a region dominated by Puritan influence throughout the 18th century, resisted Anglican evangelization more unyieldingly, but even there influence was perceptible. A most notable example involved the "Great Defection" of several well-known Puritan divines, including Timothy Cutler, president of Yale College, to the Church of England in 1722. After Cutler's ordination, he returned to America as a missionary for the SPG.

The SPG also aspired to bring the Gospel to the "heathen" inhabitants of North America, particularly American Indians (see NATIVE AMERICAN RELIGIONS) and African-Americans (see AFRICAN-AMERICAN RELIGION). While the mission to Native Americans quickly proved to be unworkable, hampered as it was by a lack of native cooperation and periodic Euro-Indian warfare, slave populations were an easier audience to isolate and organize, and thus Anglican energy shifted to the instruction and baptism of blacks. Ironically, the greatest obstacle to success, in the eyes of many missionaries, was the resistance of slaveowners to having their chattel officially recognized by the church. While some masters were merely indifferent to slave baptism, a significant number protested that bringing African-Americans into the Christian communion would imperil the legitimacy of their enslavement, and take time away from their work. They assumed that baptism, as a public acknowledgement of the slave's spiritual equality, would necessitate manumission, or the freeing of slaves. Evangelization was thus often left to the discretion of individual slaveowners, and consequently missionaries spent a substantial amount of time trying to reassure property owners that slavery and Christianity were compatible institutions. While some African-Americans were baptized, their small numbers were soon dwarfed by the many slaves who joined "New Light" (see NEW LIGHTS/OLD LIGHTS) congregations after the 1730s.

Anglican missionary activity in the New World was disrupted when the colonies declared their independence from Britain. Church of England priests joined the Loyalist exodus, signaling the end of the American phase of SPG activity.

LMK

Bibliography: C. F. Pascoe, *Two Hundred Years of the SPG: An Historical Account of the Society for the Propagation of the Gospel in Foreign Parts, 1701–1900* (London: The Society, 1901); H. P. Thompson, *Into All Lands* (New York: Macmillan, 1951).

Society of Jesus See JESUITS.

Sojourners Fellowship During the late 1960s a group of evangelical Christians from Chicago's Trinity Evangelical Divinity School formed a community, later named Sojourners Fellowship. The fellowship founders—viewing economic and racial justice, and peacemaking, as central Christian vocations—had joined the resistance to the VIETNAM WAR. Pledging loyalty only to the kingdom of God, they named their initial 1971 tabloid the *Post-American*. In the mid-1970s the fellowship relocated to Washington D.C.'s inner city, renaming the magazine *Sojourners*. Within 10 years *Sojourners* had become the most important voice for radical Christian pacifism in North America.

Sojourners' political positions usually parallel those found in the so-called alternative or leftist press. Since liberal Protestantism has also been significantly influenced by religious radicalism such as LIBERATION THEOLOGY, the liberal Protestant press and *Sojourners* often agree about United States foreign and domestic policy. But there are several things that have distinguished *Sojourners* from its liberal Protestant counterparts such as *Christian Century* and *Christianity and Crisis,* which ceased publication in 1993. Among the most important are *Sojourners'* advocacy of pacifism, relative biblical and theological conservatism, and an emphasis on spiritual discernment in the Christian moral life.

Sojourners rejected Reinhold NIEBUHR's Christian Realism and CIVIL RELIGION, the public Protestantism that viewed United States power as an important tool in the pursuit of social justice. *Sojourners* express a comprehensive skepticism about government, reflecting affinity more with Anabaptist distrust of government than with Calvinist hopes for the Christianization of human culture.

Sojourners takes the Bible as the central moral authority. But it rejected Christian fundamentalism's (see FUNDAMENTALISM) assertions about the inerrancy of scripture. The central themes expressed in *Sojourners* and in movement texts such as John Yoder's *The Politics of Jesus* and Jim Wallis's *Agenda for a Biblical People* are: Jesus' life and teachings are the model for Christian life; Jesus resisted the political powers of his day, promoting nonviolently an earthly kingdom of God that required land reform and the redistribution of wealth; early Christians followed Jesus until co-opted when the Roman emperor made Christianity the empire's official religion; Christians should return to the original kingdom mission, living simply, eschewing consumerism, and promoting justice; since the Bible does not illuminate every contemporary moral quandary, Christians must grow spiritually, and thereby cultivate a Christian conscience able to "discern the times" (i.e., perceive that which deviates from the kingdom) and act courageously.

Sojourners has evolved into an ecumenical journal, adding liberal Protestants and radical Catholics to its readership. It has taken positions controversial to many of its readers. Most notably, it has promoted a "consistent life ethic" opposed to abortion, thereby offending many liberal Protestants and Christian feminists who otherwise share *Sojourners'* views.

Sojourners illustrates that evangelical Christianity is not a monolithic, right-wing tradition. It also has played a central role in Christian resistance to United States policies. It has supported war tax resistance, and civil disobedience against nuclear weapons facilities. It has come to the defense of those incarcerated for such actions, including the Plowshares Witnesses, who infiltrated weapons sites, symbolically beating weapons into agricultural implements, sometimes drawing long prison terms.

During the 1980s, the fellowship played a leading role in developing a "Pledge of Resistance," in which thousands promised to resist any escalation of the United States-sponsored insurrection against Nicaragua's leftist regime. Sojourners also spawned "Witness for Peace"—an organization placing volunteers in violence-torn countries to document and deter or at least displace such violence through their presence. Although its impact in the past two decades is difficult to measure, the resistance of *Sojourners* and others to United States military interventions and proxy wars abroad may have prevented even bolder forms of intervention during the COLD WAR era.

(See also CATHOLIC WORKER MOVEMENT; DAY, DOROTHY.)

BRT

Bibliography: Bron Taylor, "Authority in Ethics: a Portrait of the Methodology of Sojourners Fellowship," *Encounter* 46.2 (1985) 139–155.

Soloveitchik, Joseph Dov (1903–1993)

One of the most important Orthodox Jewish theologians of the second half of the 20th century, Joseph Dov Soloveitchik remains largely unknown beyond that community. That a man who was asked to be the chief Ashkenazic rabbi of Israel could be nearly unknown in his own country says much about Orthodox insularity. It also speaks to the absence of attention that American society has paid to ORTHODOX JUDAISM. Soloveitchik exercised such tremendous influence on Orthodox Judaism that he universally was referred to as *Rav*, the rabbi's rabbi.

Born February 27, 1903 in Pruzhan, Poland where his maternal grandfather was chief rabbi, Joseph Dov Soloveitchik grew up in Haslovitz, Belorussia where his father served as rabbi. Tutored privately by his father, after it was discovered that the schoolmaster was instructing him in Hasidic texts (see HASIDISM) rather than the Talmud, Soloveitchik had a purely religious education, although his mother introduced him to modern literature. His education was in the "Brisker" method, called after his paternal grandfather, the "Brisker [Brest-Litovsk] Rav." This method, with its emphasis on incisive analysis, exact definition, precise classification, and critical independence, carried over into Soloveitchik's work at the University of Berlin and in later years.

At Berlin he studied physics, mathematics, and philosophy, receiving his doctorate in 1931. The following year, Soloveitchik and his wife came to the United States, settling in Boston where he was named chief rabbi. In 1941 he succeeded his father as professor of Talmud at Yeshiva University in New York City, commuting regularly from his home in Boston.

In the 1970s he was asked to become the chief Ashkenazic rabbi of Israel, a position he refused. When asked about this refusal he stated that he could not be an officer of the state, claiming that "a rabbinate linked up with the state cannot be completely free." Although favorably disposed toward Israel (he was honorary president of the RELIGIOUS ZIONISTS OF

AMERICA for over four decades), Soloveitchik did not view *aliya* (immigration to Israel) as a religious imperative. He believed Orthodox Judaism could thrive in the United States, and understood exile as part of the essence of the Jewish people.

Given the significance of Soloveitchik's theological and philosophical work, the relative dearth of published works is surprising. Soloveitchik acknowledged this as a family malady, since neither his grandfather nor father published much despite their reputations as scholars. A demand for perfection underlay this failing, and Soloveitchik claimed that he wrote little that seemed sufficiently complete. His public lectures, however, were filled to overflowing and like many Orthodox rabbis he could speak for hours at a time. Often recorded by listeners, his talks circulated widely as either tapes or transcripts.

Two themes dominated Soloveitchik's thought. The first was the question, what does the man of faith have to say "to a functional, utilitarian society?" Drawing from Søren Kierkegaard and Immanuel Kant, Soloveitchik argued that the religious life is fundamentally one of loneliness, not emotionally but factually. The individual comes before God alone, thereby affirming her or his existence as a subject. Only the individual who has ceased to be an object of societal demands and roles can call upon God and respond to the divine commands.

The religious life is a process of developing self-awareness, self-assertion, and self-creativity. This process is made possible through the Halakhah, the religious law that regulates personal, social, and ritual conduct. Only through Halakhah is "the apprehension and fulfillment of God's will" possible. The centrality of Halakhah to Jewish life is the second theme of Soloveitchik's thought. It both creates and defines the communal and religious existence of the Jew. Halakhah serves two fundamental purposes. The first of these is the sacralizing (sanctification) of human life and human existence. Halakhah "enables man to bend the realm of eternity into the temporal universe." The second purpose of Halakhah is to bring humanity into a knowledge of the will of the Creator, to bring the individual to awareness of God. For Soloveitchik, Halakhah was purely objective. It is "an a priori system in need of no validation and not contingent upon human personality or subjectivity."

As chief rabbi of Boston, professor at Yeshiva University, and preeminent authority on Halakhah, Soloveitchik exercised tremendous influence on Orthodox Judaism in America. Although one voice among many, his erudition, learning, and depth made it an audible one. His philosophical defense of religious law as the basis of Orthodox Judaism made him a substantial figure in American and international circles.

Soloveitchik's practical involvement with decisions about Halakhah made his work of particular significance for Orthodox Jews throughout the United States. As the leading arbiter of religious law—of questions involving food, marriage, divorce, and ritual—Soloveitchik's importance extended far beyond that of most philosophers and theologians. Until his death on April 8, 1993, his decisions regarding the application of religious law to specific cases affected the daily lives of many thousands.

EQ

Bibliography: Eugene Borowitz, *A New Jewish Theology in the Making* (Philadelphia: Westminster Press, 1968); Robert G. Goldy, *The Emergence of Jewish Theology in America* (Bloomington: Indiana University Press, 1990); Joseph Soloveitchik, *Reflections of the Rav: Lessons in Jewish Thought* (Hoboken: KTAV, 1972); ———, *The Halakhic Mind: An Essay on Jewish Tradition and Modern Thought* (Ardmore, Pa.: Seth Press, 1986); ———, *The Lonely Man of Faith* (New York: Doubleday, 1992).

South, the The American South, the Confederate states plus Oklahoma and Kentucky, has a distinctive history and religious heritage. With the exception of the state of Utah, no section of the United States is as religiously homogeneous as the American South nor as religiously observant.

Bethany Church, Siloam, Greene County, Georgia, one of the oldest churches in the county. (Library of Congress)

Neither of those two realities marked the early period of settlement (see COLONIAL PERIOD). Most southern colonies originally had the Church of England (see ANGLICANISM; EPISCOPAL CHURCH) as their religious establishment. This was a nominal establishment at best, and became increasingly weak during the 1700s with the growing secularization of the elite class that dominated the Anglican Church. Influenced by the ENLIGHTENMENT and the cultural milieu of the times, this class was often deistic in outlook.

The other major source of southern religion was the increasing immigration into the back country primarily by Presbyterian or unchurched Scots-Irish. Later these immigrants would be reached by Baptist and Methodist preachers. The Anglican Church was weakened further by its opposition to the AMERICAN REVOLUTION while the Presbyterians and Baptists were aided by their support of it.

The religious movement that dramatically transformed southern religion was the SECOND GREAT AWAKENING, known in the South as the Great Revival. The emotionalism, egalitarianism, and experientialism that marked the REVIVALISM of the Awakening indelibly marked the region. In the South religion is characterized by low-church Protestantism, those denominations that are nonsacramental and nonconfessional. BAPTISTS, METHODISTS, Presbyterians (see PRESBYTERIANISM), and DISCIPLES OF CHRIST predominate. These churches, emphasizing the importance of an individual conversion experience, personal morality, and the equality of all believers, constitute an overwhelming majority of church members in the American South. Their dominance is so profound that other denominations deviate from traditional observances to place themselves more in line with these emphases.

While religion in the South has been theologically conservative, FUNDAMENTALISM has not dominated the region. Although some southerners were important fundamentalists, notably J. Frank Norris (1877–1952) and Bob Jones (1883–1968), fundamentalism's impact has been limited. The experientialism of southern religion has argued against an emphasis on doctrine, and the region's predominant denomination—the SOUTHERN BAPTIST CONVENTION—historically has de-emphasized doctrinal rigidity in favor of evangelism and denominational unity.

This low-church Protestantism has deeply affected the cultural milieu. Codes of personal behavior formulated by those denominations, especially the Baptists and Methodists, have become normative for the society as a whole. While not necessarily defining how people actually behave, they do define the norms from which people deviate. Protestantism in particular and religion in general dominate the culture. The level of religious knowledge in the South is surprisingly high and for many people the church remains the centerpiece of the social life.

The other inescapable fact of southern religion is that it is a bi-racial phenomenon, just as the region is a bi-racial culture. Despite racism, hostility, and violence, blacks and whites in the

South have been linked throughout history. SLAVERY and the large black population have defined southern religion as well as southern culture.

This is true on several levels. Slavery brought about the most determinative event of southern history—the CIVIL WAR. The sectional tensions that divided the nation also divided religion. Baptists, Methodists, Presbyterians, and Episcopalians split into northern and southern denominations. The Episcopal Church reunited shortly after the war, the Methodists not until 1939, and the Presbyterians in 1983. The Baptists never reunited, and the identification of the Southern Baptist Convention with the South and its ethos became increasingly strong.

Churches in the South provided the white population with a source of solace and refuge following the South's defeat in the war. Many white southerners were convinced that they had been defeated not because they were wrong, but because God desired that a region of pure religion remain in the country in order to convert it. The white churches served as a bastion of southern nationalism, albeit translated into the spiritual realm. Southern religion was a creature of southern society and history, but southern society was equally a creature of southern religion (see LOST CAUSE MYTH).

This was not all that the churches did, however. Despite religion's captivity by the culture, religion and the region were haunted by its sins. Guilt in southern religion is palpable. Not only is this guilt spiritual and moral, but much of it has been attributed to the South's failure to deal justly with its black population.

For the wronged blacks, religion provided solace of another sort. Black religion in the South is as rooted in the same low-church Protestantism as that of southern whites. Evangelized primarily by Methodists and Baptists during the first half of the 1800s, blacks quickly adapted the Christian message to the situation of slavery, despite white oversight.

Following the Civil War and emancipation, blacks left the white churches to form their own black-led denominations (see AFRICAN-AMERICAN RELIGION). These churches, primarily Baptist and Methodist, provided the black community with a gathering-place free of white control and oversight. As a source of independent black thought and activity, they supplied the black community with leadership and organizational centers, best exemplified by the role of the black church in the CIVIL RIGHTS MOVEMENT, itself a product of southern black religion.

Beyond the general rule of religious homogeneity, the American South also shares in the American history of diversity. ROMAN CATHOLICISM played, and plays, a major role in Louisiana (see NEW FRANCE), Texas, and southern Florida (see NEW SPAIN). JUDAISM arrived early in the region. Charleston, South Carolina has one of the nation's oldest Jewish congregations, and the nation's first Reform congregation (see REFORM JUDAISM). Other religious groups have maintained a separate identity over the years while integrating culturally into the region. Examples of these are MORAVIANS and Quakers (see FRIENDS, THE RELIGIOUS SOCIETY OF) in North Carolina, and German Lutherans (see LUTHERANISM) in central Texas.

The South is also home to several distinctive forms of American religion. These include the small Baptist groups of Appalachia—Primitive, Old Regular, Union, Missionary, and Free Will Baptists. Although differing in doctrine, these small denominations share many characteristics, including an emphasis on foot-washing as an ordinance of the church and a distinctive fast-paced preaching style. The snake-handlers (see SNAKE-HANDLING) are another unique element of Appalachian religion. Rooted in PENTECOSTALISM, church members take literally the scriptural statement that those "who believe . . . will pick up serpents; and if they drink any deadly thing, it will not hurt them." (Mark 16:17–18). Although snakebites are infrequent, they have been sufficient in number that several states have outlawed the practice.

Despite the centralizing tendencies of television, franchises, and interstate highways, the South continues to remain a separate and identifiable region. Religion plays a continuing and important role in this distinctiveness. The relationship between southern society and southern religion creates a religious environment unique in the 20th-century United States.

(See also CAROLINAS [COLONY]; COMMITTEE OF SOUTHERN CHURCHMEN; EVANGELICALISM; PROSLAVERY THOUGHT; VIRGINIA [COLONY]).

EQ

Bibliography: Kenneth K. Bailey, *Southern White Protestantism in the Twentieth Century* (New York: Harper & Row, 1964); Karen W. Carden and Robert W. Pelton, *The Persecuted Prophets* (South Brunswick, N.J.: A. S. Barnes, 1976); Samuel S. Hill, ed., *Religion in the Southern States: A Historical Study* (Macon, Ga.: Mercer University Press, 1983); ———, *The South and North in American Religion* (Athens: University of Georgia Press, 1980); C. Eric Lincoln and Lawrence H. Mamiya, *The Black Church in the African American Experience* (Durham, N.C.: Duke University Press, 1990); Donald G. Mathews, *Religion in the Old South* (Chicago: University of Chicago Press, 1977); Albert J. Raboteau, *Slave Religion: The "Invisible Institution" in the Antebellum South* (New York: Oxford University Press, 1978).

Southern Baptist Convention

The Southern Baptist Convention was organized in Augusta, Georgia on May 8, 1845 when BAPTISTS in the North and South split over the issue of slavery. Since that time it has grown to become the largest Protestant denomination in the United States. Numbering close to 16 million members in 1993 with churches in every state of the union, the denomination retains its identification with and has its greatest strength in the South (see SOUTH, THE), where it is the largest denomination in every state except Louisiana.

The Convention has retained the classical Baptist commitment to the individual congregation as the only form and type of the true church and technically has no control over the activities of individual congregations. The Convention itself, which technically exists only during its annual meeting every year, was formed to function as a center for evangelization, i.e., the conversion of people to Christianity. Evangelism has been at the forefront of the denomination's life and to a great extent has been the source of its unity and identity.

During the latter part of the 19th century, Southern Baptists—and the South as a whole—slowly recovered from the destruction of the CIVIL WAR and worked to construct the institutions necessary to support their work. These included a seminary—Southern Baptist Theological Seminary (now located in Louisville, Kentucky), organized in 1859 but not in operation until after the war—the Women's Missionary Union (1888), and the Sunday School Board (1891). Even greater growth took place between 1900 and WORLD WAR II with the establishment of three more seminaries (Southeastern Baptist Seminary, Wake Forest, N.C.; New Orleans Baptist Seminary, New Orleans; Southwestern Baptist Seminary, Dallas, Texas) and several boards and commissions with responsibility for home and foreign missions (See MISSIONS, HOME; MISSIONS, FOREIGN), social and political issues, as well as denominational history. All of this work remained centered in the southern states, and the Convention, headquartered in Nashville, Tennessee, was understood and understood itself as a southern denomination.

Following World War II, however, the denomination began to expand throughout the country and by the mid-1970s had churches in every state in the union, even organizing a seminary to serve the Midwest, Midwestern Baptist Seminary, Kansas City, Missouri, in the 1950s. The denomination also became increasingly swept up in the social and political turmoil in the 1960s and 1970s, despite its struggle to focus primarily on the task of evangelism. To a great extent the denomination was successful in doing the latter and experienced phenomenal growth in the 20th century from 1.7 million members in 1900 to 7.1 million in 1950, to nearly 16 million by 1990.

These changes were not without consequences. The expansion of the denomination and its increasing engagement with the wider world brought a heightened awareness of the diversity within the denomination. There were some who felt that this theological diversity meant the denominational bureaucracy and the seminaries were harboring theological liberals (see LIBERALISM, THEOLOGICAL) and were failing to accommodate the concerns and desires of the more conservative and fundamentalist members (see FUNDAMENTALISM).

The result was a concerted effort by Fundamentalists to take control of the Convention and of its operations. Begun in 1976 and led by Paul Pressler and Paige Patterson, this movement desired to make biblical INERRANCY and political conservatism hallmarks of the denomination. They achieved their first success in 1979 with the election of a Convention president committed to their theological and political positions. Through the 1980s and into the 1990s, with the support of 52 to 55 percent of those voting at the Convention's annual meeting, the fundamentalists managed to gain control of the boards of the Convention's operating agencies and its seminaries.

The results were mass resignations at Southeastern Baptist Seminary and numerous resignations from Southern Baptist Seminary, the denomination's flagship school. Those opposed to the fundamentalists formed two organizations—the Southern Baptist Alliance and the Association of Southern Baptists—to act as counterweights to the fundamentalist-controlled Convention. Two seminaries separate from those controlled by the Convention also were organized. These conflicts and tensions severely affected morale throughout the denomination and the number of new members added each year began to decline.

Although the Convention has faced numerous crises in its existence, this one has been the longest-lasting and remains unresolved. Whether the denomination can regain the theological center that controlled it for so long is questionable. As it approaches the end of the 20th century, the Southern Baptist Convention faces the need to address significant changes in its identity and the possibility of a major division. Although the fundamentalists retain control of the denomination, the final implications remain unknown.

EQ

Bibliography: Nancy Tatom Ammerman, *Baptist Battles: Social Change and Religious Conflict in the Southern Baptist Convention* (New Brunswick, N.J.: Rutgers University Press, 1990); William Wright Barnes, *The Southern Baptist Convention, 1845–1953* (Nashville: Broadman Press, 1954); John Lee Eighmy, *Churches in Cultural Captivity: A History of the Social Attitudes of Southern Baptists* (Knoxville: University of Tennessee Press, 1972); Bill J. Leonard, *God's Last & Only Hope: The Fragmentation of the Southern Baptist Convention* (Grand Rapids: Eerdmans, 1990); Edward L. Queen II, *In the South Baptists Are the Center of Gravity: Southern Baptists and Social Change, 1930–1980* (Brooklyn: Carlson Publishing, 1991).

Southern Christian Leadership Conference (SCLC)

Based on the work of the Montgomery Improvement Association (see CIVIL RIGHTS MOVEMENT), an organization created to lead the bus boycott against the city's segregated buses, the Southern Christian Leadership Conference was organized in January 1957. Sixty black ministers attending the Negro Leaders Conference on Nonviolent Integration at the Ebenezer Baptist Church in Atlanta voted to create a South-wide organization designed to further the cause of nonviolent approaches to overcoming segregation. After several name changes, this organization eventually became the Southern Christian Leadership Conference.

The weekend of its birth was to be representative of its life, for during the conference the black community of Montgomery, Alabama was racked by bombings. These racist attacks hit hardest at the backbone of the SCLC, the churches. The SCLC was, and has remained, a movement rooted in the black church. Calling upon African-Americans to "assert their human dignity by refusing further cooperation with evil," the SCLC urged a process of nonviolent, direct resistance to segregation.

Under the leadership of Martin Luther KING, JR., the SCLC gained the attention of the black community, many white Americans, and the world. Although it suffered several setbacks, notably in Albany, Georgia (1962) and Chicago, Illinois (1966), the SCLC achieved tremendous success in such segregated bastions as Birmingham (1963) and Selma, Alabama (1965). The sight of African-American men, women, and children responding not violently, but prayerfully, to police dog attacks, fire hoses, and beatings aroused the conscience of the nation. The SCLC's demonstrations paved the way for the passage of the Civil Rights Act of 1964 and the Voting Rights Act of 1965.

King's assassination in April 1968 was a tremendous blow to the SCLC. Although King's successor, Ralph David ABERNATHY, a colleague of King since the Montgomery Improvement Association days, attempted to continue the movement, many forces worked against it. A long-planned Poor People's March on Washington in 1968 sank into a sea of poor planning, internal conflicts, indifference, and poor weather. The SCLC faced growing challenges to its philosophy of nonviolence and nonracialism. The Black Power movement and the growing rhetoric of violence would soon replace the SCLC's emphases on nonviolence and brotherhood.

Chastened and smaller, the SCLC continued to press for greater gains for blacks, primarily in the South, where it was strongest. Under the leadership of both Abernathy and his successor, Joseph Lowery, the SCLC has worked to expand its scope. Concern about the black family led it to institute in 1980 the Martin Luther King, Jr. Memorial Weekend, an annual conference designed to strengthen black family life. The SCLC also has developed King's interest in foreign affairs and is quite outspoken on issues involving Africa and the Middle East.

These concerns have not overshadowed its work for black political rights. When the Voting Rights Act of 1965 was up for renewal in 1982, the SCLC led a reenactment of the 1965 march from Selma to Montgomery that had been instrumental in the act's original passage. The political activities of the SCLC, along with its interest in black economic development, have kept it in the forefront of the struggle for "Jobs, Freedom, and Justice" that was its hallmark from the beginning.

EQ

Bibliography: Taylor Branch, *Parting the Waters: America in the King Years, 1954–1963* (New York: Simon & Schuster, 1988); David Garrow, *Bearing the Cross: Martin Luther King, Jr. and the Southern Christian Leadership Conference, 1955–1968* (New York: William Morrow, 1986); Thomas R. Peake, *Keeping the Dream Alive: A History of the Southern Christian Leadership Conference from King to the Nineteen-Eighties* (New York: Peter Lang, 1987).

Southern Methodists   See UNITED METHODIST CHURCH.

Southern Presbyterians   See PRESBYTERIAN CHURCH (U.S.A.); PRESBYTERIANISM.

Spalding, Martin John (1810–1872)   As a leading Catholic apologist and primate of the American Roman Catholic hierarchy as archbishop of Baltimore, Martin John Spalding was a dominant figure in 19th-century American Catholicism. Born on May 23, 1810 on a small farm near Lebanon, Kentucky and raised in a devout Roman Catholic family (see ROMAN CATHOLICISM). Martin, along with his brother Benedict, committed himself early to the priesthood. Educated at St. Mary's College (B.A. 1826), St. Thomas Seminary in Bardstown (B.D. 1830), and the Urban College in Rome (S.T.D. 1834) he returned to Kentucky in 1834. There he served as a pastor in Bardstown (1834–1838, 1841–1844) and Lexington (1840–

1841) as well as president of St. Joseph's College (1838–1840).

Appointed vicar-general (1844), then bishop (1848) of the diocese of Louisville, Spalding soon brought his intellectual and diplomatic abilities to bear in defense of the Catholic faith. A prolific writer and popular lecturer, Spalding gained national attention as an apologist for Catholicism. A collection of his lectures, *General Evidences of Catholicity,* was one of the most popular Catholic apologetical works of the time. Equally significant were his pastoral letters, especially on education, which he saw as central to maintaining the Catholic faith in America and promoting citizenship. He championed parochial schools and supported the establishment of the American colleges in Louvain and Rome as well as the Catholic University of America. Spalding also promoted the Catholic Publication Society (founded 1866, now Paulist Press), feeling that a Catholic publishing house was necessary to stem the overwhelming tide of Protestant books and pamphlets flooding the United States.

Like most of his contemporary co-religionists, Spalding believed that the Catholic faith was compatible with American citizenship. He understood this to mean that a grounding in Catholic doctrine prepared one for the responsibilities of citizenship and for one's civic duties. For this reason he supported strong Roman statements on doctrine, and was one of the few American bishops to defend Pius IX's "Syllabus of Errors," with its condemnation of religious liberty, freedom of the press, and democracy. Named archbishop of Baltimore in 1864, he attended VATICAN COUNCIL I in 1870, where he advocated the promulgation of the doctrine of papal infallibility, thinking that such a centralizing doctrine would aid priests in their work.

In the United States, Spalding used his authority to increase doctrinal and institutional order in the Roman Catholic Church by convening the Second Plenary Council of Baltimore (1866) (see BALTIMORE, COUNCILS OF). This conference not only issued rules regularizing Church procedures throughout the country, but also articulated several theological positions. Its documents included statements on the Trinity, creation, redemption, veneration of Mary, and the doctrine that outside the Church there is no salvation. Equally significant was the council's attention to the problems of the Catholic immigrant population for whom the Church's responsibility was not only religious but to "provide for every want of suffering humanity."

The council was perhaps the finest achievement of Spalding's career. He guided its meetings through several difficult moments and achieved agreement on the most important articles, many of which he had written. Long hampered by poor health and weakened by the trip to Rome in 1870, Spalding died on February 7, 1872, in Baltimore.

EQ

Bibliography: Adam A. Micek, *The Apologetics of Martin John Spalding* (Washington, D.C.: Catholic University of America Press, 1951); John L. Spalding, *The Life of the Most Rev. M. J. Spalding, D. D., Archbishop of Baltimore* (New York: Catholic Publication Society, 1873); Martin John Spalding, *The Evidences of Catholicity, a Series of Lectures* (Baltimore: John Murphy, 1874); Thomas W. Spalding, *Martin John Spalding: American Churchman* (Washington, D.C.: Catholic University of America Press, 1973).

Spangenberg, Augustus Gottlieb   See MORAVIANS.

Spellman, Francis Joseph (1889–1967)

As archbishop of New York for over a quarter-century, Francis Spellman was the preeminent Roman Catholic leader of his time (see ROMAN CATHOLICISM). Although his fellow bishops often resisted his leadership, Spellman's Vatican contacts and long-time personal friendship with Eugenio Pacelli (the Vatican secretary of state who later became Pope Pius XII) provided him with great influence in Rome.

The son of a grocer from Whitman, Massachusetts, Spellman was born on May 4, 1889. He took great pride in the fact that his parents were American-born and resented being called an Irishman. Educated in the public schools of Whitman, he attended Fordham College (now University), deciding on the priesthood shortly before graduating in 1911. After entering the archdiocesan seminary in Boston, he was sent to the North American College in Rome, where he received his doctorate in 1916. He was ordained in May of that year.

Returning to Boston, he spent two years as a parish priest until Archbishop William O'Connell assigned him to the staff of the *Pilot,* the archdiocesan paper. After his appointment to the diocesan chancery (the bishop's staff) in 1922, conflicts developed with O'Connell who over the next three years assigned Spellman to numerous insignificant positions.

Spellman made the best of this time, translating two books and gaining the support of the apostolic delegate to the United States. In 1925 he accompanied a group of pilgrims to Rome, where he became acquainted with several prominent people, including Pacelli, who arranged for his appointment as the first-ever American attaché to the Vatican secretary of state. Spellman's most important activity in this position was smuggling Pope Pius XI's condemnation of fascism, *Non Abbiamo Besogno,* out of the country and passing it on to the Associated Press.

The following year, Spellman was consecrated auxiliary bishop of Boston (September 8, 1932), much to the consternation of Archbishop O'Connell, who made no secret of the fact that he had not requested an auxiliary, especially Spellman. Relations between the two were strained at best, and conflicts repeatedly emerged.

This situation ended on April 15, 1939, when the newly elected pope, Pius XII, appointed Spellman archbishop of New York. As a relatively unknown bishop, Spellman's name had not even been among those originally considered for the position. But with the appointment

he was now the leader of the most influential archdiocese in America with an old friend sitting on the papal throne.

This power was important as the winds of war swirled around the world. Spellman was central to convincing President Franklin Roosevelt to appoint a personal representative to the Vatican, arguing that the United States could use the diplomatic information available to the Vatican as well as its European contacts. Although he had lobbied Roosevelt to establish official diplomatic relations with the Vatican since 1936, Spellman was willing to accept a personal representative as a temporary measure. As a reward for this accomplishment, Pius XII appointed Spellman vicar for the armed forces of the United States, a position Spellman relished and used to its fullest.

After the outbreak of WORLD WAR II, Spellman was an outspoken supporter of the war effort, identifying the allied forces as fighting for the cause of Christian civilization. He visited American troops throughout the European theater and helped to convince Spain's Francisco Franco to remain neutral. Following the liberation of Rome, Spellman advised Pius XII on American Church affairs, suggesting Richard J. CUSHING as successor to the recently deceased Archbishop O'Connell.

Named a cardinal in 1946, after refusing an appointment as Vatican secretary of state, he emerged from the war years as the most visible American bishop. Feeling that the struggle against COMMUNISM was central to the preservation of Christian civilization, he was an outspoken anti-Communist and a supporter of Senator Joseph McCarthy. Spellman used his position as vicar to the military as a platform for his anti-Communism, visiting American troops in Korea and Vietnam (see VIETNAM WAR), remaining outspoken in his support for the war in Vietnam until his death on December 2, 1967.

Although generally described as a conservative, Spellman had complex political views. He was sensitive to racial and ethnic inequality and supported priests and nuns who were active in the civil rights movement. He included the liberal John Courtney MURRAY among his advisors to VATICAN COUNCIL II, and was instrumental in gaining the council's adoption of the declaration on religious liberty.

As archbishop Spellman was an able administrator and oversaw massive growth in the New York archdiocese. The Catholic population of the city doubled during his tenure. Spellman ensured that there were sufficient schools, churches, and hospitals to serve its needs. All this work was guided by Spellman's deep commitment to a life of prayer that he said provided him with the strength to meet the demands placed upon him.

EQ

Bibliography: James Cooney, *The American Pope: The Life and Times of Francis Cardinal Spellman* (New York: Times Books, 1984); Gerald P. Fogarty, *The Vatican and the American Hierarchy from 1870–1965* (Stuttgart: Hiersemann, 1985); Robert I. Gannon, *The Cardinal Spellman Story* (Garden City: Doubleday, 1962).

spirit baptism   See PENTECOSTALISM.

spiritualism   The core affirmation of spiritualism, a new religious movement that arose in mid-19th-century America, is that spirits of the dead can and do communicate with the living through the agency of mediums.

Though spiritualists trace their movement back to visions of Samuel in the Hebrew Bible and the oracles of Delphi in ancient Greece, American spiritualism is usually dated from March 31, 1848, when mysterious rappings first emanated from beneath the kitchen table of Margaret and Kate Fox, two young girls in Hydesville, New York. As spiritualism spread, the spirit rappings of the Fox sisters yielded to more extravagant spiritual manifestations such as slate-writing, levitations, table-tilting, and the materialization of spirits in small theatrical stages called seance cabinets.

Thanks to the writing of Andrew Jackson DAVIS (1826–1920), the "Poughkeepsie Seer"

who soon became the most prolific medium in antebellum America, and to New York *Tribune* editor Horace Greeley's undying devotion to the cause, spiritualist seances became popular entertainment not only in the BURNED-OVER DISTRICT on the frontier but also in Canada and California. Among the famous folk who joined spiritualist circles in the 1850s were Harriet Beecher STOWE, William Lloyd Garrison, George RIPLEY, Lydia Maria Child, William Cullen Bryant, James Fenimore Cooper, and Angelina and Sarah GRIMKÉ. Perhaps because of the tendency of mediums (many of them women) to speak the language of gender equality, many early women's rights advocates, including Susan B. Anthony, Elizabeth Cady STANTON, Frances WILLARD, and Victoria Woodhull, also sympathized with the movement.

Still spiritualism remained for the most part a popular pastime, spread more effectively by P. T. Barnum, who took the Fox sisters on tour, than by New York literati. Letters of ordinary Americans in the antebellum period demonstrated an astonishing fascination with mediums and their messages. "Spiritualism is democratic," a mid-century adherent affirmed. "It is addressed to the common people, and we are all common people."

Although spiritualists evinced a common philosophical interest in the writings of the Swedish seer Emmanuel Swedenborg (1688–1772) and the Austrian physician Franz Antoine Mesmer (1733–1815), practices rather than beliefs have united their community. Nineteenth-century spiritualists agreed on the efficacy of their core ritual—namely, spiritual communication between living beings and disembodied spirits facilitated by trance mediums—which provided for them empirical proof of the existence of the individual soul beyond the grave. But they were dogmatic about little else.

Nonetheless, writings in spiritualist periodicals like *The Spiritual Telegraph* (1852–1860) and the *Banner of Light* (1857–1907) did tend toward religious liberalism. In general, spiritualist authors rejected such orthodox Christian teachings as the absolute sovereignty of God, the total depravity of human beings and the atonement in favor of an immanent and impersonal God, a free and perfectible humanity, and a human Jesus. Like the transcendentalists, they rejected miracles as violations of an inviolable natural law. And like Universalists they rejected hell as unjust and hoped that in the end everyone would be saved. Spiritualists joined religious populists of all stripes in criticizing the privileged knowledge of learned clergy and in their appeal to the natural wisdom of unlettered folk. They posited no external authorities mediating between themselves and God or Truth. Each individual, whether clerical or lay, male or female, was free to follow her or his conscience wherever it might lead. And more often than not the individual consciences of spiritualists led to notions of liberty, equality, democracy, and progress.

Accusations of fraud bedeviled the spiritualist movement almost from its inception. In 1888 Margaret and Kate Fox confessed to having fabricated their famous spirit rappings. Margaret retracted her confession one year later, but the damage done to the movement by the controversy could not be reversed. Spiritualists were also accused by their despisers of immorality. Fixing on the advocacy of "free love" by spiritualists such as Andrew Jackson Davis and Victoria Woodhull, these critics contended that affirming spiritualism would lead one to promiscuity and even prostitution.

The spiritualist boom of the mid-19th century subsided in the late 1850s, but spiritualism has endured both as an alternative and a supplement to more mainstream religious expressions. Spiritualism has also exerted an important influence on THEOSOPHY, which emerged as a reform movement out of spiritualism in 1875, and on the contemporary New Age movement (see NEW AGE RELIGION).

There were numerous attempts to organize the spiritualist impulse, which was by design as anti-institutional as it was anti-creedal. The most successful such attempt was the National Spiritualist Association, which was founded in Chicago in 1893 and at one time boasted 50,000 members.

Spiritualism made its way into the 20th century in part through the activities of the Universal Hagar's Spiritual Church, organized by Father George W. HURLEY in Detroit in 1923. Like other churches in the predominantly black Spiritual movement, Hurley's sect mixes elements from spiritualism—the seance, communication with spirits of the dead, etc.—with cultural and religious elements borrowed from ROMAN CATHOLICISM, black Protestantism, FREEMASONRY, VODOU, astrology, black nationalism, and Afrocentrism.

This recent development in spiritualism may be taking the movement full circle, since some believe that 19th-century American spiritualism was itself influenced by West African traditions of spirit possession.

SRP

Bibliography: Hans A. Baer, *The Black Spiritual Movement: A Religious Response to Racism* (Knoxville: University of Tennessee Press, 1984); Ann Braude, *Radical Spirits: Spiritualism and Women's Rights in Nineteenth-Century America* (Boston: Beacon Press, 1989); R. Laurence Moore, *In Search of White Crows: Spiritualism, Parapsychology, and American Culture* (New York: Oxford University Press, 1977).

Spyrou, Athenagoras (1886–1972)

One of the most influential Orthodox hierarchs of the 20th century, Athenagoras Spyrou served critical terms as Greek Orthodox archbishop of North and South America and subsequently as ecumenical patriarch of Constantinople.

Born Aristocles Spyrou in 1886, in the Ottoman province of Epirus (now in northern Greece), he studied at the patriarchal seminary at Halki, outside Istanbul. Ordained to the diaconate in 1910, he took the monastic name Athenagoras. He then served as a church administrator in the Balkans before being appointed in 1919 to the important post of archdeacon to Meletios Metaxakis, the reformist archbishop of Athens.

On good terms with both conservative and liberal factions in Greece, Athenagoras was consecrated as a bishop in 1922 and served as metropolitan of Kerkyra and Paxoi from 1922 until his election as archbishop of North and South America in 1930.

Charged with the formidable task of bringing peace and order to a church splintered by 10 years of extreme factional struggles, Athenagoras arrived in New York in 1931. A tall, imposing figure, Athenagoras slowly rallied the Greek community and forged a cohesive and relatively tranquil archdiocese.

Traveling almost continually, he often resolved conflicts by arriving in a town and summoning all the factions to meet with him. He loved to visit Greek families and many Greek-Americans treasure stories about the time Athenagoras drank coffee in their grandparents' living room.

Despite vigorous objections, Athenagoras centralized administration at the expense of independent diocesan bishops and struggled to give parish priests more authority than parish councils. By the early 1940s, he had gained enough support to put the archdiocese on a sound financial footing and organize several key church institutions and groups, including the Holy Cross Seminary outside Boston.

Elected patriarch of Constantinople, the senior hierarchical see in the Orthodox world, Athenagoras returned to Turkey in 1948. During an eventful 23-year-long patriarchate, he became one of the most prominent and effective proponents of the ECUMENICAL MOVEMENT. At the same time, he saw the domestic base of the patriarchate sapped, as the Greek population of Istanbul fell from more than 100,000 to a handful as the result of Turkish pressure.

Under Athenagoras, the patriarchate pressed for Orthodox unity and encouraged Orthodox participation in the WORLD COUNCIL OF CHURCHES. In the difficult period after 1945, when almost all of the world's Orthodox Christians lived in states where the church suffered persecution, he also served as an effective spokesman for world Orthodoxy.

His ecumenical activities reached their zenith in 1964, when he met Pope Paul VI in Jerusalem. There the two bishops lifted the mutual decrees of excommunication leveled by their predecessors after the 11th-century schism between Rome and Constantinople. Athenagoras spoke frequently about his hopes for church reunion and encouraged joint commissions of scholars and theologians, but at the time of his death in 1972 church union remained a distant prospect.

AHW

Bibliography: George Papaioannou, *From Mars Hill to Manhattan: The Greek Orthodox Church in America Under Patriarch Athenagoras I* (Minneapolis: Light and Life Publishing Co., 1976).

Stanton, Elizabeth Cady (1815–1902)

A prominent 19th-century social reformer who agitated for abolitionism, temperance, women's rights, and female suffrage, Elizabeth Cady Stanton was a pioneer in feminist criticism of the Bible and one of her century's most outspoken critics of the contributions of institutional Christianity to women's bondage.

Stanton was born to a wealthy family in Johnstown, New York, on November 12, 1815. As a child she first became aware of "the defect of her sex" when, after all her brothers had died, her father remarked to her, "Oh, my daughter, I wish you were a boy!" She graduated from the Johnstown Academy (1830) and the Troy Female Seminary (1831).

Stanton began her work as a social reformer in the antislavery movement (see ABOLITIONISM). In 1840 she married abolitionist Henry Stanton, but demonstrated her independence of mind by supporting her husband's rival, William Lloyd Garrison, an abolitionist who also favored women's rights. In 1848 Stanton hosted Ameri-

Elizabeth Cady Stanton, a social, political, and religious reformer who oversaw the publication of *The Woman's Bible* in 1895. (Library of Congress)

ca's first Women's Rights Convention at her home in Seneca Falls, New York and contributed to the preparation of that convention's influential Declaration of Sentiments asserting the equality of women. Her interest in women's issues was encouraged by her friend and mentor, the Quaker reformer Lucretia Mott.

Despite her early contributions to the women's rights movement, Stanton did not appear in public often until later in her life. She wrote regularly and lectured occasionally when she was not pregnant or raising her seven children, but her public activity truly began only after her children were older.

Stanton's main work as a religious reformer was overseeing the publication of *The Woman's Bible* (see WOMAN'S BIBLE, THE) in 1895 and 1898. Stanton was raised in a tradition of con-

servative PRESBYTERIANISM, but her political views led her to criticize Christianity for what she saw as its contributions to the enslavement of women. In *The Woman's Bible*, which she co-authored with a Revising Committee of female scholars, Stanton criticized biblical passages that demeaned women and praised passages that celebrated them.

As an adult, Stanton was attracted, along with many other women's rights activists, to SPIRITUALISM. One factor that may have informed her interest in spiritualism was the tendency of spirits of the dead to agitate through the avenue of mediums (most of them women) for the rights of living women. "The only religious sect in the world . . . that has recognized the equality of woman," she wrote in *The History of Woman Suffrage,* "is the Spiritualists."

Stanton died on October 26, 1902. At the time, she was heralded as one of the mothers of the women's suffrage movement. But because of her pioneering work on *The Woman's Bible,* many now remember her as well as one of the mothers of FEMINIST THEOLOGY.

TP

Bibliography: Ellen Carol DuBois, ed., *Elizabeth Cady Stanton/Susan B. Anthony: Correspondence, Writings, Speeches* (New York: Schocken Books, 1981); Elisabeth Griffith, *In Her Own Right: The Life of Elizabeth Cady Stanton* (New York: Oxford University Press, 1984); Elizabeth Cady Stanton, *Eighty Years & More; Reminiscences, 1815–1897* (New York: Schocken Books, 1971).

Stoddard, Solomon (1643–1729)

Best known as the grandfather of Jonathan EDWARDS, one of the United States's preeminent colonial theologians, Solomon Stoddard (born September 27, 1643 in Boston, Massachusetts) was a significant figure in his own right. His influence among Congregationalists (see CONGREGATIONALISM) along the Connecticut River Valley was such that he was jokingly referred to as the "pope of the West."

To a great extent Stoddard's career can be seen as a working-out of the implications of the

HALF-WAY COVENANT. Approved by a ministerial synod in 1662 (the year Stoddard received his B.A. from Harvard), the covenant allowed for an extension of BAPTISM to the children of those whose only connection to a church was that of their own infant baptism. Stoddard's understanding of the covenant led him to relax the standards for both church membership and admission to the Lord's Supper.

Following his graduation from Harvard, Stoddard spent five more years at the school—first doing graduate work, later as a tutor and librarian. In 1667 he accepted a chaplaincy in Barbados, where he remained until 1670. In that year he returned to Massachusetts (see MASSACHUSETTS BAY COLONY), becoming the minister in the town of Northampton, at that time the western frontier. Stoddard would labor at the Northampton church until his death on February 11, 1729.

While Stoddard was at Northampton, the church experienced several periods of religious "refreshening," viewed by some historians as precursors to the GREAT AWAKENING. His alterations in the requirements for church membership and admission to the sacraments generated much controversy and brought him into conflict with Increase and Cotton MATHER. The Mathers denounced "Stoddardeanism" as a violation of church order, bemoaning it as the end of Puritan (see PURITANISM) orthodoxy.

Stoddard's alterations were caused by a deep pastoral concern. Firmly committed to the doctrines of human depravity and the inscrutable workings of God's grace in bringing about salvation, he rejected the idea of limiting church membership only to those who could give evidence of a conversion experience. Stoddard returned to the older views of both the Presbyterians (see PRESBYTERIANISM) and early Congregationalists, making church membership available to all who assented to the church's doctrines and excluding only those who led an openly scandalous life.

Stoddard did differ from his Puritan forebears in his understanding of the Lord's Supper, viewing it as a means of awakening faith. Along with the sermon and prayer, it was a way of effecting divine grace within those God chose to save. For this reason, Stoddard rejected restricting it only to the saved.

Pastoral concern led Stoddard to other innovations as well. He felt that traditional forms should be altered to meet new circumstances, and judged in light of their success. All his activities were designed to increase religious vitality and personal faith. While conservative Boston looked askance at these innovations, they were widely copied by other churches in the Connecticut River Valley.

In 1726, Stoddard was joined in his pastoral work at Northampton by his grandson Jonathan Edwards. Edwards continued this work after Stoddard's death. By 1748, however, Edwards had become disturbed by the relaxation of standards introduced by his grandfather. When he attempted to strengthen the requirements for church membership, the depth of his grandfather's 59-year pastorate was seen. The congregation rebelled, forcing Edward's resignation.

EQ

Bibliography: Ralph J. Coffman, *Solomon Stoddard* (Boston: Twayne Publishers, 1978); James William Jones, *The Shattered Synthesis: New England Puritanism Before the Great Awakening* (New Haven: Yale University Press, 1973); Harry S. Stout, *The New England Soul: Preaching and Religious Culture in Colonial New England* (New York: Oxford University Press, 1986).

Stone, Barton Warren (1772–1844) Barton Stone, a Presbyterian minister, initiated the great 1801 revival at Cane Ridge, Kentucky. This event helped inaugurate the western phase of the SECOND GREAT AWAKENING and symbolized the critical importance of CAMP MEETINGS in spreading Christianity in the early 19th century. Eventually breaking away from the Presbyterian Church, Stone helped shape the "Stonite" wing of the RESTORATION MOVEMENT. Stone and his followers later united with the forces of Alexander CAMPBELL to form the denomination that became known as the CHRISTIAN CHURCH (DISCIPLES OF CHRIST).

Stone was born on December 24, 1772 near Port Tobacco, Maryland. He was converted to Christianity at the age of 19 and dedicated himself to the ministry. After studying theology privately, he was granted a license to preach in 1796. Stone served for two years as an itinerant minister in North Carolina, Virginia, and Tennessee, and in 1798 he was called to the small Presbyterian congregations at Concord and Cane Ridge, Kentucky. Having learned revival techniques from fellow Presbyterian James McGready, Stone organized at Cane Ridge a camp meeting that attracted thousands of worshipers. That event not only established Stone's reputation as a religious leader, but also demonstrated the usefulness of extended revivals in furthering the cause of Christianity under the fluid social conditions of the western frontier.

The CANE RIDGE revival, on the other hand, raised problems for Stone in relation to his own denomination. The bizarre "religious exercises" (dancing, falling, jerking, laughing, and even barking) that many people observed at the western camp meetings were a cause for obvious alarm among conservative Presbyterians. While Stone admitted that such practices were unusual, he staunchly defended their efficacy as genuine expressions of the Holy Spirit's work. Since numerous unchurched settlers in Kentucky and Tennessee were incorporated into the Methodist, Baptist, and Presbyterian denominations as a result of the revivals, Stone did not wish to see the successes that he and other evangelists achieved simply dismissed out of hand.

By 1803, Presbyterians questioned as well the theology that underlay the revivals and the emotional excesses they encouraged. Wishing both to preserve traditional Calvinist emphasis on the divine initiative in salvation and to counter the ARMINIANISM implicit in the revivalists' stress on human free will, they scrutinized Stone's work. Stone and four other dissidents, however, quickly preempted any possibility of disciplinary action. First, they formed their own independent Presbyterian body. Then, abandoning the Presbyterian denominational label altogether, they chose in 1804 to call themselves simply "Christians." They affirmed the independence of local congregations, eschewed all creeds except the Bible, and practiced adult baptism by immersion, as in New Testament times.

Stone became the principal spokesman for this intentionally nonsectarian movement. He traveled extensively to build up its membership and published a monthly journal, the *Christian Messenger,* which ran from 1826 until the time of his death. The theme of radical separation from the world appears consistently in Stone's writings. As he advised his followers in 1841, they ought never to conform themselves to earthly concerns. "Here you have no abiding place," he said, "but are as strangers and pilgrims seeking a better country." After meeting Alexander Campbell in 1830 and finding common ground with the Campbellites' desire to restore apostolic simplicity to American church life, Stone merged most of his movement with Campbell's.

Despite being hampered by paralysis, Stone continued his evangelistic work for another decade. He died while on a preaching tour at Hannibal, Missouri on November 9, 1844.

GHS, Jr.

Bibliography: William G. West, *Barton Warren Stone: Early American Advocate of Christian Unity* (Nashville: Disciples of Christ Historical Society, 1954).

Stowe, Harriet Beecher (1811–1896)

Harriet Beecher Stowe was a writer who published over 30 books during the course of her life. She is best remembered for the 1852 bestseller *Uncle Tom's Cabin,* which galvanized abolitionist (see ABOLITIONISM) sentiment in the North and was an important factor in the coming of the CIVIL WAR. As President Abraham Lincoln quipped when he first met Stowe, she was "the little woman who wrote the book that made this great war."

Stowe was born in Litchfield, Connecticut on June 14, 1811. One of 11 children of the famed

Abolitionist and novelist Harriet Beecher Stowe. Her 1852 *Uncle Tom's Cabin* sold more than 300,000 copies in its first year of publication and enormously influenced Americans' views of slavery. (Library of Congress)

Congregational minister Lyman BEECHER, she belonged to the nation's most renowned Protestant household whose members all played significant roles in the development of American Christianity in the 19th century. The Beechers moved to Cincinnati, Ohio in 1832 when Harriet's father was named president of the newly formed Lane Theological Seminary. In 1836 Harriet married Lane professor Calvin E. Stowe. The Stowes later lived at Bowdoin College in Maine and at Andover Theological Seminary in Massachusetts, where Calvin held teaching posts.

The passage of the Fugitive Slave Act outraged Stowe and occasioned her composition of *Uncle Tom's Cabin*, which was serialized in 1851 and published as a book the next year. Drawing on her earlier experiences in Cincinnati and her observations of slavery in nearby Kentucky, she vividly depicted that institution's many evils. Although long after her death the character Uncle Tom would come under severe criticism as a symbol of black passivity in the face of white oppression, Stowe intended Tom as a Christlike figure who symbolically redeemed America from the sin of slavery. *Uncle Tom's Cabin* sold more than 300,000 copies in its first year of publication. While the book provoked angry rebuttals throughout the South, it mirrored the North's feelings of guilt about captured fugitive slaves.

Obsessed by the Calvinist theology she had learned from her father, Stowe was devastated in 1857 when her eldest son, Henry, died without formally joining a church. Two years later in *The Minister's Wooing*, her most explicitly autobiographical novel, she excoriated the cruel teachings of Calvinism that consigned unconverted men and women like Henry to hellfire. Even writing, however, could not fully exorcise Stowe's feelings about the beliefs of the church of her youth. In 1864, she bought a pew at St. John's Episcopal Church in Hartford, Connecticut. Although she never officially joined the denomination, the aesthetic sense and theological flexibility of Episcopalianism proved well suited to Stowe's religious temperament.

After the Civil War, Stowe bought a house in Florida, where she spent most of the rest of her life. Despite being overcome by senility in 1890, she kept one idea clear in her mind: "Trust in the Lord and do good." Near the end of her life, Stowe returned to Hartford, where she died on July 1, 1896.

GHS, Jr.

Bibliography: Joan D. Hendrick, *Harriet Beecher Stowe: A Life* (New York: Oxford University Press, 1993).

Strong, Josiah (1847–1916) Josiah Strong was an early leader in both the ECUMENICAL and SOCIAL GOSPEL MOVEMENTS. Born in

A pioneer reformer, Josiah Strong analyzed the social problems caused by the industrial revolution and advocated ways for churches to solve them. (New-York Historical Society)

Naperville, Illinois on January 19, 1847, he attended college and seminary in Ohio, Western Reserve College (B.A. 1869) and Lane Seminary (1869–1871). Ordained as a Congregational minister in 1871 (see CONGREGATIONALISM), Strong spent the first 15 years of his career as regional secretary of the Congregational Home Missionary Society (1881–1884) and as a pastor in Wyoming and Ohio. While serving as a minister in Cincinnati he achieved national prominence with the publication in 1885 of his first book, *Our Country: Its Possible Future and Its Present Crisis,* an analysis of urban social problems and suggestions for their alleviation.

In that year Strong's church in Cincinnati held an interdenominational conference on the role of the churches in solving social problems. Many Protestant leaders of the time attended this and succeeding conferences held in 1887, 1889, and 1893. The last took place in Chicago in conjunction with the WORLD'S PARLIAMENT OF RELIGIONS.

Upon becoming general secretary of the EVANGELICAL ALLIANCE in 1886, Strong attempted to transform that institution into a leader in social affairs. Finding it too restrictive and conservative for his purposes, he left in 1898 and founded the American League (Institute after 1902) for Social Service.

Strong was one of the first American church leaders concerned with the problems of the cities. He pioneered in analyzing social problems and in articulating ways in which the churches could solve them. Coordinated effort by local churches was a major goal of Strong's work, which brought him into the nascent ecumenical movement. While preeminently a proponent of federation from the bottom up, feeling that churches in the same area had more in common with each other than with churches of the same denomination miles away, Strong was active in the Federal Council of Churches and served on its Commission on the Church and Social Service (see NATIONAL COUNCIL OF CHURCHES).

Despite, or perhaps because of, his commitment to social service, Strong's books were filled with the racism of the time. Part of the churches' goal in rectifying social evils was the "Anglo-Saxonizing" of the world (see NATIVISM). For Strong, the Anglo-Saxons were privileged above other "races," possessing superior spiritual, intellectual, and governmental faculties.

Although those attitudes limit the usefulness of his ideas, Strong is remembered today as a pioneer in the movement for Christian unity and in the development of Protestant social concern and action. He died in New York City on April 28, 1916.

EQ

Bibliography: Josiah Strong, *Our Country: Its Possible Future and Its Present Crisis* (New York: Baker & Taylor for the American Home Mission Society, 1885); ———, *The New Era, or The Coming Kingdom* (New York: Baker and Taylor, 1893); ———,

Religious Movements for Social Betterment (New York: Baker and Taylor, 1900); ———, *The Challenge of the City* (New York: Presbyterian Home Missions Literature Department, 1907); ———, *My Religion in Every-Day Life* (New York: Baker and Taylor, 1910).

Student Nonviolent Coordinating Committee

Of all the civil rights organizations (see CIVIL RIGHTS MOVEMENT) of the 1960s none was more courageous and controversial than the Student Nonviolent Coordinating Committee, or "Snick" as it was popularly known after its initials, SNCC. Intentionally nonorganizational, SNCC was determined, in the words of Ella Baker (its sage but not its leader), to "work with people where they are." Although marked by racial separatism toward the end, SNCC's early and most successful years were defined by nonracialism, grass-roots democracy, and innovative activism.

SNCC's formal creation took place over Easter weekend 1960 (April 15–17) at Shaw University in Raleigh, North Carolina. At this meeting of the Southwide Student Leadership Conference on Nonviolent Resistance, several different student movements fused into the Temporary Student Nonviolent Coordinating Committee. In its early years SNCC revolved around two poles. The first, originally centered in Nashville, was religiously grounded and viewed nonviolence as a comprehensive world view. The second, centered in Atlanta, was more secular in its orientation and viewed nonviolence more tactically.

SNCC's guiding principles can be summed up as direct action, nonviolent resistance, and local control. Early on the committee decided to remain separate from the SOUTHERN CHRISTIAN LEADERSHIP CONFERENCE (SCLC). While maintaining a working relationship with Martin Luther KING, JR. and the SCLC, SNCC viewed itself as more committed than the SCLC. SNCC's "jail, no bail" policy, along with its long-term commitment to community organization, represented major differences in orienta-

tion. Many members resented the elitist role of the ministers who comprised the SCLC, and often referred to King as "De Lawd."

The real force in SNCC, its field directors, lived in a local community, organizing people around local concerns and needs. Drawing a weekly salary of $10, the field directors rarely were better off than the people with whom they worked. The SNCC field directors were harassed, jailed, beaten, and even killed by local authorities. Although spread throughout the SOUTH, SNCC's major activities were in southwest Georgia; Danville, Virginia; and the Mississippi Delta.

SNCC's work in Mississippi began in 1960. Originally centered on voter education, it expanded to include direct action to achieve integration of public facilities and services. As part of COFO (Council of Federated Organizations), SNCC provided the organizers while the SCLC, the NAACP, and CORE (Congress of Racial Equality) provided the money for a massive project designed to bring blacks into the political system. Part of this project was the "Freedom Summer" of 1964. In that year, hundreds of white volunteers went to Mississippi to help run freedom schools to aid in community organizing, and to experience the racism and violence of the region.

In May 1964 an event occurred that focused national and international attention on the Delta when three SNCC workers disappeared. By the time the bodies of Andrew Goodman, James Chaney, and Michael Schwerner were discovered a month and a half later, Congress had passed an omnibus civil rights bill and growing numbers of voices were being raised against continued repression of African-Americans. That it took the murder of two white men (Schwerner and Goodman) to bring about such an outcry when blacks had been beaten and murdered for years created much bitterness within SNCC.

The year 1964 was significant for SNCC in other ways as well. In August the racially integrated Mississippi Freedom Democratic Party

(MFDP) nearly managed to unseat the state's regular delegation at the Democratic convention. The eloquence and dignity of the members of the MFDP during their struggle seared the demands for racial justice into the consciousness of many Americans.

The deaths of Goodman, Schwerner, and Chaney, the media attention on the white volunteers, and the failure of the Democratic convention to seat the MFDP strained SNCC to the breaking point. An organizational vote in 1966 replaced the older SNCC staff with newer members, most of whom were northern-born blacks, several of whom felt that SNCC should be racially exclusive. This group—led by Stokely Carmichael, a SNCC organizer in Lowndes County, Alabama—adopted a militant Black Power stance that forced out both the white organizers and many of the older members. They also centralized the movement, erasing its grass-roots power base.

As the leadership of SNCC moved into the Black Panther Party, it became increasingly northern and urban in orientation. Legal problems and violent conflicts with the police weakened the movement further. By 1970 it was virtually defunct.

EQ

Bibliography: Taylor Branch, *Parting the Waters: America in the King Years, 1954–1963* (New York: Simon & Schuster, 1988); Mary King, *Freedom Song: A Personal Story of the 1960s Civil Rights Movement* (New York: Morrow, 1987); Howard Zinn, *SNCC, the New Abolitionists* (Boston: Beacon, 1965).

Student Volunteer Movement One of the most ambitious and influential student voluntary associations to promote world missions, the Student Volunteer Movement (SVM), founded in 1888, claimed to have enrolled more than 20,000 North American college students as evangelical Protestant missionaries before its demise in the 1960s. In the summer of 1886, the itinerant revivalist Dwight L. MOODY, recently returned from a preaching tour of the schools which are now part of the Ivy League,

convened a month-long conference of the Intercollegiate YMCA at the Mount Hermon Academy in Northfield, Massachusetts. In the course of the meeting, Moody led 100 students, the "Mount Hermon Hundred," to take the pledge to become foreign missionaries. Over the next few years, various supporters carried the pledge to other colleges and universities. In 1888 the SVM was formally organized to direct student energies toward foreign mission service. The movement appointed John R. MOTT, a Methodist leader of the YMCA, as its first president, and Robert E. Speer, a Presbyterian supporter of missions, as traveling secretary.

Taking as its watchword "the evangelization of the world in this generation," the society sought to organize students at all major American universities. The movement also spread abroad quickly, leading to the establishment of the British Student Volunteer Missionary Union (1892) and the World Student Christian Federation (1895). Self-consciously interdenominational and evangelical, the SVM based its appeal on the authority of Scripture, particularly the "Great Commission" of Jesus Christ that was interpreted as calling individuals to "Go ye into all the world and preach the Gospel." In its many mission books and study programs the movement emphasized the importance of personal conversion and holiness and the salvation of individual souls as the avenue to social regeneration.

At the same time, the movement also had an anti-intellectual dimension that incited spiritual passions and encouraged students to take their pledge as an act of faith. The SVM connected the spiritual conquest of the globe, as indicated by the organization's watchword, to popular American patriotism. Leaders such as Mott made extensive use of militant rhetoric, envisioning himself as a global commander-in-chief, encouraging the image of the SVM as a military camp in training, and lending an added sense of urgency to the cause. The SVM thus drew upon popular late 19th-century conceptions of American superiority and MANIFEST DESTINY to further its religious goals and convince students to take the pledge. Through its long series of large conventions or "Quadrennials," held every four years beginning in 1891, the SVM vowed to reach every generation of college students with its message.

The effects of the SVM at home were perhaps even more significant than its work abroad. The movement's organizational strategies produced and trained many talented leaders in world missions who raised money, published widely, and promoted the ideal of overseas Christian service during the first half of the 20th century. Mott, Speer, Arthur T. Pierson, Kenneth Latourette, and other leaders wrote widely influential texts about world missions, helped to establish missionary collections at colleges and universities, endowed mission chairs and lectureships, founded Bible institutes and colleges, and created supporting organizations to raise funds for foreign missions, including the Laymen's Missionary Movement (1906). All these efforts directly aided the growth of financial giving to the missionary cause, which climbed steeply from $9 million in 1906 to $45 million in 1924.

The SVM fell into rapid decline after 1920, due to a lessening of popular interest in foreign missions, as well as to organizational and leadership problems. In 1959 it merged with two other student societies to form the National Student Christian Federation, and in 1966 became part of the University Christian Movement, which disbanded in 1969.

LMK

Bibliography: Ben Harder, "The Student Volunteer Movement for Foreign Missions and Its Contribution to 20th Century Missions," *Missiology* 8 (1980): 141–154; C. P. Shedd, *Two Centuries of Student Christian Movements* (New York: Association Press, 1934).

Sunday, Billy (William Ashley) (1862–1935)

Billy Sunday was a renowned and colorful leader of revivals in the early 20th century. He now also occupies a position within the ranks of America's most successful religious leaders.

Billy Sunday, a phenomenally successful evangelist whose talent for drama drew large crowds. Tens of thousands accepted his "altar call." (Library of Congress)

Because he tended to oversimplify complicated Christian teachings, Sunday appealed to popular impulses in American religion, and thus helped play a key role in strengthening Protestant fundamentalism in his day.

Sunday was born on a farm in Ames, Iowa on November 19, 1862. He received little formal education and had a diverse early career as an undertaker's assistant, furniture salesman, and professional baseball player. Employed as an outfielder for the Chicago White-Stockings, he was converted to Christ during an urban rescue mission in front of a Chicago saloon in 1886. He gave up baseball altogether in 1891 to work for the YMCA. Sunday next served as an assistant to revival leader J. Wilbur Chapman from 1893 to 1895, and when Chapman retired in 1895, he succeeded him. Sunday remained a revivalist for the rest of his life, and he was ordained to the Presbyterian ministry in 1903.

Sunday gradually developed a tremendous following. Although his initial revivalistic campaigns had been held in small midwestern towns and cities, by the time of World War I he was preaching in large cities such as Chicago, New York, and Boston. Sunday was a great dramatist, and his flamboyant gestures, theatrical poses, and salty, everyday language attracted hordes of ordinary people. Ably assisted by Nell Sunday, his wife and business manager, he developed an elaborate machinery for raising a revival. Despite the hostility of most traditional clergy and laity, whom Sunday dismissed as "hog-jowled, weasel-eyed, . . . mushy-fisted, jelly-spined, pussy-footing, four-flushing, Charlotte-russe Christians," millions of Americans heard and were moved by both his bizarre antics and his strenuous evangelistic efforts.

Sunday turned his attention as well toward issues relating to the moral and spiritual fiber of the United States. He denounced the many evils he believed afflicted American society: immigration, socialism, political corruption, and—most heinous of all—the liquor interest. Sunday thought everyone who was not a teetotaler was a "dirty low-down, whisky-soaked, beer-guzzling, bull-necked, foul-mouthed hypocrite." From 1905 until the passage of the 18th Amendment, he regularly delivered his "Booze Sermon," in which he appealed for support of a prohibition law. On a more disturbing note, Sunday's concerns about "reform" also coalesced with those of the KU KLUX KLAN. In his southern revivals of the 1920s especially, he solicited and accepted the support of the Klan, an organization expressing the same racist, nativist (see NATIVISM), and anti-Catholic fears that Sunday and many white Protestants felt.

During the brief American involvement in World War I, Sunday added his unwavering chauvinism in support of the allied war effort.

After the war, however, failing health forced him to curtail his labors, and as a consequence his evangelistic work gradually declined. Sunday died in Chicago on November 6, 1935.

GHS, Jr.

Bibliography: Lyle W. Dorsett, *Billy Sunday and the Redemption of Urban America* (Grand Rapids: Eerdmans, 1991).

Sunday school movement The origins of the Sunday school movement in the United States were part of the widespread institutional development that occurred during the early years of the republic. Its expansion coincided with the rise of hospitals, prisons, asylums, free public schools, orphanages, and houses of refuge. Although Sunday schools later became closely associated with DENOMINATIONALISM, in its early stages the Sunday school movement expanded rapidly because of the way evangelical reformers saw education as a means to fulfill their millennial expectations (see EVANGELICALISM, EVANGELICAL UNITED FRONT).

Following the example of their British counterparts, who had begun their efforts nearly a decade earlier, Sunday schools in America made their first appearance shortly after the AMERICAN REVOLUTION. The first one was probably organized in Hanover County, Virginia in 1786 by Francis ASBURY. Others soon followed in coastal cities and factory towns such as Pawtucket, Rhode Island. The METHODISTS were the first to adopt the Sunday school as official policy, urging their establishment at or near places of worship in 1790.

These early Sunday schools were largely efforts to give children of poor working-class families a chance to become educated in both basic reading and religion and at the same time to control their perceived misbehavior on the Sabbath. New motives for establishing them emerged by the 1830s, when evangelical Protestants began supporting them. From a means of basic education and social control, they were converted into a way of evangelizing and educating young children in important Christian truths

Sunday school, such as this 1930s Congregational class in a one-room schoolhouse in Maine, promoted Sabbath observance, Bible lessons, and social behavior in both urban and rural areas. (Library of Congress)

and principles. Their growth during this period was rapid, tens of thousands of teachers and students enlisting in their cause.

Sunday schools operated alongside prayer meetings, mission chapels, and urban missionaries as ways to combat urban social problems. In addition, their growth was stimulated by changing views of childhood emphasizing the vast untapped potential that existed in every human being. They also benefited from an influx of children from Protestant church-going families. Finally, the growth of free urban schooling promoted the growth of evangelical Sunday schools.

The various denominations recognized that Sunday schools could be a significant part of their programs, but during the early 1800s, the impulse to create Sunday schools remained to a large degree an interdenominational movement. Sunday school unions or societies emerged in many towns and cities, and the American Sunday School Union was organized in Philadelphia in

1817. Its *Sunday School Magazine* became part of a vast flood of literature that publicized and promoted Sunday schools all over the country.

During the decades before the CIVIL WAR, state and denominational Sunday school societies proliferated, including the Massachusetts Sunday School Union (comprising Congregationalists and Baptists) in 1825, the Protestant Episcopal Sunday School Union the following year, and its Methodist Episcopal counterpart the year after that. The year 1832 marked the first national convention of Sunday school workers, held in New York City. While the Sunday school had its origins in urban areas as a means of access to working-class children, as the frontier pushed westward during the 19th century, it served to bring religious services and instruction to places that lacked organized denominational activities. Missionaries sent out by the American Sunday School Union and the American Home Missionary Society used the Sunday school as an interim method of bringing religious services and instruction to communities before regular churches could be set up. In frontier areas, Sunday schools were therefore not just for children but for adults as well.

In addition to promoting Sabbath observance in both rural and urban areas, Sunday schools were seen as a means of enhancing the social order in general. Memorization was the major method of instruction, as it was in the common schools of the time. The rules and rituals established by the Sunday schools carried lessons that students could practice in their everyday lives: cleanliness, neatness, punctuality, benevolence, and industry.

A uniform system of teaching, devised by John H. Vincent in 1866, helped improve the quality of teaching. The Chautauqua Assembly was begun in 1874 under his leadership, in association with Lewis Miller, as a way to bring Sunday school teachers and leaders together for systematic training. During the decades after the Civil War, the movement became a major means of recruitment for the denominations. Also, the ecumenical aspect of the early-day Sunday school gradually gave way to denominational identification, and the Sunday school became closely identified with other aspects of denominational activity in later years.

MG

Bibliography: Anne M. Boylan, *Sunday School: The Formation of An American Institution, 1790–1880* (New Haven: Yale University Press, 1988); Lawrence A. Cremin, *American Education: The National Experience* (New York: Harper and Row, 1980).

Suzuki, Daisetz Teitaro (1870–1966)

Daisetz Teitaro Suzuki, the most important and influential bearer of ZEN from Japan to the United States, served as a bridge between East and West when Asia and America were in the process of discovering one another.

Born in 1870 in a humble village in northern Japan to a samurai family, as a young man he moved to Tokyo to attend Imperial University. In Tokyo he took up Zen training. His Zen masters soon recognized his substantial accomplishments by renaming him Daisetz ("great humility"). Suzuki's career as a Japanese expositor of Zen to the modern West would leave him with few reasons to be humble, however.

His East-West work began when, as a lay disciple of Zen monk Soyen Shaku, he translated into English a speech that his master subsequently intoned at the WORLD'S PARLIAMENT OF RELIGIONS in Chicago in 1893. In 1897 Suzuki moved from his Zen monastery and his Japanese homeland to LaSalle, Illinois where for 11 years he utilized his considerable language skills as a translator for Open Court Publishing Company, run by the Buddhist sympathizer Paul Carus. Suzuki also wrote numerous articles in Carus's journals, *Open Court* and *The Monist*. He returned to Japan in 1909 but visited the United States regularly thereafter to teach and to deliver lectures to Americans interested in Zen.

While in Japan in 1911, he married Beatrice Erskine Lane, a graduate of Radcliffe and an advocate of THEOSOPHY. Together he and his wife founded *The Eastern Buddhist*, an English-language journal of the Mahayana ("Greater Vehicle") Buddhist school of northern Asia. During the 1950s, Suzuki taught for six years at Columbia University, where he helped to cultivate the interest of the Beat authors in Zen. In 1959, while living in Cambridge, Massachusetts, he founded the Cambridge Buddhist Association, which he served as its first president.

In addition to numerous English translations of Pali, Sanskrit, Chinese, and Japanese scriptures, Suzuki published a number of books that attempted to explain to western readers an Asian tradition that is according to its practitioners fundamentally inexplicable. His first Zen compendium, *Essays in Zen Buddhism,* appeared in England in 1927 and his *An Introduction to Zen Buddhism* (1954) is now the standard foreigner's guide to Zen. In the latter book, Suzuki explicates key Zen concepts like *satori* (sudden enlightenment) and key Zen practices like *zazen* (sitting meditation) and grappling with the mind puzzles called *koans.* Suzuki also counters a number of standard Christian objections to Zen. He argues, for example, that the Zen doctrine of *sunyata* or emptiness does not result, as many westerners believe, in nihilism and despair but, on the contrary, in a "higher affirmation" and a life of individual freedom and spontaneity. Zen, Suzuki asserts, is mystical yet practical, a path not only to intuitive insight but also to authentic living.

When Suzuki died in 1966 in Kamakura, Japan at the age of 96, he was, undoubtedly, the most important popularizer of Zen in the modern West. He influenced a generation of eastward-looking American intellectuals, including composer John Cage, author Philip Kapleau, Catholic theologian Thomas MERTON, Beat poet Allen Ginsberg, and Zen Episcopalian Alan WATTS. More than anyone else, Suzuki was responsible for the "Zen explosion" in America in the 1950s and 1960s.

(See also BUDDHISM.)

SRP

Bibliography: D. T. Suzuki, *An Introduction to Zen Buddhism* (New York: Grove Press, 1964); Irwin

A. Switzer III, *D. T. Suzuki: A Biography* (London: Buddhist Society, 1985).

Swedenborgianism One of the most influential vehicles for "occult" wisdom in 19th-century America, Swedenborgianism originated with the Swedish scientist-turned-seer Emmanuel Swedenborg (1688–1772).

The son of a Lutheran bishop, Swedenborg was trained not as a theologian but as a scientist. He studied geology, published several books in that field, and was rewarded for his efforts by being elected a corresponding member of the Royal Academy of Sciences in St. Petersburg, Russia. At the age of 55 he experienced a spiritual crisis precipitated by visions in which he traveled to heaven and hell and conversed with, among others, Plato and Luther.

Swedenborg resolved his crisis by resigning from his job with Sweden's Bureau of Mines in 1747 and taking up a new life as a prolific theologian-philosopher. The impressive list of works that followed this life crisis included detailed descriptions of his spiritual travels, philosophical and theological treatises, and commentaries on Christian scriptures.

At the core of Swedenborg's thought is the Neoplatonic theory of correspondences between the spiritual realm and the physical realm. Swedenborg divided the spiritual realm, which he saw as more real than the physical, into a series of spheres. After death, he argued, souls travel to the sphere that matches the level of their moral attainments on earth. They then progress onward and upward through higher and higher spheres to an eventual encounter with divinity. Swedenborg never developed these ideas systematically in his writings, perhaps because he was more intent on interpreting Christian scriptures in light of his theories than on working out the theories themselves. Many of his most intriguing works, including his eight-volume *Arcana Caelestia* (1745–1756), are biblical commentaries. Perhaps because he wrote many of his books in Latin, Swedenborg was not widely studied during his lifetime.

Following his death in London in 1772, Swedenborg's works began to be translated into English. In 1783 a core group of followers institutionalized his considerable charisma by founding in London the Church of the New Jerusalem (or "New Church"). The first Swedenborgian society in the United States was established in Baltimore in 1792.

Three branches of Swedenborgianism now exist in the United States. The first and largest of these branches, the General Convention of the New Jerusalem in the United States of America, was established in 1817. Its five key doctrines affirm a basically liberal and christo-centric theology:

1. That there is one God, in whom there is a Divine Trinity; and that He is the Lord Jesus Christ.
2. That saving faith is to believe in Him.
3. Every man is born to evils of every kind, and unless through repentance he removes them in part, he remains in them, and he who remains in them cannot be saved.
4. That good actions are to be done, because they are of God and from God.
5. That these are to be done by a man as from himself; but that it ought to be believed that they are done from the Lord with him and by him.

Probably because of its esoteric bent, Swedenborgianism has never been able to attract large numbers of adherents in the United States. Swedenborgianism proper peaked in the 1840s, when John Chapman or "Johnny Appleseed" championed the ideas of the Swedish clairvoyant across the frontier. There are now only slightly more than 2,000 members of Swedenborgian societies in the United States. The movement is significant largely because of its influence on other "occult" religious movements. Swedenborg's theories have found their way into SPIRITUALISM, THEOSOPHY, and NEW THOUGHT and today influence the New Age movement (see NEW AGE RELIGION).

SRP

Bibliography: Erland J. Brock et al., eds., *Swedenborg and his Influence* (Bryn Athyn, Pa.: The Academy of the New Church, 1988); Signe Toksvig, *Emmanuel Swedenborg: Scientist and Mystic* (New Haven: Yale University Press, 1948).

Szold, Henrietta (1860–1945)

Founder of Hadassah, author, editor, and the first woman member of the world Zionist executive committee, Henrietta Szold exerted a tremendous impact on JUDAISM and Jewish life both in the United States and in Palestine.

Henrietta Szold was born in Baltimore, Maryland on December 21, 1860. The daughter of a prominent rabbi, she early showed a concern for Jewish culture and life and in her teens began to write articles for Jewish-American newspapers. Her first career was as a teacher.

The waves of poor Russian immigrants, victims of rising ANTI-SEMITISM there, who arrived in the United States during the late 19th century affected Henrietta deeply, and she organized an evening school to serve them. Touched by their stories of persecution, she developed an interest in ZIONISM—the movement to re-establish the Jewish state in the land of Israel. In 1893, she cofounded the Zionist Association of Baltimore, one of the earliest in the United States. In the same year she became a founding editor of the Jewish Publication Society (JPS), a position she held until 1916. As an editor at JPS, Szold continued her work of preserving and disseminating Jewish culture in the United States.

Beginning in 1910 when she became secretary of the Federation of American Zionists, Szold's activities were increasingly directed toward Zionism. In 1912 she founded Hadassah, the Women's Zionist Organization of America. Dedicated to relief work among Jewish immigrants to Palestine, Hadassah centered its activities on medical and health services, supplying the immigrants with doctors, nurses, ambulances, and medical supplies. As a social organization Hadassah also made Zionism prominent in the lives of thousands of American women.

In 1927 Szold became the first woman elected to the Palestine Zionist Executive Committee, with responsibility for health and education. In that year she emigrated to Palestine, where she lived until her death on February 13, 1945.

While there, Szold made her most valuable contributions to world Jewry as director of the Youth Aliyah. From 1933 until her death, Szold was responsible for resettling thousands of youths and children who managed to escape the Nazis. Of the 30,000 young people brought to Palestine in the Youth Aliyah, many arrived as orphans. Organized into children's villages and incorporated into existing kibbutzim, they provided a significant core of Israel's population.

Still working at the time of her death at the age of 85, Henrietta Szold played a major role in two countries. A "captive to a cause," as she phrased it, Szold helped to make Zionism a significant element in American Judaism and among American Jews. By working to make Zionism a reality, she helped lay the foundations for the establishment of the state of Israel.

EQ

Bibliography: Joan Dash, *Summoned to Jerusalem: The Life of Henrietta Szold* (New York: Harper & Row, 1979); Irving Fineman, *Woman of Valor: The Biography of Henrietta Szold, 1860–1945* (New York: Simon & Schuster, 1961); Elma E. Levinger, *Fighting Angel: The Story of Henrietta Szold* (New York: Behrman House, 1946); Marvin Lowenthal, *Henrietta Szold: Life and Letters* (Westport, Conn.: Greenwood Press, 1942); Rose Zeitlin, *Henrietta Szold: Record of a Life* (New York: Dial Press, 1952).

T

Tarthang Tulku   See BUDDHISM.

Taylor, Nathaniel William (1786–1858)

Nathaniel William Taylor was a Congregational minister and theologian who, along with Yale College president Timothy Dwight, is considered to be the founder of the early 19th-century religious movement known as the New Haven Theology. The New Haven Theology, a form of American ARMINIANISM, blended many of the traditional theological doctrines of Calvinism with the emphasis on free will that typified revivalism in the United States.

Taylor was born in New Milford, Connecticut on June 23, 1786. He graduated from Yale in 1807. After starting his career as a reader and secretary for Timothy DWIGHT, Taylor served as minister of the First Church of New Haven between 1811 and 1822. He left the First Church to become professor of theology at the newly founded Yale Divinity School, which was established in 1822 to supply the increasing demand for trained and educated ministers during the SECOND GREAT AWAKENING period. Taylor remained at that post for the next 35 years.

Although Taylor insisted he never departed from Calvinist orthodoxy, his theological approach was, in fact, a novel one. He made this position clear in his *Concio ad Clerum,* an address before the annual gathering of the Congregational clergy of his state in 1828. He rejected the classic view that sin derived from humanity's connection with Adam, that is, that moral depravity was an inherited quality native to human nature itself. Rather, in Taylor's view, "sin is in the sinning." Although sin was "original" because it was inevitable and universal, men and women also had—in his famous phrase—"power to the contrary." A human being was a rational, moral agent, not a passive or predetermined part of nature, and was therefore free to choose to live according to God's laws.

Taylor's approach had a twofold significance for the development of American Christianity in his day. First, he consciously encouraged Congregationalists to engage in revivalist activities, the quintessential religious expression of the democratic ethos of Jacksonian America. After that time, revivals in America came generally to be understood less as miraculous works of God than as the achievement of preachers skillful enough to win the assent and cooperation of sinners. And second, Taylor laid a broad theoretical base for religiously motivated activities of social reform. Just as sinners had the ability to seek their own spiritual conversion, so well-

Nathaniel William Taylor, architect of the New Haven Theology, a more intellectual form of revivalism that flourished in Jacksonian America.

intentioned Christians held the power to undertake the moral regeneration of American society. The New Haven Theology provided American Protestants with a rationale for trusting God while at the same time exerting themselves in the pursuit of secular goals.

Taylor's writings were collected and published in several posthumous volumes: *Practical Sermons* (1858), *Essays, Lectures, Etc.* (1859), and *Lectures on the Moral Government of God* (1859). Still serving at Yale Divinity School at the end of his life, Taylor died in New Haven on March 10, 1858.

GHS, Jr.

Bibliography: Sidney E. Mead, *Nathaniel W. Taylor, 1786–1858: A Connecticut Liberal* (Chicago: University of Chicago Press, 1942).

Tekakwitha, Kateri (Catherine) (1656–1680) Kateri or Catherine Tekakwitha (Tegah-Kouita), the first Native American to be proposed for sainthood, was born at Gandahouhage, Mohawk Territory (near modern-day Auriesville, New York) probably in the year 1656. Her mother was a captured Christian Algonquian who had been married to one of her Mohawk captors. At the age of four Kateri was stricken in a smallpox epidemic that killed her parents and left her disfigured.

Orphaned, she was raised by a paternal uncle who was virulently anti-Christian and anti-French. Successful French military attacks on the Mohawks forced them to open up their region to Jesuit missionaries whose teaching deeply influenced the young girl. Despite the opposition of her uncle, she underwent instruction in the Christian religion and was baptized on Easter Sunday (April 18), 1675 and given the name Catherine (Kateri).

Abused and threatened because of her new faith and her refusal to marry, Tekakwitha fled to the mission of St. Francis Xavier du Sault St. Louis (Lachine Rapids, Canada). Her religious devotion was so intense that she was revered as a holy woman. Kateri practiced numerous austerities—fasting two days a week, flagellating herself, undertaking numerous penances, and praying for hours in the mission chapel.

She took a private vow of chastity and established a small convent at the mission where she became an inspiration for the converts. The austerities took their toll, however, and she died on April 17, 1680 at the age of 24. She was buried at La Prairie de la Madeleine, Canada. The story of her deep faith spread throughout the region, among both French and natives, and the grave of the "Lily of the Mohawks" soon became a site of pilgrimage. An increasing number of miracles were attributed to her intervention, and in 1884 the Third Plenary Council of the United States Catholic Church petitioned Rome to initiate steps for her canonization. In 1932, with the formal presentation of her cause for beatification, she became the first native North American to be proposed for sainthood.

EQ

Bibliography: Margaret Bunson, *Kateri Tekakwitha, Mystic of the Wilderness* (Huntington, Ind.: Our Sunday Visitor, 1992); Marie C. Buehrle, *Kateri of the Mohawks* (Milwaukee: Bruce Publishing Co., 1954); Marlene McCauley, *Adventures with a Saint: Kateri Tekakwitha, "Lily of the Mohawks"* (Phoenix: Grace House, 1992); Daniel Sargent, *Catherine Tekakwitha* (New York: Longmans, Green and Co., 1937); Ellen Walworth, *The Life and Times of Kateri Tekakwitha, the Lily of the Mohawks, 1656–1680* (Buffalo: P. Paul, 1891).

televangelism See ELECTRONIC CHURCH.

temperance Opposition to "intemperance," the heavy consumption of alcohol, has a long history within the reforming vision of evangelically minded Protestants (see EVANGELICALISM; SECOND GREAT AWAKENING). The temperance cause spread in three great waves from the 1820s onward. Institutionalized in the Women's Christian Temperance Union (1874) and the Anti-Saloon League (1893), it provided a unifying focus for a wide variety of social reform and religious groups, particularly evangelical denominations and moderate women suffragists (see WILLARD, FRANCES). The movement's national impact culminated in the 1919 ratification of the eighteenth Amendment to the Constitution, which made most production and consumption of alcohol illegal until its repeal in 1933. The temperance concern continues to be evident today in the thrust of municipal liquor laws in several regions of the country.

Contrary to the popular image of PURITANISM, New England's founders were not prudes; rum played an important part in the early trade economy. Over the course of the COLONIAL PERIOD, Americans drank enormous amounts of alcohol, especially whiskey, and by the 1820s per-capita annual consumption of distilled beverages was roughly three times that of today. Early attacks on alcohol spoke of it primarily as a danger to both health and civic life. For Lyman BEECHER, widespread consumption indicated that "our vices are digging the graves of our liberties, and preparing to entomb our glory." Beecher founded the Connecticut Society for the Reformation of Morals in 1813, the nation's first temperance group, and in the next few years the movement took on an evangelical tone, as drinking itself became associated with sin. Beecher galvanized support with the publication of *Six Sermons* on abstinence in 1826, which was widely distributed and quoted.

Other societies appeared across New England during these years, including the Boston-based American Society for the Promotion of Temperance (1826) and the American Temperance Union (1836). Temperance societies produced literature on the evils of "demon rum," organized revivals, and sent out public lecturers. By 1834 the Boston group had expanded nationally to include 5,000 branch chapters, with a million members. Following Maine's lead in 1846, the reform had produced prohibition laws in 13 states by 1855. However by the end of the CIVIL WAR in 1865, only two states remained "dry."

A second wave of reform, less focused on the earlier evangelistic concerns of Beecher and the New England societies, began in the mid-1870s. Instead temperance became a vehicle for women seeking to change the emerging industrial social order, in which they were being placed in increasingly dependent positions upon wage-earning husbands and fathers. Beginning with a spontaneous protest on December 24, 1873, led by Eliza Trimble Thompson of Hillsboro, Ohio, marchers closed in on saloons, singing, praying and pleading with occupants to return to their families. If nothing else, the protests invigorated a number of women, some of whom gathered in Cleveland during November 1874 to form the Woman's Christian Temperance Union. Eventually, under Frances Willard, the WCTU went on to exert enormous national influence on temperance as well as other pressing social issues.

Willard's own vision of ecumenical, broad-reaching social reforms was overshadowed in 1893 by the formation of the Anti-Saloon League under the leadership of Methodist minister Alpha J. Kynett, president Hiram Price, and superintendent Wayne Wheeler, who said the league represented the churches and the "decent people." Backed by national groups of METHODISTS, BAPTISTS, and Presbyterians (see PRESBYTERIANISM) (totaling nearly 40,000 congregations), the league served the growing populist sentiment: anti-urban, anti-Catholic, anti-foreign (see NATIVISM). Well financed and effective at pressure politics, the league targeted members of Congress and state legislators, resulting in the passage of dry laws in two-thirds of the states by 1916. The league's tactics were successful, but the militant national climate produced by WORLD WAR I also helped. German brewers—epitomizing everything else German—were subjected to considerable harassment by the Anglo-Saxon population. With overwhelming national support, Congress passed the Eighteenth Amendment on December 18, 1917.

The temperance movement represented perhaps the most widespread consensus of values ever achieved in American culture. In spite of the extent to which the league itself was dominated by rural-based evangelical voices, the drive for prohibition found support among socialists and progressives, who saw it as a means of derailing a powerful and socially destructive liquor industry. Catholics certainly had reason to oppose prohibitionism: Catholic ethnic groups often saw alcohol as far less than demonic; working-class Catholics viewed prohibition as a middle-class strategy to control their lives (which it was). Nevertheless, liberal Catholic leaders were supportive of temperance, if not always of outright prohibition. Catholics did however view moral persuasion rather than legislation as the most appropriate strategy for reforming American drinking patterns, and their suspicion of the league grew in conjunction with the league's public influence. Cardinal James GIBBONS, who declared in 1891 that he was "a temperate man, not a temperance man," said prior to passage of the Eighteenth Amendment that prohibition would be "a national catastrophe, little short of a crime against the spiritual and physical well-being of the American people."

Although Prohibition remained the law of the land until 1933, it proved unworkable. Laws violated more than observed, said Catholic theologian John RYAN, carried no force. Certainly the experiment united the nation's Protestants, and fueled the growing anti-Catholic and anti-Jewish nativism of the 1920s. One Protestant leader for instance labeled 1928 Catholic presidential candidate Alfred E. Smith, a "rum-soaked Romanist," who represented "the kind of dirty people you find on the sidewalks of New York . . . the Italians, the Sicilians, the Poles, the Russian Jews." But the unified values that bolstered American society at the end of World War I fragmented during the 1920s, as Protestants fought among themselves, and lost what cultural authority they had developed earlier (see SOCIAL GOSPEL; EVOLUTION). In the midst of economic and cultural crisis, drinking lost much of its sinful stature, becoming instead a sign of rebellion against a stifling social order.

MG

Bibliography: Ruth Bordin, *Woman and Temperance: The Quest for Power and Liberty, 1873–1900* (Philadelphia: Temple University Press, 1981); Norman Clark, *Deliver Us from Evil: An Interpretation of American Prohibition* (New York: W. W. Norton, 1976); K. Austin Kerr, *Organized for Prohibition: A New History of the Anti-Saloon League* (New Haven: Yale University Press, 1985); Mark Edward Lender and James Kirby Martin, *Drinking in America: A History* (New York: The Free Press, 1982); W. J. Rorabaugh, *The Alcoholic Republic: an American Tradition* (New York: Oxford University Press, 1979).

Tennent, Gilbert (1703–1764)

Gilbert Tennent was the premier Presbyterian revivalist of his day. He was also an important spokesman for the Great Awakening, the remarkable series of revivals that occurred in mid-18th-century America. Best remembered for his March 1740 sermon on "The Danger of an Unconverted Ministry," in which he attacked opponents of the Awakening, Tennent's ideas contributed greatly to the animosity that split Presbyterians into New Side and Old Side (see NEW SIDE/ OLD SIDE) factions in 1741.

Tennent was born in County Armagh, Ireland on February 5, 1703. He was the eldest son of William Tennent, Sr., then a clergyman of the Church of England. After the family emigrated to Pennsylvania in 1718, William renounced his Anglican orders and was admitted to the Presbyterian ministry. Gilbert received a master's degree from Yale College in 1725 and studied theology under his father's tutelage. He was licensed as a Presbyterian minister in 1725, served briefly at Newcastle, Delaware, and then assumed a pastorate in New Brunswick, New Jersey.

At New Brunswick, Tennent became acquainted with the famed preacher and evangelist Theodorus J. FRELINGHUYSEN, pastor of a neighboring Dutch Reformed church. Frelinghuysen convinced Tennent that no one should call himself a Christian unless he had undergone an experience of conversion and received the inward assurance that his soul had been saved. As a consequence of this belief, Tennent made evangelism the center of his ministry, and by 1729 revivals had begun to occur in churches in

Gilbert Tennent, a Presbyterian minister whose preaching of personal religious experience over strict orthodoxy shook American churches in the mid-18th century.

his area. In the meantime, churches at Freehold, New Jersey (where his brother John was pastor) and Neshaminy, Pennsylvania (where his father and his brother William, Jr. both served as clergy) also showed evidences of spiritual stirring. This was the beginning of the Great Awakening.

In the late 1720s and early 1730s, Tennent was involved with the "Log College" that his father had founded at Neshaminy to train Presbyterian ministers. Despite being derided for its lack of academic credentials by those who opposed the revivals, the Log College educated a group of clergy who continued the tradition of the Awakening. By 1739, Tennent's influence was so great that Anglican revivalist George Whitefield sought him out during his famous tour of the colonies. Whitefield asked Tennent to accompany him to New England, and Tennent obliged by leading revivals in Massachusetts and Connecticut in 1740. Tennent undercut the trust people placed in a purely formal faith—attending worship as a routine matter or adhering to doctrines and moral teachings in an unexamined way—and called them to true repentance.

As it turned out, Tennent went too far, for the Presbyterians soon divided over the appropriateness of such piety and the revivals it inspired. In 1741, Tennent's New Brunswick presbytery was expelled from the Synod of Philadelphia by the anti-revivalist Old Side party. The New Side Presbyterians, as the revival party was known, responded to their ejection by organizing a church of their own. The division in Presbyterianism continued until 1758, when the factions came together again under the dominance of the New Side. In the intervening years, Tennent moderated his views and admitted that he had erred in exacerbating the controversy over revivals.

Tennent left New Brunswick in 1743 to become pastor of the Second Presbyterian Church in Philadelphia, where he stayed for the remainder of his life. In his later years, he served as moderator of the reunited Presbyterian Church and labored to foster its growth. Tennent died in Philadelphia on July 23, 1764.

GHS, Jr.

Bibliography: Milton J. Coalter, Jr., *Gilbert Tennent, Son of Thunder: A Case of Continental Pietism's Impact on the First Great Awakening in the Middle Colonies* (Westport, Conn.: Greenwood Press, 1986).

Testem Benevolentiae   See AMERICANISM.

theosophy   One of a number of new religious movements that originated in 19th-century America, theosophy (literally, "wisdom of God") began as a reform movement within American SPIRITUALISM.

Theosophists trace their roots back through SWEDENBORGIANISM and MESMERISM, Pythagoreanism and Neoplatonism, the Jewish Kabbala and the Hindu Vedas to one common and secret source of primeval wisdom from which all people of faith drink. But despite its appeals to the ancient East, theosophy has freely adopted and adapted influences from the modern West, including spiritualism, free thought, evolutionary theory, and academic Orientalism.

The theosophical movement found institutional form when Helena Petrovna BLAVATSKY (1831–1891) and Henry Steel OLCOTT (1832–1907) co-founded the Theosophical Society in New York in 1875. Among the better-known early theosophists were inventor Thomas Edison and Abner Doubleday, who was once revered (erroneously) as the inventor of baseball. Under the leadership of William Quan Judge (1851–1896), the Theosophical Society in America split off from the original Theosophical Society in 1895. That organization made its headquarters in Point Loma, California and was led by Katherine A. Tingley (1847–1929), following Judge's death in 1896. A later schism produced the third major theosophical organization, the United Lodge of Theosophists, which was founded in Los Angeles in 1909.

Members of the Theosophical Society aimed initially to conduct spiritualist experiments and then to induce on the basis of their scientific observations the occult laws undergirding spiritual phenomena. After Blavatsky and Olcott took the Theosophical Society to India in 1878, the organization integrated a new interest in Asian religious traditions into its spiritualist agenda. In the early 1880s, the society codified its now-famous "three objects": "to form the nucleus of a Universal Brotherhood of Humanity without distinction of race, creed, or color; to promote the study of Aryan and other Eastern literature, religions and sciences; and to investigate the hidden mysteries of nature and the psychical powers latent in man."

Following the death of Blavatsky in 1891, Annie Wood Besant (1847–1933) gradually moved into the forefront of the theosophical movement. She represented theosophy at the WORLD'S PARLIAMENT OF RELIGIONS in Chicago in 1893, and became president of the Theosophical Society after Olcott's death in 1907. Although Besant distinguished herself from Blavatsky and Olcott (both of whom had converted to BUDDHISM while in Sri Lanka in 1880) by her advocacy of HINDUISM, she continued her predecessors' emphasis on the kinship of all religions.

There are at the core of theosophy two distinguishable concerns: first, the esoteric interest in investigating spiritual phenomena and discovering the occult laws undergirding them; and, second, the exoteric interest in promoting the liberal theory that all religions are essentially one. These two concerns manifest themselves, on the one hand, in the Esoteric Section, founded by the charismatic Blavatsky in 1888, and in the hoped-for but never realized pan-religious "Universal Brotherhood of Humanity" emphasized by the more organizationally minded Olcott.

Theosophical is esoteric. Theosophists claim that their truths are ancient truths, passed down through the ages by a secret occult brotherhood of Mahatmas ("Great Souls") or Masters who have preserved their hermetic tradition by initiating a select group of adepts into its mysteries. The most striking capacity of these adepts (Blavatsky included) is their ability to produce, through their knowledge of occult laws, effects that look strikingly similar to the phenomena produced during spiritualist seances by mediums communing with disembodied spirits of the dead.

The writings of Helena Blavatsky, who claimed to have been initiated into this secret occult brotherhood while traveling in the Orient, form the core of the theosophical canon. Both *Isis Unveiled* (1877), her first and most widely read book, and *The Secret Doctrine* (1888), her most systematic work, trace all religion, philosophy, and science to one ancient and universal wisdom-religion.

Theosophy is often referred to as a "harmonial religion," and theosophists do attempt to harmonize numerous entities—God and humanity, religion and science, East and West, matter and spirit. Because they believe that human beings are manifestations of the divine and are therefore fundamentally at one with God, theosophists tend to be optimistic about the ability of both human beings and human societies to evolve in positive directions. Articles in the main theosophical organ, the *Theosophist* (established 1879), have promoted concerns as disparate as women's rights, TEMPERANCE, vegetarianism, cremation, caste reform, and Esperanto.

Theosophists generally reject dualistic, anthropomorphic and transcendent notions of God in favor of an Absolute that is monistic, impersonal and immanent. Most theosophists also reject orthodox Christian notions that humans live one life and then move on to eternal rewards in heaven or everlasting punishment in hell. According to Blavatsky, human beings consist of seven bodies or sheaths. The first four, or "Lower Quaternary," are the physical body, the etheric body double, the astral body, and the mental body. These bodies cease to exist at death. But the final three bodies, the "Upper Imperishable Triad" of Mind, Soul, and Spirit, survive through numerous incarnations. In addition to reincarnation, theosophists affirm the law of karma, which states that individuals cannot escape the consequences of their actions. For this reason, most reject as unjust orthodox Christian theologies of the Atonement that affirm that Jesus Christ's death on the cross pays the debt for human sin.

Theosophists' interests in reincarnation and karma point to the fact that theosophy is religiously eclectic. Because they affirm the fundamental unity of all religious traditions, theosophists have a long history of promoting Asian religious traditions and of longing for a "Universal Brotherhood of Humanity" that will bring into harmony people of all nations, religions, and cultures. Although theosophists for a time belied this pluralistic stance with anti-Christian back-biting, theosophists today tend to be as friendly toward Christianity as Blavatsky

and Olcott were toward Hindus and Buddhists.

Because of its emphasis on the immanence of God, its cosmic optimism, its interest in social reform, its criticism of dogma and ritual, its tendency toward ARMINIANISM, and its friendliness toward both science and modernity, theosophy may be seen alongside modernistic Protestantism (see MODERNISM), REFORM JUDAISM, and Americanist Catholicism (see AMERICANISM) as a form of religious liberalism. It also stands as an important precursor to the modern New Age movement (see NEW AGE RELIGION).

Despite the kinship between theosophy and more mainstream religious movements, no theosophical organization has been able to attract a large membership. From its beginning in 1875 until today, theosophy has attracted an elite rather than a popular following. In India and Ceylon, theosophy appealed almost exclusively to British civil servants and English-speaking Indian elites. Moreover, periodic scandals—beginning with the notorious "Coulomb Case" of 1884 in which Emma Coulomb, a former colleague and friend of Blavatsky, accused her of fraud—have drained theosophical organizations of members. Despite these limitations, theosophists have been able to establish and maintain hundreds of branches on five continents.

SRP

Bibliography: Bruce Campbell, *Ancient Wisdom Revived: A History of the Theosophical Movement* (Berkeley: University of California Press, 1980); Sylvia Cranston, *Helena Petrovna Blavatsky: The Extraordinary Life and Influence of Helena Blavatsky, Founder of the Modern Theosophical Movement* (New York: G. P. Putnam's Sons, 1993); Henry S. Olcott, *Old Diary Leaves: The History of the Theosophical Society*, 6 vols. (Adyar, India: Theosophical Publishing House, 1974–75).

Thoreau, Henry David (1817–1862)

Largely unknown to contemporaries outside his circle of New England intellectuals, Thoreau devoted his energies to living and thinking as an individual. Regarded during his lifetime as an extremist for his political ideas, in later times

WALDEN;

OR,

LIFE IN THE WOODS.

By HENRY D. THOREAU,

AUTHOR OF "A WEEK ON THE CONCORD AND MERRIMACK RIVERS."

I do not propose to write an ode to dejection, but to brag as lustily as chanticleer in **the** morning, standing on his roost, if only to wake my neighbors up. — Page 92.

BOSTON:

TICKNOR AND FIELDS.

M DCCC LIV.

Henry David Thoreau, a prophet of American transcendentalism whose life and writings are as influential today as in his lifetime. Title page of *Walden*. (Library of Congress)

he influenced many Americans active in causes of political and social reform. In particular his writing on nature, especially *Walden; or, Life in the Woods* (1854), exerted a profound influence on the conservation movement that arose in the late 19th and 20th centuries. In addition, his anti-authoritarian religious views, and his appreciation for Asian thought, endeared him to subsequent generations dissatisfied with the cultural mainstream, such as the COUNTERCULTURE of the 1960s.

Born in poverty on July 12, 1817, Thoreau early on developed a love of reading, and by the time he entered Harvard College in 1833 was already well prepared in the classics. At Harvard he lived frugally and began storing his ideas in his posthumously published *Journals*. After graduation Thoreau taught sporadically, made pencils with his father, and in general developed no plans for a lucrative career. He performed odd jobs, kept house while living with Ralph Waldo EMERSON for two years, spent another year tutoring the children of Emerson's brother, and performed occasional land surveys.

Thoreau was quite critical of the style of individual life necessary to both the nascent capitalism of his day and the more traditional farming. In contrast to both, which he thought turned the human into the servant of tools and machines, he sought to live an independent life. As he put it in "Civil Disobedience": "You must live within yourself, and depend upon yourself always tucked up and ready for a start." While he made an effort to join the lyceum circuit of his fellow transcendentalists (see TRANSCENDENTALISM), he never developed the oratorical skills of Emerson or Bronson ALCOTT, and never saw the essay or the lecture as means to a livelihood. As he once put it: "My life has been the poem I would have writ, / But I could not both live and utter it." He did take an active public role in supporting ABOLITIONISM. In addition he spent a brief time in jail over his refusal to pay "poll taxes," an experience which led him to reflect on the inherent corruption of political power, and to his advocacy of civil disobedience. His death at the age of 42 from tuberculosis came May 6, 1862.

Thoreau's real life emerged in the course of his many travels throughout the Northeast, and in the year spent living alone on Walden Pond near Concord. In his daily encounters with the features of his New England environment, Thoreau found a kind of sacramental power, a communion with that which is truly real, much as his friend Emerson had suggested. But the material means of Thoreau's communion were far more particular than Emerson's. In dealing with huckleberries, woodchucks, or beans, Thoreau came to see in the diversity of nature the divine presence. For Thoreau this presence could easily be obscured by human enterprise. Thus the human task as he saw it was to keep the world new and unspoiled: "In Wildness is the preservation of the world" he wrote in "Walking."

Thoreau's appreciation for the material qualities of the world have led some to see him as a pantheist, one who believes the world itself is divine. While much in his writing reflects that leaning, at the same time he inherited enough from his New England CALVINISM to suspect that nature pointed to something higher and unseen. However in spite of this residual view of a transcendent God, Thoreau broke completely with the authority claimed by religious tradition. Even more so than Emerson, he wanted to experience divinity directly. To that end he made considerable effort to acquire a breadth of perspectives on the spiritual, becoming a student of the classical Asian works recently translated into English (see BUDDHISM, HINDUISM). Thoreau's ability to blend his own insight into natural history with a wealth of background in classical Greek and Roman literature, the Bible and works from Asia and the Mideast put his solitary pursuits in what he saw as the company of immortals.

As first and foremost an individualist, Thoreau was often disdained by his contemporaries, whom he thought lived "lives of quiet desperation." But his continuing appeal to subsequent generations suggests that his efforts to see the manifold qualities of the natural world, and to live simply amid them, reflect important yearnings for an authentic life among many Americans.

MG

Bibliography: Robert D. Richardson, Jr., *Henry Thoreau: A Life of the Mind* (Berkeley: University of California Press, 1986).

Thornwell, James Henley (1812–1862)

James Henley Thornwell was a Presbyterian minister and the most notable theologian of the antebellum South. Recognized as an articulate proslavery theorist in the years preceding the Civil War, Thornwell has often been labeled "the Calhoun of the Church" because of his theological defense of the institution of slavery.

Thornwell was born in Marlboro District, South Carolina on December 9, 1812. He graduated from South Carolina College in 1831, studied in Massachusetts at Andover Theological Seminary and Harvard Divinity School, and was licensed to preach by the Harmony Presbytery of South Carolina in 1834. Over the next 20 years, Thornwell served in several brief pastorates and as a professor at South Carolina College. In 1855 he became professor of theology at Columbia Theological Seminary, where he remained until the end of his life. He was also active in the affairs of the Old School (see NEW SCHOOL/OLD SCHOOL) Presbyterian Church as founding editor of the *Southern Presbyterian Review* (1847) and as editor of the *Southern Quarterly Review* (1855–1857).

During the 1850s Thornwell formulated the so-called "doctrine of the spirituality of the church," the theoretical basis for southern proslavery religious thought. Thornwell insisted that the church was a spiritual organization concerned with matters of heavenly, not earthly, concern. He believed the church should be apolitical and had no justification involving itself in secular affairs, even in moral reform efforts. Contrary to abolitionist crusaders in the North, who condemned slavery on Christian and biblical grounds, Thornwell maintained that the institution was a purely civil affair that the church had no authority either to condemn or commend.

After the Civil War began in the spring of 1861, Thornwell led in the formation of a separate Old School denomination in the South, the Presbyterian Church in the Confederate States of America. In his "Address to All the Churches of Jesus Christ throughout the Earth," which he composed for the southern Presbyterians' first General Assembly in December 1861, Thornwell justified his church's separation from its counterpart in the North. In his speech, he described church and state as "planets moving in different orbits." If northern Presbyterians had been willing to respect that idea and had not meddled in political matters, separation into two denominations might never have been necessary. Presbyterians in the South were grateful, he said, that they had "never mixed the issues of this world with the weightier matters that properly belong to . . . citizens of the kingdom of God."

Poor health had troubled Thornwell for several months prior to the beginning of the war. Personal tragedy further weakened him. After traveling to Virginia to visit a son who had been wounded in battle, Thornwell's health failed completely. He died in Charlotte, North Carolina on August 1, 1862.

GHS, Jr.

Bibliography: James Oscar Farmer, Jr., *The Metaphysical Confederacy: James Henley Thornwell and the Synthesis of Southern Values* (Macon, Ga.: Mercer University Press, 1986).

Tillich, Paul Johannes (1886–1965)

One of the leading American theologians of the 20th century, Paul Tillich was born on August 20, 1886 in Starzeddel, Germany (now Starosiedle, Poland). His early life was that of a small-town child of a German Lutheran minister. Called to the ministry himself, Tillich studied at the universities of Berlin, Tübingen, and Halle before receiving his Ph.D. from Breslau in 1911. He returned to Halle where he received the licentiate in theology (1912) and assumed the role of a Lutheran minister.

During World War I, Tillich served as a chaplain in the German army. The horrors of the war and his wife's desertion (she ran off with his best friend) served to undermine Tillich's assumptions about the world, as did the chaos of Weimar Germany. Tillich, having experienced

the death of liberal theology (see LIBERALISM, THEOLOGICAL) in the war, immersed himself in radical thought and politics. He formed an organization of Christian socialists, the "Kairos Circle," and became the first Lutheran minister to join the German Social Democratic Party.

With the Nazi assumption of power in 1933, Tillich was in danger because of his political views. A professor of philosophy at the University of Frankfurt-am-Main, Tillich was the first Christian removed from a teaching position by the Nazis (it was learned later that he was also on the first list of non-Jews slated for execution). Although he felt that to leave Germany in its time of need was cowardice, he heeded the advice of Reinhold NIEBUHR and accepted an invitation from Union Theological Seminary to give a series of lectures. Arriving in the United States in 1933, he was made professor of Philosophical Theology at Union, the faculty having made a place for him by voluntarily giving up 5 percent of their salary.

The difficult time Tillich and his wife Hannah had in adjusting to life at Union did not prevent him from continuing the creative work he had begun in Germany. Tillich's theology centered on three main themes. The first was that religious reality can be expressed only in cultural forms. These forms are always limited and never express the totality of religious truth. These cultural forms are given meaning and value by the fact that they participate in, are infused with, the divine reality. This complex relationship was expressed by Tillich in the phrases "religion is the substance of culture" and "culture is the form of religion."

The second major theme in Tillich's work is the analysis of the goal of religious reflection. Religion is always the expression of an "ultimate concern." This phrase of Tillich's is both analytical and normative. As analytical it describes existing religious phenomena. Human beings worship many things, some of which are idols. One can know the idols of a particular culture by asking what that culture's ultimate concern is.

As normative, the phrase always asks the question "What is truly ultimate?" The answer, for Tillich, is the God that is Being Itself. God as Being Itself is not to be confused with the idols of human creation, the gods of religion, or even the God of Christian belief. God as Being Itself stands over and above humanity's limited cultural conceptions of God. The God who is truly God is beyond the ability of human beings to grasp completely. Beyond finitude, God as Being Itself continues despite the destruction of our limited and finite attempts to make God in our image, to limit God to our conceptual understandings. The realization that everything in which we put our faith is destined for collapse leads humanity to despair, to anxiety, to estrangement. The world seems to be void and meaningless. In the midst of this rests the underlying fact of God as the ground of all being. The basic unity of the world is not destroyed in the collapse of our finite forms. Being continues and non-being is overcome.

In Christian theological terms, Jesus as the Christ provides the possibility for overcoming anxiety and estrangement. He is the New Being who shows us the power of salvation. Jesus experienced all the limits and tragedy of human existence, but through the activity of God expressed the re-union and re-conciliation of the essential unity between God and humanity, the reality of "God-manhood," in Tillich's phrase. This essential unity is seen in the resurrection where the "reality" of the New Being is ultimately seen, for in the resurrection the overcoming of estrangement and finitude is demonstrated.

By the time of his retirement from Union in 1955, Tillich was probably the most influential theologian in the United States. After leaving Union, Tillich spent seven years as University Professor at Harvard. The last three years of his life (1962–1965) were spent teaching at the University of Chicago. These years, while short, were significant for Tillich. His influence extended beyond the churchly and had a deep impact even on those who did not consider themselves religious. Tillich always had a deep appreciation for the secular world, especially the arts. While at Chicago, his friendship with Mircea Eliade, a professor of the history of religions, served to broaden his knowledge and appreciation of other religious traditions. The significance of those traditions for Christian understanding was the work in which he was engaged at the time of his death of a heart attack on October 22, 1965.

EQ

Bibliography: Rollo May, *Paulus: Reminiscences of a Friendship* (New York: Harper & Row, 1973); Wilhelm Pauk and Marion Pauk, *Paul Tillich: His Life and Thought* (New York: Harper & Row, 1976); Hannah Tillich, *From Time to Time* (New York: Stein & Day, 1973); Paul Tillich, *Systematic Theology,* 3 vols. (Chicago: University of Chicago Press, 1951–63); ———, *The Protestant Era* (Chicago: University of Chicago Press, 1957); ———, *The Courage to Be* (New Haven: Yale University Press, 1952).

Toleration, Act of (Maryland) The Act of Toleration passed by the Maryland (see MARYLAND [COLONY]) colonial assembly on April 21, 1649, known officially as "An Act Concerning Religion," was a major step forward for religious liberty. Designed to end the armed conflicts between Protestants and Catholics that had racked the colony in the first part of the decade, the law carefully proscribed behavior designed to create hostility and animosity.

The act guaranteed all persons "professing belief in Jesus Christ" to be free to exercise their religion without being "any waies troubled, Molested or discountenanced." Equally it forbade reproachfully calling anyone "heretic, schismatic, idolator, Puritan, independent, Presbyterian, popish priest, Jesuit, Jesuited papist, Lutheran, Calvinist, Anabaptist, Brownist, antinomian, Barrowist, Roundhead, or Separatist." Although a far cry from the norm of the 17th century, the act protected only those who accepted the Trinity (denial being punishable by death), forbade disparaging remarks about the Virgin Mary, Apostles, or the Evangelists, and the profanation of the Lord's day or Sabbath "called Sunday."

The act, however, failed to bring about peace in the colony. A Protestant revolt removed Maryland's acting governor from power in 1651 and after firmly establishing control, they repealed the Toleration Act in 1654. The next year, the Protestant-dominated assembly outlawed the practice of Roman Catholicism. Although Catholics regained some of their rights following the return of proprietary government, not until after the AMERICAN REVOLUTION did they regain the rights they earlier had granted to others in the colony they established.

(See also ANTI-CATHOLICISM; CALVERT, CECILIUS; ROMAN CATHOLICISM.)

EQ

Bibliography: Jay P. Dolan, *The American Catholic Experience: A History from Colonial Times to the Present* (Notre Dame: University of Notre Dame Press, 1992); John Tracy Ellis, *Catholics in Colonial America* (Baltimore: Helicon Press, 1965); James Hennesey, *American Catholics: A History of the Roman Catholic Community in the United States* (New York: Oxford University Press, 1981); Aubrey C. Land, *Colonial Maryland: A History* (Millwood, N.Y.: KTO Press, 1981); Vera A. Foster Rollo, *The Proprietorship of Maryland: A Documented Account* (Lanham: Maryland Historical Press, 1989).

Tomlinson, Ambrose Jessup (1865–1943)

A. J. Tomlinson was one of the first leaders of the 20th-century Pentecostal movement and the founder of the Church of God of Prophecy. Traveling widely throughout his career, Tomlinson's ministry reflected many of the key beliefs and practices of early PENTECOSTALISM: faith healing, speaking in tongues, and restoration of the New Testament church.

Tomlinson was born near Westfield, Indiana on September 22, 1865. He began working as the Sunday school superintendent of a Quaker congregation in Westfield around the year 1889. However, after learning about the HOLINESS MOVEMENT and its views of SANCTIFICATION, Tomlinson organized his own congregation of believers. The Holiness movement, which arose within Protestantism in the 19th century, emphasized the individual Christian's ability to attain perfection on earth through the work of the Holy Spirit. After several years of missionary preaching in eastern Tennessee and western North Carolina, Tomlinson gathered several congregations and their ministers together in 1906. By 1909 he had been elected moderator of a new denomination, the Church of God, so named to emphasize its continuity with the Christianity of biblical times. It was, Tomlinson claimed, the only true church.

Two practices set Tomlinson's movement apart from other Protestant denominations. First, after learning of the doctrine of divine healing taught by Pentecostal minister Carrie Judd Montgomery, Tomlinson began praying for the healing of the sick in his revival services. His ideas about Christian holiness convinced him that God would not merely help believers overcome sin, but would bring them physical healing as well. Second, in January 1908 Tomlinson underwent a tremendous spiritual experience that he believed symbolized baptism in the Holy Spirit. From then on, Tomlinson looked upon the ability to speak in tongues, reminiscent of the day of Pentecost described in the New Testament Book of Acts (2:1–11), as evidence of God's special favor. Spontaneous outbursts of ecstatic speech marked the worship of early Pentecostal churches like Tomlinson's.

Tomlinson held the post of general overseer of the Church of God from 1910 to 1923. He also edited the denomination's official journal, *The Church of God Evangel*, during the same period. A dispute over Tomlinson's leadership style and his refusal to share power with other church officers, however, alienated his associates and led to a schism. Accused of financial mismanagement, he was deposed from his position in 1923. Tomlinson took 2,000 adherents with him to form a new denomination, also named "Church of God." Following a lengthy period of litigation, the original denomination took the name Church of God (Cleveland, Tennessee), while Tomlinson's denomination eventually accepted the designation Church of God of Prophecy. Although Tomlinson's authoritarianism kept his denomination separate from other Pentecostal churches, the Church of God of Prophecy numbered over 30,000 members by the early 1940s and nearly 73,000 by 1991.

Tomlinson always said that his primary concern was the winning of souls and their incorporation into God's church. He worked tirelessly for the remainder of his life, building up the movement he led. Tomlinson died at Cleveland, Tennessee on October 2, 1943.

GHS, Jr.

Bibliography: Lillie Duggar, *A. J. Tomlinson* (Cleveland, Tenn.: White Wing Publishing House, 1964).

tongues, speaking in   See PENTECOSTALISM.

Torrey, Reuben Archer (1856–1928)

R. A. Torrey was the first superintendent of the Chicago Bible Institute (later Moody Bible Institute), an organization founded by the great revivalist Dwight L. MOODY in 1887. During a peripatetic career as a minister and evangelist, Torrey established himself as a prominent critic of liberal theological trends in American Protestantism. He was one of the early spokesmen for the conservative religious movement, now called FUNDAMENTALISM, that emerged in the early 20th century.

Torrey was born on January 28, 1856 in Hoboken, New Jersey. He received his bachelor's degree from Yale College in 1875 and, after graduation from Yale Divinity School in 1878, was ordained to the Congregational ministry. He served in short pastorates at the Congregational church in Garrettsville, Ohio (1878–1882) and at the Open Door Congregational Church in Minneapolis, Minnesota (1883–1886). Next, Torrey worked as superintendent of the Minneapolis City Missionary Society (1886–1889). In 1889, he was called to Chicago to head the Bible Institute. And between 1894 and 1906, he was both superintendent of the Bible Institute and pastor of the Chicago Avenue Church in that city.

Torrey conveyed neither the personal warmth nor irenic temper of his mentor Moody. His evangelistic efforts, therefore, while highly successful, placed emphasis more on the intellectual content of the Christian faith than on piety, and he proved to be a prolific writer and lecturer in support of traditional Protestant doctrines. Following a year's study (1882–1883) in Germany, where he had been introduced to advanced, but troubling, ideas on biblical criticism, Torrey returned to the United States with a determination to defend Christian orthodoxy against modern theology, which he equated with infidelity.

Torrey's most significant contributions to the cause of conservative theology were made as editor of *The Fundamentals*, the influential 12-volume paperback series published between 1910 and 1915. In *The Fundamentals*, Torrey and others championed such beliefs as the INERRANCY of the biblical text, the bodily resurrection of Jesus Christ, and the eternal punishment of sinners in hell. Torrey also rejected the Social Gospel and other liberal programs aimed at bettering human society. His premillennial (see PREMILLENNIALISM) teachings inspired conservative Christians to place their hopes exclusively in the second coming of Christ.

Although he remained nominally in charge of the Chicago Bible Institute, from 1901 to 1905 Torrey undertook a worldwide evangelistic campaign, in which he reportedly preached to over 15 million people throughout Europe, Asia, and Australia. After leaving Chicago in 1908, he worked as an independent evangelist until 1912, then served as dean of the Bible Institute of Los Angeles (1912–1924) and as pastor of the Church of the Open Door, Los Angeles (1915–1924). One of his principal concerns throughout his career was the training of students for urban missionary work.

Torrey remained active as a preacher and lecturer after retirement from the Church of the Open Door in 1924. He died at his home in Asheville, North Carolina on October 26, 1928.

GHS, Jr.

Bibliography: Roger Martin, *R. A. Torrey: Apostle of Certainty* (Murphreesboro, Tenn.: Sword of the Lord Publishing, 1976).

Transcendental Meditation

Transcendental Meditation (T.M.), a combination of Vedanta philosophy and yogic practices taught by Maharishi Mahesh Yogi and popularized by the Beatles, is the most widely practiced type of HINDUISM in America. Over half a million Americans have practiced T.M.

Much of the early life of T.M.'s founder, Maharishi Mahesh Yogi, is shrouded in secrecy. Born in India, he began his training in meditation under Guru Brahamananda Saraswati, also known as Guru Dev, shortly after he received a degree in physics from Allahabad University around 1940. After 13 years of study under Guru Dev, he retired to the Himalayas for two years of solitude. Upon his emergence from the mountains he traveled to southern India, where he began to gather followers. Following a conference of his devotees in Madras in December of 1957, Maharishi established his Spiritual Regeneration movement on January 1, 1958. This movement aimed to regenerate humanity spiritually through the teachings and practices of Transcendental Meditation.

For the next 10 years Maharishi traveled across Asia, Europe, and North America, training students in the mantra-chanting that constitutes the core of T.M. practice. Maharishi published his first book, the *Science of Being and Art of Living,* in 1963. A few years later the movement received its biggest boost when the Beatles and a number of other celebrities befriended Maharishi and extolled the virtues of T.M. In the next decade adherents of T.M. drew not on the authority of superstars but the authority of science, attempting to prove through a series of experiments that T.M. could,

among other things, lessen stress and increase one's mental capacities.

In 1972 Maharishi unveiled a World Plan that moved beyond his earlier emphasis on individual spiritual transformation to a design for reforming society. By 1975 his World Plan Executive Council had purchased a college in Fairfield, Iowa and established a second university in Switzerland.

One reason for T.M.'s popularity is that it is relatively simple to learn and to practice. An elementary version of Advaita Vedanta or non-dualistic Hinduism, T.M. shuns asceticism, emphasizes what is natural, and promises joy and happiness. Initiates typically attend an introductory lecture sponsored by the T.M.-affiliated Students International Meditation Society. After paying a fee, the practitioner is given a secret mantra by a teacher during an initiation ceremony. He or she then learns to sit and silently repeat that mantra twice a day for 20 minutes.

Practitioners frequently claim that T.M. is a science rather than a religion, but the United States Court of Appeals in Philadelphia ruled otherwise. In 1979 it banned a course in T.M. that was being taught in public schools in New Jersey on the grounds that it was, indeed, a religion. Whether science or religion or both, T.M. remains a powerful force in American culture. It is one of a handful of Hindu forms more widely practiced in the West than in India.

SRP

Bibliography: Maharishi Mahesh Yogi, *Science of Being and Art of Living* (London: International SRM Publications, 1963).

transcendentalism

The loosely bound group of New England intellectuals known as "transcendentalists" shared a fascination with the ancient mystical view of correspondence between mind or spirit and nature. Transcendentalists developed their ideas more through lectures than literature; but nevertheless they exerted a powerful written influence on contemporaries and later generations, producing a creative blending of the intellectual residue of their

New England ancestors and contemporaries—PURITANS and Unitarians (see UNITARIAN UNIVERSALIST ASSOCIATION)—with the ideas of Romantic European poets and philosophers. In the social context of an industrializing North and a slave-holding South, they brought their idealist spirituality, based on views of knowledge and nature, to bear on the most pressing social questions of their day, becoming involved in socialist communal experiments, abolition, and women's rights.

Transcendentalism had its genesis in conversation, as several members of Boston's intellectual elite gathered on September 19, 1836 for an evening of discussion with Ralph Waldo EMERSON (see ALCOTT, BRONSON; BROWNSON, ORESTES AUGUSTUS; CLARKE, JAMES FREEMAN; RIPLEY, GEORGE). These friends founded the Transcendental Club, which eventually included feminist Margaret FULLER, who came to edit *The Dial*, the short-lived but influential transcendentalist periodical; Henry David THOREAU; abolitionist preacher Theodore PARKER; and poet William Ellery CHANNING, JR.

While varied in interests and viewpoints, transcendentalists grappled with a common intellectual problem, the relation of spirit and matter, and drew on common resources in order to meet their needs. Like the Puritans, they continued to rely upon both introspection and mystical experience of nature as key to understanding the divine, and to use Platonic language to express the analogous relation between matter and spirit. From the Unitarians they took a rationalist distrust of religious dogma and a high view of human moral potential. From the European Romantics such as Johann Fichte, Johann Wolfgang von Goethe, and Samuel Taylor Coleridge they learned to view the human mind as the ultimate reality. In addition they read the mystical works of SWEDENBORGIANISM, and were among the first Americans to incorporate the teachings of Asian traditions such as HINDUISM.

As articulated by Emerson in his influential *Nature* (1836), transcendentalists thought mind and nature were one. Hence there is an inherent mystical quality in their writings, as when Emerson says, "I become a transparent eye-ball; I am nothing; the currents of the Universal Being circulate through me; I am part or particle of God." But this mysticism, for which their detractors gave them the name "transcendentalists" to begin with, led to a remarkably pragmatic set of interests.

Because of the unity between mind and nature, lawful relationships could be intuited between things natural and things spiritual. Assuming the reality of correspondence, transcendentalists viewed harmony with nature as the primary law of life. Such harmony indicated both goals for personal as well as social action. Individuals were encouraged to develop their inner selves, and they encouraged their fellow citizens in a rapidly expanding, frenetic republic to develop appropriately harmonious institutions and forms of cultural expression. To that end, while Emerson remained more interested in the task of self-cultivation, other transcendentalists sought to create harmonious communities. George Ripley began Brook Farm in 1841, and Bronson Alcott helped organize the smaller, and shorter-lived Fruitlands in 1843 (see COMMUNITARIANISM and UTOPIANISM). In further efforts to give practical form to their eclectic mysticism, transcendentalists wrote about SLAVERY and women's rights, art and architecture as frequently as they did about philosophical or religious ideas.

In addition to their practical concerns for social action, transcendentalists also developed forms of ritual action, which they thought could provide modern people with more inspiration than the empty ritual forms of the Christian churches. Communing with nature came through morning walks or ritual bathing in Walden Pond, but most importantly, through ritualized, often public, forms of conversation, in which individual spirits could be harmonized with each other and the world. Several members, particularly Orestes Brownson, Theodore PARKER, James Freeman Clarke, and William Ellery

CHANNING, JR., undertook experimental forms of ministry outside Boston's Unitarian establishment.

The impact of transcendentalism is hard to trace since the group, given its emphasis on unconstrained individual communion with nature, avoided taking on institutional form. Many thousands of individuals heard Emerson, Parker, and Alcott on the lyceum circuit, an extensive network of educational lectures held in towns across New England. And Emerson's written work circulated widely in his own day.

Its most noticeable impact is perhaps on subsequent intellectual and social movements. Theological liberalism took on the critique of dogma begun by the transcendentalists, and a wide variety of 19th- and 20th-century metaphysical movements, from CHRISTIAN SCIENCE and NEW THOUGHT on down to NEW AGE RELIGION in the present, have drawn on transcendental ideas to depict the power of mental healing. The modern environmental movement, seen in the DEEP ECOLOGY movement, carries on transcendental themes of nature worship articulated by John MUIR, who himself came under the direct influence of Emerson and Thoreau. Some have argued that transcendentalism's influence has in fact spread across American culture.

MG

Bibliography: Catharine Albanese, *Corresponding Motion: Transcendental Religion and the New America* (Philadelphia: Temple University Press, 1977); Paul F. Boller, Jr., *American Transcendentalism, 1830–1860: An Intellectual Inquiry* (New York: G. P. Putnam's Sons, 1974).

Trungpa, Chogyam (1939–1987)

Chogyam Trungpa, Rinpoche, the founder of Vajradhatu, the largest Tibetan Buddhist organization in America, did more than anyone else to popularize Tibetan Buddhism in the United States.

Born in northeastern Tibet in 1939, Trungpa was tapped at the tender age of 18 months as the reincarnation of the Tenth Trungpa Tulku (bodhisattva emanation) and thus the head of the Karmapa Kargyudpa school of Tibetan Buddhism. He became a novice when he was eight and took a guru at the age of nine. Now recognized as the Eleventh Trungpa Tulku, he received the title of Rinpoche (Precious Jewel) and served as an abbot of a number of monasteries in Tibet.

Accompanied by fellow refugees from the Chinese takeover of Tibet, Trungpa made his way in 1959 to Kalimpong, India, where he was taken in by Mrs. Freda Bedi, an Oxford graduate who would eventually become a Tibetan Buddhist nun. When Bedi moved to New Delhi to serve as the principal of a school for Tibetan exiles, Trungpa joined her as its spiritual advisor. While in India, Trungpa learned English and proved himself an adept student of western culture.

Moving to England in 1963, he enrolled at Oxford where he studied western philosophy and Japanese ZEN. He found sufficient time off from his studies, however, to found the short-lived Samye-Ling Meditation Centre in Dumfriesshire, Scotland. There he first put into practice a spiritual discipline he has called "meditation in action."

In 1970 Chogyam Trungpa renounced his monastic vows and was married to Diane Judith Pybus. In that same year he emigrated to the United States. Shortly after his arrival, he established a Tibetan Buddhist community called Karme-Choling (Tail of the Tiger) in Barnet, Vermont. Lecture tours and the publication of two books—*Meditation in Action* (1970) and *Cutting Through Spiritual Materialism* (1973)—prompted the establishment of Tibetan Buddhist meditation centers in many United States cities.

Trungpa eventually settled in Boulder, Colorado, where in 1971 he founded the Rocky Mountain Dharma Center, which aims to integrate popular Zen practices and arts into Tibetan Buddhism. In 1973, Trungpa gathered his many projects together into an umbrella organization called Vajradhatu. He expanded into Canada in

Students with Rinpoche Chogyam Trungpa, founder of the largest Tibetan Buddhist organization in the United States, at the Milarepa Center, Barnet, Vermont. (Pluralism Project of Harvard University)

1981 with the Halifax-based Vajradhatu Canada.

Trungpa was perhaps most widely known outside the Tibetan Buddhist community for his delight in upsetting Occidental stereotypes of Oriental ascetics. A practitioner of tantric Buddhism, Trungpa shunned neither alcohol nor cigarettes and was known to indulge in red meat, psychedelics, and obscenities.

Trungpa's most enduring legacy in America may be his Boulder-based Naropa Institute (established 1974), an accredited college that grants B.A. and M.A. degrees. The institute has attracted teachers such as the Harvard professor turned Hindu guru Ram Dass and the Beat poet Allen Ginsberg (see BEAT MOVEMENT).

In 1976 Trungpa tapped an American, Thomas Rich (renamed Osel Tendzin), as his chief disciple. When Trungpa died in 1987, Tendzin assumed leadership of his teacher's organizations. Trungpa's cremation in Barnet, Vermont was attended by Buddhists across America. (See also BUDDHISM.)

SRP

Bibliography: Rick Fields, *How the Swans Came to the Lake* (Boulder, Co.: Shambhala, 1981); Chogyam Trungpa, *Born in Tibet* (London: George Allen and Unwin, 1966).

trusteeism   Trusteeism was a movement within the Roman Catholic Church (see ROMAN CATHOLICISM) in the United States to place control of the individual church, including the right to choose parish priests, in the hands of lay trustees or boards. Primarily an issue in the late 18th and early 19th centuries, trusteeism emerged in the United States for several reasons. First, the American Roman Catholic Church was small and weak during that time, with little centralized control. Second, most state legislatures drew up laws of incorporation that were ill-suited to the hierarchical structure of the Catholic Church. These laws vested administration of the local parish or congregation as a legal corporation in the hands of lay people who were given wide administrative powers. A third factor was the republican ethos of the United States, which argued that political authority emanated from the people. Finally, immigrant groups who felt that the hierarchy was insensitive to their religious and cultural traditions would attempt to control a parish to ensure they had a priest fluent in their language and sympathetic to their traditions.

Although the earliest conflict over trusteeism was in New York (1785), the problem surfaced significantly in Philadelphia, New Orleans, and Norfolk, Virginia. Constantly attacked by the bishops and condemned as "novel and quite unheard of" by Pope Pius VII, trusteeism lingered well into the 19th century. It received new strength in the 1850s with the election of anti-Catholic "Know-Nothing" legislatures in New York, Pennsylvania, and elsewhere, which proceeded to adopt state laws placing church property in the hands of lay trustees (see ANTI-CATHOLICISM; NATIVISM). Following the collapse of the party at the end of the decade, these laws were later repealed or overturned by the courts.

By the end of the 19th century, trusteeism had diminished greatly, and while it reappeared among the newly immigrant Slavic Catholics, especially Poles and Ruthenians, or in times of parish crisis and conflict, the hierarchy managed to establish its legal and doctrinal rights to control the property of and appointments to individual parishes. Trusteeism remained an option, however. As urban dioceses faced declining revenues and numbers in the late 1980s and 1990s and began to close churches as a solution, some

rebellions among parishioners took on aspects of the previous century's trusteeism controversy.

EQ

Bibliography: Patrick W. Carey, *People, Priests and Prelates: Ecclesiastical Democracy and the Tensions of Trusteeism* (Notre Dame: Notre Dame University Press, 1987); James Hennesey, *American Catholics: A History of the Roman Catholic Community in the United States* (New York: Oxford University Press, 1981).

Truth, Sojourner (1797–1883)

One of the leading black abolitionists (see ABOLITIONISM) of the 19th century, Sojourner Truth achieved this position only by overcoming a life of degradation and pain. Born a slave about 1797 in Hurley, Ulster County, New York to a wealthy Dutch farmer, Truth's first language was Dutch and she always spoke English with a Dutch accent. Deeply influenced by the religious visions of her mother, Truth was devastated by their separation in 1808, when she was sold for the first time.

In 1810 Truth became the property of John Dumont, who for 16 years would be her master. During this time she suffered repeated beatings from her mistress, and was forced to serve as "breeding stock" to supply the Dumonts with labor and cash. Distraught by the sale of one son south and embittered by Dumont's failure to free her as promised, Truth ran away in 1826. She found refuge with a local family who took her in until 1827, when New York's emancipation law went into effect. In that year she walked into New York City a free woman.

Given from an early age to religious visions and divine communications, she wandered about New York looking for religious truth. In 1829 she fell in with the perfectionist (see PERFECTIONISM) religious preacher Elijah Pierson, joining him and a group of followers in organizing a religious commune in Sing Sing (now Ossining), New York. When the commune collapsed amid scandal in 1835, Truth returned to New York City.

Born a slave in upstate New York, Sojourner Truth became a powerful advocate of abolitionism and a colleague of early women's rights activists. (Billy Graham Center Museum)

For the next nine years she lived a quiet life there, but in 1843 the voices and visions returned, telling her to become a wandering preacher. Originally known as Isabella, she adopted the name Sojourner Truth and began preaching throughout New England. In 1846, a visit to the Northampton Association of Education and Industry brought her into contact with abolitionists. She soon became an ardent abolitionist and worked closely with William Lloyd Garrison, Frederick Douglass, and Wendell Phillips. This work also brought her into contact with the nascent women's rights movement in 1850 and friendships with Lucretia Mott and Elizabeth Cady STANTON.

Over six feet tall with a strong voice, Truth was a powerful draw on the lecture circuit. Many who came to gawk at a woman—a black woman at that—speaking in public, left moved by her speech. Truth gained a reputation as one capable of silencing the most belligerent of hecklers. A story is told of one meeting in Ohio where she listened to a minister belittle women as delicate and weak. This, followed by disparaging remarks about Truth's femaleness, led her to rip open her bodice to reveal her breasts. She taunted her detractor by asking whether she was not a woman and where had he been when she was forced to labor in the fields?

Following the outbreak of the Civil War, she raised funds for black regiments. In 1864 she joined the National Freedman's Relief Association and taught at the Freedman's Village in Arlington, Virginia. She also served as a nurse in the Freedmen's Hospital and distributed aid to the refugee ex-slaves who flocked to the capital.

Distressed by their suffering and unemployment, Truth began a campaign for the distribution of public lands in the West to the African-Americans that would lead to the creation of a "Negro state." Opposition to the idea by the Grant administration and growing hostility from the public forced her to relinquish the plan in 1875. In that year she retired to her home in Battle Creek, Michigan where she lived until her death on November 26, 1883.

EQ

Bibliography: Jacqueline Bernard, *Journey Toward Freedom: The Story of Sojourner Truth* (New York: The Feminist Press at the City University of New York, 1967); Olive Gilbert, *Narrative of Sojourner Truth . . . Drawn from Her Life* (New York: Vintage, 1993); Carleton Mabee, *Sojourner Truth—Slave, Prophet, Legend* (New York: New York University Press, 1993); Victoria Ortiz, *Sojourner Truth: A Self-Made Woman* (Philadelphia: Lippincott, 1974); Erlene Stetson and Linda David, *Glorying in Tribulation: The Lifework of Sojourner Truth* (East Lansing, Mich.: Michigan State University Press, 1994).

Tubman, Harriet (1821–1913) A religious visionary, seer, and leader of the Underground Railroad, Harriet Tubman was born to Benjamin Ross and Harriet Green in Dorchester County on Maryland's eastern shore. The year of her birth is disputed, with 1821 being most widely accepted. Originally named Araminta by her owner, she later adopted her mother's name.

Put to work in the fields, she developed a strength and stamina later put to use on behalf of her religious and political principles. A serious head injury during childhood produced a form of narcolepsy that afflicted her until her death. Denied an education due to slavery, she nonetheless possessed acute intelligence and judgment that aided her work in the Underground Railroad.

In 1844 her mother forced her to marry John Tubman, a free black, but in 1849 the death of her master led to rumors that his slaves were to be sold south. She and her two brothers escaped and headed north. Her brothers changed their minds and returned home, but Harriet continued until she arrived in Philadelphia.

During her escape Harriet had been helped by members of the Underground Railroad, a network of antislavery people who aided escaped slaves by sheltering, feeding, and guiding them through unfamiliar territory. Tubman soon became one of the railroad's most active "conductors," making 19 trips south and rescuing over 300 blacks from slavery. Perhaps her most daring rescue came in 1857 when she spirited away her aging parents and settled them at her home in Auburn, New York on land she had purchased from William H. Seward. This occurred at a time when the Fugitive Slave Act of 1850 imposed harsh penalties on those aiding escaped slaves and when Tubman herself had a $40,000 bounty on her head, dead or alive.

Tubman's faith in divine providence and her "inner vision" gave her legendary strength and courage. As one observer remarked, "A more heroic soul did not breathe in the bosom of Judith or Jeanne d'Arc." John Brown, whom she met in Canada in 1848, referred to her as General Tubman and described her as the "most of a man naturally that I ever met with," and obtained her support for his ill-fated attack on the federal armory at Harper's Ferry.

With the outbreak of the Civil War, Tubman continued her activities on behalf of slaves. Arriving at the liberated coastal islands of South Carolina bearing a letter of introduction from the governor of Massachusetts, she was put into the service of the Union army as a cook, nurse, scout, and spy. At the close of the war she served in the freedmen's hospital at Fortress Monroe and later spent several years organizing freedmen's schools in North Carolina.

The publication of her memoirs, *Scenes in the Life of Harriet Tubman* (1869) written as told to Sarah Bradford (Tubman remained illiterate throughout her life), provided her with a modest income that allowed her to pay off the mortgage on her Auburn property. Receiving recognition from the federal government was another matter. It took over 30 years before her war-time service was recognized with a mere $20 a month pension.

Until her death on March 10, 1913, Tubman continued her activities on behalf of African-Americans. She also was a notable proponent of women's rights and developed a close relationship with Susan B. Anthony. Her property became the Harriet Tubman Home for Indigent and Aged Negroes. This national shrine is managed by the AFRICAN METHODIST EPISCOPAL ZION CHURCH to which she belonged.

EQ

Bibliography: Sarah H. Bradford, *Harriet Tubman, The Moses of Her People* (New York: Corinth Books, 1961); Earl Conrad, *Harriet Tubman* (New York: Erikson, 1969); Dorothy Sterling, *Freedom Train, The Story of Harriet Tubman* (New York: Scholastic Books, 1954).

Turner, Nat (1800–1831) Leader of the most famous slave revolt in United States history, Nat Turner was born in Southampton County, Virginia probably on October 2, 1800, although there is some dispute about the date. His father ran away from the plantation while Turner was young and was never recaptured. Turner attained the rudiments of education on his own and became a devoted student of the Bible. Deeply religious, he preached among both slaves and whites, at least one of whom, Ethelred Brantley, he baptized (1825). Turner himself escaped successfully when in his twenties, but troubled by his conscience, he returned on his own, for which he was ridiculed by the other slaves.

His owner Samuel Turner died in 1822, and Nat was sold to a neighboring planter, Thomas Moore. In 1830 Moore's widow married Joseph Travis. It was from the Travis plantation that Turner embarked upon his religiously sanctioned rebellion.

A vision in spring 1828 convinced Turner that he was to be the instrument of God in achieving a great purpose. While working in the fields, he later reported in his confession, "I heard a loud a noise in the heavens, and the spirit instantly appeared to me and said the Serpent was loosened, and Christ had laid down the yoke he had borne for the sins of men, and that I should take it on and fight against the Serpent." On February 12, 1831 he believed the sign for which he had been waiting appeared—a solar eclipse. Turner took four other slaves into his confidence, informing them that they were to be the instruments of God's wrath against slavery. The insurrection was to begin on July 4.

When that day arrived Turner was ill and the rebellion postponed. Seeing another sign in the bluish-green sun of August 13, Turner met with his fellow conspirators on Sunday, August 21 and they decided to strike that night.

At roughly 2 A.M. on August 22, the bloodiest slave revolt in United States history began. By the morning of August 23, the rebels had slain at least 57 whites, and their number had grown to over 70. They proceeded toward Jerusalem (now Courtland), the county seat. A delay to sack the home of a wealthy planter allowed white volunteers to catch up to Turner and his men. Although originally repulsed, the whites, reinforced by militia, forced Turner and his men into retreat. Turner attempted to continue, but by the next day hundreds of state militia, United States troops, and volunteers had arrived to quell the rebellion.

The suppression occurred with the utmost savagery. Scores of innocent blacks were slaughtered according to the Richmond *Whig,* September 3, 1831, "without trial and under circumstances of great barbarity." Turner hid for two months, until he was caught on October 30, 1831. During his imprisonment he was interrogated by a local lawyer, Thomas Gray, who transcribed Turner's responses. Published as the *Confessions,* this remains the main documentary source about the rebellion. Turner rejected any suggestion that he was wrong by asking, "Was not Christ crucified?" On November 5, Turner was convicted and sentenced to be executed by hanging on November 11. Contemporary accounts state that he went to his death bravely and calmly.

The results of the Turner rebellion were many. Fear of similar revolts led to new laws against educating blacks, closer supervision of black worship, and censorship of newspapers, such as William Lloyd Garrison's *Liberator.* The rebellion also moved into the religious mythology of African-American religion, where God as a source of deliverance from captivity often took the form of an avenging angel, striking slaveowners as the angel of death struck down the Egyptian first-born.

(See also ABOLITIONISM; AFRICAN-AMERICAN RELIGION; SLAVERY; VESEY, DENMARK.)

EQ

Bibliography: Herbert Aptheker, *American Negro Slave Revolts* (New York: International Publishers, 1966); Stephen B. Oates, *The Fires of Jubilee: Nat Turner's Fierce Rebellion* (New York: Harper & Row,

1975); Albert E. Stone, *The Return of Nat Turner: History, Literature & Cultural Politics in Sixties America* (Athens: University of Georgia Press, 1992); William Styron, *The Confessions of Nat Turner* (New York: Random House, 1967); Henry Irving Tragle, *The Southampton Slave Revolt of 1831* (Amherst: University of Massachusetts Press, 1971); Nat Turner, *The Confessions of Nat Turner leader of the Late Insurrection in Southampton, Va.* (Miami: Mnemosyne Publishing, Inc., 1969).

U

Unification Church Founded by the charismatic Reverend Sun Myung MOON of Korea in 1954, the Unification Church is one of the most widely publicized new religious movements in contemporary America.

Officially named the Holy Spirit Association for the Unification of World Christianity, the Unification Church was brought to the United States by Moon's followers in 1959. Moon himself toured the United States twice before moving to America in the early 1970s. During that decade the movement grew rapidly among well-educated young people looking for religious solutions to the cultural and social problems highlighted but not solved by the political protests of the 1960s.

"Moonies," as Unification Church members have been disparagingly called, distinguished themselves sharply from their hippie counterparts by clean-shaving, clean-living, and by refusing recreational drugs and sex before marriage. Many were attracted to Moon's tendency to sacralize rather than criticize America—to see the United States as a godly nation with a divine mission for the world. During the 1970s, church members could be seen in cities across America, selling flowers to raise money for the church and making converts. Many were initially recruited by The Collegiate Association for the Research of Principles (CARP), a Unification Church-affiliate active on college campuses.

The distinctive scripture of the Unification Church is *The Divine Principle,* a collection of Moon's revelations from Jesus, Moses, Buddha, and others. Originally published in 1957, *The Divine Principle* has been repeatedly revised. In the book, Moon prophesies the coming of a "Lord of the Second Advent" who will finish what Jesus Christ began by overcoming the forces of Satan, reconciling God and humanity, and restoring the world to an Edenic state of peace.

Unification theology reinterprets key Christian myths and symbols in light of Moon's master metaphor of the family. Like orthodox Christian thinking, Moon's theology begins in the Garden of Eden with the first family. According to Moon, God intended Adam and Eve to create a sinless, "God-centered family" and to bear "perfect children" who would live harmoniously with one another and with God. But because Eve was seduced by Satan, all subsequent human beings were destined to be born to imperfection in fallen, Satan-centered families.

Jesus came into the world, Moon continues, not simply to save people from their sins but to marry, to form a "God-centered family," to have "perfect children," and thus to restore the divine lineage severed by Eve's sin. Although Jesus succeeded in his spiritual mission, he failed to marry and thus to begin to reconstruct physically the kingdom of God on earth.

The mission of the "Lord of the Second Advent" is to do what Jesus fell short of doing. Although Moon does not explicitly identify himself as this prophesied messiah, his followers generally regard him as such. Unification Church members refer to one another as "brothers" and "sisters" and to Moon as the "Father" of their spiritual family. Moon's second wife, Hak Ja Han, is revered as "Mother" and the "bride of Christ."

The Unification Church has been criticized by members of the media and by relatives of its members as a cult that "brainwashes" its devotees into believing heretical teachings and practicing unorthodox rituals. Critics have complained about Moon's tendency to mix religion and politics. He supported Richard Nixon during the Watergate scandal and was reportedly connected with the intelligence agency of anti-Communist South Korea (the KCIA). Moon's mass marriages—during one ceremony in Seoul in 1975, Moon wed 800 couples—have also been derided. But Moon's detractors have complained most vociferously about his recruiting tactics, which supposedly include "mind control."

Some have responded to these tactics with equally controversial techniques, including kidnapping and "deprogramming" converts against their will. In 1977 a state appellate court in California overturned a lower court ruling that granted custody of specified Unification Church members to their parents. Since that time, anticult activists (see ANTI-CULT MOVEMENT) have deemphasized coercive deprogramming and stepped up their efforts simply to persuade Americans to eschew Moon's organizations.

Although the Unification Church may have been helped more than hurt by the publicity surrounding the "deprogramming" controversy, Moon's movement was clearly damaged by his 1982 conviction on charges of tax evasion. American membership in the Unification Church peaked in the 1970s at an estimated 30,000 full-time members. The church probably now attracts no more than 10,000 full-time members in Europe and North America.

Thousands more, however, continue to be influenced by Reverend Moon, who maintains the Unification Theological Seminary in Barrytown, New York, controls the *Washington Times* newspaper, and recently purchased (through his World Peace Academy) Bridgeport University outside New York City.

SRP

Bibliography: David G. Bromley and Anson D. Shupe, Jr., *Moonies in America: Cult, Church and Crusade* (Beverly Hills, Calif.: Sage Publications, 1979); Michael L. Mickler, *A History of the Unification Church in America, 1959–1974: Emergence of a National Movement* (New York: Garland, 1993); Sun Myung Moon, *The Divine Principle* (Washington, D.C.: Holy Spirit Association for the Unification of World Christianity, 1973).

Unitas Fratrum   See MORAVIANS.

Unitarian Controversy   The Unitarian Controversy was a series of theological debates that began in Massachusetts in 1805 and eventually divided New England Congregational churches into orthodox Calvinist and liberal Unitarian camps. As the controversy came to an end in 1825, a new denomination, the American Unitarian Association (now the UNITARIAN UNIVERSALIST ASSOCIATION), was organized by a group of Boston-area churches. This dispute not only irreparably shattered the denominational unity of Congregationalism, but it also was a major factor in the abolition of the Massachusetts religious establishment in 1833.

The term "Unitarian" refers at its most basic level to the belief that God is one being rather than three beings. Although the doctrine of the Trinity (Father, Son, and Holy Spirit) had been central to Christian orthodoxy since the fourth century, it was by no means a universal belief of early Christianity. During the 16th century, moreover, some of the more radical Protestant reformers, such as Michael Servetus and Faustus Socinus, questioned trinitarian beliefs. As a consequence, a form of Unitarianism developed in parts of Hungary, Transylvania, and Poland after the Reformation. With the coming of the ENLIGHTENMENT in the early 18th century, Unitarian ideas also appeared in England. Unitarianism was popularized by Joseph Priestley, the scientist and philosopher, who carried his skepticism about traditional Christian doctrines to the United States after the American Revolution.

The Unitarian Controversy expressed theological tensions that had been developing in segments of American Protestantism for over 150 years. The most direct historic predecessor of Unitarianism was the strain of Arminian (see ARMINIANISM) piety that emerged out of New England Puritanism in the early 18th century. Arminians emphasized the moral capability of human beings in preparing for their conversion. During the GREAT AWAKENING, this tradition received a strong expression among rationalistic "Old Light" Congregationalists like Jonathan MAYHEW and Charles CHAUNCY. These clergymen opposed revivalism and questioned such key Calvinist doctrines as predestination and original sin. The first formal rejection of the doctrine of the Trinity occurred in 1785, when King's Chapel in Boston rejected its Anglican heritage and removed all trinitarian references from the prayer book used.

The initial phase of the Unitarian Controversy began after the death of David Tappan, the Hollis professor of divinity at Harvard College, in 1803. When Henry Ware, the Congregational minister in Hingham, Massachusetts and a well-known theological liberal, was elected as Tappan's successor in 1805, Jedidiah Morse, a minister in nearby Charlestown and an overseer of the college, raised objections. Morse, who had earlier declared that the Hollis professorship needed to be filled by an orthodox Calvinist, roused his fellow conservatives to action. In 1808 they organized Andover Theological Seminary in Andover, Massachusetts to counter the spreading liberalism at Harvard. Morse later published the pamphlet *American Unitarianism* (1815), in which he accused liberal Congregationalists of heresy and called upon conservatives to sunder ties with them. Liberals responded in turn and in 1816 formed their own program of theological education at Harvard.

The next and most involved stage of the controversy centered on the efforts of William Ellery CHANNING, minister of Boston's Federal Street Church. In a published letter to his colleague Samuel Thatcher, Channing lamented the rudeness and unfairness of Morse's charges. Samuel Worcester of Salem, an orthodox minister, counterattacked, and Channing and he exchanged several open letters in 1815. Liberals questioned the conservatives' over-attachment to doctrinal semantics and argued that religious character and moral living, not subscription to human statements about God's nature, were the key basis of the Christian faith. To the orthodox, on the other hand, the creeds and confessions of the church were not trivial at all, but divinely inspired statements that were essential for all Christians to believe.

Channing stated his position definitively in his sermon at the 1819 ordination of Jared Sparks, who had been called to be the minister of an explicitly Unitarian church in Baltimore. This sermon, later published under the title "Unitarian Christianity," articulated the basic beliefs of early Unitarianism: an optimistic view of human nature, the "essential sameness" (as Channing said) between God and humankind, and the affirmation that Jesus had come to convince men and women to lead morally perfect lives. Channing's sermon touched off another round of pamphlet exchanges with the conservatives. Andrews Norton, a professor at Harvard Divinity School, and Moses Stuart, a professor at Andover Seminary, argued over the doctrine of the Trinity. And Leonard Woods of Andover and Henry Ware of Harvard debated about human nature, Ware taking the liberal position that humanity was essentially good, and Woods the Calvinist insisting on the innate sinfulness of humankind.

At the same time these theological battles raged, the Unitarian Controversy was generating even more enduring institutional changes. The Massachusetts constitution of 1780, which had continued a truncated version of the pre-revolutionary Congregational religious establishment, required each Massachusetts town to elect "public teachers of piety, religion and morality." However, since the law did not state that the "public teachers" had to be orthodox Congregationalists, voters in some localities ignored the wishes of orthodox church members and selected liberals to lead them. Divisions between Unitarians and trinitarians soon became so heated that lawsuits resulted. In the famed "Dedham decision" of 1820, the Massachusetts Supreme Court ruled that church property belonged to the parish (that is, the town) rather than to the communicant membership of the local church. The effects of this decision were far-reaching: over 100 parishes formally became Unitarian, while numerous trinitarians withdrew from them and formed new churches. As a result, Congregational support for the Massachusetts religious establishment all but evaporated.

The Unitarian Controversy effectively came to an end in 1825 with the organization of the American Unitarian Association (AUA), a loose affiliation that sponsored joint educational, journalistic, missionary, and charitable activities. By that time approximately 125 Unitarian churches dotted the landscape in eastern Massachusetts. Although the AUA did not constitute a full denomination until after the Civil War, its formation assured that Unitarianism was not a transitory phenomenon, but had become a permanent component within American Protestantism.

GHS, Jr.

Bibliography: Conrad E. Wright, ed., *American Unitarianism, 1805–1865* (Boston: Massachusetts Historical Society, 1989).

Unitarian Universalist Association The Unitarian Universalist Association (UUA) is a denomination that represents the extreme theological left wing of Protestantism in the United States. It traces its historical roots back to two early 19th-century religious movements: Unitarianism, a rationalistic, optimistic version of CONGREGATIONALISM that emerged in eastern Massachusetts during the so-called UNITARIAN CONTROVERSY of 1805–1825; and UNIVERSALISM, a modified form of Calvinism that emphasized the salvation of all humanity. The UUA was created in 1961 by the merger of the American Unitarian Association (AUA) and the Universalist Church of America, small liberal denominations centered in New England.

The beginnings of American Unitarianism are found in the antirevivalist writings of "Old Light" Congregational ministers such as Boston minister Charles CHAUNCY who opposed the Great Awakening in the 1740s. The first open break with traditional Christian belief in the Trinity (Father, Son, and Holy Spirit) occurred in 1785. In that year, King's Chapel in Boston, an Anglican parish before the War for Independence, removed all trinitarian references from

the prayer book it used for worship. The Unitarian Controversy, which eventually split churches in eastern Massachusetts between Unitarian and orthodox factions, commenced in 1805 with the election of Henry Ware, a well-known liberal minister, to the professorship of divinity at Harvard College. And the classic exposition of early Unitarian doctrine was presented in 1819 by William Ellery CHANNING in his sermon "Unitarian Christianity" at the ordination of Jared Sparks in Baltimore.

Despite the strenuous efforts of theological conservatives to suppress the Unitarians in their midst, more and more Congregational churches in eastern Massachusetts adopted Unitarian principles between 1805 and 1825. The AUA was formed in 1825 to bring some institutional cohesion to that blossoming movement. Until the 1860s, the AUA remained simply a loose missionary federation that published religious tracts and sought to found new Unitarian churches outside the Boston area. The organization did not assume a formal denominational structure until after the Civil War. A professional bureaucracy and a regular assembly of delegates to set church policy were created with the establishment of the National Conference of Unitarian Churches in 1865.

The basic theological precept that set Unitarians apart from orthodox Congregationalists in the early 19th century was their belief in the perfectability of humankind. As Channing, the Unitarians' first great leader, declared, there is an "essential sameness" between God and humanity; the ministry of Jesus Christ was not based on overcoming innate human sinfulness (the Calvinist position), but simply on leading men and women toward a natural union with God their creator. Unitarian clergyman James Freeman CLARKE later provided the quintessential summary of Unitarian beliefs: "The fatherhood of God, the brotherhood of man, the leadership of Jesus, salvation by character, and the progress of mankind onward and upward forever." Since roughly four-fifths of the 125 oldest Unitarian churches were located within

40 miles of the city of Boston, Clarke's aphorism was also easily parodied. As some critics quipped, Unitarians really believed in "the fatherhood of God, the brotherhood of man, and the neighborhood of Boston"!

The churches and people who belonged to the AUA represented the intellectual, commercial, and civic leadership of New England, Harvard University being their academic and cultural mecca. Although most 19th-century Unitarians rejected traditional Christian claims concerning the divinity of Jesus Christ, few were prepared to abandon fully the notion that Christianity was based on divine revelation. Yet radical movements within Unitarianism during the anetebellum period soon pressed to take their liberal faith to its logical limits. Ralph Waldo EMERSON and the transcendentalists (see TRANSCENDEN-TALISM), for example, attacked the authority of the Bible and envisioned the possibility of direct communion with God apart from historically rooted institutions and beliefs. The Free Religious Association, moreover, was founded in 1867 by Octavius Brooks FROTHINGHAM and other Unitarian radicals who did not consider themselves Christians at all.

Nineteenth-century Unitarians have usually been characterized as well-to-do, urban churchgoers who rejected traditional ideas about hell because they thought human beings were too good for God to damn them. Universalists, on the other hand, tended to be rural folk repelled by the idea of hell, not because humankind was undeserving of punishment, but because they thought God was too loving to inflict it. Universalists relied strongly upon faith in the atoning sacrifice of Jesus Christ, who suffered *for* men and women rather than *instead* of them. Hosea BALLOU's 1804 *Treatise on the Atonement* was one of the earliest expressions of Universalist beliefs. An institutional structure was established through the formation of the Universalist Church of America in 1833, and Tufts College and the Divinity School in Medford, Massachusetts became the main educational centers of the denomination. Universalists, like American

Protestant evangelicals generally, grew rapidly over the course of the 19th century, numbering about 65,000 members by 1900.

However, as the 20th century began, both Universalists and Unitarians appeared to have reached the limits of their expansion, for two important religious impulses outside those denominations had circumscribed their membership. First, modernist movements within the Congregational, Baptist, and Presbyterian churches cast doubt on many traditional Protestant beliefs about the Bible. Although stiff internal opposition often met those theological challenges, religious liberalism ceased being the exclusive property of Unitarians and Universalists. A person no longer had to become a Unitarian or Universalist to be open to new theological ideas. Second, within the two liberal denominations themselves, humanism and agnosticism emerged as acceptable alternatives to the Christian theism of the early 19th century. In the minds of some Unitarians and Universalists, therefore, there was no further rationale for involvement even in a relatively progressive Christian denomination. Thus, the gradual modernization of American Protestantism produced an ironic result: The old liberal denominations lost much of their accustomed constituency.

As Unitarians and Universalists faced their dwindling membership prospects in the mid-20th century, differences between them, which had always been more sociological than theological, seemed less and less significant and a denominational merger more desirable. An initial agreement was reached in 1959, and unification was made final two years later. The resulting organization continued the congregational autonomy, non-creedal position, and commitment to liberal political causes that had always typified the two separate traditions. The denomination reported slightly over 140,000 members in about 1,000 churches in 1991. New England remains the locus of the UUA's numerical strength, and cities and academic communities in the Northeast contain the majority of the church's generally well-educated and socially progressive membership.

GHS, Jr.

Bibliography: David M. Robinson, *The Unitarians and the Universalists* (Westport, Conn.: Greenwood Press, 1985).

United Brethren in Christ, Church of the   See UNITED METHODIST CHURCH.

United Church of Christ   The United Church of Christ (UCC) was formed in 1957 by the union of the Congregational Christian Churches and the Evangelical and Reformed Church. This denomination is the heir of two distinctive ecclesiastical traditions: New England CONGREGATIONALISM and the German Reformed (see GERMAN REFORMED CHURCH) heritage of the Midwest. The UCC is one of the most theologically and socially progressive of all the churches within American mainline Protestantism today.

Throughout the colonial period, Congregationalists were the largest and most influential Christian body in English North America. Congregationalism had arrived in the New World with the PILGRIMS who came to Plymouth, Massachusetts in 1620 and with the Puritan settlers of the Massachusetts Bay Colony in 1629. At the end of the 17th century when the two colonies united, the churches within them effectively became a single denomination. The GREAT AWAKENING, which peaked in New England between 1740 and 1742, also strengthened CONGREGATIONALISM by reviving the heartfelt piety that had characterized early Puritanism. Congregational minister Jonathan Edwards, whose preaching in 1734–1735 sparked the early revivals of the Awakening, is generally recognized as one of the greatest theological minds in American religious history.

Ironically, the success of the Great Awakening also soon undermined the institutional strength of Congregationalism. The revivals spawned a rift between New and Old Light factions within the Congregational churches. The New Lights, who favored revivals, argued that their clergy and fellow church members lacked true religious conviction. Many New Lights withdrew from the Congregational establishment prior to the American Revolution and formed their own "Separate" churches. A number of those Separate congregations later organized themselves as Baptist churches. The Old Lights, on the other hand, opposed the revivals. Old Light Congregationalists tended to hold highly rationalistic, liberal views out of step with the Calvinist theological orthodoxy of their Puritan past. The Old Lights were forerunners of the Unitarian party that emerged out of New England Congregational churches in the early 1900s.

Despite the losses Congregationalism suffered between, roughly, 1760 and 1830, the church was still the fourth-largest American denomination (behind the Methodists, Baptists, and Presbyterians) at the end of that period. Congregationalists took a lead in organizing societies to evangelize the new western territories of the expanding United States. One missionary venture involved an alliance with the Presbyterian Church. The PLAN OF UNION, which effectively unified the Congregational and Presbyterian denominations in the Midwest between 1801 and 1837, helped bring the cultural and religious values of New England to upstate New York and Ohio in the period before the Civil War. Congregationalists were concerned, too, with missionary work overseas. They formed the American Board of Commissioners for Foreign Missions (ABCFM), the first American foreign mission society, in 1812. Finally, the AMERICAN MISSIONARY ASSOCIATION (AMA) was founded in 1846. Although originally organized to educate African-Americans in the South, the AMA later evangelized Native Americans in the West and evolved into the home missions department of the UCC in the 20th century.

Because of Congregationalism's adherence to the principle of strictly independent church bodies, a true denominational identity and bureaucracy did not develop until the late 19th century. Not until 1871 with the founding of the organization known as the National Council of Congregational Churches were Congregationalists organized fully on a national level. Over the course of time several smaller church bodies grafted themselves onto the larger organization, and in 1931 the denomination adopted the name General Council of Congregational and Christian Churches (or the Congregational Christian Churches). In 1938, discussions regarding a further union, this time with the Evangelical and Reformed Church, were begun.

The Evangelical and Reformed Church, itself the product of a merger of two similar German ethnic traditions, had roots extending back into the late 17th century. Although most German immigrants to America were Lutherans, some German Reformed settlers also came to the New World in the colonial period. The German Reformed community adhered to the Heidelberg Catechism, a 1563 document that mediated between the teachings of the two greatest leaders of the Reformation, John Calvin and Martin Luther. The German Reformed Church was organized in America by John Philip Boehm and Michael Schlatter in the first half of the 18th century. Following the American Revolution it freed itself completely from lingering institutional ties with the Dutch Reformed Church.

The increase of the German Reformed denomination in the East and the tremendous immigration of Germans to the Midwest states between 1830 and 1845 saw the establishment of two separate church bodies: the eastern-oriented German Reformed Church in the United States (1863) and the German Evangelical Synod of North America (1872), which strongly identified with midwestern German culture. The German Reformed heritage, however, was not vibrant enough to support two American denominations, and the churches eventually united in 1934 to form the Evangelical and Reformed Church. Although this new church then contained 600,000 members, its ethnic base continued to curtail growth, even during the heady period of Protestant church expansion in the 1940s and 1950s.

The Congregational Christian Churches and the Evangelical and Reformed Church began discussions about a possible merger in 1944. Obstacles at first presented themselves. The theological traditionalism and strong sense of interdenominational connectedness that the German Reformed tradition fostered were at odds with the relatively progressive theological attitudes and emphasis on local autonomy that marked Congregationalism. Despite those initial difficulties, leaders of the two churches pressed for union. Merger into the two-million-member United Church of Christ was finally effected at a meeting in Cleveland, Ohio in June 1957.

Most but not all Congregationalists accepted the formation of the new denomination. An association of Congregational churches adhering to a conservative interpretation of Christianity had earlier been formed by those uncomfortable with the impending merger. Known as the Conservative Congregational Christian Conference, and officially organized in 1948, this denomination upheld many of the distinctive tenets of Puritanism that modern Congregationalists had gradually modified and reinterpreted: the lordship of Jesus Christ, the necessity of a fully believing church membership, and the absolute authority of the Bible. The Conservative Congregational Christian Conference remains a small association of evangelical (see EVANGELICALISM) churches today. It reported a membership of approximately 28,000 people in 1990.

The UCC is now noted for its liberal religious views, exemplified best by its continuing commitment to the principle of an active lay membership and its early recognition (by Congregationalists in 1853) of women in the ordained ministry. Despite a decline in membership (typical of mainline Protestantism as a whole) since the 1960s, the denomination still has a major impact on American Christianity.

Strongest in the northeast quadrant of the United States, the UCC reported nearly 1.6 million members and more than 6,200 congregations in 1990.

GHS, Jr.

Bibliography: Louis H. Gunnemann, *The Shaping of the United Church of Christ: An Essay in the History of American Christianity* (New York: United Church Press, 1977); John von Rohr, *The Shaping of American Congregationalism* (Cleveland, Ohio: Pilgrim Press, 1992); J. William T. Youngs, *The Congregationalists* (Westport, Conn.: Greenwood Press, 1990).

United Lutheran Church in America
See EVANGELICAL LUTHERAN CHURCH IN AMERICA.

United Methodist Church The United Methodist Church is the largest Methodist (see METHODISTS) denomination as well as the second-largest Protestant church in the United States today. It was formed in 1968 when the Methodist Episcopal Church and the Evangelical United Brethren Church, a denomination of German Pietist (see PIETISM) origins, were joined.

The United Methodist Church traces its roots back to the ministry of 18th-century Anglican clergyman John Wesley (see WESLEYAN TRADITION, THE). Wesley, who had experienced a religious conversion in 1738, sought to change the face of British society. He traveled throughout England and preached to crowds of common people about the saving grace of Jesus Christ. He also developed an ecclesiastical system dependent on lay leadership that helped spread his religious and social views. Although he did not intend to organize a new denomination but simply wished to revive the spiritual life of the Church of England, Wesley eventually ordained clergy for service among Methodists in America. The formal organization of Methodism in the United States dates from December 24, 1784, when a gathering afterwards known as the "Christmas Conference" founded the Methodist Episcopal Church and accepted Wesley's representatives Thomas COKE and Francis ASBURY as its first superintendents.

The other major branch of present-day United Methodism grew from German-American revivalism in Pennsylvania. Phillip William Otterbein, a German Reformed minister who arrived in the colonies in 1752, served a congregation in Lancaster. In 1754 he experienced a religious conversion. Otterbein later met Mennonite Martin Boehm at a religious gathering in York, Pennsylvania in the spring of 1767. Following Boehm's sermon, Otterbein recognized Boehm as a kindred spirit and exclaimed to him: "We are brothers!" Many others were similarly attracted by the evangelical message Boehm preached. Eventually, a group of preachers met near Frederick, Maryland in September 1800. They formed a body called the United Brethren in Christ and named Boehm and Otterbein their first bishops.

Jacob Albright, a Pennsylvania farmer who was brought up in a family of pietistic Lutherans, was the founder of another related movement. The deaths of some of his children led to his intense religious conversion in 1791. Licensed as a lay Methodist preacher, he began leading revivals in eastern Pennsylvania and Maryland in 1796. Since Methodists would not institute separate German-speaking congregations, Albright organized his converts into a church in 1803 and became their bishop in 1807. Known first as "Albright's People," the group changed its name to "The Evangelical Association" in 1816. The Evangelical Association adapted the Methodist Episcopal *Discipline*, which contained the church's doctrines and administrative procedures, for its own use. (Many years later, in 1922, the Evangelical Association reconstituted itself under a new name, the Evangelical Church.)

As the 19th century dawned, American Methodism was strengthened considerably by the revivals and general religious excitement of the SECOND GREAT AWAKENING. Despite several schisms, including the defection of black members to the AFRICAN METHODIST EPISCOPAL CHURCH and the AFRICAN METHODIST EPISCOPAL ZION CHURCH, the Methodist Episcopal Church numbered over 340,000 members by 1825, and Methodists constituted the largest church body in the United States. The conflict over slavery in mid-century led to further splits, including the exodus of the Methodist Episcopal Church, South in 1845. By 1850, when the membership of the Methodist church in the North stood close to 800,000, the southern church could itself report more than 600,000 members. Even Union victory in the Civil War could not heal the sectional split in Methodism, and the two denominations remained separate throughout the rest of the century.

The spread of theological liberalism raised the greatest challenge to American Methodists in the late 19th and early 20th century. Biblical criticism and the introduction of Darwin's theory of evolution produced considerable conflict in all Protestant churches during this period. Methodist theologian Borden Parker Bowne, for example, head of the philosophy department at Boston University, was a proponent of a philosophical school called Personalism. Personalism taught that the starting point of Christianity is the human personality. Bowne was charged with heresy in 1904, but his acquittal was considered an important victory for the liberal party in his denomination.

Methodists in the North also helped shape the SOCIAL GOSPEL movement at the turn of the century. In 1908 the Methodist Episcopal Church adopted a Social Creed calling for the just treatment of American workers. Bishop Francis J. McConnell, who later served as president of the Federal Council of Churches, took an active interest in social reform. He chaired an interchurch commission investigating the steel strike of 1919 that was largely supportive of the strikers. At the same time, both northern and southern Methodists united in their opposition to the consumption of alcoholic beverages. The adoption of grape juice in the communion service during this period testified to the impor-

tance Methodists placed on the temperance ideal.

Over the half century between the end of the Civil War and the conclusion of World War I, both the Methodist Episcopal Church and the Methodist Episcopal Church, South grew roughly four-fold—reaching four million members in the North and two million members in the South by 1920. President Theodore Roosevelt in 1900 gave recognition to the centrality of Methodism in American society when he called the Methodists "the most representative church" in the United States. At the same time, serious talk of reunion between the main northern and southern branches of Methodism began in earnest. The two denominations produced a common hymnal in 1905 and 1935. Finally, at a Uniting Conference in Kansas City in the spring of 1939, the Methodist Episcopal Church, the Methodist Episcopal Church, South, and the smaller Methodist Protestant Church joined themselves together as the Methodist Church.

Over the same period, the German denominations with a revivalistic heritage similar to Methodism's also moved closer to merger with the Methodist Church. Leaders of the Evangelical Association and the Methodist Episcopal Church had discussed union between 1859 and 1871. The United Brethren in Christ and the Methodist Protestant Church had likewise considered a merger after 1900. Although those negotiations did not achieve their stated goals, groundwork was laid for later successes. German Methodist conferences, moreover, which had been launched in Ohio in 1832 under the leadership of Wilhelm Nast, were absorbed into the Methodist Episcopal Church prior to the reunion with the southern Methodists in 1939.

Bishop G. Bromley Oxnam, a Methodist leader devoted to Christian unity, was one of the figures who inspired the process that eventually brought the United Methodist Church into being. Oxnam had helped found the NATIONAL COUNCIL OF CHURCHES in 1950 and served as president of the World Council of Churches from 1948 to 1957. In 1960 the Methodists and the Evangelical United Brethren Church (the denomination that merged the United Brethren in Christ and the Evangelical Church in 1946) participated in the Consultation on Church Union, a movement that sought to bring 10 Protestant denominations into a single church. Despite the ineffectiveness of the Consultation, the Evangelical United Brethren and Methodists recognized that their theological similarities could make merger possible. After a meeting in Chicago in November 1966, the union of the Methodist Church with the Evangelical United Brethren Church, effective in April 1968, was achieved.

Although the Methodists numbered over 10 million and the Evangelical United Brethren about 775,000 in 1968, membership in the combined denomination has decreased steadily over the past 25 years. A conservative backlash against the social liberalism of the mainline Protestant denominations and simple demographic changes together have eroded the membership strength of the United Methodists in recent years. Once the largest Protestant denomination, the Methodists have now fallen into second place behind the Southern Baptists. Still, the church remains strong. At its last quadrennial conference in 1992, the denomination approved a new Book of Worship, the first revision since the 1968 merger. In 1991 the United Methodist Church reported nearly nine million members in over 37,000 congregations in the United States.

GHS, Jr.

Bibliography: Frederick A. Norwood, *The Story of American Methodism: A History of the United Methodists and Their Relations* (Nashville: Abingdon Press, 1974).

United Pentecostal Church, International   See PENTECOSTALISM.

United Presbyterian Church   See PRESBYTERIAN CHURCH (U.S.A.); PRESBYTERIANISM.

United Society of Believers in Christ's Second Appearing   See SHAKERS.

United States Christian Commission See CIVIL WAR, THE.

United States Sanitary Commission See CIVIL WAR, THE.

United Synagogue of Conservative Judaism   Founded in New York City in 1913, the United Synagogue of Conservative Judaism, formerly the United Synagogue of America, is the national organization of synagogues that comprise the movement known as CONSERVATIVE JUDAISM. The founders hoped that the United Synagogue along with the Jewish Theological Seminary (JTS), with which it was affiliated, would become unifying elements in American Judaism. As a result they eschewed party labels in the name. This hope was soon dashed, however, and the United Synagogue became another branch of American Judaism, a fact that the organization finally recognized in 1994 with its formal name change.

The goal of the United Synagogue was to formulate a Judaism responsive to its historic traditions and to the distinctive situation in the United States. The United Synagogue's statement of purpose addressed this directly. The mission of the United Synagogue was "The advancement of the cause of Judaism in America and the maintenance of Jewish tradition in its historic continuity."

Solomon SCHECTER, in his inaugural address as the United Synagogue of America's first president, stressed these points: "What we intend to accomplish is not to create a new party, but to consolidate an old one. . . . I refer to the large numbers of Jews who, thoroughly American in habits of life and modes of thinking and, in many cases, imbued with the best culture of the day, have always maintained Conservative principles and remained aloof from the Reform movement which swept over the country." (See REFORM JUDAISM.) According to Schecter, these Jews do not constitute a new development in Jewish life, but mirror the state of Sephardic Jews in Spain prior to the 15th century.

While advocating a Judaism that maintained Sabbath observance, the dietary laws, traditional ritual forms such as the use of Hebrew, and prayers for the restoration of the Jewish state, the United Synagogue allowed some alterations in ritual, including greater use of English and the abolition of gender-segregated seating. While permitting ritual latitude by its member synagogues, the United Synagogue requires all men to cover their head during services, use either a Conservative or Orthodox prayer book, and maintain a kosher kitchen.

From its small beginnings, the United Synagogue grew into the largest of the three branches of American Judaism. It experienced phenomenal expansion during the 1940s and 1950s. Much of this growth resulted from its attractiveness to former Orthodox Jews who, uncomfortable with the extremes of Reform, found within the United Synagogue an atmosphere both sufficiently traditional and modern. By 1980 the United Synagogue had 824 member synagogues representing about 1.5 million members.

In the 1970s, however, conflicts within the United Synagogue and changed external circumstances had caused the movement to flounder. Preeminent was the longstanding tension between the members of the United Synagogue and the leaders of Conservative Judaism, primarily the faculty at the Jewish Theological Seminary. The latter were nearly Orthodox in their life and practice, while the majority of the former were nearly indistinguishable from Reform Jews in their practice regarding the Sabbath and dietary laws. This meant that the faculty at JTS, who traditionally had dominated Conservative Judaism, were increasingly out of touch with the reality of its members' lives and with their concerns. It also became difficult for Conservative Judaism to present itself as a distinctive movement. As the edges separating Reform and Conservative on one end of the spectrum and Orthodox and Conservative at the other began to blur, Conservative Judaism seemed to lose its reason for existence.

The secession in the 1960s of many of the movement's most dynamic thinkers to form RECONSTRUCTIONIST JUDAISM exacerbated the situation. Although far from traditional in their thinking, the Reconstructionists articulated a coherent ideology of practice and action that had infused a vibrancy into Conservative Judaism. Their departure contributed to the movement's crisis of identity.

Despite these problems, the United Synagogue experienced several positive developments during the last quarter of the 20th century. Its educational and youth programs, although producing a number of defectors to Orthodoxy, created a cadre of members committed both to the institution and to its ideological bases. Most important, the United Synagogue relied less and less on Orthodox "dropouts" to maintain and increase its membership. Growth now came from Reform and unaffiliated Jews, as well as converts to Judaism.

Despite periods of flux and demoralization, the United Synagogue succeeded in developing a second- and third-generation membership steeped in its doctrines and values. Committed to Conservative Judaism's continued existence, these members have accepted the challenge of maintaining and furthering the Jewish traditions while responding to changing intellectual, social, and historical conditions.

EQ

Bibliography: *American Jewish Year Book* (Philadelphia: Jewish Publication Society of North America, 1988, 1989, 1990); Nathan Glazer, *American Judaism,* 2nd ed., rev. (Chicago: University of Chicago Press, 1972); Abraham J. Karp, *A History of the United Synagogue of America, 1913–1963* (New York: United Synagogue of America, 1964).

United Synod South   See EVANGELICAL LUTHERAN CHURCH IN AMERICA.

Unity School of Christianity   See NEW THOUGHT.

Universalism Universalism, or the belief that all people will eventually be delivered from the penalties of sin and receive salvation, has had a long history in the United States, both as a doctrine espoused by various peoples and groups, and later as an organized religious movement. In post-Reformation England and in Europe, the Calvinist stress on predestination, the notion that God has already consigned some people to heaven and others to hell, was rejected by many people who nonetheless remained within the Protestant Church. Some German pietist sects also believed in universal salvation.

Starting in the mid-18th century, people espousing Universalist doctrines became more organized in their professions of faith, just as official toleration of their views declined. In Britain in the 1750s, James Relly and his followers called themselves Universalists and spread their convictions of a benevolent God and eventual freedom from the wages of sin. One of Relly's followers was John Murray (1741–1815), who later became known as the father of American Universalism. But even before Murray's efforts to organize a religious society bore fruit, numerous liberal Protestant colonists promoted the concept of universal salvation.

Universalism as a loosely organized religious movement began haltingly in the late 18th century. Murray, an English convert to Methodism who had been banished from fellowship because of his association with Relly, arrived in New Jersey in 1770. He began preaching Universalist doctrines all along the Atlantic coast, often to hostile and violent crowds. His efforts eventually led to the formation of the first Universalist church in America in Gloucester, Massachusetts. Organized in 1779 when a group of members of the Congregationalist First Church of Gloucester withdrew to form a separate society, the group endured a prolonged legal battle in order to exempt its members from paying taxes for the support of their former church.

The transformation from a disorganized movement to an established denomination proceeded very slowly, for a variety of reasons.

On the whole, people who were attracted to Universalist views were a fiercely independent group that had come to hold unpopular beliefs in the face of extreme hostility and opposition, and often without benefit of clerical guidance. Suspicious of centralized organization, some overtly resistant to the idea of forming a church, Universalists throughout the late 18th century established societies on an informal and local basis. Many believed that individual interpretation of the Scriptures was the only sound basis for belief, because they were highly optimistic about the rational capabilities of human beings to discern God's will. Universalists also battled many adversaries on the road to organization. The Gloucester Congregationalists had criticized the apostates for being a "mere jumble of detached members," and for holding the dangerous view that, because all would eventually be saved, people would have no incentive to act morally. This latter charge proved to be most frequently leveled against Universalists, because many Calvinists believed that the promise of selective salvation was the only way to guarantee right behavior, and thus the lack of ultimate punishment raised the frightening specter of social chaos.

In the early 19th century the scattered Universalist societies in the northeastern states gradually attained a higher degree of interdependency. These efforts were helped by early leaders such as Murray and Elhanan Winchester (1751–1797), a preacher from Brookline, Massachusetts who formed the first Society of Universal Baptists in Philadelphia. In 1803 a group of Universalists met to standardize and clarify points of doctrine in the "Winchester Profession," a brief statement that served as a basis of belief for the remainder of the century. The declaration affirmed that the Bible is the revealed word of God; asserted that a benevolent God, revealed in the person of Jesus Christ, would restore all humanity to holiness and happiness; and admonished believers to maintain order and practice good works. In addition, by the early 19th century, most Universalists adhered to a Unitarian understanding of the Godhead (as opposed to the orthodox trinitarian view of God as Father, Son, and Holy Spirit), and stressed the primacy of freedom of conscience and the separation of church and state. These basic beliefs came to characterize the Universalist Church, formally organized into the Universalist Church of America in 1833.

Universalists experienced their swiftest expansion between 1820 and 1850, when the evangelical REVIVALISM of the SECOND GREAT AWAKENING spawned an equally powerful liberal backlash. Universalists rejected the enthusiasms of the evangelicals (see EVANGELICALISM), but shared in their commitment to social reform, actively participating in the temperance, antislavery, and women's rights movements. The Universalist Olympia Brown (1835–1926) was among the first Protestant women ordained to the ministry in 1853. The church also spread to the South and West during this period. By 1870, 21 state conventions of the church had been organized. Although Universalism reached its maximum strength at the beginning of the 20th century with some 65,000 members, its growth was fastest during the earlier period in part because its common-sense, rational approach to scriptural interpretation appealed to people moving westward, out of established religious communities.

In 1961 the Universalists officially merged with the Unitarian Church to form the UNITARIAN UNIVERSALIST ASSOCIATION. Historically, the two groups had held a wide variety of beliefs in common. But Unitarianism had been much more influential among the elite and cosmopolitan classes along the eastern seaboard. Universalism, with its implicit anti-authoritarianism and individualism, appealed more widely to the working classes, particularly those in small-town New England and along the line of westward settlement. These social differences prevented the commonalities of liberal Protestant theology from bringing the movements together at an earlier point, although attempts at union had previously been considered.

After the 1961 merger, the membership of the resultant UUA stood at just under 200,000, with approximately 1,100 clergy. Three seminaries identify themselves with the denomination: Harvard Divinity School, Meadville-Lombard (Chicago), and Starr King (Berkeley). The UUA retained the early Universalist commitment to social reform, and today stands on the liberal end of both the political and theological spectra of Protestant denominations in America.

LMK

Bibliography: Ernest Cassara, *Universalism in America* (Boston: Beacon Press, 1971); Russell E. Miller, *The Larger Hope* (Boston: Unitarian Universalist Association, 1979); George Huntston Williams, "American Universalism: A Bicentennial Historical Essay," *Journal of the Universalist Historical Society* 9 (1971).

Universalist Church in America   See UNITARIAN UNIVERSALIST ASSOCIATION; UNIVERSALISM.

utopianism   The search for utopia, or a perfect society, has been a constant theme in Judeo-Christian thought. In America, the availability of land and the relative lack of constraints on free religious expression have intensified this search; indeed, some people would argue that American history, with its optimistic narratives of individual and social progress, and the constant effort to break free from the bonds of tradition and history, is itself a narrative of a utopian experiment. The term "utopian" derives from the Greek, meaning "no place." It frequently refers to an unrealizable quest, and the history of utopianism in America is filled with examples of the conflict between high ideals and mixed outcomes, dreams realized and dreams deferred. Utopianism is often a matter of perspective: What seems possible to some people may seem naively unattainable to others.

Several assumptions have characterized most American utopias. The first is the belief that either individuals, or the social system, or both,

The Welsh industrialist Robert Owen founded the famous nonsectarian utopian community in New Harmony, Indiana in 1826. The emphasis on education, free thinking, and human idealism could not hold the community together.

were perfectible and malleable, that is, they could be brought into harmony so that society would be characterized by a lack of friction. Not all utopians have believed that both society and human beings could be made perfect at once, but most have asserted that if one or the other could reach that state, it would necessarily lead to the maximal betterment of the other. The Puritans, for example, believed that original sin prevented individuals from attaining a state of perfect holiness here on earth, but they also contended that by living in a community of God, a theocracy, people would grow in grace and achieve as much as was possible in this life. Utopian schemes often have been distinguished

by the corollary assumption that this perfection could take place without direct supernatural intervention. In other words, utopians are not always millennialists, or followers of the belief that God must return to earth in order to create a perfect society. Humans, perhaps with help or guidance from a divine being, can themselves achieve the perfect society.

In America, utopian experiments have thrived from the early colonial period to the present. During the Renaissance, the New World itself was characterized by many Europeans as an earthly paradise, a garden before the fall. In turn, explorers came west looking for the perfect land. The Puritans were only one of a number of Euro-American religious groups that migrated on the expectation of finding an ever-bountiful region, one that would allow them to establish settlements where they could live unhindered by the social, economic, and religious constraints of their native countries. All hoped for a better world, although not all believed that perfection on earth was possible.

But it was in the decades immediately following the American Revolution that the utopian impulse in America gained momentum. With the acquisition of new western lands, the collapse of traditional religious and political lines of authority, and the potential for immediate social change exemplified by the birth of the republic itself, reformers came to see America as an empty space, a social void ripe for experimentation. Along with this renewed sense of possibility came a declining emphasis among Protestants on the devastating effects of original sin on human behavior; increasingly, 19th-century reformers downplayed the inescapability of human sin, and highlighted the consequent possibility of earthly holiness. The resulting utopian impulse most often took communitarian form (see COMMUNITARIANISM). By the 1830s and 1840s dozens of utopian communities were established to test the human capacity for perfection, including the SHAKERS, the EPHRATA COMMUNITY, Amana, the Mormons (see CHURCH OF JESUS CHRIST OF LATTER-DAY

SAINTS), the Oneida Community (see NOYES, JOHN HUMPHREY), Fruitlands, Brook Farm, Fourierist phalanxes, Jerusalem, New Harmony, and many more. Although most died out fairly rapidly, new ones continued to proliferate, demonstrating a remarkable American capacity for optimism even in the face of probable failure.

Utopianism tended to follow lines of westward settlement, as social pioneers sought open space on which to etch their plans for paradise. By the late 1890s, California was the state with the largest number of utopian communities in the country, including an Icarian community, Point Loma, Fountain Grove, Llano del Rio, and the Kaweah Cooperative Commonwealth. Although the 20th century has not seen the same number of social experiments as appeared in the previous century, waves of utopian interest, most recently in the late 1960s and early 1970s, continue to characterize American culture.

LMK

Bibliography: Arthur Bestor, *Backwoods Utopias* (Philadelphia: University of Pennsylvania Press, 1950); Michael Fellman, *The Unbounded Frame: Freedom and Community in Nineteenth Century American Utopianism* (Westport, Conn.: Greenwood Press, 1973); Robert V. Hine, *California's Utopian Colonies* (New Haven: Yale University Press, 1966); Mark Holloway, *Heavens on Earth: Utopian Communities in America, 1680–1880,* 2nd ed. (New York: Dover Publications, Inc., 1966).

V

Vajradhatu   See TRUNGPA, CHOGYAM.

Vatican Council I   Called by Pope Pius IX, the First Vatican Council opened on December 9, 1869 and closed on September 1, 1870. The council's original agenda involved the consideration of 52 statements dealing with matters such as church organization, the relationship between religion and reason, and the preparation of a universal catechism. Only one of these statements, however, the one on the relationship between religion and reason, which affirmed the dignity and importance of human reason while stressing its limitations and its subordination to revelation, was adopted, as the council turned its attention increasingly to the issues of papal primacy and infallibility.

The promulgation of the latter as dogma was undoubtedly the most significant event of the council not only for the Roman Catholic Church as a whole but particularly for the Church in the United States. For while this dogma technically applied to papal pronouncements made *ex cathedra* (literally, from the chair or throne) in the pope's role as head of the Church, in the popular mind the doctrine involved all issues and made it appear that Catholics would be forced to act according to the wishes of the pope.

The council was also important because it was the first Church council attended by American Roman Catholic bishops (see ROMAN CATHOLICISM). Although the Americans had little overall impact on the deliberations, the size of the delegation—48 bishops and archbishops and one abbot—well illustrated the growth of the Church in the United States.

Most of the American bishops opposed, on both theological and practical grounds, the adoption of the doctrine of papal infallibility. But even with European allies they found it impossible to stem the tide in its favor. When the vote was taken to declare papal pronouncements on doctrine infallible, the tally was 433 in favor and 2 opposed. One of the negative votes came from Bishop Edward Fitzgerald of Little Rock. Twenty-five of the yes votes came from Americans; the remaining American bishops had already left the council in order to avoid casting a negative vote in the pope's presence.

For the next century papal infallibility would remain the largest source of Protestant ANTI-CATHOLICISM. Most American Protestants were convinced that Catholics holding public office would be unable to act according to their consciences but would be forced to vote according to the dictates of the pope. While such concerns were largely groundless, they were part of the Protestant consciousness and helped to explain why few Roman Catholics held high public office in the United States until the second half of the 20th century.

(See also VATICAN COUNCIL II.)

EQ

Bibliography: *Dogmatic Canons & Decrees of the Council of Trent, Vatican Council I, Plus the Decree on the Immaculate Conception & the Syllabus of Errors* (Rockford, Ill.: T A N Books & Publishers, Inc., 1977); James Hennesey, *The First Council of the Vatican, The American Experience* (New York: Herder & Herder, 1963); William L. Portier, *Isaac Hecker and the First Vatican Council, Including Hecker's Notes in Italy: 1869–1870* (Lewiston, N.Y.: Edwin Mellen Press, 1985).

Vatican Council II   The Second Vatican Council, probably the most important event in the history of ROMAN CATHOLICISM since the Reformation, had its beginnings on January 25, 1959 when the recently elected pope, John XXIII, announced that he would call an ecumenical council. After over three years of preparation the council began on October 11, 1962. By the time of its close by John's successor, Pope Paul VI, on December 8, 1965, the council had taken long-lasting steps that radically transformed Roman Catholicism.

Although the council's decisions made changes in the daily practice of Roman Catholics, ending the requirement that they abstain from meat on Fridays for example, its most significant outcome involved a changed understanding of the Church itself. The new definition of the Church as the whole people of God, a community of the faithful, rather than a hierarchy of bishops, priests, religious, and laity was a radical transformation in Catholic thought.

The Church also changed its relationship to both Protestants and non-Christians. With the Declaration on the Relationship of the Church to Non-Christian Religions (*Nostra Aetate*) and the Declaration on Religious Freedom (*Dignitatis Humanae*), the Roman Catholic Church altered its traditional relationship to other religious traditions and its historical opposition to religious liberty and church-state separation. Both of these documents were major new statements on Catholic doctrine and dispensed with the dogmatic claim that there was no salvation outside the Roman Catholic Church. *Nostra Aetate* also explicitly condemned ANTI-SEMITISM and implicitly recognized the role of Catholic doctrine in promoting it. More positively, the documents opened the way for discussions between Catholics and Protestants and Catholics and non-Christians. The Declaration on Religious Liberty also dispelled any lingering suspicions of Catholicism as a religion committed to religious coercion.

The American bishops and their advisors were central in bringing about the adoption of these documents. Although relatively unfamiliar with the most advanced trends in European theology during the 1940s and 1950s, the American bishops knew and were comfortable with both non-Catholics and non-Christians. Unlike most of their European counterparts, the Americans were committed to republican and democratic government and could make a strong case from experience that religious liberty, freedom of the speech and press, and democracy were not hostile to the welfare of the Roman Catholic Church. As a result they actively worked for the adoption of these declarations and, in the case of *Nostra Aetate,* overcame a conservative scheme to prevent a vote on the document. The Americans' intervention forced the vote that brought about its adoption.

Such radical changes in the Church's traditions and dogmas were not without major consequences. Many conservative Catholics saw the entire conciliar enterprise as an unfortunate surrender to the claims of the secular world. The more liberal felt that it had not gone far enough in transforming the nature of authority and power in the Church. The changes in authority it did make were quickly seized upon, however, and by 1976 thousands of priests and nuns had left the religious life, Church attendance had declined by a third, and confessions by over half. Despite this, the Church retained the loyalty and commitment of millions of lay people who, along with thousands of priests, nuns, and monks, struggled to realize the implications of Vatican II for their religious life. The council wrought a tremendous change on Roman Catholicism in the United States, the full implications of which remained contested into the 1990s.

(See also MURRAY, JOHN COURTNEY; VATICAN COUNCIL I.)

F.Q

Bibliography: Walter M. Abbot, S.J., ed., *Documents of Vatican II: With Notes and Comments by Catholic, Protestant, and Orthodox Authorities* (New York: America Press, 1966); Rodger Charles and Drostan Maclaren, *The Social Teaching of Vatican II—Its Origin and Development: Catholic Social Ethics: an Historical and Comparative Study* (San Francisco: Ignatius Press, 1982); Jay P. Dolan, *The American Catholic Experience* (Garden City, N.Y.: Doubleday, 1992); Adrian Hastings, ed., *Modern Catholicism: Vatican II and After* (New York: Oxford University Press, 1990); James Hennesey, S.J., *American Catholicism: A History of the Roman Catholic Community in the U.S.* (New York: Oxford University Press, 1981); René Latourelle, ed., *Vatican II: Assessment and Perspectives 25 Years After,* 2 vols. (Mahwah, N.J.: Paulist Press, 1988).

Vedanta Society   The first Hindu missionary organization in America, the Vedanta Society aims to spread the truths of Hindu philosophy to the West.

Two Hindu philosophers figured prominently in the establishment of the Vedanta Society in New York in 1894: Sri Ramakrishna (1836–1886) and Swami VIVEKANANDA (1863–1902). Ramakrishna was a priest in a temple to Kali, the Hindu goddess who is both feared as a bloodthirsty dweller of cremation grounds and revered as the divine Mother and protectress. Vivekananda was Ramakrishna's most accomplished disciple. Before coming to the United States, Vivekananda gathered Ramakrishna's students into a brotherhood of monks who aimed not merely at individual spiritual liberation but also at social reform.

Vivekananda traveled to the United States as a Hindu representative to the WORLD'S PARLIAMENT OF RELIGIONS, convened as part of the World's Columbian Exposition in Chicago in 1893. He captured the hearts of many of his listeners with his refined demeanor and impeccable English. And he impressed at least a few religious liberals with his argument that all gods and all religions are but differing manifestations of one divine principle and one universal religion.

After establishing the Vedanta Society in New York in 1894, Vivekananda lectured across the country, founding centers in other major cities. Upon returning to India in 1897, he founded the Ramakrishna Mission. Both the Ramakrishna Mission and the Vedanta Society aim to spread Hindu philosophy and to reform society through love and devotion.

Members of the Vedanta Society tend to practice *jnana yoga*, the "discipline of wisdom" that invokes an impersonal Absolute, but their spiritual lives typically also incorporate *bhakti yoga*, the more popular "discipline of devotion" to a personal divinity.

Their nondualistic philosophy affirms that Brahman, the impersonal Absolute, is ultimately indistinguishable from the individual soul, or Atman. The goal of their spiritual practice, therefore, is to pierce the veil of Maya (illusion) that promotes the separateness of God and humanity, and thus to realize that all people are essentially and equally divine.

The writers Aldous Huxley and Christopher Isherwood were adherents of Vedanta. Two of Isherwood's books, *Vedanta for the Western World* (1945) and *Ramakrishna and His Disciples* (1965), did much to popularize Hinduism among western intellectuals. But the Vedanta Society's philosophical bent has prevented it from achieving widespread popularity. There are now 13 active United States branches and approximately 1,500 lay and monastic members of the Vedanta Society in America. The organization maintains its headquarters in Los Angeles.

SRP

Bibliography: Christopher Isherwood, *Ramakrishna and His Disciples* (New York: Simon and Schuster, 1965); Carl T. Jackson, *Vedanta for the West: The Ramakrishna Movement in the United States* (Bloomington: Indiana University Press, 1994).

Verot, Jean Pierre Augustin Marcellin (1805–1876)   One of the many French Sulpician priests who served the Roman Catholic Church (see ROMAN CATHOLICISM) in the United States, Augustin Verot served as vicar apostolic of Florida, and bishop, first of Savannah and later of St. Augustine. In these positions he struggled to revive Florida's moribund Catholicism and to encourage Roman Catholic evangelism among blacks (see AFRICAN-AMERICAN RELIGION).

Born in Le Puy, France on May 23, 1805, Verot attended the Sulpician Seminary at Issy from 1821 to 1828, followed by two years as a teacher there. Sent to the United States in 1830, he spent 22 years as professor of mathematics at St. Mary's College in Baltimore. After serving six years as a pastor in several Maryland parishes, Verot was appointed vicar apostolic of Florida (consecrated April 25, 1858), to which position was added the bishopric of Savannah in July 1861.

A sympathizer with the southern cause, he defended SLAVERY, although condemning abuses within the system. He approved of secession, yet was the only religious leader to send chaplains to work among the Union prisoners-of-war at Andersonville, Georgia. Believing that the defeat of the Confederacy was God's punishment on the South for the failures of the slave system, he argued against repeating the same mistakes following emancipation. He therefore initiated strong evangelistic work among the newly freed slaves, and insisted upon integrated services as well as an end to racial prejudice. Concerned about education for blacks, Verot brought several Sisters of St. Joseph from France to organize schools for them.

Verot was one of the most active American bishops at VATICAN COUNCIL I, where his opposition to the definition of papal infallibility earned him the designation of *enfant terrible*. He also urged the council to publicly state that blacks had souls. When it became obvious that the vote on papal infallibility would pass, Verot, like many other American bishops, absented himself in order to avoid casting a negative vote.

He managed to reconcile himself to the decision and defended the doctrine to his priests and parishioners. Appointed bishop of St. Augustine, Florida in March 1870, he continued his efforts on behalf of blacks, the Seminole Indians, and the progress of the Church until his death from a stroke on June 10, 1876.

EQ

Bibliography: Michael V. Gannon, *Rebel Bishop: The Life and Era of Augustin Verot* (Milwaukee: Bruce Publishing Co., 1964).

Vesey, Denmark (1767–1822)

Leader of one of the several slave revolts in the southern United States with distinctly religious roots, Denmark Vesey was born around 1767, probably on the island of St. Thomas, although some authorities claim Africa. Purchased by Captain Joseph Vesey of Saint-Domingue in 1781, he became the captain's personal servant, traveling with him on the African slave trade. In 1783 Captain Vesey left the trade and moved to Charleston, South Carolina.

During the slave revolt in Saint-Domingue in 1791, Captain Vesey's home became a relief center for slaveowners fleeing the rebellion. At this time Denmark Vesey absorbed the tales of the slave rebellion that would provide the model for his own uprising.

A winning lottery ticket enabled him to purchase his freedom in either 1799 or 1800 and to set up a carpentry shop. He soon became financially secure and a dominant force among Charleston's blacks, both free and slave. He defiantly refused to step aside as whites walked by, and chastised those blacks who did. An active member and lay preacher in the African Methodist Church of Charleston, he likened the blacks to the ancient Israelites whom God had delivered out of bondage, and so affected other members of the church that he was regarded as a prophet.

This religious element was strengthened by a confederate of Vesey's, Gullah Jack. Regarded as a sorcerer, Gullah Jack was believed to be invulnerable to bullets and to be able to produce charms that protected others. Late in 1821 a plan was developed for a revolt, and July 14 established as the date. Many of the white residents would have left town for the summer, and the presence of large numbers of blacks from the country on a Sunday would attract little attention. By May the number involved had grown to nearly 9,000.

One follower, ignoring Vesey's injunction against including house servants, caused the secret to be let out. Two leaders were arrested, but they were released when interrogation failed to produce any information. Vesey pushed the date ahead to June 16, but when another follower informed, the authorities flooded Charleston with troops. On June 17, 10 leaders of the insurrection were arrested, and one named Vesey as the organizer. This led to his immediate arrest. Convicted of plotting an insurrection, Denmark Vesey was hanged on July 2, 1822. In total 37 blacks were hanged in connection with the thwarted revolt. Forty-three others were deported.

The foiled rebellion led to strengthened laws against slaves and freed blacks in South Carolina. Instruction of blacks was outlawed, free blacks were forbidden to enter the state, and strict limits imposed upon the unsupervised movement of slaves. Slaves could no longer congregate without white supervision, severely restricting black-led religious worship. In fact, Bishop Moses Brown of the African Methodist Church in Charleston was forced to leave the state.

Vesey became a model and martyr for black liberation during the 19th century. He supposedly inspired John Brown's plan for a slave rebellion, and during the Civil War Frederick Douglass urged blacks to enlist in the Union army with the slogan "Remember Denmark Vesey." And while white southerners attempted to use Christianity to produce quiescence among their slaves and freed blacks, the actions of Vesey and his confederates revealed that blacks reinterpreted white preaching in light of their distinctive historical and social conditions. What in the eyes of white southerners produced social stability, could, in the hands of oppressed slaves, produce rebellion.

(See also ABOLITIONISM; AFRICAN-AMERICAN RELIGION; SLAVERY; TURNER, NAT.)

EQ

Bibliography: Herbert Aptheker, *American Negro Slave Revolts* (New York: International Publishers, 1966); John Lofton, *Denmark Vesey's Revolt: The Slave Plot that Lit a Fuse to Fort Sumter* (Kent: Kent State University Press, 1984); *The Trial Record of Denmark Vesey* (Boston: Beacon Press, 1970).

Victorious Life   See HIGHER CHRISTIAN LIFE MOVEMENT.

Vietnam War   Direct United States military involvement in Vietnam, extending from 1961 to 1973, produced enormous strain within American culture, damaging the national consensus of CIVIL RELIGION. For many the war, fought in a South Asian country far from American shores, upset longstanding assumptions about the nation's identity as a champion of democracy and freedom abroad and a haven for equality at home. Vietnam certainly failed to conform to the general pattern for making war that had come to predominate throughout American history (see AMERICAN REVOLUTION; WORLD WAR I; WORLD WAR II; COLD WAR). During the years of social turmoil sparked by the war, Americans took on, and bitterly contested, an enormous program of reform (see CIVIL RIGHTS MOVEMENT; FEMINIST THEOLOGY; COUNTERCULTURE). Given the lasting tensions stemming from Vietnam, which continue to affect many aspects of American religious and cultural life, some have compared it to other watershed periods of social change.

American interest in Vietnam dates back to the closing months of World War II, when President Roosevelt entertained the idea of supporting Vietnamese postwar independence. In those early Cold War days however, American foreign policy embraced two goals that sometimes became contradictory in practice. As leaders of "the free world," presidents and their administrations saw their global role in the postcolonial era as encouraging national independence, human dignity, and free economic development. But at the same time, they found themselves having to confront what they saw as Communist aggression (see COMMUNISM). Thus during the late 1940s and early 1950s American leaders gave support to French colonial rule. Following French defeat in 1954 the United States found itself the chief ally of the newly created anti-Communist South Vietnamese state. In 1965 President Lyndon B. Johnson expanded John F. Kennedy's program of support for South Vietnam. Without a formal declaration of war, Johnson approved a bombing campaign over North Vietnam, and then deployed an ever-increasing number of ground troops, reaching a cumulative total of over three million. For Johnson, although originally opposed to United States involvement and perhaps more committed to his own Great Society program to combat poverty at home, Vietnam became the place where American national character would be defined.

Initially support, reflected in bumper stickers like "America, Love It Or Leave It" and such popular songs as "The Ballad of the Green Berets," was strong among the Roman Catholic leadership and Protestant evangelicals such as Billy GRAHAM. Both groups championed the anti-Communist concerns motivating Cold War United States foreign policy, as when Cardinal Francis Joseph SPELLMAN in a 1966 visit to Vietnam referred to the war as a "war for civilization."

Public support for the war began wavering early, and eventually "doves" would outnumber "hawks." Opposition among college students and clergy spread widely, harnessing growing support for civil rights as well as the rather amorphous cultural dissatisfaction expressed by the counterculture. To many students involved in civil rights organizations such as the SOUTHERN CHRISTIAN LEADERSHIP CONFERENCE or THE STUDENT NONVIOLENT COORDINATING COMMITTEE, America was thoroughly corrupt. Suspicion of the government's unwillingness to sufficiently address racial issues led to the conclusion voiced by student leader Robert Moses: "The country is unwilling yet to admit it has the plague, but it pervades the whole society." Accordingly both the war's supporters and its opponents came to see Vietnam as a symbol of what was either right or wrong with the American way of life.

From their experience in the civil rights movement, students learned techniques of passive resistance, media mobilization, and picketing. Beginning with a student-faculty walkout and "teach-in" at the University of Michigan in March 1965, opponents used university campuses across the country to spark debate and at times confrontations over the war. While a national movement coalesced rapidly, members resisted the impetus to organize, in part because of the great ideological diversity among opponents. New Left Marxians, like the Students for a Democratic Society, saw the war primarily as an issue from which to build a general revolutionary movement. Black leaders debated the wisdom of diverting attention from the civil rights struggle, although Martin Luther KING, JR. came out in full opposition by 1967, and champion boxer and Black Muslim Muhammad Ali (see NATION OF ISLAM) went to prison rather than face draft induction.

Religious and peace groups also splintered over the goals and tactics of opposition. Most dramatic among the religious opposition was the "Catholic Left" associated with the Berrigan brothers, Daniel and Phillip (see CATHOLIC WORKER MOVEMENT). Catholic Workers burned draft cards, and one member, Roger LaPorte, immolated himself in front of the United Nations building in New York. The Berrigans and others began campaigns of sabotage, eventually staging raids of "symbolic witness" against Selective Service offices in Baltimore and Catonsville, Maryland, pouring blood on registration files and performing other ritual actions to subvert what they saw as American idolatry. Other, more traditional pacifists associated with the American Friends Service Committee (see FRIENDS, THE RELIGIOUS SOCIETY OF; PEACE REFORM) objected to the Catholic Left's dramatic symbolic attacks on state property.

Beginning in 1968 the climate of dissent and frustration increased, all the while denounced by the government, which continued to escalate the war. The FBI began an extensive campaign to infiltrate the movement. Assassins struck down Martin Luther King, Jr. and presidential candidate Robert J. Kennedy. Massive demonstrations erupted in New York and Washington, and during the Democratic National Convention in Chicago. At the same time many other urban centers dissolved in violence, capped by riots in over 100 cities on the night of King's death.

In response to the increasing violence and unrest, many at home, though frustrated by the war, blamed the protesters. In support of a growing conservatism, which even resulted in self-censorship by TV networks, President Nixon praised what he called "the silent majority" of loyal Americans, deliberately seeking to isolate the war's opponents. As animosities hardened, student support for radicals increased. According to a 1970 Harris poll 76 percent of the nation's students thought the country required basic structural change. Strikes disrupted 448 campuses that spring; 286 of them were still shut down at semester's end. New York City construction workers held counter demonstrations. Government officials spoke of students as if they were anarchists rather than citizens, leading to a use of force that culminated in the Ohio National Guard killing four students at Kent State University on May 4, 1970. Such reaction did little to quell the protest; in April 1971 over one million opponents gathered in the national capital, at the time the largest demonstration in United States history.

The war ended slowly. The last draftees were inducted in late 1972. United States troops had already been withdrawing, turning the ground war over to the beleaguered South Vietnamese army. Nixon increased bombing in North Vietnam, during the same months in which negotiations proceeded in Paris, culminating in a settlement on January 27, 1973. The final United States withdrawal came in April 1975, as the North Vietnamese entered the streets of Saigon.

Withdrawal from Vietnam did not end the conflict within American life. President Gerald Ford, taking the place of the disgraced Nixon, who resigned in 1974, put a benign view on the war's end, claiming "our long national nightmare is over." Ford was premature; the public

divisions created by the war lasted well into the next two decades. Returning veterans found themselves treated poorly, and experienced greater difficulty in readjusting to civilian life than did the veterans of earlier wars. Rumors of missing prisoners provided the fuel for a new national mythology. The vision of a defeated America led to a strong revival of conservative Protestant religion, which culminated in the election of Ronald Reagan to the presidency in 1980 (see MORAL MAJORITY). Conservative voices called for the end of national self-doubt, dubbed "the Vietnam Syndrome." To that end the administrations of Presidents Ronald Reagan and George Bush placed renewed emphasis on military power to solve global political problems.

Some protesters entered careers in universities, churches, politics, and the media, and continued to question the goals of American foreign policy during subsequent years of nuclear buildup and intervention in Central America. Families and relatives, scarred by at least 58,022 American deaths (the number of names carved into the Vietnam War Memorial, constructed in 1982), have endured years of grief, aggravated by the frequently voiced doubts over the war's lack of purpose.

MG

Bibliography: Walter C. Capps, *The Unfinished War: Vietnam and the American Conscience,* 2nd ed. (Boston: Beacon Press, 1990); Myra MacPherson, *Long Time Passing: Vietnam and the Haunted Generation* (New York: Doubleday, 1984); Charles A. Meconis, *With Clumsy Grace: The American Catholic Left, 1961–1975* (New York: Seabury, 1979).

Virginia (Colony)   The site of the first permanent British colony in the present-day United States, colonial Virginia had a complex and varied religious history. It moved from a colony where strict religious observance was judicially enforced to a colony where dissenting Protestant and deistic views were increasingly important. As a result, Virginia's most apparent claim to religious fame is its position as the home of Thomas JEFFERSON and James MADISON, both

John White's map depicts the arrival of Englishmen in America to establish a colony at Jamestown in 1607. (Library of Congress)

of whom were instrumental in obtaining the passage of the FIRST AMENDMENT to the United States CONSTITUTION prohibiting the establishment of religion by the federal government. This Virginia was a long way from the its colonial roots, however.

The life of the Virginia colony began on May 2, 1607 when three ships bearing 105 colonists anchored at the mouth of the James River. Organized by a group of London and Plymouth, England businessmen as a joint stock company, the Virginia colony exhibited the combination of economic, political, and religious motives that fueled most European colonialism at this time. Englishmen viewed their New World colonies as bulwarks against Spanish and Catholic expansionism—the terms were nearly synonymous—

as well as opportunities to gain great wealth such as Spain was extracting from her colonies in Mexico and South America.

As a result the expedition's commander had been directed to find either a route to the South Sea, gold, or the lost colonists from Roanoke (see CAROLINAS [COLONY]) or never return to England. Its organizers saw fit to ensure that an Anglican priest accompanied the expedition to establish the Church of England (see ANGLICANISM) in North America.

Although the priest attempted to fulfill his duty, offering Holy Communion the day after landfall, most of the colonists were more interested in easy money than religious observance or hard work. The colony, named Jamestown, faced many difficult years. Starvation and disease took their toll on the settlers, who were prepared to abandon the colony in 1610 when supply ships led by the new governor, Lord De La Warr, convinced them to stay. Although De La Warr did much to strengthen the colony, another epidemic again reduced its population and nearly killed De La Warr, causing him to return to England. In 1611 the arrival of two more groups of colonists under Thomas Dale and Thomas Gates helped to solidify the colony and make it permanent.

As governor, Dale figures prominently in the history of colonial Virginia. His *Lawes Divine, Morall and Martiall* ended the conflicts and instilled the discipline that the colony needed. These laws and their successors, after Virginia received its own colonial assembly in 1619, required church attendance on Sundays, outlawed idleness and gaming, and punished immoderate dress, swearing, and disrespect for superiors. The assembly also set aside land for the support of the church and required each community to educate several Indians to prepare them for college. Although many of these laws were steadfastly ignored or impossible to realize in the colony's unsettled state, they provide a good view of the type of society the English desired.

Problems persisted for the colony, however. Conflicts among the directors and King James I's fear that the company was infected with PURITANISM led him to revoke the colony's charter in 1624. Following on the heels of an Indian war in 1622 that had left hundreds of colonists dead, this brought turmoil to the colony from which it had just begun to recover in 1644 when another Indian war killed over 500 colonists.

Religious life in the colony suffered as a result of war and disease, although the colonists were well served by ministers such as Robert Hunt, Alexander Whitaker, and James Blair. Blair, who served in Virginia for 58 years, was responsible for the establishment of the College of William and Mary and also served as the overseer of the Church of England in the colony.

While the goal was to reconstruct in the colony the parish-based life of the Church of England, two factors mitigated against it. The first of these was the introduction of tobacco as a cash crop and the attendant development of slave labor. This led to the creation of large plantations separated from each other by vast distances. Such a social organization made it exceedingly difficult for people to travel to church services on Sundays and greatly increased the area for which one priest was responsible.

Even more significant, however, was the way in which the vestries, or church trustees, dominated parish affairs in Virginia. In the absence of a resident bishop and the ability to enforce church law, the vestrymen were capable of controlling the activities and even the payment of the priests. Many priests were never appointed to permanent positions but were kept on a temporary basis. This severely weakened their ability to enforce discipline, as they remained dependent upon the parish trustees for their livelihood. Simultaneously, the notorious stinginess of many vestries made service in Virginia, already a difficult proposition, even more unappealing to young priests.

Although institutional religion was weak, the colony was vigorous in its attempts to suppress dissent. This was particularly true following the Stuart restoration. As early as 1643 the colony required all those not in conformity with the Church of England to leave, and by the end of that decade, nearly a thousand Puritan-inclined colonists had migrated. In March 1661 the colonial assembly passed several severe laws against BAPTISTS and Quakers (see FRIENDS, THE RELIGIOUS SOCIETY OF) and in the following year expelled one of its own members for Quaker tendencies.

These laws seem to have had their intended outcome. No evidence exists for any Baptist congregations in the colony during the 1600s, and while some priests appear to have had Presbyterian (see PRESBYTERIANISM) tendencies, none moved to visible dissent.

The Quakers, while maintaining a low profile, seem to have been little deterred by the law. They arrived in the colony in the 1650s and by 1662 had a regular Meeting. When George Fox, the movement's founder, toured the colony in 1672, he was warmly received and spoke to several large gatherings until he was deported to Maryland (see MARYLAND [COLONY]).

The 18th century saw a gradual change in this atmosphere. The "Glorious Revolution" of 1688 and changes in English law increased the pressure on the colonies to allow tolerance for nonconforming Protestants. This pressure bore some fruits and Virginia became less hostile to dissenters. Among the earliest were the Scots Presbyterians who settled in the inland, mountain area of Virginia, but they were soon followed by Baptists. The first Baptist congregations were formed in the 1720s. These early congregations were Particular (Calvinist) Baptist Churches (see CALVINISM), but they were soon joined by General (Arminian) Baptists whose evangelistic fervor resulted in great expansion (see ARMINIANISM). At the outbreak of the AMERICAN REVOLUTION these General Baptists had over 3,000 members in nearly 40 congregations.

By the mid-18th century these dissenters formed a significant power bloc within the colony, one willing to make common cause with Deists and revolutionaries against both the entrenched political and ecclesiastical establishments. This alliance was felt during the Revolution when Baptists and Presbyterians strongly supported the colonial side.

The revolution itself illustrated the deep divisions within colonial Anglicanism. On one hand it was the bastion of those loyal to the British monarch and the existing social and political structures. On the other hand much of colonial Anglicanism had been affected by the ENLIGHTENMENT, and many leaders of the American Revolution were, nominally at least, Anglicans. Many indeed were vestryman who served as the trustees of their parishes. Enlightenment

thought deeply influenced the ways that these men saw religion and the relationship between religion and the government. All were committed to religious tolerance and many to religious liberty. Combined with a growing commitment to republican and representative government, these men took the lead in the American Revolution.

The result was not only the alliance of Deists, Baptists, and Presbyterians in support of the revolution, but also an alliance that enshrined religious freedom in Virginia law. Thomas Jefferson's "Bill for Establishing Religious Freedom," strongly supported by Baptists and Presbyterians and aided by James Madison's *Memorial and Remonstrance,* became Virginia law in 1786. Three years before the adoption of the United States Constitution, Virginia had shown the way for what many have seen as the genius of American life and religion.

EQ

Bibliography: Wesley F. Craven, *The Southern Colonies in the Seventeenth Century, 1607–1689* (Baton Rouge: Louisiana State University Press, 1949); Samuel S. Hill, Jr., *The Encyclopedia of Religion in the South* (Macon: Mercer University Press, 1984); Rhys Isaac, *The Transformation of Virginia, 1740–1790* (Chapel Hill: University of North Carolina Press, 1982).

Vivekananda, Swami (1863–1902)

The cultivated orator from "heathen" India who became the most dashing delegate to the WORLD'S PARLIAMENT OF RELIGIONS, Swami Vivekananda was the first great Hindu missionary to the West (see HINDUISM). He is recognized in India as the founder of the Ramakrishna Mission and in the United States as the founder of the VEDANTA SOCIETY.

Born Nerendra Nath Datta to a well-to-do Bengali family in Calcutta, India, Swami Vivekananda was destined by his birth into the Kshatriya caste for a life in either government or the military. In 1879, however, a devotee of the Hindu goddess Kali persuaded him to seek spiritual insight instead of political or military success.

As a young man, Vivekananda received his B.A. at the University of Calcutta. He was also initiated into the ways of the Brahmo Samaj, a Hindu reform movement led by Rammohan Roy. But his most important training came from Sri Ramakrishna, the Bengali mystic who taught him the principles of non-dualistic Advaita Vedanta Hinduism. Chief among those principles were the affirmations that Brahman or God is impersonal and ultimately indescribable, and that this Brahman is the same as the Atman or soul of the individual human being. The goal of Vedanta, therefore, is for the individual to realize that his or her Atman is indistinguishable from Brahman—that one's spiritual essence is one with Ultimate Reality.

After Ramakrishna's death in 1886, Vivekananda gathered his guru's devotees into a monastic community that would become the Ramakrishna Order. He then joined them in taking the vows of the *sannyasin* or world renunciant and took the name of Swami Vivekananda ("he who has the bliss of spiritual discrimination").

In 1893 Vivekananda traveled to the United States as a delegate to the World's Parliament of Religions, convened in Chicago in conjunction with the World's Columbian Exposition. There Hinduism's first great missionary to the West impressed his listeners with his erudition, his fluent British English, and his dashing good looks. Delegates were especially taken with his insistence that all religions were manifestations of one sublime Truth and that Brahman had incarnated not only as Krishna but as Buddha and Jesus as well.

After the Parliament, Vivekananda lectured widely in the United States and England. He founded the Vedanta Society, the first Hindu organization in the United States devoted to attracting Occidental converts, in New York in 1894 and the Ramakrishna Mission, an outgrowth of the Ramakrishna Order that championed both monasticism and social reform, in

India in 1897. Both organizations survived his death in India in 1902, and remain active today.

SRP

Bibliography: Carl T. Jackson, *Vedanta for the West: The Ramakrishna Movement in the United States* (Bloomington: Indiana University Press, 1994); Romain Rolland, *The Life of Vivekananda and the Universal Gospel* (Calcutta: Advaita Ashrama, 1931); Swami Vivekananda, *The Complete Works of Swami Vivekananda . . . ,* 7 vols. (Mayavati, India: Advaita Ashrama, 1924–32).

Vodou   Forged in the slave plantations of 18th-century Haiti, Vodou (or Vodon) is the religion of the majority of the people of Haiti and of a growing number of Haitian immigrants in American cities such as New York and Miami.

Rarely understood and frequently criticized, Vodou is, like the SANTERÍA tradition of Cuba, a "creole" religion rooted in the religions of West Africa. Unlike Santería, however, which mixes elements of West African religions with the beliefs and behaviors of Spanish Catholicism, Vodou blends West African religions and French Catholicism (see ROMAN CATHOLICISM).

Vodou maintains a public face at *botanicas* that dot the Haitian neighborhoods of American cities. These apothecaries sell votive candles, roots and stones, oils and alcohols, icons of saints, and crosses of the crucified Jesus. But Vodou in the United States is practiced largely in the privacy of the homes of the neighborhood priest (*oungan*) and priestess (*manbo*), who are believed to possess the ability to heal not only the diseases but also the work and love woes of their largely poor clients.

Practitioners of Vodou affirm a high god, but they interact chiefly with ancestors and spirits who are more concerned than the largely aloof deity on high with the troubles of individuals on earth. Each of these spirits, called *iwa*, are likened to Catholic saints. Thus Ogou the warrior, for example, is represented as St. James. And the Virgin Mary appears in three guises, as Lasyrenn (the mermaid), Ezili Danto (the solitary mother), and Ezili Freda (a sexy and flirtatious spirit). Like the Catholic saints with whom they are identified, each of these spirits functions as a mediator who intercedes on behalf of an individual to bring extraordinary power to bear in the everyday world. These spirits, however, do not always act "saintly." They are permitted to get angry and to perform mischief at times. Papa Gede, a spirit not only of death but also of sexuality, is undoubtedly the greatest of the Vodou tricksters.

Vodou spirits make their way into the world through rituals of spirit possession. In these rituals, the spirit "mounts" and then "rides" the priest or priestess who then speaks and acts on behalf of the spirit. These trance events provide opportunities for Vodou practitioners to interact with the spirits even as they demonstrate the exceedingly thin line that exists in Vodou between the sacred and the profane.

Because of its trance rituals, its cultivation of mystery, and its not-so-holy spirits, Vodou is often maligned as a religion bereft of ethics. But Vodou does affirm an ethic that centers around relationships of proper giving and grateful receiving. These relationships are cultivated by practitioners of Vodou between people and spirits and among people themselves.

SRP

Bibliography: Karen M. Brown, *Mama Lola: A Vodou Priestess in Brooklyn* (Berkeley: University of California Press, 1991).

voluntaryism   Voluntaryism refers to the circumstance where churches and other religious institutions must rely on persuasion rather than state coercion to prompt individuals to join and support them. It is, therefore, a corollary of the principles of religious liberty and the separation of church and state (see CHURCH AND STATE RELATIONSHIP BETWEEN).

At least since the appearance of Alexis de Tocqueville's *Democracy in America* in the 1830s, scholars have viewed voluntaryism as a distinguishing mark of American religion. Historians from Robert Baird (1844) to Sydney Ahlstrom (1972) have described the voluntary

principle as typically and uniquely American. If in Europe the state coerced individuals to join and support churches, these historians contended, in the United States the churches were forced to enlist members through persuasion. Today scholars are less likely to see voluntaryism either as uniquely American or as the characteristic feature of American religious life, but most recognize its importance in shaping the country's religious institutions.

The American transition from religious establishments to voluntary churches was gradual. Some colonies, such as Rhode Island, operated from the beginning under the voluntary principle, but in most colonies either Anglicanism or Congregationalism was legally established. Although the FIRST AMENDMENT to the United States Constitution, which stipulated that "Congress shall make no law respecting the establishment of religion, or prohibiting the free exercise thereof," prohibited a national religious establishment, it left state establishments intact. Not until 1833 when Congregationalism was officially disestablished in Massachusetts were church and state legally separated in all states.

It has been a longstanding conviction among both theologians and philosophers in the West that the cohesion of a society depends on the shared religious convictions of its citizens, so it was with some trepidation that Americans adopted the voluntary principle. Among the more celebrated opponents of voluntaryism was the Congregationalist evangelist Lyman BEECHER, who argued vociferously that the demise of the "standing order" in Connecticut would lead, first, to widespread infidelity and immorality and, later, to the collapse of civilization itself.

Voluntaryism, however, apparently did just the opposite. Americans, rather than forgetting about religion and morality after disestablishment, emphasized both with vigor. Revivalists brought new Christians into the churches and reinvigorated the piety of their members, and reformers and humanitarians organized to persuade Americans to do voluntarily the good actions that would demonstrate their "disinterested benevolence" and help to usher in the kingdom of God on earth.

Voluntaryism spawned a number of important religious innovations in the United States. First, it made necessary new techniques for religious recruitment. Chief among these new techniques was a novel form of REVIVALISM, which unlike the revivalism of the colonial GREAT AWAKENING, emphasized the ability of individuals freely to choose to commit themselves to God.

Voluntaryism also contributed to the politicization of the churches and the ministry. Because ministers were as dependent on the consent of their congregations as politicians were on the consent of the citizens they governed, they were forced to appeal to the tastes of the people in their pews. This transformation makes sense both of Tocqueville's observation that in America "you meet with a politician where you expected to find a priest" and of the argument of historian Nathan Hatch that in the late 18th and early 19th centuries American Christianity was radically democratized.

Another important development associated with voluntaryism was the proliferation of voluntary associations proper, organizations comprised of free individuals voluntarily gathering together to promote a specific end. Before the dawn of the 19th century, Americans had founded numerous local voluntary associations, but in the first decades of the 19th century, a myriad of national voluntary associations sprung up, including the American Education Society (1815), the American Bible Society (1816), the American Colonization Society (1817), and the American Temperance Society (1826). These societies focused on different objectives, but each hoped to extend the influence of the Christian churches into American society.

A fourth and final result of the shift from religious establishments to voluntaryism was the infusion of a spirit of interdenominational cooperation among Protestants of competing denominations. Because of their common com-

mitment to the strategies of revivalism and the goal of Christianizing America, Protestants of the early 19th century were able to knit their disparate associations together into one vast "benevolent empire" (see EVANGELICAL UNITED FRONT). Leaders of this empire hoped to recover whatever cultural authority they had lost (or thought they had lost) by fashioning a "quasi-establishment" that would reestablish Protestant authority as a matter of fact if not a matter of law. At least some historians believe that this effort to construct a "Christian America" was successful. They refer to the years leading up to the CIVIL WAR as the "era of republican Protestantism."

Because of the success that revivalists and reformers enjoyed in bringing individuals into the Christian fold and in Christianizing America in the wake of disestablishment, Lyman Beecher was happy to withdraw his objections to voluntaryism. As he looked back on his life in his autobiography, he referred to the end of religious establishment in Connecticut in 1818 as "the best thing that ever happened to the State of Connecticut." "They say ministers have lost their influence;" Beecher concluded, "the fact is, they have gained. By voluntary efforts, societies, missions, and revivals, they exert a deeper influence than ever they could by queues, and shoe-buckles, and cocked hats, and gold-headed canes."

SRP

Bibliography: Sydney E. Ahlstrom, *A Religious History of the American People* (New Haven: Yale University Press, 1972); Robert Baird, *Religion in America,* (New York: Harper & Brothers, 1844); Robert Handy, *A Christian America: Protestant Hopes and Historical Realities* (New York: Oxford University Press, 1984); Winthrop S. Hudson, *The Great Tradition of the American Churches* (New York: Harper & Row, 1953); Sidney E. Mead, *The Lively Experiment: The Shaping of Christianity in America* (New York: Harper & Row, 1963); Alexis de Tocqueville, *Democracy in America* (New York: A. A. Knopf, 1945).

W

Walther, Carl Ferdinand Wilhelm (1811–1887)

Carl F. W. Walther was a German-born Lutheran minister. He was chosen in 1847 to be the first president of the denomination now known as the LUTHERAN CHURCH—Missouri Synod. His theological and biblical conservatism, strict adherence to traditional beliefs and values, and insistence on the central role of divine grace in salvation all remain distinctive characteristics of Missouri Synod Lutherans today.

Walther was born on October 25, 1811 at Langenchursdorf in Germany. For his undergraduate education, he attended the University of Leipzig. At Leipzig he became increasingly disillusioned with the religious rationalism of 19th-century German Lutheranism. He was introduced at the same time to the Pietist movement, which stressed individual spiritual renewal and attention to godly living. After carefully reading the writings of the great Protestant reformer Martin Luther, Walther dedicated himself to the revival of Lutheran orthodoxy. Following his graduation in 1833, he worked as a private tutor for two years. He was then ordained to the ministry and served as pastor of a parish in Braunsdorf until 1838.

Conflicts with members of his parish left Walther despondent about the state of religion in his native Saxony. As a result, he joined a band of Saxon emigrants traveling to the United States under the leadership of Martin Stephan. This group eventually settled in Perry County, Missouri in 1839, and Walther assumed the pastorate of two churches there. After Stephan was expelled from the community for misconduct, Walther emerged as its leader. He was called in 1842 to his deceased brother's congregation in St. Louis, where he served for the rest of his life. In 1844 he began a popular periodical, *Der Lutheraner*. This journal, which adopted a conservative stance on church matters, won a loyal following and quickly became the leading theological voice of midwestern Lutheranism.

Walther and others attracted to his views formed the German Evangelical Lutheran Synod of Missouri, Ohio, and Other States in 1847. Distrustful both of a centralized bureaucracy and of clerical authority generally, Walther's group developed a democratic polity for their church. They advocated the autonomy of local congregations and the need for laity to have voice in church affairs. This placed the synod in opposition to other American Lutheran synods that gave primary authority to the clergy. With its pragmatic organization, the Missouri Synod soon became the largest of the immigrant Lutheran church bodies in the United States. Walther served as its president, first, from 1847 to 1850 and, later, from 1864 to 1878.

Walther's theological world view combined seemingly contradictory emphases. On the one hand, he preached fervently about the need for Christians to accept God's gracious forgiveness of their sins. On the other hand, Walther utterly opposed the American Protestant tendency to reduce faith to feelings. Upholding an objective rule of faith, he believed that the Bible and his denomination's doctrinal system contained all the essentials of salvation. Walther looked, therefore, to the Scriptures and to the confessional statements of Martin Luther both to foster personal piety and to combat heresy. His stress on the literal interpretation of the Bible, moreover, helped make INERRANCY a major theme of Missouri Synod doctrine in the 20th century.

Walther was instrumental in creating the Evangelical Lutheran Synodical Conference in 1872. This organization united several independent German Lutheran synods in the Midwest. The principle of pan-Lutheran unity did not last long, however, and by the end of the 1870s the conference split apart over theological questions. Although Walther defended what he conceived as the classic Lutheran position on the inability of sinners to choose faith for themselves, his emphasis on God's grace alone in saving sinners led him to be accused of "crypto-Calvinism." As a consequence of this abortive attempt at Christian reunion, the Missouri Synod refused to engage in prayer fellowship with other Lutherans.

Walther's organizational and intellectual contributions to the Missouri Synod were immense. He served as professor of theology at the denomination's Concordia Seminary in St. Louis from 1850 until his death. He was president of Concordia as well after 1854. In 1853 he founded the theological periodical *Lehre und Wehre*, which he also edited until he died. He wrote several books including *Die rechte Unterscheidung von Gesetz und Evangelium (The Proper Distinction Between Law and Gospel)*, his most widely read work, which was published posthumously in 1897. Walther's teaching and writings instilled a distinctively militant approach to Lutheran beliefs in the many students he instructed over the course of his long career. He died in St. Louis on May 7, 1887.

GHS, Jr.

Bibliography: Lewis W. Spitz, *The Life of Dr. C. F. W. Walther* (St. Louis: Concordia, 1961).

War for Independence   See AMERICAN REVOLUTION/REVOLUTIONARY WAR.

Warfield, Benjamin Breckinridge (1851–1921)

Benjamin B. Warfield was a Presbyterian minister and theologian at Princeton Theological Seminary in New Jersey. The greatest contribution he made to American religious thought was his insistence that God was the author of every statement contained in the Bible. This belief, known as the doctrine of the INERRANCY of Scripture, has served as the intellectual foundation of conservative Protestant theology from the late 19th century to the present day.

Warfield was born near Lexington, Kentucky on November 5, 1851. He graduated from the College of New Jersey (now Princeton University) in 1871 and from Princeton Seminary in 1876. During his seminary period, he studied with Charles HODGE, the greatest Presbyterian theologian of that time. After traveling and studying in Europe, Warfield was ordained and served for a year as assistant minister of the First Presbyterian Church in Baltimore. He left his parish work in 1878 to teach New Testament studies at Westminister Seminary in Allegheny, Pennsylvania. When A. A. Hodge, with whom he had earlier collaborated, died in 1887, Warfield succeeded him as professor of didactic and polemic theology at Princeton.

Warfield defended the literal truth of the Bible against assault on two fronts: first, against liberal rationalists who wished to substitute human reason for God's self-revelation in the words of Scripture; and second, against conservative "perfectionists" who preferred individual experiences of revelation to the objective standards of the biblical text. In Warfield's mind, theology ought to be grounded not on human reason or experience, but solely on a grammatical analysis of the self-interpreting statements the Bible contains. Denying the modern contention that the past is largely irretrievable, Warfield upheld the philosophical positions of SCOTTISH COMMON SENSE REALISM, which taught that "facts" about the past are immediately available to the understanding of present-day observers. He acknowledged that current scriptural texts include mistakes and discrepancies but asserted that the original edition of the Bible had been wholly free of error.

Warfield trained an entire generation of Presbyterian clergy in Princeton's conservative theology. His ideas, moreover, dominated the denomination's General Assembly in the late 19th and early 20th centuries. Over that period the General Assembly declared on several occasions that belief in the inerrancy of the original manuscript of the Bible was necessary for membership in the church. Warfield also insisted that the Westminster Confession, the classic statement of English-speaking CALVINISM, was the finest statement of Christian theology ever composed. As a consequence, he resisted all attempts by liberals to modify or modernize the wording of the confession.

Warfield published numerous books on the textual criticism and authority of the Bible, as well as many articles and book reviews. His 1881 article on "Inspiration," written with A. A. Hodge, contained his most critical affirmation of biblical inerrancy. He also edited *The Princeton Review* between 1890 and 1903. Warfield's thought had a tremendous influence on the development of FUNDAMENTALISM in the 20th century. His mantle was eventually assumed by his student J. Gresham MACHEN, who became the chief spokesman for conservative Presbyterians in the 1920s.

Warfield remained for over three decades in his post as professor of theology at Princeton. He died there on February 17, 1921.

GHS, Jr.

Bibliography: W. Andrew Hoffecker, *Piety and the Princeton Theologians: Archibald Alexander, Charles Hodge, and Benjamin Warfield* (Grand Rapids: Baker Book House, 1981).

Warner, Daniel Sidney   See HOLINESS MOVEMENT.

Washington, Booker Taliaferro (1856–1915)

The work of Booker T. Washington, perhaps the most prominent black American of his day, is difficult to judge. Accused by critics of dooming blacks to perpetual second-class citizenship, his program of black economic independence appealed to later black nationalists such as Marcus GARVEY. Although Washington argued that blacks should avoid political agitation, he was a significant political force during the presidencies of Theodore Roosevelt and William Taft. Publicly opposed to the judicial maneuvering of the NAACP, he surreptitiously aided several major court challenges to segregation laws. Throughout his life, Washington was driven by the view that moral development was integral to economic and political improvement.

Born on April 15, 1856 in Hale's Ford, Virginia of a slave mother and a white man from a neighboring plantation, Booker (he would choose the name Washington himself at a later date) spent the first nine years of his life in bondage. Following the end of the CIVIL WAR his mother moved to West Virginia, where he attended school while working at a salt furnace and in the coal mines. Overhearing two miners talk about a new school for blacks, he resolved to attend. In 1872 he traveled to Hampton Institute. Walking most of the distance, Washington arrived penniless and dirty. Washington worked his way through Hampton as a janitor, learning the trade of brick-masonry. Graduating in 1875, he returned home to West Virginia where he ran a school for blacks until 1878, when he entered Wayland Seminary in Washington, D.C.

The academic year of 1879 saw Washington back at Hampton where he was placed in charge of the school's program for American Indians and served as secretary to Hampton's president, General Samuel Chapman Armstrong. The connections he made with northern philanthropists while holding this position served him well in the future.

In May 1881 he was asked to head a Negro Normal School recently chartered by the State of Alabama. As head of this school, Tuskegee Institute, Booker T. Washington emerged as the dominant black leader in the United States, a position he retained until his death on November 14, 1915. From a school with 40 students and one building, Washington transformed Tuskegee Institute into a leading black institution of 2,000 students. Concerned with providing blacks with the skills needed to make their way in the world, Washington emphasized economic development and trades at Tuskegee, often speaking disparagingly of black colleges and blacks who could speak French but could not make a living.

A popular public speaker, Washington gave his most important address on September 18, 1893 at the Cotton States and International Exposition in Atlanta, Georgia. There he argued that blacks and white should "cast down their buckets" in working to improve their lives. He also suggested that social integration and equality were not necessary. "In all things that are purely social we can be as separate as the fingers, yet one as the hand in all things essential to mutual progress." The speech was interpreted as a public acceptance of segregation and second-class citizenship. Washington often sounded as though the overcoming of legal and social barriers was the obligation of blacks and not those who discriminated against them.

This brought him into conflict with other black leaders, most notably W. E. B. DU BOIS, who argued that Washington was consigning blacks to manual labor and political impotence. This was reinforced by Washington's tendency to speak disparagingly of ignorant blacks in public addresses and to claim that agitation in favor of the franchise was folly. On the other hand, Washington publicly criticized the inferior quality of black schools and felt that laws limiting suffrage should be applied to all unqualified persons, whites as well as blacks.

Although recent research suggests that Washington was not as politically quiescent as previously supposed, Washington's faith in the eventual white acceptance of black political development was misplaced. While his goal undoubtedly was black self-sufficiency, the charge that he was educating a black underclass to operate the white economic machine seems valid. Despite the failure of his goal of black economic security, it is important that Washington be recognized a major African-American leader, clear on the problems facing Southern blacks and desirous of providing immediate solutions to those problems. These solutions, based upon black self-reliance and economic security, were shared by his opponents and drew increased attention as political equality failed to ease the chains of racism binding blacks to an inferior condition.

(See also AFRICAN-AMERICAN RELIGION; CIVIL RIGHTS MOVEMENT.)

EQ

Bibliography: Louis R. Harlan, *Booker T. Washington: The Making of a Black Leader* (New York: Oxford University Press, 1972); ———, *Booker T. Washington: The Wizard of Tuskegee, 1901–1915* (New York: Oxford University Press, 1972); Basil Mathews, *Booker T. Washington, Educator and Interracial Interpreter* (London: SCM Press, 1949); August Meier, *Negro Thought in America, 1880–1915: Racial Ideologies in the Age of Booker T. Washington* (Ann Arbor: University of Michigan Press, 1963); Booker T. Washington, *The Future of the American Negro* (Boston: Small, Maynard, 1899); ———, *The Negro in the South: His Economic Progress in Relation to His Moral and Religious Development* (Northbrook: Metro Book, 1972); ———, *Up from Slavery: An Autobiography* (New York: Dodd, Mead, 1901).

Watchtower Bible and Tract Society

See JEHOVAH'S WITNESSES.

Watts, Alan Wilson (1915–1973)

One of the most important popularizers of ZEN in America, Alan Watts was born into a middle-class home in Kent, England in 1915. As a young man, he introduced himself to BUDDHISM through books, especially the works of the Japanese Rinzai Zen master D.T. SUZUKI. At the age of 15, the already independently minded Watts repudiated Christianity and announced his conversion to Buddhism.

He moved to London where he introduced himself to a small but active contingent of Occidental Buddhists centered around the Buddhist Lodge. At the age of 19, he wrote his first book on Zen. Watts entered into the first of his three marriages in 1938 when he was wed to Eleanor Everett, the daughter of the prominent Zen Buddhist Ruth Fuller Everett. Watts and his wife moved to New York, where Watts joined the First Zen Institute of America (then the Buddhist Society of America) and took up Zen study with its founder, the Japanese Rinzai Zen master Shigatsu Sasaki (Sokei-an).

While in America, Watts reacquainted himself with the Christian tradition and gradually came to believe that Buddhism and Christianity were mutually compatible, if not coequal, religions. He enrolled in the Seabury-Western Theological Seminary at Northwestern and emerged in the mid-1940s as an Episcopal priest (see EPISCOPAL CHURCH). He worked for a time as a chaplain at Northwestern, but quit in 1950. That same year he also left his wife. In 1951 he moved to the West Coast, joined the faculty of the American Academy of Asian Studies and recommitted himself to Buddhist work. Through his writing and lecturing, Watts helped to spawn the Zen vogue of the 1950s and 1960s.

Before his death in California in 1973 at the age of 58, Watts had published 25 books—including his widely read autobiography, *In My Own Way* (1972)—on topics ranging from Zen to Christian spirituality to mysticism to psychotherapy. In a short book called *Beat Zen, Square Zen and Zen* (1959), Watts chastised Beat writers (see BEAT MOVEMENT) like Allen Ginsberg and Jack Kerouac for flirting with Zen rather than devoting themselves to its disciplined practice. But Watts, who once described himself as a "genuine fake," might as well have been criticizing himself. He left Sokei-an after only two weeks when he became frustrated with koan study, and his attempts to engage with a psychotherapist were equally short-lived.

After his death on November 16, 1973, and his subsequent cremation, Watts's admirerers gave him a new name, "Profound Mountain, Subtle Light," and a new title, "Great Founder, Opener of the Great Zen Samadhi Gate." The Society for Comparative Philosophy (1962) keeps alive his legacy by discussing his work at seminars and publishing the *Alan Watts Journal*. Watts stands with D. T. Suzuki as one of the two most important pioneers of Zen in America.

SRP

Bibliography: Monica Furlong, *Zen Effects: The Life of Alan Watts* (Boston: Houghton Mifflin, 1986); Alan Watts, *In My Own Way: An Autobiography* (New York: Vintage Books, 1972).

Webb, Muhammad Alexander Russel (1846–1916)

Muhammad Alexander Russel Webb was the first Occidental American to convert to ISLAM. Born into a Presbyterian family (see PRESBYTERIANISM) in Hudson, New York in 1846, Webb repudiated Christianity at the age of 20. After an American career as a journalist and newspaper editor, Webb moved to Manila in 1887 to serve as United States consul to the Philippines. There he was introduced to Islam, which appealed to him as a religion that, unlike Christianity, did not contravene either reason or science.

While in the Philippines, Webb submitted to Allah and became a Muslim. He resigned his federal appointment in 1892 and departed for a lecture tour that took him, first, to India and later to the United States. While in India, Webb stated that he was not only a Muslim but also a theosophist (see THEOSOPHY). After returning to New York, he issued Muslim tracts through his Oriental Publishing Company, published an ill-fated periodical entitled *Moslem World* and organized an equally short-lived mosque.

Webb achieved international recognition as a Muslim delegate to the WORLD'S PARLIAMENT OF RELIGIONS held in Chicago in 1893. There he ruffled the feathers of many Christians with his strident defense of Islam against its missionary despisers and created another stir among women's rights advocates with his traditionalist discussions of the role of women in Islam.

Unlike the Hindu missionary Swami VIVEKANANDA and the Buddhist reformer Anagarika DHARMAPALA, both of whom founded enduring organizations in America following their appearances at the parliament, Webb was not able to organize an abiding Muslim society in America. When he died in Rutherford, New Jersey in 1916, his American Islamic Propaganda Movement (1893) died with him. However, Webb did leave behind three books, including *Islam in America* (1893), which introduced Americans to the Muslim faith.

SRP

Bibliography: Muhammad A. R. Webb, *Islam in America; a Brief Statement of Mohammedanism and an Outline of the American Islamic Propaganda* (New York: The Oriental Publishing Company, 1893).

Weld, Theodore Dwight (1803–1895)

Theodore Dwight Weld was a revivalist and one of the most active of the early antislavery advocates. He helped organize the famous debates over slavery at Lane Seminary in Cincinnati and was part of the first group of students at Oberlin College in Ohio, a school founded on the principles of religious and moral reform.

The son of a Congregational minister, Weld was born in Hampton, Connecticut on November 23, 1803. He studied at Hamilton College where, in 1825, he came under the influence of revivalist Charles Grandison FINNEY. After several years of leading revivals and lecturing on temperance and antislavery, Weld enrolled at Lane Seminary in 1832. In the spring of 1834 he convinced the majority of students at Lane to join the abolitionist cause. Although his extremism caused the school's trustees to expel him, Weld and others (labeled the "Lane Rebels") departed for newly opened Oberlin College, where they were able to continue their work unhindered. Oberlin, moreover, under the leadership of Finney and with financial backing from wealthy social reformers Arthur and Lewis Tappan of New York, soon became a center for both ABOLITIONISM and REVIVALISM.

Weld served as an agent of the new American Anti–Slavery Society. His emphasis on moral suasion and the necessity of immediately renouncing slavery as a sin, characteristics of the revivals he led, placed him in the forefront of the abolitionists' ranks. Weld eventually trained a number of disciples, including his future wife, Angelina GRIMKÉ, and sent them out to proclaim the radical message he championed. When he suffered damage to his voice, he turned his energies to tracts and composed *The Bible Against Slavery* (1837) and *American Slavery As It Is* (1839). These works won many sympa-

thizers to his cause, most notably, Harriet Beecher STOWE, later author of *Uncle Tom's Cabin*. Weld also assisted the antislavery faction of the Whig Party in Washington, D.C.

Weld's career with the American Anti–Slavery Society, however, came to a sudden halt in 1840. After that organization split over both the propriety of advocating women's rights and abolitionist William Lloyd Garrison's insistence on nonpolitical moral suasion, Weld chose to retire from public life. He worked as a farmer in Belleville, New Jersey from 1840 to 1854, then taught school in Perth Amboy, New Jersey and in Lexington, Massachusetts between 1854 and 1867. Weld retired to Hyde Park, Massachusetts in 1867, and although he lived for 28 more years, he rarely participated in reform activities again. He died at Hyde Park on February 3, 1895.

GHS, Jr.

Bibliography: Robert H. Abzug, *Passionate Liberator: Theodore Dwight Weld and the Dilemma of Reform* (New York: Oxford University Press, 1980).

Wesleyan Church   See METHODISTS.

Wesleyan tradition, the

The Wesleyan tradition refers to a type of Protestantism that traces its historical and theological roots to 18th-century Anglican clergyman John Wesley. Organized at first as societies under lay leadership within the Church of England, Wesleyanism eventually developed into a separate denomination after the American Revolution. This tradition finds its primary institutional expression today within the various Methodist (see METHODISTS) denominations in the United States. Wesleyan emphases appear as well within Holiness (see HOLINESS MOVEMENT) churches, heirs of a movement that emerged out of Methodism in the late 19th and early 20th centuries.

John Wesley (along with his younger brother Charles, a famed writer of hymns) was the son of Anglican priest Samuel Wesley. Born in Epworth, Lincolnshire, England in 1703, John was

John Wesley's emphasis on saving grace and the possibility of attaining perfection quickly took root in the fields and forests of 18th-century frontier territories.

educated at Oxford University and ordained a priest of the Church of England in 1728. He served briefly as an assistant to his father, then returned to Oxford in 1729, where he joined a small group of students seeking to deepen their religious faith. Calling itself the "Holy Club," though also known derisively as "Methodists," Wesley's society held its members accountable to one another for a daily devotional life, regular attendance at worship, and acts of charity. Wesley met with the group and directed their activities for the next five years.

In late 1735, Wesley left England and traveled to the newly established colony of Georgia, where he worked as a missionary of the Society for the Propagation of the Gospel. His stay in Georgia provided him important opportunities to experiment with practices that soon distinguished the Methodist movement: extempore prayer, outdoor preaching, and hymn singing. He also encountered MORAVIANS there, members of a German Pietist sect who stressed the need for personal conversion. As a whole, however, Wesley's missionary tour in Georgia was a disaster. Following a bungled love affair with the niece of a prominent official, he had to flee the colony to avoid a lawsuit. Depressed and spiritually confused, he returned to England in 1738.

The humiliating failure in Georgia proved to be a prologue to the dramatic conversion that ever afterward impelled Wesley's ministry. Wesley was then in turmoil, seeking pardon for his sins. On his way to a Moravian service on Aldersgate Street in London on May 24, 1738, he felt what he had never known before: a heart "strangely warmed." While reading a passage from the great reformer Martin Luther, Wesley sensed for the first time that God truly loved him. "I did trust in Christ, Christ alone for salvation," he wrote in his journal for the day, "and an assurance was given me that he had taken away *my* sins, even *mine,* and saved *me* from the law of sin and death." When Wesley returned home that evening, he declared simply to his brother Charles, "I believe."

A few weeks later, Wesley left for Germany to visit the Moravian headquarters at Herrnhut. After he returned to England, he read with approval American theologian Jonathan ED-WARD's account of the spiritual awakening at his parish in Massachusetts. Meanwhile, both John and Charles began to travel about and preach in fields, in prisons and workhouses, and at public executions. The style they adopted differed profoundly from an ordinary Anglican clergyman's concern for order and decency in worship. Even John himself worried initially about the propriety of his actions, admitting he had "submitted to be more vile." Despite the opposition that was aroused against his novel practices, Wesley became convinced that his course was correct.

Wesley preached and organized revivals throughout the British Isles. He became a successful leader who claimed to regard "all the world as my parish." He was clearly not a systematic theologian, but a busy itinerant minister who considered religious dogmas to be the least essential aspect of Christianity. The Wesleyan movement has always been marked by an emphasis on the theological doctrine of SANCTIFI- CATION and by the activistic style and concern for holiness that Wesley embraced. He taught that genuine Christians would lead lives of visible sanctity, continually manifesting to others the divine love in which they professed to believe. They might even reach a state of moral perfection (see PERFECTIONISM), he said—not complete sinlessness, certainly, but freedom from all conscious sin—in the present life.

Another significant aspect of the Wesleyan tradition is the organization that evolved to support Wesley's desire of reforming his nation. Since his movement arose within the institutional framework of the Church of England, Wesley urged Methodists to attend Anglican services as well as their own religious meetings. He also organized "bands," later called "classes," small groups that met regularly for mutual support under the leadership of a lay person. Above the "class" was the "circuit," a collection of societies within a particular geographic region. A lay itinerant preacher, or circuit rider, visited each class every month or two. Finally, a "conference," which eventually included all the itinerant preachers and met annually, was formed in 1744.

An enthusiastic and committed lay leadership was absolutely essential to the early Methodist movement. Wesley did not wish to challenge the Anglican hierarchy of bishops, priests, and deacons, and so his preachers were not clergy but simply laity with extraordinary administrative and pastoral oversight. Wesley traveled extensively, setting up and maintaining this lay

organization in England. He also sent missionaries, the most prominent being Francis ASBURY, to strengthen Methodism among American Anglicans. Although Wesley eventually violated Anglican procedure by ordaining Methodist clergy for service in America, he remained a priest of the Church of England throughout his life.

Other Methodists, however, were not as loyal to their Anglican roots as Wesley, and a new denomination soon was organized out of the movement he inspired. The first formal rift between Methodists and Anglicans occurred in America at the "Christmas Conference" of December 1784. At that meeting in Baltimore, Maryland, Methodist preachers assembled for their annual conference established a new denomination, the Methodist Episcopal Church, and elected Asbury and Thomas COKE to be the church's first superintendents (a title changed to "bishop" in 1787). Despite disobeying Wesley's wish that they stay within the Anglican fold, those assembled at the Christmas Conference approved a statement of purpose otherwise consistent with their leader's religious aims: "To reform the continent, and spread scriptural holiness through these lands." After Wesley's death in 1791, moreover, English Methodism followed the pattern that had developed in the United States and soon emerged as a movement entirely separate from the Church of England.

By the mid-1900s, Methodists had become the largest American Christian denomination. Although issues relating to race and slavery divided the Methodists along racial (the AFRICAN METHODIST EPISCOPAL CHURCH was organized in 1816 and the AFRICAN METHODIST EPISCO- PAL ZION CHURCH formed in 1821) and regional (the Methodist Episcopal Church, South separated in 1845) lines, the Wesleyan tradition remained strong in the United States throughout the 19th century.

The quest for personal holiness, a concern that has consistently characterized Wesleyanism, led to a prolonged theological debate within Methodism in the 1870s and 1880s. While most

Methodists believed that sanctification was a gradual process, lasting over a lifetime, others insisted that holiness was really an instantaneous experience, a "second blessing" received from God in the aftermath of a person's conversion. Because of Wesley's own stress on Christian perfection, Methodist advocates of holiness believed they were justified in separating from the more "worldly" members of their churches. The so-called Holiness movement soon inspired the formation of several new denominations, the SALVATION ARMY and the CHURCH OF THE NAZARENE being the two most prominent.

The largest Methodist denomination in the United States today is the UNITED METHODIST CHURCH with nearly nine million members. It is third in size of all American Christian denominations (behind the Roman Catholic Church and the Southern Baptist Convention). The African Methodist Episcopal Church is the leading black Methodist denomination with over two million members. And the Church of the Nazarene, which contains approximately 570,000 members, is now the largest Holiness denomination in America.

GHS, Jr.

Bibliography: Thomas A. Langford, *Wesleyan Theology: A Sourcebook* (Durham, N.C.: Labyrinth Press, 1984); Henry D. Rack, *Reasonable Enthusiast: John Wesley and the Rise of Methodism* (Philadelphia: Trinity Press International, 1989); Kenneth E. Rowe, ed., *The Place of Wesley in the Christian Tradition* (Metuchen, N.J.: Scarecrow Press, 1976).

White, Alma Bridwell (1862–1946)

The first female bishop in Christendom and the founder of a holiness church called the Pillar of Fire, Alma Bridwell White stands alongside Aimee Semple MCPHERSON as one of the most influential women in the Holiness-Pentecostal movement in the United States (see HOLINESS MOVEMENT and PENTECOSTALISM).

Born on a farm in Louis County, Kentucky in 1862, White was raised in the Methodist church (see METHODISTS). She began her march in the direction of the Holiness movement in

Ellen White, the "Adventist Prophetess" whose visions and unorthodox views on health, medicine, and diet led to the establishment of the Seventh-day Adventist Church in Battle Creek, Michigan in 1855.

1878 when she was converted at a revival conducted by preacher W. B. Godbey. In the midst of this conversion experience, she discerned a call to the Christian ministry, but initially pursued a career as a teacher instead. She studied at Vanceburg Seminary and Millersburg Female College, both in Kentucky, and subsequently took a teaching job at Bannack, Montana. There, in the winter of 1882–1883, she met Kent White, who was studying at the time for the Methodist ministry. The two married in 1887. When Kent White was called to the pastorate of a small church in Lamar, Colorado, his wife took a secondary but increasingly controversial role in that church's congregational life.

Her conspicuously public work as both a song-leader and lay exhorter struck many church members as inappropriate for a woman.

In 1893, Alma White received the "second blessing" of SANCTIFICATION that characterizes the Methodist and Holiness traditions. Remembering her earlier call to the ministry and weary of the objections to her prominence in her husband's church, she struck out on her own, becoming an itinerant preacher. She derived her theology from dreams, visions, and esoteric interpretations of biblical prophecy. Her exhortations focused on denouncing the heartless sort of piety that she had seen in her own parents and commending a more rigorous and enthusiastic faith originally preached and exemplified by the founder of the Methodists, John Wesley (see WESLEYAN TRADITION, THE).

Alma White's successes on the evangelistic circuit caused her husband to leave his church ministry and to join his wife on the road. From their center in Denver, they conducted camp meetings and revivals in western states such as Colorado, Montana, and Wyoming. This time, however, she was in charge and he was her helper. In 1901, the Whites left the Methodist Episcopal Church to found the Pentecostal Union Church. White became an elder in her new-found church in the year of its establishment. When she was ordained to the episcopate in 1918, she became the first female bishop in the history of the Christian tradition. Following a series of successful revivals in England, which began in 1904, she transferred her church's headquarters to Zarephath, New Jersey. Her association came to be known as the Pillar of Fire after 1917.

White's church shared much with other Holiness sects. Members were forbidden to smoke tobacco or consume alcohol and were called to act and dress modestly. Preachers emphasized the imminence of the second coming of Jesus Christ, and practiced spiritual healing. Her church distinguished itself from mainstream Holiness groups, however, by its strict Wesleyan discipline and the military-style uniforms of its members. White and her followers generally regarded mainstream Holiness denominations such as the CHURCH OF THE NAZARENE as backsliding accommodators to modernity. Not surprisingly, they ordained both male and female ministers.

White's church also resembled Pentecostal churches in many respects. It too attracted everyday folks and made a place in its worship services for strong emotions and loud music. But White herself was a strident critic of the Pentecostal movement; "spiritual gifts" such as speaking in tongues she denounced as sorcery.

Like other 20th-century evangelists, White utilized the mass media to great effect. Shortly after her Pentecostal Union Church was founded, White was publishing the *Pentecostal Union Herald,* which after 1904 appeared as *The Pillar of Fire.* Another publication, *Woman's Chains,* argued for women's rights from a biblical perspective. In addition to these and other periodicals, White's church also produced numerous books and tracts and maintained two radio stations. Among the many books that White published were *The Story of My Life,* a six-volume autobiography that appeared from 1919 to 1934, and a controversial tome, *The Ku Klux Klan in Prophesy* (1925). In the latter book, White argued for a populist theology in which anti-Catholic NATIVISM was presented as both scriptural and American.

White was aided in her evangelistic efforts not only by her husband but by two sons, Arthur Kent White and Ray Bridwell White, who both served as ordained ministers for the Pillar of Fire. Her husband, however, eventually separated from both his wife and her church, becoming a Pentecostalist and joining the Apostolic Faith Church, based in Great Britain. Alma Bridwell White died in 1946 in Zarephath, New Jersey at the age of 84, leaving her sons to continue her ministry.

SRP

Bibliography: Alma Bridwell White, *The Story of My Life,* 6 vols. (Zarephath, N.J.: Pillar of Fire, 1919–34).

White, Ellen Gould (Harmon) (1827–1915) Ellen Gould White, *née* Harmon, was the principal founder of the SEVENTH-DAY ADVENTIST CHURCH. As a teenager she had accepted the predictions of William MILLER that the second coming of Jesus Christ was to occur in 1843. Although the reign of Christ failed to materialize as Miller foretold, White refused to be discouraged. She soon experienced the first of over 2,000 spiritual visions that brought her to prominence. She began to write and teach about what she believed were the true tenets of the faith, including the observance of Saturday as the Christian Sabbath and the advocacy of health reforms such as vegetarianism.

Harmon was born in Gorham, Maine on November 26, 1827. Her father was a hat-maker, farmer, and lay preacher in a Methodist church in nearby Portland. After William Miller passed through that city in March 1840 and warned of the coming of Christ, Harmon counted herself among the converted. Following the eventual, uneventful passing of October 22, 1844, Miller's revised date for the approaching cataclysm, she became extremely ill with what was reported to be tuberculosis and heart disease. At a prayer meeting in December, however, she felt "surrounded by light" and received a vision that became the basis of her call to prophesying.

Harmon began next to travel among the various Millerite groups. She met her future husband, James White, an Adventist preacher, who worked with her in consolidating their movement. They married in 1846. Both Whites became convinced that Saturday ought to replace Sunday as the day for Christians to worship and they influenced others to adopt this practice. Although Ellen had received little formal education, she produced numerous publications interpreting the Bible and explaining the revelations God had made to her. James started publishing the *Review and Herald* in 1850, and Ellen's major work, *The Great Controversy between Christ and Satan during the Christian Dispensation,* appeared in 1888.

The Whites moved from Rochester, New York to Battle Creek, Michigan in 1855, and the new location became the Adventists' headquarters. The name "Seventh-day Adventist" was accepted as the denominational title in 1860, and in 1863 separate Adventist churches were gathered into a general conference. Ellen White's own struggle with illness was instrumental in assuring that health would be one of the new denomination's central concerns. Through her efforts, the Western Health Reform Institute, a prototype of many later sanatoriums, was established in 1866. She also advocated vegetarianism and opposed the use of coffee, tea, and alcohol, while John H. Kellogg, one of her disciples, was eventually to make Battle Creek the breakfast-cereal capital of the United States.

Mrs. White believed strongly in education, and she oversaw the founding of Battle Creek College (later Andrews University) in 1875 and the College of Medical Evangelists (later Loma Linda University) in 1906. After her husband died in 1881, she traveled extensively in both Europe and Australia. On her return to the United States she settled in California in 1900. Active until the very end of her life, White was instrumental in moving the denomination's central offices to the outskirts of Washington, D.C. in 1903 and continued to write extensively. She died on July 16, 1915 at St. Helena, California.

GHS, Jr.

Bibliography: Ronald L. Numbers, *Prophetess of Health: Ellen G. White and the Origins of Seventh-Day Adventist Health Reform,* rev. ed. (Knoxville: University of Tennessee Press, 1992).

Whitefield, George (1714–1770) George Whitefield, an Anglican clergyman known as the "Grand Itinerant," was unquestionably the most famous revivalist in America during the GREAT AWAKENING of the mid-18th century. He journeyed from England to America on seven occasions between 1738 and 1770. In the course of those evangelistic preaching tours,

George Whitefield. The Anglican missionary's whirlwind preaching tours of the colonies established him as the first public "American" figure.

Whitefield traveled tirelessly throughout the American colonies between New Hampshire and Georgia.

Whitefield was born on December 27, 1714 in Gloucester, England. He studied at Pembroke College at Oxford University, where he befriended the brothers John and Charles Wesley, later founders of the Methodist denomination. Although he remained a Calvinist (see CALVINISM) in his theological orientation and rejected the Wesley's emphasis on the freedom of the human will, Whitefield absorbed their ideas about the need for heartfelt piety and spiritual regeneration. After graduating from Oxford, he was ordained into the ministry of the Church of England in 1737 and began his life's work as an evangelist.

Rejecting the formalistic theology and practice of the established church, Whitefield was immediately successful in his preaching. He played down his connection to the Church of England and focused instead on the availability of God's grace to people of all denominational affiliations. When many Anglican churches were closed to him as a result of this message, Whitefield resorted to preaching in fields. The novelty of this approach, combined with his extemporaneous style and reliance on direct inspiration, attracted thousands of hearers wherever he went. He seldom remained long in one town or region but moved about, always seeking new congregations and audiences.

Whitefield's restlessness and religious enthusiasm inevitably led him to North America, where his greatest triumphs were to occur. His first American trip to Georgia in 1738 was a modest success despite the opposition of Anglican officials in the colony. His second tour of America, however, which lasted from 1739 to 1741, established the reputation he now holds as a revivalist. Then just 25 years old, Whitefield hurried from town to town, from crowded church to busy market, wherever people would listen to his message. He estimated that 20,000 people heard him preach on Boston Common in October 1740. At Northampton, Massachusetts, his preaching made Jonathan EDWARDS, the minister who had begun the Awakening in New England in 1734, weep with emotion. And at Philadelphia in November 1740, he preached to thousands in an auditorium specially built for his visit.

Despite the positive response Whitefield elicited, many clergy in America still expressed resentment about his mission. Timothy Cutler, for example, an Anglican minister in Boston, complained that the enthusiasm he generated amounted to madness. Whitefield's evening sermons, he said, were "attended with hideous yellings, and shameful revels, continuing . . . till break of day." Worst of all, Cutler reported, Whitefield encouraged laity in the colonies to turn against their proper leaders and question established religious beliefs and customs. Another opponent, Congregationalist Charles

CHAUNCY, leader of the antirevival Old Light (see NEW LIGHTS/OLD LIGHTS) faction in New England, openly criticized the revivals. He led the faculty of Harvard College to reject Whitefield's work in 1744.

Whitefield came to America again on five occasions: 1744–1748, 1751–1752, 1754–1755, 1763–1765, and 1769–1770. Over that period, controversy gradually subsided, and by the end of his life, he was widely respected as the greatest Anglo-American preacher of the day. No other clergyman had his gift for addressing people of every social class and moving them spiritually. Whitefield died while in Newburyport, Massachusetts on September 30, 1770.

GHS, Jr.

Bibliography: Harry S. Stout, *The Divine Dramatist: George Whitefield and the Rise of Modern Evangelicalism* (Grand Rapids, Mich.: Eerdmans, 1991).

Walt Whitman, the great poet of the American spirit. (Library of Congress)

Whitman, Walt (1819–1892)

Whitman—journalist, poet, and tramp—exerted an enormous influence on the shape of modern literature, although in his own lifetime his poetry was generally greeted with derision. He was regarded by his earliest admirers as the founder of a new, truly modern religious vision, focusing on the potential of a divinely infused democratic America. In the years since his death, he has inspired many who continue to see America as a land of infinite possibility.

Whitman, born to a farming family on New York's Long Island, May 31, 1819, moved to Brooklyn with his parents while still young. He grew up with little formal schooling, which ended when he was 11 years old, but his access to the fields and beaches of Long Island instilled a deep appreciation of the natural world that would mark his poetry. His first job, serving as a local lawyer's errand-boy, enabled him to spend considerable time in the library. Considered indolent by several of his elders, Whitman had little in the way of material ambition, or what he later called "the mania of owning things."

He learned writing through his apprenticeship to various newspapers in Brooklyn and New York City, where he lived periodically from 1835 onward, intrigued with the textures and sights of the city. Journalism, which he eventually abandoned as a full-time pursuit after two years as the editor of the Brooklyn *Eagle* (1846–1848), eventually enabled him to set aside the clichés that he came to see affecting American poetry at the time. Like a newspaper, his own poetry recorded the plethora of sights, sounds, ideas, and people of an America infused with a divine spark.

Whitman composed his great work, *Leaves of Grass,* first published in 1855 at his own expense, while working part-time as a carpenter for his father. Read at first primarily by transcendentalist intellectuals (see TRANSCENDENTALISM) such as EMERSON and THOREAU, Whitman developed a revolutionary literary form, a coarse, sensual, direct poetry, celebrating the ordinariness of American life as well as what he saw as its unique democratic promise. In subsequent years, while working on revisions and expansions of *Leaves,* he often subsisted hand to mouth. He volunteered in a Washington, D.C. hospital during the CIVIL WAR, and remained there, working in government offices until 1873. Suffering a stroke, he remained disabled the rest of his life, although still capable of an occasional public reading or lecture. In the 1880s, having found a publisher for *Leaves,* Whitman finally attracted enough readers to enable him to buy a small house in Camden, New Jersey, which became a place of pilgrimage for those who valued his poetic vision. Ravaged by tuberculosis and a number of other ailments, Whitman managed to oversee the 10th edition of *Leaves* before his death on March 26, 1892.

Whitman's work has been analyzed from a number of perspectives. His poems, glorifying working-class lives and expressing a mystical view of both self and society, were taken by early readers as the core of a new religious vision for a truly democratic people. Whitman strove to express the American genius which, as he emphasized in the preface to the first edition, lay not in leaders, but "always most in the common people." Viewing America in a post-Christian light, his faith in a democratic future nevertheless shared much in common with the POST-MILLENNIALISM of the mid-19th century, which he heard preached by Henry Ward BEECHER and others.

But Whitman's own religious influences also came from sources outside the evangelical Protestant mainstream of his day. Brought up in a liberal Quaker (see FRIENDS, RELIGIOUS SOCIETY OF) household, Whitman also learned from his father's appreciation of the deist (see ENLIGHTENMENT, THE) ideas of Tom PAINE to distrust authority and orthodoxy, to have faith in human nature, and to respect non-Christian religions. As an adult Whitman was attracted to various forms of HARMONIAL RELIGION. Reading Emerson's transcendentalism and the SPIRITUALISM of Andrew Jackson DAVIS provided much of the philosophical foundation for the immanent view of divinity, incarnate in the experience of the American people, which he developed in his poetry.

MG

Bibliography: Roger Asslineau, *The Evolution of Walt Whitman,* 2 vols. (Cambridge: Harvard University Press, 1960, 1962); David Kuebrich, *Minor Prophecy: Walt Whitman's New American Religion* (Bloomington: Indiana University Press, 1989).

Wilkinson, Jemima (1752–1819)

Considered the first American-born woman to found a religious society, Jemima Wilkinson was one of the most notable and controversial religious innovators of the revolutionary and early national eras. Born and raised on a farm in Cumberland, Rhode Island, Wilkinson was the eighth of 12 children born to Amey and Jeremiah Wilkinson, the latter a well-to-do farmer and member of the Society of Friends (see FRIENDS, RELIGIOUS SOCIETY OF). Her mother died when Jemima was 12 years old, and the young woman thereafter immersed herself in reading the Bible and the works of George Fox and William PENN, well-known Quaker leaders.

The tumultuous political and religious events surrounding the Revolutionary War had a tremendous impact upon the young woman. Her family became embroiled in the battle against Britain; two of her brothers joined the militia and were consequently suspended from the local Society of Friends meeting. Jemima's own spiritual questioning led to her involvement with the "New Lights" (see NEW LIGHTS/OLD LIGHTS) in the region, evangelicals who promoted revivalism and an intense form of religious devotion. In 1776, the Quaker meeting expelled her from membership for not attending meetings and for not using plain language, presumably a result of her leanings toward the evangelicals.

During this period of psychological and communal upheaval, Wilkinson took to her bed with a fever for a period of several weeks. Shortly after her recovery, she claimed that she had experienced physical death, and that her body had been resurrected as a new spirit sent from God to fulfill a special earthly mission. Although she herself never asserted that she represented the prophesied return of Christ, many of her believers apparently interpreted her ordeal in this way. Calling herself the "Publick Universal Friend," Wilkinson began traveling as an itinerant, preaching a message that combined biblical axioms, prophecies, dream interpretation, and faith healing. Self-consciously avoiding doctrinal disputes, Wilkinson nonetheless drew both upon the New Light themes of repentance and future judgment, and on the Quaker rejection of predestination and election. She also donned dress that mirrored both evangelical and Quaker patterns: she traveled in long, loosely flowing gowns akin to clerical garb, and wore a large-brimmed fur hat like those worn by male members of the Society of Friends. The overall effect was described by observers as "masculine" in appearance.

In the late 1770s and 1780s, Wilkinson attracted growing numbers of New Englanders with her simple, direct preaching style and her creative blending of popular beliefs. Many of her followers came from Quaker backgrounds, like herself, and a significant number were quite wealthy and financed her work. After 1782, when she took her message into Pennsylvania and western New York, she increased her following considerably, but she also faced mob violence and charges of blasphemy in Philadelphia. By 1785, she and a group of loyal supporters made plans to establish a separate community in the Genesee country of New York. In 1790, she joined some 260 settlers in a community based on independent landholding and a devotion to her teachings. "New Jerusalem" was the largest communitarian settlement in western New York in its day. Wilkinson remained there for the rest of her life, although an on-going legal battle over land rights, as well as her encouragement of celibacy, prompted a gradual decline in membership. After her death the movement died out, but she continues to oc-

cupy an important role in American religious history as a creative and dynamic spiritual leader who appealed to the popular spiritual yearnings of her contemporaries.

LMK

Bibliography: Herbert A. Wisbey, Jr., *Pioneer Prophetess: Jemima Wilkinson, the Publick Universal Friend* (Ithaca: Cornell University Press, 1964).

Willard, Frances Elizabeth Caroline (1839–1898)

Willard, the "Queen of American Democracy" according to noted British reformist William T. Stead, became one of the best known activists of the 19th century through her work as president of the Woman's Christian Temperance Union (WCTU), a position which she used to great advantage in cementing wide-ranging support for a number of reform issues: TEMPERANCE, women's suffrage, labor reform, the improvement of family life, as well as the

As president of the WCTU (1879–1898) Frances Willard expanded the union's concern to a wide range of social issues including women's suffrage. (Library of Congress)

socialist views of Edward Bellamy (1850–1898), Henry George (1839–1897), and the Knights of Labor. Her political skills contributed also to the growth of the Prohibition Party as a potential third force in American politics during the presidential elections of 1884 and 1888.

Born September 28, 1839 near Rochester, New York, Willard grew up on a farm near Janesville, Wisconsin where her family had moved. Willard went away to school in Milwaukee and Evanston, Illinois, and upon graduation taught school, traveled abroad, and served as secretary of the Methodist Centenary Fund. She became president of Evanston College for Ladies in the early 1870s, and was then appointed dean of Northwestern University, resigning in 1874 after conflicts over the extent of her authority.

Willard rose to political prominence after accepting the position of secretary of the WCTU later in 1874. At the time the organization was divided between theological conservatives and liberals (see LIBERALISM, THEOLOGICAL), with the conservative group supporting a narrow focus on the prohibition issue. Willard left the WCTU over these disputes, and moved on to work for evangelist Dwight L. MOODY's ministry in Boston. Again she found the theological orthodoxy confining, returned to Evanston, and was elected president of the Illinois chapter of the WCTU. From there she moved to the national presidency in 1879, and held that post until her death in 1898.

As president, Willard was responsible for the WCTU becoming the largest women's organization in the country during the 19th century. Though allied with various church groups active in the temperance cause, the WCTU remained independent of denominational, and male, control. Willard's own theology was eclectic, but she was quite willing to work within the fold of evangelical Christianity, igniting in countless thousands of conservative church-women a willingness to undertake public action in the name of broad-reaching social reforms. She urged her followers to "Do Everything," launching effective campaigns for prison reform, child care, job training for the young, and social welfare. Toward the end of her career, she championed world peace and what she spoke of as "Christian Socialism." Part of her genius must be attributed to her ability to make use of the rhetoric of domesticity. She portrayed the enormous social costs accompanying America's transformation into an industrial, corporate society as a threat to home, motherhood, and family life, thus making it possible for women to exert effective political power without having to contradict the accepted notion of women's domestic role.

MG

Bibliography: Ruth Bordin, *Frances Willard: A Biography* (Chapel Hill: University of North Carolina Press, 1986); Mary Earhart, *Frances Willard: From Prayers to Politics* (Chicago: University of Chicago Press, 1944); Frances Willard, *Glimpses of Fifty Years: The Biography of an American Woman*. Reprint. 1889. New York: Source Book Press, 1970.

Williams, George M.   See NICHIREN SHOSHU ACADEMY.

Williams, Roger (1603–1683)   Remembered today as the founder of Rhode Island and a proponent of religious freedom, Roger Williams was seen by his contemporaries as an inveterate troublemaker and threat to the social order. Born in London, probably in 1603, Williams attended Pembroke College, Cambridge, receiving his B.A. in 1627. He continued for two years of postgraduate work, during which time he also took religious orders. After leaving Cambridge, he served as private chaplain to the family of Sir William Masham of Essex.

Although early involved in the planning of the MASSACHUSETTS BAY COLONY, Williams did not come to America until 1631. Massachusetts welcomed the bright, personable, and charming young minister. The Boston Church asked Williams to replace its minister while he returned to England for his family. Williams refused, claiming that the Boston Church was not pure. He already had moved beyond PURITANISM and

Exiled by the Massachusetts Bay Colony for his radical religious views, Roger Williams found asylum among the Narragansett Indians in what became the colony of Rhode Island. (Library of Congress)

embraced separatism. Since all Massachusetts Bay churches, including the Boston Church, considered the Anglican churches to be true churches, they were corrupt in Williams's eyes and he refused to serve in them.

Despite these dangerous ideas, his standing in the colony remained high. In Salem he found a church more willing to adopt his ideas on separation and accepted their offer to serve as teacher. Only the intervention of Governor John WINTHROP, who feared the divisiveness separatism might create, caused the offer to be withdrawn.

After this incident, Williams left for the separatist colony of Plymouth—expecting the Pilgrims to be more receptive to his views. They were not, and in 1634 Williams returned to Massachusetts Bay. By this time he had devel-

oped ideas even more dangerous than separatism. Williams denounced the colony's charter as illegal, claiming the king had no right to give the land away. This threatened the very existence of the colony, and under pressure Williams was forced to back down.

This respite was temporary, however, and soon Williams was expressing the same view. To this he added rejection of the charter's description of Europe as Christendom and objection to oaths, and claimed that the colony should return the charter to the king, asking him to correct it.

If that were not bad enough, Williams also declared that the civil law had no right to enforce religious behavior. These views were too much for the colony's leaders, and they ordered Williams to appear before the General Court.

At this hearing he refused to admit his errors and was banished from the colony in October 1635. The sentence was stayed until spring on the condition that he remain silent. This, Williams was unwilling to do. He resumed his speaking, and to silence him, several of the colony's administrators planned to ship him back to England. Forewarned by John Winthrop, Williams escaped into the country where he took up with the Narragansett Indians. From them he bought land for his own colony. This colony grew quickly, and in 1643–1644 he traveled to England to obtain official recognition for the colony.

While there, he published his first book against religious persecution, *The Bloudy Tenent of Persecution*. This book, to which John COTTON published a rebuttal, was followed by a sequel in 1652. In these books Williams rejected the commonly held view that religious uniformity was necessary for social peace. Many states maintain civil peace without true religion he argued, and many states claiming to have true religion are in constant conflict.

Williams argued that not only is the enforcement of religious beliefs by the civil law unnecessary, it is dangerous as well. If the spiritual realm were to maintain its purity, it must be separate from the civil realm. The use of material weapons in waging the battles of the spirit only sullies religion. Christ came to save men's souls not to destroy their bodies. Spiritual weapons are sufficient for fighting spiritual battles.

Despite these views, Williams did not believe all religious views were equally acceptable. Williams particularly opposed Quakers (see FRIENDS, THE RELIGIOUS SOCIETY OF) and Catholics (see ROMAN CATHOLICISM), but both groups were welcome in the colony of Rhode Island and Providence Plantations. Jews, BAPTISTS (which Williams became long enough to help them establish their first church in the United States), and refugees from Massachusetts Bay also found homes in the colony. All were allowed to practice their beliefs as long as they did not violate the civil peace.

At the time of his death in March 1683, Williams had spent four decades as a seeker. He had left all established denominations and despaired of finding the pure church on earth. While he died without finding his pure church, he helped to enshrine religious liberty in America.

(See also CHURCH AND STATE, RELATIONS BETWEEN; COLONIAL PERIOD.)

EQ

Bibliography: Samuel H. Brockunier, *The Irrepressible Democrat: Roger Williams* (New York: Ronald Press, 1940); James E. Ernst, *Roger Williams: New England Firebrand* (New York: Macmillan, 1932); John Garrett, *Roger Williams: Witness Beyond Christendom* (New York: Macmillan, 1970); Edwin Gaustad, *Liberty of Conscience: Roger Williams in America* (Grand Rapids: Eerdmans, 1991); William Clark Gilpin, *The Millenarian Piety of Roger Williams* (Chicago: University of Chicago Press, 1979); Perry Miller, *Roger Williams: His Contribution to the American Tradition* (Indianapolis: Bobbs-Merrill, 1953); Edmund S. Morgan, *Roger Williams: The Church and the State* (New York: Harcourt Brace & World, 1967); Roger Williams, *The Bloudy Tenent of Persecution* (London: s.n., 1644); ———, *The Bloudy Tenent of Persecution Yet More Bloudy* (London: G. Calvert, 1652).

Winthrop, John (1588–1649)

John Winthrop, the first and oft-reelected governor of the MASSACHUSETTS BAY COLONY, was born in Edwardstone, England at Groton Manor on January 22, 1588. In 1603 he entered Trinity College, Cambridge. While at Cambridge he came under Puritan influence and soon was completely Puritan in his religious orientation (see PURITANISM).

Winthrop left Cambridge in 1605 without receiving a degree. In that year he married and became justice of the peace for the area around his ancestral home. Eight years later, in response to the increasing financial pressures of his large family, Winthrop turned to the law to increase his income, entering Grays Inn, one of the Inns of the Court where gentlemen studied law, in October 1613. By 1619 Winthrop was a success-

The first governor of the Massachusetts Bay Colony, John Winthrop led English Puritans to plant a colony in New England in June 1630. (Boston Public Library)

ful lawyer, dividing his time between the family estate at Groton Manor and London where he had a law practice.

Following the accession of Charles I in 1625, the situation for Puritans worsened. The Puritans, who rejected both the existence of bishops and royal absolutism on religious grounds, found themselves at odds with the king, who favored both. For an ambitious and able man like Winthrop, who as a Puritan found doors to advancement closed to him, England became a hostile place. Facing increasing persecution, many Puritans, including Winthrop, began to consider planting a colony in America to serve as a refuge.

Using their remaining influence at court, a group of Puritans obtained a charter for an American colony from the king. Winthrop, a leading member of the corporation that organized the colony, led the first group of colonists. They left England on April 7, 1630, arriving in New England on June 12. While still on board the *Arbella,* Winthrop spoke to the new colonists about their obligations to God and each other. This lecture, "A Modell of Christian Charity," reminded the emigrants that social distinctions were ordained by God. In the New World, these distinctions must be observed even more strictly to decrease the possibility of failure. These distinctions, however, did not mean that there were not mutual duties and obligations. All the colonists must work together for the good of the whole. They would be as a "citty on a hill" and all the world could see whether they succeeded or failed.

Winthrop served as governor of the Massachusetts Bay Colony through 17 one-year terms between 1629 and 1649. In 1635 he lost the election due to his leniency toward violators of the colony's ordinances. Winthrop felt that harsh dealings with offenders invited division and conflict in a new colony. Leniency, however, was to be extended only to those who admitted their errors. Persisting in error was punished with severity.

Roger WILLIAMS and Anne HUTCHINSON learned this when they were banished from the colony for violating the religious and civil peace of the colony. The threats they posed were, in Winthrop's mind, too great for leniency, especially given their refusal to admit their errors and to cease teaching them. In Williams's case, Winthrop exercised some leniency, informing Williams of a plan to ship him back to England and advising him to leave the colony. Although active in pushing for Williams's banishment, Winthrop retained his friendship and the two remained correspondents until Winthrop's death.

This, along with his numerous terms as governor, says much for Winthrop's character. While he could be self-righteous and vindictive, as he was in the case of Anne Hutchinson, Winthrop was also forgiving of human foibles and a tireless laborer for the good of the colony. When he died on March 26, 1649, governor again, Massachusetts was a thriving colony, secure in its economic and political life. Under Winthrop's leadership the Massachusetts Bay Colony would not only survive, but prosper as a model of a God-centered society.

(See also COLONIAL PERIOD.)

EQ

Bibliography: Edmund Morgan, *The Puritan Dilemma: The Story of John Winthrop* (Glenview, Ill.: Scott, Foresman, 1958); Robert G. Raymer, *John Winthrop, Governor of the Company of Massachusetts Bay in New England* (New York: Vantage Press, 1963); Robert C. Winthrop, *Life and Letters of John Winthrop, From His Embarkation for New England in 1630 to His Death in 1649* (Boston: Little, Brown and Company, 1895).

Wisconsin Evangelical Lutheran Synod
See LUTHERANISM.

Wise, Isaac Mayer (1819–1900)

Isaac Mayer Wise was one of the most important figures in American JUDAISM. While the intellectual content of REFORM JUDAISM owes more to men like David EINHORN and Kaufmann KOHLER, the institutional structure of the movement must be credited largely to Wise. His organizational bent, along with his unrelenting drive to create a modern and American Judaism, means that Wise more than anyone deserves the title "founding father" of American Judaism.

Born in Steingrub, Bohemia on March 29, 1819, Isaac Mayer Wise grew up in a freer atmosphere than that of most Central European Jews. Dissuaded by a teacher from reading the texts of the Kabbala (Jewish mystical literature), he immersed himself in German literature and philosophy. He studied at various *yeshivas* (religious schools) in Prague, Jenikau, (Bohemia) and Vienna and in 1843 became rabbi in the Bohemian town of Radnitz. By this time Wise had become increasingly discontented with traditional Judaism and with Europe. He saw the United States as a place where a reformed Judaism could take root, and where Jews could live free from prejudice and tradition. He became, in his words, "a naturalized American in the interior of Bohemia."

Arriving in the United States with his family in 1846, Wise first lived in Charleston, South Carolina. After several months of traveling, however, they finally settled in Albany, New York, where Wise became rabbi of Congregation

Isaac Mayer Wise, an ardent advocate of Reform Judaism who helped found and became the first president of Hebrew Union College in 1875.

Beth-El. Wise's efforts to move Beth-El toward reform were controversial. The hostility between the traditionalists and reformers became so great that one year at High Holy Day services Wise was assaulted in the synagogue. The arrival of the sheriff and a posse failed to end the fighting between his supporters and opponents. As the violence moved outside, Wise found himself arrested by the constable and charged with leading a mob. He had been set up by his opponents.

Such a division was untenable, and in 1850 Wise resigned and led part of his congregation in founding Anshe Emeth. There he remained until 1854 when Congregation B'nai Jeshurun in Cincinnati, Ohio called him as their rabbi. In the West, Wise found the openness to new ideas he desired. Soon, under his leadership, Cincinnati became the center of Reform Judaism in the United States. An ardent American-izer, Wise began publishing an English-language newspaper, *The Israelite,* designed to spread the views of Reform Judaism. Recognizing, however, that most of his audience was German, he also published a German language weekly, *Die Deborah.* In 1857 he issued a revision of the prayer book *Minhag America* (American Ritual), in which he shortened many of the prayers, eliminated others, and tried to bring the service more in line with the times.

Wise's vision of Judaism and religion drove his reforming activities. He wanted to remove from Judaism everything that did not elevate, or which opened it to ridicule. He taunted those Jews who followed the dietary laws, calling them "overseers of the kitchen" and "taskmasters of the stomach." Judaism, for Wise, did not reside "in victuals," but in "fear of the Lord and the love of many in harmony with the dicta of reason." He believed that "only such observances and practices which might and should become universal because they would be beneficial to all men, are with us inherent elements of Judaism."

With this language, and when speaking of God as the "central Vital Force," Wise sounds little different from any liberal religionist (see LIBERALISM, THEOLOGICAL) of the late 19th century. The same Wise, however, firmly believed in the revealed character of the Torah, and refused to allow the teaching of higher biblical criticism (see BIBLICAL INTERPRETATION) at Hebrew Union College while he was president—even firing a professor for doing so.

Wise was a practical man. As he put it, "Reform was never an end in itself; I considered it only a necessary means to clarify the teachings of Judaism, and to transfigure, exalt, and spread those teachings." He was the prime force behind the creation of the Union of American Hebrew Congregations (UAHC) in 1873 and Hebrew Union College in 1875. Wise served as the college's president until his death on March 26, 1900, carefully shepherding the school through its early years, enabling it to become the first permanent center of Jewish higher education in the United States.

Although the UAHC and Hebrew Union College were designed to serve traditionalists and reformers, the differences between these two groups were too great. Alienated by Wise's indifference to the dietary laws, and the radical statement of reform principles enunciated in the PITTSBURGH PLATFORM of 1885, the traditionalists abandoned the school and the Union, leaving both to the reformers. By 1889, when the third basic institution of Reform Judaism, the Central Conference of American Rabbis (CCAR), was created, the Reform movement dominated American Judaism. This predominance owed much to Wise's skills as an institutional builder and a popularizer. Although others may have been better at developing Reform Judaism's theological principles, none matched Wise's ability to turn those principles into organizations.

EQ

Bibliography: Israel Knox, *Rabbi in America: The Story of Isaac Mayer Wise* (Boston: Little Brown, 1957); Max B. May, *Isaac Mayer Wise: The Founder of American Judaism, a Biography* (New York: G. P. Putnam's Sons, 1916); Sefton Temkin, *Isaac Mayer Wise, Shaping American Judaism* (Oxford: Oxford University Press, 1992); Isaac Mayer Wise, *Reminiscences* (New York: Arno Press, 1973).

Wise, Stephen S. (1874–1949)

Rabbi, social reformer, and Zionist (see ZIONISM), Stephen Wise was a leading figure in American JUDAISM during his long and distinguished career. Born in Budapest, Hungary on March 14, 1874, Wise came to America as a young child. After receiving his B.A. from Columbia University (1892) he studied privately for the rabbinate in New York, Oxford, and Vienna. Between 1893 and 1906, Wise served pulpits in New York and Portland, Oregon while completing his Ph.D. at Columbia. In 1906 Wise, who had moved away from the Orthodoxy of his youth to embrace REFORM JUDAISM, accepted the position of rabbi at New York's Free Synagogue, where he served until his death on April 19, 1949.

An unabashed activist, Wise was one of the founders of the National Association for the Advancement of Colored People (1909), the American Civil Liberties Union (1920), the American Jewish Congress (1916), and the World Jewish Congress (1936). He was a vocal opponent of governmental corruption and with John Haynes Holmes, minister of the independent Community Church in New York, exposed the magnitude of corruption within New York City's political machine.

Of all the causes in which he was involved, none consumed Wise as much as Zionism. One of the few leaders of Reform Judaism to embrace the Zionist movement, Wise was active in all the major Zionist organizations. To combat the anti-Zionism of Hebrew Union College while maintaining Reform Judaism's liberalism, Wise founded the Jewish Institute of Religion (1922) in New York. He was a forceful proponent of Jewish rights and one of the first public figures to warn against Hitler's anti-Semitic policies (see ANTI-SEMITISM).

His vigor, commitment, and rhetorical skills made him a powerful religious figure in his day and a major influence on the development of Reform Judaism.

EQ

Bibliography: Melvin Urofsky, *A Voice That Spoke for Justice: The Life and Times of Stephen S. Wise* (Albany: SUNY Press, 1982); Carl H. Voss, ed., *Stephen S. Wise: Servant of the People, Selected Letters* (Philadelphia: Jewish Publication Society, 1969); Stephen S. Wise, *Challenging Years: The Autobiography of Stephen Wise* (New York: Putnam's Sons, 1949).

witchcraft   See NEO-PAGANISM.

womanist theology   A "womanist," according to the novelist Alice Walker who popularized the term, refers to "a Black feminist or feminist of color" who engages in "outrageous, audacious, courageous, or willful" behavior. Womanist theology is, therefore, the courageous and sometimes audacious theology of contemporary black feminists and feminists of color.

Womanist theologians such as Delores S. Williams, Jacquelyn Grant, and Katie G. Cannon are critical of much FEMINIST THEOLOGY, which they perceive as racist, and of much black LIBERATION THEOLOGY, which they perceive as sexist. They see feminist theology as white theology and black liberation theology as male theology. Though womanist theologians clearly aim to correct what they view as the racism of white feminist theology, they stand alongside rather than against the feminist theological tradition they hope to reform. To borrow language from Walker, womanist theology is to feminist theology not as black is to white but as "purple" is to "lavender."

Womanist theology shares with feminist theology a critique of the sexism of dominant theologies. It also criticizes the male-centered symbols and rituals of the Christian church. Like feminist theologians, womanist theologians aim to construct theologies that present positive images of women, that celebrate the role of women in religious history (or "herstory"), and that aim to construct nonsexist religious institutions as alternatives to dominant androcentric ones. But womanist theology differs from feminist theology in four significant ways.

First, womanist theology draws heavily on black folklore and black women's literature. Thus the womanist ethicist Katie G. Cannon, for example, searches for moral wisdom not in the theoretical ethical treatises of male thinkers of the past but in the practical moral admonitions passed down over the generations by black women to their daughters and preserved today in the literary tradition of black women.

Second, womanist theology resists the separatist strain prominent in some white feminist theology. Black women typically see themselves as engaged with black men in a common struggle, and they eschew more radical critiques of men as disruptive of the black community.

Third, womanist theologians tend to emphasize class issues more than their feminist counterparts. Jacquelyn Grant, for example, has argued that while feminist theologians have been preoccupied with bourgeois concerns such as self-fulfillment, womanist theologians have been tackling more basic issues such as the economic survival of the black community.

Fourth, womanist theologians are typically more reticent than their white feminist counterparts to jettison the religious traditions in which they have been raised. Though they willingly criticize portions of the Bible, or dominant interpretations thereof, as oppressive, they are not willing to get rid of Christian scripture altogether. Its God they typically view as a comforter and liberator who takes God's people out of bondage and into freedom, and its Jesus they see as a divine incarnation who suffers with the oppressed even as he redeems them from that oppression. Recognizing the historical importance of the black church as both a place of personal refuge and a rallying point for political action, womanist theologians are reluctant to move outside the Christian community to the sort of "post-Christian" feminist "thealogy" commended by Mary DALY and others.

Like feminist theology, womanist theology begins with the experience of women rather than the inherited dictates of men. What distinguishes womanist theology is its emergence out of the experience, both in church and in society, of black women and women of color.

SRP

Bibliography: Katie G. Cannon, *Black Womanist Ethics* (Atlanta: Scholar's Press, 1988); Jacquelyn Grant, *White Women's Christ and Black Women's Jesus: Feminist Christology and Womanist Response* (Atlanta: Scholar's Press, 1989); Delores S. Williams, *Sisters in the Wilderness: The Challenge of Womanist God-Talk* (Maryknoll, N.Y.: Orbis, 1992).

Woman's Bible, The *The Woman's Bible* (1895 and 1898) is an early and influential commentary on the Bible written by Elizabeth Cady STANTON and a committee of 19th-century women's rights reformers. Focusing on biblical passages pertaining to women, it attempts both to criticize the degradation of women in the Bible and to offer alternative, woman-affirming readings of key biblical texts.

Officially written by Elizabeth Cady Stanton and what came to be known as the Revising Committee, the first volume of *The Woman's Bible,* which focused on the Pentateuch, was published in 1895. The second volume, which commented on Judges, Kings, the Prophets, and Apostles, came out in 1898.

In her effort to staff the Revising Committee, Stanton wrote many women, asking them to participate, but only a few were willing. Some responded that the Bible was too sacred to criticize; others believed the Bible was too hostile to women to revise. Susan B. Anthony was sympathetic to the latter group, but she believed that a rereading of certain biblical stories traditionally used against women would help to improve women's place in the church. Despite the difficulties she had in recruiting willing commentators, Stanton was able to bring into her Revising Committee scholars in Greek, Hebrew, and Latin. *The Woman's Bible* they produced thus drew on the best historical critical scholarship of the time.

Stanton's main interest was tracing the roots of woman's 19th-century bondage to biblical passages. Rather than arguing, as have some 20th-century feminist theologians (see FEMINIST THEOLOGY), that the Bible teaches the equality of men and women, Stanton contended that the Bible does not "exalt and dignify woman." Though she celebrated the virtuous and heroic women in the Bible, she concluded that, on the whole, the text functioned to enslave rather than to liberate women.

Because of her conviction that God would not inspire inequality, Stanton rejected the doctrine of the divine inspiration of the Jewish and Christian scriptures. But she did find some hope for women imbedded in those texts. For example, she and her colleagues reread the creation myth in Genesis as a story that exalts Eve as the original matriarch and contains no direct commandment for men to rule over women.

Stanton also found some biblical warrants for envisioning God as both heavenly Father and Mother, as did Christian Scientist Mary Baker EDDY.

Reviews of *The Woman's Bible* were both positive and negative, but the book sold widely. Conservative participants in the women's suffrage movement objected to the commentary, and some thought that dealing with the Bible only diverted energy from more important issues. Ultimately, the National American Suffrage Association passed a resolution disassociating itself from *The Woman's Bible,* even though Susan B. Anthony herself gave a speech in support of the work. What divided Stanton from some of her fellow suffragists was her conviction that women could not fight the battle for equal rights simply on the political front. Religious questions, she was convinced, also had to be raised.

At least some of today's feminists apparently agree with Stanton. They have produced two feminist biblical commentaries commemorating the 100th anniversary of Stanton's work.

TP

Bibliography: Elisabeth Schüssler Fiorenza, ed., *Searching the Scriptures: A Feminist-Ecumenical Commentary,* (New York: Crossroad Press, 1993); Carol A. Newsom and Sharon H. Ringe, eds., *The Women's Bible Commentary* (Louisville: Westminster/John Knox Press, 1992); Elizabeth Cady Stanton, *The Woman's Bible.* 1895, 1898. Reprint. Boston: Northeastern University Press, 1993.

Woolman, John (1720–1772)

A leading American Quaker (see FRIENDS, THE RELIGIOUS SOCIETY OF) of his time and a staunch opponent of slavery, John Woolman was born on October 19, 1720 in Rancocas, New Jersey. Woolman originally supported himself as a shopkeeper in Mt. Holly, New Jersey, but felt that the wealth he gained from the work distracted from his spiritual development. He took up tailoring instead, since that trade provided him sufficient time to reflect upon spiritual matters.

A minister in the Society of Friends, Woolman spent much of his time traveling up and down the Atlantic coast and to England speaking about Quaker principles. Woolman not only preached these principles but tried to live them out as completely as possible. In order to open himself fully to the inner divine light, he attempted to avoid worldly distractions. An outspoken pacifist, he refused to pay taxes to support the French and Indian War of 1755. Convinced that governmental service forced people to violate their consciences, he advocated that all Quakers resign from the various colonial assemblies.

Woolman was one of the earliest and most vocal American opponents to slavery, publishing the first part of his *Considerations on the Keeping of the Negroes* in 1754. During his trips through the colonies he often visited slaveowners and attempted to convince them of the immorality of their actions. Symbolic of his refusal to recognize the validity of slavery was the fact that he always paid slaves for the services done him on these visits.

His efforts bore some fruit. In 1758 the Yearly Meeting of the Society Friends passed a resolution urging Quakers to free their slaves and threatening to expel any Quaker involved in the slave trade. In 1776, four years after Woolman died while traveling in England (October 7, 1772), the Quakers became the first denomination to make slaveowning a bar to membership, a fitting memorial to Woolman's life.

EQ

Bibliography: Edwin H. Cady, *John Woolman* (New York: Twayne Publishers, 1965); Janet Payne Whitney, *John Woolman, American Quaker* (Boston: Little, Brown and Company, 1942); John Woolman, *The Journal and Major Essays of John Woolman* (New York: Oxford University Press, 1971).

World Council of Churches

The World Council of Churches is the international, institutional expression of the ECUMENICAL MOVEMENT. Founded in 1948, the World Council was the result of the 1938 merger of the Committee on Life and Work and the Committee on Faith and Order into the World Council of

Churches in the Process of Formation. With the outbreak of WORLD WAR II, the process of formation would take 10 years. Finally, in Amsterdam on August 23, 1948, the World Council of Churches officially was constituted. The work of the council was furthered in 1961 when the International Missionary Council merged its interdenominational work into the W.C.C., becoming its Committee on World Missions and Evangelism.

At its founding, the World Council consisted of 150 member churches. The original constitution of the World Council defined itself as "composed of Churches which acknowledge Jesus Christ as God and Savior." This definition was refined at the council's third assembly in New Delhi in 1961: "The World Council of Churches is a fellowship of Churches which confess the Lord Jesus Christ as God and Savior according to the scriptures and therefore seek to fulfill together their common calling to the glory of one God, Father, Son and Holy Spirit."

The World Council has never understood itself as a super-church, or an organization to supplant existing denominational organizations. Its primarily goal is to serve the churches themselves and to facilitate interdenominational cooperation in various areas. The World Council, however, has continued the work of the old Faith and Order Conference in its ongoing discussion of the doctrinal and theological differences that separate the various churches.

Perhaps the most controversial work of the World Council has been related to the so-called younger churches, those of Asia and Africa. As a world body the council has been sympathetic to criticisms of the West and the heritage of imperialism. The creation of the Program to Combat Racism at the council's 1968 assembly in Uppsala, Sweden illustrates that concern. As a result the World Council has been a target of criticism because of its monetary grants to organizations struggling against oppression, especially in Africa, that many have seen as Communist-infiltrated and fomenters of violence. While such charges have never been proven,

they have provided critics of the council with a volatile issue that detracted from its more important activities.

The W.C.C.'s work has been weakened by the refusal of the Roman Catholic Church to join. Still, the Roman Church has participated in the council's activities. It has sent observers to every assembly since 1961 and is an official participant in the Commission on Faith and Order. Despite criticisms, financial problems, and doctrinal disputes, the World Council has grown steadily throughout its existence. By 1990 it had over 300 member churches representing over 400 million members on all six inhabited continents.

EQ

Bibliography: *Dictionary of the Ecumenical Movement* (Geneva: World Council of Churches/Grand Rapids: Eerdmans, 1991); Ruth Rouse and Stephen C. Neill, *A History of the Ecumenical Movement,* 2nd ed. (Philadelphia: Westminster Press, 1967); Geoffrey Wainwright, *The Ecumenical Moment: Crisis and Opportunity for the Church* (Grand Rapids: Eerdmans, 1983).

World War I   America entered "The Great War" on April 6, 1917, two and a half years after the conflict began. In doing so Americans drew upon their religions to mobilize the resources necessary for support of the troops, as well as the patriotic spirit to sustain warmaking, and to a much lesser extent, to resist the movement toward war. As a consequence of their support, many American religious groups emerged from the war with a greater cooperative spirit for ministry and a new vision of America as a world leader.

Traditionally most Americans were ambivalent about involvement in European conflicts. In the early 20th century, peace groups had grown in membership, leading billionaire Andrew Carnegie to offer a $2-million endowment to establish the ecumenical Church Peace Union in early 1914 (see PEACE REFORM). Even though Woodrow Wilson was elected president in 1916 under the slogan "He kept us out of the war," isolationism declined sharply following the sinking of the liner *Lusitania* by a German submarine on May 7, 1915. Americans, particularly those of Anglo-Saxon heritage, began mobilizing in support of the war effort.

With Wilson's declaration of war, April 6, 1917, American religious groups established organizational settings for the home front effort as well as a means of providing the troops with supplies, morale, and chaplains. Like the outbreak of other wars (see CIVIL RELIGION) the beginnings of World War I created an opportunity for Americans to find common cause, in particular tabling the bitter religious differences wracking the society in the early 20th century (see MODERNISM; FUNDAMENTALISM). The Federal Council of Churches quickly established a General Wartime Commission, chaired by Presbyterian Robert E. Speer, to coordinate the efforts of over 30 different denominations and organizations, such as the YOUNG MEN'S CHRISTIAN ASSOCIATION and the American Bible Society (see BIBLE SOCIETIES). The commission established a Committee of One Hundred, including notable clergy, such as Harry Emerson FOSDICK, and lay leaders like the YMCA's John MOTT, to serve as a liaison between the churches and the government. The Young Men's Christian Association, the Red Cross, and the SALVATION ARMY all served as distribution centers for the tons of Bibles, tracts, and other literature sent by Protestant denominations to training camps across the country.

Catholics and Jews also gave unstinting support to the war. Without any institutional body corresponding to the FCC, they turned to existing organizations such as the Knights of Columbus or the Young Men's Hebrew Association to provide logistical means to further the war effort. Catholics, under the leadership of Cardinal James GIBBONS gave official form to their wartime ministry by forming the National Catholic War Council (later reorganized into the NATIONAL CATHOLIC WELFARE CONFERENCE), however, which provided the spur to involve the previously neutral bishops in questions of public policy (see AMERICANISM; ROMAN CATHOLICISM; RYAN, JOHN). Coordination of support efforts led to a level of cooperation among Catholics, Jews, and Protestants previously unknown, and also provided Catholics and Jews with the opportunity to demonstrate their American loyalty.

In addition to religious groups supplying chaplains, civilian aides, supplies, and morale to troops, Americans also drew upon religious symbolism to articulate their rationales for participation in the war and to mobilize public opinion. Countless broadsides, books, and sermons echoed Woodrow Wilson's contention that America, "the disinterested champion of right," had to enter the fight. The son of a Presbyterian minister, Wilson saw America as a redeeming force in history and drew on millennial themes (see MILLENNIALISM) in rallying the nation to struggle "for a universal dominion of right by such a concert of free peoples as shall bring peace and safety to all nations and make the world free at last." While Wilson saw no other choice than entry into the conflict, he did so with apprehension, confessing his fears to one journalist that "the spirit of ruthless brutality will enter into the very fibre of our national life, infecting congress, the courts, the policeman on the beat, the man in the street."

Ministers and theologians of all persuasions were able to extend Wilson's view of America's unique moral status among nations, and for some the war became a holy war. "It is Christ, the King of Righteousness, who calls us to grapple in deadly strife with this unholy and blasphemous power," claimed one. Religion provided many Americans with the means to depict the enemy as especially demonic, contributing to a hostile anti-German climate across much of the country. A professor at Yale Divinity School urged YMCA staff members to exhort inductees with the thought: "I would not enter this work until I could see Jesus himself sighting down a gun barrel and running a bayonet through an enemy's body," hence making Christ a fellow, divinely inspired warrior doing God's work. Shailer MATHEWS, epitome of theological MODERNISM, said in *Patriotism and Religion* (1918) that it was un-Christian for Americans to refuse service. At the same time, opponents of modernism, such as Billy SUNDAY, also lent their rhetorical services to the cause, some finding in biblical prophecies proof that Germany was the Antichrist. Others, such as the famed Cyrus SCOFIELD, though supporting the war, doubted Wilson's millennial linking of the war and the creation of a permanent peace, finding biblical warrant only for the view that the war foreshadowed a catastrophic end to history (see PREMILLENNIALISM).

The peace movement, which had been so active prior to the war, was not completely stilled, although reduced to its bare-bones contingent of Quakers (see FRIENDS, RELIGIOUS SOCIETY OF), MENNONITES, and other members of "historic peace churches." Though legally allowed alternative forms of service, leading to the formation of the American Friends Service Committee in 1917, pacifists were frequently subject to public abuse. One Methodist minister told the local Rotary Club "if you have one (a pacifist), shoot him." Given the tenor of the times, expressed in Congress's passage of the Alien and Sedition Acts, pacifists were forced to keep their dissent quiet.

The war's end found Americans confronted with a changed world, and an uncertain future. The unity produced by the war effort dissolved, as the 1920s brought Americans back into conflict with each other over economic and cultural issues, particularly the challenges posed by the continued waves of immigrants and the growing influence of SECULARISM (see DARWINISM; NATIVISM; SCOPES TRIAL). Denominations now possessed much greater organizational capability and political muscle than they had earlier, which many religious leaders sought to use in charting the way ahead. Some of the revivalistic excitement generated by the cause of war remained,

enabling religious organizations to finally make headway with the TEMPERANCE issue.

The sense of global responsibility heightened by the war also soon dulled, though the idea that America's destiny involved a readiness to exert moral force on international affairs did not evaporate completely. Many liberal Protestant and Catholic religious leaders supported Woodrow Wilson's internationalism in the establishment of the League of Nations, and in the ensuing years they established relief agencies for the Belgians and French, and became quite active in the work of postwar reconstruction.

MG

Bibliography: Ray H. Abrams, *Preachers Present Arms* (New York: Round Table Press, 1933); John F. Piper, Jr., *The American Churches in World War I* (Athens: Ohio University Press, 1985); Michael Williams, *American Catholics and the War* (New York: Macmillan, 1921).

World War II   In fighting their second global war in a little more than two decades, Americans again drew on religion, as they had during WORLD WAR I, though without quite the same fervor. Again, Americans used religious symbolism to mobilize patriotic sentiment and religious organizations to supply troops with spiritual sustenance, and, in some circles, to resist the war itself. Ironically, the less strident religious participation in the war effort yielded a much more long term equation of nationalism and religion than emerged from World War I, one enabling the population to readily accept America's postwar role as global leader (see COLD WAR). In addition the unity of national purpose created by the war carried over into a sustained postwar religious revival.

The Japanese attack on Pearl Harbor on December 7, 1941 hurled America into a war that had already been raging across Europe since 1939 and Asia since 1937. Prior to the attack, Americans viewed events on the other continents from the comfort of their geographic and ideological isolation. Indeed, a great number of

Despite the pacifist trend after World War I, most churches and synagogues unreservedly supported the American war effort after Pearl Harbor. U.S. Army Chaplain School graduates. (Library of Congress)

American religious groups and public opinion leaders responded to German, Italian, and Japanese military actions during the 1930s with little concern over reported atrocities. In large measure such restraint was a self-imposed effort to avoid the bloodthirsty rhetoric by which some American preachers had rallied the nation during World War I. Pacifism had been especially pronounced during the 1920s and 1930s, not only among Quakers (see FRIENDS, RELIGIOUS SOCIETY OF) and members of "historic peace churches" (see PEACE REFORM) but also among SOCIAL GOSPEL liberals such as Harry Emerson FOSDICK and socialists, including Norman Thomas. Admittedly some American religious figures, such as the Niebuhr brothers (see NIEBUHR, HELMUT RICHARD; NIEBUHR, REINHOLD), concerned by Hitler's demolition of democracy in Germany and Japan's invasion of

China in 1937, were suspicious of what they saw as the easy convenience of pacifism. The widespread confusion over America's response to the war even led to alliances in the "America First" neutrality campaign between isolationists such as Charles Lindbergh, Christian socialists, and anti-Semites like Father Charles Edward COUGHLIN (see ANTI-SEMITISM).

The soul-searching confusion of America's religious leaders vanished immediately after Pearl Harbor. While Americans could not agree on the moral need to enter a war to deter aggression against others, they united around what appeared a treacherous act against their own "peace-loving nation," as President Franklin Delano Roosevelt put it in his address to the nation on December 8. Unlike the earlier war, in which America's sacred soil had not been threatened, the attack on Pearl Harbor symbolized just how vulnerable America was in an era of technologically advanced weaponry. Accordingly, mobilization proceeded rapidly. Industry geared up to produce "the arsenal of democracy" called for by Roosevelt, over 100,000 Japanese-Americans were herded off to relocation camps (though with some protest from the Fellowship of Reconciliation, other pacifist groups, and the journal *The Christian Century*), and the population embarked on an energetic, sacrificial campaign to ration and recycle materials needed for wartime production.

There are some obvious parallels in the role played by religious groups and religious symbolism between the First and Second World Wars. Protestant, Catholic, and Jewish religious groups created a supply of approximately 8,000 military chaplains for the troops and marshalled inspirational resources such as Bibles and other literature. Congregations were urged to respond to extensive wartime rationing with the attitude of cheerful sacrifice. The extensive network of interchurch agencies created during the previous war and the Great Depression remained in place, and easily mobilized their efforts for the new war. But the new war also produced new conditions calling for religious response.

One key difference in the role played by religion in the wars stems from the loss of cultural authority by the churches during the 1920s and 1930s (see EVOLUTION; FUNDAMENTALISM; MODERNISM; SCOPES TRIAL). Churches had been crucial carriers of the patriotic message during the previous war. But by World War II the Protestant unity of the TEMPERANCE and Social Gospel period had dissolved. In addition, the war sparked considerable tension between Protestants and Catholics, as when the Federal Council of Churches (see NATIONAL COUNCIL OF CHURCHES in 1944 denounced Washington's establishment of diplomatic relations with the Vatican.

A further indication of conflictual inter-religious relations was the American response to Hitler's persecution and extermination of European Jews (see JUDAISM). Prior to America's entry into the war, the Roosevelt administration was ambivalent about Jewish immigration, even prohibiting some 700 Jewish refugees on the liner *St. Louis* from landing in United States harbors during the spring of 1939. Although eventually allowing more Jewish immigration during 1941, and even though some Protestants criticized government inaction, administration officials were still primarily concerned that highlighting the Jewish plight would increase public support for the ravings of Father Coughlin and other anti-Semites.

American Jews themselves were divided over how the United States should respond to German persecution of European Jews, particularly in the period prior to Hitler's 1942 decision to send the Jews to death factories. The Reform rabbi Stephen S. WISE urged Jews to uphold British blockades of Nazi Europe, and to stop their shipments of aid to Polish relatives. Other Jews, particularly the Orthodox, protested United States inaction throughout the war. A group of 400 Orthodox rabbis marched on the White House on October 6, 1943, "to protest the silence of the world when an entire people is being murdered." As it was, Roosevelt chose to focus on defeating the Nazis, and naturally Jews were supportive of this goal. But many continued to question Roosevelt's passive acceptance of the mass murders. In the end, Roosevelt mentioned the Jews only once during the course of his wartime speeches and vetoed several plans to rescue Jews from the death camps.

Thus although there was broad ideological support for the war among many religious leaders, interreligious conflict, combined with the country's shifting intellectual climate, tended to reduce the extent to which the religious groups themselves were seen as centers of moral leadership. Even though the Niebuhrs and other Neo-orthodox theologians (see NEO-ORTHODOXY) played a notable public role during the war years, their influence was far from dominant.

Instead the growing national popular culture, centered in the media of radio, film, and weekly news magazines, as well as a more secular group of intellectuals (see SECULARISM), served to define American norms and values, as can be seen in the shifting symbolism of war rhetoric. Americans adopted a new approach to the propaganda task in their Voice of America radio broadcasts to Europe. The Roosevelt administration abandoned the moralism of Woodrow Wilson, or the outright sensationalism of German and Japanese propaganda, in favor of news broadcasts emphasizing "facts and figures" and incorporating the public opinion and marketing research of contemporary social scientists. By such an approach, Americans became inspired not primarily by the thought of their moral superiority, but of their productive superiority, such as turning 48,000 airplanes out of American factories in one year.

Another difference between the wars lies in the sort of moral justifications advanced by the war's supporters. While the righteous indignation over Pearl Harbor never left American war rhetoric, Americans were more likely to speak of their task as laboring for the bare survival of "Christian civilization," leaving behind the triumphalism of "the Great War." In popular music the tone shifted from the early patriotism of Kate Smith's "God Bless America" and Danny Kaye's "Remember Pearl Harbor" to the more practical, can-do "Praise the Lord and Pass the Ammunition." After 1942 and a few American victories in the Pacific islands of Midway and Guadalcanal, outright patriotism took a back seat to songs of love, longing, and commitment, such as "In the Mood" and "Don't Sit Under the Apple Tree With Anyone Else But Me." Hollywood and Tin Pan Alley were evidently more effective channels for such patriotic mobilization than the churches.

Broadly speaking, Americans were more tolerant of individuals who refused to support the war than they were in World War I, during which all objectors were inducted and then imprisoned. The Selective Service Act of 1940 provided grounds for refusal to serve for anyone who "by reason of religious training and belief is conscientiously opposed to participation in war in any form." While this created problems

for those whose objection did not stem from any recognized religious tradition, it paved the way for alternative service programs run by churches themselves. Approximately 4,000 MENNONITES, 1,000 Quakers, and members of the CHURCH OF THE BRETHREN engaged in alternative service, while 5,000 JEHOVAH'S WITNESSES chose prison.

Surprisingly, nearly 90 percent of the draft-eligible Quakers and Church of the Brethren actually enlisted.

In addition to the tolerance of conscientious objection, Americans were also more willing to allow dissent. While there was significant censorship of war reporting, the costs of the Allied effort to smash Germany did lead many religious leaders to question military policies in ways unthinkable during World War I. Catholics largely opposed the bombing of Rome; and the saturation bombing of Germany and Japan, in which many hundreds of thousands of civilians died in urban infernos, reduced the extent to which Americans could argue that their own form of war-making was morally superior to that of their enemies. The prominence given to Reinhold Niebuhr's writing, with its emphasis on sin and the critique of moral self-delusion, at least dampened the rhetorical excesses of those Americans who viewed the war as God's work. Niebuhr's active pen, in journals such as *Christianity and Crisis,* produced countless cautionary exhortations: "If we should give ourselves to the illusion that this war was a simple contest between right and wrong, and that the victory was a simple triumph of right over wrong . . . we shall be bound to corrupt the peace by vindictiveness."

With the war's end in August 1945, American life was transformed completely. As a result of wartime mobilization America had emerged as the world's economic and military giant. Willingness to use that power to pulverize totalitarian enemies gave new life to the longstanding Puritan (see PURITANISM) faith that America was morally superior to other nations, though now it was expressed in ways that were self-consciously "mature" and "realistic." Finally, Americans emerged from the war with a heady mixture of confidence and anxiety, responsive to the pull of a national popular culture—conditions that impelled them into full-fledged religious revivals during the postwar years and the most dramatic church growth in American history (see GRAHAM, BILLY; MAINLINE PROTESTANTISM; REVIVALISM).

MG

Bibliography: John Morton Blum, *V Was for Victory: Politics and American Culture during World War II* (New York: Harcourt, Brace, Jovanovich, 1976); Geoffery Parrett, *Days of Sadness, Years of Triumph: The American People, 1939–1945* (Madison: University of Wisconsin Press, 1983); Richard Polenberg, *War and Society: The United States, 1941–1945* (Philadelphia: J. P. Lippincott, 1972).

World's Parliament of Religions   The World's Parliament of Religions, held in Chicago in September of 1893 as part of the World's Columbian Exposition, was a watershed event in the history of American religion. By paving the way for Asian religious traditions in the United States, the parliament functioned as a rite of passage from a predominantly Judeo-Christian to a more religiously plural America (see PLURALISM).

Before the parliament, Christian missionaries and academic Orientalists represented (and misrepresented) Asian religions without much input or correction from Asians themselves. At the parliament, well-educated Asian missionaries arrived in the United States for the first time to make their case for their respective traditions and, in many cases, against Christian missions. These pioneering Asians then established enduring institutions in their wake.

Inspired by Charles C. Bonney, a Chicago attorney and lay Swedenborgian (see SWEDENBORGIANISM), the parliament was organized by John Henry Barrows, the liberal minister of the First Presbyterian Church of Chicago. Bonney and Barrows promoted the event as the greatest ecumenical gathering in world history, and a wide array of delegates attended. Christians and

Jews were joined on the parliament's podium by 12 Buddhists (see BUDDHISM), eight Hindus (see HINDUISM), two Muslims (see ISLAM), two Zoroastrians, two Shintoists, two Confucians, one Taoist, and one Jain. The parliament was attended, however, for the most part by liberal religionists. Among those who joined the sultan of Turkey and the archbishop of Canterbury in declining to commingle with the "heathen" were numerous Protestant evangelicals (see EVANGELICALISM), Orthodox Jews (see ORTHODOX JUDAISM), and conservative Catholics (see ROMAN CATHOLICISM).

The parliament did not conclude without a considerable number of ironies. On the morning of its opening day, the Columbian Liberty Bell tolled 10 times (once for each of the 10 great religious traditions), but the parliament itself began with the Lord's Prayer and ended with "America the Beautiful." Barrows admitted after the parliament that he had secretly hoped that the event that he had publicly billed as an ecumenical gathering would, in the last analysis, serve to vindicate Christianity to the other religions of the world. By most accounts the parliament did just the opposite, contributing to what historians have termed "the spiritual crisis of the Gilded Age" by promoting Asian religions as legitimate alternatives to Christianity.

When the archbishop of Canterbury sent back his invitation with a "no," he wrote that he did not see how anyone could take part in the parliament without presupposing (as many delegates did) the equality of religions. And the parliament does seem to have advanced the cause of the "all religions are one" school. Delegate after delegate underscored the commonalities rather than the differences between Christianity and other religions. At least a few blasted the overseas Christian missionary effort as immoral and non-Christian.

Following the parliament, two of its most flamboyant delegates, the Hindu reformer Swami VIVEKANANDA and the theosophical Buddhist Anagarika DHARMAPALA, traveled around the United States on lecture tours. Vivekananda brought the work of his Ramakrishna Order to the United States in the form of the VEDANTA SOCIETY, while Dharmapala transplanted his Maha Bodhi Society to American soil. A third Asian delegate, the Rinzai Zen master Soyen Shaku (1859–1919), returned to his homeland shortly after the parliament. But he dispatched his student and the translator of his parliament speeches to America, and that student-translator, D. T. SUZUKI (1870–1966), became the most important popularizer of ZEN in the modern West.

Although the parliament was probably not, as one witness claimed, "the greatest event so far in the history of the world," it did play an important role in undermining the exclusivism that had marked the Christian missionary effort and in making a place for Asian religions in the American landscape. The parliament also provided important models for the contemporary movement for interreligious dialogue.

SRP

Bibliography: John Henry Barrows, ed., *The World's Parliament of Religions,* 2 vols. (Chicago: The Parliament Publishing Company, 1893); Richard H. Seager, *The World's Parliament of Religions: The East/West Encounter.* 1893. Reprint. Bloomington: Indiana University Press, 1994.

Worldwide Church of God

Founded in 1933 in Oregon by Herbert W. Armstrong (1892–1986), the Worldwide Church of God is perhaps best known to non-members for its radio show, "The World Tomorrow," and its magazine, *The Plain Truth.*

Members of the Worldwide Church of God echo Protestant evangelicals (see EVANGELICAL-ISM) and fundamentalists (see FUNDAMENTAL-ISM) in affirming the divine inspiration of the Bible and denying the theory of EVOLUTION. But they distinguish themselves by denying the Trinity. Their most controversial belief is that Anglo-Saxons are descended from the lost tribes of Israel and thus inherit both the promises and the responsibilities that issued from the covenant established between God and the ancient Israe-

lites. Members of the Worldwide Church of Christ observe the sabbath on Saturday (see SABBATARIANISM) and keep Jewish holy days such as Passover; they generally denounce as pagan and un-Christian holidays such as Christmas and Halloween. Because of their belief that the Anglo-Saxons rather than the Jews are the rightful inheritors of God's promises and commandments, they have been charged with ANTI-SEMITISM. And because the Anglo-Saxonism of the church has also been criticized as tending toward racism, the movement reportedly has also attracted sympathy from Ku Klux Klansmen and neo-Nazis. These unsavory connections have prompted denunciations from the Anti-Defamation League and allegations that the church is a dangerous "cult."

Born into a Quaker (see FRIENDS, THE RELIGIOUS SOCIETY OF) family in Des Moines, Iowa in 1892, Herbert W. Armstrong became a member and then a preacher in an Adventist sect shortly after moving to Oregon in 1924. In 1933 he struck out on his own, founding a multimedia religious empire that he took to Pasadena, California in 1947. In 1968 Armstrong's creation would came to be known as the Worldwide Church of God.

The church has endured a number of scandals and schisms. In 1974, allegations of sexual improprieties among church leaders and a bitter controversy regarding the remarriage of divorced church members precipitated splits into several independent churches. The most notable schismatic was Garner Ted Armstrong, Armstrong's son and one of the church's most popular preachers, who separated from his father's church and founded the Church of God International in 1978. Following the death of Herbert W. Armstrong in 1986, Joseph W. Tkach ascended to leadership of the Worldwide Church of God.

Despite its troubles, the church maintains a membership of approximately 100,000 in over 100 countries. Most of its adherents, however, live in the United States. In addition to producing radio programs and publishing periodicals, the organization maintains colleges in both Pasadena and Big Sandy, Texas. It also vigorously promotes its founder's books. Armstrong's best-known work, *The United States and Britain in Prophecy* (1980), articulates his controversial brand of what has been called "Anglo-Israelism."

SRP

Bibliography: Herbert W. Armstrong, *The United States and Britain in Prophecy* (Pasadena, Calif.: Worldwide Church of God, 1980).

Wovoka (1856?–1932)

Wovoka, a Paiute religious leader, received visions leading to the development of a new religion in the late 19th century. Beginning with his own people, Wovoka's teachings of a new world spread among many Native Americans across the American West.

Wovoka, born between 1856 and 1858 in the Walker River country of western Nevada, lived in a world that had been radically altered in the years since Americans began streaming across the Great Basin of Nevada and Utah in search of gold. Great Basin Native Americans (see NATIVE AMERICAN RELIGION: INTERMONTANE/CALIFORNIA) had developed successful strategies for surviving in balance with the fragile environment of the arid region. Archeological evidence indicates that historic tribes had dwelt in the basin for several hundred, or in some cases thousands, of years. But after the California Gold Rush, the massive influx of whites, exposure to new diseases, war, and expropriation of tribal lands had placed severe economic and cultural constraints upon the Paiutes and other basin native peoples. Wovoka himself spent most of his life in Mason Valley, Nevada, working as a hand on the Dick Wilson ranch.

Wovoka's father, Tavibo, was influenced by an earlier Paiute dreamer, Wodziwob (some reports state that Tavibo and Wodziwob were the same person). In the early 1870s Wodziwob had dreamed of an imminent end to the world, followed by a renewal of life for native people in a lush, plentiful land. Wodziwob's message spread among both basin tribes and whites, receiving support from Mormons such as Orson Pratt (see CHURCH OF JESUS CHRIST OF LATTER-DAY SAINTS). Wodziwob's vision had included a version of the traditional Paiute round dance, which became known as the GHOST DANCE.

Apocalyptic expectations diminished somewhat among the Paiutes as the years went by. But throughout the region millennial fears and hopes frequently surfaced among many tribes, as they did among the dominant culture. Wovoka learned from his father both the traditional Paiute creation story, which speaks of the renewal of human life and a blooming of the desert, and the similar teachings of Wodziwob. Evidence suggests that he also may have come in contact with disciples of John Slocum, a Squaxin prophet and founder of what is now the Indian Shaker Church, who combined traditional and Christian themes to speak of cultural rebirth by adhering to a strict moral code.

By the mid-1880s Wovoka, who claimed to have inherited his father's dreaming powers, had already been taken to heaven in a vision, and given miraculous powers, such as prediction and control of the weather. A bout with scarlet fever in late 1888 left him near death until he made a dramatic recovery on January 1, 1889, at the same time as the sun was emerging from a total eclipse. Wovoka then announced a new vision, which rapidly spread across the basin, into California, and eastward across the plains.

In his vision Wovoka talked with God. He saw the dead in a pleasant land, looking young and engaging in traditional activities. God told him the world would be renewed. The dead would rise, game would be plentiful, the earth green. He must prepare his people by encouraging them to live morally upright lives. They were to love one another, to avoid war with the whites and fighting with each other, and be honest and hardworking—accepting work with the whites. God gave Wovoka a dance that the people were to perform monthly for four consecutive nights and the morning of the fifth day. The dance would help hasten the time of world renewal and bring the people happiness by providing contact with their dead relatives.

Throughout 1889 and 1890 Wovoka received delegations from many tribes, who took messages from the prophet back to their homes. As the new religion spread among tribes, its adherents incorporated Wovoka's teachings along with their own religious symbols, rituals, and sacred stories. In the wake of the massacre at Wounded Knee, South Dakota on December 29, 1890, in which approximately 200 Lakotas were killed, the pacifist Wovoka urged people to stop the dancing. While many did, the dance continued in recognizable forms into the 20th century. Wovoka worked on the Wilson ranch for many years, and served as a holy man among the northern Paiutes. He died September 20, 1932 in Yerington, Nevada.

MG

Bibliography: James Mooney, *The Ghost-Dance Religion and the Sioux Outbreak of 1890,* abridged ed. (Chicago: University of Chicago Press, 1965).

Y

Yogananda, Paramhansa See SELF-REAL-
IZATION FELLOWSHIP.

Young, Brigham (1801–1877) The second president of the CHURCH OF JESUS CHRIST
OF LATTER-DAY SAINTS, Brigham Young was responsible for transplanting Mormonism to the
American West. The most influential figure in
Mormon history after founder Joseph SMITH,
JR., the bureaucratic Young led the church
through its "pioneer period" in the West just as
the charismatic Smith inspired its founding and
early growth on the FRONTIER.

Young was born in 1801 in Whitingham,
Vermont. Over the course of his lifetime, Young
would move frequently—with his family, in

The successor of Joseph Smith, Jr., Brigham
Young led the great exodus of Mormons to flee
persecution in the Midwest and establish a new
Zion in Salt Lake City, Utah.

search of economic advantage, and with his
church, to escape persecution. The ninth of 11
children born to John and Abigail Howe Young,
he moved with his family from Whitingham to
Sherburn in central New York in 1804 and then
farther west in the state to Auburn in 1813.
He was raised, therefore, in the BURNED-OVER
DISTRICT, so-called because the fires of various
forms of religious enthusiasm were scorching
the area at the time.

Young was raised in a strict Reformed Methodist household, and many of his brothers
eventually became leaders in Methodist congregations. But Young himself mistrusted the emotionalism of frontier revivals, and did not join
the Methodist church until he was 23 years old.
At the age of 16 he moved to Auburn, New
York and struck out on his own. There Young,
who had received little formal education, served
as an apprentice and learned the carpentry, glaz-
ing, and painting trades. Following his marriage
in October of 1824 to Miriam Angeline Works
of Aurelius, New York, Young continued his
peripatetic ways. He moved in 1829 with his
wife and his first child, Elizabeth, to Mendon,
New York, only 40 miles from where Joseph
Smith, Jr. was putting the final touches on what
would become the *Book of Mormon.*

After studying Smith's controversial translation of the ancient gold plates he had discovered
buried in the Hill Cumorah near Manchester,
New York, Young determined, along with many
of his closest relatives, that the *Book of Mormon*
was indeed divine writ and that Smith was the
prophet he claimed to be. Young was baptized
into the Church of Jesus Christ of Latter-day
Saints and ordained an elder in Mendon, New
York on April 15, 1832. Tragically, his first
wife died that same year of tuberculosis. Young
responded to the misfortune by devoting himself
wholeheartedly to the Mormon cause.

During his early years with the LDS church,
Young served as a missionary in the United

States and Canada and as a volunteer in Zion's Camp, a Mormon militia organized by Smith to defend Mormons from persecution. Because of his success in bringing converts into the Mormon fold and his zeal in defending his Mormon brothers and sisters, Young quickly became one of Smith's most valued advisors. When Smith formed in February of 1835 the Council of the Twelve Apostles as a governing body just below the First Presidency of the prophet himself, Young was in its ranks. And when Smith, because of his imprisonment, needed someone to organize the Mormon evacuation from Missouri to Illinois in 1838, he turned to Young.

Between the time of his appointment to the Council of the Twelve Apostles in 1835 and Smith's death in 1844, Young faithfully served Smith in many different capacities. In 1840, the same year he would ascend to the presidency of the Council of the Twelve Apostles, he led a successful Mormon mission to England. And in 1841 he followed Smith's lead and became a Mason. Finally, following Smith's announcement of his candidacy for the United States presidency in 1844, Young campaigned vigorously for Smith across the country.

Following Smith's murder in a jail cell in Carthage, Illinois in 1844, Young struggled for and won his mentor's mantle as the spiritual and political leader of the Church of Jesus Christ of Latter-day Saints. But that victory did not come without cost. A significant minority, which objected to polygamy and insisted that Smith's successor come from his bloodline, refused to recognize Young. In 1860 they formed under the leadership of Joseph Smith III, the REORGANIZED CHURCH OF JESUS CHRIST OF LATTER-DAY SAINTS, now centered in Independence, Missouri.

Young's most celebrated action as president of the LDS church was leading the Mormon exodus (1846–48) from the persecution that had been their lot in New York, Ohio, Missouri, and Illinois to a new Mormon "Zion" outside the United States in Mexico in the Great Salt Lake basin. Because this act is seen by many Mormons as a modern-day recapitulation of the Hebrew exodus out of Egypt, through the wilderness and to the promised land, Young is often viewed as an "American Moses," leading God's "chosen people" from persecution to freedom.

From the new Mormon base in Utah, Young built a vast Mormon empire in the American West, overseeing the establishment and maintenance of hundreds of LDS settlements as far away as San Bernardino, California. In Utah, Young organized missions to the Indians, negotiated contracts that led to the completion of the transcontinental telegraph and the transcontinental railroad, and founded a university in Salt Lake City that would become the University of Utah. Elected governor of what was then the independent state of "Deseret" in 1849, he was appointed, after the incorporation of the Utah territory into the United States in 1850, territorial governor and superintendent of Indian affairs.

Young was a controversial leader whose theocratic rule many denounced as an affront to American political traditions. His ban, instituted in 1847, on ordaining African-Americans to the priesthood and his successful campaign to legalize slavery in the Utah territory served to dissuade blacks from joining the Mormon church in significant numbers. But Young's most controversial practice was his polygamy. Though he had initially resisted Smith's 1841 revelation affirming what Mormons refer to as "plural marriage," Young had been among the first Mormons to follow Smith's teaching on the subject. Young took his first "plural wife," Lucy Ann Decker, in 1842. He would eventually marry 55 times; and 16 of his wives would bear him a total of 57 children.

Mormons practiced polygamy for over a decade before Young proclaimed publicly Smith's revelation on plural marriage in 1852. This announcement led, after the incorporation of the Utah territory into the United States in 1850, to a series of clashes with federal officials. In 1857, Democratic President James Buchanan responded to demands by the newly formed Republican Party to outlaw in American territories "those twin relics of barbarism—Polygamy and Slavery" by deciding to replace Young with non-Mormon administrators. The president then mobilized 2,500 United States troops to enforce his decision. Young responded by considering yet another Mormon exodus, this time to places as far away as Central America or Alaska, but in the end he decided to stand his ground. In September of 1857 the resolves of Buchanan and Young conspired to create a slaughter that haunted the LDS church for decades. In what came to be known as the "Mountain Meadows Massacre," 120 non-Mormon emigrants were killed by Indians and Mormons.

Buchanan did relieve Young of his governmental responsibilities in Utah, but the Mormon leader remained the most powerful man in the American West. In 1861 Congress aimed to undercut both Young's power and his church's most controversial practice by passing the Morrill Anti-Bigamy Bill outlawing polygamy. Young himself was arrested on bigamy charges in 1863 and again in 1871. Following a Mormon challenge on FIRST AMENDMENT grounds, the Supreme Court upheld the law in *United States v. Reynolds* in 1879. That action, however, like Young's arrest, only served to solidify Young's authority among his Mormon followers.

By the time of Young's death at the age of 76 on August 29, 1877 in Salt Lake City, the LDS church claimed approximately 150,000 members, about half of them recruited from overseas. Young is still criticized by opponents of Mormonism as a lecher and a tyrant. But he is remembered by his followers for steering the Mormons through the difficult period of their founder's death, for transplanting the Mormon church to a new "Zion" in the desert West, for sustaining that church in the face of massive persecution, for heading one of America's

largest and most influential families, and for spearheading the highly successful worldwide mission work of the Church of Jesus Christ of Latter-day Saints.

SRP

Bibliography: Leonard J. Arrington, *Brigham Young: American Moses* (New York: Alfred A. Knopf, 1985).

Young Men's Christian Association (YMCA)

The YMCA has grown from an evangelical mission to the newly urban middle class into a worldwide ecumenical organization with associations in many countries concerned with breaking down barriers of understanding between people of all races and religions.

The original YMCAs emerged out of the wave of evangelical reform stemming from the SECOND GREAT AWAKENING of the early 19th century. The initial idea for a voluntary society (see VOLUNTARYISM) devoted to the welfare of young urban men was English, developed by George Williams in 1844. Brought to Boston in 1851 by T. V. Sullivan, who had encountered the English forerunner during a visit to the London World's Fair, the earliest YMCAs were allied with the city's Protestant churches. Eventually YMCAs became autonomous, each association funded independently, and with lay leadership frequently drawn from the local business community. Expansion came rapidly. An 1854 international convention held in Buffalo, New York had representatives from 40 American associations, and by 1860 there were 205, enrolling 25,000 members. Early associations provided room and board for youths moving into urban areas, and various programs that contributed to their educational and spiritual well-being. While the outbreak of the CIVIL WAR disturbed the movement, YMCAs provided religious literature to soldiers, and expanded their operations to include campus associations by 1857.

After the war the YMCA responded to rapid growth in American cities, establishing chapters

For half a century, beginning in the 1870s, the YWCAs and YMCAs served young people in the cities, emphasizing physical, educational, social, and religious activities. Scenes from *Harper's Weekly*, 2/8/1879. (Billy Graham Center Museum)

across the country. Under the leadership of men like Chicago revivalist Dwight L. MOODY (see REVIVALISM) the YMCAs had placed particular significance on religious development, through Bible studies and evangelistic meetings. By the 1870s, however, YMCAs were being built with residential facilities, gymnasiums, and swimming pools in an effort to minister to the "wholeness" of life, and to compete with saloons and other urban temptations. The triangular symbol adopted by the YMCA in 1895 emphasized the unity of body, mind, and spirit. Increasingly the YMCA projected an ideal of character-building, healthy Christianity, and in the crowded, tumul-tuous environments of a burgeoning urban America, the YMCAs became islands sheltering white, middle-class Protestant youths moving into the cities in search of opportunity. One YMCA member in the 1870s, Connecticut dry-goods salesman Anthony Comstock, began a national campaign to eradicate obscene litera-ture, funded by upper-class business leaders on the national YMCA's board, which culminated in federal legislation suppressing obscene mate-rials.

The YMCA spread worldwide by the turn of the century, under the leadership of John R. MOTT. In the United States the YMCA contin-ued to serve the interests of middle-class Protes-tants, largely sequestering youths from contact with immigrants, blacks, or the urban lower-class. At the same time, black YMCAs were beginning to be founded. Within the context of the times, the separate-but-equal facilities, which remained until the 1940s, were often seen as the high point in racial equality.

During WORLD WAR I and WORLD WAR II the YMCA, already nationally organized, played an important auxiliary role both in training camps and overseas at the request of the War Depart-ment (staffing 1,397 stations in France during World War I), providing lay ministers and reli-gious literature, aiding prisoners, and serving as part of the United Services Organizations (USO) during World War II.

In the years since World War II, the YMCA has continued to grow in membership, totaling close to 14 million, with 2,000 associations in 1995. Responding to changing social condi-tions, YMCAs grew increasingly concerned about providing services for lower-class urban youth in the 1960s, and abolished gender barri-ers as well. Organizational goals have shifted from making a home away from home for mid-dle-class Protestants in the cities to meeting the goal of enhancing global cooperation and world peace by developing Christian personality and building a Christian society through cultivating spirit, mind, and body.

MG

Bibliography: Charles Howard Hopkins, *History of the YMCA in North America* (New York: Association Press, 1951); David I. Macleod, *Building Character in the American Boy: The Boy Scouts, The YMCA and Their Forerunners, 1870–1920* (Madison: University of Wisconsin Press, 1983).

Young Women's Christian Association (YWCA)

This organization, originally founded to provide single women with a safe moral haven in growing American cities, has expanded worldwide and includes over one million members and associates in the United States. Developing out of the 19th-century evangelical reform movement, the YWCA is now an ecumenical organization, focusing its efforts on a wide variety of social problems in addition to the traditional effort to provide spiritual, educational, and physical nurture.

Like its counterpart, the YOUNG MEN'S CHRISTIAN ASSOCIATION, the YWCA was originally an expression of the reform-minded EVANGELICALISM that dominated American life in the decades prior to the CIVIL WAR. Both organizations began in the efforts of British evangelicals to improve the conditions of young people moving into the cities to find wage-labor in the wake of the Industrial Revolution. The YWCA came out of an 1855 merger of two earlier efforts, the Prayer Union established by Emma Roberts and the General Female Training Institute established by Mary Jane Kinnaird.

The first American Ladies' Christian Association formed in 1858 at New York University for the "temporal, moral and spiritual welfare of the self-supporting young woman." However the movement did not begin to spread until after the Civil War, when the first YWCA was established in Boston. The various associations began not only to supply shelter and spiritual instruction, but also to meet educational needs, offering practical classes in bookkeeping and domestic arts, but also in such subjects as astronomy and physiology.

As the number of associations grew, expanding into midwestern cities during the 1870s, the YWCA continued to model its approach on the YMCA when possible. Following the YMCA lead, the new YWCA facilities were also constructed with goals of physical education in mind. Regular Bible classes drew many women as well. Expanding onto campuses in the 1870s, associations were established at several normal schools—devoted to training teachers—and women's colleges. Under the leadership of Emily Huntington and Grace Dodge, the YWCA continued to expand its emphasis on domestic education.

Prior to the 20th century the YWCA did little work with younger girls. In response to changing social conditions, middle-class children under 16 became the focus of reformers, eager to insure that changing economic conditions would not disturb gender roles seen as God-given. In 1909 the YWCA expanded its program of domestic arts and athletic activities to serve young girls. Veteran YWCA and YMCA workers Dorothy and Luther Gulick began the Camp Fire Girls' program in 1912. While obviously patterned upon the new Boy Scouts of America, the Gulicks believed that a direct copy would be "fundamentally evil," since girls needed to learn how "to be womanly." While YMCA workers saw their task as steering boys toward careers in business, YWCA leaders on the other hand strove to inculcate a spirit of self-sacrifice in girls, encouraging them to take up domestic and service roles, "to be happy" as the Camp Fire Girls' final law put it. YWCA workers were also concerned to ward off "moodiness" and dissatisfaction, while YMCA staff, seeking to channel frustrations into successful economic endeavor, paid little attention to the moods of boys other than to diffuse what they saw as rampant adolescent SEXUALITY.

Like the YMCA, the YWCA over the 20th century has expanded both geographically and in terms of its perceived mission in American life, taking an active part in providing support services during WORLD WAR I and WORLD WAR II. Responding to the longstanding demands of black women to end the YWCA's policy of segregation, the YWCA came to see itself as an ecumenical organization, open to all, concerned with ending institutional racism on a global scale as well as establishing a network of understanding to increase the potential for world peace. Membership in 1993 stood at 358,546; this figure excludes 646,421 participating but unregistered members (associates).

MG

Bibliography: Grace H. Wilson, *The Religious and Philosophical Works of the YWCA* (New York: Teachers College Press, 1933).

Z

Zen Zen Buddhism arrived in America in the 19th century from Japan via China and India. The term "Zen" is a Japanese transliteration of the Chinese term "Ch'an," which itself is a Chinese rendering of the Sanskrit term "Dhyana." Each of these words means "meditation." Zen is a school of the Mahayana ("Great Vehicle") Buddhist school of northern Asia that seeks Satori, or sudden, immediate, and intuitive enlightenment, through meditation (see BUDDHISM). Its practitioners have cultivated into sophisticated spiritual practices arts such as the tea ceremony and flower arranging.

Zen Buddhism is typically divided into two schools: Rinzai Zen, founded by Eisai (?–1215) in the 12th century, and Soto Zen, founded in the 13th century by Dogen (?–1253). One key difference between these two schools is that while Rinzai Zen masters emphasize koans, or mind puzzles, Soto Zen masters stress zazen, or sitting meditation. Both of these schools are represented in the hundreds of Zen centers scattered across America.

Just as Zen practitioners in Asia credit Bodhidharma, the first Zen patriarch, with bringing Zen out of India to China, so do American Zen practitioners credit Soyen Shaku (1859–1919) with making of Zen a gift to the West. It was he who introduced Americans to Zen by addressing the WORLD'S PARLIAMENT OF RELIGIONS in Chicago in 1893 and by instructing the first non-Asian American Zen practitioner, Mrs. Alexander Russell of San Francisco, in zazen and koan study some years later.

The most important figure in American Zen, however, is not Shaku but his lay student and translator, D. T. SUZUKI (1870–1966). By translating its scriptures into English and its practices into American cultural idioms, Suzuki made Zen accessible to everyday Americans. Suzuki's presence as a professor at Columbia University in the 1950s helped to precipitate the Zen boom of the 1950s and 1960s.

During those decades, Beat poets and novelists like Allen Ginsberg, Jack Kerouac, and Gary Snyder sought to popularize Zen even as they integrated its ideas and, to a lesser extent, its practices into their lives and literature. Though another Zen sympathizer, Alan WATTS, eventually dismissed Beat Zen as "phony Zen," the Beats did much to arouse the popular interest in Zen that peaked in the 1960s.

If Suzuki can be credited with introducing Americans to Zen thought, much credit for introducing Americans to Zen practice must go to Philip Kapleau, an American businessman turned Zen priest who spent 13 years in a Zen monastery in Japan. In *The Three Pillars of Zen* (1965) and other books, Kapleau supplanted what he saw as Suzuki's intellectual approach to Zen with an emphasis on three key Zen acts: zazen, or sitting meditation, dokusan, or the student's private encounter with the Zen master, and teisho, the master's commentaries. Kapleau institutionalized his approach to Zen in 1966 when he founded the Zen Meditation Center of Rochester.

Additional contributors to American Zen include, on the side of Rinzai Zen, Shigemitsu Sasaki or Sokei-an (1882–1945) and his wife, Ruth Fuller Sasaki (1893–1967), and, on the side of Soto Zen, Shunryu Suzuki (1904–1971).

The Japanese-born Sokei-an first came to America in 1906. After a failed farming experiment in northern California, he made his way to Seattle and then, in 1916, to New York City. There he founded in 1931 the Buddhist Society of America (later renamed the First Zen Institute of America). He also edited a Zen magazine, *Cat's Yawn*, until he was imprisoned, along with many other Japanese-Americans, in a wartime internment camp. During his year-long imprisonment, Sokei-an married Ruth Fuller Everett Sasaki (1893–1967), an American-born member of the Zen Institute who was an important contributor to American Zen in her own right.

In a secular age, the direct, practical bent of Zen Buddhism appeals to many Americans. The Zen Center, Providence, Rhode Island. (Pluralism Project of Harvard University)

After his death in 1945, Ruth Fuller Sasaki continued her husband's work. She lived out her last years in Japan, where she translated Zen texts into English.

Shunryu Suzuki, a Soto Zen master, came to America in the late 1950s and helped to build the San Francisco Zen Center into the largest Zen center in the United States. In 1967 he established Zen Mountain Center at Tassajara Hot Springs. Upon his death in 1971 he handed over leadership of his organization to an American-born Roshi, Richard Baker.

Zen masters and students in America have conspired in numerous ways to "Americanize" Zen. Like Jack Kerouac's *Dharma Bums* (1958), which preceded it, Robert M. Pirsig's best seller, *Zen and the Art of Motorcycle Maintenance* (1974), forged Zen insights into a new vision that incorporated, among other things, the American myth of the self-reliant man on the open road. A less masculine but equally "American" adaptation of Zen has been effected by the British-born Soto Zen master Jiyu KENNETT. The founder of the Shasta Abbey monastery in northern California, Kennett has worked to divorce Zen from Japanese culture and to wed it to American cultural forms, including feminism.

In addition to being "Americanized," Zen has also been "Christianized" by sympathizers eager to find common ground between Christianity and Zen. Books that attempt this difficult task include *Mystics and Zen Masters* (1967) by the Roman Catholic monk Thomas MERTON and *Zen Catholicism* (1963) by another Roman Catholic, Dom Aelred Graham.

By westernizing Zen, American Zen practitioners have made an exceedingly elusive religious tradition more accessible to everyday Americans. But despite these efforts, Zen is studied and practiced in the United States almost exclusively by students and intellectuals. Its influence in American culture is far greater, however, than the numbers of converts to Zen. Both in its syncretistic and in its more pristine forms, Zen continues to influence American literature and popular culture.

SRP

Bibliography: Robert S. Ellwood, Jr., *Alternative Altars: Unconventional and Eastern Spirituality in America* (Chicago: University of Chicago Press, 1979); Rick Fields, *How the Swans Came to the Lake: A Narrative History of Buddhism in America* (Boston: Shambhala, 1986); Helen Tworkov, *Zen in America* (New York: Kodansha International, 1994).

Zinzendorf, Nicolas Ludwig von (1700–1760)

An important Moravian leader on both sides of the Atlantic Ocean, Count Nicolas

Ludwig von Zinzendorf lent to the Renewed Moravian Church its missionary fervor, its emphasis on ecumenism (see ECUMENICAL MOVEMENT), and many of its distinctive hymns.

Born in Dresden, Saxony on May 26, 1700 into an aristocratic family, Zinzendorf was the godson of Philipp Jakob Spener, the so-called father of pietism. He studied theology under August Hermann Franke, Spener's most important pupil, so his roots in Lutheran pietism are as impeccable as they are well established. But Zinzendorf initially opted, apparently at the urging of insistent parents, for a career devoted to law rather than religion. He obtained a legal education at Wittenberg, then went to work in 1721 at the court in Dresden. At Dresden he first encountered the MORAVIANS, members of a pietistic Protestant sect rooted in the Hussite movement of 15th-century Moravia. Drawn to the Moravians' christocentric "heart-religion" and concerned about their persecution in Bohemia and Moravia, Zinzendorf offered a group of Moravians sanctuary at his estate in Saxony. There they established in 1722 a religious settlement that they called Herrnhut.

The success of this experiment prompted Zinzendorf to leave behind his legal career and to take up a post at the helm of the Moravians' Unitas Fratum or "Unity of the Brethren." Zinzendorf converted to the Moravian tradition, but following his conversion he devoted as much of his energy to attempting to introduce his Moravian brethren to his style of christocentric Lutheran piety as he did attempting to make Moravians out of his Lutheran kin. Zinzendorf's major project, in fact, during his early years at Herrnhut was to find common ground between Moravians and Lutherans, and indeed among all Protestants. This project met with some success. Zinzendorf, who was ordained to the Lutheran ministry in 1734, persuaded the Herrnhut Moravians to join the local Lutheran parish. But Lutheran authorities remained wary of the Moravians' almost erotic emphasis on the bodily passion of Jesus Christ, and when in 1737 Zinzendorf announced his appointment as a Moravian bishop, the understanding of local Lutheran leaders came to an end.

In addition to attempting to foster kind relations between Lutherans and Moravians, Zinzendorf worked to instill in his brethren at Herrnhut a commitment to Christian missions. Ultimately, this missionary work met with more success than Zinzendorf's ecumenical efforts. As early as 1732, the Moravians sent missionaries to the Caribbean to minister to slaves. Soon they had expanded their missionary field to include Africa, India, and North and South America.

Banished from Saxony in 1734, Zinzendorf came to America in 1741. He assisted in the establishment of the Moravians' settlement at Bethlehem, Pennsylvania in that same year, and subsequently founded the First Moravian Church in Philadelphia. During his New World sojourn, Zinzendorf also contributed to the establishment of numerous missions among Native Americans. And he saw semicommunal settlements of Moravians established from Maine to the Carolinas.

While in America, he also continued to pursue his ecumenical vision, especially among the German-speaking "Pennsylvania Dutch." In the 1740s, Zinzendorf succeeded in enlisting pastors from the German Reformed, Lutheran, and Moravian traditions into an ecumenical community of Christians called the "Congregation of God in the Spirit." Seven times he brought together members of his "Pennsylvania synods," but eventually his unstable union, which emphasized the experience of conversion over doctrinal correctness, collapsed over creedal and liturgical differences.

Zinzendorf's banishment from Saxony was lifted in 1747, and he did return to his homeland long enough to effect a rapprochement between Moravians and Lutherans there. This short-lived union was unable, however, to survive Zinzendorf's death at Herrnhut in 1760.

Zinzendorf is justly remembered as a pioneer in both ecumenism and missions. He was also a prolific writer of hymns. The Moravian Church in America has perpetuated his legacy by continuing to sing his music and to support missions across the globe. Apparently Zinzendorf's ecumenical vision persists also. The Moravian Church in America was one of the founding members of both the NATIONAL COUNCIL OF CHURCHES and the WORLD COUNCIL OF CHURCHES.

SRP

Bibliography: Arthur J. Lewis, *Zinzendorf, The Ecumenical Pioneer: A Study of the Moravian Contribution to Christian Mission and Unity* (London: SCM Press, 1962); John R. Weinlich, *Count Zinzendorf* (Nashville: Abingdon Press, 1956).

Zionism   Zionism, the movement for the reestablishment of a Jewish state in the historical land of Israel, has had a complex and ambiguous existence in the United States. It has involved both Christians and Jews, national policy and individual feelings, hostility and support. More than anything, its religious significance has complicated greatly people's views and understanding of Zionism.

To some extent Zionism began with the failure of the Jewish revolts against Roman rule in 70 C.E. and 125 C.E. The former led to the destruction of the Jewish temple and the end of Jewish worship there. The latter resulted in the expulsion of all Jews from Jerusalem. Both these events furthered the diaspora, or dispersal, of the Jews throughout the world that had begun with the Babylonian captivity in 586 B.C.E. The dispersal of the Jews, the loss of their homeland, and the destruction of the Jewish temple gave birth to Jewish hopes for the reestablishment of Israel and the rebuilding of the temple with the coming of the Messiah. The restoration of Zion to those whom God had given it became part of the religious life of the Jewish people.

For 1,700 years, it remained just a hope. Although Jews individually and in groups returned to their Holy Land, many to die and be buried there, there was no movement for the creation of a Jewish state. Roman, Byzantine, Muslim, Christian, and (again) Muslim rulers in succession dominated the land, with the fortunes of Palestine's Jews waning or waxing according to the whims of the various rulers.

The 19th century saw the emergence of various schemes to reestablish a Jewish homeland. While some, like that of the American Mordechai Noah, involved locations other than Palestine, most centered on the historic land of the Jews—at the time a part of the Ottoman Empire. These schemes had various sources and supporters. The romantic vision of uniting a people with their land was one such source. In England it was seen as a means of furthering British influence in the region, in preparation for the demise of the Ottoman Empire. Others viewed the establishment of a Jewish state as a necessity, given ANTI-SEMITISM and religious persecution.

For despite decreasing legal restriction in Western Europe, events such as the treason trial of Alfred Dreyfus in France on trumped-up charges (1894) made Jews realize that their fates were not completely secure. In Eastern Europe, especially in the Russian Empire, violent persecutions made many Jews view flight as the only alternative. For most, this flight was to the United States, but others looked toward the establishment of a Jewish state, where Jews would not be dependent on Gentile sufferance.

As a result, numerous organizations dedicated to that cause emerged, of various types and ideologies. Some emphasized the cultural and spiritual elements of such a state. A Jewish return to Israel would allow for a flowering of Jewish culture, freed from the oppression of Christian Europe. Others desired the formation of a socialist utopia; still others sought a state run according to religious laws with rule by the high priests.

All these views were transformed in 1896 with the publication of *Die Judenstaat*. Theodor Herzl, its author—an accomplished satirist, journalist, and playwright—previously had shown little interest in Jewish affairs. His newfound commitment to the establishment of a Jewish state, preferably in Palestine, became his life, and led to the creation of political Zionism, which in 1948 resulted in the establishment of the state of Israel.

Zionism in the United States has had a less tumultuous history, resulting from the view that the United States is a qualitatively different place for Jews and Judaism. Whether valid or not, this view developed early, and in the 19th century one can find Jews of all stripes claiming that the United States was the new Holy Land. Although traditionally religious Jews did not abandon their hope for the restoration of Israel and the temple, as did their Reform counterparts, both groups viewed the United States as particularly suited for the revitalization of Judaism.

With Herzl's establishment of the World Zionist Organization (WZO) in 1897 and the emergence of political Zionism, the relationship between American Jews and Palestine became even murkier. The dominant movement in American Judaism at that time, REFORM JUDAISM, opposed it vigorously, having officially renounced any desire for the restoration of the Jewish state and removed the prayers for the restoration of Zion from their services. In the same year as the first World Zionist Congress (1897), the CENTRAL CONFERENCE OF AMERICAN RABBIS (CCAR)—the Reform rabbinical conference—issued a statement denouncing Zionism. This opposition was reaffirmed in 1917 and 1919, when the CCAR and the Union of American Hebrew Congregations (UAHC) denounced the British government's Balfour Declaration that committed the British government to a Jewish homeland in Palestine.

Reform's opposition to Zionism was more than a statement of policy. It was a statement of theology, rooted in their view of Judaism's mission to the world. To disagree was heresy and several professors at Hebrew Union College (HUC) were fired for their Zionist inclinations.

Some Reform rabbis resisted the norm, most notably Abba Hillel Silver and Stephen WISE, both of whom served as president of the Zionist Organization of America (ZOA). These men assailed the Reformers' rejection of a central tenet of Judaism, as well as their failure to recognize the needs of persecuted Jews. Silver's and Wise's activities on behalf of Zionism were aided greatly by the public support given the movement by Louis Brandeis. A respected lawyer and later justice of the United States Supreme Court, Brandeis made Zionism respectable.

While Silver and Wise, along with others, helped keep the idea of Zionism alive within Reform Judaism, the rise of Nazism made it dominant. The persecution of the Jews in Hitler's Germany forced both the CCAR (1935, 1937) and the UAHC (1937) to reverse their historical positions and urge all Jews "to unite in the activities leading to the establishment of a Jewish homeland in Palestine."

The response of ORTHODOX JUDAISM to Zionism was even more complex than that of Reform. Theologically committed to the restoration of their ancestral homeland, many believed that it would be brought about through the supernatural intervention of God. To them, political Zionism was a blasphemous attempt to force the hand of the Messiah.

For the Orthodox Jew, an Israel without religious law would be like a body without a soul. Seeking to counter the secular influence within the WZO, Orthodox Jews in Europe founded Mizrahi, one of the constituent members of the organization. The foundation of Mizrahi in the United States dates from 1903, when the Orthodox-dominated United Zionists of America affiliated with the wider European movement. Now known as RELIGIOUS ZIONISTS OF AMERICA (RZA), it is the main Orthodox Zionist organization in the United States. Affiliated with Israel's National Religious Party (NRP), the RZA looks toward the implementation of religious law within the land of Israel. It demands the cessation of public transportation on the Sabbath, the serving of only kosher food in public accommodations and institutions, and religious laws in matters of marriage and divorce.

Although a minority in Israel, the nature of Israeli politics gives NRP disproportionate clout and they have been able to achieve several of their goals.

The complexity of the relationship between Orthodox Judaism and Zionism is illustrated by the existence of AGUDATH ISRAEL. An international organization of Orthodox Jews, it is non-Zionist in orientation. It rejects the establishment of a secular state in the land of Israel, yet exists as a political party in Israel and has on occasion joined in the coalition governments. Much smaller than the RZA, Agudath Israel has a noticeable presence in the United States. Organized in 1922, Agudath Israel of America is strongest among the ultra-Orthodox who came to the United States following World War II. Although numerically insignificant, it illumines the difficulty Orthodox Jews have in coming to terms with the existence of the entity for which they pray.

There is no such difficulty among the Satmar HASIDIM. For them Zionism is an unmitigated evil. After arriving in the United States in the 1940s, Joel Teitelbaum, Satmar's founder, continued his anti-Zionist diatribes begun decades earlier. Teitelbaum, who ironically owed his wartime survival to the actions of the Zionists, believed that Zionism and secular Jews caused the Holocaust. Their blasphemous behavior engendered God's anger and punishment upon the Jews. Although numbering no more than 9,000 in the United States and 1,500 to 2,000 in Israel, the Satmars keep up a constant harangue against the state of Israel.

If there has been one segment in American Judaism consistently in the Zionist camp, it has been CONSERVATIVE JUDAISM. The leading proto-Conservatives—Isaac LEESER, Henry Pereira MENDES, and Sabato MORAIS—engaged in early Zionist activities. The founder of Hadassah (the Women's Zionist Organization of America), Henrietta SZOLD was the daughter of a Conservative rabbi, and several Conservative leaders were founding members of the ZOA.

Solomon SCHECHTER, president of the Jewish Theological Seminary (JTS), was responsible for bringing Conservative Judaism into the Zionist fold. Although more concerned with the cultural and religious aspects of Zionism and suspicious of secular Zionists, he argued that Zionism "recommended itself as a great bulwark against assimilation . . . loss of identity, and disloyalty to Israel's history and its mission." This announcement in December 1905 coupled with Schechter's membership in the ZOA had immediate repercussions. Jacob Schiff, a major contributor to the school, published a letter in the *New York Times* accusing Schechter of dual loyalty. Schechter, however, prevailed and the Jewish Theological Seminary and the Conservative movement were committed to Zionism.

The increasing secularism of political Zionism and the WZO/ZOA after the death of Schechter disturbed many faculty members at JTS. Although Cyrus ADLER, Schechter's successor at JTS, resigned from the Federation of American Zionists (the precursor of the ZOA) due to its secular orientation, he actively supported colonization schemes. The conflict between political and religio-cultural Zionism dogged the seminary, and until the creation of the state of Israel, the faculty was split over the issue. After 1948, a change in the school's administration brought it openly into support for the Jewish state.

With the creation of the state of Israel in 1948, the debate over Zionism changed dramatically. For many Jewish-Americans, Israel's creation seemed to be the actualization of Zionism, so the movement no longer seemed necessary. Membership in the ZOA waned. Israel was a welcome but inconsequential reality for much of American Jewry. Indeed, a symposium on Jewish belief, sponsored by the magazine *Commentary* in 1966, saw little emphasis on Israel or the Holocaust. The Arab-Israeli war of 1967 changed that and dramatically transformed Israel's significance within American Judaism. Arthur Hertzberg, writing in the *American Jewish Year Book, 1968* noted this change: "The immediate reaction of American Jewry to the crisis was far more intense and widespread than anyone could have foreseen. Many Jews would never have believed that the grave danger to Israel would dominate their thoughts and emotions to the exclusion of all else."

The threat to Jewish survival presented by the war, coming just over 30 years after the Holocaust, transformed Zionism and Israel from a philanthropic interest into a religious value. Nowhere was this more obvious than within Reform Judaism. Meeting in Los Angeles immediately after the war, the CCAR adopted a resolution announcing its solidarity with Israel, declaring that "their triumphs are our triumphs. Their ordeal is our ordeal. Their fate is our fate." After moving from hostility to Zionism to grudging acceptance, Reform Judaism would make Israel's existence a tenet of religious faith. In 1969 the CCAR declared Israeli Independence Day a religious holiday and instructed the liturgical committee to create a liturgy for the festival. The New Reform prayer book restored many of the references to Zion and included special prayers for the state of Israel. Zionism and Israel constitute a major portion of the curriculum of Reform education, and Hebrew Union College now requires all rabbinical students to spend one year studying in Israel.

Conservative Judaism adopted a similar course. Both it and the Reformers have attempted to establish a presence in Israel. As a result several Reform and Conservative synagogues have been established there, both HUC and JTS have branches in Jerusalem.

This has led to problems, however. Religion in Israel is dominated by the Orthodox. Neither Reform nor Conservative rabbis are recognized as legitimate rabbis. They cannot perform weddings, for example, and conflicts have occurred. In 1987, a small Reform congregation in Jerusalem was attacked physically by a group of ult. Orthodox during the celebration of Simchat Torah for allowing women to touch the holy scrolls.

Reform Jews in the United States also have been critical of Israeli governmental policy, and have called upon the Israeli government to show more flexibility in dealing with both the Palestinians and the Arab governments. This criticism increased following the 1982 Israeli invasion of Lebanon. Leaders of American Reform Judaism have been most active in calling for a negotiated settlement, and for trading land for peace. Although Reform Judaism strongly supports Israel, political and religious conflicts have exacerbated the tensions between secular and Reform Jews in America (who provide substantial sums to the Zionist cause) and certain segments of Israeli society.

Despite these differences, American Jewry is not about to end its support for Israel. Linked by ties of culture, religion, and often family, Jewish-Americans, while occasionally in disagreement with Israeli attitudes and policy, are committed to Israel's security and existence. Israel has become a constant source of revitalization for Jewish culture and religion in the United States.

EQ

Bibliography: *American Jewish Yearbook, 1968;* (Philadelphia: Jewish Publication Society, 1968); Nathan Glazer, *American Judaism,* 2nd ed., rev. (Chicago: University of Chicago Press, 1972.); Menahem Kaufman, *Ambiguous Partnership: Non-Zionists and Zionists in America* (Jerusalem: Magnes Press, Hebrew University, 1984); Aaron S. Klieman and Adrian L. Klieman, eds., *American Zionism: A Documentary History*, 17 vols. (New York: Garland, 1990); Robert Silverberg, *If I Forget Thee O Jerusalem: American Jews and the State of Israel* (New York: Morrow, 1970).

AFRICAN-AMERICAN RELIGION

Abernathy, David Ralph
African-American religion
African Methodist Episcopal Church
African Methodist Episcopal Zion Church
Allen, Richard
Black Jews
Christian Methodist Episcopal Church
Church of God in Christ
civil rights movement
Crumwell, Alexander
Divine, Father
Drew, Timothy (Noble Drew Ali)
Du Bois, W. E. B.
Fard, W. D.
Farrakhan, Louis (Abdul)
Garvey, Marcus
Grace, Sweet Daddy (Charles Emmanuel)
Hurley, George Willie
Jones, Absalom
King, Martin Luther, Jr.
Lee, Jarna
Malcolm X (Malcolm Little)
Moorish Science Temple
Muhammad, Elijah
Muhammad, Warith Deen
Nation of Islam (Black Muslims)
National Baptist Convention of America, Inc.
National Baptist Convention, U.S.A., Inc.
Pennington, James William Charles
Powell, Adam Clayton, Jr.
Powell, Adam Clayton, Sr.
Progressive National Baptist Convention, Inc.
Washington, Booker Taliaferro
Webb, Muhammad Alexander Russell
Womanist theology

BAPTISTS

American Baptist Churches in the U.S.A.
Backus, Isaac
baptism
Baptists

Canwell, Russell Herman
Furman, Richard
Graham, Billy (William Franklin)
Graves, James Robinson
Leland, John
Mathews, Shailer
National Baptist Convention of America, Inc.
National Baptist Convention, U.S.A., Inc.
Progressive National Baptist Convention, Inc.
Southern Baptist Convention
Williams, Roger

CHRISTIAN CHURCH (DISCIPLES OF CHRIST)

Ames, Edward Scribner
Campbell, Alexander
Christian Church (Disciples of Christ)
Churches of Christ
Lipscomb, David
primitivism
restoration movement
Stone, Barton Warren

CHURCH AND STATE

American Revolution/Revolutionary War
church and state, relationship between
civil religion
Cold War
Communism
Constitution
education, public school
First Amendment
Jefferson, Thomas
Madison, James
Mann, Horace
Murray, John Courtney
peace reform
sexuality
Spellman, Francis Joseph
Vietnam War
World War I
World War II

CIVIL RIGHTS MOVEMENT

Abernathy, David Ralph
civil rights movement
Committee of Southern Churchmen
Garvey, Marcus
King, Martin Luther, Jr.
Koinonia Farm
Ku Klux Klan
Malcolm X (Malcolm Little)
Powell, Adam Clayton, Jr.
Powell, Adam Clayton, Sr.
segregation
Southern Christian Leadership Conference (SCLC)
Student Nonviolent Coordinating Committee (SNCC)
Washington, Booker Taliaferro

CONGREGATIONALISTS

Abbott, Lyman
Beecher, Henry Ward
Beecher, Lyman
Bellamy, Joseph
Cambridge Platform
Congregationalism
Dwight, Timothy
Edwards, Jonathan
Half-way Covenant
Hopkins, Samuel
Mather, Cotton
Mather, Increase
Mayhew, Jonathan
New Divinity
New Lights/Old Lights
Plan of Union
Stoddard, Solomon
Strong, Josiah
Taylor, Nathaniel William
United Church of Christ

EASTERN ORTHODOX

Belavin, Tikhon
Coucouzes, Iakovos

Greek Orthodox Archdiocese of North and South America
Orthodox Christianity
Orthodox Church in America
Schmemann, Alexander
Spyrou, Athenagoras

EASTERN RELIGIONS

Baha'í Faith
Beat movement
Blavatsky, Helena Petrovna
Buddhism
Buddhist Churches of America
Dharmapala, Anagarika
Hinduism
Hunt, Ernest Shinkaku
International Society for Krishna Consciousness
Islam
Kennet, Jiyu
Nichiren Shoshu Academy
Olcott, Henry Steel
Prabhupada, A. C. Bhaktivedanta Swami
Self-Realization Fellowship
Sikhism
Suzuki, Daisetz Teitaro
Transcendental Meditation
Trungpa, Chogyam
Vedanta Society
Vivekananda, Swami
Watts, Alan Wilson
World's Parliament of Religions
Zen

ECUMENISM

ecumenical movement
Evangelical Alliance
Mott, John Raleigh
National Council of Churches
World Council of Churches

EPISCOPALIANS

Anglicanism
Anglo-Catholicism
Brooks, Phillips

Crummell, Alexander
DuBose, William Porcher
episcopacy
Episcopal Church
Hobart, John Henry
Jarratt, Devereaux
Jones, Absalom
Seabury, Samuel
Society for the Propagation of the Gospel in Foreign Parts

EVANGELICALISM

Arminianism
biblical interpretation
Calvinism
conversion
election
Evangelical Alliance
Evangelical United Front
evangelicalism
justification
National Association of Evangelicals
preachers, Protestant
Reformation, the
Sabbatarianism
sanctification
voluntaryism

FEMINISM

Daly, Mary
feminist theology
Fuller, Sarah Margaret
Grimké, Angelina Emily and Sarah Moore
Harkness, Georgia Elma
Hutchinson, Anne
Stanton, Elizabeth Cady
Truth, Sojourner
Willard, Frances Elizabeth
womanist theology
Woman's Bible, The

FRIENDS

Dyer, Mary
Friends, the Religious Society of (Quakers)

Keithian controversy
Penn, William
Woolman, John

FUNDAMENTALISM

Bible schools
Bryan, William Jennings
creationism
dispensationalism
Dixon, Amzi Clarence
evolution
fundamentalism (Protestant)
Fundamentals, The
Henry, Carl Ferdinand Howard
Hodge, Charles
inerrancy
Machen, John Gresham
Princeton Theology
Scofield, Cyrus Ingerson
Scopes trial
Scottish Common Sense Realism
Torrey, Reuben Archer
Warfield, Benjamin Breckinridge
Worldwide Church of God

HARMONIAL RELIGION

Blavatsky, Helena Petrovna
Christadelphians
Christian Science
Davis, Andrew Jackson
Deep Ecology
Eddy, Mary Baker
Hopkins, Emma Curtis
mesmerism
Muir, John
nature religion
New Age religion
positive thinking
Quimby, Phineas Parkhurst
Rosicrucians
Scientology
spiritualism
Swedenborgianism
theosophy
Transcendental Meditation

HOLINESS CHURCHES

Church of the nazarene
Higher Christian Life movement
Holiness movement
Mahan, Asa
Palmer, Phoebe Worrall
perfectionism
Salvation Army
White, Alma Bridwell

HUMANISM

American Humanist Association
atheism and free thought
Dewey, John
Enlightenment, the
Ethical Culture
freemasonry
Humanist Manifesto
Ingersoll, Robert Green
James, William
Kallen, Horace Meyer
Mencken, Henry Lewis
New Thought
O'Hair, Madalyn Murray
Paine, Thomas
Royce, Josiah
secular humanism
secularism
Small, Albion Woodbury
Whitman, Walt

JUDAISM

Adler, Cyrus
Adler, Felix
Agudath Israel
anti-Semitism
Black Jews
Central Conference of American Rabbis
Conservative Judaism
Einhorn, David
Hasidism
Heschel, Abraham Joshua
Judaism
Kaplan, Mordecai M.

Kohler, Kaufmann
Leeser, Isaac
Mendes, Henry Pereira
Morais, Sabato
Orthodox Judaism
Pittsburgh Platform
Reconstructionist Judaism
Reform Judaism
Religious Zionists of America
Schechter, Solomon
Schneerson, Menachem Mendel
Soloveitchik, Joseph Dov
Szold, Henrietta
United Synagogue of Conservative Judaism
Wise, Isaac Mayer
Wise, Stephen S.
Zionism

LUTHERANS

Evangelical Lutheran Church in America
Krauth, Charles Porterfield
Lutheran Church—Missouri Synod
Lutheranism
Muhlenberg, Henry Melchior
Schmucker, Samuel Simon
Walther, Carl Ferdinand Wilhelm

METHODISTS

African Methodist Episcopal Church
African Methodist Episcopal Zion Church
Allen, Richard
Asbury, Francis
Cartwright, Peter
Christian Methodist Episcopal Church
Coke, Thomas
Harkness, Georgia
Lee, Jarena
Methodists
United Methodist Church
Wesleyan tradition, the

MILLENNIALISM/ADVENTISM

dispensationalism
eschatology

Jehovah's Witnesses
Miller, William
postmillennialism
premillenialism
rapture, the
Russell, Charles T.
Seventh-day Adventist Church
White, Ellen Gould (Harmon)

MISSIONS

American Missionary Association
Haystack Prayer Meeting
Judson, Adoniram
Kino, Eusebio Francisco
missions, foreign
missions, home
Mott, John Raleigh
Serra, Junipero
Student Volunteer Movement

MODERN RELIGIOUS THOUGHT—CONSERVATIVE

Buchman, Frank Nathan Daniel
Christian Right
electronic church
fundamentalism
Graham, Billy (William Franklin)
Henry, Carl Ferdinand Howard
innerancy
Moral Majority
National Association of Evangelicals
Roberts, Granville Oral
Scopes trial

MODERN RELIGIOUS THOUGHT—LIBERAL

Ames, Edward Scribner
biblical interpretation
death of God theology
Fosdick, Harry Emerson
Koinonia Farm
liberalism, theological
liberation theology
Mathews, Shailer

Merton, Thomas
Metropolitan Community Church
modernism (Protestant)
Neo-orthodoxy
Niebuhr, Helmut Richard
Niebuhr, Reinhold
science and religion
Tillich, Paul

MORMONS

Book of Mormon
Church of Jesus Christ of Latter-day Saints
Reorganized Church of Jesus Christ of Latter-day Saints
Smith, Joseph, Jr.
Young, Brigham

NATIVE AMERICANS

American Indian Religious Freedom Act (AIRFA)
assimilation and resistance, Native American
Ghost Dance
Handsome Lake
Native American Church
Native American religions
Native American religions: Eastern Woodlands
Native American religions: Intermontane/California
Native American religions: Northwest
Native American religions: Plains
Native American religions: Southwest
Wovoka

NEW RELIGIOUS MOVEMENTS

anti-cult movement
International Society for Krishna Consciousness
Jesus movement
Jones, James Warren (Jim)
Moon, Sun Myung
Neo-paganism
satanism
Santería
Unification Church
Vodou

ORGANIZED CHURCH LIFE

baptism
Bible schools
Bible societies
ecumenical movement
episcopacy
establishment, religious
Federal Council of Churches
heresy
mainline Protestantism
National Council of Churches
preachers, Protestant
Sunday school movement
World Council of Churches

PENTECOSTALS

Assemblies of God
Azusa Street revival
Church of God (Cleveland, Tennessee)
McPherson, Aimee Semple
Parham, Charles Fox
Pentecostalism
Seymour, William Joseph
snake-handling
Tomlinson, Ambrose Jessup
White, Alma Bridwell

PIETISTS/SECTARIANS

Amish, the
Church of the Brethren (Dunkers)
Ephrata Community
Hutterites
Mennonites
Moravians
Pietism
Zinzendorf, Nicolas Ludwig von

PLURALISTIC CULTURE

ethnicity
immigration
nativism
pluralism

PRESBYTERIANS/REFORMED

Briggs, Charles Augustus
Calvinism
Christian Reformed Church
German Reformed Church
Huguenots
Nevin, John Williamson
New School/Old School
New Side/Old Side
Presbyterian Church (U.S.A.)
presbyterianism
Reformed Church in America
Reformed Tradition, the
Schaff, Philip

PURITANS/PILGRIMS

Antinomian Controversy
Bradford, William
Cambridge Platform
colonial period
Cotton, John
Covenant Theology
Eliot, John
Half-way Covenant
Hooker, Thomas
Hutchinson, Anne
Massachusetts Bay Colony
Mather, Cotton
Mather, Increase
Mayflower Compact
Pilgrims
Puritanism
Salem witchcraft trials
Saybrook Platform
Stoddard, Solomon
Williams, Roger
Winthrop, John

REVIVALISM

Azusa Street revival
Burned-Over District
camp meetings
Cane Ridge revival

Davies, Samuel
Dwight, Timothy
Edwards, Jonathan
Finney, Charles Grandison
Frelinghuysen, Theodorus Jacobus
Graham, Billy (William Franklin)
Great Awakening
Jones, Samuel Porter (Sam)
Moody, Dwight Lyman
revivalism
Sankey, Ira David
Second Great Awakening
Sunday, Billy (William Ashley)
Tennent, Gilbert
Whitefield, George

ROMAN CATHOLICISM

Americanism
anti-Catholicism
Baltimore Catechism
Baltimore, Councils of
Brownson, Orestes Augustus
Cabrini, Francesca Xavier
Cahenslyism
Calvert, Cecilius
Carroll, John
Catholic Worker movement
Columbus, Christopher
Coughlin, Charles Edward
Cushing, Richard James
Day, Dorothy
Gibbons, James
Hecker, Isaac
Ireland, John
Jesuits
Kino, Eusebio Francisco
Longinqua Oceani
Marechal, Ambrose
Marquette, Jacques
Merton, Thomas
Murray, John Courtney
National Catholic Welfare Conference
National Conference of Catholic Bishops
Old Catholic movement

Roman Catholicism
Ryan, John Augustine
Serra, Junipero
Seton, Elizabeth Ann Bayley
Sheen, Fulton J.
Spalding, Martin John
Spellman, Francis Joseph
Tekakwitha, Kateri (Catherine)
trusteeism
Vatican Council I
Vatican Council II
Verot, Jean Pierre Augustin Marcellin

SETTLING OF AMERICA—NON-NEW ENGLAND

Calvert, Cecilius
Carolinas (Colony)
colonial period
Columbus, Christopher
frontier
Kino, Eusebio Francisco
Manifest Destiny
Marquette, Jacques
Maryland (Colony)
New France
New Netherlands
New Spain
Penn, William
Pennsylvania (Colony)
Serra, Junipero
Toleration, Act of (Maryland)
Virginia (Colony)

SLAVERY/CIVIL WAR

abolitionism
American Missionary Association
Civil War, the
Dabney, Robert Lewis
Du Bois, W. E. B.
Fourteenth Amendment
Grimké, Angelina Emily and Sarah Moore
Haygood, Atticus Greene
Howe, Julia Ward
Jones, Charles Colcock

Jones, John William
Lincoln, Abraham
Lost Cause Myth
Pennington, James William Charles
Phelps, Elizabeth Stuart (Ward)
proslavery thought
slavery
South, the
Stowe, Harriet Beecher
Thornwell, James Henley
Truth, Sojourner
Tubman, Harriet
Turner, Nat
Verot, Jean Pierre Augustin Marcellin
Vesey, Denmark
Weld, Theodore Dwight

SOCIAL REFORM

Catholic Worker movement
Conwell, Russell Herman
Day, Dorothy
Evangelical Alliance
Evangelical United Front
Gladden, Solomon Washington
Gospel of Wealth
peace reform
Rauschenbusch, Walter
Ryan, John Augustine
Sheldon, Charles Monroe
Sojourners Fellowship
Strong, Josiah
Sunday school movement
temperance
Willard, Frances Elizabeth Caroline
Young Men's Christian Association
Young Women's Christian Association

THEOLOGICAL MODERNISM (19TH CENTURY)

Abbott, Lyman
Ames, Edward Scribner

Beecher, Henry Ward
Briggs, Charles Augustus
Bushnell, Horace
Clarke, William Newton
evolution
Gray, Asa
Mathews, Shailer
modernism (Protestant)
science and religion
Smyth, Newman

UNITARIANISM/UNIVERSALISTS

Ballou, Hosea
Channing, William Ellery
Chauncy, Charles
Clarke, James Freeman
Emerson, Ralph Waldo
Frothingham, Octavius Brooks
Mayhew, Jonathan
Parker, Theodore
transcendentalism
Unitarian Controversy
Unitarian Universalist Association
Universalism

UTOPIANISM

Alcott, Amos Bronson
communitarianism
counterculture
Lee, (Mother) Ann
Noyes, John Humphrey
Owen, Robert Dale
Rapp, George
Ripley, George
Shakers
Thoreau, Henry David
utopianism
Wilkinson, Jemima

WESTWARD EXPANSION

frontier
Manifest Destiny

GENERAL INDEX

This index is designed to be used in conjunction with the extensive A-to-Z encyclopedia entries. Page references to titles, names and terms that have their own encyclopedia entry are **boldfaced** below; for additional references, see their text entries. Other titles, names and terms that are not the subjects of the A-to-Z entries are generally given fuller citations here. *Italicized* page references indicate illustrations.

A

Abbott, Lyman (1835–1922) **1**
ABCFM *see* American Board of Commissioners for Foreign Missions
Abdu'l-Bahá 51
Abernathy, David Ralph (1926–1990) **1–3**, 138, 531, 640
Abif, Hiram 241
Abilene Christian University (Abilene, Texas) 132
abolitionism **3–5**, *4*
   African-American religion 10
   American Missionary Association 24
   biblical interpretation 71
   civil rights movement 136
   Civil War 139
   evangelicalism 227
   Evangelical United Front 226
   Holiness movement 296
   Methodists 402
   New School/Old School 465
   peace reform 497
   people
      Alcott, Amos Bronson 17
      Allen, Richard 18
      Beecher, Henry Ward 63
      Channing, William Ellery 110
      Crummell, Alexander 171
      Einhorn, David 201
      Grimké, Angelina Emily and Sarah Moore 272, 273, 274
      Howe, Julia Ward 301
      Leland, John 359
      Mahan, Asa 377
      Parker, Theodore 495
      Pennington, James William Charles 499
      Stanton, Elizabeth Cady 645
      Stowe, Harriet Beecher 648, 649
      Thoreau, Henry David 666
      Truth, Sojourner 676, 677
      Tubman, Harriet 678
      Weld, Theodore Dwight 714
   perfectionism 505, 506
   preachers, Protestant 520

proslavery thought 531
   Quakers 243
   slavery 624
abortion 573, 574, 615
Abourezk, James 23
ABS *see* American Bible Society
academic freedom 574, 575
Accommodation Plan (1808) 512
acculturation *see* assimilation and acculturation
"Acres of Diamonds" (Russell Conwell sermon) 262
Adams, Hannah 86, 288
Adams, John 212, 388
Adena Indians 439, 442
Adler, Cyrus (1863–1940) *5*, **5–6**, 158, 488, 754
Adler, Felix (1851–1933) **6–7**
   atheism 47
   Ethical Culture 219
   Judaism 338
   Reform Judaism 544
   secularism 607
Adler, Margo 459
Adopting Act (1729) 466
adult baptism
   baptism 55, 56, 57
   Baptists 57
   Church of the Brethren (Dunkers) 129
   Mennonites 397
adultery 613
Advaita Vedanta 316, 672
Adventism *see* Seventh-Day Adventist Church
AELC *see* Association of Evangelical Lutheran Churches
Africa 15, 407, 408, 432, 733
African-American religion **7–14**
   African Methodist Episcopal Church (A.M.E.) 10, 14–15, 402, 410, 520, 689, 717
   African Methodist Episcopal Zion Church (A.M.E.Z.) 10, 15–16, 402, 410, 689
   American Baptist Churches in the U.S.A. 21
   American Missionary Association 24

anti-Semitism 39
   Bahá'í Faith 52
   Baptists 59
   biblical interpretation 71
   Black Jews 12, 73–74
   Carolinas 104, 105
   Christian Methodist Episcopal Church (C.M.E.) 115–116, 403
   Church of God in Christ (COGIC) 125–127, 503, 505
   civil rights movement *see* civil rights movement
   Civil War 142
   Committee of Southern Churchmen 151
   communitarianism 155
   counterculture 167
   ethnicity 221
   feminist theology 234
   immigration 311, 312
   Koinonia Farm 352
   Ku Klux Klan 354
   liberation theology 361
   literature and Christianity 367
   Methodists 402, 403
   missions, foreign 406
   missions, home 410
   Moorish Science Temple 320, 415–416
   National Baptist Convention, U.S.A., Inc. 11, 59, 61, 432–433, 531
   National Baptist Convention of America, Inc. 60, 61, 431–432, 432
   Nation of Islam (Black Muslims) (NOI) 11, 12, 39, 320, 321, 427–431, *428*
   Nichiren Shoshu Academy 471
   Pentecostalism 503
   people
      Abernathy, David Ralph 1–3, 138, 531, 640
      Allen, Richard 14, *14*, 15, 18–19, 136, 402, 520
      Crummell, Alexander 171–172

Divine, Father 11, 12, 185–186
   Drew, Timothy (Noble Drew Ali) **187–188**, 320, 415, 427
   Du Bois, W. E. B. 11, 12, 137, **188–190**, 432
   Fard, W. D. 12, **231–232**, 320, 415, 427, 430
   Farrakhan, Louis Abdul 13, 39, **232–233**, 321, 429, 431
   Garvey, Marcus 12, 73, **253–254**, 320, 415
   Grace, Sweet Daddy (Charles Emmanuel) 263
   Hurley, George Willie **305–306**, 644
   Jones, Absalom 10, 14, **328–329**
   King, Martin Luther, Jr. *see* King, Martin Luther, Jr.
   Lee, Jarena **356–357**
   Malcolm X (Malcolm Little) 12, 13, 138, 320, **379–381**, 427, 429
   Muhammad, Elijah *see* Muhammad, Elijah
   Muhammad, Warith Deen 321, **422–423**, 429
   Pennington, James William Charles **499–500**
   Powell, Adam Clayton, Jr. **516–517**, *517*–**518**
   Truth, Sojourner 16, **676–677**, *677*
   Tubman, Harriet 16, **678**
   Turner, Nat 10, 59, 71, 520, 531, **678–680**
   Vesey, Denmark 10, 520, 531, **699–700**
   Washington, Booker Taliaferro 24, 137, 432, **711–712**
pluralism 513
preachers, Protestant 520
Progressive National Baptist Convention, Inc. (PNBC) 60, 61, 433, 531
proslavery thought 532

Reorganized Church of Jesus Christ of Latter Day Saints 554
Roman Catholicism 566
segregation *see* segregation
slavery *see* slavery
Society for the Propagation of the Gospel in Foreign Parts 632, 633
South 636, 637
Southern Christian Leadership Conference (SCLC) 639, 640
spiritualism 644
Student Nonviolent Coordinating Committee 651
United Church of Christ 686
womanist theology 234, 730–731, 731
Young Men's Christian Association (YMCA) 746
Young Women's Christian Association (YWCA) 747–748
African Methodist Episcopal Church (A.M.E.) **14–15**
African-American religion 10
Methodists 402
missions, home 410
preachers, Protestant 520
United Methodist Church 689
Wesleyan tradition 717
African Methodist Episcopal Zion Church (A.M.E.Z.) 10, **15–16**, 402, 410, 689
Agenda for a Biblical People (Jim Wallis) 633
Age of Reason, The (Tom Paine) 210
Agudath Israel **16–17**, 754
Ahavath Chesed (New York City synagogue) 158
Ahimsa (nonviolence) 290
Ahlstrom, Sydney 462, 470, 707
AIDS (acquired immune deficiency syndrome) 404, 573, 615
AIM *see* American Indian Movement
AIRFA *see* American Indian Religious Freedom Act
Aitken, Robert 69
Alabama *see also specific city (e.g., Selma)*
Christian Methodist Episcopal Church 116
Ku Klux Klan 354
New France 463
Roman Catholicism 568
secular humanism 605
Alamo (San Antonio, Texas) 469
Alaska 484, 485

Albanian Orthodox Church 272, 482, 485
Albany, Georgia 640
Albany, New York 372, 464, 488, 548, 549
Albigenses (medieval sect) 154
Albright, Jacob **17**, 508, 688
ALC *see* American Lutheran Church
alcohol *see* temperance
Alcott, Amos Bronson (1799–1888) **17–18**, 673, 674
Alcott, Louisa May 140
Alexander, Archibald 529
Algonquian Indians 442, 443
Ali, Muhammad (Cassius Clay) 321, 429, 701
Alien and Sedition Acts (1798) 452, 735
Allen, Charles B. 33
Allen, Ethan 210
Allen, Richard (1760–1831) *14,* **18–19**
African Methodist Episcopal Church 14, 15
civil rights movement 136
Methodists 402
preachers, Protestant 520
Alpert, Richard *see* Ram Dass, Baba
Alphabetical Compendium of the Various Sects, An (Hannah Adams) 86, 288
Altizer, Thomas J. J. 180
Alton, Illinois 3
AMA *see* American Missionary Association
Amana (utopian community) 154
A.M.E. Church *see* African Methodist Episcopal Church
AME Review (magazine) 15
America (magazine) 328, 572
America First 736
"America Must Return to the Faith of Our Fathers" (Jerry Falwell sermon) 418
American and Foreign Bible Society 69
American Association for the Advancement of Atheism 48
American Association of Bible Colleges 68
American Atheists 48
American Baptist Association 61
American Baptist Churches in the U.S.A. **19–21**, 61
American Baptist Convention *see* American Baptist Churches in the U.S.A.
American Baptist Home Mission Society 20, 58, 59, 409
American Bible Society (ABS)
Bible societies 68, 69
ecumenical movement 194

Evangelical United Front 226
missions, home 409
National Council of Churches 435
voluntaryism 708
World War I 734
American Bible Union 69
American Board of Commissioners for Foreign Missions (ABCFM) 194, 281, 407, 435, 686
American Catholic Church 480
American Catholic Church (Syro-Antiochean) 480
American Christian Missionary Society 114
American Civil Liberties Union 597, 599
American Colonization Society 3, 136, 708
American Council of Christian Churches 431
American Education Society 708
American Episcopal Church 31
American Ethical Union 220
American Fabian Society 631
American Family Foundation, Inc. 36
American Foreign Missionary Society 408
American Friends Service Committee 244, 497, 701, 735
American Home Missionary Society 194, 226, 409, 435, 655
American Humanist Association **21–22**, 48, 605
American Indian Movement (AIM) 46, 258
American Indian Religious Freedom Act (AIRFA) **22–24**
American Indians *see* Native Americans
American Islamic Propaganda Movement 320
Americanism **27–28**, 285, 566, 567, 595
American Israelite, The (periodical) 335
American Jewish Congress 16
American Jewish Year Book, 1968 754
American Judaism (Nathan Glazer) 338
American Lutheran Church (ALC) 223, 225, 374
American Missionary Association (AMA) **24–25**, 686
American Missionary (journal) 24
American Muslim Mission (A.M.M.) 320, 321, 429
American Muslim Scientists and Engineers 320

American Muslim Social Scientists 320
American National Baptist Convention 432
American Party 33, 34
American Peace Society 496
American Prayer Book 214
American Protective Association 34, 453
American Reform Judaism 755
American Republican Party 33
American Revolution/Revolutionary War (1775–1783) **25–27**
Anglicanism 31
anti-Catholicism 32
biblical interpretation 70
church and state, relationship between 122
civil religion 133
colonial period 148
episcopacy 212
Episcopal Church 213
establishment, religious 217
German Reformed Church 255
Great Awakening 270
Massachusetts Bay Colony 388
Roman Catholicism 563
Virginia 705
American Ritual (Minhag America) (Hebrew prayer book) 336
American Slavery as It Is (Theodore Dwight Weld) 3
American Society for the Prevention of Cruelty to Animals 586
American Society for the Promotion of Temperance 661
American Sunday School Union 194, 226, 409, 435, 655
American Temperance Society 708
American Temperance Union 661
American Tract Society 226, 409
American Unitarian Association (AUA) 684
American Unitarianism (Jedidiah Morse) 683
"American Way of Life" 146, 153
Americus, Georgia 352
Ames, Edward Scribner (1870–1955) **28–29**, 411
A.M.E.Z. Church *see* African Methodist Episcopal Zion
Amida Buddha 86, 89
amillennialism 215
Amish **29–30**, 500
A.M.M. *see* American Muslim Mission
Ammann, Jakob 29

Amoskeag, New Hampshire *271*
Anabaptists
Amish 29
baptism 56
Baptists 57
Church of the Brethren
(Dunkers) 129
communitarianism 154
Hutterites 307
Mennonites 397, 398
Reformation 548
anarchism 453
Anasazi Indians 439, 450
Ancient and Mystical Order
Rosae Crucis (A.M.O.R.C.)
576
Andover (Massachusetts)
Theological Seminary 281, 683
Andreae, Johann Valentin 575
Andrew, James O. 402
Angelus Temple (Los Angeles,
California) 504
Anglicanism **30–31** *see also*
Society for the Propagation of
the Gospel in Foreign Parts
African-American religion 9
American Revolution/
Revolutionary War 26
Anglo-Catholicism 31
Carolinas 104, 105
colonial period 148
Enlightenment 210
episcopacy 212
Episcopal Church 212, 213
establishment, religious 216,
217, 218
Great Awakening 268, 270
Keithian controversy 346
Massachusetts Bay Colony
388
missions, foreign 406
Pilgrims 509
Reformation 547, 548
Reformed Church in America
549
South 636
Virginia 703, 705
Anglo-Catholicism **31–32**, 213
Anglo-Israelism 608, 741
Anglo-Saxons
Evangelical Alliance 222
Ku Klux Klan 354, 355
nativism 453
segregation 608
Worldwide Church of God
740
animal magnetism 400
animal sacrifice 238, 586
Anishenabeg (Chippewa)
Indians 46, 443
Anne (queen of England) 217
Annunciation Greek Orthodox
Church (Milwaukee,
Wisconsin) 484
anointing of the sick 129

Anshe Emeth, Congregation
(Albany, New York) 543
Anthony, Susan B.
feminist theology 233
Quakers 244
sexuality 614
spiritualism 643
Woman's Bible, The 731, 732
anthropocentrism 180
anti-Catholicism **32–35**
American Revolution/
Revolutionary War 26
biblical interpretation 71
Ku Klux Klan 355
Longinqua Oceani 368
Maryland 386
nativism 452, 453
Roman Catholicism 564,
568, 571
Antichrist 25, 523, 538, 735
anticlericalism 47, 209
anti-Communism
Christian Right 118
Cold War 145, 146
Communism 152, 153
nativism 454
Roman Catholicism 571
Vietnam War 701
anti-cult movement **35–36**,
292, 682
Anti-Defamation League 740
Anti-Imperialist League 497
anti-moderns 29
Antinomian Controversy
36–38, 387
antinuclear activists 497
Antiochian Orthodox Christian
Archdiocese of North America
483
*Anti-Romanist, Priestcraft
Unmasked* (periodical) 33
Anti-Saloon League 660, 661
anti-Semitism **38–40**
Christian Right 117, 118
Communism 153
Judaism 338
Nation of Islam (Black
Muslims) 431
Reform Judaism 545
Roman Catholicism 570
Vatican Council II 697
World War II 737
Worldwide Church of God
740
antislavery *see* abolitionism
Anti-Slavery Almanac 4
"anxious bench" 245, 520
Apache Indians 448, 450, 451
apocalypticism *see* eschatology
Apology for the Anglican Church
(John Jewel) 30
Apostolic Advocate (periodical)
113
Apostolic Faith Movement 42,
502, 504

*Appeal to the Public for Religious
Liberty Against the Oppression of
the Present Day, An* (Isaac
Backus) 217
Aquinas, Thomas 571
Arab Americans 482, 485
Arab-Israeli War (1967) 339,
545, 754–755
Arapaho Indians 135, 257, *450*
Arawak Indians 22
Arbella (ship) 386, 387, 519
Arcana Caelestia (Emmanuel
Swedenborg) 657
Archdale, John 104
Arikara Indians 448
Aristotle (Greek philosopher)
594
Arizona 451, 469
Ark (ship) 385
Arkansas 170, 171, 230, 596
Arminianism **40–41**
Calvinism 98
conversion 162
election 203
evangelicalism 227
Higher Christian Life
movement 288
justification 343
revivalism 558
Second Great Awakening 603
Arminius, Jacobus (James
Harmens) 40, 97, 202, 227,
342
Armstrong, Garner Ted 740
Armstrong, Herbert W. 740
Arndt, Johann 507
Arnold, Sir Edwin 87
Aryan Nations 608
Asbury, Francis (1745–1816)
41, **41–42**
African Methodist Episcopal
Church 14
Methodists 401, 402
preachers, Protestant 519,
520
Sunday school movement 654
United Methodist Church
688
Wesleyan tradition 716
Ashkenazi Jews 334, 335, 336,
486, 487 *see also* Eastern
European Jews
Asian Americans *see also specific
group (e.g.,* Chinese Americans)
Buddhism 85
ethnicity 221
immigration 312
missions, home 410
nativism 454
pluralism 514
Asian Exclusion Act (1917)
290, 291, 622
Asian religions *see also specific
religion (e.g.,* Hinduism)
anti-cult movement 35

Beat movement 61, 62
counterculture 167
pluralism 513
World's Parliament of
Religions 739
asiento (possession) 586
Assemblies of God **42–44**, 504,
505
assimilation and acculturation
23, 89, 221, 482
assimilation and resistance,
Native American **44–46**
Assiniboine Indians 257
Associate Reformed Presbyterian
Church 528
Association for International
Development 408
Association of American Hebrew
Congregations 337
Association of American
Orthodox Hebrew
Congregations 488
Association of Evangelical
Lutheran Churches (AELC)
223, 225, 371, 374
Association of Independent
Methodists 608
Association of Orthodox Jewish
Scientists 489
Association of Pentecostal
Churches 130
Association of Southern Baptists
639
astrology 461
atheism **46–48**, 606, 607
Athenagoras, Patriarch 272
Atkinson, William Walker 291
Atlanta, Georgia *621*
African-American religion 12
anti-Semitism 39
Hinduism 293
National Baptist Convention,
U.S.A., Inc. 432
Nation of Islam (Black
Muslims) 428
Student Nonviolent
Coordinating Committee
651
Atlanta (Georgia) University 24
Atlantic Monthly (magazine)
569
atman (*individual* soul) 698
atomic weapons *see* nuclear
weapons
AUA *see* American Unitarian
Association
Auburn Declaration (1837) 466
"auditing" (Scientology) 596
Augsburg Confession (1530)
224, 372
Augusta, Georgia 59, 638
Augustine of Hippo, St. 97,
202, 234, 547, 613
Austin, Ann 243
Austria 308

Austro-Hungarian Empire 482
"Authority of Holy Scripture, The" (Charles Augustus Briggs address) 285
Autobiography (Malcolm X) 429
Autobiography of a Yogi (Paramahansa Yogananda) 609
Awful Disclosures of Maria Monk (Rebecca Reed) 33
Aztecs 62, 437
Azusa Street revival **48–49**
  Assemblies of God 42, 43
  Church of God (Cleveland, Tennessee) 124
  Church of God in Christ 126
  Holiness movement 298
  Pentecostalism 502, 503, 504
  perfectionism 506
  sanctification 584

B

Baal Shem Tov 340
Baba, Meher 321
Baba, Satya Sai 291
babalawo (diviner) 586
Babbitt, Irving 22
"back to Africa" movement 320
Back to Godhead (magazine) 316
Backus, Isaac (1724–1806) *50,* **50–51**
  American Baptist Churches in the U.S.A. 19
  baptism 56
  Baptists 58
  establishment, religious 217
  Great Awakening 269
  secularism 606
Bacon, Francis 209, 313, 529, 600
Baconianism *see* Scottish Common Sense Realism
Badger, Joseph 409
Bahá'í Faith **51–53,** 321
Bahá'í House of Worship (Wilmette, Illinois) 52
Bahá'u'lláh, Mírzá Husayn 'Alí 51, 321
Baird, Robert 221, 707
Baker, Ella 651
Baker, Richard 750
Bakker, Jim and Tammy 43, 204, 205
Bald and Golden Eagle Protection Act (1940) 23
Balfour Declaration (1917) 753
Ballou, Hosea (1771–1852) *53,* **53–54,** 685
Baltimore, Maryland *565*
  Orthodox Judaism 488
  Roman Catholicism 563
  Swedenborgianism 657
  Vietnam War 701
  Wesleyan tradition 716

Baltimore, Councils of (1791, 1810) 54, **54–55**
Baltimore, Lord *see* Calvert, George
Baltimore Catechism **54**
Banner of Holiness (periodical) 296
Banner of Light (periodical) 643
Bannock Indians 257
baptism **55–57** *see also* adult baptism; spirit baptism
  American Baptist Churches in the U.S.A. 19
  Assemblies of God 43
  Bible societies 69
  Churches of Christ 132
  Half-way Covenant 275
  Pentecostalism 504
  restoration movement 556
Baptism of the Holy Spirit, The (Asa Mahan) 505
Baptist Board of Foreign Missions 407
Baptist Foreign Mission Convention of the U.S.A. 432
Baptist General Conference 60
Baptist General Tract Society 20, 58
Baptist Missionary Training School (Chicago, Illinois) 67
Baptists **57–61** *see also* American Baptist Churches in the U.S.A.; National Baptist Convention, U.S.A., Inc.; National Baptist Convention of America, Inc.; Progressive National Baptist Convention, Inc. (PNBC); Southern Baptist Convention
  abolitionism 4
  African-American religion 9, 11
  American Revolution/Revolutionary War 26
  Arminianism 41
  baptism 56, 57
  Bible societies 69
  Burned-Over District 91
  Calvinism 99
  camp meetings 101
  Cane Ridge revival 103
  Carolinas 104, 105
  church and state, relationship between 123
  Civil War 139
  colonial period 148
  Congregationalism 156
  establishment, religious 216, 217, 218
  evangelicalism 228
  frontier 245
  Great Awakening 269, 270
  Higher Christian Life movement 287
  Holiness movement 296

missions, foreign 407
missions, home 409
New Lights/Old Lights 464
Pennsylvania 500
Pentecostalism 503
people
  Backus, Isaac *see* Backus, Isaac
  Conwell, Russell Herman 162–163, *163,* 262
  Furman, Richard **251–252**
  Graham, Billy *see* Graham, Billy (William Franklin)
  Graves, James Robinson 57, 60, 61, **265–266**
  Leland, John 217, 218, **358–359**
  Mathews, Shailer 20, **391–392,** 411, 630, 735
  Williams, Roger *see* Williams, Roger
perfectionism 505
preachers, Protestant 520
primitivism 528
restoration movement 555
secularism 606
slavery 623
Social Gospel 631
South 636, 637
Sunday school movement 655
temperance 661
Virginia 704, 705
Barker, James W. 33
Barnes, Albert 71, 284, 465
Barnum, P. T. 643
Barrows, John Henry 739
Barth, Karl 179, 456
base communities 360, 361
Bates College (Lewiston, Maine) 20, 59
Baton Rouge, Louisiana 205
Battersby, T. D. Harford 288, 296
Battle Creek, Michigan 612
Battle for the Bible, The (Harold Lindsell) 314
Battle for the Mind (Tim LaHaye) 605
"Battle Hymn of the Republic" 140, 624
Bavarian Illuminati 452
B.C.A. *see* Buddhist Churches of America
Beachy, Moses 30
Beachy Amish Mennonite Churches 30
Bean, Scipio 15
Beatles (musical group) 292, 672
Beat movement **61–62**
  Buddhism 87, 88
  counterculture 167
  Deep Ecology 181
  Zen 749

"Because I Could Not Stop for Death" (Emily Dickinson poem) 366
Beecher, Henry Ward (1813–1887) **62–64,** *63,* 520
Beecher, Lyman (1775–1863) **64–65**
  anti-Catholicism 33
  education, public school 198, 199
  establishment, religious 218
  Evangelical Alliance 221, 222
  Evangelical United Front 226
  heresy 284
  revivalism 557
  Second Great Awakening 603
  temperance 661
  voluntaryism 707, 708
"Beecher's Bibles" 520
Be Here Now (Baba Ram Dass) 292
Beissel, Johann Conrad 129, 211, 581
Belavin, Tikhon (1865–1925) **65–66,** 485
Bellah, Robert N. 133
Bellamy, Joseph (1719–1790) **66–67,** 462
Belleville, Virginia 73
Bellows, Henry Whitney 140
Beloved (Toni Morrison) 367
Beman, Nathan 466
Benedict XV, Pope 433
Ben Eliezer, Israel 278
benevolence, Christian 19, 20, 140, 226, 604, 708
Benezet, Anthony 26
Bennett, Dennis 111, 504
Bennett, William W. 141
Berg, Allen 39
Berkeley, California 167, 293
Berkeley, George 600
Berlin Wall (1961) 146
Bernard, Pierre 291
Bernardin, Joseph Cardinal 573
Berrigan, Daniel 327, 701
Berrigan, Phillip 701
Besant, Annie Wood 290, 664
Besht (Master of the Good Name) *see* Ben Eliezer, Israel
bestiality 613
Bethany Church (Siloam, Georgia) *636*
Bethany College (West Virginia) 114
Beth B'nai Abraham (New York City) 73, 74
Beth-El, Congregation (Albany, New York) 543
Bethel-Aurora (utopian community) 154
Bethel Church 10, 14
Beth Elohim, Congregation (Charleston, South Carolina) 543

Bethlehem, Pennsylvania 419
Beth Shalom, Temple (Cambridge, Massachusetts) *333*
Bethune, Mary McLeod *8*
"Bewitched" (TV show) 581
"Beyond Modernism" (Harry Emerson Fosdick sermon) 457
Beyond the Gates (Elizabeth Stuart Phelps) 366
Beyond the Melting Pot (Daniel Moynihan and Nathan Glazer) 513
Beza, Theodore 547
Bhagavad-Gita As It Is (Hindu text and commentary) 316
Bhagavad Gita (Hindu text) 288, 289
Bhajan, Yogi 291, 622
Bhaktipada, Kirtanananda Swami 316
bhakti yoga 316, 698
Bible *see also* biblical interpretation
   Bible schools 68
   creationism 170
   evolution 229, 230
   feminist theology 234
   fundamentalism (Protestant) 249
   Fundamentals, The 251
   heresy 285
   inerrancy 312, 313
   liberalism, theological 359
   Lutheran Church—Missouri Synod 371
   Lutheranism 372
   Neo-orthodoxy 456
   Pittsburgh Platform 511
   Presbyterian Church (U.S.A.) 525
   presbyterianism 527
   Princeton Theology 530
   Puritanism 534
   Reformation 546
   Reformed Tradition 551
   restoration movement 554, 556
   science and religion 594
   Scottish Common Sense Realism 600
   segregation 608
   slavery 624
   Sojourners Fellowship 633
   Woman's Bible, The 731
   Worldwide Church of God 740
Bible Against Slavery, The (Theodore Dwight Weld) 3, 71
Bible Institute (Houston, Texas) 48
Bible Institute (Topeka, Kansas) 42
Bible Institute of Los Angeles 204

"Bible *Is* a Textbook of Science, The" (Henry M. Morris) 170
Bible Presbyterian Church 118, 527
Bible schools **67–68**
Bible societies **68–70**, 70
biblical interpretation **70–73**
   dispensationalism 184
   evangelicalism 227, 228
   feminist theology 234
   fundamentalism (Protestant) 248, 249
   liberalism, theological 359
bicentennial celebration (1976) 118, 119, 417
Bickerdyke, Mary Ann 140
Bierce, Ambrose 366
Bigelow, William Sturgis 87
"Big Fellow in the Sky" (song) 146
Big Foot (Lakota leader) 258
Big Sandy, Texas 741
Bill for Establishing Religious Freedom (Virginia) 123, 218, 705
Bill of Rights 123, 160, 218 *see also* First Amendment
Billy Budd (Herman Melville) 365
Billy Graham Evangelistic Association 228
"biocentrism" 180
biofeedback 461
Bioregionalism 181
Birmingham, Alabama 13, 136, 138, 640
birth control *see* contraception
Birth of a Nation, The (film) 354
Bishop Hill (utopian community) 154
"Bishops' Program on Social Reconstruction" (John Ryan) 433
bison (buffalo) 258, 448, 449
Black, Hugo 121
Black Americans *see* African-American religion
Blackfoot Indians 448
Black Israelites 74
Black Jews 12, **73–74**
blacklisting 153
"Black Manifesto" 13
black mass 587
Black Muslims *see* Nation of Islam
Black Panther Party 138, 652
Black Power 13, 138, 652
Black Star shipping lines 12
Blair, James 704
Blavatsky, Helena Petrovna (1831–1891) **74–76**, *75*
   Buddhism 87
   Hinduism 290
   theosophy 664, 665

Bliss, William Dwight Porter 631
blue laws 580
B.M.N.A. *see* Buddhist Mission of North America
B'nai Jeshurun (Cincinnati, Ohio synagogue) 335, 543
B'nai Jeshurun (New York City synagogue) 487
B'nei Akivah (Zionist youth organization) 552
boarding schools 45
Boardman, William Edwin 287, 288, 296, 297
Bodhidharma (Zen master) 749
Boehm, John Philip 255, 687
Boehm, Martin 688
Boff, Leonardo 361
Bogardus, Everardus 464
Bohemia 418
Bole Maru (Native American movement) 446
Boll, Robert H. 132
Bolsheviks 152, 453
Bonhoeffer, Dietrich 179
Bonino, Jose Miguez 361
Bonney, Charles C. 739
Book of Common Prayer (Episcopal Church) 212, 214
Book of Common Prayer, The (Anglican Church) 31
Book of Mormon **76–77**, 127, 128, 554
Book of Shadows (Doreen Valiente) 458
Booth, Ballington and Maud 583
Booth, Evangeline 583
Booth, William and Catherine Mumford 297, 582–583
"born again" experience 508
Borresen, Kari 234
Boston, Massachusetts
   Antinomian Controversy 37, 38
   Christian Science 120
   Congregationalism 156
   Ethical Culture 220
   Great Awakening 268, 269
   Huguenots 303
   Nation of Islam (Black Muslims) 428, 429
   nativism 452
   preachers, Protestant 519
   Quakers 243
   Second Great Awakening 604
   Social Gospel 631
   temperance 661
   transcendentalism 673
   Unitarian Universalist Association 685
   Young Women's Christian Association (YWCA) 747
Boston Massacre (1770) 25

Boston Missionary Training School 67
Boston Platform 156
botanicas (retail shops) 586, 706
Boudinot, Elias 69
Bound, Nicholas 580
Bowers, Henry 34
Bowne, Borden Parker 689
Boyd, Richard Henry 432
Bradford, William (1590–1657) **77–78**, 364, 509
Bradstreet, Anne 364–365
"Brahma" (Ralph Waldo Emerson poem) 289
Brahman (Hindu impersonal Absolute) 698
Brainerd, David 406
brainwashing 36
Branch Davidians 36
Brandeis, Louis 753
Bray, Thomas 632
breathwork 461
Brent family 562
Bresee, Phineas Franklin 130, 297
Brethren Church (Progressive Dunkers) 129
Brethren Volunteer Service 130
Brewster, William 509
Bridgeport (Connecticut) University 682
Briggs, Charles Augustus (1841–1913) **78–80**, *79*
   biblical interpretation 72
   heresy 285
   inerrancy 313
   Presbyterian Church (U.S.A.) 525
British and Foreign Bible Society 69
British North America *see* colonial period
British Student Volunteer Missionary Union 652
broadcasting, religious *see* electronic church
Brook Farm (Massachusetts utopian community) 154, 560, 673
Brooklyn, New York 278, 279, 326
Brooks, John P. 296
Brooks, Phillips (1835–1893) *80*, **80–81**, 213, 521
Brotherhood of Sleeping Car Porters 137
Brown, Olympia 693
Brownson, Orestes Augustus (1803–1876) *81*, **81–83**, 673
Brown University (Providence, Rhode Island) 20, 58, 59
Brown vs. the Board of Education (1954) 134, 137
Bruderhofs (Hutterite colonies) 308

Bryan, William Jennings
 (1860–1925) *83*, **83–84**
  biblical interpretation 72
  creationism 170
  evolution 229–230
  inerrancy 314
  peace reform 497
  science and religion 595, 596
  Scopes trial 598, 599
Bryant, William Cullen 643
Bubba Free John (Franklin
 Jones) 291
Buchman, Frank Nathan Daniel
 (1878–1961) **84–85**
Bucknell University (Lewisburg,
 Pennsylvania) 59
Buddha's Universal Church (San
 Francisco, California) 86
Buddhism **85–89**, *90 see also*
 Kennett, Jiyu; Nichiren Shoshu
 Academy; Trungpa, Chogyam
  Beat movement 62
  communitarianism 155
  feminist theology 234
  pluralism 514
  World's Parliament of
   Religions 739
Buddhist Bible (Dwight
 Goddard) 89
Buddhist Brotherhood of
 America 90
Buddhist Catechism (Henry Steel
 Olcott) 87
Buddhist Churches of America
 (B.C.A.) 86, **89–90**
Buddhist Mission of North
 America (B.M.N.A.) 86, 90
Buddhist Promoting Foundation
 90
Buddhist Vihara Society
 (Washington, D.C.) 89
buffalo *see* bison
Buffalo, New York 745
Bulgarian Americans 482, 485
Bullinger, Heinrich 547
Bulwer-Lytton, Sir Edward 576
Bureau of Indian Affairs 438
Bureau of Land Management 24
Burke, John J. 433, 567
Burma 407
Burned-Over District **90–92**,
 127, 602, 604, 643
Burnouf, Eugene 87
Bush, George 119, 574, 702
Bushnell, Horace (1802–1876)
 92, **92–93**, 141, 198, 199
Byzantine Empire 481

C

cabildos (socio-religious clubs)
 586
Cabrini, Francesca Xavier
 (1850–1917) **94**
Caddo Indians 257

Cahensly, Peter Paul 94
Cahenslyism **94–95**
"Cain, curse of" 608
Caitanya (Indian saint) 292, 316
Calabasas, California 293
California *see also specific city*
 (e.g., San Francisco)
  Buddhism 86
  Church of the Nazarene 130
  Ghost Dance 257
  Islam 321
  Jesus movement 328
  National Baptist Convention
   of America, Inc. 432
  Native American Church 439
  Native American religions:
   Inter-montane/California
   444, 445
  nativism 454
  New Spain 467, 469, 470
  Reformed Church in America
   550
  Roman Catholicism 561,
   564, 565
  spiritualism 643
  Unification Church 682
  utopianism 695
California Gold Rush (1849)
 445
Calvary Episcopal Church
 (Pittsburgh) 204
Calvert, Cecilius (1606–1675)
 (Second Lord Baltimore) *95*,
 95–96
  colonial period 147
  establishment, religious 217
  Maryland 385, 386
Calvert, George (First Lord
 Baltimore) 385, 386, 562
Calvert, Leonard 385
Calvin, John
  Calvinism 96
  election 202, 203
  German Reformed Church
   255
  Huguenots 302
  justification 342, 343
  Reformation 547
  Reformed Tradition 550
  United Church of Christ 687
Calvin College and Theological
 Seminary (Grand Rapids,
 Michigan) 117, 229
Calvinism **96–99**
  Revolutionary War 25
  Arminianism 40
  election 202
  Enlightenment 209, 211
  Higher Christian Life
   movement 288
  justification 343
  Scottish Common Sense
   Realism 600
Cambodian Americans 52, 312

Cambridge Platform **99–100**,
 155
Campbell, Alexander
 (1788–1866) **101–103**, *102*
  baptism 56
  Book of Mormon 77
  Christadelphians 113
  Christian Church (Disciples of
   Christ) 114
  Churches of Christ 131
  primitivism 528, 529
  restoration movement 555,
   556
Campbell, Thomas 70, 131,
 554, 555
Campbell, Will D. 150, 151
Camp Creek, North Carolina
 124, 503
Camp Fire Girls 747
camp meetings *100*, **100–101**
  Cane Ridge revival 103
  counterculture 168
  frontier 245
  Methodists 402
  preachers, Protestant 520
  Second Great Awakening 602
Canada 25, 308, 463, 643
Cane Ridge (Kentucky) revival
 103
  baptism 56
  camp meetings 101
  frontier 245
  preachers, Protestant 520
  restoration movement 555
  Second Great Awakening 603
Cannon, Katie G. 234, 730
Canons (Synod of Dort) 97, 202
Cantwell v. Connecticut (1940)
 123, 160, 238, 240
Capers, William 532
capitalism 152
Caribbean region 15, 312, 432
Carlisle Industrial Training
 School 45
Carmichael, Stokely 652
Carnegie, Andrew 262, 497,
 733
Carnegie, Dale 471, 514
Carnell, Edward John 228
Caro, Joseph 157, 486
Carolinas **103–105**, 224, 398
 see also North Carolina; South
 Carolina
CARP *see* Collegiate Association
 for the Research of Principles
Carpatho-Russian Orthodox 272
Carroll, Charles 563
Carroll, John (1735–1815)
 105–107
  anti-Catholicism 32
  Baltimore, Councils of 54
  episcopacy 212
  Roman Catholicism 563, 564
Carter, Jimmy 61, 138
Carthage, Illinois 128

Cartwright, Peter (1785–1872)
 107, 603
Carus, Paul 87
Cashwell, Gaston B. 503
*Catechism of Christian Doctrine,
 A* (Roman Catholic Church) 54
Cathars (medieval sect) 154
Catherine of Aragon 30, 547
Catholic Congress (Chicago,
 1893) 27
"Catholic Hour, The" (radio
 show) 204, 572
"Catholic Left" 701
Catholic University of America
 (Washington, D.C.) 55, 574
Catholic Worker (newspaper)
 108, 570, 572
Catholic Worker movement
 108, 569, 572, 701
Catonsville, Maryland 701
CBN *see* Christian Broadcasting
 Network
CBN University 205
CCAR *see* Central Conference
 of American Rabbis
celibacy 614, 616, 617, 618
Central American immigrants
 312, 454, 467, 470, 561
Central Conference of American
 Rabbis (CCAR) **108–109**
  Cold War 145
  Judaism 338
  Pittsburgh Platform 511
  Reform Judaism 543, 544
  Zionism 753, 755
Ceylon *see* Sri Lanka
"Challenge of Peace: God's
 Promise and Our Response,
 The" (Roman Catholic pastoral
 letter) 435
Chaney, James 138, 651, 652
channeling 461
Channing, William Ellery
 (1780–1842) *109*, **109–110**,
 683, 684
Channing Jr., William Ellery 673
chaplains, military 140–141,
 736, 737
Chapman, John 657
Chapter of Perfection 575
charismatic movement
 110–112, 504
Charles I (king of England)
 386, 534, 562
Charles II (king of England)
 217, 500
Charleston, South Carolina
  African-American religion 10
  Carolinas 104
  Huguenots 303
  Judaism 334, 335
  South 637
Chauncy, Charles (1705–1787)
 112, **112–113**
  Arminianism 41

Great Awakening 269
Half-way Covenant 275
New Lights/Old Lights 464
Unitarian Controversy 682
Unitarian Universalist
    Association 684
Chautauqua, New York 101
Chautauqua Assembly 655
Cherokee Indians 23, 419, 442,
    443, 444
Cherry, Prophet F. S. 73
Cheyenne Indians 24, 135, 257,
    450
Chicago, Illinois
    African-American religion 12
    Bahá'í Faith 52
    Black Jews 74
    Ethical Culture 220
    Greek Orthodox Archdiocese
        of North and South America
        270
    Hinduism 293
    Islam 320
    Moorish Science Temple 415
    Nation of Islam (Black
        Muslims) 427, 429
    Nichiren Shoshu Academy
        472
    Roman Catholicism 564
    Sikhism 622
    Southern Christian
        Leadership Conference
        (SCLC) 640
    spiritualism 644
Chicago Evangelization Society
    67
Chicago-Lambeth Quadrilateral
    214
"Chicago Statement on Biblical
    Inerrancy, The" (Lutheran
    Church's Missouri Synod) 314
Child, Lydia Maria 643
childhood 198, 654, 655
China 407
Chinese Americans 85, 86, 312
Chinese Exclusion Act (1882)
    85, 453
Chinigchinich (Native American
    spirit) 445
Chippewa Indians see
    Anishenabeg
Chiricahua Apache Indians 451
chosenness 542
Christ, Carol 235
Christadelphians 113–114
Christ and Culture (H. Richard
    Niebuhr) 256
Christian and Missionary
    Alliance 298
Christian Association of
    Washington 555
Christian Beacon (newspaper)
    118
Christian Broadcasting Network
    (CBN) 119, 205

Christian Century (journal) 34,
    115, 737
Christian Church (Disciples of
    Christ) 114–115 see also
    Churches of Christ
    baptism 56
    ecumenical movement 195
    eschatology 216
    fundamentalism (Protestant)
        249
    Methodists 402
    people
        Ames, Edward Scribner
            28–29, 411
        Campbell, Alexander see
            Campbell, Alexander
        Lipscomb, David 131,
            363–364, 556
        Stone, Barton Warren see
            Stone, Barton Warren
    restoration movement 554,
        555, 557
    South 636
Christian Churches and
    Churches of Christ
    (Independent) 131, 556
Christian Coalition 119
Christian Connection 556
Christian Crusade Newspaper
    (journal) 118
Christian Holiness Association
    296
Christianity see also specific
    churches; specific denominations;
    specific topics (e.g., justification)
    assimilation and resistance,
        Native American 44
    feminist theology 233
    missions, foreign 405
    pluralism 513, 514
    slavery 623, 624
    womanist theology 731
Christianity and Crisis
    (magazine) 256, 738
Christianity and Liberalism (J.
    Gresham Machen) 314
Christianity and the Social Crisis
    (Walter Rauschenbusch) 631
Christianity Today (magazine)
    228
Christian Manifesto, A (Francis
    Schaeffer) 605
Christian Methodist Episcopal
    Church (C.M.E.) 115–116,
    403
Christian Nationalist Crusade
    117
Christian Philosopher, The
    (Cotton Mather) 209
Christian Reconstructionism see
    dominion theology
Christian Recorder (newspaper)
    15
Christian Reformed Church 99,
    116–117, 550, 552

Christian Right 117–120
Christian Science 120–121, 470
Christian Science Monitor
    (newspaper) 120
Christian Science Theological
    Seminary 470
Christian's Secret of a Happy
    Life, The (Hannah Smith) 287
Christian unity see ecumenical
    movement
Christian World Liberation
    Front 328
Christ in the Camp (John
    William Jones) 141, 369
Christmas Conference
    (Baltimore, Maryland, 1784)
    401, 688, 716
Christ Orthodox Catholic
    Exarchate of the Americas and
    the Eastern Hemisphere 480
Christ Seminary-Seminex 371
Chumash Indians 445
church and state, relationship
    between 121–124 see also
    establishment, religious;
    Toleration, Act of (Maryland);
    voluntaryism
    Cambridge Platform 99
    Christian Right 119
    Church of the Brethren
        (Dunkers) 129
    Constitution, U.S. 160, 161
    Jefferson, Thomas 324, 325
    Longinqua Oceani 368
    Madison, James 375, 376,
        377
    Mann, Horace 383
    Murray, John Courtney 425,
        426
    Roman Catholicism 571
    Sabbatarianism 580
Church and the Second Sex, The
    (Mary Daly) 234
Churches of Christ 114,
    131–133, 556
church government and
    organization see
    Congregationalism; episcopacy;
    presbyterianism; Saybrook
    Platform; trusteeism
Church of Christ (Scientist) see
    Christian Science
Church of England see
    Anglicanism
Church of God (Anderson,
    Indiana) 297
Church of God (Black Jews) 73
Church of God (Cleveland,
    Tennessee) 124–125, 503, 630
Church of God Evangel (journal)
    125
Church of God in Christ
    (COGIC) 125–127, 503, 505
Church of God International
    740

Church of God of Prophecy
    125, 503
Church of Jesus Christ, Christian
    608
Church of Jesus Christ of
    Latter-day Saints 127–128,
    128 see also Book of Mormon;
    Smith Jr., Joseph; Young,
    Brigham
    Burned-Over District 91
    Communism 152
    eschatology 216
    frontier 245
    premillennialism 523
    sexuality 614
Church of Lukumi Babalu Aye v.
    City of Hialeah, The (1993)
    238
Church of Satan 586, 587
Church of Scientology see
    Scientology
Church of Sweden (Lutheran)
    147
Church of the Brethren
    (Dunkers) 128–130, 139,
    211, 223, 738
Church of the Higher Life 470
Church of the Nazarene
    130–131
    Holiness movement 295, 297
    Methodists 403
    perfectionism 506
    sanctification 584
    Wesleyan tradition 717
Church of the New Jerusalem
    657
Church of the United Brethren
    in Christ see United Methodist
    Church
Church Peace Union 733
"church-shopping" 91
Church World Service 436
Cincinnati, Ohio 293, 297,
    531, 564
circuit riders 519, 716
City of God, The (Augustine of
    Hippo) 613
civic virtue 606
civil religion 133–135
    American Revolution/
        Revolutionary War 25
    atheism 47
    Cold War 144
    Constitution, U.S. 160
    Freemasonry 241
Civil Rights Act (1964) 138,
    640
civil rights movement 135–139
    African-American religion 12
    American Indian Religious
        Freedom Act (AIRFA) 23
    assimilation and resistance,
        Native American 46
    Committee of Southern
        Churchmen 151

counterculture 167
Hinduism 290
immigration 311
Koinonia Farm 352
Ku Klux Klan 355
people
  Abernathy, David Ralph 2, 3
  King Jr., Martin Luther
    347, 348, 349
  Malcolm X (Malcolm Little)
    379, 380
  Powell Jr., Adam Clayton
    516, 517
  preachers, Protestant 522
  Progressive National Baptist
    Convention, Inc. 531
  Reform Judaism 545
sexuality 615
South 637
Southern Christian
  Leadership Conference
  (SCLC) 639, 640
Student Nonviolent
  Coordinating Committee
  651, 652
Civil War, U.S. (1861–1865)
  139–142
African-American religion 10
African Methodist Episcopal
  Church 15
American Baptist Churches in
  the U.S.A. 20
anti-Catholicism 34
Baptists 59
Christian Church (Disciples of
  Christ) 114
civil rights movement 136
literature and Christianity 366
New School/Old School 466
presbyterianism 527
Roman Catholicism 566
slavery 624
South 637
Clansman, The (Thomas Dixon)
  354
Clarke, James Freeman
  (1810–1888) 142–143, 289,
  673, 684
Clarke, John 57
Clarke, William Newton
  (1841–1912) 20, 143
Clay, Cassius see Ali, Muhammad
"Clean Up America" campaign
  417
"clearing" (Scientology) 596
Clemens, Samuel see Twain,
  Mark
Clement VII, Pope 30
Clement XIV, Pope 327
Cleveland, Ohio 661, 687
Cleveland, Tennessee 125, 503
Cleveland, Grover 569
Clifton, Richard 509
Clinton, Iowa 34
Clinton, Bill 418

Clymer, R. Swinburne 576
C.M.E. see Christian Methodist
  Episcopal Church
Codde, Peter 480
COFO see Council of Federated
  Organizations
COGIC see Church of God in
  Christ
Coke, Thomas (1747–1814)
  143–144, 212, 401, 688, 716
Colby College (Waterville,
  Maine) 20, 59
Colchester, Connecticut 486
Cold War 144–147, 152, 497
Coleridge, Samuel Taylor 673
Colgate, William 69
Colgate University (Hamilton,
  New York) 20
Collegiate Association for the
  Research of Principles (CARP)
  681
Collegiate Church (New York
  City) 549
Collier, John M. 23, 45
colonial period 147–148
  African-American religion 7
  anti-Semitism 38
  Carolinas see Carolinas
  church and state, relationship
    between 122
  colonial period 147
  education, public school 198
  Jesuits 327
  Maryland 385–386
  Pennsylvania 500–501
  Roman Catholicism 562
  sexuality 613
  slavery 623
  Society for the Propagation of
    the Gospel in Foreign Parts
    632
  South 636
  temperance 661
  Virginia 702–705
Colored Cumberland
  Presbyterian Church 11
Colored Methodist Episcopal
  Church 10, 403
Colored Primitive Baptists 11
Color Purple, The (Alice Walker)
  367
Columbia University (New York
  City) 39, 632
Columbus, Ohio 225
Columbus, Christopher
  (1451–1506) 148–150
  American Indian Religious
    Freedom Act (AIRFA) 22
  anti-Semitism 38
  Judaism 334
  Native American religions 440
  New Spain 467
Comanche Indians 23, 257,
  437, 438
Comfort, Alex 615

Commandment Keepers
  Congregation of the Living
  God 73
Commentary (magazine) 754
Commentary on Romans (Karl
  Barth) 456
Commission on Faith and Order
  733
Committee of One Hundred
  734
Committee of Southern
  Churchmen 150–151
Committee on Faith and Order
  732
Committee on Life and Work
  732
Common Faith, A (John Dewey)
  607
Common Sense philosophy see
  Scottish Common Sense
  Realism
Commonweal (periodical) 572
communal marriage 614
Communism 151–153 see also
  anti-Communism
  Orthodox Christianity 482
  peace reform 497
  Roman Catholicism 570
  Vietnam War 700
Communist Party of the United
  States 152
communitarianism 153–155
  see also Shakers
  Burned-Over District 91
  Catholic Worker movement
    108
  Communism 152
  Hutterites 307, 308
community 13, 14, 154, 168
Comparison of the Institutions of
  Moses with Those of the Hindoos
  and Other Ancient Nations, A
  (Joseph Priestley) 86, 288
"Compensation" (Ralph Waldo
  Emerson essay) 289
"complex marriage" 506
Comstock, Anthony 746
Conch, Oklahoma 450
Concordia Seminary (St. Louis,
  Missouri) 371
Confederacy see Civil War
Conference of Black Churchmen
  13, 138
Conference on Faith and Order
  (Lausanne, Switzerland, 1927)
  195
confirmation (rite) 213
Confucianism 85, 739
Congregational American
  Missionary Association 410
Congregational Christian
  Churches 686
Congregationalism 155–156
  see also United Church of Christ

American Baptist Churches in
  the U.S.A. 19
American Revolution/
  Revolutionary War 26
Baptists 57
Burned-Over District 91
Cambridge Platform 99, 100
colonial period 147, 148
conversion 161
ecumenical movement 194,
  195
establishment, religious 216,
  217, 218
Evangelical United Front 226
Great Awakening 269
Half-way Covenant 275
Haystack Prayer Meeting 281
Higher Christian Life
  movement 287
Holiness movement 296
missions, foreign 407
National Council of Churches
  435
nativism 452
New Divinity 462
New Lights/Old Lights see
  New Lights/Old Lights
people
  Abbott, Lyman 1
  Beecher, Henry Ward
    62–64, 63, 520
  Beecher, Lyman see
    Beecher, Lyman
  Bellamy, Joseph 66–67, 462
  Dwight, Timothy 191,
    191–192, 211, 226, 453,
    602
  Edwards, Jonathan see
    Edwards, Jonathan
  Hopkins, Samuel 98, 226,
    300–301, 301, 462
  Mather, Cotton see Mather,
    Cotton
  Mather, Increase 161, 275,
    389–391, 390
  Stoddard, Solomon 161,
    646–647
  Strong, Josiah 221, 222,
    631, 649–651, 650
  Taylor, Nathaniel William
    603, 659, 659–660
Plan of Union 511, 512
Presbyterian Church (U.S.A.)
  524
presbyterianism 527
Puritanism 533, 534
Saybrook Platform 587
Second Great Awakening 602
Social Gospel 631
Sunday school movement 655
Unitarian Controversy see
  Unitarian Controversy
Congregation Fide (Roman
  Catholic office) 361
Congress, U.S. 122, 238

Congress of Racial Equality (CORE) 651
Connecticut *see also specific cities (e.g.,* New Haven)
American Baptist Churches in the U.S.A. 19
Baptists 58
Congregationalism 156
Constitution, U.S. 160
establishment, religious 216, 218
Great Awakening 268, 269
Half-way Covenant 275, 276
missions, home 409
New Divinity 462
Saybrook Platform 587
Second Great Awakening 602
voluntaryism 707, 708
Connecticut Missionary Society 409
Connecticut Society for the Reformation of Morals 661
consciousness, transformation of 461
Conservative Baptist Association 21, 60
Conservative Congregational Christian Conference 156, 687
Conservative Judaism **156–159** *see also* United Synagogue of Conservative Judaism
immigration 309
Judaism 337, 338, 339, 340
Zionism 754, 755
Consistent Calvinism 98
Constantine (Roman emperor) 216, 580
Constantinides, Michael 272
Constitution of the United States **159–161** *see also specific amendments (e.g.,* First Amendment)
anti-Catholicism 32
anti-Semitism 38
atheism 46, 47
church and state, relationship between 121, 123
civil religion 134
education, public school 199
establishment, religious 218
Judaism 335
secularism 606
Consultation on Church Union 115, 690
"contextualization" 361
Continental Army 210
Continental Congress 26, 210, 563
contraception 573, 614
conversion **161–162,** 275, 557
Conwell, Russell Herman (1843–1925) **162–163,** *163,* 262
Cook, James 447
Coolidge, Calvin 34, 454

Cooper, James Fenimore 643
Copernicus, Nicolaus 594
CORE *see* Congress of Racial Equality
corporativism 569
correspondences, theory of 657
Corrigan, Michael 27, 567
Cotton, John (1584–1652) 37, 99, **163–165,** *164*
Coucouzes, Iakovos (1911–) **165,** 272
Coughlin, Charles Edward (1891–1979) **165–166**
Christian Right 117–118
electronic church 204
Roman Catholicism 570
World War II 736, 737
Coulomb, Emma 665
Council of All Beings 181
Council of Federated Organizations (COFO) 651
counterculture **166–169**
anti-cult movement 35
Bahá'í Faith 52
Deep Ecology 181
Hinduism 291
International Society for Krishna Consciousness 316
Jesus movement 328
secular humanism 605
sexuality 615
Vietnam War 701
Counter-Reformation 327, 418
Court of Indian Offenses 23, 449
Covenant, the Sword, and the Arm of the Lord (C.S.A.) 608
"covenant of grace" 37
Covenant Theology 169
Cramer, Malinda 470
creationism 124, **169–171,** 230, 596
Creation Research Society 596
Creation Science Research Center 596
Cree Indians 442
Creek Indians *see* Muskogee (Creek) Indians
"creole" religions *see* Santería; Vodou
Crisis (journal) 137
crisis theology *see* Neo-orthodoxy
Critique of the Gotha Program (Karl Marx) 152
Cross and the Flag (magazine) 117
cross burning 354
"Cross Fire Way" (peyote ritual) 438
Crowdy, William 73
Crow Indians 449
Crucible, The (Arthur Miller play) 581
Cruise, Tom 597

Crummell, Alexander (1819–1898) **171–172**
Crystal Cathedral (Garden Grove, California) 206, 515, 522
crystal healing 461
C.S.A. *see* Covenant, the Sword, and the Arm of the Lord
Cuban Americans 467, 561, 586
Cuban Missile Crisis (1962) 146
cults *see* anti-cult movement
Cumberland Presbyterian Church 524, 527, 528, 603
Cummins, George David 213
Cuomo, Mario 573
Curran, Charles 574, 575
Cushing, Richard James (1895–1970) **172–174**
Custer, George Armstrong 135
Cutler, Timothy 268, 632
Cutting Through Spiritual Materialism (Chogyam Trungpa) 88
Czech Americans 47

D

Dabbs, James McBride 151
Dabney, Robert Lewis (1820–1898) **175,** 369
Dahl, Robert A. 513
Daily Examiner (newspaper) 368
Dakotas, Canadian 258
Dalai Lama 88
Dale, Thomas 704
Daly, Mary (1928–) **175–176,** 234, 615, 731
"Danger of an Unconverted Ministry, The" (Gilbert Tennent sermon) 268, 524
Danish American Evangelical Lutheran Church 225
Danish Americans 20, 224, 373
Danville, Virginia 651
Darby, John Nelson 184, 185, 523
Darrow, Clarence 48, 72, 596, 598, 599
Darwin, Charles
creationism 169
evangelicalism 227, 228
evolution 229, 230
fundamentalism (Protestant) 249
Gospel of Wealth 262
inerrancy 313, 314
nativism 453
science and religion 595
Scopes trial 598
secularism 607
Davenport, James 269
Davenport, John 275
David, Christian 418

David Lipscomb College (Nashville, Tennessee) 132
Davies, Samuel (1723–1761) **176–177,** 217
Davis, Andrew Jackson (1826–1910) **177–178,** 400, 643, 644
Davis, John W. 34
Dawn Horse Fellowship 292
Day, Dorothy (1897–1980) 108, **178–179,** 569, 572
Dayton, Tennessee *see* Scopes Trial
Dearborn Independent (newspaper) 39
Death of God, The (Gabriel Vahanian) 179
death of God theology **179–180**
Deborah (periodical) 335
Declaration of Independence (1776)
American Revolution/ Revolutionary War 26
civil religion 134, 135
Enlightenment 210
Episcopal Church 213
Roman Catholicism 563
Declaration on Religious Freedom *(Dignitatis Humanae)* (Roman Catholic Church) 697
Declaration on the Relationship of the Church to Non-Christian Religions *(Nostra Aetate)* (Roman Catholic Church) 697
Dedham decision (1820) 218, 683
Deep Ecology **180–182,** 459
Defender Magazine (journal) 117
Defenders of the Christian Faith 117
Deists 123, 210, 606, 705
Delaware 14, 19, 58, 216, 632
De La Warr, Lord 704
Democracy in America (Alexis de Tocqueville) 707
Democratic National Convention (Chicago, 1968) 168, 702
Democratic Party 34, 568
Democratic-Republican Party 452
Democratic Review (periodical) 381
"demon rum" 661
Denominationalism 654
Denver, Colorado 293
Department of Defense 24
depravity, human
Calvinism 97
Christian Science 121
Covenant Theology 169
heresy 284

literature and Christianity
365, 366
New Divinity 462
Reformed Tradition 551
revivalism 558
spiritualism 644
deprogramming 36, 292, 682
Descartes, René 209
Descent of Man, The (Charles
Darwin) 227, 595
"Deseret" 128
Detroit, Michigan 12, 415,
427, 564, 644
Dev, Guru 672
Dewey, John (1859–1952)
182–183, 199, 304, 607
Dharma Bums (Jack Kerouac)
62, 750
Dharmapala, Anagarika
(1864–1933) 87, **183–184,**
739, 740
Dial (magazine) 87, 673
dialectical theology *see*
Neo-orthodoxy
dialectics 457
*Dianetics, The Modern Science of
Mental Health* (L. Ron
Hubbard) 596
"diaspora" 334
Dickinson, Emily 366
Diderot, Denis 209
Diegueno Indians 445
dietary laws 157, 159, 337, 612
Dietrich, John H. 22
Diggers (San Francisco street
actors) 168
Disciples of Christ *see* Christian
Church (Disciples of Christ)
*Discipline (Methodist Episcopal
Church)* 688
disestablishment 217, 218
dispensationalism **184–185,**
215, 248, 249, 523 *see also*
rapture
divination 586
Divine, Father
(1877/82?–1965) 11, 12,
185–186
divine justice, doctrine of 169
Divine Light Mission 291
Divine Principle, The (Sun
Myung Moon) 681
Divine Science 470
Dixon, Amzi Clarence
(1854–1925) 185, **186–187,**
251
Dixon, Thomas 354
Doane, George Washington 31
Doctrine and Covenants
(Mormon text) 77
"doctrine of the spirituality of
the church" 532
*Doctrine of Transcendental
Magic, The* (Eliphas Levi)
575–576

Dodge, Grace 747
Dodge, William E. 222
Does Civilization Need Religion?
(Reinhold Niebuhr) 456
Dogen (Zen master) 749
dokusan (Zen) 749
Domestic and Foreign
Missionary Society 409
dominion theology 118
"Don't Sit Under the Apple
Tree With Anyone Else But
Me" (song) 738
Douay Translation (Bible) 71
Doubleday, Abner 664
Douglass, Frederick *139*
abolitionism 3
African-American religion 13
African Methodist Episcopal
Zion Church 16
civil rights movement 136
slavery 624
Dove (ship) 385
"doves" 701
"do your own thing" 167
Dresden firebombing (1945)
570
Dresser, Julius and Annetta 470
Drew, Timothy (Noble Drew
Ali) (1886–1929) **187–188,**
320, 415, 427
Dreyfus, Alfred 752
Drinan, Robert 327
dry laws 661
Du Bois, W. E. B. (1868–1963)
11, 12, 137, **188–190,** 432
DuBose, William Porcher
(1836–1918) *190,* **190–191,**
213
"due process" clause
(Fourteenth Amendment) 240
Dunkers *see* Church of the
Brethren (Dunkers)
Duquesne University
(Pittsburgh, Pennsylvania) 111
Durham, William 43, 504
Dutch Americans 116, 117,
372, 550
Dutch Reformed Church
Arminianism 40
Calvinism 98
church and state, relationship
between 122
colonial period 147
Huguenots 303
missions, home 409
New Netherland 464, 465
Pietism 508
Reformation 547, 548
Reformed Tradition 551
Dutch West India Company 464
Dwight, Timothy (1752–1817)
191, **191–192**
Enlightenment 211
Evangelical United Front 226
nativism 453

Second Great Awakening 602
Dyer, Mary (1591–1660)
192–193

E

Earth First! (environmental
group) 181
Earth Lodge religion 446
Eastern European Jews
Central Conference of
American Rabbis 109
Conservative Judaism 158
immigration 309
Judaism 334, 337, 338
Orthodox Judaism 487, 489
Reform Judaism 542, 544,
545
Zionism 752
Eastern Orthodoxy *see*
Orthodox Christianity
Eastern religions *see also* Asian
religions
Bahá'í Faith 51–53, 321
Buddhism *see* Buddhism
Buddhist Churches of
America (B.C.A.) 86, 89–90
Hinduism *see* Hinduism
International Society for
Krishna Consciousness
(ISKCON) 35, 292, 293,
316–317
Islam *see* Islam
Nichiren Shoshu Academy
(N.S.A.) 86, 471–472
people
Blavatsky, Helena Petrovna
74–76, *75,* 87, 290, 664,
665
Dharmapala, Anagarika 87,
183–184, 739, 740
Hunt, Ernest Shinkaku 90,
304–305
Kennett, Jiyu 89, **346–347,**
750
Olcott, Henry Steel 87,
290, **478–480,** *479,* 664
Prabhupada, Abhay
Charanaravinda
Bhaktivedanta Swami 292,
316, **518**
Suzuki, Daisetz Teitaro 87,
89, **656–657,** 740, 749
Trungpa, Chogyam 88,
674–675, *675*
Vivekananda, Swami 290,
291, 609, 698, **705–706,**
739, 740
Watts, Alan Wilson 87,
712–713, 749
Self-Realization Fellowship
(S.R.F.) 291, 609
Sikhism *621,* 621–623
Transcendental Meditation
35, 292, 672

Vedanta Society 290, 698,
740
World's Parliament of
Religions (Chicago, 1893)
see World's Parliament of
Religions
Zen 61, 88, 740, 749–750
Eastern Rite Catholics 482,
484, 485
Easton, Pennsylvania 487
Ebenezer Baptist Church
(Atlanta, Georgia) 639
"ecclesia" 113
"ecocentrism" 180
"ecological consciousness" 180
economic justice 138, 435
"Economic Justice for All:
Catholic Social Teaching and
the U.S. Economy" (Roman
Catholic pastoral letter) 435
ecumenical movement **194–196**
Evangelical Alliance 221, 222
Hinduism 293
Moravians 419
Mott, John Raleigh 420
National Council of Churches
435, 436, 437
Neo-orthodoxy 458
Orthodox Christianity 483
Orthodox Church in America
485
secularism 607
World Council of Churches
732, 733
Eddy, Mary Baker (1821–1910)
120, *196,* **196–198,** 470–471,
732
Edict of Nantes (1598) 302–303
Edison, Thomas 664
education *see also* education,
public school; Sunday school
movement
assimilation and resistance,
Native American 45
church and state, relationship
between 123
ethnicity 221
evangelicalism 227
Jesuits 327
education, public school
198–200
biblical interpretation 70
church and state, relationship
between 124
evolution 230
Mann, Horace 382, 383
Roman Catholicism 571
Edward VI (king of England)
547
Edwards, Jonathan (1703–1758)
200, **200–201,** 267
conversion 161
election 203
Enlightenment 209
Great Awakening 268

literature and Christianity 365
missions, foreign 406
New Divinity 462
New Lights/Old Lights 463
postmillennialism 515
preachers, Protestant 519
revivalism 558
science and religion 594, 595
Second Great Awakening 603
United Church of Christ 686
Wesleyan tradition 715
Edwards Jr., Jonathan 462
Effendi, Shoghi 51, 52
Eiberg, Amy 159
Eighteenth Amendment 661,
662
Einhorn, David (1809–1879)
201–202, 336, 487, 543, 544
Eisai (Zen master) 749
Eisenhower, Dwight D. 23,
146, 521
Elan Vital (Hindu mission) 291
ELCA *see* Evangelical Lutheran
Church in America
El Centro, California 622
Elchanan Theological Seminary,
Rabbi Isaac 488
election 97, 162, 169,
202–203, 342
electronic church **203–206,** 522
Eliot, John (1604–1690) 22,
68, **206–207,** 406
elixir of immortality 576
Elizabeth I (queen of England)
31, 533, 547
Elliott, Stephen 140
Elliott, Walter 28
Elpis Israel (John Thomas) 113
Ely, Richard T. 631
Emancipation Proclamation
(1863) 59
Emanu-El, Temple (New York
City) 543
Emerson, Mary Moody 289
Emerson, Ralph Waldo
(1803–1882) **207–208,** *208*
Beat movement 62
Buddhism 87
Christian Science 121
Hinduism 289
literature and Christianity 365
positive thinking 514
transcendentalism 673, 674
Unitarian Universalist
Association 685
Emet Ve-Emunah (Conservative
Judaism statement of principles)
159
Emmaus, Pennsylvania 419
Emmons, Nathanael 462
emotionalism
African-American religion 9
Baptists 58
frontier 245
Holiness movement 296

Presbyterian Church (U.S.A.)
524
Second Great Awakening 603
South 636
Employment Division vs. Smith
(1990) 439
Encyclopedia of Social Reform
(William Dwight Porter Bliss)
631
Engel v. Vitale (1962) 123
England
anti-Semitism 38
Arminianism 40
Calvinism 97
Enlightenment 209
establishment, religious 216
Freemasonry 241
Higher Christian Life
movement 287
Holiness movement 296
Reformation 547
England, John 566
England, Mabel and Martin 352
"engrams" (Scientology) 596
Enlightenment **208–211**
American Revolution/
Revolutionary War 25
atheism 46
church and state, relationship
between 123
civil religion 133
Constitution, U.S. 160
Freemasonry 241
inerrancy 313
Judaism 335
nature religion 455
peace reform 496
Reform Judaism 542
Scottish Common Sense
Realism 600
secularism 606
sexuality 613
environmental movement *see*
Deep Ecology
Ephrata Community 129, 211,
211, 580
episcopacy **212**
Episcopal Church **212–215** *see
also* Anglo-Catholicism
African-American religion 10
African Methodist Episcopal
Church 14
Anglicanism 30, 31
Calvinism 99
charismatic movement 111
episcopacy 212
Great Awakening 270
missions, foreign 407
people
Brooks, Phillips *80,* **80–81,**
213, 521
Crummell, Alexander
171–172
DuBose, William Porcher
190, **190–191,** 213

Hobart, John Henry 31,
213, **293–294**
Jarratt, Devereux 270,
323–324
Jones, Absalom 10, 14,
328–329
Seabury, Samuel 26, 212,
213, *601,* **601–602**
Social Gospel 631
South 637
Episcopal Synod of America 31
Epistle to the Romans, The (Karl
Barth) 457
e pluribus unum ("one out of
many") 134
equality of all believers 9, 636
Equal Rights Amendment 128
eschatology **215–216** *see also*
dispensationalism;
postmillennialism;
premillennialism
Deep Ecology 182
New Age religion 461
*Essay Concerning Human
Understanding, An* (John
Locke) 209
Essenes 154
establishment, religious
216–219
"establishment" clause (First
Amendment) 160, 238, 240
Ethical Culture 21, 47,
219–220, 338, 544
Ethiopian Jews 73, 74
ethnicity **220–221,** 309, 312,
513
Etiwanda, California 472
Etz Chaim Academy 488
Evangelical Alliance **221–222**
Evangelical and Reformed
Church 686, 687 *see* German
Reformed Church
Evangelical Association 688
Evangelical Church 688
Evangelical Friends Alliance 244
evangelicalism **227–229** *see also*
Finney, Charles Grandison
anti-cult movement 36
Arminianism 41
Bible schools 67
biblical interpretation 72
Burned-Over District 91
Calvinism 98
conversion 161
electronic church 205
frontier 245
Great Awakening 267
Higher Christian Life
movement 288
Jesus movement 328
Manifest Destiny 382
missions, foreign 408
New Divinity 462
New Lights/Old Lights 463
Pietism 507

positive thinking 515
Quakers 244
sanctification 584
Sunday school movement 654
Young Women's Christian
Association (YWCA) 747
Evangelical Lutheran Church
225
Evangelical Lutheran Church in
America (ELCA) **222–226,**
371, 372, 374
Evangelical Synod of North
America 255
Evangelical Theological Society
228
Evangelical United Brethren
Church 403, 688, 690
Evangelical United Front 69,
226–227
Evans, Clement A. 369
Evans, Warren Felt 470
Everson v. Board of Education
(1947) 160, 238, 240
evil and sin 360, 412, 456, 471
evolution **229–230** *see also*
creationism; Scopes trial; social
Darwinism
biblical interpretation 72
evangelicalism 227, 228
fundamentalism (Protestant)
248, 249
liberalism, theological 359
modernism (Protestant) 411
Worldwide Church of God
740
Ezili Danto (Vodou spirit) 706
Ezili Freda (Vodou spirit) 706

F

Fagal, William A. 204
Fairfield, Iowa 672
Faith and Order Conference
(Edinburgh, 1937) 195
"Faith for Today" (TV show)
204
*Faithful Narrative of the
Surprising Work of God, A*
(Jonathan Edwards) 268, 365,
558
faith healing 125, 503, 504
Falashas *see* Ethiopian Jews
Falwell, Jerry
Baptists 61
Christian Right 119
electronic church 204, 205
fundamentalism (Protestant)
250
Moral Majority 417, 418
preachers, Protestant 522
premillennialism 523
secular humanism 605
*Fama Fraternitas of the
Meritorious Order of the Rosy*

Cross, The (Johann Valentin Andreae) 575
Fard, W. D. (?–1934) **231–232**
  African-American religion 12
  Islam 320
  Moorish Science Temple 415
  Nation of Islam (Black Muslims) 427, 430
Farm, the (Tennessee commune) 168
Farrakhan, Louis Abdul (1933–) **232–233**
  African-American religion 13
  anti-Semitism 39
  Islam 321
  Nation of Islam (Black Muslims) 429, 431
Faulkner, William 366
Fayette, New York 127
Federal Bureau of Investigation (FBI) 701
Federal Communications Commission (FCC) 205
Federal Council of Churches *see also* National Council of Churches
  American Baptist Churches in the U.S.A. 20
  Baptists 60
  Christian Church (Disciples of Christ) 115
  ecumenical movement 194
  electronic church 204
  Evangelical Alliance 222
  National Association of Evangelicals 431
  National Catholic Welfare Conference 433
  Reformed Church in America 550
  Social Gospel 631
  World War I 734
  World War II 737
Federalist Party 452, 453
Federation of Islamic Associations of the United States and Canada (F.I.A.) 320
Federation of Polish Jews 16
Fellowship of Reconciliation 497, 737
Fellowship of Reconstructionist Congregations 541
Fellowship of Southern Churchmen 151
female castration 614
feminism and women's rights *see also* womanist theology
  evangelicalism 227
  Friends, the Religious Society of (Quakers) 244
  National Council of Churches 436
  people
    Daly, Mary **175–176**, 234, 615, 731

Fuller, Sarah Margaret **246–248**, *247*, 673
Grimké, Angelina Emily and Sarah Moore 136, 226, 233, **272–274**, *273*, 643
Harkness, Georgia Elma **277–278**
Stanton, Elizabeth Cady 233, 643, **645–646**, *646*, 731, 732
Truth, Sojourner 16, **676–677**, *677*
Willard, Frances Elizabeth Caroline 497, 643, 661, *723*, **723–724**
perfectionism 506
sexuality 615
spiritualism 643
Woman's Bible, The 732
feminist theology **233–235**, 361, 730
Fenollosa, Ernest 87
Ferdinand I (king of Spain) 38, 334
Ferraro, Geraldine 573
Fichte, Johann 673
Fifteenth Amendment 240
Fillmore, Charles and Myrtle 470
Finney, Charles Grandison (1792–1875) *235*, **235–237**
  Burned-Over District 91
  Calvinism 98
  conversion 162
  election 203
  evangelicalism 227
  Evangelical United Front 226
  frontier 245
  Higher Christian Life movement 287
  Holiness movement 295
  perfectionism 505, 506
  preachers, Protestant 519, 520
  Presbyterian Church (U.S.A.) 524
  revivalism 557, 558
  sanctification 584
  Second Great Awakening 602, 604
Finish Americans 47, 224, 372, 373
Finnish Evangelical Lutheran Church 225
Fiorenza, Elisabeth Schuessler 234
Fire-Baptized Holiness Church 503
fire-handling 630
First African Baptist Church of Charleston 10
First Amendment **237–238**
  American Indian Religious Freedom Act (AIRFA) 22, 23

anti-Semitism 38
church and state, relationship between 121
Constitution, U.S. 160
establishment, religious 218
Sabbatarianism 580
voluntaryism 707
First Methodist Wesleyan Church (Washington, D.C.) *401*
First Vatican Council *see* Vatican Council I
Fisher, Mary 243
Fisk University (Nashville, Tennessee) 24
Fitzgerald, Edward 696
Flint, Timothy 409
"flood geology" 170
Florida 432, 467, 469, 561, 637 *see also specific city* (*e.g.*, Miami)
Florovsky, George 483, 485
flower arranging 749
Flushing, New York 293
Followers of Buddha 89
foot-washing 29, 129, 637
Ford, A. J. 73, 74
Ford, Gerald 702
Ford, Henry 39
Foreign Missions Conference 436
Forman, James 13
Forrest, Nathan Bedford 354
Fort Caroline (Florida) 468
Fort Sumner (New Mexico) 452
Fosdick, Harry Emerson (1878–1969) **238–239**
  American Baptist Churches in the U.S.A. 21
  Baptists 60
  Neo-orthodoxy 457
  preachers, Protestant 521
  World War I 734
  World War II 736
Fountain Grove (California utopian community) 695
Foursquare Gospel *see* International Church of the Foursquare Gospel
Fourteen Lessons in Yoga Philosophy and Oriental Occultism (William Walker Atkinson) 291
Fourteenth Amendment 123, 136, 160, 238, **239–240**
Fox, George 243, 346, 705
Fox, Margaret and Kate 643, 644
France *see also* New France
  anti-Semitism 38
  atheism 46
  Enlightenment 209, 211
  presbyterianism 526
  Reformation 547
  Reform Judaism 543

Zionism 752
Franciscans (Roman Catholic order) 22, 468, 469
Frank, Leo 39
Franke, August Hermann 507–508
Frankel, Zechariah 157
Franklin, Benjamin
  atheism 47
  Enlightenment 210
  Freemasonry 241
  Great Awakening 268
  Native American religions 441
  Roman Catholicism 563
  secularism 606
Fraternitas Rosae Crucis (Rosicrucian association) 576
Frederick, Maryland 688
Frederick William III, Elector of the Palatinate 254
Free African Society 14
Free Church Tradition *see* Amish, the; Church of the Brethren (Dunkers); Hutterites; Mennonites; Moravians; Pietism
"Freedom Summer" (1964) 138, 651
"free exercise" clause (First Amendment) 238, 240
Free Inquiry (magazine) 22, 606
free love 613, 614, 644
Freemasonry 26, 116, 210, **241–242**, 455
Free Methodist Church 402, 506
Free Religious Association 21, 685
Free Soil 5
Free Speech Movement 167
free thought *see* atheism
Free Will Baptists 20, 637
Frelinghuysen, Theodorus Jacobus (1691–1748) **242–243**, 267, 508, 549, 558
French America *see* New France
French and Indian War (1754-63) 25, 243, 463
French Reformed Church *see* Huguenots
French Revolution (1789-99) 209, 452
Friends, the Religious Society of (Quakers) **243–244** *see also* Dyer, Mary; Penn, William; Woolman, John
  abolitionism 3
  Revolutionary War 26
  assimilation and resistance, Native American 44
  Carolinas 104, 105
  civil rights movement 136
  colonial period 147
  establishment, religious 216
  Evangelical United Front 226

Higher Christian Life
  movement 287
Holiness movement 296
Keithian controversy 346
New Netherland 464
peace reform 496
Pennsylvania 500, 501
perfectionism 505
slavery 623
South 637
Virginia 704, 705
World War I 735
World War II 736, 738
Froeligh, Solomon 116
Fromm, Erich 166
frontier **244–246,** 258
Frothingham, Octavius Brooks
  (1822–1895) **246,** 685
Fruitlands (Massachusetts
  utopian community) 17, 154,
  673
Fruit of Islam 427, 430
Fuller, Charles E. 204
Fuller, Linda and Millard 352
Fuller, Sarah Margaret
  (1810–1850) **246–248,** *247,*
  673
Fuller Theological Seminary
  (Pasadena, California) 204,
  229, 314
Full Gospel Business Men's
  Fellowship International 111,
  504
fundamentalism (Protestant)
  248–250 *see also*
  Fundamentals, The
  American Baptist Churches in
    the U.S.A. 20
  Bible schools 67
  biblical interpretation 72, 73
  Christian Right 117
  Churches of Christ 132
  creationism 170
  eschatology 215
  evangelicalism 228
  evolution 230
  heresy 285
  inerrancy 312, 314
  liberalism, theological 360
  people
    Bryan, William Jennings *see*
      Bryan, William Jennings
    Dixon, Amzi Clarence 185,
      186–187, 251
    Henry, Carl Ferdinand
      Howard 228, **283–284,**
      431
    Machen, John Gresham
      314, **375,** 525, 527, 529,
      530, 605
    Scofield, Cyrus Ingerson
      185, 249, 523, 539,
      597–598, 735
    Torrey, Reuben Archer 185,
      251, **671–672**

Warfield, Benjamin
  Breckinridge 229, 313,
  529, 600, **710–711**
positive thinking 515
Presbyterian Church (U.S.A.)
  525
restoration movement 556
science and religion 595
Scopes trial 598
Scottish Common Sense
  Realism 599
sexuality 615
South 636
Southern Baptist Convention
  639
Fundamentals, The (pamphlets)
  72, **250–251**
Furfey, Paul 145
Furman, James 531
Furman, Richard (1755–1825)
  251–252
Furman University (Greenville,
  North Carolina) 59

G

Gabrielino Indians 445
Gage, Matilda Joslyn 233
Galicia 337
Galileo Galilei 594
Gandhi, Mohandas K. 290
Garden Grove (California)
  Community Church 206
Gardner, Gerald 458, 459
Garrison, William Lloyd
  abolitionism 3
  civil rights movement 136
  Evangelical United Front
    226, 227
  peace reform 497
  spiritualism 643
Garvey, Marcus (1887–1940)
  12, 73, **253–254,** 320, 415
Gasper River, Kentucky 100,
  101, 103
Gates, Thomas 704
Gates Ajar, The (Elizabeth Stuart
  Phelps) 366
Gayarre, Charles 452
gay men *see* homosexuality
Gemara (Jewish text) 486
General Association of Regular
  Baptist Churches 21, 60
*General Catechism of the
  Christian Doctrine* (Roman
  Catholic Church) 54
General Conference Mennonite
  Church of North America 398
General Convention of the New
  Jerusalem in the United States
  of America 657
General Council of
  Congregational and Christian
  Churches 687

General Council of the
  Evangelical Lutheran Church
  224
General Court of Connecticut
  276
General Court of Massachusetts
  37, 38, 99, 275
General Female Training
  Institute 747
General Missionary Convention
  see Triennial Convention
General Synod of the Evangelical
  Lutheran Church 224, 373
General Synod of the German
  Reformed Church 255
General Wartime Commission
  734
"generation gap" 167
*Genesis Flood: The Biblical Record
  and Its Scientific Implications,
  The* (Henry Morris and John C.
  Whitcomb, Jr.) 596
Geneva, Switzerland 97, 547,
  550
Geneva Version (Bible) 534
Gentleman's Agreement (1908)
  453
geology 359
George II (king of England) 632
Georgetown University
  (Washington, D.C.) 565
Georgia *see also specific cities
  (e.g.,* Atlanta)
  Anglicanism 31
  Christian Methodist Episcopal
    Church 116
  colonial period 148
  establishment, religious 216,
    217
  Moravians 419
  Society for the Propagation of
    the Gospel in Foreign Parts
    632
  Student Nonviolent
    Coordinating Committee
    651
  Wesleyan tradition 715
German Americans
  American Baptist Churches in
    the U.S.A. 20
  atheism 47
  Baptists 60
  Cahenslyism 94
  Carolinas 104
  Evangelical Lutheran Church
    in America 224
  German Reformed Church
    255, 256
  immigration 310
  Judaism 335
  Lutheran Church—Missouri
    Synod 369, 370
  Lutheranism 371, 372, 373
  Mennonites 398
  Pennsylvania 500, 501

Reformation 548
Roman Catholicism 564
temperance 661
United Church of Christ 687
German Evangelical Lutheran
  Synod of Missouri, Ohio, and
  Other States 370
German Evangelical Synod of
  North America 687
German Reformed Church
  254–256
  Calvinism 98
  Ephrata Community 211
  Evangelical Lutheran Church
    in America 223
  Pennsylvania 500, 501
  Reformation 547
  Reformed Tradition 551
German Reformed Church in
  the United States 255, 687
German Seventh-Day Baptists
  130, 211
Germantown, Pennsylvania 129,
  398
Germany
  biblical interpretation 71
  fundamentalism (Protestant)
    249
  Hutterites 308
  Mennonites 397
  Reformation 546, 547
  Reform Judaism 543
  World War I 735
  World War II 736
Geronimo (Apache leader) 452
Gestalt psychology 461
Gettysburg Address (Abraham
  Lincoln) 135
Ghose, Sri Aurobindo 291
Ghost Dance **256–258,** 444,
  449
Gibbons, James (1834–1921)
  258–260
  Americanism 27, 28
  Cahenslyism 95
  heresy 285
  Roman Catholicism 567
  temperance 662
  World War I 734
Giddings, Salmon 409
Gideons International 68, 70
Gidolim (Torah leaders) 489
Gilded Age 215, 249, 516, 739
Gimbutas, Marija 458
Ginsberg, Allen 61, 62, 87,
  167, 749
Gitlow v. New York (1925) 240
"give away" (Native American
  mourning ceremony) 23
Gladden, Solomon Washington
  (1836–1918) 152, **260–262,**
  261, 521, 630
Glazer, Nathan 338, 513
Glorious Revolution (1688)
  209, 217, 386

glossolalia *see* tongues, speaking in
Gloucester, Massachusetts 692
gnosticism 62
"God Bless America" (song) 738
Goddard, Dwight 89
goddess-centered religions 235
Goddesses and Gods of Old Europe, The (Marija Gimbutas) 458
God of the Witches, The (Margaret Murray) 458
Godspell (musical) 328
Goethe, Johann Wolfgang von 673
Gohonzon (Nichiren Buddhist mandala) 472
golden tablets 76
Gold Mountain Dhyana Monastery (San Francisco, California) 86
Goldstein, Joseph 88
Goldwater, Julius 90
Goodman, Andrew 138, 651, 652
Gordon, A. J. 67
Gordon, John Brown 369
Gordon College (Wenham, Massachusetts) 68
Gospel Advocate (periodical) 132
Gospel of Christian Atheism, The (Thomas J. J. Altizer) 180
Gospel of Wealth **262**
grace 97, 202, 342
Grace, Sweet Daddy (Charles Emmanuel) (1881–1960) **263**
Graham, Billy (William Franklin) (1918–) **263–265**
    Cold War 146
    electronic church 205
    evangelicalism 228
    fundamentalism (Protestant) 250
    preachers, Protestant 521, 522
    revivalism 559
    Vietnam War 701
Graham, Dom Aelred 88, 750
Graham, Sylvester 614
Graham cracker 614
Grant, Jacquelyn 234, 730, 731
Granth Sahib (Sikh text) 621
Graves, James Robinson (1820–1893) 57, 60, 61, **265–266**
Gray, Asa (1810–1888) 170, 229, **266–267**
Great Awakening **267–270**
    American Baptist Churches in the U.S.A. 19
    American Revolution/Revolutionary War 25
    baptism 56
    Baptists 58
    biblical interpretation 70

Calvinism 98
Congregationalism 156
conversion 161, 162
Enlightenment 210
establishment, religious 217
Methodists 402
missions, foreign 406
Moravians 419
New Lights/Old Lights 463
New Side/Old Side 466
Pietism 508
postmillennialism 515
preachers, Protestant 519
Presbyterian Church (U.S.A.) 524
presbyterianism 527
Reformed Tradition 552
revivalism 558
Unitarian Controversy 682
United Church of Christ 686
Great Awakening, Second *see* Second Great Awakening
Great Britain *see* England; Scotland
"Great Defection" 632
Great Depression 569, 570, 583
"Great Migration" 19
Great Revival *see* Second Great Awakening
Greek Americans 270, 271, 453, 482, 483
Greek Orthodox Archdiocese of North and South America **270–272,** *271,* 483
Greeley, Andrew 575
Greeley, Horace 643
Green, Byron 281
Green Corn Ceremony 440, 442, 443
Green Egg (journal) 459
Griffith, D. W. 354
Grimké, Angelina Emily (1805–1879) and Sarah Moore (1792–1873) **272–274,** *273*
    civil rights movement 136
    Evangelical United Front 226
    feminist theology 233
    spiritualism 643
Griswold, Alexander Viets 213
Grof, Stanislav 461
Gross, Rita 234
group marriage 506, 614
Guale Rebellion (1597) 468
Guideposts (magazine) 515
Guide to Confident Living, A (Norman Vincent Peale) 515
Gulick, Dorothy and Luther 747
Gurdjieff, Georgei Ivanovitch 321
gurdwara (temple) 622
Gurney, John 244
gurus 88, 291, 321, 622
Gutierrez, Gustavo 361
Gyatso, Tendzin 88
"gyn/ecology" 615

H

Habad *see* Lubavitchers
Habitat for Humanity 228, 352
Hadassah (Women's Zionist Organization of America) 754
Haiti 15, 706
hajj (pilgrimage) 429
Halachah (Jewish law) 159, 485, 488
"Half Moon Way" (peyote ritual) 438
Half-way Covenant 56, 99, **275–276**
Hall, Gordon 281
Halle, University of (Germany) 507
"Hallelujah Lasses" 583
hallucinogens 437, 445, 461
"Hamatreya" (Ralph Waldo Emerson poem) 289
Hamilton, William 179
Hamilton College (Clinton, New York) 20, 59
Hampton (Virginia) Normal and Agricultural Institute 24
Han, Hak Ja 681
Hand, W. Brevard 605
Handsome Lake (Ganio'dai'io) (1735–1815) 45, **276–277,** 441
Hanover County, Virginia 269, 654
Hanuman Foundation 292
Hapoel Hamizrahi (Zionist labor organization) 552
Happy/Healthy/Holy Organization 291
Harding College (Searcy, Alabama) 132
Hare Krishna movement *see* International Society for Krishna Consciousness
Hargis, Billy James 118
Harkness, Georgia Elma (1891–1974) **277–278**
Harmens, James *see* Arminius, Jacobus
Harmonial Religion *see* Christadelphians ; Christian Science; Mesmerism; New Age Religion; New Thought; Positive Thinking; Rosicrucians; Scientology; Spiritualism; Theosophy; Transcendental Meditation
Harper, William Rainey 20
Harris, Barbara 214
Har Sinai, Temple (Baltimore) 335, 336, 543
Hartford, Connecticut 415
Harvard, John 70
Harvard College (Cambridge, Massachusetts)
    anti-Semitism 39

biblical interpretation 70
Enlightenment 209
Great Awakening 269
Massachusetts Bay Colony 388
science and religion 594
Unitarian Controversy 683
Unitarian Universalist Association 684, 685
Harvard Divinity School (Cambridge, Massachusetts) 693
Ha Shomer Hatzair (Zionist movement) 338
Hasidism 155, **278–280,** 340, 489
Haskalah (Jewish Enlightenment) 542–543
Hassan, Riffat 234
Hatch, Nathan 708
"Hate that Hate Produced, The" (TV documentary) 428
havuroth (religious communities) 159, 340
Hawaii 86, 407
"hawks" 701
Hawthorne, Nathaniel 365
Haygood, Atticus Greene (1839–1896) **280–281**
Haystack Prayer Meeting (1806) **281,** 407
healing *see also* faith healing
    Christian Science 120, 121
    Holiness movement 295, 298
    mesmerism 400
    Native American religions: Southwest 451
    New Age religion 461
    primitivism 529
health reform 612
Healthy, Happy, Holy Organization (3HO) 622
Hearn, Lafcadio 87
Hebrew (language) 109, 337, 338
Hebrew Theological College 488
Hebrew Union College (HUC) (Cincinnati, Ohio)
    Conservative Judaism 157
    Judaism 336
    Pittsburgh Platform 511
    Reform Judaism 543
    Zionism 753, 755
Hecker, Isaac (1819–1888) 28, **281–283,** *282*
Hegel, Georg W. F. 180, 457
Heidelberg Catechism (1563) 254, 687
Henry IV (king of France) 302
Henry VIII (king of England) 30, 216, 533, 547
Henry, Carl Ferdinand Howard (1913–) 228, **283–284,** 431
Henry, Patrick 217

Hensley, George W. 629
Herberg, Will 34, 146, 561
herem (excommunication) 541
heresy 72, **284–285,** 525
Heritage USA (Charlotte, North
  Carolina theme park) 205
Herman, Lebrecht Frederick
  255
Herron, George D. 631
Hertzberg, Arthur 754
Herzl, Theodor 752, 753
Heschel, Abraham Joshua
  (1907–1972) **286–287**
Heyward, Carter 234
Hick, Elias 244
Hicksite controversy 244
Hidatsa Indians 448
high-church tradition *see*
  Anglo-Catholicism
Higher Christian Life, The
  (William E. Boardman) 287,
  296, 297
Higher Christian Life movement
  287–288
higher criticism *see* biblical
  interpretation
Highland Park, Michigan 320
Hill, D. H. 369
Hindu Festival of India (Edison,
  New Jersey) *289*
Hinduism **288–293** *see also*
  International Society for
  Krishna Consciousness;
  Transcendental Meditation;
  Vedanta Society
  Beat movement 62
  pluralism 514
  transcendentalism 673
  World's Parliament of
    Religions 739
Hinkletown, Pennsylvania *397*
hippies 167
Hiroshima, bombing of (1945)
  145, 571
Hispanic Americans
  Assemblies of God 43
  Bahá'í Faith 52
  ethnicity 221
  immigration 312
  liberation theology 361
  Nichiren Shoshu Academy
    471
  Pentecostalism 505
  Roman Catholicism 574
"Historical School"
  (Conservative Judaism) 157
History of Plymouth Plantation
  (William Bradford) 364
Hitler, Adolf
  Judaism 339
  nativism 454
  Roman Catholicism 570
  World War II 736, 737
  Zionism 753

Hobart, John Henry
  (1775–1830) 31, 213,
  293–294
Hobbes, Thomas 209
Hodge, Archibald A. 313, 529,
  600
Hodge, Charles (1797–1878)
  294–295
  biblical interpretation 71
  Calvinism 99
  evolution 229
  inerrancy 313
  Princeton Theology 529
  Scottish Common Sense
    Realism 600
Hoffman, Melchior 398
Hohokam Indians 450, 451
Holiness movement **295–298**
  see also Mahan, Asa; Palmer,
  Phoebe Worrall; White, Alma
  Bridwell
  African-American religion 11,
    13
  camp meetings 101
  Church of God (Cleveland,
    Tennessee) 124
  Church of the Nazarene 130
  Higher Christian Life
    movement 287
  Methodists 402
  missions, foreign 408
  National Association of
    Evangelicals 431
  Pentecostalism 502
  perfectionism 505
  Salvation Army 582
  sanctification 584
  Wesleyan tradition 714, 717
Hollywood (motion picture
  industry) 153, 614, 615
Holmes, Ernest 470
Holocaust
  Agudath Israel 16
  anti-Semitism 39
  Central Conference of
    American Rabbis 108
  death of God theology 179
  Judaism 339
  Reform Judaism 545
  World War II 737
  Zionism 754
holy kiss 129
Holy Koran (Noble Drew Ali)
  415
Holy Spirit Association for the
  Unification of World
  Christianity *see* Unification
  Church
Home Missionary Society 20
Home Missions Council 436
homosexuality *see also* lesbians
  Episcopal Church 214
  Judaism 340
  Metropolitan Community
    Church 404

Reform Judaism 545, 546
  Roman Catholicism 573
  sexuality 614, 615
Honolulu, Hawaii 472
Hooker, Thomas (1586–1647)
  99, 169, **298–299**
Hoover, Herbert 569
Hoover, J. Edgar 497
Hope, New Jersey 419
Hopedale (utopian community)
  154
Hopewell Indians 439, 442
Hopi Indians 23, 45, 441, 451,
  452
Hopkins, Emma Curtis
  (1853–1925) **299–300,** 470
Hopkins, Samuel (1721–1803)
  98, 226, **300–301,** *301,* 462
Horton, Douglas 457
Horton, Walter Marshall 457
Hosier, Harry 520
Hospital Sketches (Louisa May
  Alcott) 140
"Hour of Decision, The" (radio
  show) 521
"Hour of Power" (TV show)
  205, 522
Housatonic Indians 406
House of Acts (San Francisco
  Christian commune) 328
House Un-American Activities
  Committee 153
Houston, Texas 43, 293, 622
Howard University
  (Washington, D.C.) 24, 531
Howe, Julia Ward (1819–1910)
  139, **301–302,** *302,* 614, 624
"Howl" (Allen Ginsberg poem)
  61–62
How Should We Then Live?
  (Francis Schaeffer) 605
*How to Stop Worrying and Start
  Living* (Dale Carnegie) 515
*How to Win Friends and
  Influence People* (Dale
  Carnegie) 471, 515
*How You Can Help Clean Up
  America* (Jerry Falwell) 417
Hubbard, L. Ron 596, 597
Hudson, Henry 464
Hudson's Bay Company 447
Hughes, Charles Evans 240
Hughes, John 33
Huguenots (French Reformed)
  302–303
  Calvinism 98
  Carolinas 104
  Reformation 547
  Reformed Tradition 551
Huichol Indians 437
Humanae Vitae (papal
  encyclical) 573
humanism

American Humanist
  Association *see* American
  Humanist Association
Enlightenment *see*
  Enlightenment
Ethical Culture 21, 47,
  219–220, 338, 544
Freemasonry 26, 116, 210,
  241–242, 455
Humanist Manifesto *see*
  Humanist Manifesto
New Thought 120, 470–471
people
  Dewey, John **182–183,**
    199, 304, 607
  Ingersoll, Robert Green 47,
    219, **315–316**
  James, William 121, *322,*
    322–323, 412, 470, 607
  Kallen, Horace Meyer
    344–345, 513, 607
  Mencken, Henry Louis 47,
    250, **395–396,** 614
  O'Hair, Madalyn Murray
    478
  Paine, Thomas 47, 198,
    210, 211, **492–493,** 606
  Royce, Josiah **576–577**
  Small, Albion Woodbury
    625–626
  Whitman, Walt 167, *721,*
    721–722
secular humanism *see* secular
  humanism
secularism 222, 303, 606–607
Humanist, The (journal) 22
humanistic psychology 461
Humanist Manifesto **303–304**
Humbard, Rex 204, 205
Hume, David 210, 600
Hungary 308, 682
Hunt, Ernest Shinkaku
  (1878–1967) 90, **304–305**
Hunt, Robert 704
Huntington, Emily 747
Huntington, William Reed 214
Hurley, George Willie
  (1884–1943) **305–306,** 644
Huron Indians
  American Indian Religious
    Freedom Act (AIRFA) 22
  assimilation and resistance,
    Native American 44
  Native American religions:
    Eastern Woodlands 443
  New France 462, 463
  Roman Catholicism 562
Hurston, Zora Neale 367
Hus, Jan 418
Hussites 418
Hutchinson, Anne (1591–1643)
  37, 38, **306–307,** 387, 464
Hutchison, William 407
Hutter, Jacob 308
Hutterites **307–308**

Huxley, Aldous 698
Hydesville, New York 643
hymns, gospel 585

I

"I Believe" (TV show) 204
Icaria (California utopian
community) 695
iconography 484
Identity Movement 355, 608
Ignatius of Loyola 327
Igram, Abdullah 320
"I Have a Dream" (Martin
Luther King Jr. speech) 522
Illinois 321, 512, 550 see also
specific city (e.g., Chicago)
"Illusions" (Ralph Waldo
Emerson essay) 289
"I Love America" rallies 417
immanence of God 411, 412,
644, 665
immigration 309–312
anti-Catholicism 33, 34
atheism 47
Baptists 60
church and state, relationship
between 123
Evangelical Alliance 222
Ku Klux Klan 354
missions, home 410
nativism see nativism
pluralism 513
Roman Catholicism 565,
568, 574
Immortale Dei (papal encyclical)
569
incarnation 180
In Darkest England and the Way
Out (William Booth) 297, 583
indentured servants 7, 8
Independence, Missouri 553
India 87, 291, 316, 621, 665
India American Cultural Center
622
India Christiania (Cotton
Mather) 288
Indiana
Amish 30
Friends, the Religious Society
of (Quakers) 244
Ku Klux Klan 354
Mennonites 398
Plan of Union 511, 512
Indian Affairs, Office of 258,
449
Indian Americans 289
Hinduism 290, 292
immigration 312
International Society for
Krishna Consciousness 316
Sikhism 622
Indian National Congress 290
Indian Rights Association 439

Indian Territory (Oklahoma)
444
inductive method 68
inerrancy 312–315
biblical interpretation 71
creationism 170
fundamentalism (Protestant)
248, 249
heresy 285
Lutheran Church—Missouri
Synod 371
Princeton Theology 529,
530, 531
Scottish Common Sense
Realism 600
Southern Baptist Convention
639
"I Never Saw a Moor" (Emily
Dickinson poem) 366
infallibility, papal 480, 696
Ingersoll, Robert Green
(1833–1897) 47, 219,
315–316
"In God We Trust" 146
In His Steps (Charles M.
Sheldon) 631
initiation rites 445
inner light, doctrine of the 243
Inquisition 38, 147
Insight Meditation Society
(Barre, Massachusetts) 88
Inskip, John 296
"Inspiration" (Archibald A.
Hodge and Benjamin B.
Warfield article) 313
Institute for Creation Research
170
Institutes of the Christian
Religion (John Calvin) 97,
547, 550
I.N.T.A. see International New
Thought Alliance
interdenominational cooperation
see ecumenical movement
Interdenominational Theological
Center (Atlanta, Georgia) 116
Internal Revenue Service 597
International Catholic Congress
(Fribourg, 1897) 28
International Church of the
Foursquare Gospel 504, 505
International Congress of
Religious Liberals (Boston,
1920) 291, 609
International Council of
Religious Education 436
International Journal of Ethics
220
international law 496
International Missionary
Conference (Edinburgh, 1910)
194
International Missionary Council
195, 733

International Muslim Society
320
International New Thought
Alliance (I.N.T.A.) 470
International Society for Krishna
Consciousness (ISKCON) 35,
292, 293, 316–317
Interseminary Missionary
Alliance 194, 436
Inter-Seminary Movement 436
"In the Mood" (song) 738
In Tune with the Infinite, or,
Fullness of Peace, Power, and
Plenty (Ralph Waldo Trine)
471, 514
Iowa 34, 116, 550, 672
Iranian Americans 52, 312
Iraqi Americans 312
Ireland 100
Ireland, John (1838–1918) 27,
317, 317–318, 567
Irish Americans 310
anti-Catholicism 33
Cahenslyism 94
immigration 310
Presbyterian Church (U.S.A.)
523
Roman Catholicism 564
Iroquois Indians
Native American religions:
Eastern Woodlands 442,
443, 444
New France 462, 463
Roman Catholicism 562
Irving, John 367
Irwin, B. H. 503
Isabella (queen of Spain) 38,
334
Isherwood, Christopher 698
Isis Unveiled (Helena Blavatsky)
664
ISKCON see International
Society for Krishna
Consciousness
Islam 318–321, 319
anti-Semitism 38
feminist theology 233, 234
pluralism 513
slavery 623
World's Parliament of
Religions 739
Islamic Medical Association 320
Islamic Society of North
America (I.S.N.A.) 320
Islamic Teaching Center 320
Islam in America (Muhammad
Alexander Russell Webb) 320
I.S.N.A. see Islamic Society of
North America
Israel
Agudath Israel 16
anti-Semitism 39
Bahá'í Faith 51
Black Jews 74

Central Conference of
American Rabbis 108–109
Hasidism 279
Judaism 333, 339, 340
Reform Judaism 545
Religious Zionists of America
552
Zionism 752, 753, 754, 755
Italian Americans 453, 564
Ives, Levi Silliman 31
iwa (spirit) 706

J

Jackson, Jesse 13, 39, 60, 429
Jackson, Joseph H. 13, 432,
433, 531
Jackson, Stonewall 141
Jainism 290, 739
James, William (1842–1910)
322, 322–323
Christian Science 121
modernism (Protestant) 412
New Thought 470
secularism 607
James I (king of England) 386,
534, 562, 704
Jamestown, Virginia 7, 562,
703, 703–704
Janakananda, Swami Rajasi
(James J. Lynn) 609
Jansen, Cornelius 480
Jansenism 480
Japan 87, 453, 471, 735, 736
Japanese Americans
Buddhism 86
Buddhist Churches of
America 89, 90
immigration 312
nativism 453, 454
Nichiren Shoshu Academy
471
World War II 737
Jarratt, Devereux (1733–1801)
270, 323–324
Jastrow, Marcus 157
Jastrow, Morris 337
Jefferson, Thomas (1743–1826)
324, 324–325
American Revolution/
Revolutionary War 26
atheism 47
church and state, relationship
between 121, 123
civil religion 135
education, public school 198
Enlightenment 210
establishment, religious 218
secularism 606, 607
Virginia 702, 705
Jefferson Airplane (musical
group) 167
Jeffersonian (newspaper) 39
Jehovah's Witnesses 123, 216,
325–327, 523, 738

Jemison, Theodore J. 433
"jeremiads" 388, 519
Jesuits 327–328
    assimilation and resistance,
        Native American 44
    liberation theology 361
    Maryland 385
    missions, foreign 408
    Native American religions:
        Eastern Woodlands 443
    New France 462
    New Spain 468
    Old Catholic movement 480
    Roman Catholicism 562, 563
Jesus Christ Superstar (rock
    opera) 328
Jesus movement 35, 328, 529
Jewel, John 30
Jewish Centers 541
Jewish Daily Forward
    (newspaper) 338
Jewish Defense League 340
Jewish Enlightenment see
    Haskalah
Jewish Horizon (periodical) 553
Jewish Reconstructionist
    Foundation 541
Jewish Theological Seminary
    (JTS) (New York City)
    Conservative Judaism 158,
        159
    Judaism 337
    Reconstructionist Judaism
        541
    United Synagogue of
        Conservative Judaism 690
    Zionism 754, 755
Jewish Welfare Board 433
Jicarilla Apache Indians 451
"Jim Crow" laws 136, 142
"Jimmy Swaggart Show, The"
    (TV show) 205
jimson weed 445
jnana yoga 698
Jodo Shinshu (Buddhist sect)
    86, 89
John XXIII, Pope 572, 696
"Johnny Appleseed" 657
John Paul II, Pope 361
Johns Hopkins University
    (Baltimore, Maryland) 47
Johnson, Andrew 55, 566
Johnson, Lyndon B. 138, 497,
    700, 701
Johnson, Samuel 289, 290
John Street Church (New York
    City) 15
Jones, Abner 555
Jones, Absalom (1746–1816)
    10, 14, 328–329
Jones, Bob 250, 636
Jones, Charles Colcock
    (1804–1863) 329–330, 532
Jones, Charles Price 125, 126

Jones, Franklin see Free John,
    Bubba
Jones, James Warren (Jim)
    (1931–1978) 330–331
Jones, John William
    (1836–1909) 141, 331–332,
    369
Jones, Samuel Porter (Sam)
    (1847–1906) 332–333
Jones, Sir William 288
Jonestown Massacre (1978) 36
Jordan, Clarence 352
Joseph, Jacob 337, 488
Joy of Sex, The (Alex Comfort)
    615
Judaism 333, 333–341
    Agudath Israel 16–17, 754
    anti-cult movement 36
    anti-Semitism see
        anti-Semitism
    Black Jews 12, 73–74
    Carolinas 104
    Central Conference of
        American Rabbis (CCAR)
        see Central Conference of
        American Rabbis (CCAR)
    church and state, relationship
        between 123
    Cold War 145
    Communism 153
    Conservative Judaism 156
        see Conservative Judaism
    death of God theology 179,
        180
    ecumenical movement 196
    education, public school 199
    feminist theology 233, 234
    Freemasonry 241
    Hasidism 155, 278–280,
        340, 489
    immigration 309, 312
    Ku Klux Klan 354, 355
    nativism 453
    New Netherland 464
    Orthodox Judaism 487 see
        Orthodox Judaism
    people
        Adler, Cyrus 5, 5–6, 158,
            488, 754
        Adler, Felix 6–7, 47, 219,
            338, 544, 607
        Einhorn, David 201–202,
            336, 487, 543, 544
        Heschel, Abraham Joshua
            286–287
        Kaplan, Mordecai M.
            345–346, 540–541, 542
        Kohler, Kaufmann
            350–352, 351, 510, 543,
            544
        Leeser, Isaac 157, 336,
            357–358, 488, 754
        Mendes, Henry Pereira 157,
            337, 396–397, 488, 754

    Morais, Sabato 157, 337,
        416, 416–417, 754
    Schechter, Solomon 158,
        588–590, 589, 690, 754
    Schneerson, Menachem
        Mendel 16, 279, 280, 340,
        592–594
    Soloveitchik, Joseph Dov
        553, 634–635
    Szold, Henrietta 658, 754
    Wise, Isaac Mayer see Wise,
        Isaac Mayer
    Wise, Stephen S. 729–730,
        737, 753
    Pittsburgh Platform 157,
        336, 510–511, 544, 545
    pluralism 513
    positive thinking 515
    Reconstructionist Judaism
        158, 540–542, 691
    Reform Judaism see Reform
        Judaism
    Religious Zionists of America
        (RZA) 552–553, 753
    secularism 607
    sexuality 615
    slavery 623
    Social Gospel 631
    South 637
    United Synagogue of
        Conservative Judaism
        690–691
    World's Parliament of
        Religions 739
    World War I 734
    World War II 737
    Zionism 108, 338, 339, 544,
        752–755 see Zionism
Judaism as a Civilization
    (Mordecai M. Kaplan) 541
Judenstaat (Theodor Herzl) 752
Judge, William Quan 664
Judson, Adoniram (1788–1850)
    341, 341–342
    American Baptist Churches in
        the U.S.A. 20
    Baptists 58
    Haystack Prayer Meeting 281
    missions, foreign 407
Jumping Dance (Native
    American ceremony) 445
justification 342–343
    Antinomian Controversy 37
    conversion 161
    Great Awakening 268
    Lutheranism 371, 372
    Reformation 546
just war doctrine 571

K

Kabbala (Jewish mystical
    tradition) 279
kachina (spirits) 451
Kali (Hindu goddess) 698

Kallen, Horace Meyer
    (1882–1974) 344–345, 513,
    607
Kansas City, Missouri 131, 689
Kant, Immanuel 209, 219
Kaplan, Mordecai M.
    (1881–1983) 345–346,
    540–541, 542
Kapleau, Philip 89, 749
karma, law of 665
Karok Indians 257
kashrut (Jewish dietary laws) 157
Katallagete—Be Reconciled
    (journal) 151
Kaweah Cooperative
    Commonwealth (California
    utopian community) 695
Kaye, Danny 738
Keith, George 346, 632
Keithian controversy 346
Kellogg, John Harvey 612, 614
Kennedy, John F.
    anti-Catholicism 32, 35
    civil religion 134
    Nation of Islam (Black
        Muslims) 428
    Roman Catholicism 561, 572
    Vietnam War 700
Kennedy, Robert J. 701
Kennett, Jiyu (1924–) 89,
    346–347, 750
Kenrick, Francis Patrick 70
Kent (Ohio) State University
    702
Kentucky 224, 245, 524, 527
    see also Cane Ridge revival
Kerouac, Jack 61, 62, 87, 749,
    750
Keswick Grove, New Jersey 288
Keswick movement 287, 288,
    296
Khrushchev, Nikita 146
Kicking Bird (Lakota leader) 258
Kierkegaard, Soren 457
King, Coretta Scott 522
King Jr., Martin Luther
    (1929–1968) 347–350
    African-American religion 12,
        13
    Baptists 60
    civil rights movement 137,
        138
    Hinduism 290
    National Baptist Convention,
        U.S.A., Inc. 433
    preachers, Protestant 519,
        522
    Progressive National Baptist
        Convention, Inc. 531
    Southern Christian
        Leadership Conference
        (SCLC) 640
    Student Nonviolent
        Coordinating Committee
        651

Vietnam War 701, 702
Kingdom of God in America, The
(H. Richard Niebuhr) 457
King James Version (Bible) 69,
70, 71, 534
King Ludwig's Mission Society
(Bavarian organization) 565
King Philip's War (1675) 406
King's Chapel (Boston,
Massachusetts) 683, 684
Kinnaird, Mary Jane 747
Kino, Eusebio Francisco
(1645–1711) 327, **350**, 469
Kiowa Indians 23, 257, 437,
438, 448
Kirpal Light Satsang (Sikh
group) 622
Kirtland, Ohio 127
Kishkovsky, Leonid 436
"Kitchen Debate" (1959) 146
kivas (ceremonial centers) 22,
451
klal Yisrael (universal Israel) 158
Klamath Indians 23, 257
Klein, Abbé Felix 28
Knapp, Martin Wells 297
Knights of Columbus 734
Knights Templar 241
Knitter, Paul 513
Knorr, Nathan H. 326
Know-Nothing Party 33, 452,
453, 676
Knox, John 97, 523, 526, 547,
550
Kodiak Island, Alaska 484
Kohler, Kaufmann (1843–1926)
350–352, *351*, 510, 543, 544
Kohut, Alexander 157
Koinonia Farm (Georgia)
352–353
Kontoglou, Photios 484
Korean Americans 43
Koresh, David 36
Kornfield, Jack 88
Kosciusko, Tadeus 563
kosher food *see kashrut* (Jewish
dietary laws)
Kourides, Peter 271
Krauth, Charles Porterfield
(1823–1883) 224, *353,*
353–354
Krishna (Hindu god) 292, 316,
317
Krishna Consciousness *see*
International Society for
Krishna Consciousness
kriya yoga 291, 609
Ku Klux Klan 34, 352,
354–355, 454, 568
kundalini (spiritual power) 291,
609
Kurtz, Paul 22, 606
Kwakiutl Indians 446, 447
Kynett, Alpha J. 661

L

Labadists (Protestant sect) 154
Lafayette, Marquis de 134, 563
LaHaye, Tim 605
Lakota (western Sioux) Indians
American Indian Religious
Freedom Act (AIRFA) 24
assimilation and resistance,
Native American 46
civil religion 135
Ghost Dance 257, 258
Native American religions:
Plains 448
Lamont, Corliss 22
Lancaster County, Pennsylvania
29, 303, 398, 688
Landmark movement 56, 57, 61
Laotian Americans 52, 312
LaPorte, Roger 701
Lasyrenn (Vodou spirit) 706
Late Great Planet Earth, The
(Hal Lindsey) 185, 523, 539
Latin America 360, 408 *see also*
South America; *specific countries*
(*e.g.,* Mexico)
Latinos *see* Hispanic Americans
Latourette, Kenneth 653
Laud, William 98
LaVey, Anton S. 586
*Lawes Divine, Morall and
Martiall* (Thomas Dale) 704
Lawrence, William 262
Lawrenceburg, Kentucky *557*
Laws, Curtis Lee 249
Laws of Manu, The (Hindu text)
288, 289
Laymen's Missionary Movement
653
Lay Mission Helpers 408
League for Social Service 222
League of Nations 735
Leary, Timothy 167, 292
Lebanese Americans 312, 320
Lebanon, Connecticut 406
Lectures on Preaching (Phillips
Brooks) 521
Lee, Ann (1736–1784) **356,**
616, *617*
Lee, Jarena (1783–?) **356–357**
Lee, Robert E. 141, 369
Leeser, Isaac (1806–1868) 157,
336, **357–358**, 488, 754
legislative enactment 158
Leisler, Jacob 563
Leland, John (1754–1841) 217,
218, **358–359**
Lenin, Vladimir Illych 152
Leo XIII, Pope 27, 94, 285,
567, 569
Leopold, Aldo 180
Leopoldine Foundation
(Austria) 565
lesbians 234, 403

Let Our Children Go! (Ted
Patrick) 36
Levi, Eliphas 575
Levin, David 452
Lewis, Edwin 457
Lewis, John 137
Lexington, Kentucky 555
liberal feminist theology 234
liberalism, theological **359–360**
see also modernism (Protestant)
evangelicalism 228
fundamentalism (Protestant)
248
missions, foreign 408
United Methodist Church
689
liberal Protestantism *see*
mainline Protestantism
liberation theology **360–362,**
730
Liberator (newspaper) 3, 136,
226
Liberia 15
Liberty Party 5
"Liberty Tree" 26
Liebman, Joshua 515
"life, liberty and the pursuit of
happiness" 135
"Life Is Worth Living" (TV
show) 204
Light of Asia (Sir Edwin Arnold)
87
Lincoln, Abraham (1809–1865)
362, **362–363**
civil religion 134, 135
Civil War 139, 141
literature and Christianity 366
slavery 624
Lindbergh, Charles 736
Lindsell, Harold 314
Lindsey, Hal 185, 523, 539
Lipan Indians 437
Lipscomb, David (1831–1917)
131, **363–364**, 556
Listen, America! (Jerry Falwell)
417
literalism, biblical *see* inerrancy
literature and Christianity
364–367
Lithuania 337, 487
Little, Malcolm *see* Malcolm X
Little Big Horn, Battle of
(1876) 135
Liuseno Indians 445
Livingston, John Henry 549
Llano del Rio (California
utopian community) 695
Locke, John
American Revolution/
Revolutionary War 25
Carolinas 104
Enlightenment 209, 210
primitivism 528
Scottish Common Sense
Realism 600

Loehe, Wilhelm 370
"Log College" 267, 268, 466,
467
Lollards, English 154
Loma Linda, California 612
Lomax, Louis 428
London Missionary Society 407
Long, Huey 117
Longinqua Oceani (papal
encyclical) 27–28, 285,
367–368, 567
Long Island, New York 526,
549
Loomis, Harvey 281
Los Angeles, California
Azusa Street revival 48, 49
Buddhism 88
charismatic movement 111
Church of God in Christ 126
Hinduism 291, 293
International Society for
Krishna Consciousness 316
Orthodox Judaism 488
Scientology 597
Self-Realization Fellowship
609
theosophy 664
Vedanta Society 698
*Lost Cause: A New Southern
History of the War of the
Confederates, The* (Edward A.
Pollard) 368
Lost Cause Myth 141, 366,
368–369, 637
lost tribes of Israel 73, 74
Lotus Sutra (Buddhist text) 86,
87, 471, 472
Louis XIV (king of France) 303
Louisiana *see also specific city*
(*e.g.,* New Orleans)
African-American religion 9
anti-Semitism 38
creationism 171
evolution 230
New France 463
Roman Catholicism 564, 566
South 637
Southern Baptist Convention
638
Louisiana Purchase (1803) 463
Louisville, Kentucky 402
love feast 129
Lovejoy, Elijah P. 3
Lowery, Joseph 640
Loyalists (American Revolution)
26
LSD (lysergic acid diethylamide)
167
Lubavitcher Hasidim 279–280,
340
Lucumi (Santería) 586
Lumbrozo, Jacob 38
Lusitania (ship) 734
Luther, Martin
Bible societies 69

Evangelical Lutheran Church in America 224
German Reformed Church 255
justification 342, 343
Lutheran Church—Missouri Synod 370
Lutheranism 371, 372
Reformation 546
United Church of Christ 687
Lutheran Church in America (LCA) 223, 225, 374
Lutheran Church—Missouri Synod 369–371
  biblical interpretation 72
  electronic church 204
  Evangelical Lutheran Church in America 223, 224–225
  fundamentalism (Protestant) 250
  inerrancy 314
  Lutheranism 372, 373, 374
Lutheraner (periodical) 370
Lutheran Free Church 225
Lutheranism 371–374
  Carolinas 104
  charismatic movement 111
  church and state, relationship between 122
  Evangelical Lutheran Church in America 222
  Lutheran Church—Missouri Synod 369
  National Council of Churches 436
  New Netherland 464
  Pennsylvania 500, 501
  people
    Krauth, Charles Porterfield 224, 353, 353–354
    Muhlenberg, Henry Melchior 26, 223, 224, 373, 423–424, 501
    Schmucker, Samuel Simon 221, 222, 224, 373, 591, 591–592
    Walther, Carl Ferdinand Wilhelm 370, 373, 709–710
  Pietism 507
  Reformation 548
  South 637
Lutheran Laymen's League 370
Lutheran Woman's Missionary League 370
Luther Seminary (St. Paul, Minnesota) 225
lyceum circuit 674
Lyford, John 510
Lynchburg, Virginia 417
lynchings 39, 142
Lyng v. Northwest Indian Cemetery Protective Association (1988) 24

Lynn, James J. see Janakananda, Swami Rajasi

M

Machen, John Gresham (1881–1937) 375
  inerrancy 314
  Presbyterian Church (U.S.A.) 525
  presbyterianism 527
  Princeton Theology 529, 530
  secular humanism 605
Macintosh, Douglas Clyde 411
Mack Sr., Alexander 129
Macy, Joanna 181
Madison, James (1751–1836) 375–377, 376
  Constitution, U.S. 160
  establishment, religious 218
  secularism 606
  Virginia 702, 705
magic 459
Magnalia Christi Americana (Cotton Mather) 519
Maha Bodhi Society 740
Mahan, Asa (1799–1889) 377–378
  Higher Christian Life movement 287, 288
  Holiness movement 295, 296
  perfectionism 505, 506
  sanctification 584
Maharaj-ji (boy guru) 291
Maharishi Mahesh Yogi 292, 672
Mahatmas ("Great Souls") 664
Mahayana Buddhism 85, 89, 471 see also Zen
Maimonides (Moses ben Maimon) 486
Maine 20, 59, 218, 320, 632, 661
mainline Protestantism 72, 215, 378–379 see also American Baptist Churches In the U.S.A.; Christian Church (Disciples of Christ); Episcopal Church; Evangelical Lutheran Church in America; Presbyterian Church (U.S.A.); United Church of Christ; United Methodist Church
"Make Love, Not War" 168
Makemie, Francis 523, 526
Malcolm Shabazz Temple (New York City) 428
Malcolm X (Malcolm Little) (1925–1965) 379–381
  African-American religion 12, 13
  civil rights movement 138
  Islam 320
  Nation of Islam (Black Muslims) 427, 429

manbo (priestess) 706
Manchester, New York 76
Mandan Indians 448
Manhattan Island (New York City) 372, 464
Manifest Destiny 381–382
  assimilation and resistance, Native American 44
  civil religion 135
  Native American religions: Eastern Woodlands 444
  nature religion 455
  Student Volunteer Movement 652
manitou (spiritual powers) 443
Mann, Horace (1796–1859) 382–383
Manning, James 59
mantras 316
Manual of the Mother Church (Mary Baker Eddy) 120
Marcuse, Herbert 166, 167
Marechal, Ambrose (1764–1828) 383–384, 564
Marquette, Jacques (1637–1675) 327, 384–385
marriage for eternity 553
Marshall, Daniel 269
Martha's Vineyard 406
Martin, Clarice 234
Martin Luther King Jr. Center for Nonviolent Social Change 531
Martin Luther King Jr. Memorial Weekend 640
Marty, Martin 223, 481
Marx, Karl 152, 457
Marxism 361
Mary (queen of England) 97, 547
Mary II (queen of England) 217, 386
Maryknoll Order 408
Maryland see also specific city (e.g., Baltimore)
  African Methodist Episcopal Church 15
  Anglicanism 31
  anti-Semitism 38, 39
  church and state, relationship between 122
  colonial period 147, 385–386
  Constitution, U.S. 160
  establishment, religious 216, 217
  Roman Catholicism 562, 563, 566
  Society for the Propagation of the Gospel in Foreign Parts 632
  Toleration, Act of see Toleration, Act of
Maslow, Abraham 22
Mason, C. H. 125, 126, 503

Masonic Order see Freemasonry
Massachuset Indians 406
Massachusetts see also specific city (e.g., Boston)
  American Baptist Churches in the U.S.A. 19
  American Indian Religious Freedom Act (AIRFA) 22
  Baptists 57, 58
  church and state, relationship between 122, 123
  Congregationalism 156
  education, public school 199
  Episcopal Church 212
  establishment, religious 216, 218
  Great Awakening 269
  Half-way Covenant 275
  missions, home 409
  Native American religions: Eastern Woodlands 443
  Reformation 548
  Unitarian Controversy 682, 683, 684
  voluntaryism 707
Massachusetts Bay Colony 386–389
  anti-Catholicism 32
  Antinomian Controversy 36–37
  colonial period 147
  Congregationalism 155
  Friends, the Religious Society of (Quakers) 243
  Half-way Covenant 275
  Puritanism 534
  Roman Catholicism 562
Massachusetts Metaphysical College 120
Massachusetts Sunday School Union 655
massage 461
mass marriages 681
mass suicide 331
Mata, Sri Daya (Faye Wright) 609
Mather, Cotton (1663–1728) 389
  Enlightenment 209
  Half-way Covenant 275
  Hinduism 288
  missions, foreign 406
  preachers, Protestant 519
  Salem witchcraft trials 582
  science and religion 594
Mather, Eleazar 275
Mather, Increase (1639–1723) 161, 275, 389–391, 390
Mather, Richard 99, 275
Mathews, Shailer (1863–1941) 20, 391–392, 411, 630, 735
Matthew, Wentworth Arthur 73, 74
Maurin, Peter 108, 569
Mayan Indians 62

Mayflower (ship) 509
Mayflower Compact (1620) **392,** 509
Mayhew, Jonathan (1720–1766) 41, **392–394,** *393,* 682
Mayhew Jr., Thomas 406
Mayo, Katherine 292
Mays, Benjamin 531
McCarthy, Carlton 369
McCarthy, Joseph 146, 153, 454, 571, 572
McCollum v. Board of Education (1948) 123
McConnell, Francis J. 689
McFague, Sallie 235
McGiffert, Arthur Cushman 313
McGready, James 100, 101, 103
McIntire, Carl 118, 250, 527
McKinley, William 34
McPherson, Aimee Semple (1890–1944) 204, *394,* **394–395,** 504
McQuaid, Bernard 27, 567
McQuilkin, Robert C. 288
Meacham, Joseph 617
Meade, William 213
Meadville-Lombard Seminary (Chicago, Illinois) 693
Medellín, Colombia 360
medical establishment 614
Medicine Lodge (Cheyenne ceremony) 449
meditation 461, 749
mehitzah (curtain) 158, 337
Melanchthon, Philip 372
Melville, Herman 365
Memorial and Remonstrance (James Madison) 218, 705
Memphis, Tennessee 126, 293, 503
Mencken, Henry Louis (1880–1956) 47, 250, **395–396,** 614
Mendes, Henry Pereira (1852–1937) 157, 337, **396–397,** 488, 754
Menendez de Aviles, Pedro 468, *562*
Mennonites *397,* **397–398**
  American Revolution/ Revolutionary War 26
  Amish 29
  Civil War 139
  Mennonites 398
  Pennsylvania 500
  Reformation 548
  World War I 735
  World War II 738
Menominee Indians 23
Mercersburg, Pennsylvania 255
Mercersburg Theology 255
Mercer University (Macon, Georgia) 59
Merton, Thomas (1915–1968) 88, 146, **399–400,** 750

Mescalero Apache Indians 437, 451
Mesmer, Franz Anton 400, 401, 643
mesmerism **400–401**
MEST (Matter, Energy, Space, and Time) 597
Metaxakis, Meletios 271
Methodist Episcopal Church
  Civil War 139
  Great Awakening 270
  Holiness movement 296
  Methodists 401
  perfectionism 506
  Sunday school movement 655
  United Methodist Church 688, 689
  Wesleyan tradition 716
Methodist Episcopal Church, South 4, 116, 402, 403
Methodist General Conference (1844) 4
Methodist Protestant Church 402, 403, 689
Methodists **401–403** *see also* African Methodist Episcopal Church; African Methodist Episcopal Zion Church; Christian Methodist Episcopal Church (C.M.E.); United Methodist Church
  abolitionism 3, 4
  African-American religion 9, 10, 13
  American Revolution/ Revolutionary War 26
  Arminianism 41
  Burned-Over District 91
  camp meetings 101
  Cane Ridge revival 103
  charismatic movement 111
  colonial period 148
  election 203
  episcopacy 212
  establishment, religious 218
  Evangelical United Front 226
  frontier 245
  Holiness movement 295
  justification 343
  missions, foreign 407
  people
    Allen, Richard 14, *14,* 15, **18–19,** 136, 402, 520
    Asbury, Francis *see* Asbury, Francis
    Cartwright, Peter **107,** 603
    Coke, Thomas **143–144,** 212, 401, 688, 716
    Harkness, Georgia Elma **277–278**
    Lee, Jarena **356–357**
    perfectionism 505, 506
    Pietism 507
    preachers, Protestant 519, 520

primitivism 528
  sanctification 584
  Second Great Awakening 603
  slavery 623
  Social Gospel 631
  South 636, 637
  Sunday school movement 654
  temperance 661
  Wesleyan tradition 714, 715
Methodist Soldiers' Tract Association 141
Metropolitan Community Church (M.C.C.) **403–404,** 615
Mexican Americans 312, 454, 470
Mexico 437, 438, 467, 561
Meyendorff, John 485
Meyer, Louis 251
Miami, Florida 586, 706
Michaelius, Jonas 464, 549
Michigan 117, 512, 550 *see also specific city* (*e.g.,* Detroit)
Michigan, University of 111, 701
Middleborough, Massachusetts 19, 56, 58
middle classes
  Bahá'í Faith 52
  charismatic movement 111
  Cold War 146
  counterculture 167
  temperance 662
  Young Men's Christian Association (YMCA) 746
"middle way" 31, 156, 158, 548
Midewiwin (medicine societies) 443
Midwestern Baptist Seminary (Kansas City, Missouri) 638
mikveh (pool for ritual purification) 487
Milarepa Center (Barnet, Vermont) *675*
Miles, William H. 116
millennialism *see* dispensationalism; eschatology; postmillennialism; premillennialism; rapture
  American Revolution/ Revolutionary War 25, 26
  Civil War 139
  Communism 152, 153
  Miller, William 404, 405
  Native American religions: Inter-montane/California 446
  New Age religion 460
  Russell, Charles Taze 577, 578
  White, Ellen Gould (Harmon) 719
  World War I 734
Miller, Arthur 581
Miller, John Peter 211

Miller, Lewis 655
Miller, William (1782–1849) 113, **404–405,** *405,* 612
Millerites (adventist group) 92
Mills, Samuel J. 281
Milwaukee, Wisconsin 564
"mind control" 36, 682
Minhag America (Jewish prayer book) 544
Minneapolis, Minnesota 46
Minnesota 46, 225, 308
minyan (quorum) 158–159, 487
miracles 210
Miscavige, David 597
Mishna (Jewish text) 486
Mishneh Torah (Jewish text) 486
misogyny 234
missionaries
  American Indian Religious Freedom Act (AIRFA) 22
  Buddhism 86, 87
  Hinduism 290
  Judson, Adoniram 20, 58, 281, *341,* 341–342, 407
  Kino, Eusebio Francisco 327, **350,** 469
  Native American religions: Inter-montane/California 445
  Native American religions: Northwest 447
  New France 462, 463
  New Spain 469
  Serra, Junipero 469, *610,* **610–611**
Missionary Baptists 637
Missionary Training Institute (New York City) 67
missions, foreign (Protestant) **405–408** *see also* Society for the Propagation of the Gospel in Foreign Parts; Student Volunteer Movement
  African Methodist Episcopal Church 15
  assimilation and resistance, Native American 44
  Church of the Nazarene 131
  Haystack Prayer Meeting 281
  Moravians 419
  National Baptist Convention of America, Inc. 432
  Seventh-day Adventist Church 612
missions, home (Protestant) **408–411**
  African-American religion 9
  African Methodist Episcopal Church 15
  Baptists 60
  Burned-Over District 91
  Church of Jesus Christ of Latter-day Saints 128
  Church of the Nazarene 131
  Evangelical United Front 226

Manifest Destiny 382
Native American religions:
   Inter-montane/California
   445
Native American religions:
   Northwest 447
proslavery thought 532
Mississippi 116, 432, 463, 651
Mississippian Indians 442
Mississippi Freedom Democratic
   Party (MFDP) 138, 651–652
Missouri 127, 409 *see also*
   specific city (*e.g.,* St. Louis)
Missouri Compromise (1820) 3
"Missouri Mormons" 553
Missouri Synod Lutherans 374
mitzvoth (religious laws) 279,
   486
Mizrahi (Zionist group) 552,
   753
Mizrahi Hatzhair (Zionist youth
   organization) 552
Mizrahi Women's Organization
   552
Moby Dick (Herman Melville)
   365
"Model of Christian Charity, A"
   (John Winthrop sermon) 519
modernism (Protestant)
   411–412
   American Baptist Churches in
      the U.S.A. 20
   fundamentalism (Protestant)
      248
   Humanist Manifesto 303
   liberalism, theological 360
   people
      Abbott, Lyman **1**
      Ames, Edward Scribner
         28–29, 411
      Beecher, Henry Ward
         62–64, *63,* 520
      Briggs, Charles Augustus
         72, **78–80,** *79,* 285, 313,
         525
      Bushnell, Horace *92,*
         92–93, 141, 198, 199
      Clarke, William Newton 20,
         143
      Gray, Asa 170, 229,
         266–267
      Mathews, Shailer 20,
         391–392, 411, 630, 735
      Smyth, Newman **628–629**
   science and religion 595
Modoc Indians 257
Mojave Indians 257, 451
moksha (spiritual liberation) 609
monasticism 31, 211, 665
"Monkey Trial" *see* Scopes trial
Mono Indians 444
Montana 308
Monteagle, Tennessee 151
Montgomery, Alabama 639
Montgomery, Carrie Judd 125

Montgomery Improvement
   Association 137, 639
Moody, Dwight Lyman
   (1837–1899) **412–414,** *413*
   Bible schools 67
   conversion 162
   Fundamentals, The 251
   Higher Christian Life
      movement 288
   preachers, Protestant 521
   revivalism 558
   Student Volunteer Movement
      652
   Young Men's Christian
      Association (YMCA) 746
Moody Bible Institute (Chicago,
   Illinois) 67, 68, 431
Moon, Sun Myung (1920–)
   414–415, 681
Mooney, James 438
Moore, Jennie 48, 502
Moorish Science Temple 320,
   415–416
Morais, Sabato (1823–1897)
   157, 337, **416–417,** 754
Moral Majority **417–418**
   Baptists 61
   Christian Right 119
   electronic church 205
   fundamentalism (Protestant)
      250
   preachers, Protestant 522
   satanism 587
   secular humanism 605
   sexuality 615
Moral Re-Armament 84, 85
Moravia 308
Moravians **418–420**
   American Revolution/
      Revolutionary War 26
   Carolinas 105
   Evangelical Lutheran Church
      in America 223
   Pennsylvania 500
   Pietism 507, 508
   South 637
   Wesleyan tradition 715
Morehouse College (Atlanta,
   Georgia) 433, 531
Morgan, Marabel 615
Mormons *see* Church of Jesus
   Christ of Latter-day Saints;
   Reorganized Church of Jesus
   Christ of Latter Day Saints
Morris, E. C. 432
Morris, Henry M. 170, 596
Morrison, Toni 367
Morse, Jedidiah 452, 683
Morton, Thomas 510
Mosaic laws 511
Moses, Robert 701
"Mother Ann's Work" (spiritual
   revival) 617
Mother India (Katherine Mayo)
   292

motion picture industry 614 *see
   also* Hollywood
Mott, John Raleigh
   (1865–1955) **420**
   ecumenical movement 194
   missions, foreign 407
   Student Volunteer Movement
      652, 653
   World War I 734
   Young Men's Christian
      Association (YMCA) 746
Mott, Lucretia 244
"Mount Hermon Hundred"
   652
Mt. Sinai Holy Church 11
Moynihan, Daniel 513
muckrakers 630
Muhammad (founder of Islam)
   319
Muhammad, Abdul 427
Muhammad, Elijah
   (1897–1975) **420–422**
   African-American religion 12
   Islam 320, 321
   Nation of Islam (Black
      Muslims) 427, 428, 429,
      430
Muhammad, Warith Deen
   (1933–) 321, **422–423,** 429
Muhlenberg, Henry Melchior
   (1711–1787) **423–424**
   American Revolution/
      Revolutionary War 26
   Evangelical Lutheran Church
      in America 223, 224
   Lutheranism 373
   Pennsylvania 501
Muir, John (1838–1914) *424,*
   424–425, 674
multiculturalism 221
Münster, Germany 548
Murray, John Courtney
   (1904–1967) 145, 327,
   425–426, 692
Murray, Margaret 458
music 131, 556 *see also* Gospel;
   hymns
Muskogee (Creek) Indians
   American Indian Religious
      Freedom Act (AIRFA) 23
   assimilation and resistance,
      Native American 45
   Moravians 419
   Native American religions:
      Eastern Woodlands 442,
      443, 444
Muslim Americans 221
Muslim Journal 321
Muslim Student Association 320
Mussolini, Benito 570
mysticism 62, 278, 279, 455,
   673
Mystics and Zen Masters
   (Thomas Merton) 750

N

NAACP *see* National
   Association for the
   Advancement for Colored
   People
Nagasaki, bombing of (1945)
   145, 571
Nanak, Guru 621
Napoleon Bonaparte 543
Naropa Institute (Boulder,
   Colorado) 88
Narragansett Indians *725*
*Narrative of the Great Revival
   Which Prevailed in the Southern
   Armies, A* (William W.
   Bennett) 141
Nashville, Tennessee
   Committee of Southern
      Churchmen 150
   Hinduism 293
   National Baptist Convention,
      U.S.A., Inc. 433
   Roman Catholicism 564
   Southern Baptist Convention
      638
   Student Nonviolent
      Coordinating Committee
      651
Nast, Wilhelm 689
National American Suffrage
   Association 732
National Association for the
   Advancement of Colored
   People (NAACP) 137, 432,
   651
National Association of
   Evangelicals 43, 228, **431**
National Baptist Convention,
   Unincorporated 432
National Baptist Convention,
   U.S.A., Inc. 11, 59, 61,
   432–433, 531
National Baptist Convention of
   America, Inc. 60, 61,
   431–432, 432
National Baptist Educational
   Convention of the U.S.A. 432
National Baptist Sunday Church
   School 432
National Camp Meeting
   Association for the Promotion
   of Christian Holiness 101
National Catholic War Council
   567, 734
National Catholic Welfare
   Conference **433–434,** 569,
   734
National Catholic Welfare
   Council 567
National Conference of Catholic
   Bishops (NCCB) 434,
   434–435
National Conference of
   Unitarian Churches 684

National Congress of American Indians 45
National Council of Churches 435–437
  African-American religion 13
  Baptists 60
  Church of the Brethren (Dunkers) 130
  Cold War 145
  Communism 153
  ecumenical movement 196
  Metropolitan Community Church 404
  Reformed Church in America 550
  Scientology 597
  Social Gospel 631
  United Methodist Church 689
National Council of Churches of Christ in the U.S.A. 195
National Council of Congregational Churches 156, 687
National Evangelical Lutheran Church 370
National Forest Service 24
National Holiness Association 130
National Indian Youth Council 45
National League for Decency 614
National League for the Protection of American Independence 453
National Lutheran Council 225, 373
National Missionary Baptist Convention of America 432
National Origins Act (1927) 454
National Park Service 24
National Religious Party (NRP) 552, 753
National Right to Life Committee 615
National Spiritualist Association 644
National Student Christian Federation 653
Nation of Islam (Black Muslims) (NOI) 427–431, 428
  African-American religion 11, 12
  anti-Semitism 39
  Islam 320, 321
Native American Church 45, 437–439
Native American religions 439–442
  Eastern Woodlands 442–444
  Inter-montane/California 444–446
  Northwest 446–448
  Plains 448–450

Southwest 450–452
Native American Rights Fund 45
Native Americans see also Ghost Dance; Handsome Lake; Wovoka
  American Missionary Association 24
  assimilation and resistance see assimilation and resistance, Native American
  Bahá'í Faith 52
  Beat movement 62
  Bible societies 69
  Book of Mormon 76
  civil religion 135
  frontier 245
  Massachusetts Bay Colony 388
  missions, foreign 405, 406
  missions, home 408, 409, 410
  Moravians 419
  nature religion 455
  New Age religion 461
  New France 463
  Orthodox Church in America 485
  Penn, William 498
  Pennsylvania 500
  Pilgrims 509
  sexuality 613
  Society for the Propagation of the Gospel in Foreign Parts 632
  United Church of Christ 686
nativism 452–454, 661, 662
  see also Ku Klux Klan
naturalism-supernaturalism debate 542
natural philosophy 210
natural selection 229
natural theology 209
"Nature" (Ralph Waldo Emerson essay) 365, 673
nature religion 454–456
Nauvoo, Illinois 127
Navajo Indians 23, 439, 450, 451, 452
Nazareth, Pennsylvania 419
Nazism
  Agudath Israel 16
  anti-Semitism 39
  Christian Right 118
  death of God theology 179
  Hasidism 279
  Judaism 339
  Ku Klux Klan 355
  modernism (Protestant) 412
  nativism 454
  Roman Catholicism 570, 571
  World War II 737
  Zionism 753
NCCB see National Conference of Catholic Bishops
Neale, Leonard 564

Negro Improvement Association (UNIA) 12
Negro Leaders Conference on Nonviolent Integration (1957) 639
neo-evangelicalism 228, 431
Neolin (Delaware Indian leader) 45
neo-Nazis 39
neo-orthodoxy 179, 360, 456–458
neo-paganism 235, 458–460
neo-Pentecostalism 111
Neoplatonism 657
Netherlands see also New Netherland
  Mennonites 397
  presbyterianism 526
  Puritanism 534
  Reformation 547, 548
Nettleton, Asahel 603
neutrality 26
Nevada 257, 444
Nevin, John Williamson (1803–1886) 255, 460
New Age religion 456, 460–461, 513, 644
New Amsterdam (Dutch settlement that became New York City) 303, 334, 464, 486, 549
Newark, New Jersey 74, 320, 415
New Brunswick, New Jersey 466, 467
New Brunswick (New Jersey) Theological Seminary 549
New Deal 23, 117, 569
New Divinity 461–462
Newell, Samuel 281
New England see specific state (e.g., Massachusetts)
New France 462–463
  anti-Semitism 38
  Carolinas 104
  church and state, relationship between 122
  colonial period 147
  Jesuits 327
  Native American religions: Eastern Woodlands 443
  Roman Catholicism 561, 562
New Hampshire
  anti-Catholicism 32
  church and state, relationship between 123
  establishment, religious 216, 218
  Second Great Awakening 602
  Sikhism 622
New Harmony, Indiana 47
New Haven, Connecticut 275, 534, 580, 602
New Haven Theology 659–660
New Humanist (periodical) 304

New Jersey see also specific city (e.g., Newark)
  African Methodist Episcopal Church 14
  American Baptist Churches in the U.S.A. 19
  anti-Catholicism 32
  Baptists 58
  Christian Reformed Church 116
  establishment, religious 216
  missions, foreign 406
  Moravians 419
  presbyterianism 528
  Reformed Church in America 549, 550
  Roman Catholicism 563
  Society for the Propagation of the Gospel in Foreign Parts 632
  Transcendental Meditation 672
  Universalism 692
New Jerusalem (New York utopian community) 91, 723
New Lebanon, New York 617
New Left 167
New Lights/Old Lights 463–464
  American Baptist Churches in the U.S.A. 19
  Congregationalism 156
  establishment, religious 217
  Society for the Propagation of the Gospel in Foreign Parts 633
  Unitarian Controversy 682
  United Church of Christ 686
"New Measures" (revivalism) 245
New Mexico 450, 469, 564, 565
New Netherland 122, 147, 464–465, 501, 548
New Orleans, Louisiana
  anti-Semitism 38
  Greek Orthodox Archdiocese of North and South America 270
  Hinduism 293
  New France 463
  Roman Catholicism 565
  trusteeism 676
New Orleans (Louisiana) Baptist Seminary 638
New Paltz, New York 303
"new physics" 456
Newport, Rhode Island 58, 334, 486, 580
New Religious Right 118, 119, 417, 523, 605
New Rochelle, New York 303
New School/Old School 465–466
  abolitionism 4
  Civil War 139

heresy 284
missions, foreign 407
Plan of Union 512
Presbyterian Church (U.S.A.)
    524, 525
presbyterianism 527
Princeton Theology 529
New Side/Old Side **466–467**
    Great Awakening 268–269
    Presbyterian Church (U.S.A.)
        524
    presbyterianism 527
New South 368
New Spain **467–470**
    anti-Semitism 38
    Carolinas 104
    church and state, relationship
        between 122
    colonial period 147
    Jesuits 327
New Sweden 122, 147, 501
New Thought 120, **470–471**
Newton, Sir Isaac 209, 210, 594
New Vrindaban (Hare Krishna
    commune) 316
New York Bible Society 69
New York City
    Anglicanism 31
    anti-Catholicism 33
    anti-Semitism 39
    Black Jews 73, 74
    Christadelphians 113
    establishment, religious 217
    Ethical Culture 219
    Greek Orthodox Archdiocese
        of North and South America
        270
    Hinduism 293
    Huguenots 303
    International Society for
        Krishna Consciousness 316
    Methodists 402
    Moorish Science Temple 415
    Nation of Islam (Black
        Muslims) 428, 429
    New Netherland 465
    New Side/Old Side 467
    Nichiren Shoshu Academy
        472
    Orthodox Judaism 488
    Pennsylvania 501
    Reconstructionist Judaism
        541
    Reformation 548
    Reformed Church in America
        549
    Religious Zionists of America
        552
    Santería 586
    Second Great Awakening 604
    Sikhism 622
    Sunday school movement 655
    theosophy 664
    trusteeism 676

United Synagogue of
    Conservative Judaism 690
Vedanta Society 698
Vodou 706
New York Missionary Society
    409
New York State *see also specific
    city (e.g., New York City)*
    Anglo-Catholicism 31
    anti-Catholicism 33
    Burned-Over District 90
    Christian Reformed Church
        116
    education, public school 199
    establishment, religious 216
    Evangelical Lutheran Church
        in America 224
    frontier 245
    Islam 321
    Lutheranism 372
    Methodists 401
    Native American Church 439
    New Netherland 464
    New Side/Old Side 466
    Plan of Union 511, 512
    Reformed Church in America
        550
    Roman Catholicism 563
    Society for the Propagation of
        the Gospel in Foreign Parts
        632
    United Church of Christ 686
New York Times (newspaper)
    605, 754
Nichiren Daishonin (Buddhist
    reformer) 86, 471
Nichiren Shoshu Academy
    (N.S.A.) 86, **471–472**
Niebuhr, Helmut Richard
    (1894–1962) 256, 457,
    472–473, 736, 737
Niebuhr, Reinhold (1892–1971)
    473–475
    Cold War 145
    German Reformed Church
        256
    Neo-orthodoxy 456, 457
    Sojourners Fellowship 633
    World War II 736, 737, 738
Nietzsche, Friedrich 249
Nims, Jerry 418
Ninza, Marcos de 451
Niskeyuna, New York 617
Nixon, E. D. 137
Nixon, Richard
    American Indian Religious
        Freedom Act (AIRFA) 23
    civil rights movement 138
    Cold War 146
    peace reform 497
    Unification Church 681
    Vietnam War 702
Noah, Mordechai 752
nonviolence 13, 138, 290, 496,
    501

Norfolk, Virginia 676
Norris, J. Frank 250, 636
North American Baptist
    Conference 60
North American Christian
    Convention 115, 132, 556
North American Old Roman
    Catholic Church 480
North American Review 262
Northampton, Massachusetts
    268
North Carolina *see also specific
    city (e.g., Salem)*
    African-American religion 10
    Anglicanism 31
    anti-Semitism 39
    Carolinas 104, 105
    church and state, relationship
        between 123
    Church of God (Cleveland,
        Tennessee) 124, 125
    colonial period 148
    Constitution, U.S. 160
    establishment, religious 216,
        217
    Evangelical Lutheran Church
        in America 224
    Moravians 419
    Pentecostalism 503
    presbyterianism 528
    Society for the Propagation of
        the Gospel in Foreign Parts
        632
    South 637
North Dakota 308
Northern Baptist Convention
    20, 60, 249
Norton, Andrews 683
Norwegian Americans 224, 373
Notre Dame (Indiana),
    University of 111, 565
Nott Jr., Samuel 281
novus ordo seclorum ("new order
    of the ages") 134
Noyes, John Humphrey
    (1811–1886) **475–477,** *476,*
    506, 614
N.S.A. *see* Nichiren Shoshu
    Academy
NSA Quarterly (periodical) 471
nuclear weapons 145, 146, 435
Nyingma Institute (Berkeley,
    California) 88

O

Oak Bluffs, Massachusetts 101
Oakland, California 293
oaths, rejection of 243, 308
Oblate Sisters of Providence 566
Occident (periodical) 336
occult *see* Freemasonry;
    mesmerism; Neo-paganism;
    New Age religion; Rosicrucians;
    Santeria; satanism; spiritualism;

Swedenborgianism; theosophy;
    Vodou
Ockenga, Harold John 228, 431
O'Connell, Denis 28
O'Connor, Flannery 367
O'Connor, John Cardinal 573,
    574
Ogou (Vodou spirit) 706
Ogun (Yoruba god) 586
O'Hair, Madalyn Murray
    (1919–) **478**
Ohio *see also specific city (e.g.,
    Cincinnati)*
    Amish 30
    Cane Ridge revival 103
    Evangelical Lutheran Church
        in America 224
    Friends, the Religious Society
        of (Quakers) 244
    Mennonites 398
    missions, home 409
    Plan of Union 511, 512
    restoration movement 555
    Second Great Awakening 603
    United Church of Christ 686
    United Methodist Church
        689
O'Kelly, James 402, 554, 555
Oklahoma 23, 257, 437, 438,
    444
Oklahoma City, Oklahoma 503
Olat Tamid (Jewish prayer
    book) 544
Olcott, Henry Steel
    (1832–1907) 87, 290,
    478–480, *479,* 664
Old Catholic movement
    480–481
Old Colony Mennonites 398
"Old Fashioned Revival Hour,
    The" (radio show) 204
Old German Baptist Brethren
    (Old Order Dunkers) 129
Old Lights *see* New Lights/Old
    Lights
Old Lutheran Church
    (Philadelphia, Pennsylvania)
    223
Old Order Amish Mennonite
    Church 30
Old Order Dunkers *see* Old
    German Baptist Brethren
Old Regular Baptists 637
Old School *see* New
    School/Old School
Old Side *see* New Side/Old Side
Old South *see* proslavery
    thought; slavery; South
"Old-Time Gospel Hour" (TV
    show) 205, 417, 522
Olivet Baptist (Chicago) 11
Olodumare (Yoruba god) 586
Onanharoia (Huron/Iroquois
    ritual)

Native American religions:
Eastern Woodlands 443
Onderdonk, Benjamin Tredwell
31
Onderdonk, Henry Ustick 31
Oneida Community (New York
State) 91, 152, 154, 506, 614
Ontario, Canada 398
On the Origin of Species (Charles
Darwin)
creationism 170
evangelicalism 227
evolution 229
inerrancy 313
science and religion 595
Scopes trial 598
On the Road (Jack Kerouac) 61
"Operating Thetans" (O.T.s)
597
optimism 412, 471
Order, the (segregationist
group) 608
Order of Knights Templar 241
Order of the Star Spangled
Banner *see* Know-Nothing Party
ordination 213 *see also* women
and religion
Oregon
Hinduism 291
Ku Klux Klan 354
Native American Church 439
Native American religions:
Inter-montane/California
445
Roman Catholicism 568
Worldwide Church of God
740
Oregon City, Oregon 564
Organization of the Star
Spangled Banner 33
Organization of United
American Mechanics 453
Organization of United
Americans 453
*Oriental Religions and their
Relation to Universal Religion*
(Samuel Johnson) 290
Original Hebrew Israelite Nation
74
orishas (spiritual beings) 586
Orthodox Christianity
481–484 *see also* Greek
Orthodox Archdiocese of
North and South America;
Orthodox Church in America
baptism 57
Communism 152
ecumenical movement 194,
195
episcopacy 212
people
Belavin, Tikhon 65–66, 485
Coucouzes, Iakovos 165,
272

Schmemann, Alexander
484, 485, 590–591
Spyrou, Athenagoras
271–272, 644–645
Zionism 755
Orthodox Church in America
(OCA) 436, 483, 484–485
Orthodox Judaism 485–490
see also Religious Zionists of
America
Black Jews 74
Hasidism 280
immigration 309
Judaism 338, 339, 340
Zionism 753, 754
Orthodox Presbyterian Church
99, 525, 527, 528
Osborn, William B. 296
Osceola (Seminole leader) 45
O'Sullivan, John 381
Oto Church of the First Born
438
Otterbein, Phillip William 688
oungan (Vodou priest) 706
Our Country (Josiah Strong)
631
"Oversoul" (Ralph Waldo
Emerson essay) 289
Owen, Robert Dale
(1801–1877) 47, 490–491,
694
Oxford, England 287–288,
296, 401
Oxford Movement 31
Oxnam, G. Bromley 689

P

Pacific Coast Khalsa Diwan
Society 622
pacifism
American Revolution/
Revolutionary War 26
Catholic Worker movement
108
Christadelphians 113
Church of the Brethren
(Dunkers) 129, 130
Friends, the Religious Society
of (Quakers) 243
Hutterites 308
Mennonites 397
peace reform 496
Sojourners Fellowship 633
World War II 736
paganism *see* neo-paganism
Pagels, Elaine 234
Pai Indians 451
Paine, Thomas (1737–1809)
492–493
atheism 47
education, public school 198
Enlightenment 210, 211
secularism 606
Paiute Indians 257, 444

Palestine 407
Palmer, A. Mitchell 153
Palmer, Elihu 47, 210, 211, 606
Palmer, Phoebe Worrall
(1807–1874) 493–494
Higher Christian Life
movement 287
Holiness movement 295–296
Pentecostalism 502
perfectionism 505
sanctification 584
Palmer Raids (1917) 453
Papa Gede (Vodou spirit) 707
Papago Indians 451
Papal Volunteers for Latin
America 408
Parham, Charles Fox
(1873–1929) 494
Assemblies of God 42, 43
Azusa Street revival 48
Pentecostalism 502, 504
perfectionism 506
Parker, Quanah 438
Parker, Theodore (1810–1860)
494–496, 495, 673, 674
Parker, William 137
Parliament, English 30
Parris, Samuel 581
Parris Island, South Carolina
104
Pasadena, California 404, 741
Passamoquoddy Indians 444
Pastorius, Francis Daniel 398
patriarchy 615
Patrick, Ted 36
patriotic faith *see* civil religion
Patriotism and Religion (Shailer
Mathews) 735
patroons (landed gentry) 464
Patterson, James O. 126
Patterson, Paige 639
Patton, Francis 284, 285
Patwin Indians 445
Paul, Saint 71, 532, 623, 630
Paul VI, Pope 573, 696
Pawnee Indians 23, 257, 258,
448
Pawtucket, Rhode Island 654
Payne, Daniel 15
peace churches *see* Amish;
Church of the Brethren;
Friends, the Religious Society
of; Hutterites; Mennonites;
Moravians
Peace Mission Movement 11
peace reform 496–497
Bahá'í Faith 53
Catholic Worker movement
108
perfectionism 506
World War I 733, 735
"peak experiences" 461
Peale, Norman Vincent 120,
146, 471, 514, 550

Pearl Harbor, attack on
(December 7, 1941) 735, 736,
738
Pearl of Great Price, The
(Mormon text) 77
Pendleton, William Nelson 141
Penn, William (1644–1718)
497–499, 498
establishment, religious 217
Friends, the Religious Society
of (Quakers) 243
Keithian controversy 346
Mennonites 398
Pennsylvania 500, 501
Pennington, James William
Charles (1807–1870) 499–500
Pennsylvania *see also specific city*
(*e.g.,* Philadelphia)
African Methodist Episcopal
Church 14
American Baptist Churches in
the U.S.A. 19
Amish 30
Baptists 58
colonial period 147,
500–501
establishment, religious 216
Friends, the Religious Society
of (Quakers) 243
German Reformed Church
255, 256
Lutheranism 372
Mennonites 398
Moravians 419
New Side/Old Side 467
peace reform 496
Pietism 508
presbyterianism 528
Reformation 548
Roman Catholicism 563
Rosicrucians 575
Society for the Propagation of
the Gospel in Foreign Parts
632
trusteeism 676
Pennsylvania Ministerium 373,
501
Penobscot Indians 444
Pensacola, Florida 469
Pentecostal-Charismatic
Churches of North America
505
Pentecostal Evangel (periodical)
43
Pentecostal Fellowship 505
Pentecostal Holiness Church
503, 505
Pentecostal Holiness Church,
International 503
Pentecostalism 501–505 *see
also* Assemblies of God; Azusa
Street revival
African-American religion 13
charismatic movement 111

Church of God (Cleveland, Tennessee) 124, 125
Church of God in Christ 126
Holiness movement 298
missions, foreign 408
National Association of Evangelicals 431
people
McPherson, Aimee Semple 204, *394*, **394–395**, 504
Parham, Charles Fox 42, 43, 48, **494**, 502, 504, 506
Seymour, William Joseph *see* Seymour, William Joseph
Tomlinson, Ambrose Jessup 124, 125, 503, 630, **670–671**
White, Alma Bridwell **717–718**
perfectionism 506
positive thinking 515
primitivism 529
sanctification 584
snake-handling 629, 630
Peoples Temple 330–331
Pepperdine University (Los Angeles, California) 132
Pequot Indians 443
Percy, Walker 367
Perez, Juan 447
perfectionism **505–506**
Arminianism 41
Church of God (Cleveland, Tennessee) 124
Church of the Nazarene 130
Enlightenment 209
Evangelical United Front 226
Higher Christian Life movement 287
Holiness movement 295, 296
revivalism 558
sanctification 584
Second Great Awakening 604
Unitarian Universalist Association 684
utopianism 694
Wesleyan tradition 716
Perry, Commodore Oliver 87
Perry, Troy D. 403
Perry County, Missouri 370, 373
Personalism (philosophical school) 689
Petersburg, Virginia 402
peyote religion 23, 45, 449
Pharisees (ancient Jewish group) 334
Phelps, Elizabeth Stuart (Ward) (1844–1911) 366, **506–507**
Philadelphia, Pennsylvania
African-American religion 9–10
anti-Catholicism 33
biblical interpretation 70, 71
Black Jews 74

Ethical Culture 220
Great Awakening 268
Judaism 335
Keithian controversy 346
Methodists 402
Moorish Science Temple 415
Moravians 419
Nation of Islam (Black Muslims) 428
Pennsylvania 500, 501
Pietism 508
preachers, Protestant 519, 520
Presbyterian Church (U.S.A.) 523
presbyterianism 526
Roman Catholicism 563
Second Great Awakening 604
Sunday school movement 655
trusteeism 676
Universalism 692
Philadelphia Association 19, 58, 500
Philadelphia Bible Society 69
Philadelphia Yearly Meeting (Quakers) 243
Phillips Seminary (Atlanta, Georgia) 116
philosopher's stone 576
Phipps, Sir William 582
Pia Desideria (Pious Longings) (Philipp Jakob Spener) 507
Pierce v. Society of Sisters (1925) 568
Pierson, Arthur T. 408, 653
Pietism 60, 370, **507–509** *see also* Moravians; Zinzendorf, Nicolas Ludwig von
Pike, James 214
Pilgrim Holiness Church 297, 403
Pilgrims 155, 364, 392, **509–510**, 534
"Pilgrim's Hour, The" (radio show) 204
Pilot Point, Texas 130
Piman Indians 450, 451
Pirsig, Robert M. 750
Pittsburgh, Pennsylvania 415, 552
Pittsburgh Platform 157, 336, **510–511**, 544, 545
Pius VI, Pope 563
Pius VII, Pope 327, 676
Pius IX, Pope *32*, 34, 55, 566, 696
Pius XI, Pope 569
Plain Account of Christian Perfection (John Wesley) 287
Plains Indians *see* Native American religions: Plains
Plain Truth (magazine) 740
Plan of Union **511–512**
ecumenical movement 194

National Council of Churches 435
New School/Old School 465, 466
Presbyterian Church (U.S.A.) 524
presbyterianism 527
United Church of Christ 686
Plaskow, Judith 234
Plea for the West (Lyman Beecher) 33, 198
"Pledge of Allegiance" 146
"Pledge of Resistance" 634
Plessy v. Ferguson (1896) 136
Plowshares Witnesses 634
pluralism **512–514**
atheism 47
Christian Right 119
immigration 309
missions, home 411
secular humanism 606
World's Parliament of Religions 739
Plymouth, Massachusetts
Congregationalism 155
Half-way Covenant 275
Huguenots 303
Mayflower Compact 392
Pilgrims 509
Puritanism 534
Plymouth Brethren 184
Point Loma, California 664, 695
Poland 16, 337, 487, 682
Polish Americans 564, 676
Polish National Catholic Church of America 480, 481
politics, religion and *see* Christian Right; church and state, relationship between; civil religion; Constitution
Politics of Jesus, The (John Yoder) 633
Polk, James 381
Polk, Leonidas 141
Pollard, Edward A. 368
polygamy
American Indian Religious Freedom Act (AIRFA) 23
Church of Jesus Christ of Latter-day Saints 127, 128
Reformation 548
Reorganized Church of Jesus Christ of Latter Day Saints 553, 554
Pomo Indians 257
Pope's Day (anti-Catholic holiday) 26
populism, religious 26
Portsmouth, Rhode Island 59
positive thinking 120, 146, **514–515**, 550
poskita (thanksgiving ceremony) 443
possession 586, 707
"possibility thinking" 206

postmillennialism 70, 215, **515–516**, 554, 604
potlatch 446
"Poughkeepsie Seer" *see* Davis, Andrew Jackson
Powell Jr., Adam Clayton (1908–1972) **516–517**, **517–518**
Power of Positive Thinking, The (Norman Vincent Peale) 471, 515
Power of Prayer on Plants, The 146
powwow (shaman) 443
Poyen, Charles 400
Prabhupada, Abhay Charanaravinda Bhaktivedanta Swami (1896–1977) 292, 316, **518**
pragmatism 121
"Praise the Lord and Pass the Ammunition" (song) 738
Pratt, Captain Richard 45
Prayer for Owen Meany, A (John Irving) 367
Prayer Union 747
Pray Your Weight Away 146
preachers, Protestant **518–522**
predestination
Arminianism 40
Calvinism 97, 98
election 202, 203
justification 342
Reformation 547
"preferential option for the poor" 361
premillennialism **522–523**
Assemblies of God 42
Churches of Christ 132
Church of God (Cleveland, Tennessee) 125
Cold War 145
eschatology 215
fundamentalism (Protestant) 248, 249
Jehovah's Witnesses 326
revivalism 559
Seventh-day Adventist Church 612
World War I 735
preparationism 37, 203
Presbyterian Church (U.S.A.) 99, **523–526**, 528, 552
Presbyterian Church in America 99, 527, 528
Presbyterian Church in the Confederate States of America 525
Presbyterian Church in the United States 523, 525, 527
Presbyterian General Assembly 285, 603
presbyterianism **526–528** *see also* Briggs, Charles Augustus;

Nevin, John Williamson;
Presbyterian Church (U.S.A.)
  abolitionism 4
  American Revolution/
    Revolutionary War 26
  Arminianism 41
  biblical interpretation 72
  Burned-Over District 91
  camp meetings 100, 101
  charismatic movement 111
  church and state, relationship
    between 123
  Civil War 139
  colonial period 147
  ecumenical movement 194
  establishment, religious 217
  evangelicalism 228
  Evangelical United Front 226
  fundamentalism (Protestant)
    249
  German Reformed Church
    256
  Great Awakening 267, 268
  heresy 284
  Higher Christian Life
    movement 287
  Holiness movement 296
  inerrancy 313, 314
  missions, foreign 407
  missions, home 409
  National Council of Churches
    435
  nativism 452
  New School/Old School *see*
    New School/Old School
  New Side/Old Side *see* New
    Side/Old Side
  Pennsylvania 500
  perfectionism 505
  Pietism 508
  Plan of Union 511, 512
  Princeton Theology *see*
    Princeton Theology
  Puritanism 533
  Reformation 547
  Saybrook Platform 587
  Scottish Common Sense
    Realism 600
  Second Great Awakening 604
  South 636, 637
  temperance 661
  Virginia 704
Pressler, Paul 639
Preus, J. A. O. 371
Price, George McCready 170
Price, Hiram 661
Priestcraft Exposed (periodical)
  33
Priestley, Joseph 86, 210, 288,
  682
Primitive Baptists 59, 637
Primitive Church of Divine
  Communion 292

primitivism 113, 114,
  528–529, 546 *see also*
  restoration movement
Princeton Theological Review
  170
Princeton Theology 98–99,
  529–531, *530*
Princeton (New Jersey)
  University 210, 467, 600
Principia Mathematica (Isaac
  Newton) 209
pro-choice movement 615
Program to Combat Racism 733
progress 209, 360, 411
Progressive Dunkers *see*
  Brethren Church
Progressive National Baptist
  Convention, Inc. (PNBC) 60,
  61, 433, **531**
Prohibition 661, 662
pro-life movement 128, 615
property 152, 153, 307, 548
proslavery thought **531–532**
prostitution 614
Protestant (periodical) 33
Protestant-Catholic-Jew (Will
  Herberg) 34, 146
Protestant Episcopal Church
  195, 409
Protestant Episcopal Sunday
  School Union 655
"Protestant ethic" 167
Protestant Film Commission
  436
Protestantism *see also* mainline
  Protestantism; *specific
  denomination* (*e.g.,* Baptists);
  specific topic (*e.g.,* justification)
  abolitionism 3
  American Indian Religious
    Freedom Act (AIRFA) 22
  baptism 55
  Bible societies 68
  biblical interpretation 70
  charismatic movement 111
  church and state, relationship
    between 122
  Communism 153
  dispensationalism 184, 185
  education, public school 198,
    199
  electronic church 203
  Enlightenment 211
  episcopacy 212
  Evangelical Alliance 221
  Evangelical United Front 226
  evolution 229
  frontier 244, 245
  fundamentalism *see*
    fundamentalism
  Haystack Prayer Meeting 281
  heresy 285
  Higher Christian Life
    movement 287
  Holiness movement 295

  immigration 311, 312
  inerrancy 313
  liberalism, theological 359
  liberation theology 361
  Manifest Destiny 381
  Maryland 386
  missions, foreign 406, 407
  missions, home 408, 410
  Native American religions:
    Inter-montane/California
    445
  Native American religions:
    Northwest 447
  nativism 452
  Pentecostalism 501
  positive thinking 515
  preachers *see* preachers
  primitivism 528
  Reformation *see* Reformation
  revivalism *see* revivalism
  satanism 587
  science and religion 595
  Scottish Common Sense
    Realism 599
  secularism 607
  sexuality 613, 615
  Social Gospel 630
  temperance 660, 662
  Unitarian Universalist
    Association 684
  Vietnam War 701
  voluntaryism 708
  Wesleyan tradition *see*
    Wesleyan tradition
  World War I 734
  World War II 737
Protestant Radio Commission
  436
Protestants and Other Americans
  United for Separation of
  Church and State 34, 571
Protocols of the Elders of Zion, The
  39
Providence, Rhode Island 19,
  56, 57
Provoost, Samuel 213
psychedelic drugs 167 *see also*
  hallucinogens
psychic powers 461
"PTL Club" (TV show) 205
Ptolemy (Greek astronomer)
  594
public lands 24
public religion *see* civil religion
public school *see* education,
  public school
Pueblo Indians 22, 450, 469
puha (spiritual power) 444
Pulaski, Tennessee 354
Pulaski, Casimir 563
Purcell, John 566
Puritanism **532–535,** *533 see
also* Pilgrims
  American Baptist Churches in
    the U.S.A. 19

  American Revolution/
    Revolutionary War 25, 26
  anti-Catholicism 32
  Antinomian Controversy *see*
    Antinomian Controversy
  baptism 56
  Baptists 57
  biblical interpretation 70
  Calvinism 96, 98
  Cambridge Platform 99, 100
  Carolinas 104
  church and state, relationship
    between 122
  civil religion 133
  colonial period 147
  Congregationalism 155
  conversion 161
  Covenant Theology 169
  election 203
  Enlightenment 209
  establishment, religious 216
  Half-way Covenant 275, 276
  immigration 309, 312
  justification 343
  literature and Christianity 364
  Massachusetts Bay Colony
    386, 387
  missions, foreign 406
  Native American religions:
    Eastern Woodlands 443
  nature religion 455
  New Lights/Old Lights 463
  people
    Bradford, William **77–78,**
      364, 509
    Cotton, John 37, 99,
      163–165, *164*
    Eliot, John 22, 68,
      206–207, 406
    Hooker, Thomas 99, 169,
      298–299
    Hutchinson, Anne 37, 38,
      306–307, 387, 464
    Mather, Cotton *see* Mather,
      Cotton
    Mather, Increase 161, 275,
      389–391, *390*
    Stoddard, Solomon 161,
      646–647
    Williams, Roger *see*
      Williams, Roger
    Winthrop, John *see*
      Winthrop, John
  primitivism 528
  Reformation 548
  Reformed Tradition 550
  Sabbatarianism 580
  Salem witchcraft trials *see*
    Salem witchcraft trials
  Separatists *see* Separatists

Q

Qaddafi, Muammar 39

Quadregesimo Anno (papal encyclical) 569
Quakers *see* Friends, the Religious Society of
Quebec Act (1774) 25
Quechan Indians 451
Quimby, Phineas Parkhurst (1802–1866) 120, 470, *536,* **536–537**
Qur'an (Islamic text) 234, 319

R

Rabbinical Assembly of America 158
Rabbinic Council of America 488, 489
Race, Alan 513
race and racism *see also* Ku Klux Klan
  African-American religion 11, 13
  Bahá'í Faith 52
  counterculture 167
  immigration 311, 312
  nativism 453
Radhasoami Satsang (Sikh-influenced movement) 622
radical feminist theology 234, 235
Radical Reformation 29, 548 *see also* Anabaptists
radio ministry 118, 204
Rajneesh, Bhagwan 291
Rajneeshpuram (Oregon) 291
Raleigh, Sir Walter 104
Rama (Hindu god) 316
Ramakrishna, Sri 290, 698
Ramakrishna and His Disciples (Christopher Isherwood) 698
Ram Dass, Baba (Richard Alpert) 292
Randolph, A. Philip 12, 137
Rapp, George (1757–1847) **538**
rapture 184, 523, **538–539**
rationalism and reason 209, 463, 544
Ratzinger, Josef 361
Rauschenbusch, August 60
Rauschenbusch, Walter (1861–1918) *539,* **539–540**
  American Baptist Churches in the U.S.A. 20
  Communism 152
  preachers, Protestant 521
  Social Gospel 631
Ravenscroft, John Stark 213
Ray, John 209
Reagan, Ronald
  Christian Right 118, 119
  civil religion 135
  civil rights movement 138
  fundamentalism (Protestant) 250

liberation theology 361
  Moral Majority 417
  Vietnam War 702
Reasonableness of Christianity, The (John Locke) 209
Reasonable Religion (Cotton Mather) 209
Reason the Only Oracle of Man (Ethan Allen) 210
rebbe (Jewish spiritual authority) 340, 489 *see also zaddik*
Reconstruction (historical period) 10, 136, 239, 368, 410
reconstructionism, Christian *see* dominion theology
reconstructionism, feminist 234
Reconstructionist (magazine) 541
Reconstructionist Judaism 158, **540–542,** 691
Reconstructionist Rabbinical College (Philadelphia, Pennsylvania) 541
Reconstructionist Rabbinical Fellowship 541
Red Cross 734
Red River, Kentucky 100, 103
"Red Scare" 153
Reed, Ralph 119
Reed, Rebecca 33
reform, social *see* Social Gospel
Reformation **546–549**
  Anglicanism 30
  atheism 46
  communitarianism 154
  ecumenical movement 194
  episcopacy 212
  inerrancy 313
  presbyterianism 526
  Reformed Tradition 550
  Sabbatarianism 580
Reformed Church in America 99, **549–550,** 552
Reformed Church in the United States *see* German Reformed Church in the United States
Reformed Episcopal Church (REC) 213
Reformed Protestant Dutch Church 549
Reformed Society of Israelites 543
Reformed Tradition **550–552** *see also* Christian Reformed Church; German Reformed Church; Huguenots; Reformed Church in America
  Calvinism 99
  election 202
  Huguenots 302
  presbyterianism 526
  Reformation 547
Reform Judaism **542–546** *see also* Central Conference of American Rabbis

Ethical Culture 219
  immigration 309
  Judaism 335, 336, 337, 338, 339, 340
  Pittsburgh Platform 510
  South 637
  Zionism 753, 755
Reform Vereine (Reform Societies) 543
Regulator movement 105
Reid, Thomas 210, 313, 600
reincarnation 459, 461, 665
Reines, Isaac 552
"Relationship of the Church to Non-Christian Religions, The" (Roman Catholic document) 196
religious nationalism *see* civil religion
Religious Science 470
religious tolerance 104, 122, 147 *see also* First Amendment; Toleration, Act of (Maryland)
Religious Zionists of America (RZA) **552–553,** 753
Relly, James 692
"Remember Pearl Harbor" (song) 738
Remond, Charles Lenox 136
"Remonstrants" 40
Reorganized Church of Jesus Christ of Latter Day Saints 128, **553–554**
repentance-struggle (*Busskampf*) 508
Republican Methodist Church 402, 554
Republican Party
  abolitionism 5
  anti-Catholicism 34
  Christian Right 118, 119
  electronic church 205
  Moral Majority 417
Rerum Novarum (papal encyclical) 27, 569
resistance 136 *see also* assimilation and resistance, Native American
restoration movement 56, 113, 114, 131, **554–557**
Reuther, Rosemary Radford 234
Revere, Paul *25,* 303
revivalism 557, **557–559**
  Azusa Street revival *see* Azusa Street revival
  Burned-Over District 90
  camp meetings 100
  Cane Ridge revival 103
  conversion 161
  evangelicalism 227
  frontier 245
  Great Awakening *see* Great Awakening
  people

Davies, Samuel **176–177,** 217
Dwight, Timothy *191,* **191–192,** 211, 226, 453, 602
Edwards, Jonathan *see* Edwards, Jonathan
Finney, Charles Grandison *see* Finney, Charles Grandison
Frelinghuysen, Theodorus Jacobus **242–243,** 267, 508, 549, 558
Graham, Billy *see* Graham, Billy (William Franklin)
Jones, Samuel Porter (Sam) **332–333**
Moody, Dwight Lyman *see* Moody, Dwight Lyman
Sankey, Ira David **585,** *585*
Sunday, Billy 558, *653,* **653–654,** 735
Tennent, Gilbert *see* Tennent, Gilbert
Whitefield, George *see* Whitefield, George
perfectionism 505
presbyterianism 527
Second Great Awakening *see* Second Great Awakening
Shakers 617
voluntaryism 708
Revolutionary War *see* American Revolution/Revolutionary War
Rhode Island *see also specific city (e.g.,* Providence)
  anti-Semitism 38, 39
  church and state, relationship between 122
  colonial period 147
  establishment, religious 216
  Friends, the Religious Society of (Quakers) 243
  voluntaryism 707
Rice, Abraham 487
Rice, Luther 20, 58, 281, 407
Richards, James 281
Richmond African Baptist Missionary Society 59
Right, Christian *see* Christian Right
Right to Life movement 615
Rinzai Zen 87, 749
Ripley, George (1802–1880) **559–560,** 643, 673
Riverside Church (New York City) 13, 521
Roanoke Island, North Carolina 104
Robbins, Francis 281
Roberts, Emma 747
Roberts, Granville Oral (1918–) 111, 205, 504, 515, **560–561**
Robertson, Marion Gordon (Pat) 119, 204, 205, 515, 523

Robinson, Ida 11
Robinson, John 509
Robinson, William 269
Rochester, New York 88
Rochester (New York),
  University of 20
Rockefeller Jr., John D. 219,
  521
Rock Island, Illinois 60
rock music 168
Rodeph Shalom (Philadelphia,
  Pennsylvania synagogue) 487
Roe v. Wade (1973) 118, 573,
  615
Roger's Version (John Updike)
  367
Roman Catholicism *149,*
  561–575, *565*
  African-American religion 7
  Americanism 27–28, 285,
    566, 567, 595
  American Revolution/
    Revolutionary War 25
  Anglo-Catholicism *see*
    Anglo-Catholicism
  anti-Catholicism *see*
    anti-Catholicism
  Baltimore, Councils of 54–55
  Baltimore Catechism 54
  baptism 57
  biblical interpretation 70, 72
  Cahenslyism 94–95
  Carolinas 104
  Catholic Worker movement
    108, 569, 572, 701
  charismatic movement 111
  Christian Right 117
  church and state, relationship
    between 122
  Cold War 145
  colonial period 147
  Communism 153
  communitarianism 155
  Constitution, U.S. 160
  ecumenical movement 195,
    196
  education, public school 199
  episcopacy 212
  eschatology 215
  establishment, religious 217
  Evangelical Alliance 222
  feminist theology 234
  heresy 285
  immigration 310, 311, 312
  Jesuits *see* Jesuits
  Ku Klux Klan 354
  liberation theology 360
  Longinqua Oceani (papal
    encyclical) 27–28, 285,
    367–368, 567
  Maryland 385, 386
  missions, foreign 408
  National Catholic Welfare
    Conference 433–434, 569,
    734

National Conference of
  Catholic Bishops (NCCB)
  434–435
Native American religions:
  Eastern Woodlands 443
Native American religions:
  Inter-montane/California
  445
Native American religions:
  Northwest 447
Native American religions:
  Southwest 451, 452
nativism 454
New France 462
New Spain 467, 470
Old Catholic movement
  480–481
Pennsylvania 500
people
  Brownson, Orestes Augustus
    81, **81–83,** 673
  Cabrini, Francesca Xavier **94**
  Calvert, Cecilius (Second
    Lord Baltimore) *95,*
    95–96, 147, 217, 385, 386
  Carroll, John 32, 54,
    105–107, 212, 563, 564
  Columbus, Christopher 22,
    38, **148–150,** 334, 440,
    467
  Coughlin, Charles Edward
    117–118, **165–166,** 204,
    570, 736, 737
  Cushing, Richard James
    172–174
  Day, Dorothy 108,
    178–179, 569, 572
  Gibbons, James *see*
    Gibbons, James
  Hecker, Isaac 28, **281–283,**
    282
  Ireland, John 27, *317,*
    317–318, 567
  Kino, Eusebio Francisco
    327, **350,** 469
  Marechal, Ambrose
    383–384, 564
  Marquette, Jacques 327,
    384–385
  Merton, Thomas 88, 146,
    399–400, 750
  Murray, John Courtney
    145, 327, **425–426,** 692
  Ryan, John Augustine 433,
    569, 570, *578,* **578–579,**
    662
  Serra, Junipero 469, *610,*
    610–611
  Seton, Elizabeth Ann Bayley
    565, *611,* **611–612**
  Sheen, Fulton J. 145, 204,
    515, 572, **618–619**
  Spalding, Martin John 28,
    55, **640–641**

Spellman, Francis Joseph
  571, 572, **641–643,** 701
Tekakwitha, Kateri
  (Catherine) 463, **660**
Verot, Jean Pierre Augustin
  Marcellin **698–699**
positive thinking 515
Santería 586
satanism 587
science and religion 595
secularism 607
sexuality 613, 614, 615
Social Gospel 631
South 637
temperance 662
trusteeism 564, 675–676 *see*
  trusteeism
Vatican Council I 55, 480,
  696
Vatican Council II 35, 54,
  195, 196, 310, 572,
  696–697
Vietnam War 701
World War I 734
World War II 737, 738
Roman Empire 134, 333
Romania 308, 337, 487
Romanian Americans 482, 483,
  485
Rome, New York 604
Roosevelt, Eleanor 137
Roosevelt, Franklin D.
  American Indian Religious
    Freedom Act (AIRFA) 23
  Christian Right 117, 118
  civil religion 134
  civil rights movement 137
  electronic church 204
  Roman Catholicism 569, 570
  Vietnam War 700
  World War II 736, 737, 738
Roosevelt, Theodore 453, 689
Rosenberg, Ethel and Julius 153
Rosenkreuz, Christian 575
Rosicrucians **575–576**
Ross, South Dakota 320
Round Dance (Paiute ceremony)
  257
Rousseau, Jean-Jacques 133
Roy, Rammohan 289
Royce, Josiah (1855–1916)
  576–577
Rubenstein, Richard 179, 339
Rublev, Andrei 484
Ruhani Satsang 622
"Rum, Romanism, and
  Rebellion" 34
Rush, Benjamin 198
Rushdoony, R. J. 118
Russell, Charles Taze
  (1852–1916) 325, 326,
  577–578
Russell, Mrs. Alexander 87, 749
Russia
  Hutterites 308

immigration 309
Judaism 337
Orthodox Christianity 481
Orthodox Judaism 487
Zionism 752
Russian Americans 482, 483
Russian Orthodox Church 482,
  485
Russian Orthodox Church
  Abroad 485
Russian Orthodox Greek
  Catholic Church of America
  485
Russian Revolution (1917) 152
"Russification" 308, 398
Rutgers University (New
  Brunswick, New Jersey) 549
Ruthenian Americans 676
Rutherford, Joseph Franklin
  ("Judge") 326
Ryan, Abram Joseph 368
Ryan, John Augustine
  (1869–1945) *578,* **578–579**
  National Catholic Welfare
    Conference 433
  Roman Catholicism 569, 570
  temperance 662

S

Sabbatarianism **580–581,** 612,
  740
Sabbathday Lake, Maine 616
sacred relatedness
  Beat movement 62
  Deep Ecology 180
  Native American religions:
    Plains 449
  Neo-paganism 458, 459
  New Age religion 461
Sadanaga, Masayasu *see*
  Williams, George M.
Sadducees (ancient Jewish
  group) 334
St. Augustine, Florida 468, 469
St. Bartholomew's Day Massacre
  (1572) 302
St. George's Methodist Church
  (Philadelphia, Pennsylvania) 14
St. Herman's Pastoral School
  (Alaska) 485
St. Louis (ship) 737
St. Louis, Missouri 220, 552,
  564, 565
St. Nicholas Cathedral
  (Washington, D.C.) 484
St. Thomas (Philadelphia,
  Pennsylvania congregation) 10,
  14
St. Vladimir's Seminary (New
  York City) 485
Saints of Christ 73
SAJ *see* Society for the
  Advancement of Judaism
SAJ Review 541

Salem, Massachusetts 581
Salem, North Carolina 105, 419
Salem witchcraft trials (1692)
  581, **581–582**
Salt Lake City, Utah *128*
salvation 37, 40, 97
salvation, universal *see*
  Universalism
Salvation Army *582*, **582–583**
  Holiness movement 295, 297
  Methodists 403
  missions, home 410
  perfectionism 506
  Social Gospel 631
  Wesleyan tradition 717
  World War I 734
San Antonio, Texas 293
sanctification **583–585**
  Antinomian Controversy 37
  Assemblies of God 43
  Azusa Street revival 48
  Church of God (Cleveland,
    Tennessee) 124
  Church of God in Christ 126
  Church of the Nazarene 130
  election 203
  Higher Christian Life
    movement 287
  Holiness movement 295,
    296, 297, 298
  Methodists 403
  Pentecostalism 502
  perfectionism 505
  Salvation Army 583
  Wesleyan tradition 716, 717
Sand County Almanac, A (Aldo
  Leopold) 180
Sandeen, Ernest R. 67
Sandwich Islands *see* Hawaii
Sandy Creek, North Carolina
  105
Sandy Creek Association 105
Sanford, Edward 240
San Francisco, California *582*
  Buddhism 85, 86, 88
  Buddhist Churches of
    America 90
  counterculture 168
  Hinduism 293
  International Society for
    Krishna Consciousness 316
  Jesus movement 328
  Roman Catholicism 564
San Francisco Zen Center 750
Sanger, Margaret 614
Sanitary Commission *see* United
  States Sanitary Commission
San Juan, Puerto Rico 467
San Juan Bautista Mission
  (California) *468*
Sankey, Ira David (1840–1908)
  585, *585*
sannyasin (ascetic) 316, 609
Santa Fe, New Mexico 469
Santa Monica, California 471

Santayana, George 304
Sant Bani Ashram 622
Santería **586**
San Xavier Del Bac Mission
  (Arizona) 469
Sasaki, Ruth Fuller 750
Satanic Bible, The (Anton S.
  LaVey) 587
satanism **586–587**
Satmar Hasidim 279, 754
Satolli, Francesco 27
Satori (enlightenment) 749
Sauer, Christopher 129
Savannah, Georgia 486
Sawan Kirpal Mission (Sikh
  group) 622
Saxony, Germany 418, 546
Saybrook, Connecticut 155
Saybrook Platform 155, 156,
  526, 527, **587**
Scandinavian American Lutheran
  Church 374
Scandinavian Americans 224,
  371, 373
Scarlet Letter, The (Nathaniel
  Hawthorne) 365
Schaeffer, Francis 605
Schaff, Philip (1819–1893)
  255, **587–588**
Schechter, Solomon
  (1847–1915) 158, **588–590**,
  589, 690, 754
Schiff, Jacob 754
Schlatter, Michael 255, 501, 687
Schleiermacher, Friedrich 419
Schmemann, Alexander
  (1921–1983) 484, 485,
  590–591
Schmucker, Samuel Simon
  (1799–1873) *591*, **591–592**
  Evangelical Alliance 221, 222
  Evangelical Lutheran Church
    in America 224
  Lutheranism 373
Schneerson, Joseph Isaac 279
Schneerson, Menachem Mendel
  (1902–1994) 16, 279, 280,
  340, **592–594**
*School District of Abington
  Township v. Schempp* (1963)
  123
Schuller, Robert 206, 515, 522,
  550
Schwenkfelders 500
Schwerner, Michael 138, 651,
  652
*Science and Health, with Key to
  the Scriptures* (Mary Baker
  Eddy) 120
science and religion 411,
  594–596 *see also* creationism;
  evolution
*Science of Being and Art of
  Living* (Maharishi Mahesh
  Yogi) 672

Science of Judaism movement
  157, 543
Scientific Creationism (Henry
  M. Morris) 170
"scientific racism" 34, 453
Scientology 35, **596–597**
SCLC *see* Southern Christian
  Leadership Conference
Scofield, Cyrus Ingerson
  (1843–1921) **597–598**
  dispensationalism 185
  fundamentalism (Protestant)
    249
  premillennialism 523
  rapture 539
  World War I 735
Scofield Reference Bible (Cyrus
  Scofield) 185, 249, 523, 539
Scopes, John T. 72, 230, 250,
  596, 599
Scopes trial **598–599**, *599*
  biblical interpretation 72
  creationism 170
  evolution 230
  science and religion 595
Scotch Americans 98, 524, 528,
  705
Scotch-Irish Americans 98, 500,
  552, 636
Scotland 100, 241, 526, 547,
  550
Scott, Orange 296, 402
Scott, Walter 555
Scottish Common Sense Realism
  599–601
  biblical interpretation 71
  creationism 170
  inerrancy 313
  Princeton Theology 529
  science and religion 595
Scranton, Pennsylvania 481
Scripture *see* Bible; biblical
  interpretation
*Scripture Doctrine of Christian
  Perfection* (Asa Mahan) 295,
  505, 584
Seabury, Samuel (1729–1796)
  26, 212, 213, *601*, **601–602**
seances 643
*Seasonable Thoughts on the State
  of Religion in New England*
  (Charles Chauncy) 269, 464
"second blessing" 717
Second Coming of Christ *see*
  eschatology
Second Great Awakening *602*,
  602–604
  African-American religion 9
  American Baptist Churches in
    the U.S.A. 19
  American Revolution/
    Revolutionary War 26
  Arminianism 41
  baptism 56
  Baptists 58

biblical interpretation 70
Burned-Over District 91
Calvinism 98
camp meetings 100
Cane Ridge revival 103
civil rights movement 136
conversion 162
education, public school 198
election 203
Enlightenment 211
Evangelical United Front 226
Holiness movement 295
justification 343
Methodists 401
missions, foreign 407
missions, home 409
New School/Old School 465
perfectionism 505
postmillennialism 515
preachers, Protestant 520
Presbyterian Church (U.S.A.)
  524
presbyterianism 527
revivalism 558
sanctification 584
secularism 606
South 636
United Methodist Church
  688
Universalism 693
Young Men's Christian
  Association (YMCA) 745
Secret Doctrine, The (Helena
  Blavatsky) 664
*Secret Ritual of the Nation of
  Islam* (W. D. Fard) 430
sectarianism 250
secular humanism 22, **605–606**
"Secular Humanist Declaration"
  606
secularism 222, 303, **606–607**
secularization 606
Seed, John 181
segregation 117, **607–609**
Selective Service 701
Selective Service Act (1940) 738
self-flagellation 565
self-realization 167, 168, 609
Self-Realization Fellowship
  (S.R.F.) 291, **609**
Seligman, Joseph 220
Sellars, Roy Wood 304
Selma, Alabama 13, 138, 640
Seminole Indians 443, 444
Seneca Indians 44
Separate Baptists 19, 56, 58, 269
"separate but equal" 136
separatism, religious 248, 250,
  509
separatism and nationalism,
  African-American
  African-American religion 11
  Black Jews 73, 74
  Islam 320, 321

Nation of Islam (Black Muslims) 429
Separatists, Puritan 147, 155, 533, 534
Sephardic Jews
    Conservative Judaism 157
    Judaism 334, 336
    Orthodox Judaism 486, 487
    United Synagogue of Conservative Judaism 691
Serbian Americans 482
Serb Orthodox Church 485
Sergeant, John 406
sermons 534, 535, 551
Serra, Junipero (1713–1784) 469, *610*, **610–611**
Servetus, Michael 682
Seton, Elizabeth Ann Bayley (1774–1821) 565, *611*, **611–612**
Seventh-day Adventist Church **612–613**
    electronic church 204
    eschatology 216
    premillennialism 523
    Sabbatarianism 581
    sexuality 614
Seventh-day Baptist Church 58, 580
Sewall, Samuel 406
sexuality **613–616**
    electronic church 205
    Neo-paganism 459
    Orthodox Judaism 486
    Roman Catholicism 573
    Shakers 616
sexual revolution 168, 573, 613, 615
Seymour, William Joseph (1870–1922) **616**
    Assemblies of God 43
    Azusa Street revival 48, 49
    Church of God in Christ 126
    Holiness movement 298
    Pentecostalism 502, 503
Shahadah (Muslim creed) 319
Shakarian, Demos 111
Shakers **616–618**, *617*
    Burned-Over District 91
    Communism 152
    communitarianism 154
    counterculture 168
    eschatology 216
    frontier 245
    sexuality 614
Shaku, Soyen 87, 740, 749
"Shallow and the Deep, Long-Range Ecology Movements, The" (Arne Naess article) 180
"Shall the Fundamentalists Win?" (Harry Emerson Fosdick sermon) 21, 60, 521
shamanism 443, 445, 447, 451, 461

Shango (Yoruba god) 586
Shankara (Hindu philosopher) 292
Sharing the Light of Faith: National Catechetical Directory for Catholics of the United States 54
Shasta Abbey (California) 89, 750
Shasta Indians 257
Shearith Israel, Congregation (New York City) 334, 335, 487
Sheba, queen of (Biblical figure) 73
Sheen, Fulton J. (1895–1979) 145, 204, 515, 572, **618–619**
shehitah (ritual slaughterer) 487
Sheldon, Charles Monroe (1857–1946) **619–621**, *620*, 631
Shensin Temple (Los Angeles, California) *90*
shiatsu 461
Shi'ite Muslims 320, 321
Shinran (Japanese reformer) 86
Shintoism 739
Shiva (Hindu god) 293
Short Bull (Lakota leader) 258
Shoshone Indians 257, 444, 448
Shreveport, Louisiana 117, 432
shtetls (communities) 487
Shulhan Aruch (Jewish law code) 157, 486
shuls (synagogues) 487
shunning *(Meidung)* 29
Sikh Council of North America 622
Sikhism *621*, **621–623**
Silver, Abba Hillel 753
Silver Spring, Maryland 613
Simons, Menno 397, 548
Simpson, A. B. 67, 68, 297, 298
sin *see* evil and sin; sanctification
Singh, Gobind 621
Singh, Jaimal 622
Singh, Kirpal 622
Singh, Seth Shiv Dayal 622
Sinhalese Buddhism 87
"Sinners Bound to Change Their Own Hearts" (Charles G. Finney sermon) 98, 162
"Sinners in the Hands of an Angry God" (Jonathan Edwards sermon) 365, 519
Sino-American Buddhist Association 86
Sioux Indians *see* Lakota (western Sioux) Indians
Sisters of Charity 565
Sisters of Loretto 565
Sisters of the Holy Family 566
Sisters of the Sacred Heart 565
Six Months in a Convent (Rebecca Reed) 33

Six Sermons (Lyman Beecher) 661
slave preachers 520
slave rebellions 10, 624
slavery **623–625**, *624 see also* abolitionism; proslavery thought
    African-American religion 8–9, 10
    Baptists 59
    biblical interpretation 71
    Civil War 139
    Fourteenth Amendment 240
    Islam 319
    literature and Christianity 366
    Lost Cause Myth 369
    missions, foreign 406
    Roman Catholicism 566
    South 637
    United Methodist Church 689
    Virginia 704
Slavic Americans 453, 482, 485
Slocum, John 257
Slovak Evangelical Lutheran Church 370
Small, Albion Woodbury (1854–1926) **625–626**
smallpox inoculations 595
Smith, Adam 210
Smith, Alfred E. 34, 117, 568, 662
Smith, Elias 555
Smith, Emma 553
Smith, Gerald L. K. 117
Smith, Hannah Whitall 287, 288, 296
Smith, Henry Preserved 313
Smith, Hyrum 128
Smith Jr., Joseph (1805–1844) *626*, **626–628**
    Book of Mormon 76
    Church of Jesus Christ of Latter-day Saints 127, 128
    Reorganized Church of Jesus Christ of Latter Day Saints 553, 554
Smith III, Joseph 128, 554
Smith, Kate 738
Smith, Kelly Miller 14
Smith, Robert Pearsall 287, 288, 296
Smithsonian Institution (Washington, D.C.) 23
Smohalla (Wanapum leader) 257, 446
Smyth, John 57
Smyth, Newman (1843–1925) **628–629**
snake-handling **629–630**, 637
SNCC *see* Student Nonviolent Coordinating Committee
Snyder, Gary 62, 87, 89, 181, 749
Social Contract, The (Jean-Jacques Rousseau) 133

Social Creed 689
social Darwinism 249, 262
Social Gospel **630–631**
    American Baptist Churches in the U.S.A. 20
    Committee of Southern Churchmen 151
    Communism 152
    Ethical Culture 219
    Evangelical Alliance 221
    Gladden, Solomon Washington 260
    modernism (Protestant) 412
    preachers, Protestant 521
    Rauschenbusch, Walter 539, 540
    Sheldon, Charles Monroe 619
    Strong, Josiah 649
    United Methodist Church 689
    World War II 736
socialism 338
social reform *see also* peace reform; Social Gospel
    Catholic Worker movement *see* Catholic Worker movement
    Day, Dorothy 178, 179
    Evangelical United Front 226
    Gladden, Solomon Washington 261
    Ryan, John Augustine 578, 579
    Sheldon, Charles Monroe 620
    Sojourners Fellowship 633, 634
    Strong, Josiah 650
    Sunday School movement *see* Sunday School movement
    temperance *see* temperance
    Universalism 693
    Willard, Frances Elizabeth Caroline 723, 724
    Young Men's Christian Association (YMCA) 745, 746
    Young Women's Christian Association (YWCA) 747
Society for Ethical Culture *see* Ethical Culture
Society for the Advancement of Judaism (SAJ) 541
Society for the Promotion of Christian Knowledge (Church of England) 69, 213
Society for the Propagation of the Faith (French organization) 565
Society for the Propagation of the Gospel in Foreign Parts (SPG) **631–633**
    African-American religion 9
    Anglicanism 31
    Episcopal Church 213
    missions, foreign 406

slavery 623
Society of Christian Socialists 631
Society of Jesus *see* Jesuits
Society of the Brethren 281
Society of Universal Baptists 692
Socinians 548
Socinus, Faustus 548, 682
sodomy 613, 614
Sojourners (magazine) 228, 633, 634
Sojourners Fellowship **633–634**
Soka Gakkai (Buddhist movement) 86, 471
Solomon (Biblical monarch) 241
Soloveitchik, Joseph Dov (1903–1993) 553, **634–635**
Some Thoughts Concerning the Present Revival of Religion in New England (Jonathan Edwards) 267
Soto Zen 749
Souls of Black Folk, The (W. E. B. Du Bois) 11
South **635–638** *see also specific states* (*e.g.,* Mississippi)
abolitionism 3
African-American religion 10
African Methodist Episcopal Church 15
American Baptist Churches in the U.S.A. 20
American Missionary Association 24
Bahá'í Faith 52
Baptists 59
Christian Church (Disciples of Christ) 114
Civil War 139, 140, 141
Committee of Southern Churchmen 151
establishment, religious 217
Friends, the Religious Society of (Quakers) 243
Great Awakening 269
heresy 285
Ku Klux Klan 354
literature and Christianity 367
Lost Cause Myth *see* Lost Cause Myth
Presbyterian Church (U.S.A.) 524
proslavery thought 531, 532
segregation 608
slavery 623
Southern Baptist Convention 638
South Africa 39
South America 312, 407, 467, 470, 561
South Carolina *see also specific city* (*e.g.,* Charleston)
African-American religion 9
Anglicanism 31
anti-Semitism 38

Bahá'í Faith 52
Carolinas 104
colonial period 148
establishment, religious 216, 217
Evangelical Lutheran Church in America 224
National Baptist Convention of America, Inc. 432
Pentecostalism 503
presbyterianism 528
Society for the Propagation of the Gospel in Foreign Parts 632
South Dakota 308 *see also* Wounded Knee Massacre
Southeast Asia 407, 408
Southeastern Baptist Seminary (Wake Forest, North Carolina) 638, 639
Southern Baptist Alliance 639
Southern Baptist Convention **638–639**
abolitionism 4
American Baptist Churches in the U.S.A. 20
baptism 56, 57
Baptists 59, 61
biblical interpretation 72
charismatic movement 111
Civil War 139
electronic church 204
fundamentalism (Protestant) 249, 250
South 636, 637
Southern Baptist Theological Seminary (Louisville, Kentucky) 638, 639
Southern Christian Leadership Conference (SCLC) 137, 138, **639–640**, 701
Southern Methodists 689
Southern Presbyterian Church *see* Presbyterian Church in the United States
Southwestern Baptist Seminary (Dallas, Texas) 638
Southwide Student Leadership Conference on Nonviolent Resistance (1960) 651
sovereignty, divine
Arminianism 40
Calvinism 96
Christian Science 121
Church of Jesus Christ of Latter-day Saints 127
Committee of Southern Churchmen 151
dispensationalism 184
election 203
Enlightenment 210
evolution 229
justification 342
Neo-orthodoxy 456, 458
New Divinity 462

Reformed Tradition 551
revivalism 558
spiritualism 644
Soviet Union 135, 570 *see also* Cold War
Spain 38, 334, 561 *see also* New Spain
Spalding, Martin John (1810–1872) 28, 55, **640–641**
Spangenberg, Augustus Gottlieb 419, 508
Spanish Americans 453
Spanish-American War (1898) 28, 382, 497
Sparks, Jared 683, 684
Speedwell (ship) 509
Speer, Robert E. 408, 652, 653, 734
Spellman, Francis Joseph (1889–1967) 571, 572, **641–643,** 701
Spellman College (Atlanta, Georgia) 433
Spener, Philipp Jakob 507
spirit baptism
Assemblies of God 42, 43
charismatic movement 110, 111
Church of God (Cleveland, Tennessee) 124, 125
Church of God in Christ 125
Holiness movement 298
Pentecostalism 502, 504
perfectionism 506
primitivism 529
sanctification 584
Spiritual Advancement of the Individual Foundation, Inc. 291
Spiritual Counterfeits Project 36
Spiritual Exercises (Ignatius of Loyola) 327
spiritual gifts *see* charismatic movement
spiritualism 400, **643–644,** 663
Spiritual Regeneration Movement (S.R.M.) 292
Spiritual Telegraph (periodical) 643
Spong, John 214
Springfield, Missouri 43
Spyrou, Athenagoras (1886–1972) 271–272, **644–645**
Squanto (Native American friend of the Pilgrims) 509
Sri Aurobindo Society 291
Sri Lanka (Ceylon) 87, 89, 665
Sri Venkateswara Temple (Pittsburgh, Pennsylvania) 293
Stalin, Josef 153
Stamp Act (1765) 26
Stanton, Elizabeth Cady (1815–1902) **645–646,** *646*
feminist theology 233

spiritualism 643
Woman's Bible, The 731, 732
Starhawk (feminist writer) 235, 459
Starr King Seminary (Berkeley, California) 693
State and the Church, The (John Ryan) 569
Statement of Fundamental Truths (Assemblies of God) 43
states *see also specific state* (*e.g.,* California)
Constitution, U.S. 160
education, public school 199
establishment, religious 218
First Amendment 238
Fourteenth Amendment 240
Stearns, Shubal 105, 269
Stephan, Martin 370
Stewart, Dugald 210
Stewart, Lyman 251
Stewart, Milton 251
Stiles, Ezra 26
Stiles, Robert 369
Stillpoint Institute (San Jose, California) 88
Stockbridge, Massachusetts 406
Stockton, California 622
Stoddard, Solomon (1643–1729) 161, **646–647**
Stone, Barton Warren (1772–1844) **647–648**
baptism 56
camp meetings 101
Cane Ridge revival 103
Christian Church (Disciples of Christ) 114
Churches of Christ 131
primitivism 528, 529
restoration movement 555
Second Great Awakening 603
Stone, William 385
Stonewall Riot (New York City, 1969) 615
Stowe, Harriet Beecher (1811–1896) **648–649,** *649*
abolitionism 4, 5
biblical interpretation 71
literature and Christianity 366
spiritualism 643
Strauss, C. T. 87
Stromberg v. California (1931) 240
Strong, Augustus Hopkins 20
Strong, Josiah (1847–1916) 221, 222, 631, **649–651,** *650*
Stuart, George H. 140
Stuart, Moses 602, 683
Student Nonviolent Coordinating Committee (SNCC) 138, **651–652,** 701
Students for a Democratic Society 701
Students International Meditation Society 672

Student Volunteer Movement (SVM) 407, 436, **652–653**
Stuyvesant, Peter 464
Subordination and Equivalence: The Nature and Role of Woman in Augustine and Thomas Aquinas (Kari Borresen) 234
Subuh, Muhammad 321
suburbs 146, 167, 545
Sufism 321
Sujata, Anagarika 88
Sullivan, T. V. 745
"Summer of Love" (1967) 168
sumptuary laws 387
Sun Dance (Native American ceremony)
   American Indian Religious Freedom Act (AIRFA) 23
   Ghost Dance 258
   Native American religions 440
   Native American religions: Plains 448, 449
   Native American religions: Southwest 451
Sunday, Billy (William Ashley) (1862–1935) 558, *653*, **653–654**, 735
Sunday School Board 638
Sunday School Magazine 655
Sunday school movement **654–656**, *655*
Sunday School Times (periodical) 288
Sunni Muslims 320, 321, 429
Supremacy, Act of (England, 1534) 30
Supreme Court, U.S.
   Brown vs. the Board of Education (1954) 134, 137
   Cantwell v. Connecticut (1940) 123, 160, 238, 240
   Church of Lukumi Babalu Aye v. City of Hialeah, The (1993) 238
   Employment Division vs. Smith (1990) 439
   Engel v. Vitale (1962) 123
   Everson v. Board of Education (1947) 160, 238, 240
   Gitlow v. New York (1925) 240
   Lyng v. Northwest Indian Cemetery Protective Association (1988) 24
   McCollum v. Board of Education (1948) 123
   Pierce v. Society of Sisters (1925) 568
   Plessy v. Ferguson (1896) 136
   Roe v. Wade (1973) 118, 573, 615
   School District of Abington Township v. Schempp (1963) 123

Stromberg v. California (1931) 240
West Virginia State Board of Education v. Barnette (1943) 123
Wisconsin v. Yoder (1972) 30
Suzuki, Daisetz Teitaro (1870–1966) 87, 89, **656–657**, 740, 749
Suzuki, Shunryu 750
Swaggart, Jimmy 43, 204, 205
Swaminarayan, Sri 291
Swaminarayan Mission and Fellowship 291
Sweden *see* New Sweden
Swedenborg, Emmanuel 643, 657
Swedenborgianism **657–658**, 673
Swedish Americans 20, 60, 224, 372, 548
Swedish Augustana Synod 225
Sweet, William Warren 245
Swing, David 284, 285, 525
Swiss Americans 104
Swiss Reformation 547
Switzerland 308, 397, 526, 550, 672
Syllabus of Errors (papal document) 55, 566
Synagogue Council of America 145
syncretic practices 586
Synod of Dort (1619) 40, 97, 202
Synod of Philadelphia 466, 467, 523
Synod of the Free German Reformed Congregations 255
Synod of the Reformed German Church in the United States of America 255
Syrian Americans 482, 483
Syrian Orthodox Church 485
Szold, Benjamin 157
Szold, Henrietta (1860–1945) **658**, 754

T

takhanah (legislative enactment) 158
Takoma Park, Maryland 613
Talmud (Jewish text) 278, 334, 486
Tanoan Pueblo Indians 452
Tantrik Order in America 291
Taoism 85, 739
Taos Pueblo Indians 23
Tappan, David 683
Tar Baby (Toni Morrison) 367
Tarthang Tulku (Buddhist monk) 88
tatanka lowanpi (puberty rite) 448

Taylor, Nathaniel William (1786–1858) 603, *659*, **659–660**
tea ceremony 749
"teach-in" 701
Teaching for the Lost-Found Nation of Islam in a Mathematical Way (W. D. Fard) 430
Teachings of Buddha 90
Tecumseh (Shawnee leader) 444
teisho (Zen) 749
Teitelbaum, Joel 279, 754
Tekakwitha, Kateri (Catherine) (1656–1680) 463, **660**
television broadcasting 203, 204, 205, 572
Teller, Henry M. 23
temperance 227, 410, 506, **660–662**, 689
Ten Commandments, The (film) 146
Ten Great Religions: An Essay in Comparative Theology (James Freeman Clarke) 290
Tennent, Gilbert (1703–1764) **662–663**, *663*
   Great Awakening 267, 268
   New Side/Old Side 466, 467
   Pietism 508
   Presbyterian Church (U.S.A.) 524
   presbyterianism 527
   revivalism 558
Tennent, John 466
Tennent Jr., William 466, 508
Tennent Sr., William 267
Tennessee *see also specific city* (*e.g.,* Nashville)
   Cane Ridge revival 103
   Christian Methodist Episcopal Church 116
   Churches of Christ 132
   Church of God (Cleveland, Tennessee) 124
   Evangelical Lutheran Church in America 224
   Pentecostalism 503
   Presbyterian Church (U.S.A.) 524
   presbyterianism 527
   Scopes trial 599
   Second Great Awakening 603
   snake-handling 629
Tenskwatawa (Shawnee leader) 45
Tenth Muse, Lately Sprung up in America, The (Anne Bradstreet) 365
"termination" policy 23
Testem Benevolentiae (papal encyclical) 28, 285, 567
Texas *see also specific city* (*e.g.,* Houston)
   Assemblies of God 42

Churches of Christ 132
National Baptist Convention of America, Inc. 432
Native American Church 437
New Spain 469
Pentecostalism 504
South 637
Thanksgiving (holiday) 510
Thatcher, Samuel 683
"thealogians" 235
Their Eyes Were Watching God (Zora Neale Hurston) 367
theology *see also* death of God theology; heresy; liberalism, theological; Neo-orthodoxy; New Divinity
   African-American religion 13
   Bahá'í Faith 51
   Covenant Theology 169
Theology Digest 328
Theology of Liberation, A (Gustavo Gutierrez) 361
Theology of the Social Gospel, A (Walter Rauschenbusch) 521
Theosophical Society 290, 664
Theosophical Society in America 664
Theosophist (periodical) 665
theosophy 87, 290, 644, **663–665**
Theravada Buddhism 85, 87, 89
"thetan" (Scientology) 596
Third Order Dominicans 565
Thirteenth Amendment 240, 624
"This Is the Life" (TV show) 204
Thomas, Clarence 574
Thomas, John 113
Thomas, Norman 736
Thomas Road Baptist Church (Lynchburg, Virginia) 417
Thompson, Eliza Trimble 661
Thompson River Indians 445
Thoreau, Henry David (1817–1862) **665–667**, *666*
   Buddhism 87
   counterculture 167
   Hinduism 289
   Huguenots 303
   literature and Christianity 366
   transcendentalism 673, 674
Thornwell, James Henley (1812–1862) 525, 532, **667–668**
3HO *see* Healthy, Happy, Holy Organization
Three Pillars of Zen, The (Philip Kapleau) 749
Thurman, Robert 88
Tibetan Americans 312
Tibetan Buddhists 88, *675*
Tibetan Nyingma Meditation Center (Berkeley, California) 88

Tillich, Paul Johannes (1886–1965) 179, 457, **668–669**
Tillotson, John 209
Time (magazine) 146, 179, 204, 328
Tingley, Katherine A. 664
Tituba (West Indian slave) 582
Tkach, Joseph W. 740
Tobias, Joseph 38
Tocqueville, Alexis de 604, 707, 708
Toleration, Act of (Maryland) (1649) 147, 217, 385, **669–670**
Tomlinson, Ambrose Jessup (1865–1943) 124, 125, 503, 630, **670–671**
Tomlinson, Milton 125
tongues, speaking in (glossolalia)
    Assemblies of God 42
    Azusa Street revival 48
    charismatic movement 110, 111
    Church of God (Cleveland, Tennessee) 124, 125
    Church of God in Christ 125, 126
    Holiness movement 298
    Pentecostalism 502, 504
    perfectionism 506
    primitivism 529
Topeka, Kansas 506
Torah (Jewish scriptures) 486
Torrey, Reuben Archer (1856–1928) 185, 251, **671–672**
Total Woman, The (Marabel Morgan) 615
Touro Synagogue (Newport, Rhode Island) 334
Toy, Crawford 285
Tracy, Joseph 267
Transcendental Club 673
transcendentalism **672–674**
    Buddhism 87
    Christian Science 121
    Hinduism 289
    literature and Christianity 365
    positive thinking 514
    Unitarian Universalist Association 685
Transcendental Meditation 35, 292, **672**
transpersonal psychology 461
Transylvania 682
Travolta, John 597
Traynor, William J. H. 34
Treatise on the Atonement (Hosea Ballou) 685
tref (opposite of kosher) 157, 337
Trible, Phyllis 234
tribulation 523, 538
"trickster" figure 449

Triennial Convention (General Missionary Convention) 20, 58, 59
Trine, Ralph Waldo 471, 514
Trinity College (Bannockburn, Illinois) 68
Trinity Evangelical Divinity School (Chicago, Illinois) 633
Troy, New York 604
True Christianity (Wahre Christentum) (Johann Arndt) 507
True Doctrine of the Sabbath (Nicholas Bound) 580
True Holland Reformed Church 550
Truman, Harry S. 145, 153
Trumbull, Charles G. 288
Trungpa, Chogyam (1939–1987) 88, **674–675**, *675*
trusteeism 564, **675–676**
Truth, Sojourner (1797–1883) 16, **676–677**, *677*
tsetega (winter ceremony) 447
Tubman, Harriet (1821–1913) 16, **678**
Tufts College (Medford, Massachusetts) 685
Turner, Frederick Jackson 244
Turner, Nat (1800–1831) **678–680**
    African-American religion 10
    Baptists 59
    biblical interpretation 71
    preachers, Protestant 520
    proslavery thought 531
"turn on, tune in, drop out" 167
Turretin, Francois 313, 529
Twain, Mark (Samuel Clemens) 47, 219
"Twentieth-Century Reformation Hour" (radio broadcast) 118

U

Udall, Morris 23
Ukraine 308, 481
Ukrainian Americans 482
Ukrainian Orthodox Church 272
Uncle Tom's Cabin (Harriet Beecher Stowe) 4, 5, 71, 366
unconditional surrender policy 570
Uneasy Conscience of Modern Fundamentalism, The (Carl F. H. Henry) 228
Unification Church 35, **681–682**
Unification Theological Seminary (Barrytown, New York) 682
Union Baptists 637

Union for Traditional Conservative Judaism 159, 340
Union of American Hebrew Congregations (UAHC) 336, 543, 753
Union of Orthodox Jewish Congregations 488, 489
Union of Orthodox Rabbis (Augudat ha-Rabbanim) 488
Union Theological Seminary (New York City) 285
"Unitarian Christianity" (William Ellery Channing sermon) 683, 684
Unitarian Controversy 156, **682–684**, 684
Unitarianism
    anti-Semitism 38
    Christadelphians 114
    Enlightenment 210, 211
    establishment, religious 218
    Humanist Manifesto 303, 304
    New Lights/Old Lights 464
    people
        Channing, William Ellery 109, **109–110**, 683, 684
        Chauncy, Charles *see* Chauncy, Charles
        Clarke, James Freeman **142–143**, 289, 673, 684
        Frothingham, Octavius Brooks 246, 685
        Parker, Theodore **494–496**, *495*, 673, 674
        Reformation 548
    Unitarian Universalist Association 684
    Universalism 693
Unitarian Universalist Association (UUA) 156, 682, **684–686**, 693
Unitas Fratrum *see* Moravians
United Brethren in Christ 688, 689
United Church of Christ (UCC) **686–688**
    American Missionary Association 24
    Calvinism 99
    Congregationalism 156
    German Reformed Church 256
    Reformed Tradition 552
United Evangelical Lutheran Church 225
United House of Prayer for all People 11
United Lodge of Theosophists 664
United Lutheran Church in America 225
United Methodist Church 403, 508, **688–690**, 717
United Nations 118

United Pentecostal Church, International 43, 504
United Presbyterian Church in the United States of America 523
United Presbyterian Church of North America 525, 528
United Services Organizations (USO) 746
United Society of Believers in Christ's Second Appearing *see* Shakers
United States and Britain in Prophecy, The (Herbert W. Armstrong) 741
United States Catholic Conference (USCC) 434
United States Catholic Missions Council 408
United States Christian Commission 140
United States Sanitary Commission 140
United Synagogue of America 158
United Synagogue of Conservative Judaism **690–691**
United Synod South (Lutheran) 224
United Zionists of America 552
Unity of Brethren *see* Moravians
Unity School of Christianity 470
Universal Christian Conference on Life and Work (Stockholm, 1925) 195
Universal Hagar's Spiritual Church 644
Universal House of Justice (Bahá'í Faith) 51
Universalism 360, 684, 685, **692–693** *see also* Ballou, Hosea; Chauncy, Charles
universal Israel *(klal Yisrael)* 158
Universalist Church of America 684, 685, 693
Universal Negro Improvement Association (UNIA) 73, 320
Universal Peace Congress (Paris, 1889) 497
University Christian Movement 653
Unvanquished, The (William Faulkner) 367
Updike, John 367
"Upon the Burning of Our House" (Anne Bradstreet poem) 365
Ursuline Convent (Charlestown, Massachusetts) 33
Ursulines (Roman Catholic order) 565
Utah 128, 444
"Utah Mormons" 554
Ute Indians 257, 444
Utica, New York 604

utopianism **693–695**
 Alcott, Amos Bronson 17
 Burned-Over District 91–92
 communitarianism 154
 counterculture 168
 frontier 245
 Noyes, John Humphrey 475,
  476, 477
 Rapp, George 538
 Shakers *see* Shakers
 Wilkinson, Jemima 723

V

Vahanian, Gabriel 179
Vaishnava Hinduism 316, 317
Vajrayana Buddhism 85, 88
Valiente, Doreen 458
Van Buren, Paul 179
Vanderhorst, Richard H. 116
Van Dusen, Henry P. 457
Vane, Henry 37
van Mecklenburg, Jan 464
Varick, James 402
Varieties of Religious Experience
 (William James) 607
Varlet, Dominique 480
Vatican Council I 55, 480, **696**
Vatican Council II **696–697**
 anti-Catholicism 35
 Baltimore Catechism 54
 ecumenical movement 195,
  196
 immigration 310
 Roman Catholicism 572
Vedanta for the Western World
 (Christopher Isherwood) 698
Vedanta Hinduism 290
Vedanta Society 290, **698**, 740
Veniaminov, John 484
Vermont 675
Verot, Jean Pierre Augustin
 Marcellin (1805–1876)
 698–699
Vesey, Denmark (1767–1822)
 10, 520, 531, **699–700**
Victorious Life conferences 288
Vietnamese Americans 52, 312
"Vietnam Syndrome" 702
Vietnam War (1961–1975)
 700–702
 civil religion 135
 Cold War 146
 counterculture 167, 168
 peace reform 497
 Reform Judaism 545
Vietnam War Memorial
 (Washington, D.C.) 702
Vincennes, Indiana 564
Vincent, John H. 655
Vineland, New Jersey 101, 296
Virginia *see also specific city (e.g.,*
 Norfolk)
 African-American religion 10
 Anglicanism 31

 church and state, relationship
  between 123
 colonial period 147, 148,
  702–705
 education, public school 199
 Episcopal Church 212
 establishment, religious 216,
  217, 218
 Great Awakening 269, 270
 Huguenots 303
 Mennonites 398
 Methodists 401
 New Side/Old Side 467
 Reformation 548
 Sikhism 622
Virginia Baptist Foreign Mission
 Society 4
Virginia Beach, Virginia 205
Virginia House of Burgesses 8
Vishnu (Hindu god) 291, 292,
 293, 316
Vivekananda, Swami
 (1863–1902) **705–706**
 Hinduism 290, 291
 Self-Realization Fellowship
  609
 Vedanta Society 698
 World's Parliament of
  Religions 739, 740
Vodou **706–707**
Voice of America 738
voluntaryism 19, 226,
 707–708, 745
Volunteers of America 583
Voting Rights Act (1965) 138,
 640

W

Wabokieshiek (Winnebago
 Indian leader) 45
Waco, Texas 36
wakan tanka (life-sustaining
 powers) 258
Wake Forest University
 (Winston-Salem, North
 Carolina) 59
Walden (Henry David Thoreau)
 366, 666
Walden Pond (Massachusetts)
 673
Waldenses (medieval sect) 154
Walker, Alice 367, 730
Wallace, Mike 428
Wallis, Jim 228, 633
Walther, Carl Ferdinand
 Wilhelm (1811–1887) 370,
 373, **709–710**
Wampanoag Indians 443
Ware, Henry 683, 684
Warfield, Benjamin Breckinridge
 (1851–1921) 229, 313, 529,
 600, **710–711**

War for Independence *see*
 American Revolution/
 Revolutionary War
Warner, Daniel Sidney 297
Washington (state) 308
Washington, D.C. 293, 472,
 622
Washington, Booker Taliaferro
 (1856–1915) 24, 137, 432,
 711–712
Washington, George 26, 47,
 134, 241
Washington County,
 Pennsylvania 555
Washington Times (newspaper)
 682
Washoe Indians 257
Watchman-Examiner
 (periodical) 249
Watchtower (magazine) 326
Watchtower Bible and Tract
 Society 326
Watson, Tom 39
Watts, Alan Wilson
 (1915–1973) 87, **712–713,**
 749
Wayland, Francis 59
"Wealth" (Andrew Carnegie
 article) 262
Webb, Muhammad Alexander
 Russel (1846–1916) 319, 320,
 713–714
Weems, Renita 234
Weld, Theodore Dwight
 (1803–1895) 3, 71, 136, 226,
 714
Wesley, Charles 268, 270, 401
Wesley, John 715
 Arminianism 41
 Church of the Nazarene 130
 election 203
 episcopacy 212
 Great Awakening 268, 270
 Higher Christian Life
  movement 287
 Holiness movement 295
 justification 343
 Methodists 401, 402, 403
 Moravians 419
 Pentecostalism 502
 perfectionism 505
 Pietism 508
 preachers, Protestant 519
 Salvation Army 583
 Society for the Propagation of
  the Gospel in Foreign Parts
  632
 United Methodist Church
  688
 Wesleyan tradition 714, 716,
  717
Wesley, Samuel 714
Wesleyan Church 297, 402
Wesleyan Methodist Church 4,
 296, 506

Wesleyan tradition 40, 130,
 714–717
West African religions 311, 586,
 706
West Indies 73, 419
Westminister Assembly
 (London, 1643) 551
Westminister Theological
 Seminary (Philadelphia,
 Pennsylvania) 525, 530
Westminster Confession (1646)
 Baptists 58
 Cambridge Platform 99
 heresy 284
 New Side/Old Side 466
 Presbyterian Church (U.S.A.)
  524
 Puritanism 534
 Reformed Tradition 551
West Virginia 114, 123, 316
*West Virginia State Board of
 Education v. Barnette* (1943)
 123
What Is Darwinism? (Charles
 Hodge) 229
Wheaton, Illinois 431
Wheaton (Illinois) College 228
Wheeler, Wayne 661
Wheelock, Eleazer 406
Wheel of Dharma (periodical) 90
Wheelwright, John 37
whiskey 661
Whitaker, Alexander 704
Whitcomb Jr., John C. 596
White, Alma Bridwell
 (1862–1946) **717–718**
White, E. E. 438
White, Ellen Gould (Harmon)
 (1827–1915) 581, 612, 614,
 717, **719**
White, John *703*
White, Walter 137
White, William 213
White Deerskin Dance (Native
 American ceremony) 445
Whitefield, George
 (1714–1770) **719–721,** *720*
 Great Awakening 268, 269,
  270
 Moravians 419
 preachers, Protestant 519
 revivalism 558
White Goddess, The (Robert
 Graves) 458
white supremacist groups 355
Whither? (Charles Augustus
 Briggs) 72
Whitman, Walt (1819–1892)
 167, *721*, **721–722**
Whittier, John Greenleaf 303
Who Governs? (Robert A. Dahl)
 513
wicca *see* witchcraft
Wichita Indians 23, 438, 448
Wieman, Henry Nelson 411

wilderness 455
Wilkins, Charles 288
Wilkins, Roy 12, 137, 138
Wilkinson, Jemima (1752–1819) 91, **722–723**
Willard, Frances Elizabeth Caroline (1839–1898) 497, 643, 661, *723,* **723–724**
William III (king of England) 217, 386
William and Mary, College of (Williamsburg, Virginia) 210, 704
Williams, Delores S. 730
Williams, George (English reformer) 745
Williams, George M. (Buddhist leader) 471, 472
Williams, Peter 402
Williams, Roger (1603–1683) **724–726,** *725*
  American Baptist Churches in the U.S.A. 19
  baptism 56
  Baptists 57, 58
  church and state, relationship between 122
  colonial period 147
  establishment, religious 216
  Massachusetts Bay Colony 387
Williams College (Williamstown, Massachusetts) 281
Wilmette, Illinois 52
Wilson, David 257
Wilson, Edward O. 22
Wilson, John 437
Wilson, Woodrow 453, 569, 733, 734, 735
Winchester, Elhanan 692
Winchester Profession (1803) 692
Winrod, Gerald B. 117
Winthrop, John (1588–1649) **726–728,** *727*
  Antinomian Controversy 37
  civil religion 133
  Congregationalism 155
  Massachusetts Bay Colony 386, 387
  preachers, Protestant 519
Wisconsin 512, 550 *see also specific city (e.g.,* Milwaukee)
Wisconsin Evangelical Lutheran Synod 372, 373, 374
Wisconsin v. Yoder (1972) 30
Wisdom of God Manifest in the Works of Creation (John Ray) 209
Wise, Isaac Mayer (1819–1900) *728,* **728–729**
  Central Conference of American Rabbis 108
  Conservative Judaism 157
  Judaism 335

Pittsburgh Platform 510, 511
Reform Judaism 543, 544
Wise, Stephen S. (1874–1949) **729–730,** 737, 753
Wise, Ted 328
witchcraft 235, 458, 459 *see also* Salem witchcraft trials
Witchcraft Today (periodical) 458
Witch-Cult in Western Europe, The (Margaret Murray) 458
Witches of Eastwick, The (John Updike) 367
Witherspoon, John 26, 210, 600
Witness for Peace 634
Wittenberg, Germany 546
Wollaston, Massachusetts 37
womanist theology 234, **730–731**
Woman's Bible, The (Elizabeth Cady Stanton) **731–732**
women and religion *see also* feminism and women's rights; feminist theology
  Bible schools 68
  Buddhism 89
  Christian Science 121
  Conservative Judaism 158
  Evangelical United Front 227
  Friends, the Religious Society of (Quakers) 244
  Judaism 340
  missions, foreign 407
  missions, home 409
  ordination
    Anglo-Catholicism 31, 32
    Central Conference of American Rabbis 109
    Conservative Judaism 159
    Episcopal Church 214
    Judaism 340
    Lutheran Church—Missouri Synod 371
    Reform Judaism 545
    Reorganized Church of Jesus Christ of Latter Day Saints 554
    Roman Catholicism 574
    United Church of Christ 687
    Universalism 693
  people
    Blavatsky, Helena Petrovna **74–76,** *75,* 87, 290, 664, 665
    Daly, Mary **175–176,** 234, 615, 731
    Day, Dorothy 108, **178–179,** 569, 572
    Dyer, Mary **192–193**
    Eddy, Mary Baker 120, *196,* **196–198,** 470–471, 732
    Fuller, Sarah Margaret **246–248,** *247,* 673

Grimké, Angelina Emily and Sarah Moore 136, 226, 233, **272–274,** *273,* 643
Harkness, Georgia Elma **277–278**
Hopkins, Emma Curtis **299–300,** 470
Howe, Julia Ward 139, **301–302,** *302,* 614, 624
Hutchinson, Anne 37, 38, **306–307,** 387, 464
Kennett, Jiyu 89, **346–347,** 750
Lee, Ann **356,** 616, *617*
Lee, Jarena **356–357**
McPherson, Aimee Semple 204, *394,* **394–395,** 504
O'Hair, Madalyn Murray **478**
Palmer, Phoebe Worrall 287, 295–296, **493–494,** 502, 505, 584
Phelps, Elizabeth Stuart (Ward) 366, **506–507**
Seton, Elizabeth Ann Bayley 565, *611,* **611–612**
Stanton, Elizabeth Cady 233, 643, **645–646,** *646,* 731, 732
Stowe, Harriet Beecher 4, 5, 71, 366, 643, **648–649,** *649*
Szold, Henrietta **658,** 754
Tekakwitha, Kateri (Catherine) 463, **660**
Truth, Sojourner 16, **676–677,** *677*
Tubman, Harriet 16, **678**
White, Alma Bridwell **717–718**
White, Ellen Gould (Harmon) 581, 612, 614, *717,* **719**
Wilkinson, Jemima 91, **722–723**
Willard, Frances Elizabeth Caroline 497, 643, 661, *723,* **723–724**
Reconstructionist Judaism 542
Reform Judaism 546
Roman Catholicism 573, 574
sexuality 614, 615
temperance 661
"women-church" movement 234
Women's Christian Temperance Union 410, 497, 615, 660, 661
Women's Missionary Union 638
Women's Zionist Organization of America *see* Hadassah
Woodhull, Victoria 643, 644
Woodrow, James 285
Woodruff, Wilford 128
Woods, Leonard 683

Woodstock (music festival, 1969) 168
Woolman, John (1720–1772) **732**
Worcester, Samuel 683
Word of God and the Word of Man, The (Karl Barth) 457
work, meaning of 168, 617
World Christian Fundamentals Association 249
World Council of Churches **732–733**
  Christian Church (Disciples of Christ) 115
  Church of the Brethren (Dunkers) 130
  Cold War 145
  ecumenical movement 195, 196
  Orthodox Christianity 484
World Peace Academy 682
World Series, baseball (1919) 39
World's Parliament of Religions (Chicago, 1893) **739–740**
  Americanism 27
  Buddhism 87
  Hinduism 290
  Islam 319
  theosophy 664
  Vedanta Society 698
  Zen 749
World's Student Christian Federation 194, 436
World Student Christian Federation 652
"World Tomorrow, The" (radio show) 740
World Tribune (periodical) 471
World War I (1914–1918) **733–735**
  Evangelical Lutheran Church in America 225
  fundamentalism (Protestant) 249
  Lutheranism 373
  National Council of Churches 436
  Orthodox Christianity 482
  Roman Catholicism 567
  Salvation Army 583
  science and religion 595
  temperance 661
  Young Men's Christian Association (YMCA) 746
  Young Women's Christian Association (YWCA) 747
World War II (1939–1945) **735–739,** *736*
  Jehovah's Witnesses 327
  nativism 454
  Roman Catholicism 570, 571
  Young Men's Christian Association (YMCA) 746
  Young Women's Christian Association (YWCA) 747

Worldwide Church of God **740–741**

World Zionist Congress (1897) 753

World Zionist Congress (1903) 552

World Zionist Organization (WZO) 552, 753

Wounded Knee, Siege at (1973) 46

Wounded Knee Massacre (South Dakota, 1890) 257, 258, 449

Wovoka (1856?–1932) 257, 441, **741–742**

Wright, Faye *see* Mata, Sri Daya

Wright, Frances 614

Wright, Frank Lloyd 484

Wright, George Frederick 170, 229

Wright, Lucy 617

Wyneken, F. C. D. 370

Y

Yad Ha-Hazaka ("The Mighty Hand") (Jewish text) 486

Yale University (New Haven, Connecticut) 111

Yaqui Indians 451, 452

yeshivas *(yeshivoth)* (religious schools) 16, 280, 489

YMCA *see* Young Men's Christian Association

Yoder, John 633

Yogananda, Swami Paramahansa 291, 609

Yoga Sutras 291, 609

Yogoda Satsanga Society of India 609

York, Pennsylvania 688

Yoruba (West African ethnic group) 586

Young, Brigham (1801–1877) 128, 553, *743*, **743–745**

"Young Goodman Brown" (Nathaniel Hawthorne story) 365

Young Men's Buddhist Association 86

Young Men's Christian Association (YMCA) **745–747**, *746*
  ecumenical movement 194
  missions, home 410
  National Catholic Welfare Conference 433

National Council of Churches 436
  Social Gospel 631
  World War I 734

Young Men's Hebrew Association 734

Young Women's Christian Association (YWCA) 194, 410, 436, 631, **747–748**

Yuba City, California 622

Yuchi Indians 444

Yukteswar, Swami Sri 609

YWCA *see* Young Women's Christian Association

Z

zaddik (spiritual teacher) 279, 280

Zahm, John 28

Zalman, Schneur 279

Zanoni (Sir Edward Bulwer-Lytton) 576

Zarahemla, Wisconsin 554

zazen (meditation) 749

Zealots (ancient Jewish group) 334

Zeeland, Michigan 116, 550

Zen 61, 88, 740, **749–750**

Zen and the Art of Motorcycle Maintenance (Robert M. Pirsig) 750

Zen Catholicism (Dom Aelred Graham) 750

Zen Center (Providence, Rhode Island) *750*

Zen Meditation Center (Rochester, New York) 89, 749

Zen Mountain Center (Tassajara Hot Springs) 750

Zinzendorf, Nicolas Ludwig von (1700–1760) **750–752**
  Lutheranism 372
  Moravians 418, 419
  Pennsylvania 500
  Pietism 508

Zionism 108, 338, 339, 544, **752–755**

Zionist Organization of America (ZOA) 753

Zoroastrians 739

Zuni Indians 451

Zurich, Switzerland 546, 547, 550

Zwingli, Ulrich 398, 546, 550